THE AMERICAN BIBLIOGRAPHY

OF

CHARLES EVANS

VOLUME 14—INDEX

---

by

ROGER PATTRELL BRISTOL

AMERICAN ANTIQUARIAN SOCIETY

WORCESTER, MASSACHUSETTS

1959

GLOUCESTER, MASS.

PETER SMITH

1967

Whatsoever errors have escaped the
Authour or Printer, as the commission of them speaks a man, so
let the pardon shew a good man.

Preface

During the period of fifty-two years over which the thirteen volumes of Charles Evans' *American Bibliography* were being printed, great improvements were made in the techniques of constructing bibliographies and indexes. Evans himself made changes in his methods from volume to volume as experience with the earlier units of the series suggested improvements, such as shifting from personal to institutional entries for some kinds of material. The net result is that booksellers and bibiographers are constantly describing as "not in Evans" items which he entered under some odd heading.

Another difficulty in the use of Evans has been the lack of a cumulative index, frequently making it necessary to take down thirteen large volumes to answer one question. We have several times worn the bindings off one of our sets of Evans. During the past year the possession of a set of the galleys of the present book has checked that wear and tear, has greatly expedited our work, and has (thanks to cross-indexing) turned up hundreds of items we would have missed had we relied on the old indexes.

The institutions behind the production of this volume have been the American Philosophical Society and the University of Virginia, but it would have been confusing, as John Cook Wyllie pointed out, to have volume fourteen of Evans brought out by anyone other than the American Antiquarian Society. So we are publishing it, using the revolving fund established by George Francis Booth and Harry Galpin Stoddard for such good works. It will, we hope, be followed eventually by a checklist of not-in-Evans items (also prepared by Mr. Bristol) and by a short-title revision of the entire work.

Clifford K. Shipton

American Antiquarian Society

ERRATA

Introduction

As Mr. Shipton has said, the volumes of Charles Evans' *American Bibliography* which contain the fruits of his single-handed attempt to locate and describe everything printed in America up to 1800 have long posed problems for bibliographers trying to discover whether a particular item has or has not already been described. Not only was Evans wont to put certain items under entries which often hide them successfully; he also sometimes placed in the wrong year (and hence on occasion in the wrong volume) items he had heard of but had not seen. Again, an item of an earlier year often appears out of chronological sequence in a later volume, because it was discovered later. These flaws, incidental to the publication of a work which we can only call a *magnum opus,* sometimes baffle the best endeavors of researchers to run down a specific item.

Futhermore, because Evans died before he could see his work to completion (the thirteenth and concluding volume of entries was brought out by Shipton in 1955), the indexes provided are inadequate. Each volume has its own set of indexes, nowhere cumulated. Evans provided an author index, a not very helpful subject index, and an index of printers and publishers. There is no title index. Shipton in his thirteenth volume purposely included only an author index, in the knowledge that the present volume was in preparation.

The need for a general index to the set of volumes has been widely felt, but it would be folly to pretend that its preparation has been an exciting task. Nevertheless there have been moments when the necessity of reconciling discrepancies in authorship and in biographical dates gave some rein to the detective spirit that lurks in every bibliographer, and once in a while Mr. Evans' humor shot up like a crocus amid the bibliographical dust of scholarship.

The premise on which this index is built is that the typical user will have in hand an early American imprint, which may or may not be one of the 39,162 items already described by Evans or Shipton. The in-

v

dex entries are intended to provide the quickest and surest check as to whether a particular item is recorded in the thirteen volumes of the *American Bibliography*.

To that end, this is an author-title index, with certain additions, in a single alphabet. Among "authors" have been included all pseudonyms and all attributed authors suggested by Evans. Corporate authors have been shown as indicated in Evans; but under most governmental bodies, breakdowns have been added under **Governor, Laws,** and so on, when to do so seemed to make for easier finding of an item. Separate laws of the United States have been entered both by topic and by date of promulgation; most of them are thus entered twice. Similarly, items issued by governors are entered both under the person and under the governmental body; for example, under both **Hancock, John, 1737-1793** and **Massachusetts. Governor.**

Entries have been made for all titles except those beginning with **Sermon** or **Speech,** which are shown only under author unless anonymous. There are entries for running titles and half-titles when given by Evans, for anonymous works, for distinctive titles, and for non-distinctive titles, especially those troublesome ones beginning with **Report, Letter, Proceedings, Address, Message.** Almanacs and newspapers appear not under specific title in the main alphabet, but in special sections headed **ALMANACS** and **NEWSPAPERS.**

Entries have been made also for names of people, names of ships, and Indian tribes, whenever brought out in the title as transcribed by Evans. Inclusion of these entries has been based on the assumption that only too often a newly acquired item may lack all or part of a title page, and that a name mentioned elsewhere in the piece (possibly menem may lack all or part of a title page) may lead to adequate identification. "Items about" follow "items by" in a separate alphabet under the person named, and are distinguished by the use of lower-case initial letters, as follows:

> **Clap, Thomas, 1703-1767**
> Conjectures, 5362, 17113
> Letter (to Edwards), 5561
> Religious constitution, 7171
> death, 10597
> letter (from Edwards), 5582

Except for the possible subject value of such entries, no subject coverage has been attempted. Any historical or biographical side-effects of this index may be attributed to the power of serendipity that often inheres in bibliographical endeavor.

It is obvious from the foregoing that anyone attempting to identify an item will be likely to obtain the quickest answer by searching first under title, next under personal author given on the title page, next under person (not author) given on the title page, and last under corporate author. As all bibliographers know, dubious items require checking in every possible and impossible place.

Acknowledgments are due to many: to John Cook Wyllie, at whose instigation the project was undertaken; to the several bibliographers who gave advice and encouragement at the inception of the project; to the American Philosophical Society for a grant which during 1954 got the work off to a good start; to Mrs. Hilda Z. Floam, who during that year labored as valiantly as if the project were her own; and to all those who have borne with the endless clutter of preparation and printing and who have had a hand in reducing chaos to order.

Roger Pattrell Bristol

University of Virginia

A

A., C.
Bussfertige beicht-vater, 23100
(tr.) Wunderbahre bussfertige, 6950
A., P. Three curious, 17447
A., R. see **Allen, Richard**
A . . . n, F. see **Allison, Francis, 1705-1777**
A. B. C. des chretiens, 1493
A, B, C. oder namenbucher, 10514
A, B, C of religion, 1614
A. B. C. und buchstabierbuch, 4331, 9047
A. B. C. with the catechism, 20345, 21409
A. B. C. with the Church, 19208, 28631
A son excellence, 16177
Aan den eerwaarden, 9504
Aanbiddelyke, 2820
Aanspraak van de vergadering, 15470
Aaron, priest of Babel, 23100
Aaron, Margalitha. Wunderbahre bussfertige, 6950
Abaellino, 25073
Abailard see **Abélard**
Abbot, Rev. —, hand of fellowship, 6955
Abbot, Abiel, d. 1739, death, 4336
Abbot, Abiel, 1770-1828
Discourse, 35070
Eulogy, 36751
Memorial of divine, 33262
Traits of resemblance, 35071
ordained at Coventry, 30425
ordained at Haverhill, 28711
Abbot, Hull, 1702-1774
Awakening calls, 4214
Disswasive against, 5898
Duty of God's people, 5724
Jehovah's character, 3860
hand of fellowship, 6955?
Abbot, Jacob, ordained, 33737
Abbot, John. Know all men, 28075
Abbot, Moses, d. 1734. Diary, 3762
Abbot, Priscilla. At her shop, 26529
Abbot, Samuel, petition by, 33005
Abbot, Stephen, orders court martial, 34080
Abbott, Joshua, pardoned, 24540
Abdias. Historia, 9863
Abeel, David, deposition by, 17633
Abeel, David G. Inaugural dissertation, 26530
Abeel, Garret. Committee-chamber, New-York, 14927
Abeel, John N., ordained, 28731

Abeille françoise, 24566
Abel, lamentations for, 28483-84
Abel, Thomas. Subtensial plain trigonometry, 8777
Abélard. Letters, 13787, 29945
Aber, Israel. Art of manufacturing, 29946
Abercrombie, James, 1758-1841
Sermon, 33263
prayer by, 27259
Abercrombie, Robert
Account of the proceedings, 7142
Remarks on a late, 7826
ordained, 5385
proceedings against, 7720
reply to, 8224
Abermahlige treue, 5134
Abermalige vorschlag, 4888
Abgeforderte relation, 8778
Abgenothigter bericht, 4420
Abhandlungen über die natur, 19923
Ability of God, 13237
Ability to and fidelity in, 5145
Abingdon, Willoughby Bertie, earl of, 1750-1799
Thoughts, 15740-41
Able and faithful, 13079
Abolition societies
Address of a convention, 26531
Committee to whom was referred, 26532
Minutes, (1794) 26533, (1795) 28146, (1796) 29947, (1797) 31686, (1798) 33264, (1800) 37969
To the free Africans, 29948
To the society, 31687
Abounding grace, 13870
Abraham in arms, 256
Abraham the passenger, 1205
Abraham's humble intercession, 111
Abridgement of Mr. Hopkins's, 7916

VOL.	ITEMS	VOL.	ITEMS
1	1-3244	8	22298-25074
2	3245-6623	9	25075-28145
3	6624-9891	10	28146-30832
4	9892-13091	11	30833-33261
5	13092-16176	12	33262-25854
6	16177-19448	13	35855-39162
7	19449-22297		

VOL.	ITEMS	VOL.	ITEMS
1	1-3244	8	22298-25074
2	3245-6623	9	25075-28145
3	6624-9891	10	28146-30832
4	9892-13091	11	30833-33261
5	13092-16176	12	33262-25854
6	16177-19448	13	35855-39162
7	19449-22297		

concerning the territory, 23847
contained in this, 9432
of Assembly for the regulation, 37889-90
of incorporation, 23146
of the rebels, 6058-60
passed at the first session, 27724
passed at the second session, 29551
Adam, Alexander, 1741-1808. Rudiments of Latin, 35073
Adams, ———. Sketches of the history, 31688
Adams, ———. satire on, 16697
Adams, Amos, 1728-1775
  Character of a Christian, 7605
  Concise, historical, 11130, 13092
  Expediency, 8289
  Ministerial affection, 11131
  Only hope, 10534
  Pleasures peculiar, 10809
  Religious liberty, 10810
  Sermon, (1761) 9048, (1766) 10221
  Songs of victory, 8290
Adams, Daniel, 1773-1864
  Inaugural dissertation, 35074
  Oration, 36754
Adams, Ebenezer
  (ed.) New and complete, 32692
  True and wonderful, 23461
Adams, Eliphalet, 1676-1753
  Brief discourse, 2830
  Connecticut election sermon, 1442
  Discourse, (1706) 1238, (1717) 1864, (1731) 3740, (1733) 3741
  Eminently good, 2090
  Funeral discourse, (Adams), 6274, (Bulkley) 6450, (Saltonstall) 2498
  God sometimes, 3861
  Gracious presence, 3245
  Ministers must, 2723
  Sermon, (1721) 2198, 36755, (1738) 4215
  Short discourse, 6625
  Work of ministers, 2599
Adams, Eliza, d. 1800, death, 37639
Adams, George, d. 1773. Astronomical essays, 36756
Adams, George, 1750-1795
  Astronomical & geographical, 36756
  Essay on the use, 36757
Adams, Hannah, 1755-1832
  Alphabetical compendium, 18319
  Summary history, 35075
  View of religions, 23102
Adams, James, of Dorchester, ordained, 35753
Adams, James, of Wilmington. To the public, 19449
Adams, John, 1704-1740
  Jesus Christ, 2982
  Poems on several, 5527, 6275
Adams, John, 1735-1826
  Defence of the Constitution, (1787) 20176-77, (1788) 20910, (1797) 31689-91
  Essay on canon, 17975-76
  Farewel address, 31946
  Letter (to Pinckney), 38370
  Message, 34811, 34827
  President's answer, 34836
  President's speech, 34833, 34835
  Proclamation, (1797) 33046-47, (1798) 34797
  Reflexions, 33928
  Speech, (1797) 33058-59, (1798) 34831-32, (1799) 36589
  Thoughts on government, 14639-40, 20911

Twenty-six letters, 21624-25
  address to, 33436
  administration denounced, 38657
  approves law, 22969, 32953, 32956, 34697, 36472, 36475, 38693
  committee to meet Howe, 15168
  conduct of, 37170, 37566-70
  dedication to, 32817, 32886, 34162
  defended, 30293-94, 31212-13, 32853, 38643
  delegate to Congress, 13425
  draws up resolution, 15141
  election favored, 30472, 37093
  election opposed, 30984
  letter (from Washington), 34828-29
  letters (from Mably), 19065
  minister plenipotentiary, 18231, 20789
  moderator at Faneuil Hall, 13159
  observations on, 38152-53
  political opinions, 29982, 30411
  recommends fast day, 34401, 34414-16
  reply to, 20465
  report by, 20775
  satire on, 16697?
  services of, 34116
  strictures on, 31909, 32140
  subscribes to book, 22380
  vindicated, 38941
Adams, John, 1750-1814
  Flowers of ancient, 28149
  Flowers of modern, 29950, 31692
Adams, John Quincy, 1767-1848
  Oration, 25076-77
  (tr.) Origin and principles, 37501
Adams, Joseph, 1719-1783
  Blessedness, 3246
  Death of the righteous, 7827
  Duty of professors, 10811
  Letter (to Barnard), 5110-11
  Necessity and importance, 11132
Adams, Lydia Pygan, d. 1749, death, 6274, 6625
Adams, Moses, d. 1819. Sermon, (1798) 33265, (1799) 35076
Adams, Nathaniel, worshipful master, 31798
Adams, Phineas, 1741-1801
  Sermon, 21626
  hand of fellowship, 28533
Adams, Samuel, of Boston. For sale, 31693
Adams, Samuel, of Pennsylvania, accounts of, 19893
Adams, Samuel, of Wilmington. To the public, 19449
Adams, Samuel, 1722-1803
  Appeal to the world, 11133
  Appendix to the American, 11134
  Boston, Mar. 30, 1773, 12688
  Proclamation, (1794) 27279-80, (1796) 30759-60, (1797) 32442
  approves resolution, 27283
  dedication to, 21879, 22560, 23431, 24384, 25589, 27098, 28809, 30545
  delegate to Congress, 13425
  denied pardon, 14184-86
  insolence of, 13840
  member donations committee, 13161
  moderator of meeting, 17480
  portrait, 15451
  pres. Mass. Senate, 17222-23, 19424
  satirized, 35400
  secy. House of repres., 14197, 15901, 16857
  sermon before, 22506, 23741, 24841, 26855, 28686,

VOL.	ITEMS	VOL.	ITEMS
1	1-3244	8	22298-25074
2	3245-6623	9	25075-28145
3	6624-9891	10	28146-30832
4	9892-13091	11	30833-33261
5	13092-16176	12	33262-25854
6	16177-19448	13	35855-39162
7	19449-22297		

inhabitants of the city, 31695
inhabitants of the colony, 11860
inhabitants of the county, 15717
inhabitants of the district, 23313
inhabitants of the New Hampshire, 16163
inhabitants of the new settlements, (1793) 25329, (1795) 28463
inhabitants of the province, 5900
inhabitants of the state of Mass., 16228-29
inhabitants of the state of Vermont, 15720
inhabitants of the towns, 23270
legislature, 23165
living, 24753
members of Congress, 28153
members of the Mass. Charitable, (1795) 29086, (1797) 33195
members of the Protestant Episcopal, (1784) 18742, (1792) 24025, (1793) 25836, (1795) 29374, (1799) 35761
merchants, freeholders, 10812
merchants of Philadelphia, 17076
ministers, (1790) 22880, (1797) 32815
Negroes, 20400
numerous, 23105
people called Quakers, 18802
people of England on the subject, 14173
people of England, Scotland, 23726
people of Gt. Brit., (1791) 24231-33, (1798) 34961-62
people of Kentucky, 30739
people of Maine, 27539
people of Maryland, 33626, 35619
people of New England occasioned, 6954
people of New England representing, 7917
people of North Carolina (Maclaine), 20594
people of North Carolina (Publicola), 21041
people of Pennsylvania, 22735
people of South Carolina, 26784, 27092
people of the congressional, 31045
people of the state of N.Y. on the subject, 21175
people of the state of N.Y. shewing, 21465
people of the U.S., (1796) 31532, 31534, (1800) 36917-20
people of Virginia, 33702
President, 28387
principal, 9356
public, (Gardiner) 10622, (Hopkins) 14803, (Magruder) 37881, (Matthews) 24533
public containing some remarks, 19470, 20179
Republicans, 36070
Rev. Dr. Alison, 9892
Rev. Moses, 27769
Roman Catholics, 18390
second, 20213
senior class, 31234
soldiers, 14168
speakers, 18523
stockholders, 23970-71
students at Phillips, 35837
students of Dickinson, 19865
Unitarian, 23713
United States, 18439-40
vestrymen, 10814
voters for electors, 36773-74
voters of Anne-Arundel, 33272
young people, 35338

youth, 27522
to those of the people, 17160
to those persons, 19154
to those Quakers, 7606
to young men, 28690
to young people, 3732
to young persons, 33153
Addresse an die freyen, 35082
Addresse der endsunterschriebenen, 20622
Addressed to the freeholders, 11252-54
Addresses to old men, 534
to the citizens, 20180
to young men, 19651
Addressor addressed, 31607
Adelaide of Wulfingen, 37744
Adelos. New sentiments, 19452
Ader, Israel ben. Chronicle, 7927
Adet, P. A.
Notes addressées, 30440
(tr.) Reflexions, 30440
complaints by, 31946, 31948, 34840
insolence of, 30226
notes to the secy. of state, 30208
reply to, 33064
Adgate, Andrew, d. 1793
Lecture, 28154
Mechanics lecture, 21627
Philadelphia harmony, 21629, 29953
Philadelphia songster, 21628
Rudiments of music, (1788) 20916, (1790) 22299, (1799) 35083
Select psalms, 20181
Adgate, Matthew. Northern light, 36775-76
Adiawando, sachem of the Pigwackets, 3554
Adlum, John. Geographical and hydrographical, 23104
Adminiculum puerile, (1758) 8111, (1778) 15778, (1785) 18983, (1788) 21042
Administration dare not, 13992
Administration of parochial, 22141
Administrations of providence, 27241
Admiral Byng's defence, 7865
Admiral Russel's letter, 629
Admonition to unconverted, 25088
Admonitions against swearing, 26537
Admonuere plusquam, 36777
Adopted child, 33422-23
Adopted son, 34271
Adorable ways, 2821
Adriano, 30613
Adroite princesse, 29300
Adulateur, a tragedy, 13063
Advantageous proposals, 10251
Advantages and disadvantages of a married, 25662
and disadvantages of the marriage state, (1761) 8891, (1764) 9707, (1766) 10345, (1790) 22589, (1795) 28903
and disadvantages of the married state, (1783) 17989, (1794) 27164-65, (1796) 30639
and obligations, 5562

VOL.	ITEMS	VOL.	ITEMS
1	1-3244	8	22298-25074
2	3245-6623	9	25075-28145
3	6624-9891	10	28146-30832
4	9892-13091	11	30833-33261
5	13092-16176	12	33262-25854
6	16177-19448	13	35855-39162
7	19449-22297		

(1796) 31640
reason (Paine), (1794) 27458-64, (1795) 29261-67, (1796) 30941-32, (1797) 32633
reason and revelation, 28344
reason unreasonable, 34568
superstition, 29906
Aged layman. Letter, 8635
Aged minister see **Dickinson, Moses, 1695-1778**
Aged minister's solemn appeal, 18003
Aged real friend. To the public, 17007
Aged school-mistress. Explanation, 26955
Agency and providence, 17002
Agency of God, 39113
Agnew, James, d. 1840. Inaugural dissertation, 36780
Agrarian justice, 32629-30
Agreeable admonitions, 1118
intelligence, 25800
surprise, (1786) 19878, (1793) 25939, (1794) 26558, 27437
Agreed that the principles, 21632
Agreement between William Smith, 8493
Agricola
Advertisement, 13098-99
Squabble, 9564-65
To the inhabitants, 13097
To the worthy inhabitants, 13100
Agricola, or the religious, 2905
Agricultural enquiries, 32673
Agricultural society, Boston. Inquiries, 37935
Agriculture, a poem, 28394
Agrippa. Chronicon, 19558
Agrippa, Cornelius. Appendix, 6626
Aguecheek, Andrew. Almanac see **Almanacs (Aguecheek)**
Aguilio, Pedro, life, 22402, 32380, 35299
Agur's choice, 32397
Ah can I cease to love, 26217
Ah well a day, 29956
Ahiman rezon, 17915
Aiken, Solomon, d. 1832
Charge, 35133
Sermon, 25081
Aikin, John, 1747-1822
Calendar of nature, 36782
Evenings at home, 31698-99, 35087
Juvenile trials, 31700
Letters from a father, (1794) 26541, (1796) 29957-58, (1800) 36783
View of the life, 26542-43
Aimwell, Absalom see **Adgate, Andrew, d. 1793**
Aitken, John
Compilation of the litanies, 20186, 23106
(ed.) Scots musical museum, 31701
engraver of music, 21152, 22093
Aitken, Robert, 1734-1802
Catalogue, 11140
Following books, 16179
General American register, 12299, 12638
Aix de la Chaise, François d'. Letter, 438
Akenside, Mark, 1721-1770
Pleasures of imagination, 26544, 28155
excerpts from, 23246
Akin, James, engraver, 36890
Alamoth, an address, 33962
Alarm, no. I-V, 12799-803
Alarm, oder eine erweckungs-zuschrift, 14643
Alarm, or an address, 14642
Alarm sounded desiring, 4581
Alarm sounded to prepare, 1383
Alarm; to the freemen, 18321

Alarm to the legislature, 14453
to the world, 24410
to unconverted sinners, (1727) 2832, (1739) 4332, (1741) 4663, (1743) 5112, (1764) 9567, (1767) 10538
Alarming Boston Port-act, 13306
Albaniad, 23699
Albany, N. Y.
At a . . . meeting . . . in the city, 33275
At a meeting of a number of freeholders, 36852-53
At a meeting of a number of members, 33276
Charter, (1707) 1287, (1736) 3979, (1771) 11957, (1800) 36784
Crisis; to the people, 33277
Fellow citizens, 28156
In committee; Albany, 4th March, 28157
Laws and ordinances, 12639, 23107
Order of divine, 36785
To the electors, 33278
Albany, Oct. 30, 1775, 13792
Albany centinel. News-boy's address, 35089
Albany collection, 37667
Albemarle, George Keppel, earl of, 1724-1772, Havana taken by, 9091, 9933
Albemarle district association. Minutes, 25084-85
Alberoni, Giulio, cardinal, 1664-1752, governor to King Philip, 2536
Albert and Emma, 34525
Alberthoma, Robertus, 1690-1772. Principles, 21636
Alberti, Michael. Narratio, 3656
Albertus Magnus
Anhagen an Gott, 9850
Kurzgefastes weiber-buchlein, 33311
Alcander and Rosilla, 34307
Alcuin, a dialogue, 34553
Alden, Abner, 1758-1820
Introduction to reading, 31706
Introduction to spelling, 31707, 36789
Alden, John, d. 1687, poem on, 426
Alden, Sarah, d. 1796, death, 32463
Alden, Timothy, 1736-1828, wife's death, 32463
Alden, Timothy, 1771-1839
Affection for the house, 28160
Appendix, 32463
Sermon, 36790-91
Alderman Blagge's case, 12892
Aletheleupheria, 8639
Alexander the Great. Epistles, 4660
Alexander, ———, of New York, house searched, 3716, 3848
Alexander, Ashton. Inaugural dissertation, 28161
Alexander, Caleb, 1755-1828
Columbian dictionary, 36792
Essay on the real, 23110
Grammatical elements, 25086
Grammatical institute, 26547
Grammatical system of the English, (1792) 24030, (1793) 25087, (1795) 28162, (1796) 29962, (1799) 35092

VOL.	ITEMS	VOL.	ITEMS
1	1-3244	8	22298-25074
2	3245-6623	9	25075-28145
3	6624-9891	10	28146-30832
4	9892-13091	11	30833-33261
5	13092-16176	12	33262-25854
6	16177-19448	13	35855-39162
7	19449-22297		

Odes, 37067
Oration, (1792) 24032, (1796) 29967, (1797) 31713, (1798) 33285, (1799) 35094, (1800) 36801
Allen, Richard. Narrative, 27170
Allen, S., engraver, 28930
Allen, Samuel, heirs of, 3106
Allen, T. Broke open, 20188
Allen, Thomas, of Boston. Directions for sailing, 10882
Allen, Thomas, of N.Y. New-York—1792, 24033
Allen, Thomas, of Pittsfield, ordained, 9700
Allen, Thomas, 1743-1810. Benefits of affliction, 33286, 35095
Allen, Timothy, 1715-1806
   Answer to Pilate, 9894
   Discourse, 24034
   Essay, 20921
   Main point, 9895
   Salvation for all, 17453, 17812
   Sermon, (1757) 8782, (1760) 8783, (1791) 23111
Allen, William, of N.H., ordained, 7694
Allen, William, d. 1768, murdered, 12772-73
Allen teutschen eltern, 5101
Allerneuste harfenspiel, 28623
Alley, Sarah. Account of a trance, 33287
Alleyne, John, letter (from Franklin), 34527
Allin, James, 1632-1710
   Man's self-reflection, 278, 858
   Neglect of supporting, 425
   New England's choicest, 260
   Principles, 502
   Serious advice, 261-2
   death, 1492
   reply to, 515?
Allin, James, 1691-1747 see **Allen, James, 1691-1747**
Allin, John, 1596-1671
   Animadversions, 83
   Spouse of Christ, 165
Alline, Henry, 1748-1784
   Gospel call, 28168
   Hymns, 28169, 31714
   Sermon, 31715
Alling, Roger, urges publishing of sermon, 5050
Allinson, Samuel, letter (from Wake), 13753
Allison, Burges, 1753-1827
   Oration, 32874
   Selection of psalms, 22593, 33939
Allison, Francis see **Alison, Francis, 1705-1779**
Allison, Patrick, 1740-1802
   Discourse, 36802
   Thoughts on the examinations, 10223
Allmächtige errettungshand, 9568
All's well, 9320
Allston, William. Inaugural essay, 31716
Allyn, ——, actor, 10573
Allyn, John. Their majesties colony, 686
Allyn, John, 1767-1833
   Office of a bishop, 26550
   Sermon, (1798) 35096, (1799) 36803
   ordained, 22274
Almanack of almanacks, 6805

ALMANACS

Adam astrologist, (1795) 26536, (1796) 28147-48, (1797) 29949
Aguecheek, (1760) 8291, (1761) 8526, (1762) 8781, (1763) 9050, (1764) 9319, (1765) 9566, (1766) 9893, (1767) 10222, (1768) 10537, (1769) 10813, (1770) 11139, (1771) 11545, (1772) 11956

Aitken, (1773) 12299, (1774) 12638
Albany, (1784) 17811, (1787) 20127, (1788) 20861, (1789) 21178, (1790) 22254
Alexandria, (1801) 36797
Allerneueste, (1777) 14644, (1778) 15236, (1779) 15721
Almanack, (1752) 6805, (1776) 13810-11, (1777) 14647, (1796) 28170, (1799) 33288, (1800) 35097, (1801) 36804
Americaanse, (1752) 6721, (1753) 6889, (1754) 7066, (1755) 7259, (1756) 7489, (1757) 7721, (1758) 7959, (1759) 8195, (1761) 8672, (1762) 8933, (1763) 9191, (1764) 9446, (1765) 9741, (1766) 10080, (1767) 10399, (1768) 10695, (1769) 10982, (1770) 11343, (1771) 11749
American, (1700) 861, (1701) 915, (1702) 981, (1703) 1054, (1704) 1112, (1705) 1164, (1706) 1208, (1707) 1247, (1708) 1297, (1709) 1356, (1710) 1393, (1711) 1457, (1712) 1501, (1713) 1548, (1714) 1612, 1684, (1715) 1683, (1716) 1747-48, (1717) 1814, (1718) 1889, (1719) 1962, (1720) 2028, (1721) 2126, (1722) 2227, (1723) 2345, (1724) 2439, (1725) 2543, (1726) 2647, (1727) 2755-56, (1728) 2891-92, (1729) 3046-47, (1730) 3175-76, (1731) 3292, 3294, (1732) 3430, 3432, (1733) 3555, 3558, (1734) 3631, 3671, 3674, (1735) 3754, 3783, 3876, (1736) 3876, 3918-19, (1737) 3994, 4028-29, (1738) 4125, 4147, 4150-51, (1739) 4256, 4259-60, (1740) 4372, 4374-75, (1741) 4535, 4540, (1742) 4733, 4736-37, (1743) 4978, 4985, (1744) 5219, 5222-23, (1745) 5418, 5423, (1746) 5613, 5618, 5646, (1747) 5793, 5812, (1748) 5977, 6011-12, (1749) 6171, 6195, (1750) 6341, 6369-70, (1751) 6522, 6553-54, 6719-20, (1752) 6696, (1753) 6858, 6887-88, (1754) 7029, 7064-65, (1755) 7219, 7257-58, (1756) 7438, 7492, (1757) 7690, 7724, (1758) 7928, (1759) 8158, (1760) 8378, (1767) 10457, (1768) 10741-42, (1769) 11042-43, (1770) 11418-19, (1771) 11824, (1772) 12197, (1773) 12529, 12954, (1775) 13546, (1776) 14402, (1777) 15029, (1778) 15554, (1779) 16013, (1780) 16478, 16675, (1781) 16726, 17070, (1782) 17109, 17434, (1783) 17486, (1784) 17860, (1785) 18386, (1790) 21654, (1791) 22313, (1792) 23112, (1793) 24047, (1796) 28309, (1797) 30100, 30701, (1798) 31722, 31836, 32386, (1799) 33431, 34012, (1800) 35213, (1801) 36808, 36816, 37844
Americanischer (Americanische), (1772) 11960, (1778) 15236, (1780) 16187, (1781) 16692, (1782) 17078-79, (1783) 17454-55, (1784) 17814-15, (1785) 18327-28, (1786) 18907-908, 19468, (1787) 19469, (1788) 20197-98, (1789) 20931-32, (1790) 21652-53, (1791) 22312, (1792) 23120, (1793) 24050-51, (1794) 25106-107, (1795) 26563-64, (1796) 28185-86, (1797) 29980-81, (1798) 31733, (1799) 33299-300, (1800) 35110, (1801) 36826
Ames, (1726) 2601, (1727) 2725, (1728) 2838, (1729) 2984, (1730) 3128, (1731) 3248, (1732) 3386, (1733) 3499, (1734) 3622, (1735) 3743, (1736) 3866, (1737) 3982, (1738) 4109, (1739) 4217, (1740) 4335, (1741) 4469, (1742) 4667, (1743) 4878,

VOL.	ITEMS	VOL.	ITEMS
1	1-3244	8	22298-25074
2	3245-6623	9	25075-28145
3	6624-9891	10	28146-30832
4	9892-13091	11	30833-33261
5	13092-16176	12	33262-25854
6	16177-19448	13	35855-39162
7	19449-22297		

ALMANACS

ALMANACS

(1737) 3994, (1738) 4125, (1744) 5143, (1745) 5350

Bowen, (1722) 2205, (1723) 2322, (1724) 2415, (1725) 2506, (1726) 2611-12, (1727) 2732, (1728) 2845, (1729) 2995, (1730) 3258, (1732) 3395, (1733) 3508, (1734) 3632, (1735) 3755, (1736) 3877, (1737) 3995, (1738) 4126

Bradley, (1775) 13174

Brakenbury, (1667) 113

Brattle, (1678) 245, (1682) 314, (1694) 687

Brigden, (1659) 54

Briggs, (1798) 31867-70, (1799) 33453-57, (1800) 35234-40, (1801) 37041-46

Browne, (1669) 135

Bullard, (1788) 20255, (1790) 21719, (1791) 22378, (1792) 23231, (1793) 24156, (1801) 37065

Brumbo, (1781) 16726, (1782) 17109, (1783) 17486, (1784) 17860, (1785) 18386

Burlington, (1771) 11899, (1772) 12254, (1773) 12584, (1774) 13048, (1775) 13690, (1776) 14524, (1777) 15118, (1778) 15617, (1791) 22384, (1792) 23241

Bushnell, (1793) 24167-68

Calendar of Maine, (1797) 30699

Calendrier, (1781) 17110, (1793) 25251, (1797) 30150, (1798) 31904

Cambridge, (1684) 736, (1685) 399-400, (1687) 436, (1776) 14062-63

Carey, (1801) 37100

Carleton, (1790) 21726, (1791) 22391, (1792) 23248-49 (1793) 24177, (1794) 25260-61, (1795) 26742, (1796) 28392, (1797) 30163

Carolina, (1783) 17745, (1794) 18211, (1787) 19542, (1796) 29940-42, (1797) 31682

Chandler, (1798) 31929

Chauncy, (1662) 69, (1663) 76, (1664) 87

Cheever, (1660) 57, (1661) 66

Christopher, (1754) 6978-79, (1755) 7170

Citizen and farmer's, (1800) 36296, (1801) 37185

Citizen's, (1801) 38491

Clap, (1697) 779

Clough, (1700) 861, (1701) 906, (1702) 970, (1703) 1041, (1704) 1104, (1705) 1153, (1706) 1203, (1707) 1243, (1708) 1292, 1345

Cockburn, (1772) 12012

College, (1761) 8621, (1762) 8884, (1773) 12357

Columbia, (1787 2009, (1788) 20438, (1789) 21181, (1790) 21907

Columbian, (1788) 20225, (1789) 20958, (1790) 21672, 21743, (1791) 22912, 22409-12, (1792) 23264-65, (1793) 24201-202, (1794) 25316, 25578, (1795) 26785-86, 27080, (1796) 28450, 28784-85, (1797) 30045, 30244-46, 30627-30, 30894, (1798) 32309, 32825, (1799) 33539, (1800) 35321, (1801) 37206, 38539

Concord, (1791) 22887

Connecticut, (1756) 7566, (1767) 10291, (1768) 10606, (1769) 10892, (1770) 11247, (1771) 11647, (1775) 13645, (1777) 15099, (1778) 15608, (1779) 16087-88, (1780) 16538, (1781) 17003, (1788) 20437, (1789) 21179, (1791) 23068, (1795) 27757, (1800) 36384-85, (1801) 38581

Continental, (1780) 16500, (1781) 16974-75, (1782) 17348-49, (1783) 17701, (1784) 18159, (1785) 18759-60

Copernicus, (1745) 5402, (1747) 5778, (1748) 5955, (1749) 6147, (1750) 6325, (1751) 6505, (1767) 10457, (1768) 10741-42, (1769) 11042-43, (1770) 11418-19, (1771) 11824, (1772) 12197, (1773) 12529, (1774) 12737-38, 12954, (1775) 13229-30,

13546, (1776) 13895, 14402, (1777) 15029, (1778) 15554, (1779) 16013, (1780) 16478, (1788) 21024-25, (1794) 25260

Counting-house, (1775) 13231, (1787) 19486

Countryman's, (1775) 13232

Croswell, (1800) 35165

Curtis, (1798) 32009, (1800) 35366, (1801) 37275

Daboll, (1773) 12371, (1774) 12743-44, (1775) 13235, (1776) 14001, (1777) 14724-25, (1778) 15280-81, (1779) 15777, (1780) 16250, (1781) 16755, (1782) 17131, (1783) 17507, (1784) 17902, (1785) 18432-33, (1786) 18982, 19596, (1787) 19595, (1788) 20313, (1789) 21038-39, (1790) 21779-80, (1791) 22439-40, 22544, 23420, (1792) 23305-306, (1793) 24240-41, 24366, (1794) 25368, 25564, (1795) 26841-42, 27066, (1796) 28523-24, (1797) 30308-309, (1798) 32012-13, (1799) 33595-96, (1800) 35368-69, (1801) 37279-80

Danforth, (1646) 18, (1647) 21, (1648) 23, (1649) 27, (1679) 265, (1686) 403-404

Davis, (1755) 7180, (1756) 7405, (1757) 7645, (1758) 7882

Daye, (1640) 3, (1641) 5, (1642) 8, (1643) 11, (1644) 14, (1645) 16

Delaware, (1788) 20326, (1789) 21536, (1790) 22215, (1791) 23011

Dickson, (1798) 32045, (1799) 33636, (1800) 35408, (1801) 37325

Douglass, (1743) 4935, (1744) 5168, (1745) 5380, (1746) 5575, (1747) 5763, (1748) 5935

Dudley, (1668) 121

Dunham, (1796) 28602-603, (1797) 30368, 32065

Eaton, (1688) 442, (1801) 37342

Eddy, (1760) 8341, (1761) 8588, (1762) 8846

Edes, (1769) 11078, (1770) 11479, (1771) 11870, (1796) 28615

Ehrliche kurzweiliche, (1764) 9384

Ellicott, (1781) 16770, (1782) 17145, (1783) 17527, (1784) 17920, (1785) 18457, (1786) 18999, (1787) 19619, (1788) 20341-42, (1789) 21071, (1790) 21808, (1791) 22482, (1792) 23347, (1793) 24295

Elliott, (1767) 10291, (1768) 10606, (1769) 10892, (1770) 11247, (1771) 11647

Ellsworth, (1765) 9651, (1766) 9965, (1767) 10292, (1768) 10607, (1769) 10893, (1786) 19000

Essex, (1769) 10920, (1770) 11283, (1771) 11675, (1772) 12064, (1773) 12410

Evitt, (1771) 11650, (1772) 12039

Family, (1776) 13895, (1798) 32106

Farley, (1799) 33707, (1800) 35459

Farmer's, (1714) 1724, (1716) 1793, (1717) 1863, (1718) 1937, (1719) 2008, (1720) 2087, (1721) 2195, (1722) 2304, (1723) 2405, (1724) 2494, (1725) 2593, (1726) 2718, (1727) 2827, (1728) 2975, (1729) 3119, (1730) 3235, (1791) 22618, (1792) 23496, (1793) 24470, 24847, (1794) 26254, (1795) 26962, 27792, (1796) 28250, 28647, 29626, (1797) 30400, 31294, (1798) 31786, 32114, 32922, 33172, (1799) 33389, 33708-709, 33787, 34394, 34654, 34968, (1800)

VOL.	ITEMS	VOL.	ITEMS
1	1-3244	8	22298-25074
2	3245-6623	9	25075-28145
3	6624-9891	10	28146-30832
4	9892-13091	11	30833-33261
5	13092-16176	12	33262-25854
6	16177-19448	13	35855-39162
7	19449-22297		

35167-68, 35538, 35460, 36138, 36414, 36680, (1801) 36925, 37397, 38630

Father Abraham, (1759) 8280-82, (1760) 8516, (1761) 8766, (1762) 9037, (1763) 9301, (1764) 9533, (1765) 9864, (1766) 10203, (1767) 10520, (1768) 10799, (1769) 11110, (1770) 11521, (1771) 11927-28, (1772) 12276-77, (1773) 12607-608, (1774) 13069-70, (1775) 13575-76, (1776) 14428-29, (1777) 15062-63, (1778) 15576-77, (1779) 16050-51, (1780) 16501-502, (1781) 16976, (1782) 17350-52, (1783) 17702-703, (1784) 18160-61, (1785) 18761-62, (1792) 23363, (1793) 24311, (1794) 25579, (1795) 27081-82, (1796) 28786, (1797) 30631-32, (1798) 32310, (1799) 34630, (1800) 36398, (1801) 38492

Father Hutchins, (1790) 21900, (1791) 22581, (1792) 23460, (1793) 24416-18, (1794) 25644-45, (1795) 27148

Father Richard, (1793) 26082, (1794) 26083, (1795) 27621, (1796) 29409, (1797) 31099, (1798) 32762, (1799) 34462, (1801) 38296

Father Tammany, (1786) 19391, (1787) 20160-61, (1788) 20897, (1789) 21617, (1790) 22292, (1791) 23093, (1792) 24014, (1793) 25059, (1794) 26510, (1795) 28135, (1796) 29925, (1797) 31662, (1798) 32826, (1799) 35057, (1800) 36297-98, (1801) 38493

Federal, (1788) 20860, (1789) 21083-84, 21580, (1790) 22252, 22293, (1791) 22498, 23043, (1792) 23981, (1793) 24416-18, (1794) 25472, (1795) 28065, (1797) 31614

Ferguson, (1790) 21821

Fleeming, (1772) 12043, (1773) 12391

Fleet, (1720) 2023, (1779) 15794, (1780) 16274, (1781) 16774, (1782) 17154, (1783) 17534, (1784) 17929, (1785) 18469, (1786) 19006, (1787) 19649, (1788) 20361, (1789) 21091, (1790) 21828, (1791) 22503, (1792) 23377, (1703) 24320, (1794) 25488, (1795) 26977, (1790) 28680-81, (1797) 30430-31, (1798) 32135, (1799) 33739, (1800) 35487

Flint, (1666) 107

Folger, (1790) 21830

Folsom, (1788) 21024-25, (1798) 32136-37

Foresight, (1784) 17931

Foster, (1675) 198, (1676) 212, (1677) 229, (1678) 247, (1679) 268, (1680) 283-84, (1681) 300-301

Fox, (1762) 8858, (1763) 9117, (1764) 9389, (1765) 9661, (1766) 9972, (1767) 10299, (1768) 10617, (1769) 10901, (1770) 11259, (1771) 11655, (1772) 12048, (1773) 12396, (1774) 12771, (1775) 13281, (1776) 14037, (1777) 14760, (1778) 15297, (1779) 15797, (1780) 16278, (1781) 16778, (1782) 17157, (1783) 17535, (1784) 17933, (1785) 18478, (1786) 19008, (1787) 19653, (1788) 20366, (1789) 21094, (1790) 21833, (1791) 22507, (1792) 23382, (1793) 24329, (1794) 25494, (1797) 30437

Franklin, (1741) 4511, (1801) 37100

Franklin's legacy, (1798) 32690, (1800) 35169, (1801) 36926

Freebetter, (1773) 12371, (1774) 12743-44, (1775) 13235, (1776) 14001, (1777) 14724-25, (1778) 15280, (1779) 15777, (1780) 16250, (1781) 16755, (1782) 17131, (1783) 17507, (1784) 17902, (1785) 18432, (1786) 18982, (1787) 19595, (1788) 20313, 20371, (1789) 21039, (1790) 21780, (1791) 22439, (1791) 22439, (1792) 23305

Freeman, (1767) 10305, (1768) 10620, (1769) 10902-905, (1770) 11265, (1771) 11659, 11675, (1772) 12049, (1791) 22512

Freemason, (1793) 24817

Freneau, (1795) 27018

Friend's, (1796) 28718-19

Fry, (1796) 28718-19, (1797) 30461, (1798) 32165

Fulling, (1799) 33771, (1800) 35527-29

G., G., (1752) 6672

Gaine, (1774) 12779, (1775) 13290-91, 13448, (1776) 14057-58, (1775) 14890, (1778) 15303-504, 15445, (1779) 15803, 15915-16, (1780) 16281, 16375-76, 16781, (1781) 16782, 16870-71, (1782) 17168, 17238-39, (1783) 17608-609, (1784) 18037-38, (1785) 18612-13, (1786) 19100-101, 19016, (1787) 19808-809, 19661, (1788) 20532-33, (1789) 21266-67, (1790) 21973-74, (1791) 22678-79, (1792) 23574, (1793) 24337, 24557, (1794) 25842, (1795) 27346, (1796) 29100, (1797) 30811, (1798) 32497, (1799) 34131, (1800) 35836, (1801) 37993

Gale, (1745) 5402, (1747) 5778, (1748) 5955, (1749) 6147, (1750) 6325, (1751) 6505

Gantz neue, (1776) 14430, (1777) 15064, (1778) 15578, (1779) 16052-53, (1780) 16503, (1781) 16978, (1782) 17353, (1783) 17704, (1784) 18162, (1785) 18763, (1786) 19223, (1787) 19965

Gatchell, (1715) 1741

Gemeinnützige, (1798) 32177

Gemeinüzige, (1801) 37497

General American, (1774) 12638

Gentleman and citizen's, (1762) 9016, (1763) 9278, (1764) 9520, (1765) 9847, (1766) 10175, (1767) 10502, (1768) 10775, (1769) 11079, (1770) 11480-81, (1771) 11650, (1772) 12039

Gentleman and lady's, (1775) 13229, (1781) 16784

Gentleman's, (1795) 27707, (1796) 29520, (1797) 31197, (1798) 32009, 32180, 32739, (1801) 38511

Gentlemen's, (1797) 30595, (1798) 32284, (1799) 33906, (1800) 35642, (1801) 37654

Genuine country, (1766) 10081

George, (1776) 14062-63, (1777) 14773, (1778) 15306, (1779) 15809-10, (1780) 16286, (1781) 16785, (1782) 17172, (1783) 17547, (1784) 17945-46, (1786) 19022, (1787) 19665, (1799) 33787, (1800) 35538

Georgia, (1771) 11894, (1800) 35234, (1801) 37041

German, (1791) 22532

Gillam, (1684) 359

Gleason, (1772) 12058-59, (1773) 12403-404, (1774) 12791, (1775) 13299-300, (1776) 14066, (1777) 14776-77, (1779) 15812, (1780) 16287-88, (1781) 16786, (1782) 17174-75, (1783) 17549, (1784) 17956, (1785) 18498-500, (1786) 19027, (1787) 19686, (1788) 20392, (1789) 21115, (1790) 21857, (1791) 22537, (1792) 23414-15, (1793) 24358, (1794) 25547-48, (1795) 27052-53

Goddard, (1785) 18457, (1787) 19687

Godfrey, (1730) 3168, (1731) 3284, (1732) 3422-23, (1733) 3545, (1734) 3658, (1735) 3772-73, (1736) 3907-908, (1737) 4018

Good old Thomas, (1767) 10398

Good old Virginia, (1801) 37532

Goodfellow, (1796) 28761, (1797) 30500, (1798) 32827, (1799) 33806

Grant, (1767) 10322

Green, (1789) 21038, (1790) 21779, (1791) 22544, (1792) 23420, (1793) 24366, (1794) 25564, (1795) 27066, (1796) 28767, (1797) 30510, (1798) 32207, (1799) 33817, (1800) 35566, (1801) 37545

Greenleaf, (1791) 22334, (1792) 23164, (1793) 24084, (1794) 25153, (1795) 26634-35, (1796) 28251-54, (1797) 30046-47, (1798) 31787, (1799) 33390,

ALMANACS

(1800) 35170-71, (1801) 37543
Grew, (1733) 3546, (1734) 3662, (1735) 3777, (1752) 6687-88, (1753) 6851, (1754) 7013, (1755) 7206-207, (1756) 7427-28, (1757) 7678-79, (1758) 7907-908, (1759) 8144-45, (1760) 8359, (1761) 8610, (1762) 8868, (1763) 9130, (1764) 9399, (1765) 9684, (1766) 9995, (1767) 10327
Hackley, (1794) 25577, (1795) 27079
Hale, (1794) 25578-79, (1795) 27080-82, (1796) 28784-87
Hall, (1769) 10920, (1770) 11283, (1771) 11675, (1772) 12064, (1773) 12410, (1789) 21126
Harper, (1801) 37580
Harris, (1692) 595
Harvard, (1690) 544
Haswell, (1792) 23828, (1794) 25591, (1795) 26536, (1796) 28147-48, (1797) 29949, (1798) 32236, (1800) 35600, (1801) 37596
Hobart, (1673) 175
Hoch-deutsch(e), (1739) 4253, (1740) 4370, (1741) 4528, (1742) 4728, (1743) 4972, (1744) 5210, (1745) 5411, (1746) 5611, (1747) 5788, (1748) 5970, (1749) 6159, (1750) 6332, (1751) 6518, (1752) 6695, (1753) 6855, (1754) 7022, (1755) 7212, (1756) 7431, (1757) 7682, (1758) 7913, (1759) 8152, (1760) 8371, (1761) 8619, (1762) 8881, (1763) 9139, (1764) 9404, (1765) 9699, (1766) 10004, (1767) 10333, (1768) 10645, (1769) 10927, (1770) 11292, (1771) 11682, (1772) 12075, (1773) 12417, (1774) 12810, (1775) 13332, (1776) 14119, (1777) 14800, (1778) 15364, (1779) 15852, (1780) 16304, (1781) 16798, (1782) 17189, (1783) 17560, (1784) 17974, (1785) 18528, (1786) 19041, (1787) 19715, 20095, (1788) 20415, 20826, (1789) 21146, (1790) 21890, (1791) 22571-72, (1792) 23444, (1793) 24401, (1794) 25614, (1795) 27127, (1796) 28842, (1797) 30570, (1798) 32262, (1799) 33885, (1800) 35627, (1801) 37629
Hodge, (1795) 27793, (1796) 29627, (1797) 31296, (1798) 32923, (1799) 34655, (1800) 36415, (1801) 37632
Holyoke, (1709) 1355, (1710) 1391, (1711) 1456, (1712) 1499, 1545, (1713) 1546, (1714) 1610, (1715) 1680, (1716) 1745
Houghton, (1797) 30595, (1798) 32284, (1799) 33906, (1800) 35642, (1801) 37654
Hughes, (1725) 2540, (1726) 2644, (1728) 2883
Hundertjährige, 37662
Huntington, (1761) 8621, (1762) 8884
Hutchins, (1753) 6857, (1754) 7024, (1755) 7213-14, (1756) 7435-36, (1757) 7684, (1758) 7919, (1759) 8153, (1760) 8374-76, (1761) 8622, (1762) 8886, (1763) 9145, (1764) 9411, (1765) 9704, (1766) 10023, (1767) 10341, (1768) 10656, (1769) 10931, (1770) 11298, (1771) 11690, (1772) 12083, (1773) 12420, (1774) 12815, (1775) 13345, (1776) 14125, (1777) 14807, (1778) 15369, (1779) 15854, (1780) 16308, (1781) 16807, (1782) 17192, (1783) 17562, (1784) 17980, (1785) 18531, (1786) 19047, (1787) 19725, (1788) 20423, (1789) 21165, (1790) 21900-901, (1791) 22409, 22580-81, (1792) 23460-61, (1793) 24416-19, (1794) 25644-46, (1795) 27148-50, (1796) 28873-77, (1797) 30614-17, 32296-98, (1799) 33919-20, (1800) 35172, 35649, (1801) 36927-32, 37669-70
Ivins, (1797) 30627-34, (1798) 32309-11
Jenks, (1799) 34395
Jerman, (1721) 2125, (1723) 2344, (1724) 2435, (1725) 2541, (1726) 2645, (1727) 2752, (1728) 2888, (1729) 3043, (1730) 3173, (1731) 3292, (1732) 3430, (1733) 3555, (1734) 3671, (1735) 3783, (1736)

3918, (1737) 4028, (1738) 4147, (1739) 4256, (1740) 4372, (1741) 4535, (1742) 4733, (1743) 4978, (1744) 5219, (1745) 5418, (1746) 5613, (1747) 5793, (1748) 5977, (1749) 6171, (1750) 6341, (1751) 6522, (1752) 6696, (1753) 6858, (1754) 7029, (1755) 7219, (1756) 7438, (1757) 7690, (1758) 7928, (1759) 8158, (1760) 8378
Judd, (1785) 18544-45, (1786) 19052-54, (1787) 19741-42, (1788) 20437-39, (1789) 21178-82, (1790) 21907, (1791) 22595-97, (1792) 23476, (1793) 24438-39, (1794) 25676-77, (1795) 27175
Keatinge, (1800) 35151
Keimer, (1726) 2708, (1727) 2836
Kentucky (Kentucke), (1788) 20441, (1789) 21185, (1790) 21912, (1794) 25688, (1795) 27184, (1796) 28927, (1797) 30658, (1798) 32338, (1799) 33954, (1800) 35684, (1801) 37728, 37730
Kollock, (1786) 19053
Ladd, (1794) 25934
Lady's, (1786) 19748, (1792) 23484-85
Lancaster, (1772) 12092, (1773) 12426, (1774) 12827, (1775) 13367, (1776) 14431, (1777) 15065, (1778) 15579-80, (1779) 16054-55, (1780) 16504-505
Larkin, (1796) 28947
Leavitt, (1797) 32365, (1800) 35721
Leeds, Daniel, (1687) 408, (1688) 430, (1689) 446, (1690) 473, (1691) 518, (1692) 551, (1693) 646, (1694) 692, (1695) 716, (1696) 744, (1697) 785, (1698) 821, (1700) 866, 1701) 915, (1702) 981, (1703) 1054, (1704) 1112, (1705) 1164, (1706) 1208, (1707) 1247, (1708) 1297, (1709) 1356, (1710) 1393, (1711) 1457, (1712) 1501, (1713) 1548, (1714) 1612, (1715) 1683
Leeds, Felix, (1727) 2755, (1728) 2891, (1729) 3046, (1730) 3175, (1731) 3293
Leeds, Titan, (1714) 1684, (1715) 1747, (1716) 1748, (1717) 1814, (1718) 1889, (1719) 1962, (1720) 2028, (1721) 2126, (1722) 2227, (1723) 2345, (1724) 2439, (1725) 2543, (1726) 2647, (1727) 2756, (1728) 2892, (1729) 3047, (1730) 3176-77, 3294, (1731) 3295, (1732) 3432, (1733) 3558, (1734) 3674, (1735) 3786, (1736) 3919, (1737) 4029, (1738) 4150-51, (1739) 4259-60, (1740) 4374-75, (1741) 4540, (1742) 4736-37, (1743) 4985, (1744) 5222-23, (1745) 5423, (1746) 5618
Leland, (1790) 21921, (791) 22618, (1792) 23496, (1793) 24470
Lewis, (1800) 35728
Lilly, (1801) 37829
Livermore, (1797) 30699
Lodowick, (1695) 717
Longworth, (1797) 30701, (1798) 32386, (1799) 34012, (1800) 35740, (1801) 37844
Loudon, (1786) 19499, (1787) 19500
Lover's, (1799) 34996
Low, (1762) 8906, (1763) 9164, (1764) 9422, (1765) 9714, (1767) 10358, (1768) 10664, (1769) 10951, (1770) 11317, (1771) 11704, (1772) 12100-102,

VOL.	ITEMS	VOL.	ITEMS
1	1-3244	8	22298-25074
2	3245-6623	9	25075-28145
3	6624-9891	10	28146-30832
4	9892-13091	11	30833-33261
5	13092-16176	12	33262-25854
6	16177-19448	13	35855-39162
7	19449-22297		

ALMANACS

(1773) 12438-39, (1774) 12837-38, (1775) 13384, (1776) 14168, (1777) 14829, (1778) 15381, (1779) 15870-71, (1780) 16324-25, (1781) 16821, (1782) 17202, (1783) 17575, (1784) 18004, (1785) 18561, (1786) 19063, (1787) 19760, (1788) 20466-67, (1789) 21208-209, (1790) 21925, (1791) 22623, (1792) 23511-12, (1793) 24483-84, (1794) 25732-33, (1795) 27235-37, (1796) 28988-89, (1797) 30707-708, (1798) 32391-92, (1799) 34020-21, (1800) 35746, (1801) 37854

Lyon, (1794) 26256, (1795) 27796, (1796) 29123

M'Cormick, (1792) 23520, (1793) 24489, (1794) 25738

M'Culloch, (1793) 24490, (1794) 25739, (1795) 27247, (1796) 29003, (1797) 30712, (1798) 32400, (1799) 34034, (1800) 35755, (1801) 37868

Mark Time, (1787) 20023, (1788) 20751, (1789) 21499, (1790) 22183

Maryland, (1733) 3546, (1759) 8173, (1764) 9426, (1767) 10368, (1768) 10672, (1769) 10956, (1770) 11324, (1773) 12448, (1776) 14180, (1780) 16506, (1781) 16770, (1787) 19619, (1788) 20341, (1789) 21071, (1790) 21808, (1791) 22482, (1792) 23347, (1796) 28231, (1798) 31867-69, 32433, (1800) 35151, 35235, (1801) 37897

Marylandischer, (1780) 16342

Massachusetts, (1772) 12058-59, (1773) 12403-404, (1774) 12791, (1779) 15812-13, (1780) 16288, (1781) 16786, (1782) 17174-75, (1783) 17549, 17800, (1784) 17956, (1785) 18498-500, (1786) 19027, (1787) 19686, (1788) 20392, (1789) 21115, 21126, (1790) 21857, 22073, (1791) 22537, 23044-46, 23070, (1792) 23414-15, 23962-63, 23984-85, (1793) 24358, 24994, 25018-21, (1794) 25547-48, 26441, 26463, (1795) 27052-53, 28064, (1796) 29624, (1797) 31028, 31291, (1798) 32919-20, (1799) 34652, 34969-70, 35001, (1800) 36413, (1801) 38628

Mather, (1683) 351, (1685) 395, (1686) 418

Maxwell, (1731) 3320

Meanwell, (1774) 12866, (1775) 13434, (1785) 18607

Mein and Fleeming, (1767) 10390, (1768) 10687, (1769) 10973

Melcher, (1786) 19798

Mercurius, (1743) 4935, (1744) 5168, (1745) 5380, (1746) 5575, (1747) 5763, (1748) 5935

Merlinus, (1733) 3588

Merry Andrew, (1775) 13437-38, (1776) 14258

Middlesex, (1787) 19800, (1788) 20523, (1789) 21256, (1790) 21962, (1791) 22916, (1792) 23808

Mills and Hicks, (1774) 12869-70, (1775) 13440-41, (1777) 14889, (1778) 15442, (1779) 15912, (1780) 16374

Miniature, (1787) 29487

Monmouth, (1795) 27018

Moore, R., (1762) 8932, (1763) 9190, (1764) 9445, (1765) 9740, (1766) 10077, (1767) 10394-95, (1768) 10692, (1769) 10980

Moore, T., (1761) 8671, (1770) 11341, (1771) 11747, (1772) 12130, (1773) 12467, (1774) 12871, (1775) 13447-48, (1776) 14262, (1777) 14890, (1778) 15445, (1779) 15915-16, (1780) 16375-76, (1781) 16870-71, (1782) 17238-39, (1783) 17608-609, (1784) 18037-38, (1785) 18612-13, (1786) 19100-101, (1787) 19808-809, (1788) 20532-33, (1789) 21266-67, (1790) 21973-74, (1791) 22678-79, (1792) 23574, (1793) 24557, (1794) 25842-43, (1795) 27346, (1796) 29100, (1797) 30811, (1798) 32497, (1799) 34131, (1800) 35836, (1801) 37993

More, R., (1750) 6369, (1751) 6552, (1752) 6718,

(1756) 7489-91, (1757) 7721-23, (1758) 7959-61, (1759) 8195-97, (1760) 8420-21, (1761) 8672-74, (1762) 8933-34, (1763) 9191-93, (1764) 9446-48, (1765) 9741-43, (1766) 10078-79, (1767) 10396-97, (1768) 10693-95, (1769) 10981-82, (1770) 11342-43, (1771) 11748-49, (1772) 12132, (1773) 12468

More, T., (1746) 5646, (1747) 5812, (1748) 6011-12, (1749) 6195, (1750) 6370-71, (1751) 6553-54, 6719-21, (1753) 6887-89, (1754) 7064-67, (1755) 7257-60, (1756) 7492, (1757) 7724, (1760) 8419, 8422-24, (1761) 8675, (1762) 8935, (1763) 9194, (1764) 9449-50, (1765) 9744, (1766) 10080-81, (1767) 10398-99, (1768) 10696, (1770) 11344, (1771) 11750, (1772) 12133

Moss, (1720) 2056

Mott, (1791) 22685, (1792) 23581, (1794) 25850, (1795) 27353, (1796) 29123-24, (1799) 34155

Nadir, (1743) 4935, (1744) 5168, (1745) 5380, (1746) 5575, (1747) 5763, (1748) 5935

Nathan, (1747) 5814, (1748) 6014, (1749) 6197, (1750) 6374, (1751) 6556, (1785) 18619, (1786) 19108

Nederduitsche, (1742) 4758, (1743) 5012, (1744) 5251, (1745) 5441, (1746) 5647, (1747) 5815, (1748) 6016, (1749) 6198, (1750) 6375, (1751) 6557, (1752) 6723, (1753) 6891

Neu-eingerichteter, (1747) 5816, (1748) 6017, (1749) 6199, (1750) 6376, (1751) 6558, (1752) 6724, (1753) 6892, (1754) 7069, (1755) 7263, (1756) 7497, (1757) 7725, (1758) 7962, (1759) 8198, (1760) 8425, (1761) 8677, (1762) 8938, (1763) 9198, (1764) 9452, (1765) 9746, (1766) 10083, (1767) 10403, (1768) 10697

Neue allgemein nützliche, (1801) 38030

Neue gemeinnützige, (1788) 20538-39, (1789) 21278-79, (1790) 21981, (1791) 22687, (1792) 23589, (1793) 24569, (1794) 25857, (1795) 27358, (1796) 29138, (1797) 30837, (1798) 32519, (1799) 34169, (1800) 35858, (1801) 38031

Neue hoch deutsche, (1791) 22688, (1792) 23590, (1793) 24570, (1794) 25858, (1795) 27359, (1796) 29139, (1797) 30838, (1798) 32520, (1799) 34170, (1800) 35859, (1801) 38032

Neue Lancästerischer (Lancästerscher), (1796) 29138, (1797) 30837

Neue Nord-Americanische, (1798) 32521, (1799) 34171, (1800) 35860, (1801) 38033

Neue verbessert, (1783) 17612

Neuer hauswirthschafts (hauszwirthschafts), (1798) 32525, (1799) 34174-75, (1800) 35863-64, (1801) 38037-38

Neuer Lancästerscher (Lancästersche), (1799) 34169, (1800) 35858, (1801) 38031

Neueste verbessert(e), (1763) 9199, (1764) 9453, (1765) 9748, (1766) 10084, (1767) 10404-406, (1768) 10698, (1769) 10987, (1770) 11351, (1771) 11754, (1772) 12136, (1773) 12471, (1774) 12876, (1775) 13451, (1776) 14270, (1777) 14897, (1778) 15449

Neugestellte, (1779) 15920, (1780) 16381

New, (1775) 13230, (1796) 28247

New England, (1686) 403-4, (1695) 717, (1701) 906, (1702) 970, (1703) 1041, (1704) 1104, (1705) 1153, (1707) 1243, (1708) 1292, (1722) 2205, (1723) 2322, (1724) 2415, (1725) 2506, (1726) 2611-12, (1727) 2732, (1728) 2845, (1729) 2995, (1730) 3138, 3258, (1732) 3395, (1733) 3508, (1734) 3632, (1735) 3755, (1736) 3877, (1737) 3995, (1738) 4126, (1763) 9303, (1764) 9536, (1765) 9868, (1766)

ALMANACS

10205, (1767) 10521, (1768) 10802, (1769) 11113-14, (1770) 11527, (1771) 11934, (1772) 12282-83, (1773) 12371, 12614, (1774) 12743-44, 13075, (1775) 13235, 13299-300, 13755, 13764, (1776) 14001, 14618-19, (1777) 14724-25, 15215-16, (1778) 15280-81, 15706, 15708, (1779) 15777, 16167-68, (1780) 16250, 16672, 16674, (1781) 16555, 17067-68, 19436, 19446, (1782) 17131, 17429-31, (1783) 17507, 17793-94, (1784) 17902, 18305-306, (1785) 18432, 18880, (1786) 18982, 19373, 19375-76, (1787) 19595, 20138, (1788) 20313, 20880, (1789) 21039, 21586, 21594, (1790) 21780, 22272, (1791) 22439, 23071-72, (1792) 23305, 23986-88, (1793) 24240, 24743, 24995, 25022-24, 25026, (1794) 25368, 26081, 26207, 26461, 26464-65, (1795) 26841, 27620, 27797, 28066, (1796) 28523, 29630, 29867-68, (1797) 30308, 31298, 32365, (1798) 32012, 33201, (1799) 33595, 35002, (1800) 35368, 36700, 36720-21, (1801) 36962, 37279

New Hampshire, (1786) 19798, (1791) 23047, (1793) 24764, (1794) 25933, 26117, (1795) 27379-80, 28038, (1796) 29386, (1797) 30368, 30857, 31073, (1799) 34433

New Jersey, (1742) 4670, (1743) 4885, (1744) 5123, (1745) 5333, (1746) 5533, (1747) 5736, (1748) 5903, (1749) 6092, (1750) 6281, (1751) 6460, (1752) 6634, (1753) 6811, (1754) 6958, (1755) 7146, (1756) 7352, (1757) 7614, 7745, (1758) 7838, (1759) 8077, (1768) 10798, (1769) 11109, (1776) 14524, (1777) 15118, (1779) 16095, (1780) 16549, (1781) 17010-11, (1782) 17380-81, (1783) 17748, (1784) 18217, (1785) 18811, (1786) 19276, (1787) 20034, (1788) 20852, (1789) 21569, (1790) 22007, 22238, (1791) 22716, 23031, (1792) 23613, 23955, (1793) 24596, 24980, (1794) 26417, (1795) 26608-609, 27698, (1796) 29178, 29504, (1797) 30865, (1798) 32833, (1799) 34542-43, (1800) 35214, 36302-306, (1801) 38498

New pocket, (1788) 21024-25, (1796) 29184, (1798) 32136-37

New town and country, (1796) 29505
New universal, (1764) 9450
New York, (1745) 5402, (1746) 5662, (1747) 5778, (1748) 5955, (1749) 6147, (1750) 6325, (1751) 6505, (1755) 7206, (1756) 7427, (1757) 7678, (1758) 7907, (1759) 8144, 8241, (1760) 8419, 8472, (1761) 8671, 8717, (1762) 8932, 8985, (1763) 9190, 9244, (1764) 9445, 9490, (1765) 9740, 9800, (1766) 10077, 10144, (1767) 10305, 10395, 10467, (1768) 10620, 10692, (1769) 10902-904, 10980, (1770) 11265, 11341, (1771) 11747, 11659, (1772) 12049, 12130, (1773) 12467, (1774) 12871, (1775) 13488, (1776) 14344, (1777) 14890, (1778) 15445, 15707, (1779) 15915, (1780) 16375, 16673, (1782) 17238, 17355, (1783) 17608, 17706, (1784) 18037, (1785) 18612, (1786) 19053, 19100, (1787) 19808, (1788) 20532, (1789) 21180, 21266, (1790) 21973, (1791) 22334, 22678, (1792) 23164, 23574, (1793) 24084, 24557, (1794) 25153, 25842, (1795) 26634-35, 27346, (1796) 28251-54, 29100, (1797) 30046-47, 30811, (1798) 31787, 32497, (1799) 33390, 34131, 34376, (1800) 35170-71, 35836, (1801) 37543, 37993

Newman, (1691) 544, 574, (1797) 30894
Newport, (1800) 35969, (1801) 38115
Norman, (1780) 16415
North American, (1769) 11078, (1770) 11479, (1771) 11870, (1772) 12235, (1773) 12566, (1774) 13028, (1775) 13638, (1776) 14473, (1777) 15096, 15212, (1780) 16188-89, (1781) 17069, (1782) 17432-33,

(1783) 17796-97, (1784) 18307-309, (1785) 18881, (1786) 19377-78, (1787) 20139, (1788) 20881-82, (1789) 21597, (1790) 22273, (1791) 22532, 23073, (1792) 23989, (1793) 24202, 25027, (1794) 26467, (1795) 28068, (1796) 29872, (1797) 31618, (1798) 33204, (1799) 35004

North and South Carolina, (1786) 19145, (1787) 20001, 20140, (1788) 20720

North Carolina, (1790) 22179, (1791) 22742, (1795) 27793, (1796) 29627, (1797) 31296, (1798) 32923, (1799) 34248-49, 34655, (1800) 36415, (1801) 37632

North Mountain philosopher, (1795) 28005, (1796) 29804, (1797) 31506, (1798) 33131, (1799) 34943

Norwich, (1793) 24167
Nowell, (1665) 104
Noyes, (1794) 25933-34, (1797) 30921
Oakes, (1650) 32
Oneida, (1801) 37342
Osborne, (1787) 19879, (1788) 20609, (1789) 21352
Osgood, (1801) 38171
Pack of cards, (1801) 38174
Paine, (1718) 1920, (1719) 1992
Palladium, (1788) 20905, (1796) 29940-42, (1797) 31682, (1798) 33256, (1799) 35069, (1800) 35236, (1801) 37042-44

Parsons, (1757) 7745
Partridge, (1692) 627, (1733) 3588, (1786) 19376-78
Pennsylvania, (1731) 3284, 3360, (1732) 3422, (1733) 3545, 3609, (1734) 3658, 3726, (1735) 3772, 3842, (1736) 3907, 3963, (1737) 4018, 4084, (1738) 4201, (1739) 4313, (1740) 4430, (1741) 4608, (1742) 4818, (1743) 5069, (1744) 5143, 5296, (1745) 5350, 5496, (1746) 5694, (1755) 7324, (1756) 7579, (1757) 7803, (1758) 8047, (1759) 8269, (1760) 8465, 8502-503, (1761) 8712, 8746, 8748, (1762) 8977, 9024-25, (1763) 9237, 9284, (1764) 9482, 9523, (1765) 9792, 9856, (1766) 10129, 10186, (1767) 10450, 10508, (1768) 10735, 10785, (1769) 11034, 11092, (1770) 11410, 11502, (1771) 11810, 11893, (1772) 12187, 12248, (1773) 12516, 12581, (1774) 12933, 13043, (1775) 13532, 13685, (1776) 14381, 14521, (1777) 15010, 15116, (1779) 15988, (1780) 16459, (1781) 16944, (1782) 17145, 17307, (1783) 17527, 17673, (1784) 17920, 18134, (1785) 18457, 18724, (1786) 18999, 19190, (1787) 19687, 19848, 19910, (1788) 20898, (1789) 21374, 21619, (1790) 22058, 22294, (1791) 22785, 23094, (1792) 23147, 23690, (1793) 24072, 24676, (1794) 25140, (1795) 26610-12, (1796) 28787, 29497, (1797) 30633-34, (1798) 32311, 32662, (1799) 34631, (1800) 36075-76, (1801) 38225, 38227

Pennsylvanischer, (1796) 29297, (1797) 30989, (1798) 32665, (1799) 34340, (1800) 36077

Perpetual, (1761) 8942, (1790) 22787
Perry, (1774) 12934, (1785) 18725
Philadelphia, (1775) 13648, (1776) 14482, (1778) 15553, (1779) 16012, (1800) 35728

ALMANACS

ALMANACS

Saur, (1796) 29139, (1797) 30838

Sewall, (1783) 17718, (1784) 18183, (1785) 18780, (1786) 19237, (1787) 19983, (1788) 20699, (1789) 21455, (1790) 22135, (1791) 22886-87, (1792) 23759, (1793) 24781, (1794) 26152, (1795) 27688, (1796) 29493, (1797) 31177, (1798) 32822, (1799) 34529-30, (1800) 36292-94, 36681, (1801) 38487

Sharp, (1776) 14430, (1778) 15580, (1780) 16500, 16503, (1782) 17348-49, 17353, (1783) 17701, 17704, (1784) 18159, 18162, (1785) 18759-60, 18763, (1796) 29497, (1798) 32825-27, (1799) 34535, (1800) 36296-98, (1801) 38491-93

Sheet, (1750) 6371, (1787) 19742, (1789) 21595, (1793) 25025, (1794) 25843, 26233, 26466, (1795) 26842, 27236, 27798, 28063, (1796) 28524, 28615, 29581, 29583, 29631, 29870, (1797) 30309, 30431, 30708, 31249, (1798) 32013, 32891-93, (1799) 33596, 34021, 34395, 34617, (1800) 35215, 35369, 36294, 36386, (1801) 37280

Shepard, (1672) 172

Shepherd, (1750) 6414, (1751) 6606, (1752) 6780, (1753) 6929, (1754) 7117, (1755) 7313, (1758) 8037

Sherman, (1674) 196, (1676) 223, (1677) 241, (1750) 6415-16, (1751) 6608-609, (1752) 6781-82, (1753) 6930-32, (1754) 7118-19, (1755) 7315-16, (1756) 7566, (1757) 7791, (1758) 8038, (1760) 8491, (1761) 8734

Shoemaker, (1795) 27698-99, (1796) 29504-506, (1797) 30701, 31189, (1798) 32386, 32833-34, (1799) 34012, 34542-47, (1800) 35740, 36302-307, (1801) 37543, 37844, 38498-99

Slygood, (1784) 18196

Smith, (1795) 27707, (1796) 29520, (1797) 31197, (1801) 38511

South Carolina, (1765) 10187, (1766) 10188, (1767) 10509, (1768) 10786, (1769) 11093, (1770) 11503, (1772) 12249, (1773) 12582, (1774) 13044, (1775) 13686, (1776) 14522, (1777) 15117, (1778) 15615, (1779) 16094, (1780) 16548, (1781) 17008, (1782) 17377, (1784) 18212, (1785) 18808, (1786) 19275, (1787) 19472, 20026, (1789) 21504, (1790) 22186, (1791) 22940, (1792) 23835-36, (1793) 24984, (1794) 26422, (1795) 28025, (1796) 29545, (1797) 31221, (1798) 32857, (1799) 34578, (1800) 36339-41

Southern states, (1787) 20001, (1788) 20720

Southwick, (1776) 13811, (1777) 14647, (1801) 38539

Stafford, (1739) 4311, (1740) 4428, (1741) 4607, (1742) 4815, (1743) 5065, (1744) 5294, (1745) 5495, (1776) 14479, (1777) 15098, (1778) 15609, (1779) 16088, (1780) 16539, (1781) 17004, (1782) 17374, (1783) 17732, (1784) 18202, (1785) 18799, (1786) 19264, (1787) 20015, (1788) 20733, (1789) 21482, (1790) 22170, (1791) 22917, (1792) 23809, (1793) 24827, (1794) 26232, (1795) 27755, (1796) 29582, (1797) 31250, (1798) 32892, (1799) 34594, 34618, (1800) 36354, (1801) 38550

Starry calculator, (1799) 34596, (1800) 36357

Stearns, (1769) 11078, (1770) 11479, (1771) 11870, (1772) 12235, (1773) 12566, (1774) 13028, (1775) 13638, (1776) 14473, (1777) 15096, (1783) 17727, (1784) 18196, (1787) 20007, (1788) 20725-27, (1789) 21476, (1790) 22162, (1791) 22906-907, (1792) 23798, (1793) 24817, (1794) 26207, (1795) 27740

Steuart, (1762) 9016, (1763) 9278, (1764) 9520, (1765) 9847, (1766) 10175, (1767) 10502, (1768) 10775, (1769) 11079, (1770) 11480-81

Steward, (1759) 8263, (1760) 8498, (1761) 8743

Stoddard, (1787) 20009, (1788) 20438, (1789) 21181, (1790) 21907, (1791) 22595, (1796) 29124, (1797) 30048, (1798) 31788, (1799) 33391, (1800) 35173, 36372, (1801) 37670

Storm, (1801) 38566

Stover, (1791) 22912

Strong, (1776) 14479-80, (1777) 15098-99, (1778) 15608-609, (1779) 16087-88, (1780) 16538-39, (1781) 17003-4, 19436, (1782) 17373-74, (1783) 17730-32, (1784) 18201-202, (1785) 18798-99, (1786) 19263-64, (1787) 20012-15, (1788) 20732-34, (1789) 21480-83, (1790) 22169-70, (1791) 22914-17, (1792) 23805-808, (1793) 24824-28, (1794) 26229-33, (1795) 27753-57, (1796) 29580-84, (1797) 31247-50, (1798) 32890-94, (1799) 34616-18, (1800) 36354, 36383-86, (1801) 38550, 38581

T., T., (1768) 10779, (1769) 11084, (1770) 11488

Tattle, (1799) 34630-31, (1800) 36398

Taylor, (1702) 1027, (1703) 1095, (1704) 1149, (1705) 1196, (1706) 1236, (1707) 1281, (1708) 1333, (1709) 1373, (1710) 1434, (1711) 1488, (1712) 1528, (1713) 1586, (1714) 1652, (1715) 1718, (1716) 1782, (1717) 1857, (1718) 1931, (1719) 2001, 2075, (1720) 2184, (1721) 2185, (1722) 2294, (1723) 2390, (1724) 2483, (1725) 2587, (1726) 2707-708, (1728) 2966, (1729) 3109, (1730) 3222, (1731) 3360, (1732) 3480, (1733) 3609, (1734) 3726, (1735) 3842, (1736) 3963, (1737) 4084, (1738) 4201, (1739) 4313, (1740) 4430, (1741) 4608, (1742) 4818, (1743) 5069, (1744) 5296, (1745) 5496, (1746) 5694

Telescope, (1775) 13648, (1776) 14482

Teutsche pilgrim, (1731) 3361, (1743) 3481, (1733) 3610

Thomas, I., (1775) 13299-300, (1779) 15813, (1780) 16288, (1781) 16786, (1782) 17174-75, (1783) 17549, (1784) 17956, (1758) 18498-500, (1786) 19027, (1787) 19686, (1788) 20392, (1789) 21115, (1790) 21857, (1791) 22537, (1792) 23414-15, (1793) 24358, (1794) 25547-48, (1795) 27052-53, (1796) 29624, (1797) 31291, (1798) 32919-20, (1799) 34652, (1800) 36413, (1801) 38628

Thomas, R. B., (1793) 24847, (1794) 26254, (1795) 27792, (1796) 29626, (1797) 31294, (1798) 32922, (1799) 34654, (1800) 36414, (1801) 38630

Thomas, T., (1760) 8502, (1761) 8746, (1762) 9024

Thomas, W., (1790) 22179, (1795) 27793, (1796) 29627, (1797) 31296, (1798) 32923, (1799) 34655, (1800) 34615

Thorn, (1792) 23828-29, (1794) 26256, (1795) 27796

Thornton, (1788) 20747, (1789) 21496, (1790) 22180, (1791) 22932, (1792) 23830, (1793) 24850, (1794) 26257, (1795) 27797-98, (1796) 20630-31, (1797) 31298

Time, (1787) 20023, (1788) 20751, (1789) 21499, (1790) 22183

VOL.	ITEMS	VOL.	ITEMS
1	1-3244	8	22298-25074
2	3245-6623	9	25075-28145
3	6624-9891	10	28146-30832
4	9892-13091	11	30833-33261
5	13092-16176	12	33262-25854
6	16177-19448	13	35855-39162
7	19449-22297		

ALMANACS

Tobler, (1755) 7324, (1756) 7579, (1757) 7803, (1758) 8047, (1759) 8269, (1760) 8503, (1761) 8748, (1762) 9025, (1763) 9284, (1764) 9523, (1765) 9856, 10187, (1766) 10186, 10188, (1767) 10508-509, (1768) 10785-86, (1769) 11092-93, (1770) 11502-503, (1771) 11893-94, (1772) 12248-49, (1773) 12581-82, (1774) 13043-44, (1775) 13685-86, (1776) 14521-22, (1777) 15116-17, (1778) 15615, (1779) 16094, (1780) 16548, (1781) 17008, (1782) 17377, (1783) 17745, (1784) 18211-12, (1785) 18808, (1786) 19275, (1787) 20026, (1789) 21504, (1790) 22186, (1791) 22940, (1792) 23835-36

Town and country, (1774) 12866, (1775) 13434, (1789) 21572, 21581, (1790) 22241, 22249-50, (1791) 23031, 23048-49, (1792) 23958, 23964, 23997, (1793) 23983, 25058, (1794) 25647, 26420-21, (1795) 27150, 27699, 28067, (1796) 28877, 29506, 29869, (1797) 30616, 31189, 31309, 31616, (1798) 32298, 32834, 33168, 33203, (1799) 34544-45, 35003, (1800) 36148, 36307, 36441-43, (1801) 36993, 38315, 38499, 38566, 39033

Town and countryman, (1788) 20855

Travis, (1707) 1334, (1709) 1377, (1710) 1435, (1711) 1490, (1712) 1530, (1713) 1589, (1714) 1654, (1715) 1719, (1716) 1784, (1717) 1859, (1718) 1932, (1719) 2002, (1720) 2077, (1721) 2189, (1722) 2296, (1723) 2392, (1724) 2486

Treat, (1723) 2393, (1724) 2487, (1725) 2589, (1726) 2711, (1727) 2817

True, (1798) 32941

Trueman, (1771) 11899, (1772) 12254, (1773) 12584, (1774) 13048, (1775) 13690, (1776) 14524, (1777) 15118, (1778) 15617, (1779) 16095, (1780) 16549, (1781) 17009-11, (1782) 17379-81, (1783) 17747-48, (1784) 18217, (1785) 18811, (1786) 19276, (1787) 20034

Tulley, (1687) 435, (1688) 454, (1689) 499, (1690) 548, (1691) 578, (1692) 630, (1693) 682-3, (1694) 710, (1695) 740, (1696) 776, (1697) 815, (1698) 854, (1699) 897, (1700) 955, (1707) 1028, (1702) 1097

United States, (1781) 17009, (1782) 17379, (1783) 17467, 17747, (1788) 20439, (1789) 21182, (1790) 21821, (1791) 22596, 22618, (1792) 23476, 23496, (1793) 24438, 24470, 24689-90, (1794) 24676, 25999, (1795) 27521, 27980, (1796) 28873-75, 29321, (1797) 30437,30614, 31008, 31474, (1798) 32296, 32689, 33101, (1799) 33919, 34546-47, (1800) 36599, (1801) 36934, 37934, 38912-13

Universal, (1756) 7491, (1757) 7723, (1758) 7961, (1759) 8197, (1760) 8291, 8424, (1761) 8526, (1762) 8781, (1763) 9050, (1764) 9319, (1765) 9566, (1766) 9893, (1767) 10222, (1768) 10537, (1769) 10813, (1770) 11139, (1771) 11545, (1772) 11956, (1773) 12542, 12979, (1774) 12980, (1775) 13290-91, 13577, (1776) 14057-58, 14433, (1777) 15066, (1778) 15303-304, (1779) 15803, 15916, (1780) 16281, 16376, 16781, (1781) 16782, (1782) 17168, 17239, (1783) 17609, 17727, (1784) 18038, 18196, (1785) 18613, (1786) 19016, 19101, (1787) 19661, 19809, 20007, (1788) 20533, 20725-27, (1789) 21267, 21476, (1790) 21974, 22162, (1791) 22679, 22906-907, (1792) 23798, (1793) 24337, (1801) 37065

Van Cuelen, (1789) 21536, (1790) 22215, (1791) 23011

Verbessert(e), (1785) 18851, (1786) 19339, (1787) 20095, (1788) 20826, (1789) 21539, (1790) 22216, (1791) 23012, (1792) 23932, (1793) 24954, (1794)

26374, (1795) 27992, (1796) 29786, (1797) 31485, (1798) 33113, (1799) 34916

Vereinigten Staaten, (1798) 33114, (1799) 34917, (1800) 36610, (1801) 38925

Vermont, (1784) 17931, (1785) 18725, (1792) 23828, (1794) 25591, 26256, (1795) 26536, 27079, 27796, 28095, (1796) 29123, 29895, (1797) 31637, (1798) 33228, (1799) 33707, 35031, (1800) 35459, 35600, 36723, (1801) 37596

Virginia, (1730) 3374, (1731) 3375, (1752) 6688, (1753) 6851, (1754) 7013, (1755) 7207, (1756) 7428, (1757) 7679, (1758) 7908, (1759) 8145, (1760) 8359, (1761) 6810, (1762) 8868, (1763) 9130, (1764) 9399, (1765) 9684, (1766) 9995, (1767) 10322, 10327, (1768) 10779, (1769) 11059, 11084, (1770) 11488, 11514, (1771) 11912-13, (1772) 12266-67, (1773) 12593, 13059, (1774) 12981, (1775) 13578-79, (1776) 14434, (1777) 15067, (1778) 15581, (1779) 16056-57, (1780) 16507, (1781) 16698, (1782) 17080, (1783) 17458, (1784) 17816-17, (1785) 18330, (1786) 18911-12, (1787) 19473, 19849, 20110, (1788) 20199-200, 20342, 20843, (1789) 20934, 21657, (1790) 21658, 22228, 22295, (1791) 22315-17, (1792) 23125-26, (1793) 24053, 24295, 24968-71, (1794) 25112-13, (1795) 26567-69, 28005, (1796) 28196-98, 29804, (1797) 29991, 30019-20, 31506-07, (1798) 31737, 31870, 33131-32, (1799) 33455-57, 34943, (1800) 35237-40, 36649-52, (1801) 37045-46, 37532

Wait, (1792) 23512, (1794) 25733, (1795) 27237, (1796) 28989

Waring, (1787) 20120-21, (1788) 20852-55, (1789) 21569-72, (1790) 22238-41, (1791) 23031-34, (1792) 23955-58, (1793) 24980-84, (1794) 26417-22, (1795) 28023-25

Warner, (1730) 3374, (1731) 3375

Warren, (1775) 13755, (1777) 15212

Washington, (1801) 39011

Watson, (1776) 14480, (1777) 15099

Weather-guesser, (1768) 10798, (1769) 11109

Weatherwise, (1759) 8280-82, (1760) 8516-17, (1761) (1765) 9863, (1766) 10203, (1767) 10520, (1768) 1765) 9863, (1766) 10203, (1767) 10520, (1768) 10799, (1769) 11110, 11521-22, (1771) 11927-28, (1772) 12276-77, (1773) 12607-608, (1774) 13069-70, (1775) 13575-76, (1776) 14428, (1777) 15062, (1778) 15576, (1779) 16050-51, (1780) 16501, (1781) 16976, 16979-80, (1782) 17350, 17354, (1783) 17702, 17705, (1784) 18160, 18163-64, (1785) 18761, 18764, (1786) 19224-25, (1787) 20124-26, (1788) 20859-60, (1789) 21579-81, (1790) 22249-53, (1791) 23043-49, (1792) 23962-64, (1793) 24994-95, (1794) 26441-42, (1795) 28037-38, (1796) 29846, (1797) 31583, (1798) 33168-72, (1799) 34531, 34968-70, (1800) 35529, 36679-81, (1801) 39032-34

Webster, (1785) 18545, (1786) 19054, (1787) 20127, (1788) 20861, (1789) 21586, (1790) 22254, (1791) 22597, (1792) 23829, (1793) 24439, (1794) 25677, (1795) 27175, (1796) 29871, (1797) 31617, (1798) 31789, (1799) 33392, (1800) 35174, (1801) 36935

Weems, (1799) 34996

West, (1763) 9303, (1764) 9536, (1765) 9868, (1766) 10205, (1767) 10521, (1768) 10801-802, (1769) 11112-14, (1770) 11526-27, (1771) 11933-34, (1772) 12281-83, (1773) 12613-14, (1774) 13074-75, (1775) 13763-64, (1776) 14618-19, (1777) 15215-16, (1778) 15705-708, (1779) 16166-68, (1780) 16672-75, (1781) 17067-70, 19446, (1782) 17428-34, (1783) 17792-97, 19445, (1784) 18303-309, (1785) 18873-

ALMANACS

END OF ALMANACS

VOL.	ITEMS	VOL.	ITEMS
1	1-3244	8	22298-25074
2	3245-6623	9	25075-28145
3	6624-9891	10	28146-30832
4	9892-13091	11	30833-33261
5	13092-16176	12	33262-25854
6	16177-19448	13	35855-39162
7	19449-22297		

VOL.	ITEMS	VOL.	ITEMS
1	1-3244	8	22298-25074
2	3245-6623	9	25075-28145
3	6624-9891	10	28146-30832
4	9892-13091	11	30833-33261
5	13092-16176	12	33262-25854
6	16177-19448	13	35855-39162
7	19449-22297		

Anecdotes of a little, 28201
    of the reign, 19153, 20601
Angel of Bethesda, 2352
Angelical life, 5488
Angelographia, 756
Angels ever bright, 36840
    ministering, 7417
    of the churches, 6110
    preparing, 2772
Angenehme opfer, 7372
Angenehmer geruch, 7610
Angier, Ames. Spiritual anatomizing, 1661
Angier, John, d. 1787. Sower going forth, 10821
Angier, Samuel, ordained, 10821
Anglais, Un see **Davis, John, b. 1776**
Anglus Americanus. To the citizens, 13118
Angus, John, captain Hibernia (brig), 22053
Anhagen an Gott, 9850
Anhang zu dem gesangbuch, 22495, 28641
Anhang zum widerlegten, 21604
Anhalt-Dessau, Dietrich, prince von. Letzte wylle, 6991
Animadversions critical, 9534
    on a late publication, 16519
    on a pamphlet, 10243
    on James Holland, 36841
    on Mr. Day, 25032
    on Mr. Hart, 11686
    on Mr. Paine, 29883
    on the reasons, 4895
    on the Rev. Mr. Croswell, 9371, 9903
    on The substance, 22168, 26227
    upon and the refutations, 5060
    upon the antisynodalia, 83
    with some brief, 7622
Animadversory address, 15719
Anketell, John. Poems, 28202
Anleitung zur englischen, 6455
Anmerkungen über ein noch nie, 9578
Anmerkungen über eine neuliche, 9668
Anmuthige erinnerung, 8644
Ann (ship), lawsuit over, 10945
Anna Matilda, poems by, 25807
Annals of New England, 7301, 7546-47
    of the troubles, 16059, 17707
    or history of Yale, 10262
Annan, ———, conduct of, 10152
Annan, David. Charge, 30822
Annan, Robert
    Brief animadversions, 20203
    Concise and faithful, 21659
    reply to, 23534
Annapolis
    At a meeting of the inhabitants, 13119
    Bye-laws, 11156
    Play-bill of Isabella, 19474
Annapolis, May 6; important, 17461
    May 23, 1769, 11157
    Dec. 24, 1784, 18542
    Jan. 20, 1785, 19069
    June 1, 1785, 19070
Annapolis circulating library. Catalogue, 17872
Annapolis (in Maryland) June 22, 1769, 11158
Annapolis, Maryland, Oct. 20, 13120
Anna's tomb, 22600
Anne, queen of England
    Instructions to our trusty, 1353
    Speech, 1607
Anne Arundel county
    At a full meeting, 13817
    To the inhabitants, 13816

Annerch ir cymru, 2286
Annesley, Thomas, signs ordinance, 27502
Annesley, William, life, 30728
Anningait and Ajut, 28977
Anniversary address, 22730
    oration, 17479
    sermon, (1776) 15256, (1777) 16169
Anno regni . . .
    For titles beginning thus see under colony con-
    cerned, e.g., **New York. Laws**
Annual history, 36438
    oration delivered, 34559
    oration pronounced, 36278
    pocket ledger, 30509
    register and political, 23127
    register and Victorian, 35113
    register of the Baptist, 23132, 26579-83
    report of the superintendent, 34272
Anonymous author see **March, Edmund, 1703-1791**
Anonymus's travels, 25114
Another and better, 2478
Another citizen
    Fellow citizens, 33727
    To the honest and industrious, 29644
    To the inhabitants, 13661
Another essay, 78
Another freeman. To the freeholders, 14495
Another high road, 10852
    letter, 1662
    tongue, 1307
    twig of the olive, 17820
Anrede an die deutschen, 9576
Anson, George, baron, 1697-1762. Lord Anson's voyage, 8534
Anstey, Christopher, 1724-1805. Election ball, 15724
Answer, &c., 1431
    in the form of a familiar, 11633
    of his excellency, 9973
    of several, 1517
    of the friend, 7385
        House, 1063
        pastor, 5934, 6082
    to a bill, 6808
        book entitled, 8302
        book entituled, 9340
        book lately, 2809
        dialogue, 37316
        late pamphlet, 2407
        letter from a gentleman, 7834
        letter from an aged, 8838
        letter of Dec. 26, 1763, 9579
        pamphlet containing, 20462
        pamphlet entitled, 6809
        pamphlet lately published, 12636
        piece entitled, A line, 10195
        piece entitled, An appeal, 18915
        printed letter, 4379
        small pamphlet, 2810

VOL.	ITEMS	VOL.	ITEMS
1	1-3244	8	22298-25074
2	3245-6623	9	25075-28145
3	6624-9891	10	28146-30832
4	9892-13091	11	30833-33261
5	13092-16176	12	33262-25854
6	16177-19448	13	35855-39162
7	19449-22297		

VOL.	ITEMS	VOL.	ITEMS
1	1-3244	8	22298-25074
2	3245-6623	9	25075-28145
3	6624-9891	10	28146-30832
4	9892-13091	11	30833-33261
5	13092-16176	12	33262-25854
6	16177-19448	13	35855-39162
7	19449-22297		

tions, (1731) 3388, (1732) 3500-501, (1738) 4218

Art of cheese making, 25123, 33315-16
    contentment, 7083, 31170
    courting, 28341
    curing, 31805
    excelling, 35254
    making, 14651-52
    manufacturing, 29946
    preaching, (1739) 4424, (1741) 4807, (1747) 6068, (1751) 6785, (1762) 9273
    preserving health, (1745) 5532, (1757) 7836, (1787) 20204, (1790) 22319, (1794) 26544
    preventing diseases, 28021, 33232
    reading, 38554
    rhetorick, 24404
    singing, 27204, 37787
    speaking (Burgh), (1775) 13850, (1780) 16727, (1782) 17487, (1785) 18945, (1786) 19535, (1790) 22381, (1793) 25239, (1795) 28373-74, (1800) 37068
    speaking (Webster), 21583
    war, containing the duties, 14816
    war lawful, 13276
    writing, 23469

Artaz, Hassan, humours of, 33487, 35265

Arthur (Negro), d. 1768
  Life and dying speech, 10822
  execution, 10952, 11299

Arthur, John. Genealogy of Jesus, 9057
Arthur, Thomas, 1724-1751. Sermon, 6457
Arthur, William. Family religion, 26576
Arthur Mervyn, 35243, 37053

Articles agreed upon by the archbishops, 448
    agreed upon by the foederal, 20791
    agreed upon by those, 11904
    and bye-laws . . . list of members, 38252
    and bye laws of the Friendship Fire, 38248
    and regulations of the Augusta, 35122
    and regulations of the Relief, 14347
    and rules, 5137
    containing the rules, (1793) 26507, (1798) 35056
    de confédération, 15628
    drawn up, 2896
    for the Boston, 3989
        Old, 22125
        government, 24065
    in addition, 24577-78
    of a treaty between, 36491-92
        treaty concluded at Fort M'Intosh, 19278
        treaty concluded at Fort Stanwix, 18817
        treaty concluded at Hopewell, 19279
        treaty concluded at the mouth, 20041
    of agreement &c., 27511, 34359
    of agreement between, 31188
    of agreement entered into, 21348
    of agreement for conducting, 30272
    of agreement made May 10, 1732, 4182
    of agreement made and concluded, 3710
    of agreement made and entered, 26586
    of agreement made on the 4th, 34849
    of agreement of the convention, 38714
    of agreement relative, 11162
    of an association, 19877, 20605
    of association, Mar. 7, 1734, 3749
    of association (Universal Tontine), 24950
    of association and agreement (Conn. land co.), 28475
      and agreement (New Eng. Miss. land co.), 34178
      and systems, 32574

    in Pennsylvania, 14370
    of the African, 36095
    of the first, 13705
    of the Havre, 32238
    of the New York, 30884
    of the trustees, 32471
  of belief professed, 13122, 30000
  of capitulation, 14540
  of confederation, (1776) 15148-49, (1777) 15619-27, (1778) 16105, (1784) 18818, (1785) 19349
  of consocation, 31970
  of faith and plan, 23009
  of faith and practice, 6504
  of faith of the Evangelical, 9968
  of faith of the holy, 7262
  of impost, 19476
  of incorporation, 7155
  of religion, 21961
  of the Amity, 31152
      Friendship, 31000
      Hibernia, 19918
      Reliance, 19919
      Social, 26125
      Star, 30896
  or by-laws for the government of the Associated, 34351
  of by-laws for the government of the Second, 36109
  published, 16145

Artifices of deceivers, 11709
Artikel der patriotischen, 12525
Artikel des bundes, 16106
Artist's assistant, 26577
Artykelen, 20792
Arundel, a novel, 37796
As a scandalous paper, 11163
As an answer, 18769
As it is generally, 11499
As the connexion, 14749

Asbury, Francis, 1745-1816
  Address to the annual, 20277
  Address to the subscribers, 21661
  Causes, evils, 24080
  Doctrines and disciplines, 34102
  Extract from the journal, 24060
  To the friends, 20206
  approves hymnbook, 22667, 29074
  conversations, 19097
  ordained, 18959
  presides conference, 20522, 21253, 21961, 22666, 23564, 24543, 30786, 32472

Ascanius see **Lowell, John, 1769-1840**
Ash, John, 1724-1779. Grammatical institutes, (1774) 13123, (1779) 16194, (1785) 18918, (1786) 19477, (1788) 20936, (1792) 24059, (1794) 26578, (1795) 38214, (1796) 30348, (1798) 33317, (1799) 35118, (1800) 36851
Ashburn, Rebecca. Three remarkable, 22320
Ashby, Joseph, reply to, 6694

VOL.	ITEMS	VOL.	ITEMS
1	1-3244	8	22298-25074
2	3245-6623	9	25075-28145
3	6624-9891	10	28146-30832
4	9892-13091	11	30833-33261
5	13092-16176	12	33262-25854
6	16177-19448	13	35855-39162
7	19449-22297		

meeting of a number of the freemen, 14654
meeting of a number of the inhabitants, 25818
meeting of a respectable, 13663
meeting of clergymen, 18743
meeting of . . . freeholders, 36672
meeting of many, 17463
meeting of . . . Republican, 36854
meeting of the board, 36493-94
meeting of the boarding-school, 30455
. . . meeting of the Boston, 19516
meeting of the committee appointed, 13396
meeting of the committee of inspection, 14141
meeting of the committee of observation, 14140
meeting of the committee of the county, 14821
meeting of the corporation, 18652
meeting of the delegates from each town, 14353
meeting of the delegates of every town, 13646
meeting of the delegates . . . of the province, 14178
meeting of the directors, 20603, 21349
meeting of the federal, 37775
meeting of the freeholders, (1766) 10245, (1767) 10564, (1774) 13160, (1781) 17105, (1782) 17480
meeting of the general, 37224
meeting of the governor and council, (1779) 16746, (1794) 26810
meeting of the governor and directors, 29032
meeting of the inhabitants of Charleston, 24186
meeting of the inhabitants of the city of Annapolis, 13119
meeting of the inhabitants of the city of Savannah, 29469
meeting of the inhabitants of the township, 37525
meeting of the Maryland, 24509
meeting of the merchants, 11576
meeting of the Middlesex, 34106
meeting of the Republican citizens, 36856
meeting of the Republican committee, 37526
meeting of the school committee, 19943
meeting of the subscribers, 29315
meeting of the true, 13126
meeting of the trustees, 20370
meeting of those, 17842
numerous meeting, 36857
publick town meeting, 2201
quarterly meeting, 21388
special General court, 347
town-council, 36180
town meeting called, 10716
town meeting held, 13498
town meeting of the freemen, 31095
treaty held with the Oneida, 33925, 36495
yearly meeting, 27021
At an adjourned town meeting, 16420
At an half-yearly, 21838
At her shop, 26529
At Pelham's book store, 30971
At the cockpit, 7676
    convention of the governour, 475, 482
    Parliament begun, 6708
    Superior court, 13426
    town house, 458
At this alarming, 11379
At this juncture, 11878
Athenian oracle, 1199
Atherton, Charles Humphrey, 1773-1853

Eulogy, 36858
Oration, (1798) 33320, (1799) 35121
Selection of the orations, 36859
Atkins, Dudley, 1760-1829. Address, 20210
Atkins, Robert, wronged, 11453
Atkins, Samuel. Kalendarium see **Almanacs (Atkins)**
Atkinson, Jonathan, ordained, 27323
Atkinson, William. Appendix of algebra, 33810, 37535
Atkinson, William King. Oration, 23123
Atlas for Winterbotham's history, 31647
Atlas minimus, 33794
Atonement of Christ, 20214
Attempt to collect, 20150
    to delineate, 31162
    to establish, 30148
    to explain, 20951
    to illustrate and confirm, 10003
    to illustrate the great, 12653
    to nip in the bud, 14684
    to point out, 8418
    to prove that digestion, 37527
    to prove the affirmative, 6093
    to shew and maintain, 17829
    to shew that America, 12861
    to translate, 26669
    to vindicate, 8538
Attention; or new thoughts, 22258
Attention to the scriptures, 29651
Atterbury, Francis, committed to Tower, 2380
Atticus. Character of Eusebius, 10547
Attorney general's answer, 3195
Attucks, Crispus, murdered, 11683, 12094
Atwater, Noah, 1752-1802
    Sermon, 20211
    hand of fellowship, 32424?
Atwell, Amos Maine. Address, 37189
Atwell, Thomas H. New York collection, 28216
Atwood, John, d. 1714, death, 1664
Atwood, John, fl. 1798, Imagination, 33321
Atwood, Joshua. Imagination, 33321
Aubin, Penelope. Noble slaves, 36861
Auborn, A. d'. French convert, (1751) 6631, (1761) 8790, (1769) 11164, (1793) 25125-26, (1794) 26587-91, (1795) 28217-18, (1796) 30003, (1798) 33322-24
Aubrey, Laetitia. Advertisement, 5039
Aubrey, William, daughter's death, 2851
Auchmuty, Samuel, 1725-1777
    Letter (to Montresor), 13818
    Sermon, (1766) 10231, (1770) 11970
    death, 15373, 15444
    letter (from C.J.), 14131
Auction of very select, 38256
Auf die einweisung, 34010
Aufforderung an das volk, 18548
Aufrère, Anthony, 1756-1833. Cannibal's progress, 33325-38
Aufrichtige nachricht, 5013

VOL.	ITEMS	VOL.	ITEMS
1	1-3244	8	22298-25074
2	3245-6623	9	25075-28145
3	6624-9891	10	28146-30832
4	9892-13091	11	30833-33261
5	13092-16176	12	33262-25854
6	16177-19448	13	35855-39162
7	19449-22297		

80, (1796) 30760, (1797) 32442-43, (1798-99)
   34065, 34067, 34069, 35789-90
Avery, John, of Truro, wife's death, 3729
Avery, Joseph, ordained, 14112
Avery, Ruth, d. 1732, death, 3729
Avery, Stephen. By permission of the legislature,
   33242
Avis au public, 15861
Awakening call, 3650, 4923
   calls, 4214
   soul-saving, 2147
   thoughts, 1549
   truths, 1470

Award and final, 7837
Awful crisis, 36638
   death, 35131
   malignant fever, 31018
Axe, ———
   Card, 10849, 11198
   reply to, 11199
Ayer, Oliver, ordained, 25932
Ayres, Capt.
   commands tea ship, 13487
   returns to England, 12945
   threatened, 12942

B

B. see **Bordley, John Beale, 1727-1804**
B., A. see **Appleton, Nathaniel, 1693-1784; Benezet,
   Anthony, 1713-1784; Byfield, Nathaniel, 1653-
   1733; Franklin, Benjamin, 1706-1790**
B****, A****.** Proposals for erecting, 11555
Babcock, Samuel, Middlesex harmony, 28221
Bach, Johann Christian, 1735-1782. Cease a while,
   28222
Bache, Benjamin Franklin, 1769-1798
   (tr.) Important state paper, 27003
   Remarks occasioned, 31759
   Sketch of the present, 32115
   attacks Cobbett, 31946
   publishes letter, 33529
   satire on, 33524
Bache, Richard. To the citizens, 16949
Bache, Theophylact, affidavit by, 14332
Bache, William. Inaugural experimental, 26598
Bacheller, Rev. ———, of Haverhill
   charges against, 8617
   defended, 8873
   doctrinal dispute, 8562
   remarks on, 8814
Bacheller, Samuel. Vindication of an association,
   8272
Bachelor's address, 23138
Bachmair, John James
   Complete German grammar, (1772) 12315, (1774)
      13127, (1793) 25128
   Erste oder theoretische, 20938
   German grammar, 20937
Back settler. Some fugitive thoughts, 13630
Backus, Azel, 1765-1817
   Absalom's conspiracy, 33348-51
   Sermon, 31761
   ordained, 23141
Backus, Charles, 1749-1803
   Afflictions improved, 25129
   Benevolent spirit, 33352

Discourse, 18920
Faithful ministers, 23141
Five discourses, 31762
Folly of man's choosing, 30008
High importance, 35133
Living warned, 35134
Man's mortality, 26599
Ministers serving God, 30009
Principal causes, 33353
Qualifications, 28223
Scripture doctrine, 36872
Sermon, (1788) 20939, (1793) 25130, (1795)
   30010, (1799) 35135
True Christian, 33354
son's death, 27119
Backus, Elizabeth, d. 1769, death, 11166
Backus, Isaac, 1724-1806
   Address to the inhabitants, 20212
   Address to the Second Baptist, 20213
   All true ministers, 7145
   Answer to Mr. Wesley, 23139
   Appeal to the public, 12654
   Atonement of Christ, 20214
   Charge, (1795) 28227, (1797) 32882
   Church history, 18336, 30011
   Discourse, 12655
   Doctrine of sovereign, 11971

VOL.	ITEMS	VOL.	ITEMS
1	1-3244	8	22298-25074
2	3245-6623	9	25075-28145
3	6624-9891	10	28146-30832
4	9892-13091	11	30833-33261
5	13092-16176	12	33262-25854
6	16177-19448	13	35855-39162
7	19449-22297		

Doctrine of the particular, 21663
Doctrine of universal, 17464
Door opened, 17824
Evangelical ministers, 12316
Family prayer, 10232
Fish caught, 10823
Godliness excludes, 18921
Gospel comfort, 11166
Government and liberty, 15727
History of New England, 15240
Infinite importance, 23140
Kingdom of God, 24061
Letter (to a gentleman), 11972
Letter (to Lord), 9587
Liberal support, 22322
Nature and necessary, 24062
Policy as well, 16195
Reply to a piece, 12317
Seasonable plea, 11556
Sermon, 7612
Short description, 7613, 11557
Sovereign decrees, 12656
Spiritual ignorance, 9330
Substance of an address, 16196-97
Testimony of the two, 19485, 25131
True faith, 10549
Truth is great, 17083
approves hymns, 23632
letter (from Holly), 12076
moderator, 20731
remarks on, 12042
Backus, Jabez, d. 1794, death, 27119
Backus, Joseph
  Proclamation, 2726
  orders whipping, 2606
Backus, Rufus. Sir, at a meeting, 33910
Bacon, Asa, 1771-1857. Oration, 35136
Bacon, Ezekiel, 1776-1870. Oration, 35137
Bacon, Sir Francis. Essaies, 447
Bacon, Friar, history of, 3668
Bacon, James. Funeral sermon, 33355
Bacon, John, 1737-1820
  Illustrations illustrated, 17084
  Letter (to Huntington), 17465
  Letters of gratitude, 17085
  Reprimander reprimanded, 17086
  Sermon, 12318
  appendix by, 17071
  ordained, 12419
  reply to, 17191
Bacon, Nathaniel, 1593-1660. Relation of the fear-
  ful, (1682) 310, (1683) 338, (1762) 9059, (1770)
  11558, (1772) 12657, (1796) 30012, (1798) 33356-
  57
Bacon, Nathaniel, 1648-1676, rebellion, 3407
Bacon, Thomas. Laws of Maryland, 10049
Bad omen, 6051
Badcock, Josiah, ordained, 17789
Badger, Stephen, 1726-1803
  Address, 18337
  Nature and effects, 13128
  ordained, 6955
Bag of nuts, 20748, 34662
Bage, Robert, 1728-1801. Man as he is, 28224
Bagg, James, d. 1766, death, 10747
Bagg, Jonathan, d. 1766, death, 10747
Bagley, Azar, petition, 33009
Bagley, Jonahan, sermon before, 7813
Bailey, ——, grammarian, 4011, 5762, 6485, 7884,
  10603
Bailey, Abner see **Bayley, Abner, d. 1798**

Bailey, Ebenezer. Funeral elegy, 31763
Bailey, Francis. Almanac see **Almanacs (Bailey)**
Bailey, Isaac, ordained, 19031
Bailey, John, 1643-1697
  Man's chief end, 456
  To my loving, 457
  death, 828, 831
Bailey, Joseph. God's wonders, 6458-59
Bailey, Kiah
  Substance of a discourse, 33359
  ordained, 33671
Bailey, Nathan, d. 1742. English and Latine, 2092
Bailey, Rhoda, d. 1797?, elegy for, 31763
Baily, James, letter (from Balch), 5735
Baily, John see **Bailey, John, 1643-1697**
Baillie, Matthew, 1761-1823. Morbid anatomy,
  28226
Baine, John, & co., type founders, 22329
Baker, ——, aerial voyage, 30099
Baker, Charles. Map of the county, 26481
Baker, Christina, letter (from Seguenot), 3216
Baker, Daniel, 1687-1731. Two sermons, 2988
Baker, Gardiner
  Notice; the subscriber, 23142
  keeper of museum, 25908
Baker, George A., petitions by, 18335
Baker, Joel, ordained, 32082
Baker, John. Hypocrite unmask'd, 33360
Baker, Joseph, 1779-1800?
  Confession, 36873
  pirate, 37391, 37781
Baker, Josiah, conference at home of, 36204
Baker, Polly. Speech, 35007
Baker, William, life, 35297, 37156
Bakewell, Robert. Method of breeding, 28247
Balance of the sanctuary, 2906
Balbani, Niccolo, d. 1587. Italian convert, 6633,
  26601
Balch, Benjamin
  Short account, 12658
  ordained, 11167
Balch, Stephen Bloomer, 1747-1833. Two sermons,
  23143
Balch, Thomas, 1711-1774
  Christ always present, 6091
  Discourse, 7838
  Preaching the gospel, 5902
  Sermon, 9331, 11167
Balch, William, 1704-1792
  Apostles St. Paul, 5121
  Duty of a Christian, 3502, 3868
  Duty of ministers, 5332
  False confidences, 5122
  Publick spirit, 6280
  Reconciliation, 4470
  Reply to the articles, 5406
  Simplicity, 8537
  Vindication of some, 5734
  Vindication of the second, 5735
  dispute over doctrine, 5738
  remarks on, 5890
Baldwin, Abraham, 1754-1807
  Review of the revenue, 26973
  memorial referred to, 32976-77
  message referred to, 33054-55, 34799
  produces papers, 24917
  reports on ratification, 21520
  reports on treasury report, 21516
Baldwin, Ashbel, 1757-1846. Discourse, 33361
Baldwin, Ebenezer, 1745-1776
  Appendix stating, 13614

VOL.	ITEMS	VOL.	ITEMS
1	1-3244	8	22298-25074
2	3245-6623	9	25075-28145
3	6624-9891	10	28146-30832
4	9892-13091	11	30833-33261
5	13092-16176	12	33262-25854
6	16177-19448	13	35855-39162
7	19449-22297		

VOL.	ITEMS	VOL.	ITEMS
1	1-3244	8	22298-25074
2	3245-6623	9	25075-28145
3	6624-9891	10	28146-30832
4	9892-13091	11	30833-33261
5	13092-16176	12	33262-25854
6	16177-19448	13	35855-39162
7	19449-22297		

Bayard, Samuel, 1767-1840. Funeral oration, 36911
Bayard, William. To the honourable, 11371
Bayley, Rev. ——, hand of fellowship, 7116
Bayley, Abner, d. 1798
  Duty of ministers, 9597
  Promises through Christ, 16708
Bayley, Daniel
  Collection of anthems, 18341
  Essex harmony, (1770) 11560, (1771) 11979, (1772) 12319, (1780) 16709, (1785) 18925
  New and complete introduction, (1764) 9598-9600, (1766) 10236, (1768) 10829
  New harmony, 20956
  New universal harmony, 12664
  Psalm singer's assistant, 18926
Bayley, Deborah, d. 1772, death, 12962
Bayley, Frye, wife's death, 12962
Bayley, Jacob. Public defence, 16391
Bayley, Josiah, ordained, 7841
Bayley, Kiah see **Bailey, Kiah**
Bayley, Richard, 1745-1801
  Account of the epidemic, 30041
  Cases of the angina, 17092
  Letter (to Bard), 23162
  Letters from the Health-office, 35161
Bayley, Samuel, book auction at shop of, 22394
Baylies, William, 1783-1865. Funeral oration, 26628
Bayly, ——, grammarian, 8582
Bayly, James
  Brief narrative, 5738
  letter (from Balch), 5735?
Bayly, Lewis, d. 1632
  Manitowompae, 95, 383
  Practice of piety, 1797, 1944
Baynum, Bartholomew, treason of, 17519
Bazin, John. John Bazin at his store, 31781
Be followers of them, 7548
Be liberty thine, 14819
Be merry and wise, (1762) 9285-86, (1786) 20028
Beach, Jesse
  Charge, 33751
  Oration, 33385
Beach, John, 1700-1782
  Appeal to the unprejudiced, 4113
  Attempt to prove, 6093
  Attempt to vindicate, 8538
  Calm and dispassionate, 6283
  Continuation, 6637
  Defence of the second, 10237
  Duty of loving, 4337
  Familiar conference, 9601
  Friendly expostulation, 9336
  Funeral sermon, 12320
  God's sovereignty, 5906
  Modest enquiry, 7355
  Second familiar conference, 9910
  Second vindication, 6094
  Sermon, 5535
  Three discourses, 10830
  Vindication of the worship, 3984
  attacked, 4237
  death, 17581
  remarks on, 5761
  reply to, 4136, 4237, 6123, 6483, 6693, 9534, 10028, 10348
  successor, 3653
Beach, Lazarus, proposals for publishing magazine, 25344
Beacon Hill, a local poem, 32512
Beadle, Lydia, d. 1782, death, 18009, 21216
Beadle, William, d. 1782, death, 17828, 17903, 18009, 21216, 26629, 28246, 30042
Beadle, William A.
  Narrative, (1783) 17828, (1794) 26629, (1795) 28246
  William Beadles lebenschreibung, 30042
Beale, Dr. ——, dialogue with, 15811
Bealer, Charles, d. 1793, death, 25617
Beall, Isaac. Funeral discourse, 36912
Beall, Joshua, letter (from Henderson), 14113
Beaman, Capt. ——, waggon master, 15343
Bean, Joseph, d. 1784. Sermon, 13136
Beane, Sauney, account of, 20132-33
Bear ye one another's burdens, 35298, 37163
Beard, Thomas, 1693-1710. Life, 3869
Bearss, Benjamin, wife's death, 24753
Beatifick vision, 3762
Beattie, Andrew, 1768-1801
  hand of fellowship, 36152
  ordained, 32625
Beattie, James, 1753-1803
  Elements of moral science, 24081, 26630
  Evidences of the Christian, 20223
  The hermit, 31953
  Minstrel, or itinerant, 18342
  Poems, 18343, 20224
  excerpts from, 23246
Beatty, ——
  reports on accounts, 18833
  reports on supplies, 19308
Beatty, Charles
  Double honor, 7843
  Sermon, 6817
  ordained, 5497
Beau metamorphized, 38011
Beaufort, James. Hoyle's games, 30598-99
Beaumarchais, Pierre Auguste, 1732-1799. Observations, 17093
Beaumont, H. New York theatre, 17635
Beaumont, William H. Ohio navigator, 33915-16
Beauties of Blair, 24121-22
  of Fielding, 24317
  of Goldsmith, 32200
  of Hervey, (1794) 27115, (1796) 30558, (1797) 32249
  of history, (1787) 20336, (1794) 27749-51, (1795) 29577, (1796) 30355
  of Madam Genlis, 23406
  of nature, 38583
  of poetry, 23246
  of Poor Richard, 8730
  of psalmody, 19749
  of religion, 21826
  of spring, 8379
  of Sterne, (1789) 22163, (1790) 22908, (1791) 23799, (1793) 26208-209
  of the Bible, 38459
    creation, (1792) 24745, (1796) 31105, (1798) 34470
    late Rev. Dr., 31574, 33161
    muses, 25149

VOL.	ITEMS	VOL.	ITEMS
1	1-3244	8	22298-25074
2	3245-6623	9	25075-28145
3	6624-9891	10	28146-30832
4	9892-13091	11	30833-33261
5	13092-16176	12	33262-25854
6	16177-19448	13	35855-39162
7	19449-22297		

studies, 36266
Beautiful appearance, 7901
Beautiful little novel, 33877
Beauty and benefits, 38605
   and loveliness, 2813
   and the monster, 19021
   of holiness, 31831
Beauvois, A. M. F. J.
   Catalogue, 36915
   Scientific and descriptive, 30967
Beaven, Samuel
   Lay-liberty, 6961
   Religious liberties, 6962
Beaven, Thomas. Essay, 3985
Beccaria, Cesare, 1738-1794. Essay on crimes,
   (1773) 12665, (1778) 15730, (1793) 25150
Bechtel, Johann, 1690-1777
   Abermaliger vorschlag, 4888
   Kort catechismus, 5126
   Kurzer catechismus, 4889
   Short catechism, 4890
Beck, John. Doctrine of perpetual, 36916
Becker, Christian Ludwig, 1756-1818. Religion
   Jesu, 30043
Beckett, William. Duty of both clergy, 3133
Beckford, ———. Speeches, 10463
Beckford, William, letters (from Brydone), 24150,
   33467-68
Beckley, John James, 1757-1807
   Address to the people, 36917-20
   Epitome of the life, 36921
   clerk U.S. House, 22007, 22200
   clerk Va. House, 19352, 20101, 20838-39
   Potomac commissioner, 19274
Beckwith, George, 1703-1794
   Adam's losing, 3871
   Attempt to show, 17829
   Christ the alone, 4891
   Infant seed, 11561
   Invalidity, 9337
   Ministers of the gospel, 6818
   Second letter, 10238
   That people, 7617
   Two sermons, 5334
   Visible saints, 11170
   Whatsoever God, 4338
   ordained, 3316
   reply to, 10646, 11279
Beddoes, Thomas, 1760-1808. Observations, 31782
Bedell, Gregory. Closet companion, 33386
Bedford, ———, duke of, attacks Burke, 30142-43
Bedford, Gunning, 1747-1812
   Funeral oration, 36922
   reports on Northwest Territory, 18264
   reports on supplies, 19308
Bedlow, Henry, trial, 26513
Bee, by William Honeycomb, 10006
Beebee, David Lewis, ordained, 23994
Beebee, Samuel. Answer to Mr. Wadsworth, 2315
Beech, ———, letter (from Jouet), 28911
Beeckley, Abraham, inspects lottery drawing,
   12192
Beedé, Thomas, d. 1848. Oration, 35163
Beelzebub see **Bourn, Benjamin**
Beeman, Anna
   Hymns, (1792) 24082, 24195, (1793) 25304
   Three letters, 26631
Beers, Andrew, 1749-1824. Almanac see **Almanacs**
   (Beers)
Beers, William Pitt, 1766-1810
   Address, 23165

Oration, 36936
Beert, Samuel see **Brett, Samuel**
Beete ———. Man of the times, 31790
Beggar and no beggar, 6284
Beggar girl, 33401
Beggarly boy, 35297
Beggar's opera, 6673
Behaim, Martin, examined, 24085
Beissel, Johann Conrad, 1690-1768
   Büchlein, 2990
   Deliciae ephratenses, 12666
   Dissertation, 9911
   Ehe das zuchthaus, 3251
   Göttliche liebes, 3253
   Jacobs kampff- und ritter-platz, 3896
   Mystische abhandlung, 5536
   Mystische und sehr geheyme, 3252
   Neu-vermehrtes gesäng, 9062
   Neun und neunzig, 2991
   Paradisisches wunder-spiel, 7147, 10239
   Urständliche und erfahrungs-volle, 5538
   Vorspiel der neuen-welt, 3503
   Zionitischen stiffte, 5537
   life, 19558
   quarrel with Saur, 4420
Bekanntmachung, (1741) 4796, (1743) 5280, (1764)
   9880
Belair, Alexandre Pierre, 1747-1819. Elements of
   fortification, 35175
Belcher, Abigail, d. 1771, death, 12555
Belcher, Jonathan
   At a conference, 3916
   Conference, 3554
   Ordinance for regulating, 7502
Belcher, Jonathan, d. 1757
   Proclamation, (1730) 3309-10, (1731) 3444,
     (1732) 3567-68, (1733) 3684, (1734) 3793, (1735)
     3926, (1737) 4160, (1738) 4269, (1740) 4553-54,
     (1741) 4746
   arrival, 3282
   death, 7861, 8097
   dedication to, 3428, 3548, 3666, 3780, 3914, 4025,
     4143, 4229, 4252, 4369, 4525, 4726, 4968
   epistle (from Byles), 3999
   made governor, 4068
   memorial to, 7508
   sermon before, 3262, 3417, 4026, 4153, 4321
   wife's death, 3999, 4067, 12555
Belcher, Joseph, 1669-1723
   Copy of a letter, 30049, 36937
   Duty of parents, 1443
   God giveth, 2316
   Singular happiness, 968
   Worst enemy, 816
   death, 2454
   paper in possession of, 4242
Belcher, Mary, d. 1736, death, 4067
Belcher, Samuel, 1640-1714
   Concio ad magistratum, 1288
   Essay tending to promote, 1289
Belcher, Supply, 1751-1836
   Harmony of Maine, 26636
   Ordination anthem, 31791
Belden, Elizur, d. 1786, death, 19714
Belden, Jonathan, 1774-1844. Oration, 36938
Belding, Anne, d. 1773, death, 13264
Belding, Joshua, wife's death, 13264
Belgrove, William. Treatise upon husbandry, 7356
Believer in politicks. Political creed, 11047, 11420
Believer's espousals, 4506
   gain, 1632

golden chain, 5170
   happy change, 802
Believers in Christ, 4989
   invited, 1852
   most sure freedom, 8051
   proved to be, 33588
Believer's redemption, 3115
   triumph in God's promises, 21638
   triumph over death, 7545, 18406
Believing Gentile's sure, 6431
Belisarius, (1770) 11715, (1795) 28652, (1796) 30737
Belknap, Daniel, 1771-1815
   Evangelical harmony, 36939
   Harmonist's companion, 28255, 31792
Belknap, Jeremy, 1744-1798
   Account of John Clarke, 34642
   American biography, 26637, 33393
   Boston, Dec. 22, 1796, 30050
   Charge, 22275
   Discourse, 24085
   Dissertations, 28256
   Eclogue, 9338
   Election sermon, 18927
   Foresters, 24086, 30051
   History of New Hampshire, (1784) 18344, (1791) 23166, (1792) 24087-88
   Jesus Christ, 24089
   Memoirs of the lives, 25154
   Plain and earnest, 11980
   Proposal for printing, 22336
   Proposal of Joseph Belknap, 23167?
   Queries, 28257
   Sacred poetry, 28258, 31793
   Sermon, (1772) 12667, (1789) 21673, (1796) 30052, (1798) 33394-95
   Subscriber being engaged, 22335
   death, 33964
   ordained, 10641
   reply to, 16989, 24343
Belknap, Joseph. Proposal, 23167
Bell, Abraham, petition, 38901
Bell, Benjamin, 1749-1806
   System of surgery, 23168-70
   Treatise on gonorrhoea, 28259
   Treatise on the theory, (1791) 23171, (1795) 28260, (1797) 31794
Bell, Benjamin, 1752-1836
   Character of a virtuous, 26638-39
   Folly of sinners, 24090
   Impartial history, 31795
   Nature and importance, 23172
   Sleepy dead sinners, 25155
   ordained, 18793
Bell, John
   Short sketch of General George Washington, 17436
   Short sketch of General Washington, (1779) 16677, (1781) 17131, (1782) 17801
Bell, Robert, auctioneer, 11242
Bell, Robert, d. 1784
   Address to every, 18345-46
   Catalogue of a collection, 16710
   Catalogue of a gentleman's, 17470
   Catalogue of a small collection, 15731
   Catalogue of books, (1768) 10831, (1770) 11562, (1771) 11981-82, (1774) 13138-40, (1775) 13829, (1777) 15241, (1778) 15732-34, (1781) 17094, (1782) 17468-69, 17471, (1783) 17831-35, (1784) 18348-50
   Catalogue of jewels, 19544
   Catalogue of new and old, 13137

   Catalogue of old physical, 11563
   Catalogue of second hand, 11564
   Catalogue of several hundred, 18351
   Illuminations for legislators, 18352
   Jewels and diamonds, 15735
   Just published and now selling, 17830
   Memorial on the free, 18347
   Observations relative to the manufacture, 12668
   Philadelphia, Jan. 17, 1774, 13141
   Proposals for reprinting, (Catholic Christian) 13142, (Gregory) 13830, (Lectures) 13143, (Leland) 12669
   Proposals for reprinting, (Ferguson) 11983, (Hume) 11984
   Sale catalogue, 12670
   To the encouragers, 12321
   To the honorable the representatives, 17836
   To the sons, 12671
Bell, Samuel. Oration, 33736
Bell, Thomas, tr. Proof of the true, 31666
Bell, William, petition, 34751, 34800
Bell, William, 1731-1816. Practical inquiry, (1793) 25156, (1799) 35176, (1800) 36940
Bellamy, Joseph, 1719-1790
   Blow at the root, 9339
   Careful and strict, 9539, 11565
   Dialogue on the Christian, 9063
   Early piety, 6095
   Essay on the nature, (1762) 9064, (1797) 31796, (1798) 33397
   Great evil, 6963
   Half-way covenant, 11171-72, 11236
   Inconsistence of renouncing, 11173
   Law our school-master, 7618
   Letter to Scripturista, 8540, 8794
   Letter to the reverend author, 8080
   Millennium, 26594
   Remarks, 9340
   Sacramental controversy, 11566
   Sermon, 9065
   Sermons, 8081
   That there is but one, 11174
   Theron, Paulinus, and Aspasio, 8297, 33396
   True religion, 6462
   Wisdom of God, 8541
   death, 22339
   letter (from committee), 9846
   letter (from Davies), 6657
   letter (from Devotion), 11630-31
   remarks on, 9099, 11742
   reply to, 8418, 9100, 9945, 12635
Bellamy, Thomas. Fatal effects, 34307
Belle's stratagem, 26559, 26824
Bellew, Henry. His majesty's ship, 15829
Bellinger, John Skottowe. Inaugural dissertation, 35177
Bellingham, Richard. Book of the general lawes, 28
Bellomont, Richard Coote, earl of
   Account of the proceedings, 834

VOL.	ITEMS	VOL.	ITEMS
1	1-3244	8	22298-25074
2	3245-6623	9	25075-28145
3	6624-9891	10	28146-30832
4	9892-13091	11	30833-33261
5	13092-16176	12	33262-25854
6	16177-19448	13	35855-39162
7	19449-22297		

VOL.	ITEMS	VOL.	ITEMS
1	1-3244	8	22298-25074
2	3245-6623	9	25075-28145
3	6624-9891	10	28146-30832
4	9892-13091	11	30833-33261
5	13092-16176	12	33262-25854
6	16177-19448	13	35855-39162
7	19449-22297		

Bible

The Bible, 8th ed., 26649
The Bible, 9th ed., 33410, 35190
Bible in miniature, 24100
Biblia, (1743) 5127-28, (1763) 9343, (1775) 13834, (1776) 14663
Christian's new and complete, (1788) 20960, (1789) 21680, (1790) 22347
Curious hieroglyphick Bible, 20961
History of the Holy Bible, (1786) 19507, (1793) 25174-75, (1798) 33411
Holy Bible abridged, (1782) 17474, (1786) 19506, (1790) 22350, (1791) 23182, (1793) 25173, (1794) 26650, (1795) 28269-71, (1796) 30067, (1797) 31809, (1800) 36953
Holy Bible containing, (1663) 72, (1752) 6819, (1782) 17473, (1790) 22345-46, (1791) 23180, 23183-86, (1792) 24096-98, (1793) 25171-72, (1794) 26648, (1796) 30065-66, (1797) 31806-808, (1798) 33408-409, (1799) 35188-89, (1800) 36054-55
Holy Bible in verse, 7148
Holy Bible tr. from the Latin, 21681, 22349
Kinder Bibel, 14644
Mamusse, 73, 385
Morality of the Bible, 10251
New hieroglyphical Bible, 26651, 30068
Pocket Bible, 24101
Self-interpreting Bible, (1790) 22348, (1791) 23181, (1792) 24099
Umgewendete Bibel, 5739
Verbum sempiternum, (1765) 10179, (1769) 11086

Bible. Apocrypha

Des Jüngers Nicodemi Evangelium, 9863
Evangelium Nicodemi, (1784) 18362, (1791) 23203, (1796) 30089
Testament, 23199

Bible. Daniel

Remarks on the book, 26663

Bible. Ephesians

Epistle to the Ephesians, 30088

Bible. Genesis

Genesis (Indian), 38
Genesis, chap. III, 21682

Bible. Gospels

Four gospels, 30086, 35200

Bible. Isaiah

Isaiah, a new translation, 26662
Paraphrase on eight chapters, 28284

Bible. Job

Paraphrase on some parts, 28273
Poetical paraphrase, 30070

Bible. Matthew

Gospel of Matthew (Indian), 39
Poetical paraphrase, 30087
Spiegel für alle menschen, 35202

Bible. N.T.

Catholic liturgy, 31819
Collection of the New Testament commands, 15244
Concise history, 30083
Expository notes, 26668, 30084-85
Ganz Neue Testament, 20235
Geschichte von der marterwoche, 35201
Harmony of the gospels, 9348
History of the New Testament, 28288
Neue Testament, (1743) 5127-28, (1745) 5542, (1755) 7359, (1761) 8799, (1763) 9347, (1769) 11181, (1775) 13837, (1783) 17846, (1787) 20236, (1788) 20969, (1791) 23202, (1794)

26667, (1795) 28286-87, (1796) 30081-82, (1800) 36956
New Testament, (1661) 64-65, (1777) 15243, (1778) 15743, (1780) 16715, (1781) 17101-102, (1782) 17476-77, (1786) 19511, (1788) 20966-68, (1789) 21689-90, (1790) 22358-59, (1791) 23200-201, (1792) 24109-10, (1793) 25191, (1794) 26664-66, 28285, (1796) 30080, (1797) 31817-18, (1798) 33415-17, (1799) 35197-99, 35912, (1800) 36957
Novum Testamentum, 36952
Several texts, 28289
Testament abridged, 36959
Wusku wuttestamentum, 279

Bible. O.T.

Selectae e profanis, 20227
Selectae e Veteri Testamento, (1787) 20226, (1789) 21683, (1795) 28272, (1796) 30069

Bible. Proverbs

Proverbs of Solomon, 20965

Bible. Psalms

Collection of Psalms, 4207
Dr. Watts's Imitation, (1785) 18931, (1786) 19510, (1790) 22352-53, (1791) 23188-90, (1795) 28275, (1800) 36950-51
Few Psalmes in meeter, 50
Gantze Psalter, 10556
Hundert und neunzehnte Psalm, 23198
Imitation of the Psalms, 31810
Kleine Davidische Psalterspiel, (1744) 5340, (1760) 8548, (1764) 9602, (1777) 15242, (1781) 17100, (1791) 23197, (1795) 28283, (1797) 31815-16
Massachusee Psalter, 1380
New England Psalter, (1744) 5336, (1745) 5541, (1760) 8543, (1761) 8795-96, (1764) 9603, (1768) 10834-35, (1770) 11567-68, (1771) 11986-87, (1773) 12672, (1774) 13148, (1784) 18358
New version, (1710) 1444, (1713) 1594-95, (1720) 2094, (1725) 2603, (1733) 3625, (1737) 4114, (1740) 4471, (1752) 6820, (1754) 7149, (1755) 7358, (1756) 7619, (1757) 7846, (1760) 8544, (1762) 9068-69, (1763) 9344-45, (1765) 9913-14, (1766) 10241, (1767) 10557-58, (1769) 11180, (1770) 11569-70, (1771) 11988-91, (1773) 12673-77, (1774) 13149-51, (1775) 13835, (1787) 20228, (1788) 20962, (1790) 22351, (1791) 23187, (1793) 25176, (1795) 28274
Psalms carefully suited, (1787) 20229-30, (1788) 20963, (1789) 21684-86, (1790) 22354, (1791) 23191, (1792) 24102-104, (1793) 25177-80, (1794) 26652-54, (1795) 28276-78, (1797) 31811-12, (1799) 35191
Psalms, hymns, and spiritual songs, (1651) 33, (1658) 49, (1665) 96, (1695) 714, (1698) 817, (1702) 1039, (1706) 1239-40, (1707) 1290, (1709) 1381, (1714) 1666, (1715) 1725, (1716) 1798, (1717) 1867, (1718) 1945, (1720) 2095, (1722) 2317, (1726) 2729, (1729) 3134, (1730) 3255, (1737) 4115, (1742) 4892, (1744) 5337-39, (1750) 6464, (1758) 8082, (1762) 9070, (1773) 12678, (1785) 18929, (1796) 30071
Psalms of David according to the version, 36958
Psalms of David imitated, (1729) 3135, (1741) 4672-73, (1743) 5129, (1753) 6965, (1754) 7150, (1756) 7620, (1757) 7847, (1760) 8545-47, (1761) 8797-98, (1763) 9346, (1766) 10242, (1767) 10559-60, (1768) 10836, (1770) 11571, (1771) 11992, (1772) 12324-26, (1773) 12679-81, (1774) 13152, (1775) 13836, (1778) 15742, (1780) 16714, (1781) 17097-99, 19399, (1782)

17475, (1783) 17844, (1784) 18357, (1785) 18930, (1786) 19508-509, (1787) 20231-32, (1789) 21687, (1791) 23192-93, (1792) 24105-106, (1793) 25181-85, (1794) 26655-58, (1795) 28279-81, (1796) 30072, (1798) 33413, (1799) 35192-96, (1800) 39030

Psalms of David in meeter, (1725) 2604, (1736) 3987, (1747) 5907

Psalms of David in metre, (1783) 17843, (1787) 20233, (1788) 20964, (1790) 22355, (1791) 23194, (1792) 24097, (1793) 25186, (1794) 26659, (1797) 31813, (1798) 33414

Psalms of David with hymns, (1789) 21688, (1792) 24107, (1798) 33412

Psalms of David with the Ten Commandments, 10561

Psalter Davids, 7848

Psalter des königs, (1746) 5740, (1760) 8549, (1762) 9071-72, (1768) 10837-38, (1773) 12682, (1783) 17845, (1784) 18361, (1790) 22357, (1791) 23195-96, (1793) 25189-90, (1796) 30074-77, (1797) 31814

Psalter for children, 311

Psalter or Psalms of David, (1734) 3746, (1784) 18359-60, (1787) 20234, (1795) 28282, (1796) 30073

Psalterium Americanum, 1946

Select Psalms, 26660

Selection of Psalms, 24108, 26661

Translation of sundry, 18932

Up-bookum, 74-75

Version of the book, 30078

Wame ketoohomae, 85, 312

Watt's Psalms carefully suited, 21685

Whole book of Psalms, (1640) 4, (1647) 20, (1790) 22356, (1791) 23721, (1793) 25187-88, 26042-43, (1794) 27575-78, (1795) 29363, (1796) 30079, (1797) 32727, (1798) 34420, (1800) 36960

Bible. Revelation
Attempt to translate, 26669

Bible. Song of Solomon
Paraphrase, 5130

Bible Baptist, 21919
  in miniature, 24100
  needs no apology, 30603
  the word of God, 38672

Biblia, das ist, die ganze, 13834, 14663

Biblia, das ist, die heilige, 5127-28, 9343

Bibliotheca curiosa, 3765

Bicheno, James, d. 1831
Explanation of scripture, 30090
Friendly address, 28290
Signs of the times, (1794) 26670, (1795) 28291-92, (1797) 31820-21

Bickerstaffe, Isaac, 1735-1787
Hypocrite, a comedy, 28293
Life and adventures of Ambrose, (1795) 28294, (1798) 33418, (1800) 37561
Lionel and Clarissa, 26671, 31175
Love in a village, 26672, 31175
Maid of the mill, 22360
Padlock, 28295-96
Romp, a musical, 24111, 25192
Thomas and Sally, 23204
dedication by, 9701

Bickham, George, secy. Council of safety, 14751

Bicknell, Alexander, d. 1796
English hermit, 31822, 35203
Hermit, (1795) 28297-98, (1797) 31823

Biddle, Clement, 1740-1814
Advertisement, 18363

Philadelphia directory, 23205
notary, 29220

Biddle, James
To the freeholders, 9915
reply to, 9973

Biddle, N., poem on, 17159

Biddle, Owen
Oration, 17103
Plan for a school, 22361

Bidpai. Instructive and entertaining, 18364

Bidwell, Barnabas, 1763-1833
Copy of a letter, 30516
Mercenary match, 18365
Oration, (1789) 21691, (1795) 28299
Susquehannah title, 30091

Bielby, bp. of London see **Porteus, Bielby, 1731-1808**

Big puzzling cap, 20337, 25193-94

Big Tree, speech by, 28887

Bigelow, Jacob, ordained, 12370

Bigelow, Timothy, of Worcester. Thirty dollars reward, 15440

Bigelow, Timothy, 1767-1821
Eulogy, 36965, 37383, 37453
Oration, (1796) 31824, (1798) 33419

Biglow, William
Child's library, 36966-67
(ed.) Massachusetts magazine, 30774

Biglow, William, 1773-1874
Education, a poem, 35204
To the patrons, 34511

'Bijah in pandemonium, 35400

Biles-Island lottery, 11993

Bill authorizing the transfer, (1793) 26330, (1795) 29712
  concerning the high, 38950
  entitled, An act, 7530
  for ascertaining, 7055
  for establishing religious, 19350
  for establishing the constitution, 20716
  for raising a supply, 9170
  for regulating, 29040
  for the ascertainment, (1794) 27900, (1795) 29713
    better raising, 4409
    better regulating, 5270
  in the chancery of New Jersey, (1747) 6021, (1767) 10654
  in the chancery of New York, 12159
  making further provision, 29714
  of complaint, 8550
  of rates, 35292
  of rights, 22202, 22845
  prohibiting for a limited, 32962
  relative to the compensations, 29715
  supplementary to the act for enrolling, 29717
    to the act intituled, 29716
    to the several, 29718
  to amend an act, 38951
  to amend the act, 27899

VOL.	ITEMS	VOL.	ITEMS
1	1-3244	8	22298-25074
2	3245-6623	9	25075-28145
3	6624-9891	10	28146-30832
4	9892-13091	11	30833-33261
5	13092-16176	12	33262-25854
6	16177-19448	13	35855-39162
7	19449-22297		

to establish an uniform mode, 38715
    an uniform system, (1798) 34712-13, (1800)
      38716-19
    offices, 29719
to prevent citizens, 32963
to prevent disorderly, 7110
to promote the progress, 22192
to provide for organizing, (1795) 29720-21,
  (1798) 34715
    for the better establishment, 38720
    for the more convenient, 38721
to regulate and restrain, 6686
which requires, 6491
Billing, Edward, installation, 7202
Billings, Nathaniel
  New Year's song, 28650
  Republican harmony, 28300
Billings, William. Vision, 38627
Billings, William, fl. 1733. Warning to God's cove-
  nant, 3626
Billings, William, 1746-1800
  Anthem for Thanksgiving, 25196
  Bird and the lark, 22362
  Continental harmony, 26673
  Easter anthem, 28301
  Massachusetts harmony, 18366, 18933
  Music in miniature, 16205
  New-England psalm-singer, 11572
  Psalm-singers amusement, 17104
  Singing master's assistant, (1778) 15744, (1779)
    16206, (1780) 16716
  Suffolk harmony, 19512
Billmeyer, Michael, letter (from Blaeser), 18368
Bingham, Caleb, 1757-1817
  American preceptor, (1794) 26674, (1795) 28302,
    (1796) 30092, (1797) 31825, (1798) 33420, (1799)
    35205-207, (1800) 36969-70
  Astronomical and geographical, (1795) 28303,
    (1796) 30093, (1797) 31826, (1798) 33421, (1800)
    36971
  Child's companion, 24112-13, 30094
  Columbian orator, (1797) 31827, (1799) 35208,
    (1800) 36972
  Rules and articles, 33438
  Young lady's accidence, (1785) 18934, (1789)
    21692, (1790) 22363, (1791) 23206, (1792) 24114,
    (1793) 25197, (1794) 26675, (1796) 30095, (1797)
    31828, (1799) 35209
Bingham, William, 1752-1804
  Description of the situation, 25720
  Letter from an American, 18367
  Letters on American commerce, 27328, 29484
  preface by, 38328
  proposes amendment, 38706
  reports on Indian affairs, 20770
  reports on treasury report, 21516
Binney, Barnabas. Oration, 13153
Biographical and political, 3557
  history, 21498
  memoirs, 37222-23
  sermons, 23352, 26944
  sketch of George Washington, 35334
  sketch of the life, 26234-35
Birch, Samuel, 1757-1841
  Adopted child, 33422
  Songs in the musical, 33423
Birch, Thomas Ledlie, d. 1808. Letter from an
  Irish, 33424, 35210
Birch, William, & Son. City of Philadelphia, 38259
Bird, Benjamin. Jacobites catechism, 587
Bird, Benjamin, petition, 38849

Bird, John. To the honorable, 31829
Bird, Jonathan, 1746-1813
  Discourse, 36974
  Jesus knocking, 15745
  Parable of the unclean, 24115
  Sermon, 28304
Bird, Joseph, d. 1754, death, 7447
Bird, Samuel. Importance of the divine, 8299
Bird and the lark, 22362
Birge, Samuel, d. 1792, death, 27242
Birkett, William. Almanac see **Almanacs (Birkett)**
Birth, life, and character, 30647, 32325
Birth, parentage, and education, 10339-40
Bisco, Abijah, d. 1801. Address, 36975
Bishop, Abraham, 1763-1844
  Connecticut republicanism, 36976-79
  Georgia speculation, 31830, 33425
  Oration, 36980
  Triumph of truth, 23207
  unmasked, 39049
Bishop, Samuel G. Eulogium, 36981
Bishop Jarvis's charge, 33932
  of London's last, 4518
  of London's pastoral, 3283
  Seabury's first, 19207
  Seabury's second, 19981
Bishop's office, 17448
Bisse, Thomas, 167--1731. Beauty of holiness, 31831
Bissell, Hezekiah, d. 1783, death, 18168
Bisset, James. Abridgment and collection, 8391
Bissett, George, d. 1788
  Sermon, 11994
  Trial of a false, 12683
Bissett, John, 1761-1810. Sermon, (1788) 20970,
  (1791) 23208
Bitter afflictions, 3664
Bixby, Samuel. Word of counsel, 16207
Black, John, 1750-1802
  Duty of Christians, 22364
  Examination of the Reverend, 24116
Black, Robert. Inaugural dissertation, 31832
Black, W. Short account, 30096
A black. Sermon, (1772) 12557, (1782) 17717
Black book of conscience, (1732) 3556, (1742) 4890-
  81, (1771) 12089
    Giles the poacher, 35298, 37142-43
    Prince, 37164
Blackburn, Henry, d. 1796, execution, 30424
Blackburne, Francis, 1705-1787. Critical commen-
  tary, 11995
Blacket, Belinda, series of letters, 35084
Blackness of sins, 1450
Blacksmith. Letter (to the ministers), 10215, 22574
Blacksmith, A. T. see **Witherspoon, John, 1722-1794**
Blackstock, William, ordained, 31114
Blackstone, Sir William, 1723-1780
  Commentaries on the laws, (1771) 11996, (1772)
    12327, (1790) 22365, (1799) 35211
  Interesting appendix, 12328, 12684
  Palladium of conscience, 13154
  Rules for interpreting, 32214
  Treatise on the law, 9775, 10721
  commentaries advertised, 12321
  letters (from Furneaux), 13154
Blackwell, Thomas, 1660-1728
  Forma sacra, 13155
  Schema sacrum, 14665
Bladensburgh, 2 August, 14113
Blaeser, Peter, 1735-1813. Brief (to Billmeyer),
  18368
Blagge, Benjamin

alderman, 12892
justice of peace, 14336
Blagrave, J. Laws for the regulating, 20238
Blair, Judge ———, opinion by, 25370-71
Blair, Rev. ———, of Doningham. Life of faith, 24117
Blair, Hannah, d. 1792, death, 26596
Blair, Hugh, 1718-1800
  Account of Robert Walker, 31520, 33144
  Beauties of Blair, 24121-22
  Critical dissertation, 22633
  Essays on rhetoric(k), (1788) 20971, (1789) 21693, (1793) 25198-99, (1797) 31833, (1798) 33426
  Lectures on rhetoric(k), (1784) 18369, (1793) 25200-201, (1800) 36982
  Select sermons, 28306
  Sermons, (1790) 22366, (1791) 23209, (1792) 24118-20, (1793) 25202, (1794) 26676-77, (1795) 28305
Blair, John, 1720-1771
  Animadversions, 10243
  Essays, (1771) 11997, (1789) 21694
  New creature, 10562
  Sermon, 8800
  Synod of New York, 7151
Blair, John Durbarrow, 1759-1823. Sermon, 36983
Blair, Robert, 1699-1746. The grave, a poem, (1753) 6966-67, (1772) 12329, (1773) 12685, (1787) 20239, (1791) 23210, (1793) 25203-205, 26014, (1797) 31834, 31953
Blair, Samuel, 1712-1751
  Animadversions, 4895
  Doctrines of predestination, 4896
  Gospel method, 4117
  Particular consideration, 4675-76
  Persuasive to repentance, 5132
  Sermon, 4340
  Sermons, 4438
  Short and faithful, 5342
  Vindication of the brethren, 5343
  Works, 7152
  death, 6843
Blair, Samuel, 1741-1818
  Discourse delivered . . . May 9, 1798, 33427
  Discourse on psalmody, 21695
  Funeral discourse, 35212
  Oration, 8801
Blair, Thomas. Some short and easy, 2096
Blair, William. The grave, 6966-67
Blake, Francis, 1774-1817. Oration, 30097
Blake, George, 1769-1841
  Masonic eulogy, 36984-85, 37383
  Oration, 28307
Blake, James, 1750-1771. Six sermons, 12330
Blake, John, signs capitulation, 14540
Blake, John M. Plaster of Paris, 35538
Blake, Joseph, 1768-1802. Oration, 24123
Blake, Lemuel. Catalogue of American, 31835
Blake, William P. Catalogue, (1793) 25206, (1796) 30098, (1797) 31835, (1798) 33428, (1800) 37000
Blakney, William, 1672-1761. New manual exercise, (1746) 5742-43, (1747) 5909, (1754) 7153, (1756) 7621, (1759) 8300?
Blakes, James, Jun.
  Account of the author, 3403
  Grace of our Lord, (1771) 12046, (1772) 12395, (1773) 12768, (1780) 16777, (1783) 17932, (1784) 18475, (1792) 24327
Blakeslee, Edward, d. 1797?, death, 33385
Blakeslee, Enos. System of astronomy, 26678
Blakesley, Solomon see **Blakslee, Solomon, 1762-**

1835
Blakslee, David, wife's death, 33825
Blakslee, Lucy, d. 1797, death, 33825
Blakslee, Solomon, 1762-1835
  Oration, 36986
  Sermon, 28308
Blameless and inoffensive, 2418
  bishop, 6841
  Christian, 1335
Blanchard, Edward, account of, 27889
Blanchard, Jean Pierre Baptiste, 1753-1809
  Journal, 25207
  Principles, history, & use, 30099
Blanchard, Jonathan, 1738-1788, reports on Penobscot expedition, 18838, 19312
Blanchard, Joseph. Map of the province, 8898
Blanchard, Joshua. Sober reply, 4897
Blanchard's balloon, 30099
Blanchet, François. Reserches, 36987
Bland, Humphrey, 1686-1763
  Abstract of military, (1743) 5133, (1744) 5344-45, (1747) 5910, (1754) 7154, (1755) 7360-61
  Evolutions of the foot, (1746) 5742-43, (1747) 5909, (1754) 7153, (1756) 7621
  New manual exercise, 8300
Bland, Priscilla, suit by, 12159
Bland, Richard, 1710-1776
  Inquiry into the rights, 10244
  Letter (to the clergy), 8551
  remarks on, 9359, 9922
Bland, William. Sermon, 13838
Blatchford, John. Narrative of remarkable, 20972, 26679
Blatchford, Samuel, 1767-1828
  Address, 33429
  Validity of Presbyterian, 33430
  reply to, 34562
Blauvelt, Abraham. Almanac see **Almanacs (Blauvelt)**
Blazing stars messengers, 8301
Blazing stars the messengers, 11182
Bleakley, John. Premiums, 29977
Bleecker, Ann Eliza Schuyler, 1752-1783
  History of Maria Kittle, 31837
  Posthumous works, 25208
  proposed printing of work by, 26241
Blenman, Jonathan. Remarks, 4118-20, 11573
Blessed effects, 16811
  hope and the glorious, 998
  manumission, 3145
  state of the dead, 6799
  unions, 621
Blessedness of a fixed, 8535
  of departed, 23084
  of peace-makers, 10181
  of such as trust, 7593
  of the dead, (Adams) 3246, (Chauncy) 6298, (Wigglesworth) 3493, (Williams) 31636
    godly, 24197
    liberal, 30733
    tried saint, 2859
  of those who are dead, 19756

VOL.	ITEMS	VOL.	ITEMS
1	1-3244	8	22298-25074
2	3245-6623	9	25075-28145
3	6624-9891	10	28146-30832
4	9892-13091	11	30833-33261
5	13092-16176	12	33262-25854
6	16177-19448	13	35855-39162
7	19449-22297		

of those who die, (1757) 7886, (1793) 26453, (1800) 37810
Blessing and honor, 1730
    of Abraham, 11590
    of Zebulun, 2018
Blessings bestow'd, 4360
    of a soul, 4954
    of America, 23504
    of Billy's budget, 30101
    of peace, 27525
Bligh, William, 1754-1817. Narrative of the mutiny, 22367
Blind beggar, 15288
Blind child, (1787) 20648, (1792) 24693-94, (1793) 26004, (1795) 29325, (1796) 31013
Bliss, Daniel. Gospel hidden, 7362
Bliss, Jonathan, d. 1800, death, 38633
Blockheads, or fortunate, 17478
Blockheads, or the affrighted, 15213
Blodget, Samuel, 1724-1807. Prospective plan, 7363
Blodget, William
    New and correct map, 24124-25
    New and correct table, 20973
    Topographical map, 21696
Blood, Caleb, 1754-1814. Sermon, 24126
Blood calls for blood, 13988
    of Abel, 9616
    will out, 588
Bloody buoy thrown, 30205-207
    butchery, 13839
    court, a bloody ministry, 13906-15
    Indian battle, 33432
    register, 23211
Bloomfield, Jonathan, chairman meeting, 25818
Bloomfield, Joseph. To the society, 31687
Blossoms of morality, (1795) 28479, (1796) 30277, (1798) 33568, (1800) 37248
Blount, Charles, 1654-1693. Great is Diana, 31838
Blount, Thomas, 1759-1812. Motion, 31358
Blount, William
    Letter, 32686
    Proclamation, 27725
    impeachment, 34791-93, 34785-87, 34798, 36561, 37888-90
    plea from, 36558
Blow at the root, 9339
Blowers, Thomas, d. 1729, death, 3164
Blue Beard, 38059
Blue shop, 31065
Blumenbach, Johann Friedrich, 1752-1849. Elements of physiology, 28310
Blundell, James. Inaugural dissertation, 23212
Blunt, Edmund March. New theoretic, 33433
Blunt, John, ordained, 3708
Bluster, J. see **Otis, James, 1725-1784**
Blut-fahne ausgestecket, 31944
Blutige schau-platz, 6256
Bly, John, d. 1787
    Narrative, 20974
    executed, 21598-99
Blyth, Joseph. Oration, 36990, 37383
Boaden, James, 1762-1839
    Fontainville Forest, 28311
    Secret tribunal, 31839
Boanerges, 2908
Board of commissioners appointed for the state, 34077
    of commissioners appointed in the state, 34192
    of health; commonwealth of Mass., 35788
    of health, to their constituents, (1799) 35220, (1800) 36995

of treasury, (June 1777) 15631, (Aug. 27, (1785) 19280, (Apr. 8, 1786) 20042, (June 22, 1786) 20043
    of treasury to whom it was referred, 20756
        to whom was referred a motion, 20755
        to whom was referred their letter, 20044
    of war and ordinance, 16656
Boarding school, 33748
Boardman, Mrs. ——, d. 1794, death, 29085
Boardman, Abel, court martial, 34080
Boardman, Benjamin, 1731-1802
    Sermon, 18370
    installation, 18502
Bobadill, Capt. ——. Where are ye, 18884
Bockett, Elias, 1695-1735
    Determination of the case, 2502
    Poem to the memory, 4593
Boddily, John, 1755-1802
    Sermon, 36991
    Substance of a discourse, 31840
    Substance of a sermon, 31841
    installation, 34139
Body now assembled, 18745
Body of death, 1336-37, 4099
Boehm, Johann Philip
    Abermahlige treue, 5134
    Getreuer warnungs brief, 4898
    Reformierten kirchen, 6098
    remarks on, 5013
Boehme, Anton Wilheim
    Spiritual improvement, 18935
    letter (from Webb), 17424, 18295-96, 34972-73
Boel, ——. Klagte kerk, 2605
Boel, Henricus, predicant, 2605, 6098
Boerhaave, ——, opinion on smallpox, 6689
Boerhaave, ——, rules of, 30574
Bogardus, Cornelius C., claim, 13038, 14510
Bogardus, Jacob. To be sold, 31842
Bogart, David Schuyler, d. 1839. Discourse, 20975
Bogatzky, Karl Heinrich von, 1690-1754
    God's thoughts, 16717
    Golden treasury, (1793) 25209, (1796) 30102, (1797) 31843
Bogg, F., remarks on, 1192
Boggs, Joseph. Philadelphia directory, 26680
Bogue, David. Objections against a mission, 32384
Bogue, Ebenezer see **Booge, Ebenezer**
Bogle, Samuel. Great variety, 12686
Bohun, William. Brief view, 9916-17
Boinod & Gaillard. Catalogue, 18371-72
Boissier de Sauvages de la Croix, Pierre Augustin Directions, 11574
Boissy, Louis de, 1694-1758. False appearances, 28312
Bold conscience, 16718
    push, 8083
    stroke for a husband, 26825
    stroke for a wife, 26559, 26751
Bolde, ——. Preparation for death, 3399
Bolingbroke, Henry St. John, viscount, 1678-1751
    Freeholder's political catechism, 8030, 11450
    Letters on the spirit, 6412, 7786
    epistles to (from Pope), 22809, 23707, 24702-703, 26017-18, 27535, 29337-39, 31023-26, 32701-702
    remarks on his letters, 6854, 27115, 30558
Bollan, William. Biographical history, 21498
Bolles, Eunice, d. 1786, murdered, 19547, 20264
Bolles, John, 1677-1767
    Few words, 2606
    Persecutions in Boston, 8084
    Relation of the opposition, 8802

To worship God, 7622
Bolles, Joseph, 1701-1785
  Addition to the book, 8085
  Answer to a book entitled, 8302
  Answer to a book entituled, 9349
  Answer to part, 9073
  Concerning the Christian, 7849
Bolton, ——, meeting at house of, 11785
Bolton, James. Treatise, 25210
Bolton, Robert, 1572-1631. Twenty considerations, 6968
Bolton, Thomas. Oration, 13840
Bolton, Mass. Result of an ecclesiastical, 12687
Bomb search'd, 1230
Bomb thrown, 1152
Bompard, Capt. ——, on Ambuscade, 25917
Bon ton, 26558, 27031
Bond, Benjamin. Answer to a bill, 6808
Bond, Elizabeth, marriage, 6856
Bond, Nathan. Report of a committee, 31854
Bond, Samson. Publick tryal, 313
Bond, Thomas, of Alexandria. 'Tis now near two, 25211
Bond, Thomas, of Philadelphia, lottery drawing inspected by, 12192
Bond, Thomas, 1712-1784. Anniversary oration, 17479
Bond, Tobias. Humble address, 16835
Bonds of baptism, 1934
Bonds of the covenant, 1399
Bone to gnaw, (1795) 28431-35, (1796) 30234, 31173, (1797) 31945, 31948
Bonifacius, 1460
Bonner, John, 1662-1726
  New plan, 11183
  Town of Boston, 2318
Bonnet, Charles, 1720-1793. Conjectures, 36992
Bonny Wully, 33809
Bonnycastle, John, 1750-1821. Scholar's guide, 19513, 21697
Bonsall, ——, partner of Clarkson, 13201
Booge, Ebenezer, 1716-1767. Unteachable, forsaken, 7623
Book of common prayer, (1710) 1454, (1785) 19940, (1790) 22821, (1791) 23721, (1793) 26042-43, (1794) 27575-76, 27578, (1795) 29362-63, (1797) 32727, (1798) 34420, (1799) 36175, (1800) 38334-37
  of common prayer, selections from, 26045
  of discipline, 19014
  of knowledge, (1790) 22488-89, (1793) 25454, (1794) 26948-49, (1795) 28633-34, (1796) 30393, (1797) 32089-90, (1798) 33696, (1799) 35451
  of nature, 24127
  of problems, 24057, 33312
  of songs, 27542
  of the chronicles, 5732
    general lawes, (1649) 28, (1660) 60
    general lawes, supplement, (1650) 30, (1654) 37, (1657) 46
    general laws (Plymouth), 171, 397
    revelation, 2172
Books added to the library, 5853
  for sale, 25062
  importation of May, 34165
  imported in the last vessel, 8362
  just imported, 7368
Boone, Daniel, 1735-1820, adventures, 18467, 19514, 25480, 25648
Boone, Nicholas, Constable's pocket-book, 1445, 2842
Boone, Thomas, dedication to, 8684
Booth, Abraham, 1734-1806
  Apology for the Baptists, 20976
  Commerce in the human, 24128
  Essay on the kingdom, 23213
  Glad tidings, 31844
  Reign of grace, (1793) 25212, (1795) 28313, (1798) 33434
  proposals to print his Essay, 22474
Booth, Benjamin, trial, 27076
Booth, James, clerk of convention, 14732
Booth's paedobaptism, 20977
Bordley, John Beale, 1727-1804
  Country habitations, 33435
  Essays and notes, 35216
  Hemp, 35217
  Intimations on manufactures, 26681
  On monies, 21698
  Outlines of a plan, 26682, 27512
  Purport of a letter, 21699
  Queries selected, 31845
  Sketches on rotation(s), (1792) 24129, (1796) 30103, (1797) 31846
  Summary view, 18373
  Supplement to the essay, 22368
  Yellow fever, 26683-84
Bordwell, Joel, ordained, 8384
Borrowe, Samuel. Inaugural dissertation, 25213
Boscawen, Mrs. ——, addressed, 19102, 36746
Boscawen, Edward, 1711-1761
  Journal, 8076
  captures man-of-war, 8505
Boshoo, Ram Ram, hymn by, 31107
Boss, Peter, trial, 642
Boston, Patience, d. 1735, execution, 4245
Boston, Thomas, 1676-1732
  Crook in the lot, 24130
  Human nature, 30104
  Key to heaven, 30105
  Nature and necessity, 6969
  doctrine of justification, 6302
Boston
  Anthem, hymns, 37015
  Arrangement of the performances, 26688
  Arrangement of the performances, 33437
  Articles of association, 3749
  Articles of incorporation of the Society for encouraging, 7155
  Association and articles of agreement, 26689
  At a ... meeting of the Boston Episcopal, 19516
  At a meeting of the freeholders, (1766) 10245, (1767) 10564, (1774) 13160, (1782) 17480
  At a meeting of the merchants, 11576
  At a publick, 2201
  At the town-house, 458
  Board of health, to their constituents, (1799) 35220, (1800) 36995
  Boston, (Mar. 30, 1773) 12688, (Apr. 9, 1773) 12689, (June 22, 1773) 12690, (Dec. 1, 1773) 12694-95, (Dec. 2, 1773) 12696, (May 27, 1774) 13156, (June 10, 1774) 13158, (Sept. 27, 1774)

VOL.	ITEMS	VOL.	ITEMS
1	1-3244	8	22298-25074
2	3245-6623	9	25075-28145
3	6624-9891	10	28146-30832
4	9892-13091	11	30833-33261
5	13092-16176	12	33262-25854
6	16177-19448	13	35855-39162
7	19449-22297		

13162, (June 21, 1779) 19400, (Dec. 4, 1783)
17847, (May 15, 1794) 26687, (Jan. 6, 1800)
36996
Brief account of the present state, income, 28322
Brief account of the present state of the Society,
    22369
By-laws and orders, 8086
By-laws and town-orders, 19515
By order of the selectmen of Boston, 31847
Carpenter's rules, 26685, 28318
Catalogue of W. P. & L. Blake, 37000
Catechism for the instruction, 19517
Church renewed covenant, 281
Circular letter; from a committee, 24136
Collection of Psalms, 35222
Committee consisting of the following, 13161
Compleat body of the rules, 3628
Concise view of the facts, 37021
Confession of faith, (1680) 280, (1699) 860, (1710)
    1446, (1722) 2319, (1725) 2608, (1734) 3750,
    (1750) 6466, (1757) 7850
Constitution and laws of the Boston Marine,
    24133
Constitution of the Boston Tontine, 23215
Copy of the proceedings, 16208
Directions to the selectmen, 2202
Extracts from the proceedings, 16209
Following was unanimously, 10840
Funeral dirge on the death, 37009
Gentlemen, the evils, 13157
Gentlemen, the inhabitants, 17105
Haymarket theatre, Monday evening, 31853
In consequence of a conference, 12693
Information for immigrants, 28321
Large and general assortment, 37004-5
Large and well assorted, 37006
Large collection, 37016
Large, valuable and extensive, 37019
Laws and extracts of laws, 10839
Laws for the Assistant fire society, 28314
Laws of the Relief fire society, 18939
Letter from the Presbyterian, 2503
Liturgy collected, 18938
Manifesto or declaration, 859
Massachusetts charitable, 28319
Meeting, Apr. 24, 1734, 3748
Merchants and all others, 11575
Merchants and traders, 11184
Names of the streets, 1342, 36997
Necessity of reformation, 263
Never performed in Boston, 33439
New and valuable assortment, 37022
Notice of a town meeting, 9350
Notification; freeholders and other, 21700
Notification of a meeting, (1771) 11998, (1785)
    18937
Notification of a town meeting, 18936
Notification; the freeholders, (1767) 10563, (1784)
    18374, (1796) 30106, (1797) 31848, (1799) 35218,
    (1800) 36998
Ode performed, 37008
On Saturday next, 13841
Order of performances at the old, 37010
Order of performances; instrumental, 36999
Order of procession, 25214
Orders and by-laws, 2607
Post-days at Boston, 28323
Procession; Boston, Oct. 19, 1789, 21701
Proposals; by the president, 28320
Proposals for a bank, 25216

Propositions concerning the subject, 68
Regulations for the government, 31852
Report concerning the town, 24131
Report of a committee chosen, 31854
Report of a committee of the inhabitants, 12331
Report of the committee, 24132
Report printed by order, 31849
Resolutions regulating, 30107
Rules and articles, 33438
Rules and orders of the Anti-stamp, 14666
Rules and orders to be observed, 18376
Rules and regulations of the Boston chamber,
    26686
Rules and regulations of the Scots' charitable,
    37018
Rules for a fire club, 9074
Rules of work, 37003
Schedule of the expenses, 35219
Selectmen of the town, 25215
Several rules, orders, 1040, 2843
Sir, at a meeting, 30108
Small but very valuable, 37007
Subscription assembly, 30109
System of public, 21702
Teas at auction, 37020
Testimony and advice, 5136
Testimony of a number, 5544
Testimony of the pastors, 5135
To be performed at the Brattle-street, 37002
To be performed at the Old South, 37011
To John Adams, 33436
To the freemen, 12691
Two plans, 18375
Valuable books, 37013
Valuable collection of books, (Clap) 37017,
    (Shaw) 37014
Vote at a meeting, 4899
Vote of the town, 2412
Votes and proceedings of the freeholders, 12332,
    12692
Votes and proceedings of the town, 13159
We the subscribers, 13163
William Richardson imports, 37023
Boston, Mar. 31; this morning, 17850
Boston, Dec. 19; melancholy, 23214
Boston, (Mar. 22, 1672,3) 176, (Dec. 23, 1767)
    10780, (Jan. 25, 1769) 11225, (Mar. 30, 1773)
    12688, (Apr. 9, 1773) 12689, (June 22, 1773) 12690,
    (Dec. 1, 1773) 12694-95, (Dec. 2, 1773) 12696,
    (May 24, 1774) 13156, (June 10, 1774) 13158,
    (Sept. 27, 1774) 13162, (Jan. 31, 1775) 14080,
    (Feb. 25, 1775) 14193, (June 26, 1775) 13842,
    (Jan. 4, 1777) 15245, (Oct. 23, 1777) 15438, (June
    21, 1779) 19400, (Oct. 22, 1779) 16210, (Mar. 29,
    1783) 17849, (Apr. 7, 1783) 17851, (Sept. 5, 1783)
    19109, (Oct. 16, 1783) 19421, (Dec. 4, 1783) 17847,
    (Nov. 10, 1785) 18901, (Jan. 29, 1789) 21704, (Jan.
    13, 1792) 24131, (Feb. 22, 1792) 24134, (April,
    1794) 26856, (May 15, 1794) 26687, (Sept. 24,
    1796) 29982, (Nov. 1, 1796) 30772, (Dec. 22, 1796)
    30050, (Nov. 30, 1797) 31850, (December, 1797)
    32453, (Apr. 2, 1798) 34466, (Feb. 5, 1799) 35855,
    (Apr. 15, 1799) 35340
Boston, Jan. 1, 1800; the carriers, (Columbian cen-
    tinel) 37208, (Commercial gazette) 37026, 38441
    Jan. 6, 1800, 36996
    Sept. 1800, 37215
Boston cavalry. Boston, Nov. 30, 1797, 31850
Boston directory, (1789) 22033, (1796) 31619,
    (1798) 35005, (1800) 37024
Boston dispensary. Institution of the Boston, 31851
Boston ephemeris see **Almanacs (Boston)**

Boston Episcopal charitable society. At a . . . meeting, 19516
Boston (frigate), combat, 25917
Boston gazette. Boston, Jan. 1, 1800, 37026
Boston in New-England, 115
Boston library society. Catalogue, (1795) 28317, (1800) 37001
Boston magazine, (1783) 17854, (1784) 18378, (1785) 18941, (1786) 19519
Boston marine insurance co. Act to incorporate, 35221
Boston, Mass., Feb. 28, 1792, 24135
Boston mechanic association
 Constitution, 28315
 Sir, you being, 28316
Boston paper staining manufactory, 28428
Boston Port Bill, 13303-308, 13406
Boston Presbyterian society. Articles, 3989
Boston, Sunday, Jan. 12, 1777, 15246
Boston theatre. To all people, 26690
Bostonian, preface by, 20119
Bostonian see **Haliburton, William**
Bostonian Ebenezer, 827
Bostwick, David, 1720-1763
 Brief account, 8834-36
 Character of the author, 26854
 Fair and rational vindication, (1764) 9606-607, (1768) 10844, (1774) 13166, (1790) 22371
 Self disclaimed, 8070
 extracts (from Buell), 8808
 ordained, 5549
 reply to, 10316
 synod moderator, 8035
Bostwick, Elijah, relief of, 26321
Bostwick, Nuel. First book, 35223
Bostwick, S. Address to Major-general Tryon, 16212
Bosworth, Benjamin. Signs of apostacy, 633
Botanic garden, 33600
Botanical harmony, 32795
Botanoaotia, 31323
Bothwell, David. Qualifications of rulers, 30112
Botetourt, Norborne Berkeley, baron de, 1718?-1770, dedication to, 11860
Bouchard de la Poterie, Claude Florent
 Boston, Jan. 29, 1789, 21704
 Pastoral letter, 21705
 Resurrection, 21706-707
Boucher, Jonathan, 1738-1804
 American times, 16697
 Letter from a Virginian, 13167-70
Boucher, Matthew. Almanac see **Almanacs (Boucher)**
Boudier de Villemert, Pierre Joseph, 1761-1800
 Ladies' friend, (1789) 21708, (1793) 25218, (1794) 26692, (1795) 28326-27
Boudinot, Mrs. ——, dedication to, 9888
Boudinot, Elias, 1740-1821
 Letter (to Livingston), 17850
 Oration, 25219
 Orders and directions, 31465
 Proclamation, (Jan. 23, 1783) 18231, (Apr. 11, 1783) 18238, 18240-44, (June 24, 1783) 18229, (Sept. 25, 1783) 18245, (Dec. 11, 1783) 18247
 pres. Congress, 18233
Boulanger, Nicolas Antoine
 Christianity unveiled, 28846
 reply to, 29237
Boulding, ——, miller, 32385
Boulton, Thomas. Voyage, a poem, 12699
Bounty (ship), mutiny, 22367
Bouquet, Henry, expedition under, 10167

Bouquet, a collection, 30613
Bouquier, ——. National convention, 27001
Bourdon, Leonard. National convention, 26999
Bourignon, Antoinette de, observations on, 4097
Bourk, Thomas
 Letter (to Chamberlaine), 15747
 letter (from Chamberlaine), 15757
Bourke, Michael. Review of the subject, 24138
Bourn, Benjamin, of Boston. Sure guide to hell, 6643-44, 10568
Bourn, Benjamin, 1755-1808
 Account of the settlement, 18942
 appointed judge, 31096
Bourn, Melatiah, 1755-1808. Proposals for carrying, 10828
Bourne, Silvanus. Dangerous vice, 21736
Bournonville, ——. Letters, 28090
Bours, John, 1734-1815
 Appeal to the public, 21709
 Town tax, 23628
 misrepresentations by, 21450
Bowden, John, 1751-1817
 Address, 24139
 Letter (to Stiles), 20979
 Letter from a weaver, 21710
 Second letter, 21711
Bowdoin, James, 1727-1790
 Additional observations, 11583
 Address, 20500
 Colony of Massachusetts-Bay, 14840
 Paraphrase, 8307
 Philosophical discourse, 16720, 19520
 Proclamation, (1785) 19085-86, (1786) 19787-90, (1787) 20501-506
 Short narrative, 11580-82
 commissioner, 7025
 daughter's marriage, 18205
 death, 23824-25
 dedication to, 19035, 19703, 19751
 delegate to Congress, 13425
 eulogy on, 23513, 25092
 order on Mass. constitution, 16844
 pres. convention, 16846
 pres. Council, 14868
 sermon before, 20142, 20469
Bowdoin, James, 1752-1811
 Opinions respecting the commercial, 31857
 arrival in Boston, 17850
Bowdoinham association. Minutes, (1790) 22372, (1791) 25220-21, (1792) 24140, (1794) 26693, (1795) 28328, (1796) 30113, (1797) 31858, (1798) 33442, (1799) 35224, (1800) 37027
Bowen, Daniel
 Collection of funny, 20241
 Columbian museum, 33443-44, 35225, 35227
 Museum head of the mall, 35226
Bowen, Jabez, 1739-1815
 To the freemen, 19521
 dedication to, 21432, 22113, 22850, 23739, 24740,

VOL.	ITEMS	VOL.	ITEMS
1	1-3244	8	22298-25074
2	3245-6623	9	25075-28145
3	6624-9891	10	28146-30832
4	9892-13091	11	30833-33261
5	13092-16176	12	33262-25854
6	16177-19448	13	35855-39162
7	19449-22297		

VOL.	ITEMS	VOL.	ITEMS
1	1-3244	8	22298-25074
2	3245-6623	9	25075-28145
3	6624-9891	10	28146-30832
4	9892-13091	11	30833-33261
5	13092-16176	12	33262-25854
6	16177-19448	13	35855-39162
7	19449-22297		

Discourse, 17855
Examination of and some answer to, 3996
Letter (to Hobby), 6645
Letter from the elders, 11586
Past dispensations, 18381
Sermon, 39104
answered, 6694
death, 18552
ordained, 4007
pastor at Springfield, 4044
Brent, Richard, 1757-1814, message referred to, 31406, 34807
Brethren and fellow citizens, this is, 13358
    and fellow citizens, you may, 13358
    dwelling, 1972
    of St. John's, 24724
Breton, William
    Military discipline, 4225
    Militia discipline, 3634
Brett, Samuel
    Relation of the great, 30301
    True relation, 28342
Brett, Silas, ordained, 6225
Bretz, Guy de. Rise, spring and foundation, 119
Brevitt, Joseph. History of anatomy, 35232
Brevoort, Henry. To the freemen, 13846
Brewer, Daniel, 1669-1733. Gods help, 2507
Brewer, John, sermon at house of, 33304
Brewerton, George, witness, 11226
Brewster, Martha. Poems, 7855, 8093
Briant, Lemuel, 1722-1754
    Absurdity, 6291
    Some friendly remarks, 6472
    Some more friendly, 6646
    slandered, 6975
Brice, John, reply to, 10253
Bricket, John, portrait, 27563
Bricklayers corporation. Charter, 32678
Bride's burial, 30317
Bridge, Rev. ———. Charge, 33265, 35076
Bridge, Ebenezer, clerk of meeting, 13439
Bridge, Ebenezer, d. 1792. Sermon, (1752) 6825, (1767) 10569
Bridge, Josiah, 1740-1801
    Sermon, 20242, 21713
    ordained, 8817
Bridge, Matthew, d. 1775
    Sermon, 8806
    ordained, 5733
Bridge, Thomas, 1657-1715
    Jethro's advice, 1448, 3635
    Knowledge of God, 1202
    Mind at ease, 1540
    What faith can do, 1597, 3396
    character, 1767
    death, 1731, 1754, 1767, 1790
Bridge, William, 1600-1690. Word to the aged, 264
Bridger, ———, letter (from Cooke), 2022
Bridgham, James, ordained, 4058
Bridgham, Samuel Willard, 1774-1840. Oration, 31865, 33452
Bridgewater's monitor, (1717) 1888, (1768) 10940
Bridle for sinners, 9548, 17804
Bridle for the ass, 8807
Brief account of a religious, 17681
    account of an ecclesiastical, 10788
        God's dealings, 5401
        some, 7590-91
        the Associated, 31040
        the deluded, 9120
        the epidemical, 28538

the formation, 6507
the late revivals, (1799) 35139-42, (1800) 36875-76, 37523-24
the life, 9515
the occasion, 5518
the pious, 5144
the present state, income, 28322
the present state of the Society, 22369
the revenues, 2613
the rise and progress, 11661, 18083
the rise, principles, 21415
the rise, progress, 5886-87, 6292
the Society, 34639
the state, 1896
and candid, 1022
and general account, 4626-29, 4844
and plain discourse, 2881
and plain essay, 5666, 6037
and plain exhortations, 6255
and remarkable, 19612
and true narrative, 613
animadversions, 309, 20203
answer to a small, 266
answer to two, 589
apology, 2016
attempt to set, 17928, 19406
catechisme, 63, 110
concordance or table, 22472, 23184
concordance to the Holy, (1791) 23185, 23225, (1792) 24148
consideration, 30472, 34116
considerations, 12701
decent but free, 17543
declaration, 2187
directions, 3976
directory, 33515
discourse, Feb. 6, 1727, 2830
discourse at the ordination, 3486
    concerning futurities, 8048
    concerning prayer, 1183
    concerning regular, 2614
    concerning the lawfulness, 1592
    concerning the unlawfulness, 490
    deliver'd at North-Haven, 8768
    of justification, 423
    proving, 341
display, 2870
dissertation on the three, 3887
dissertation on the venereal, 35304
dissertations, 10572
eines priester, 30782
enquiry, 1801
essay on the number, 3879
essay, or an attempt, 21102
examination of Lord Sheffield, 23294-95
examination of the practice, 3212
exhortation, 586
explications, 468
exposition, 29010
history and vindication, 7386, 7873
    of epidemic, 36687
    of the country, 3066
    of the Pequot, 4033
    of the rise, 7569
    of the settlement, 18885
    of the warr, 220
illustration and confirmation, (1746) 5759-60, (1763) 9376, (1781) 17136, (1793) 25395
illustration of infant, 27785
memorial, 2449
narration of the captivity, 11684

narration of the sufferings, 911
narrative of some, 5738
    of the captivity, 10652-53
    of the case, (1736) 4107, (1739) 4330, (1756) 7824, (1770) 11952, (1799) 36749
    of the life, 16756
    of the proceedings of the Eastern, 9871
    of the proceedings of the government, 13102
    of the success, 701
    of the trial, 37039
    or poem, 13289
observations on the doctrine, 18455, 28617
of the claim, 11356
of the governor, 1970
of the titles, 23376
paraphrase, 16215
recognition, 160
remarks on a number, 11285
    on the common, 12257
    on the defence, 10116
    on the saytrical, 12022
remembrancer, 9611
reply to a pamphlet, 33945
    to Mr. George, 1150
    to the grand, 16276
review of the campaigns, 8556
review of the rise, 13177
rule to guide, 242, 1096
statement of opinions, 37428
statement . . . of the sentiments, 36666
summe, 77
testimony against tale-bearers, 1024
testimony to the great, 2588, 2710
van de wel erwarde, 10029
van de weleerwaarde, 12309
view of ecclesiastical, 9916-17
    the accounts, 18679
    the distresses, 11595
    the manner, 12463
vindication of the duty, 19480
    of the particular, 26602-603, 35143
    of the proceedings, 7282
    of the purchassors, 5792
weiland von Peter, 18368
Briefs in the controversy, 4345
Briefwechsel, 17568
Brigden, Zechariah. Almanac see **Almanacs (Brigden)**
Briggs, Ephraim, of Chatham, ordained, 31866
Briggs, Ephraim, d. 1799. Sermon, 31866
Briggs, Isaac, 1775-1862. Sermon, 35233
Briggs, John, 1765-1811. Oration, 37047
Briggs, Richard. New art of cookery, 24145, 33458-59
Brigham, Benjamin, d. 1799, death, 37810
Brigham, Lucy, d. 1793, death, 37810
Brigham, Paul, sermon before, 33220, 34513
Bright, Michael, d. 1792, death, 24364
Bright side, 1453
Brigitte, St., prophecies, 9318
Brigstock, William, defendant, 38723
Brimshead, William, d. 1701. Mass. election sermon, 298
Bringhurst, Joseph, poems by, 25104
Brisco, Joseph, d. 1657, death, 48
Brissot de Warville, Jacques Pierre, 1754-1793
    Commerce of America, 28343
    Critical examination, 20981
    Discourse, 23222
    New travels, 24146, 31871

    Oration, 21001, 21739
    To his constituents, 26700
    supports impeachment of Lafayette, **25497,** 26996
Bristol (Negro), 1747-1763
    Dying speech, 9355
    execution, 9616
Bristol, Simeon, d. 1782, death, 17914
Bristol, Eng. Guildhall, Bristol, 13847
Bristol, R. I.
    Bristol church lottery, 37048
    By-laws and catalogue, 37049
Bristol gazette. From the Bristol gazette, 17506
Bristol tragedy, 4681
Britain's mercies, 5883-84
Britain's remembrancer, (1747) 5915, (1748) 6104-105, (1759) 8311
Britannia's intercession, 11191
Britannus Americanus. Liberty, property, 10041
British album, 25807
    and American physician, 31323
    and American register, (1773) 12869-70, (1777) 15442, (1778) 15912, (1779) 16374, (1780) 16869
British Bostonian
    Watchman's alarm, 13757
    see also **Skillman, Isaac, 1740-1799**
British grammar, 18382
    honour, 31255
    prison ship, 17159
British tar company. Account of coal tar, 20982
Briton in New York. Loyal and humorous, 16326
Britton, David. List of prices, 16514
Broaddus, Andrew, 1770-1848
    Age of reason, 28344
    Selection of hymns, 33460
Broadgrin, Billy. Merry fellow's pocket, 35241
Broadhurst, Miss ———, sings song, 28591, 29501-502, 30239, 30371, 30969, 33214, 34489, 35618
Broadstreete, Mr. ———, answer to, 459
Broadwell, Mary, d. 1730, death, 3276-77
Brockett, Titus, d. 1773, death, 12648
Brockway, Thomas, 1745-1807
    America saved, 18383
    European traveller, 18944
    Gospel tragedy, 28345
    Sermon, 31872
    Virtue its own, 26701
    ordained, 12726
Brockwell, Charles. Brotherly love, 6473
Broddeck, Christian. Geistiges wetter-glöcklein, 24147
Broderick, Admiral ———, expedition, 8138-39
Brogden, William. Freedom and love, 6474
Broke open last night, 20188
Broken heart, 1728
Brome, Richard, d. 1652. Jovial crew, 9079
Bromfield, Edward, requests publication of Mather epistle, 936, 1266
Bromfield, Edward, 1695?-1756, death, 7769
Bromley, Thomas. Way to the Sabbath, 8309

VOL.	ITEMS	VOL.	ITEMS
1	1-3244	8	22298-25074
2	3245-6623	9	25075-28145
3	6624-9891	10	28146-30832
4	9892-13091	11	30833-33261
5	13092-16176	12	33262-25854
6	16177-19448	13	35855-39162
7	19449-22297		

candidate, 36224
Brown, John, 1757-1837
reports on accounts, 21534
reports on invalid establishment, 21512
Brown, Joseph, of Conn. Examination into the principles, 10571
Brown, Joseph, of Exeter, N.H. Remembrancer, 32747
Brown, Joseph, of Shapleigh, Me., ordained, 30965
Brown, Mary, d. 1703?, death, 1121
Brown, Moses, fl. 1733. Scripture bishop, 3636
Brown, Moses, 1738-1836
From the meeting for sufferings, 17541
Observations, 25233
referee, 11614?
reply to, 27695
verses by, 37327
Brown, Nicholas, d. 1792, death, 23802
Brown, Peter, d. 1770, drowned, 11591
Brown, Richard, d. 1770, drowned, 11591
Brown, Samuel, d. 1770, drowned, 11591
Brown, Samuel, 1769-1830
Inaugural dissertation, 31881
Treatise, 37058
Brown, Samuel, fl. 1794. To all people, 26690
Brown, Samuel, fl. 1800, petition, 38827
Brown, Thaddeus, d. 1803. Address, 33464
Brown, Thomas
Plain narrative, 8557-58
ordained, 8332
Brown, William, of Glastenbury, ordained, 24291
Brown, William, of Mass., justice Superior court, 13426
Brown, William, of Penna., chairman meeting, 30985
Brown, William, of Philadelphia
Pharmacopoeia, 15750, 17108
Three rondos, 20246
Brown, William, 1764-1803
Claims of Thomas Jefferson, 37187
Oration, 35251
Brown, William, d. 1794?, death, 27531
Brown, William Hill, 1766-1793. West Point preserved, 31882
Brown, William Laurence, 1755-1830. Essay, 25234
Brown university
Act for the establishment, 9823
Catalogue, (1775) 14424, (1778) 16049, (1781) 17347, (1786) 19960, (1789) 22112, (1792) 24739, (1793) 26077, (1795) 29406, (1798) 34456
Commencement, (1795) 29407, (1796) 31097, (1797) 32760, (1798) 34457, (1799) 36226
Exhibition, 5 December, 34459
Exhibition in college chapel, 34458
Laws, 26078
Order of the exercises, 27617
Philosophemata see **Brown university.** Theses
Supplement to the laws, 26079
Theses, (1769) 11444, (1776) 15060, (1788) 21432, (1789) 22113, (1790) 22850, (1791) 23739, (1792) 24740, (1793) 26080, (1794) 27618, (1795) 29408, (1796) 31098, (1797) 32761, (1798) 34460
Browne, Arthur, 1700-1773
Advantages of unity, 8095
Doctrine of election, 7856
Excellency of the Christian, 4227
Folly and perjury, 5749
Necessity of reformation, 7857
Religious education, 4478
Remarks on Dr. Mayhew, 9357
Universal love, 7370

Browne, Isaac Hawkins. On the immortality, 30813
Browne, John. Discourse, 10248
Browne, Joseph, 1646-1678. Almanac see **Almanacs (Browne)**
Browne, Joseph, fl. 1798
Treatise on the yellow, 31883, 33465
memoir of, 35941
Browne, William. Whereas a report, 11433
Brownell, Abner
Enthusiastical errors, 17856?
Worship of God, 17484
Brownell, Benjamin, letter (from A. Brownell), 17856
Brownell, George, schoolmaster, 1741
Brownrigg, Dr. ——, extract from, 14651-52
Brown's gazette extra, 32686
Brownson, David, ordained, 10180
Brownson, Oliver
New collection, 31884
Select harmony, 17857, 23227
Bruce, ——, captain tea-ship, 12913
Bruce, James, 1730-1794
Account of the simoon, 35721?
Interesting narrative, 23228, 33466
Bruderliebe in Philadelphia, 27107
Bruderlied oder ein ausfluss, 7627
Bruno, John see **Brown, John, 1735-1788**
Brunswick, Duke of, retreats, 24169
Brunswick, Me. Answer to the remarks, 6976
Brunt, Jonathan. Few particulars, 31885
Brush, Abner, ordained, 8244
Brush, Crean
Speech, 13848
chairman NY Assembly, 13239
commission to, 14191
Brush of sound reason, 30131
Brute, Sir John, dedication to, 10022
Brutus
English advice, 2335
Important doubts, 12335
To John de Noyellis, 12337
To the foremen, 36429
To the free and loyal, 11588, 13180
To the public, (1770) 11589, (1772) 12336
Two curious and important, 11587
Bryan, George, 1731-1791
Proclamation, 16436
death, 23359
Bryan, Hugh, surveys by, 13240
Bryan, Samuel
An die einwohner, 20250
Centinel no. I-II, 20248-49
Letters on the constitution, 21344
Mein herr, in befolgung, 36064
measures against, 38557
Bryant, ——. To the curious, 22375
Bryant, Lemuel, 1722-1754
slandered, 6975?
vindicated, 6902
Bryant, William. Account of the electric eel, 28989
Brydone, Patrick, 1743-1818

VOL.	ITEMS	VOL.	ITEMS
1	1-3244	8	22298-25074
2	3245-6623	9	25075-28145
3	6624-9891	10	28146-30832
4	9892-13091	11	30833-33261
5	13092-16176	12	33262-25854
6	16177-19448	13	35855-39162
7	19449-22297		

Tour through Sicily, 24150, 33467-68
selections from, 31692
Buchan, Alexander. Last solemn confession, 13369
Buchan, David Stewart Erskine, earl, 1742-1829,
    correspondence with Washington, 39007
Buchan, William, 1729-1805
    Domestic medicine, (1772) 12338, (1774) 13181,
        (1778) 15751, (1784) 18384, (1789) 21715, (1790)
        22376, (1792) 24151, (1793) 25235-36, (1795)
        28365-66, (1797) 31886-88, (1798) 33469, (1799)
        35252
    Family physician, 20251
    Letter to the patentees, 26707, 28367
Buchanan, Archibald. Oration, 28368
Buchanan, George, 1506-1582. De juri regni, 10249
Buchanan, George, 1763-1807
    Dissertatio physiologica, 21716
    Oration, 24152, 25237
    Treatise, 21717
Buchanan, James. Regular English syntax, (1780)
    16725, (1783) 17858, (1786) 19256, (1788) 20985,
    (1792) 24153
Buchanan, James, d. 1778, execution, 15872-73
Buchanan, John, accounts, 18702, 19173
Buchan's Family physician, 20251
Buckingham, Stephen. Connecticut election ser-
    mon, 1495
Buckingham, Thomas, d. 1731. Moses and Aaron,
    3141
Buckland, James
    Account of the discovery, 19527, 20252
    Remarkable discovery, 19528
    Surprizing account, 19529-30
    Wonderful discovery of a hermit, 19532
    Wonderful discovery of an old, 19531, 24154
Buckler, Edward. Disswasive, 503
Bucklin, Daniel. Wharfage and storage, 26047
Buckminster, Joseph, 1720-1792
    Blessing of Abraham, 11590
    Brief dissertations, 10572
    Heads of families, 8310
    Ministers to be pray'd for, 9080
    letter (from Foster), 16776
Buckminster, Joseph, 1751-1812
    Brief paraphrase, 16215
    Discourse, (1783) 18385, (1789) 21718, (1798)
        33470, (1800) 37061
    Domestic happiness, 37062
    Duty of republican, 30132
    Religion and righteousness, 37063
    Remarks, 30133
    Sermon, (1787) 20253, (1794) 26708, (1798)
        33471, (1799) 35253, (1800) 37064
    Sermons, 24540
    hand of fellowship, 37597
    love affair, 32142
    reply to, 30606
Bucknam, Nathan
    Ability to and fidelity in, 5145
    Charge, 9593
    Just expectations, 4682
    Monitor for gospel, 6293
    colleague ordained, 21035
Buckner, Samuel. American sailor, 22377
Bucks County man. True and faithful narrative,
    12253
Buckskin. Contract, being a concise, 11611
Budd, John. Dissertation, 23230
Budd, Thomas
    Brief answer, 589
    False judgments, 611
    Good order, 386

Just rebuke, 590
Plea of the innocent, 612
trial of, 642
Buds of beauty, 20268-70
Büchlein vom Sabbath, 2990
Buel, Ebenezer, 1713-1801. Index to the Holy
    Bible, 33472
Buel, William, letters (from Smith), 31593
Buell, Abel, 1750-1825
    Map of the U.S., 19533
    To the honourable, 11192
Buell, Elias
    By permission of the legislature, 33242
    Capt. John Wood's lottery, 35048
Buell, Samuel, 1716-1798
    Best New Year's gift, 13849
    Christ the grand subject, 7371
    Divine agency, 7858
    Divine support, 20254
    Epistle (to Gardiner), 7402
    Excellence and importance, 8808
    Faithful narrative, 10250
    Happiness of the blessed, 8559
    Import of the saint's confession, 24155
    Intricate and mysterious, 11592
    Life of Christ, 26709
    Sermon, 20986
    Sincere reigning, 31889
    Spiritual knowledge, 12002
    Useful instructions, 17485, 17859
    Young & old, 11591
    death, 35372
    ordained, 5766
Buell, Samuel, 1772?-1787, death, 20254
Buell's Map of the U.S., 19533
Buffet, Platt. Letter, 26710
Buffin, John. True Quaker, 9609
Buffon, Georges Louis, comte de, 1707-1788, de-
    scribes elephant, 32074-77
Bugg, Francis, 1644-
    Bomb thrown, 1152
    refuted, 1230
    remarks on, 1192?
Builder's assistant, 36941
Builder's jewel, 37778
Builder's pocket treasure, 25955
Buist, George, 1740-1808
    Collection of hymns, 30134
    Oration 28369
    Sermon, 26711
    (ed.) Version of the book, 30078
Bulfinch, Charles
    Boston, Jan. 6, 1800, 36996
    To all people, 26690
Bulfinch, Thomas
    Desultory extracts, 30574
    remarks by, 31194
Bulkeley, Gershom, 1635-1713
    People's right, 459
    Some seasonable considerations, 688
Bulkeley, John
    Voyage, 7859
    proposals for printing Voyage, 7771
Bulkley, Edward. Sermon, 226
Bulkley, Col. John, wife's death, 6625
Bulkley, John, 1678-1731
    Impartial account, 3142
    Necessity of religion, 1598
    Usefulness of reveal'd religion, 3260
    death, 3740
    preface by, 2722
    remarks on, 3484?, 3494

reply to, 3237
Bulkley, Mary, d. 1750, death, 6450, 6625
Bulkly, ——, remarks on, 3484
Bull, Amos. Responsary, 28370
Bull, George, 1634-1710. Discourse, 4479
Bull, John, 1740?-1802, reports on accounts, 20062
Bull, Jonathan. Relation, 460
Bull, Nehemiah, ordained, 3124
Bull, William, 1710-1791
  Letter (to Penn), 4480
  surveys by, 13240
Bullard, Rev. ——, hand of fellowship, 34467
Bullard, Samuel. Almanac see **Almanacs (Bullard)**
Bullen, Joseph, charge to, 35738
Buller, Francis, 1745-1800. Introduction to the law, 20987
Bullock, John, defendant, 31668
Bundle of myrrh, 9358, 9921
Bungey, ——, conjurer, 3668
Bunker, Samuel, demandent, 11614
Bunker Hill, a tragedy, 30141
Bunker Hill, or the death, 31893
Bunn, Matthew, 1772-
  Journal, 30135-36
  Short narrative, 31890
Bunyan, John, 1628-1688
  Christian pilgrim, 33473
  Come and welcome, 3002
  Divine emblems, 26712, 30138
  Doctrine of the law, 4905
  Eines Christen reise, 7162-63, 30137
  Grace abounding, (1729) 3143, (1732) 3509, (1735) 3881, (1739) 4346, (1794) 26713, (1797) 31891
  Heilige krieg, 28371
  Holy war, 3998, 26714-15
  Jerusalem sinner, 3637, 33474
  Pilgrims- oder Christen-reise, 7372
  Pilgrim's progress, (1681) 299, (1706) 1242, (1738) 4228, (1744) 5351, (1798) 21720, (1791) 23232, (1794) 26717-18, (1800) 37066
  Sighs from hell, 1344
  Solomon's temple, 22379
  Visions, 28372
  life, 32379
Buonaparte, Napoleon
  Military journal, 38024
  campaign in Italy, 34393
  instructions to, 33753
  memoirs of, 34551
  overturns government, 37411
  portrait, 31904
  soldiers' letter, 35496
  suppresses Pope, 33462
Buonaparte's march, 34660
Burch, Thomas. Free grace, 7860
Burd, James, chairman of meeting, 14142
Burdon, William. Gentleman's pocket farrier, 3882, 25238
Burges, Bartholomew
  Seaman's journal, 19534, 20988
  Series of Indostan, 22380
  Short account, 21721-22
Burges, Tristam, 1770-1853
  Art of excelling, 35254
  Cause of man, 30139
  Solitude and society, 31892
  Spirit of independence, 37067
  War necessary, 35255
Burgess, Daniel, 1645-1713
  Craftsman, 2615

Rules for hearing, 4906
Sure way to wealth, 3003
Burgh, James, 1714-1775
  Art of speaking, (1775) 13850, (1780) 16727, (1782) 17487, (1785) 18945, (1786) 19535, (1790) 22381, (1793) 25239, (1795) 28373-74, (1800) 37068
  Britain's remembrancer, (1747) 5915, (1748) 6104-105, (1759) 8311
  Dignity of human, 26719
  Political disquisitions, 13851
  Rules for expressing, 34521
  Thoughts on education, 6294
  Youth a friendly, 20256
Burgher, John. God's love, 23233
Burghley, William Cecil, baron, 1520-1598. Ten precepts, (1786) 20002, (1789) 22158, (1792) 25064-65, (1795) 29560
Burgoyne, Sir John, 1722-1792
  Blockade of Boston, 15195
  For tenderness form'd, 26720
  Lord of the manor, 22382, 23234
  Maid of the oaks, 15252
  Prologue, 13841
  Speech, 16626
  Substance of General Burgoyne's speeches, 15752
  When first this, 30140
  articles of convention with Gates, 15274
  besought by Tryon, 15095
  correspondence with Lee, 14559
  head of Cerberus, 13985
  instructions to Baum, 15686
  letter (from Lee), 14148-50
  permit to sutlers, 15336
  surrender, 15313, 15318, 15438, 15599, 16217-18, 16284, 16479, 16684, 18167, 18765
Burgundy, Duke of, letter (from Fénélon), 4246
Burk, John Daly, 1775-1808
  Bunker Hill, 30141, 31893
  Death of General Montgomery, 15248-50
  Female patriotism, 33475
  History of the late, 35256
Burke, Mrs. ——. Ela, 21723, 23235
Burke, Aedanus, 1743-1802
  Address to the freeman, 17861, 27328
  Considerations on the society, 17862-66, 18387
Burke, Edmund, 1729-1797
  Appeal from the new, 23236, 31172
  Letter (to Duke of Portland), 31894
  Letter (to member of Nat. assembly), 23237
  Letter (to noble lord), 30142-43
  Reflections on the Revolution, 23238, 24157
  Speech (conciliation), 13854-55
  Speech (dissenters), 14092
  Speech (East India bill), 18388
  Speech (taxation), 13852-53
  Two letters (to member of Parliament), 31895
  extract from, 15942
  lesson based on, 24001-2

VOL.	ITEMS	VOL.	ITEMS
1	1-3244	8	22298-25074
2	3245-6623	9	25075-28145
3	6624-9891	10	28146-30832
4	9892-13091	11	30833-33261
5	13092-16176	12	33262-25854
6	16177-19448	13	35855-39162
7	19449-22297		

letters (from Priestley), 23716
observations on, 23517
remarks on, 15740-41
reply to, 23659-65, 24495, 26050, 27466, 31174,
   32097
strictures on, 31876, 32778
Burkitt, Lemuel. Minutes of the Kehukee, 27178
Burkitt, William, 1650-1703
   Divine hymns, 20989
   Expository notes, 26668, 30084-85
   Poor man's help, (1725) 2616, (1731) 3398, (1788)
      20990, (1795) 28375
   commentary on Bible, 20960, 21680, 22347
Burkloe, Samuel. Account of burials, 10737
Burlamaqui, Jean Jacques, 1694-1748. Principles
   of natural, 24158
Burlesson, E. Lamentation, 2617
Burling, Edward. Some remarks, 2508
Burling, Thomas, petition, 38894, 38897
Burlington advertiser. News carriers' address,
   23240
Burlington library
   Additional catalogue, 31896
   Catalogue, 24159
   Charter, 8096
Burlington, Nov. 1776, 14916
Burn, Richard, 1709-1785
   Abridgment, or the American, 24160-61
   (ed.) Commentaries on the laws, 35211
   Justice, 12702
   excerpts from, 10721, 21358-59, 22754, 24661,
      27472
Burnap, Jacob, 1748-1821
   Sermon, 35257
   ordained, 12809
Burnel, Rebeckah, d. 1724?, death, 2555
Burnes, George, meeting at house of, 11263
Burnet, Ann, d. 1789, death, 22385
Burnet, George Whitefield, d. 1800. Oration, (1798)
   35258, (1799) 37069
Burnet, Gilbert, 1643-1715
   Sermon, 461
   Some account, 28376-77, 31898
   preface by, 7565, 10489-90, 29478
   remarks on, 4218
Burnet, I., dispute with Roger Williams, 228
Burnet, James, 1779-1806. Oration, 35259
Burnet, Matthias, 1749-1806. Sermon, 22385
Burnet, William, 1688-1729
   Answer to a letter, 3216
   Essay on scripture-prophecy, 2509
   Ordinance, (1721) 2276, 2278, (1722) 2376, (1723)
      2464, 2468-69, 2568, (1724) 2567
   Proclamation, (1720) 2155-56, 2158, (1721) 2274-
      75, 2277, 2279, (1722) 2367-68, (1724) 2570,
      (1726) 2788
   Speech, (1720) 2099, 2159, (1722) 2369, 2465, 2467,
      (1724) 2571, (1725) 2686, (1726) 2789, (1727)
      2934 (1728) 3073
   address to, 2377
   character of, 3147
   death, 3278
   petition to, 2790
   poem to, 3004, 3092
   sermon before, 3093, 3242
Burney, Fanny see **Arblay, Frances Burney d',
   1752-1840**
Burnham, John, 1780-1826. Oration, 33476
Burnham, Jonathan. Arithmetick, 6106
Burnham, Richard, 1749-1810. Hymns, 31899
Burnham, William. God's providence, 2323

Burning and shining light, 6493
Burning of Sodom, 4808
Burnings bewailed, 1512, 1565
Burns, Ann, seduced, 33360
Burns, Robert, 1759-1796
   Masonic song, 37491
   Poems, 20991-92, 33477
   excerpts from, 23246
Burn's justice, 12702
Burnyeat, John, 1631-1690. Epistle, 401
Burr, Aaron, 1716-1757
   (ed.) American Latin grammar, 16982-83, 27639-
      40
   Discourse, 7373
   Sermon, (1745) 5549, (1756) 7628-29
   Servant of God, 7861, 8097
   Supreme deity, 7862, 23242
   Watchman's answer, 7863-64
   death, 7933, 8162, 8259
   excerpts from, 18758, 21434, 26105, 22853
   ordained, 4304
Burr, Aaron, 1756-1836
   dedication to, 31893
   opposes ratifying treaty, 29756
Burr, Jonathan, 1757-1842
   Catechism, 25240
   Compendium, 31900
Burr, Theodosia, dedication to, 30740
Burril, John
   defended, 1663
   letter (from Dudley), 1675, 1685
Burrill, George Rawson, 1770-1818. Oration, (1796)
   30145, (1797) 31901, (1800) 37070
Burrill, James
   (ed.) Poems, 31753
   secy. convention, 31061
   secy. Providence meeting, 31060
Burrill, John, d. 1721
   death, 2224
   defended, 1663?
   letter (from Cooke), 2022
   letter (from Dudley), 1675?, 1685?
Burriss, ———, owns meetinghouse, 25559
Burroughs, Eden, 1738-1813
   Charge, 38516
   Faithful narrative, (1793) 25241, 25243-45, (1794)
      26721
   Professional and practice, 25246
   Wonderful works, 25242
Burroughs, Jeremiah, 1599-1646
   Causes, evils, 24080
   Rare jewel, 3399, 4907
Burroughs, Josiah. The assistant, 30146, 35260
Burroughs, Peleg, d. 1800. Oration, 37071
Burroughs, Stephen, 1765-1840
   Faithful narrative, 24162-66
   Memoirs, 33478
   Sermon, 33479
Burrows, Silas, pastor at Groton, 37551
Burt, John, d. 1775
   Earthquakes, 7374
   Mercy of God, 8312
Burt, Nathaniel, poem on, 7855, 8093
Burton, Asa, 1752-1836
   Discourse, 28378
   Sermon, (1785) 19536, (1800) 37072
   To be greatest, 23243
   True sources, 25247
Burton, John, 1746-1806. Lectures on female edu-
   cation, (1794) 26722-23, (1796) 30147, (1798)
   33480, (1799) 35261

Burton, Richard see **Crouch, Nathaniel, 1632-1725**
Burton, Robert. Fables of Aesop, 15231
Bury, Elizabeth Lawrence, 1644-1720. Account of the life, 5146
Bush, Philip, petition, 38849
Bushe, Gervase Parker. Case of Great Britain, 11193-94
Bushnell, Ebenezer. Almanac see **Almanacs (Bushnell)**
Bushnell, Jedediah, ordained, 38575
Business and diversion, 5285
Business, scope and end, 5892
Bussfertige beicht-vater, 23100
Busy body, a comedy, 26559, 26750
Butcher, Elizabeth, 1709-1718, early piety of, 1973, 2038, 5008
Bute, John Stuart, earl of, 1713-1792
   conduct of, 13992
   persuades Tryon, 15095
Butler, George B. Case of Great Britain, 11193-94
Butler, James, 1755-1842. Fortune's foot-ball, 31902, 33481
Butler, John. Political fugitive, 26724
Butler, Joseph, 1692-1752. Analogy of religion, 25248
Butler, Richard
   concludes treaty, 18817
   portrait, 23268
Butler, S., vision, 20351
Butterworth, James. Exhortation, 28233
Buxton, Charles
   Inaugural dissertation, 25249
   Oration, 33482
By an arrival at Newport, 24169
   express arrived at Philadelphia, 13857
     arrived yesterday, 14671
     just arrived from New York, 14789
     just arrived we have, 13856
   order from the Orphan's court, 38507
By Augustin Prevost, 16290
By authority; by the American company, 10573
By authority; copies of letters, 16788
By authority, Mr. Pool, 19196
By authority; New York, 15323
By Brigadier General Stanwix, 8459
By Charles Wilson, 12523
By command of the king, 13182
By his excellency . . . A proclamation see under name of official issuing proclamation
   excellency Edward viscount Cornbury, 1185
     George Washington, 14542
     Isaac Tichenor, 38929
     John Jay, 38076
     Robert Hunter, 1772
     the governor, 8910
     William Burnet, 2276, 2278
By-laws and catalogue, 37049
   and orders, 8086
   and regulations of the East India, 38454
   and regulations of the incorporated, 32800
   and town-orders, 19515
   of St. John's, 32765
   of the city of Hartford, 21134, 32231
   of the Merrimack, 24541
   of the Sixth Massachusetts, 35803
   of the town, 29344
   passed Aug. 8, 1792, 24715
By legislative authority, 31875
By order of his excellency . . . see under name of person (e.g., **Howe, Sir William.** Proclamation)
   of the government, 2063

of the selectmen, 31827
By permission; a list, 15824
By permission; Mr. Carleton, 20261
   of his excellency, 15336
   of the legislature, 33242
By Richard, viscount Howe, 14782-83
By Sir George Collier, 16291
By-stander. Common sense, 12359
By the Congress of the U. S.; a manifesto, 16132
   Congress of the U. S. of A.; a manifesto, 16133
   council of safety, 15511
   court in the yeares, 10
   governor . . . A proclamation see under state or colony concerned (e.g., **New York. Governor.** Proclamation)
   governour & council, 519, 533
   honourable . . . A proclamation see under name of official or under governmental body
   honourable Cadwallader Colden, 9754
     James Logan, 4183
     Major general, 19441
     Peter Schuyler, 2062
     the president, 4060
House of delegates, (1796) 30747, (1799) 35776, (1800) 37892
Lord Hyde packet, 14082
mail which arrived, 21469
mayor, aldermen, 30995
mayor, recorder, 10132
medium, 12703
Old American company, 27407
packet, 13858
president and council, (1686) 410, (1747) 6043
proprietaries, (1738) 4297, (1739) 4410
proprietary, 894
supreme executive, 15509-10
U.S. in Congress assembled, (Mar. 3, 1781) 17383, (Apr. 7, 1781) 17384, (Jan. 3, 1782) 17755, (Jan. 10, 1782) 17756, (Feb. 20, 1782) 17757-58, (Aug. 7, 1782) 17759, (Sept. 4, 1782) 17760, 19291, (Oct. 4, 1782) 17761, (Feb. 17, 1783) 18232, (Nov. 1, 1783) 18246, 18827, (Mar. 23, 1784) 18824, (Apr. 23, 1784) 19283, (Apr. 30, 1784) 18825, (June 3, 1784) 18826, (Feb. 23, 1785) 19281, (Mar. 31, 1785) 19282, (June 7, 1785) 19284, (July 27, 1785) 19285, (Aug. 17, 1785) 19286, (Sept. 27, 1785) 19287, (Sept. 30, 1785) 19288-89, (Oct. 3, 1785) 19290, (Oct. 12, 1785) 19291, (Nov. 2, 1785) 19292, (Jan. 2, 1786) 20045, (June 27, 1786) 20046, (July 14, 1786) 20047, (Aug. 2, 1786) 20048, (Aug. 7, 1786) 20049, (Aug. 8, 1786) 20050, (Sept. 18, 1786) 20051, (Oct. 20, 1786) 20052, (Oct. 23, 1786) 20053, (Mar. 23, 1787) 20757, (Apr. 21, 1787) 20758-59, (May 3, 1787) 20760, (May 7, 1787) 20761, (Oct. 3, 1787) 20762, (Oct. 11, 1787) 20763, (June 11, 1788) 21512, (June 20, 1788) 21513-14, (July 9, 1788) 21515, (Sept. 13, 1788) 21518

VOL.	ITEMS	VOL.	ITEMS
1	1-3244	8	22298-25074
2	3245-6623	9	25075-28145
3	6624-9891	10	28146-30832
4	9892-13091	11	30833-33261
5	13092-16176	12	33262-25854
6	16177-19448	13	35855-39162
7	19449-22297		

U.S. in Congress assembled, a proclamation
. . . see U. S. Proclamation
U.S. in Congress assembled, Wednesday, Aug.
20, 1788, 21516
way of a scripture interpretation, 9413
By virtue of a certain, 13366
By William Cobbett, 35316
By Winthrop Sargent, 37973
Byberry library company. Constitution, 37073
Bye-laws and ordinances, 20265
   and regulations, 29317
   for the organization, 33509
   of the city, 22708
      corporation, 11156
      Friendship fire company, 29313
   resolutions, and orders, 20579, 30881
Byerley, Thomas, d. 1826. Plain and easy introduc-
tion, 12704
Byfield, Nathaniel, 1653-1733
   Account of the late, 462
   Seasonable motives, 463
   death, 3640
   wife's death, 3402
Byfield, Sarah, d. 1730, death, 3402
Byles, Anna, death, 5352
Byles, Mather, 1706-1788
   Affections on things, 4481
   Character of the perfect, 3144, 5352
   Comet, a poem, 5353
   Conference, 3655
   Death of a friend, 12339
   Discourse on the present, 3510, 12003
   Divine power, 7375
   Elegy, 3597
   Epistle, 12555

Flourish of the annual, 4683, 11195
Glories of the Lord, 4482, 11196
Glorious rest, 5550
God glorious, 5354
God the strength, 6826
Man of God, 8098
New England hymn, 23079
On the death, 4229
Poem on the death, 2846
Poem presented, 3004
Poems on several occasions, 5355
Poems; the conflagration, 7376
Prayer and plea, 6647
Repentance and faith, 4684
To his excellency, 3999
Vanity of every man, 8809
Visit to Jesus, 4685
chaplain, 3554
conference with prisoner, 3655
dispute with New London church, 10909
introduction by, 5983
leaves New London, 11035
preface by, 4717, 5025
Byles, Mather, 1735-1814
   Christian sabbath, 8313
   Sermon, 8560
   answer to, 8302
   ordained, 8098
Byles, Samuel, 1743-1764. Pious remains, 9610
Byng, John, 1704-1757
   Defence, 7865
   Trial, 7890-92
Byrd, William, commissioner, 7689
Byrnes, Daniel. Following address, 13859
Bystander, or a series, 37074

C

C., D. see **Cornyn, Dominick**
C., E. see **Cook, Ebenezer**
C., G. Little looking-glass, 9611
C., J. see **Carey, John, 1756-1826; Cleaveland, John, 1722-1799**
C., R. see **Challoner, Richard, 1691-1781**
C., S. see **Crisp, Stephen, 1628-1692**
C., S. Almanac see **Almanacs (Cheever)**
C., T. Scheme to drive, 7377
C., W. B. see **Crafton, William Bell**
C . . . .d, A. see **Cleveland, Aaron**
C'est appeller, 28491
Ça ira; to the citizens, 29345
Cabal and love, 29470
Cabot, Marston, d. 1756
    Christ's kingdom, 5147
    Nature of religious, 3756, 3883
    Sermon, (1745) 5552, (1754) 7164
Cacique of Ontario, 36232
Cadell & Davies. London, Decr. 11, 1800, 37842
Cadet de Gassicourt, Charles Louis, 1769-1821
    Tomb of James, 31903
Cadogan, William, 1711-1797
    Dissertation on the gout, (1771) 12004, (1772)
        12338, 12340-43, (1785) 18946
    Essay upon nursing, 12344, 12705
    dedication to, 23758
Cadwalader, John, 1742-1786. Reply, 17867
Cadwalader, Lambert, 1742-1823
    reports on sundry motions, 19307
    reports on supplies, 19308
Cadwalader, Thomas, 1707-1779. Essay, 5553
Cagliostro, Giuseppe Balsamo, 1745-1785. Defence,
    21724
Cagnawaga Indians, conference with, 3916
Caine, Henrietta Maria. Catalogue of goods, 7165
Cain's lamentations, (1795) 28483-84, (1796) 30283
Caius see **Carey, Mathew, 1760-1839; Pinkney,
    William, 1764-1822**
Cajouge Indians, treaty, 702, 743
Calamy, Benjamin, letter (from De Laune), 9374,
    37309
Calcott, Wellins. Candid disquisition, 12345
Calculation exhibiting, 25250
    on the commencement, (1795) 28789, (1796)
        30126, 30530, (1797) 31877
    shewing in what, 34360
    shewing that within, 34361
Calculations on American, 14625
Calder, James. Information to aid, 32338
Caldwell, Charles, 1772-1853
    Attempt to establish, 30148

Elegiac poem, 36453, 37077-80
Elements of physiology, 28310
Eulogium, 35262
Semi-annual oration, 35263
(ed.) Zoonomia, 30312
Caldwell, James, murdered, 11683, 12094
Caldwell, John
    Answer to the appendix, 5147
    Impartial trial, 4908, 5750
    Nature, folly and evil, 4909
    Scripture characters, 4910
    answered, 4993
Caldwell, Joseph. Eulogy, 37081
Caldwell, Samuel, ordained, 28792
Caldwell, Samuel C., ordained, 24373
Caleb the flying mercury, 19077
Calef, Ebenezer, demandent, 11614
Calef, Jonathan, ordained, 28821
Calef, Robert, d. 1723
    More wonders, 30149
    answer to, 975
Calendar; James Cochran, 31950
Calendar of nature, 36782
Calendrier pour l'année 1781, 17110
    pour l'année sextile, 25251
    republicain pour l'an VI, 31904
Calet, Jean Jacques. True and minute account,
    30151, 37082
Calhoun, James, cancels subscription, 13677
Calhoun, James, mayor Baltimore, 36881
Call from heaven, 274, 393
    from Macedonia, 10910
    from the dead, 3020
    of the gospel, 413, 432
    to Archippus, 1103
    to parents, 4112
    to such as experience, 4314
    to the tempted, 2563
        unconverted, (1702) 1037, (1717) 1866,
            (1720) 2093, (1731) 3391, (1792) 24031,
            (1793) 25148, (1795) 28243-44, (1797)

Campe, Joachim Heinrich von, 1746-1818. New Robinson Crusoe, 22389, 24171
Canada forever, 8314
Canal lottery, no. two, 31167
Canal lottery; scheme, 29473
Canawese Indians, treaty with, 3041
Cancers; the following, 26021
Candid address, 37093
    and impartial account, 5917-18
    animadversions on a petition, 25444
    animadversions respecting, 17922
    considerations, 21725
    discussion, 28130
    disquisition, 12345
    examination of Dr. Mayhew, 9360
        of the address, 18389
        of the mutual, 14059
        of the objections, (1795) 29534-35, (1798) 34907
    narrative of certain, 21450
    narrative of the rise, 7112
    refutation, 13326
    remarks, 12346
    reply to the arguments, 36838
    reply to the reverend, 28625
    retrospect, 16728-29
Candidus
    Letter (to Philo-Africanus), 20993
    see also **Smith, William, 1727-1803**
Candor see **Delanoe, S.**
Caner, Henry, 1700-1792
    Candid examination, 9360
    Discourse, 6107
    Firm belief, 9923
    God the only, 6648
    Great blessing, 9361
    Joyfulness, 8811
    Nature and necessity, 8099
    Piety of founding, 6296
    True nature, 5554
    appendix by, 6283
    reflections on, 5761
    reply to, 6693
Canfield, Ithamar, relief of, 38885
Cannibal's progress, 33325-38
Cannon, James. Catalogue, 17723
Canonicus see **Chauncy, Charles, 1705-1787**
Cantata-quartette for St. Patrick's, 20611
Canterbury, Thomas, abp. of see **Secker, Thomas, 1693-1768**
Cantiques françaises, 33363
Cantrill, Stephen, petition, 34887
Capacity of Negroes, 24623
Capel, Arthur see **Essex, Arthur Capel, earl of, 1631-1683**
Capen, Hopestill. Following was written, 14672
Capen, Joseph, 1658-1725
    Funeral sermon, 1870
    Verses, 308
Capron, Henry, ed. First number of music, 25831
Captain Cook's third and last, (1793) 25346, (1795) 28476-77, (1796) 30275-76
Captain Cook's Three voyages, 31982-83
Captain in the late 72nd regiment see **Drinkwater, John, 1762-1844**
Captain James, who was hung, 37094
    John Wood's lottery, 34029, 35048
    O'Blunder, 9081
    of the Lord's, 4692
    Smith late of Maryland, 16072
    Truxton, 36246

Captives bound, 4934
Captivity, a ballad, 26218
Capture, a favorite song, 25306
Caracciolo, Galeazzo see **Vico, Galeazzo Caracciolo, marquis of, 1517-1586**
A card; Cassius presents, 14674
    Jack Bowling, 10848
    Jack Hatchway, 11199
    Mr. Axe, 10849
    New York, Sept. 9, 1774, 13184
    number I, 11594
    Robert Barclay, 10850
    the public present, 12707
    to the electors, 15753
    to the freeholders, 11198
Cardiphonia, 24620, 29212-13
Care, Henry, 1646-1688. English liberties, 2208, 13185
Care of the soul, 8842, 25408
Careful, Charles, history of, 29818
Careful and strict enquiry, 7187, 10289
    and strict inquiry, 22476
    and strict examination, 8539, 11565
Carefully to observe, 26487
Careless, Tommy, history of, 35623
Cares about the nurseries, 1065
Carew, Bampfylde Moore, 1690-1770. Adventures, 12708
Carey, Henry, 1696-1744. Contrivances, 9082
Carey, James
    Anticipation, 31914
    Collected wisdom, 35268
    He wou'd be a poet, 30154
    House of wisdom, 33490-92
    Life of skunk, 33493
    Nosegay, 33494-95
    Pill for Porcupine, 30155
    View of the New England, 35269-70
Carey, John, 1756-1826
    Catalogue of part, 24172
    Catalogue of scarce, 23245
    (ed.) Official letters, 29737
    System of short-hand, 25252
Carey, Mathew, 1760-1839
    Address of M. Carey, 26729
    Address to the House, 30156, 31172
    Address to the President, 28387
    American atlas, 28390, 37096
    American musum, 20193-95
    American pocket atlas, 30161
    American primer, 37095
    American remembrancer, 28389
    Beauties of poetry, 23246
    Catalogue, (1792) 24173-76, (1793) 25253, (1794) 26730, (1795) 28388
    Child's guide, 37098
    Columbian reading, 35271
    (ed.) Debates, 19884
    Epistle (to Oswald), 19539
    Exchange catalogue, 33497

VOL.	ITEMS	VOL.	ITEMS
1	1-3244	8	22298-25074
2	3245-6623	9	25075-28145
3	6624-9891	10	28146-30832
4	9892-13091	11	30833-33261
5	13092-16176	12	33262-25854
6	16177-19448	13	35855-39162
7	19449-22297		

Criterion, 30166
trial, 11683
Carroll, Charles, 1702-1782
Letter (to the reader), 16216
chairman of meeting, 13817
Carroll, Daniel, 1730-1796
reports on Indian affairs, 18262-63
reports on representation 18827
Carroll, John, 1735-1815
Address to the Roman, 18390
Discourse, 37108
Pastoral letter, 35284
consecrated, 23703
dedication to, 21706-707
Carroll, Nicholas. Address of the visitors, 27666
Carson, James. Practical grammar, 26744
Carson, Jemmy. Collection of ballads, 9083
Carte de l'Isle St. Domingue, 30817
Carter, ——, selections from music, 34516
Carter, George. Essay on fevers, 30167
Carter, J. Boston, Mar. 29, 1783, 17849
Carter, John. Catalogue of books, 28396
Carter, Joshua, petition, 31372
Carter, Landon
Rector detected, 9613
remarks on, 9359
Carter, Robert, recommends reprinting pamphlet, 28429
Carter, Susannah. Frugal housewife, (1772) 12348, (1774) 13186, (1792) 24180, (1796) 30168
Carter, William, account of Sweeting, 23814-15, 24836-37, 27767, 32899
Cartwright, Charlotte. Lady's best companion, 33499
Cartwright, Edmund, 1743-1823. Armine and Elvira, (1774) 13449, (1775) 14263, (1784) 18550, (1787) 20535
Cartwright, John, 1740-1824. American independence, 14673
Carver, Jonathan, 1732-1780. Three years travels, (1784) 18391, (1789) 21728, (1792) 24181, (1794) 26745, (1796) 30169, (1797) 31920
Cary, Anna, d. 1755, death, 7545
Cary, Richard, 1716?-1790
death, 22683
wife's death, 7545
Cary, Richard, 1747-1806. Charlestown, May 27, 1789, 21729
Cary, Thomas, 1745-1808
Charge, 30726
Importance of salvation, 12709
Sermon, 30170
colleague ordained, 21888
correspondence, 21507
ordained, 10825
Cary, Thomas, d. 1820
Sermon, 31921
hand of fellowship, 32625
Caryl, Benjamin, d. 1811. Duty of thanksgiving, 11200
Casca
Crisis, (no. XIII) 13976-77, (no. XV) 13980-81, (no. XVI) 13982, (no. XXI) 13987, (no. XXIV) 13990, (no. XXV) 13991, (no. XXVI) 13992
Crisis extraordinary, 13995-96
Epistle (to Mansfield), 13983
Epistle (to North), 13984
Case, Mrs. M. W., d. 1796, death, 34014
Case, Wheeler, d. 1795
Poems occasioned by several, 15754-56
Poems on several occurrences, 16217-19

Case and complaint of Mr. Samuel, 5265
and complaint of Rev. Samuel, 6548
decided, 25370-71
of a troubled mind, 1897, 4751
of conscience, 798
of George M'Intosh, 15383
of Great-Britain, 11193-94
of Heman, 7769
of his majesty's province, 6003
of James Christie, 13868
of John Nelson, 12134
of Jonathan Robbins, 36121
of Major John, 16731
of Mr. T. L., 8630
of Nathaniel Matson, 2151
of our fellow, 18353
of poor emigrants, 32714
of Satan's fiery, 5366
of the commonwealth, 21363
county of Orange, 13187, 33500
dissenting, 12865
Episcopal, 17802
Georgia sales, 35587-88
German, 6977
heir, 2735
inhabitants, 18392
late election, (1772) 12328, (1773) 12684, (1774) 13154
manor, 11201
manufacturers, 32564
muster rolls, 2135
people, 2533
provinces, 9731
Scotch, 12710
sloop, 16220
Whigs, 17900
of unclean birds, 982
put & decided, 822
relating to the southern, 7261
Trevett against Weeden, 20825
upon statute, 31672
Cases adjudged, 27391
and observations, 21296
and trials, 14655
argued, 28636
determined, 25451, 25702, 32426
of conscience about singing, 2485
of conscience concerning evil, 658
of the angina, 17092
Cash, Caleb. Account of the births, (1747) 6050, (1748) 6220, (1751) 6755, (1752) 6914, (1753) 7092, (1754) 7293, (1755) 7539, (1756) 7763, (1757) 8004, (1758) 8236, (1759) 8467, (1760) 8714, (1761) 8980, (1762) 9238, (1763) 9483, (1764) 9793, (1765) 10136, (1766) 10452, (1767) 10738, (1768) 11036, (1769) 11414, (1770) 11819, (1771) 12522, 12524
Caslon, William, type manufacturer, 19272
Caspipina, Tamoc see **Duché, Jacob, 1737-1798**
Cassem, life of, 20458, 21202, 22620
Cassius

VOL.	ITEMS	VOL.	ITEMS
1	1-3244	8	22298-25074
2	3245-6623	9	25075-28145
3	6624-9891	10	28146-30832
4	9892-13091	11	30833-33261
5	13092-16176	12	33262-25854
6	16177-19448	13	35855-39162
7	19449-22297		

VOL.	ITEMS	VOL.	ITEMS
1	1-3244	8	22298-25074
2	3245-6623	9	25075-28145
3	6624-9891	10	28146-30832
4	9892-13091	11	30833-33261
5	13092-16176	12	33262-25854
6	16177-19448	13	35855-39162
7	19449-22297		

VOL.	ITEMS	VOL.	ITEMS
1	1-3244	8	22298-25074
2	3245-6623	9	25075-28145
3	6624-9891	10	28146-30832
4	9892-13091	11	30833-33261
5	13092-16176	12	33262-25854
6	16177-19448	13	35855-39162
7	19449-22297		

Funeral oration, 37124
Oraison funebre de frere, 37125
Oraison funebre du frere George, M. de la Grange, 37126
Oraison funebre du frere George Washington, 37127
Chaudron, Simon, d. 1846. Ode, 35295
Chauncey, Dr. ——, observations on, 10934
Chauncey, Charles, 1777-1849. Oration, 31932
Chauncey, Isaac, 1671-1745
Blessed manumission, 3145
Faithful evangelist, 2618
Loss of the soul, 3515
Unprofitableness of superficial, 3516
Chauncey, Nathaniel, 1681-1756
Charge, 4460
Faithful ruler, 3757
Faithful servant, 3517
Honouring God, 2017
Regular singing, 3006, 12716
death, 7804
Chauncy, Charles, 1592-1672
Anti-synodalia, 86
God's mercy, 40
pres. Harvard, 41, 59, 92, 102, 108, 123, 140
Chauncy, Charles, 1705-1787
Accursed thing, 15759
All nations, 9088
Appeal to the public answered, 10853
Benevolence of the deity, 18397
Blessedness of the dead, 6298
Breaking of bread, 12350
Character and overthrow, 3758
Charge, 12419
Charity to the distressed, 7869
Christian love, 12717
Civil magistrates, 5919
Compleat view, 12009
Cornelius's character, 5556
Counsel of two, 5752
Discourse occasioned by the death, (Foxcroft) 11207, (Mayhew) 10254, (Sewall) 11206
Discourse on the good, 10255
Divine glory, 17870
Duty of ministers, 10256
Early piety, 3518
Earth delivered, 7634
Earthquakes, 7380
Enthusiasm described, 4912
Gifts of the spirit, 4913
Horrid nature, 7168
Idle-poor secluded, 6827
Joy the duty, 4687
Late religious commotions, 5150
Letter (to a friend), (1755) 7381, (1767) 10579, (1774) 13197
Letter (to Whitefield), 5152, 5557
Man's life, 3402
Marvellous things, 5558
Ministers cautioned, 5357
Ministers exhorted, 5358
Nathanael's character, 3640
New creature, 4688
Only compulsion, 4349
Opinion of one, 8100
Outpouring of the holy, 4914
Prayer for help, 4129
Reply to Dr. Chandler, 11598
Salvation for all, 17489-90
Seasonable thoughts, 5151
Second letter (to a friend), 7382

Second letter (to Whitefield), 5153
Sermon, (1767) 10580, (1785) 18953
Trust in God, 11599
Twelve sermons, 9925
Unbridled tongue, 4689
Validity of Presbyterian, 9089
Wonderful narrative, 4915
death, 20273
hand of fellowship, 12745
letter (from Whitefield), 5710-11
observations on, 10934?
remarks on, 21711
reply to, 11203, 12007, 22478
vindicated, 10800, 31609
Chauncy, Isaac, captain of Columbia, 24863
Chauncy, Isaac, 1671-1745 see **Chauncey, Isaac, 1671-1745**
Chauncy, Israel. Almanac see **Almanacs** (Chauncy)
Chauvet, David
Conduct of the government, 33510
Letter of a Genevan, 33511
Cheap repository; number 1-42, 37128-169
Cheap repository tracts, 35296-98
Cheapside apprentice, 34135, 37140
Cheat unmask'd, 9614
Chebacco narrative, 4303, 6113
Checkered state, 1032
Checkley, John, 1680-1753
Choice dialogue, 2100
Defence of a book, 2510
Dialogue between a minister, 4690
Letter (to Dickinson), 2619
Modest proof, 2417
remarks on, 2194, 2592
reply to, 2581
Checkley, Samuel, 1696-1769
Character and hope, 6111?
Charge, 5942
Day of darkness, 7383
Death of the godly, 2848
Duty of a people, 2847
Duty of God's people, 7384
Little children, 4691
Mercy with God, 3641
Murder a great, 3642
Prayer a duty, 5559
Sinners minded, 3643
Checkley, Samuel, 1723-1768
Character and hope, 6111
Christian triumphing, 9926, 10257
death, 11584
Cheerful songster's companion, 29541
Cheering rosary, 25966
Cheetham, James, of Gt. Brit., trial, 27076
Cheetham, James, 1772-1810
Answer to Alexander Hamilton, 37170
Dissertation, 37171
Letter (to Hamilton), 37172
Cheever, Abijah. History of a case, 26763

VOL.	ITEMS	VOL.	ITEMS
1	1-3244	8	22298-25074
2	3245-6623	9	25075-28145
3	6624-9891	10	28146-30832
4	9892-13091	11	30833-33261
5	13092-16176	12	33262-25854
6	16177-19448	13	35855-39162
7	19449-22297		

Cheever, David
  Watertown, July 6th, 14239
  chairman supply committee, 14196
Cheever, Edward, d. 1794. Ministers are to testify, 12351
Cheever, Ezekiel, 1615-1708
  Short introduction, (1709) 1384, (1724) 2511, (1767) 10767
  death, 1361, 1376, 13431
  grammarian, 4197, 6417, 6928, 7567-68, 8728, 9008, 10492, 10758, 11070, 11464, 11855-56, 12227, 13013, 16982-83, 18186, 19239-42, 27639-40
Cheever, Ezekiel, d. 1775. Scripture prophesies, 7870
Cheever, Samuel. Almanac see **Almanacs (Cheever)**
Cheever, Samuel, 1639-1724
  Gods sovereign government, 1541
  death, 2501
Cheever, Thomas, 1658-1749
  Churches duty, 1727
  Two sermons, 2736
Chemical and economical, 22757
Chemical syllabus, 36609
Chemico-medical essay, 32036
Chemico-physiological inaugural, 29431
Chemin-Dupontes, Jean Baptiste. Morality, 26764
Cheney, Thomas, accounts, 19171
Cherokee Indians
  account of, 22329, 23159-60
  campaigns against, 9242-43
  treaty, (1756) 7689, (1785) 19279, (1799) 36487, 36491-92
Cherubims explained, 29657
Cherubini, Luigi, 1760-1842. Overture, 28412
Chesapeak (favoring a canal), 10854
Cheselden, William, 1688-1752
  Anatomical tables, 28414, 30186
  Anatomy of the human, 28413
Chesnut, ——, ordained, 6817
Chesnuthiller wochenschrift, 22401
Chesselden, John. Surprising account, 18954, 30187
Chester garland, 31934
Chester, Mar. 23, 1776, 14972
Chesterfield, Philip Dormer Stanhope, earl, 1694-1773
  Accomplished gentleman, 22157
  Advice to his son, (1781) 17372, (1786) 20002, (1789) 22158, (1792) 24064-65, (1794) 27735, (1795) 29560
  Letters (to Stanhope), 14471, 16534-36
  Life, 14472
  Principles of politeness, (1778) 15914, 16077, (1782) 17726, (1785) 19258, (1786) 20003, (1788) 22159, (1791) 23326-27, 23790, (1792) 24813, (1793) 26202, (1794) 27736-37, (1795) 29561, (1796) 31229, (1798) 34595, (1800) 38553
  Select letters, 16078
  extracts from letters, 21985
  letter (from Dodsley), 28580, 28583
  letter (from Muilman), 6722
  reply to, 16802
Chesterfield's impenetrable secret, 27026, 37174
Chetwood, William Rufus, d. 1766
  Remarkable history, (1793) 25294, (1795) 28415, (1798) 33513
  Voyages and adventures, (1790) 22402, (1794) 26766, (1796) 30188, (1799) 35299
Chevalier, John, inspects lottery drawing, 12192
Chevy Chace. Hunting of Chevy Chase, 35300
Chew, Jeffery, defendant, 36396

Chew, Samuel, 1690-1744. Speech, (1741) 4708-709, 13867, (1742) 4930
Chickkemogga Indians, escape from, 20472, 27248, 30713, 32401
Child, John, d. 1684, suicide, 30012, 33357
Child, Samuel. Every man his own brewer, 30189
Child, William. Collection of hymns, 28416
Child of light, 2769
  of nature, a dramatic, 22525, 22619
  of nature, a philosophical, 13198
  of Pallas, 38316
Children foederally holy, 9984
  in the wood(s), (1785) 19401, (1795) 29114-17, (1796) 29955, (1799) 35086
  of light, 2771
  of the abbey, (1798) 34480, (1799) 36240, (1800) 38416
  of the covenant, 1840
  well imployed, 4413
Children's catechism, 24565
  friend, (1786) 19504-505, (1789) 21676, (1791) 23344, (1793) 25163-64, (1794) 26643, (1795) 28266, (1796) 30061
  magazine, 21734
  miscellany, 30190, 33611
Childs, Francis
  New-York, Nov. 1793, 25295
  letters (from Dayton), 37297
Childs, Isaac
  Geschichte, 23257
  Vision of Isaac, 10258
Childs, Thomas. Biographical memoirs, 37222-23
Child's best instructor, 29441-42
  best plaything, 10314-15
  catechism, 34049
  companion, 24112-13, 30094
  daily present, 19554
  first primer, 37176
  guide to spelling, 37098
  guide to the English, 1858
  instructor (Ely), (1792) 24298, (1793) 25445, (1794) 26939, (1796) 30387, (1797) 32080, (1800) 37361-62
  instructor (Sterling), 31236
  instructor (Waterman), (1793) 26433, (1794) 28032, (1795) 29837, (1799) 35441, 36671
  library, 36966-67
  new plaything, (1744) 5359, (1750) 6477, (1757) 7871, (1761) 8813, (1765) 9927
  plain pathway, 20162, 26512
  plaything, 19555, 28417
  pocket companion, 19556
  portion, 380
  reading book, 35301
  spelling book, 33346, 37179
  toy, 29393
Chimera, or effusions, 29022-23
Chipman, John, 1691-1775
  Remarks on some points, 5890
  Seasonable meditations, 3146
  colleague ordained, 12074
  reply to, 5734
Chipman, Nathaniel, 1752-1843
  Reports and dissertations, 25296
  Sketches of the principles, 25297-98
Chipman, William, d. 1800?, murdered, 39091
Chippewa Indians
  treaty, (1785) 19278, (1795) 29742
  vocabulary, 31920
Chisholm, Alexander, sues Georgia, 25370-71
Chisholm, Colin, 1755-1855. Essay, 35302

Chism, William, murdered, 7168
Chisolm, Robert. On the hydrocephalus, 30191
Chittenden, Abel, d. 1770, death, 11585
Chittenden, Thomas
    Proclamation, (1779) 16651-52, (1781) 17403-404, (1783) 18277, (1787) 20829-30, (1791) 23935-36, (1793) 26377, (1794) 27994, (1795) 29788, (1796) 31487, (1797) 33120
    Regulations for the order, 20832
    State of Vermont, Windsor, 17405
    discourse before, 24788, 28093, 28378, 30655
    forwards memorial, 28997
    letters (from Weare), 16391
    sermon before, 18566, 19536
Choate, John
    Reasons of dissent, 8562, 8617
    Remarks on the late, 8814
    reply to, 8873
Choctaw Indians, account of, 22329?, 23159-60?
The Choice (Fitch), 21827
The choice, a discourse, 34031
The choice, a poem, 7872
Choice collection of English, 9569
    collection of Free Masons songs, 16222
        of hymns, (1734) 5304, (1774) 13507, (1782) 17491, (1784) 18398, 18667, (1785) 19152, (1787) 20271, (1792) 24641, (1794) 26767
        of riddles, 25194
        of songs, 13124
        out of the Psalms, 4361
    dialogue, 2194
    dialogues, 2100
    drop of honey, (1667) 118, (1734) 3857, (1741) 4864-67, (1743) 5314, (1770) 11942, (1794) 28085
    emblems, 22854
    of wisdom, 2764
    tales, 37180
Chorister's companion, (1782) 17567, (1783) 17988, (1788) 21177, (1790) 22588, (1791) 23472, (1792) 24433
Chorus sung, 22093
Christ a Christian's life, 28723
    a perfect, 12816
    abolishing death, 4067
    always present, 6091
    besuchet, 6112
Christ church, Philadelphia see under Philadelphia
Christ expects, 4254
    formed in the soul, 24272
    holding, 6654
    in the clouds, (1729) 3131, (1742) 4887, (1752) 6806, (1770) 11559, (1786) 19460, (1800) 36807
    Jesus a common, 16277
    Jesus the physician, 8598
    living, 5318
    sent to heal, 12862-63
    standing, 4231
    the alone, 4891
    the Christian's hope, 21639
    the Christian's life, 12718
    the foundation, 10605
    the grand subject, 7371, 9869
    the great example, 6492
    the great subject, 2391
    the king, 5521
    the life, and death, 12756

    the life of true, 4731
    the lord, 19007
    the son, 6759
    the standard, 19621-22
    the true victim, 20704
    triumphing, 4716, 4951
    victorious, 3723
Christen gedancken, 9555
Christian, Capt. ——, on Vigilant, 15321
Christian, a poem, 17893, 26830
    A.B.C., 19042, 21891
    advice, 1720
    ambassador, 18472
    and civil liberty, 14675
    apology, 7990
    at his calling, 990
    baptism, 10324
    bravery, 4000
    charity, 35249
    churches, 3390
    confession, 2924
    conversing with himself, 1409
    conversing with the great, 1400
    courage, 2939
    covenanting, 58
    cynick, 1819
    discipline, 8515
    doctrines, 38406
    economy, 24191-92, 28418
    edifice, 19993
    education, 7169
    epistle, 580
    faith, 600
    fixed, 1190
    forbearance, 21923
    funeral, 1618
    glorying, 3983
    harmony, 27205, 30680
    history, (for 1743) 5154, 5482, (for 1744-45) 5360, 5682
    hymns, poems, (1774) 13566, (1776) 15042, (1782) 17688, (1789) 22099
    in compleat armour, 12062
    indeed, 10938
    journal, 30129
    knowledge, 19257
    laid forth, 9132, 9688
    letter, 9928
    love, 12717
    loyalty, 2909
    magnanimity, 20893
    memoirs, 31190
    minister described, 20407
    minister or faithful, 12065
    minister the good, 9540
    ministers, 25367
    monitor, 3719, 5279
    oeconomy, (1773) 12719-20, (1788) 20997, (1790) 22403-404
    panoply, 33158

VOL.	ITEMS	VOL.	ITEMS
1	1-3244	8	22298-25074
2	3245-6623	9	25075-28145
3	6624-9891	10	28146-30832
4	9892-13091	11	30833-33261
5	13092-16176	12	33262-25854
6	16177-19448	13	35855-39162
7	19449-22297		

Church, John, 1774-1809. Inaugural dissertation, 31935
Church, John Hubbard, 1772-1840
  Ministry of reconciliation, 35306
  ordained, 35322
Church, Simeon, conference at house of, 36203
Church, Thomas
  Entertaining history, 12352
  Entertaining passages, 1800
Church bells, 38058
    catechism (1767) 10610
    catechism explained, (1748) 6176, (1753) 7039, (1765) 10039, (1800) 37824
    covenant, 32266
    discipline, 10846
    God's peculiar care, 24747
    history of Geneva, 3557
    history of New England, 18336, 30011
    in the house, 22564
    membership of children, (1663) 82, (1669) 145, (1762) 9272, (1769) 11462, (1786) 19985
    mouse, 28786
    music, 19563
    of Christ a firm, 10613
    of Christ one, 18200
    of Christ vindicated, 2528
Church of England
    A.B.C., with the catechism, 20345
    A.B.C., with the Church, 28631
    Abstract of the proceedings, 12761
    Address from the clergy, 12037
    Book of common prayer, 1454
    Catechism, 24301
    Family prayer book, 10610
    Form of prayer, (1757) 7888, (1758) 8120, (1762) 9111
    Form of publick devotions, 3022
    Morning and evening prayer, 1740, 9385
    New weeks preparation, 26946
    Order for morning, 11248
    Primer, (1746) 5768, (1749) 6314, (1786) 19624
Church of England man see Searson, John
Church of Ephesus arraign'd, 11072
    of God described, 24460
    of Rome evidently, 384
Church of Scotland
    Confession of faith, 5709
    Scripture songs, 12554
Church of the New Jerusalem. Liturgy, 24599
Church renewed covenant, 281
Church wardens, 23621
Churches duty, 1727
    quarrel, (1713) 1660, (1715) 1795, (1772) 12625-26
    shall know, 1935
Churchill, George, 1752?-1796, death, 30195
Churchill, Mrs. George. Following lines, 30195
Churchill, Silas, d. 1854. Sermon, 37182
Churchman, John, 1705-1775. Account of the gospel, 16223
Churchman, John, 1753-1805
    Dissertation, 23260
    Explanation of the magnetic, 22406
    Magnetic atlas, 37183
    Map of the peninsula, 20272
Church's flight, 15082
Church's marriage, 5766
Cibber, Colley, 1671-1757
    Provoked husband, 26559, 27987
    She would, 8815
    plagiarized, 28293

Cicero
  Cato major, 5361, 8101
  De officiis, 25299
Cicero, or a discovery, 35307
Ciceronian society. Constitution, 38246
Cincinnati, Society of the see Society of the Cincinnati
Cincinnatus, L. Q.
  Letter (to freeholders), 6299
  Mote point, 16224
Cinderella, 37184
Cineas. To Luther Martin, 16225
Ciprian, life of, 9863
Circuit court of the U. S., 38723
Circuit of human life, 22395
Circulaire adressée, 28983
Circular; Boston, Mass., 24135
[Circular describing bank notes], 23147
Circular directing returns, 31439
    in council, 34938
    letter (Clarkson), 17875
    letter (Vanuxem, in French), 15690
    letter addressed, 18787
        from a committee, 24136
        from his excellency, (1783) 18257, 18260-61, (1786) 20054-55, (1797) 33148
        from the Congress, 16558-61
        from the Warren, 22242
        of his excellency, 20764
        of valediction, 23494, 27213
        on the allimportant, 19226
    letters containing, 33961
    of instruction to collectors, 31441
    of instructions relative to bonds, 31442
        relative to licenses, 27942
        relative to losses, 27939
        relative to passports, 31440
        relative to punishment, 27940
        relative to the shipment, 31437
        to collectors, 29764
    Philadelphia, (April 1792) 24414, (Feb. 20, 1796) 31208, (Sept. 25, 1796) 30985, (Sept. 22, 1797) 32897, (July 27, 1799) 36603, (May 14, 1800) 37586
    Princeton, 179-, 30863
    relating to relief, 31438
    relating to the cargoes, 31443
    relative to captured, 27941
        to duties, 27944
        to entries, 29765
        to vessels, 31436
    Richmond, Jan. 2, 1794, 28000
    Richmond, supervisor's office, 29802
    schreiben, 6828
    the ministers, elders, 26372
    to collectors, 27943
    to the collector, 34850
    to the collectors, 26342
    to the free, 24856
    Treasury department, 36502

VOL.	ITEMS	VOL.	ITEMS
1	1-3244	8	22298-25074
2	3245-6623	9	25075-28145
3	6624-9891	10	28146-30832
4	9892-13091	11	30833-33261
5	13092-16176	12	33262-25854
6	16177-19448	13	35855-39162
7	19449-22297		

Circulars to collectors, 36501
Circulating library, New York, 30412
Circumstantial narrative, 19559
Cish, Jane. Vision, (1793) 25300-301, 25515, (1797) 31936, (1798) 33516
Cist, Charles. Washington city, 39013
Citizen
  Alderman Blagge's case, 12892
  Fever, an elegiac, 35480
  Marriage of a deceased, 32423
  Observations on Mr. Justice, 11391
  Observations on the peculiar, 19151
  Stranger's assistant, 29576
  To his excellency, 14486
  To John M. S. . . . ., 13653
  To the citizens of Annapolis, 14488
  To the freeholders and freemen, 14492
  To the freeholders, freemen, 14496
  To the friend, 26264
  To the honourable the legislature, 20024
  To the inhabitants, 13659
  To the members, 29645
  To the people of New York, 13665
  To the public, 13676
  To the voters of Maryland, 22939
  To the worthy inhabitants, 13684
    see also Findley, William, 1750-1821; Livingston, Philip, 1716-1778
Citizen, a farce, 26558, 27356
Citizen and countryman's experienced farrier, 9718, 32419
Citizen of Albany. To the people, 38657
Citizen of America
  Dimension proper, 30353
  Political opinions, 22072
    see also Webster, Noah, 1758-1843
Citizen of Boston see Richards, George, 1769-1837
Citizen of Connecticut see Beers, William Pitt, 1766-1810
Citizen of Kentucky. View of the administration, 34928
Citizen of Maryland. Maria, 29264
Citizen of Massachusetts see Bowdoin, James, 1752-1811; Mann, Herman, 1772-1833; Sullivan, James, 1744-1808
Citizen of New England see Lowell, John, 1769-1840
Citizen of Newhampshire. Device devised, 26874
Citizen of New Jersey see M'Elroy, Thomas
Citizen of New York
  Commercial conduct, 19566
  Cursory review, 30305
  Observations on accidental, 32608
  Serious address, 13605
    see also Adgate, Matthew; Barlow, Joel, 1754-1812; Jay, John, 1745-1829
Citizen of Newburyport. Algerine slaves, 33747
Citizen of Pennsylvania see Carey, Mathew, 1760-1839; Gallatin, Abraham Albert Alphonse, 1761-1849
Citizen of Philadelphia
  Essay on the culture, 22491
  (tr.) Morality of the Sans-Culottes, 26764
    see also Markoe, Peter; Purdon, John, d. 1835; Rittenhouse, David, 1732-1796; Swanwick, John, 1760-1798; Webster, Pelatiah, 1725-1795; Wells, Richard
Citizen of South Carolina see Ford, Timothy, 1762-1830; Smith, William Loughton, 1758-1812
Citizen of that state see Jackson, James, 1757-1806
Citizen of the state. Address to the free, 19451,

28152
Citizen of the United States
  Cicero, or a discovery, 35307
  Columbia and Britannica, 19922
  Remarks on the treaty, 30255
    see also Coxe, Tench, 1756-1824; Duane, William; Ogden, John Cosens, 1751-1800; Phelps, Charles, 1715-1789; Witherspoon, John, 1722-1794; Wood, Silas, 1769-1847
Citizen of the world, 27057
Citizen of the world see Carey, Mathew, 1760-1839
Citizen of Trenton see Chauvet, David
Citizen of Virginia. Manual of a free, 35767
Citizen of Westmoreland county see Lee, Henry, 1756-1818
Citizen of Williamsburg see Tucker, St. George, 1752-1827
Citizen Snub see Swanwick, John, 1760-1798
Citizen's address, 11209
Citizens of Kentucky, 34650
Citoyen des Etats Unis. Essai, 28637
City-Hall, high noon, 10883
City of New York, Feb. 11, 1768, 10885
  of New York; on the first, 2162
  of New York, ss.   Jan. 6th, 11284
    ss. At a common council held on Monday, 27401
    ss. At a common council held on Thursday, 32561
    ss. Personally, 14336
  of Philadelphia; by the mayor, 10132
  of Philadelphia in the state, 38259
  of refuge, 1449, 1820
  of Washington; the advantageous, 27068
Civil and executive officer's assistant, 25556, 33807
  government, 6692
  magistrates, 5919
  military and ecclesiastical, 12047
  prudence, 14677
  ruler a dignify'd, 6989
  rulers an ordinance, 13382
    are God's, 1593
    directed, 12835
    gods by office, 9538
    raised, 3093
    the ministers, 6430
  state compared, 12712
Civis
  Following publication, 17871
  To the freemen, 12353
    see also Ramsay, David, 1749-1815
Claesse, Lawrence, tr. Morning and evening prayer, 1740, 9385
Claggett, Thomas J. Convention of the Protestant, 27569
Claggett, William. Looking-glass, 2209
Claiborne, John. Inaugural essay, 33518
Claiborne, William C. C., petition referred to, 32981
Claim and answer, (Allen) 36503, (Ingles) 36504
  of the inhabitants, 10435
  or title, 9920
Claims of Thomas Jefferson, 37187
Clairac, Louis André de la Mamie, chevalier de, 1670-1750. Ingenieur de campagne, 14678
Clandestine marriage, (1766) 10263, (1774) 13203, (1777) 15255
Clap, John. Almanac see Almanacs (Clap)
Clap, Mary, d. 1769, death, 11530
Clap, Nathaniel, 1668-1745
  Broken heart, 1728
  Duty of all, 2101, 4487

VOL.	ITEMS	VOL.	ITEMS
1	1-3244	8	22298-25074
2	3245-6623	9	25075-28145
3	6624-9891	10	28146-30832
4	9892-13091	11	30833-33261
5	13092-16176	12	33262-25854
6	16177-19448	13	35855-39162
7	19449-22297		

(1747) 6025, (1748) 6204, (1749) 6380-81,
   (1750) 6566-68, (1751) 6734
Speech, (1743) 5256-57, (1744) 5455-58, (1745)
   5655-56, (1746) 5832-33, (1747) 6027-28, (1748)
   6205, (1749) 6383-84, (1750) 6570
Treaty, 5791
address to, (1744) 5459-61, (1745) 5660-61,
   (1749) 6385-86, (1750) 6571, (1751) 6736-37,
   (1753) 7076
letter (from representatives), 5984
representation to, 5834, 6032
Clinton, George, 1739-1812
   Proclamation, (1778) 15931, 16406, (1792) 25906
   charge against, 24859
   election, 24769, 24856-57
   election favored, 20025
   election opposed, 26265
   memorial to, 18210
   proposes convention, 21431
   reply to, 15719
Clinton, George, Jr., fl. 1798. Oration, 33522
Clinton, Sir Henry, 1738-1795
   Letter (to Germaine), 15284
   Letters and other papers, 15826
   Manifesto, 15832-34
   Narrative, 17876
   Proclamation, 16790-91
   address to, 15954
   besought, 15095
   captures Fort Clinton, 15323
   head of Cerberus, 13985
   letter (from Washington), 30392
   officers under, 16295
   reply to, 18208
Clio, visions of, 23207
Clissold, Mrs. ——, diary, 1645
Clodius. To the advocates, 12727
Cloris, Pedro. Genteel & surprizing, 23263
Close, John. Discourse, 37196
Closet companion, 33386
Cloud of witnesses, 921
Clough, ——, plaintiff, 31668
Clough, Ebenezer. Boston paper staining, 28428
Clough, Samuel. Almanac see **Almanacs (Clough)**
Cloven foot discovered, 9615, 9838-39
Clowes, John, 1743-1831
   Dialogues on the nature, 26774
   (tr.) Heavenly doctrine, 27764
   Letter of exhortation, 18958, 28429
   Remarks, 37197
   (tr.) True Christian, 22172, 24835
   True end, 26775
Cloyne, George, bp. of see **Berkeley, George, 1684-
1753**
Club, or a grey, 29372
Clunn, Joseph, subscribes to sports book, 23785-86
Cluny, Alexander. American traveller, 11603
Clymer, George, 1739-1813
   letter (from Rush), 22866
   report by, 15172
Coade, George. Letter (to clergyman), 12728
Coasting pilot, 30464
Coates, Samuel. Committee appointed, 32680
Coates, William. William Coates takes this, 12354
Coats, William, accounts, 18118
Cobb, Ebenezer, sponsors sermon, 27630
Cobb, James, 1756-1818
   The capture, 25306
   Doctor and the apothecary, 28430
   Favorite songs, 25307
   Haunted tower, 26776

Lullaby, 25308
Sailor lov'd a lass, 30203
Whither my love, 25309
Cobb, William. Country trader's assistant, 35315
Cobbet, Thomas, 1608-1685. Mass. election sermon,
26
Cobbett, William, 1762-1835
   Accurate plan, 31943
   Address, 30192
   Antidote, 30204
   Bloody buoy, 30305-207
   Blut-fahne, 31944
   Bone to gnaw, 28431-35, 31945
   By William Cobbett, 35316
   (ed.) Copies of original, 34606
   Democratic judge, 33523
   Detection of Bache, 33524
   Fortgang, 33525
   French arrogance, 33526
   Gros mousqueton, 30208
   History of the American Jacobins, 30209, 31016
   History of the campaign, 36845
   Impeachment of Mr. Lafayette, 25497, 26996
   Kick for a bite, 28436, 30210
   Letter, (to Paine) 30211, (to Swanwick) 30727
   Life and adventures, 30212-13
   Little plain English, 28437-38, 30214
   New Year's gift, (1796) 30215-16, 31174, (1798)
      33527
   Observations on the emigration, (1794) 26777-
      78, (1795) 28439-40, (1796) 30217-18, (1798)
      33528
   Political censor, 30219-28
   Porcupine's Political censor, 31946-47
   Porcupine's Works, 30233, 31948
   Prospect from the Congress, 30229-30
   Remarks on the insidious, 33529
   Rush-light, 37198
   Scarecrow, 30231-32
   (tr.) Summary of the law, 29025
   Tit for tat, 30314
   Topographical and political, 30818, 34138
   Tuteur anglais, 28441
   Works of Peter Porcupine, 30234
   attacked, 31255
   cartoon of, 30820
   controversy with Carey, 35272-74
   dedication to, 31010, 33494-95
   dedication to Erskine, 32097
   defendant, 37103
   letter (from Hopkinson), 30593
   observations on, 31065
   preface by, 30143
   reply to, 29594, 30119-20, 30155, 30553, 31256
   satire on, 33493, 35275-77
Cobby, John. Poetic essays, 31949
Cochran, John. Calendar, 31950
Cochran, Johnson, executed, 10036
Cochrun, Simon. Extraordinary life, 31951
Cock-fighter, 37166

on the subject, 31593
  relative, 18255-56
  that have, 15825
of penal laws, 35921
of plays and poems, 34158
of poems by several, 5365
of poems on religious, 31953
of pretty poems, 9281
of psalm tunes, 9406
of psalms and hymns, (1737) 4207, (1781)
  17427, (1790) 22341, (1794) 27533, (1795)
  28264, (1799) 35222
of psalms, hymns, 12621
of religious tracts, (1774) 13145, (1784) 18354,
  (1799) 35518
of select biography, 33760
of sermons (Erskine), 5388, 5587
of some of the many, 991
of some papers, 2698
of some writings, 10583
of songs, 35407
of speeches, 12014
of tables, 24477, 28975
of the best and most approved, (1779) 16317,
  (1781) 17201, (1782) 17572
  best English, 16874
  best psalm tunes, 9659
  letters, 9136
  most esteemed, 33943
  New Testament, 15244
  newest and most fashionable, 21122
  newest cotillions, (1788) 21121, (1794)
    28774, (1797) 32213, (1800) 37202
  penal laws, 27478
  private acts, 27419
  proceedings, 3184
  speeches, 31402
  statutes now in force, 13309
  statutes of the Parliament, 24627, 30909
  wise and witty, 22487
  works (Chalkley), 7166, 22397
of thirty-eight, 2488
of tracts, 10857, 11212
of voyages, 20444
of wise and witty, 18459
Collections for an essay, 33377
  of the Mass. hist. soc., (1792) 24530, (1793)
    25791, (1794) 27297, (1795) 29049, (1798)
    34082, (1799) 37930
  of the testimonies, 97
College of New Jersey
Account of the college, 9752
Catalog, (1770) 11770, (1773) 12883, (1786)
  19842, (1789) 22005, (1792) 24595, (1800) 37203
Catalogue of books, 8683
Circular; Princeton, 30863
Laws, 27392
Philosophemata, 8684, 9208
To the honourable, 30864
College of New York
Additional charter, 7515
Charter, 7279
College of Philadelphia
Account of the commencement, 14395
Additional charter, 7540
Exercise containing, 9484, 14396
Exercise performed, 22798
General heads, 15994
Philosophemata, (1761) 8981, (1762) 9239, (1763)
  9485
Plan of a performance, 10140

College of physicians
Charter, 22794
Facts and observations, 34355
Proceedings, 34356
Transactions, 25992
College of Rhode Island see **Rhode Island college**
College of William and Mary
Charter, 37204
Statutes, 25038
Collegii Yalensis quod est, 6271
Collegii Yalensis . . . statuta, (1755) 7599, (1759)
  8523, (1764) 9885
Collens, Daniel. Believers triumph, 18406
Colles, Christopher, 1738-1821
Geographical ledger, 26781
Proposals for publishing a survey, 21740
Proposals for the speedy, 18960
Survey of the roads, 21741
Syllabus of a course, 12730
Colley, Thomas, 1742-1812
Discourse, 21003
Nature and necessity, 20278, 21742
Salutation, 30238
Tender salutation, 28443
Collier, Sir George. Address, 16291
Collier, John, petition, 38897
Collier, Joseph, trial, 27076
Collier, Mary see **Collyer, Mary, d. 1763**
Collier, Mrs. Nathaniel, death, 1518
Collier, William, ordained, 35145
Collin, Nicholas. Philological view, 33534
Collins, Alexander. This oration, 37205
Collins, Isaac, 1746-1817. Proposals made, 18961
Collins, John Baptist, account of, 27818
Collins, Nathaniel, d. 1684
On the much lamented, 1670
elegy on, 392
Collins, William, 1721-1759
Desponding Negro, 25313, 33535
Loose were, 30239
Ode on the passions, 28444
Passions, an ode, 28977
Poetical works, 21004
excerpts from, 26014
Colloquia selecta, 17529, 25453
Colloquiorum centura, (1786) 19588, (1792) 24228,
  (1800) 37256
Colloquiorum centuria, (1724) 2517, (1770) 11615,
  (1787) 20301, (1789) 21770
Collot, Georges Henri Victor, 1751-1805. Precis,
  25445
Collyer, Joseph, tr. Messiah, 21190, 28935
Collyer, Mary, d. 1763
(tr.) Death of Abel, (1765) 9981, (1766) 10313,
  (1770) 11667, (1787) 20390, (1790) 22535,
  (1794) 24049, (1795) 28747, (1797) 32188
Woman's labour, 25421
Colman, Benjamin, 1673-1747
Argument for, 3008
Blameless & inoffensive, 2418

VOL.	ITEMS	VOL.	ITEMS
1	1-3244	8	22298-25074
2	3245-6623	9	25075-28145
3	6624-9891	10	28146-30832
4	9892-13091	11	30833-33261
5	13092-16176	12	33262-25854
6	16177-19448	13	35855-39162
7	19449-22297		

Blessing and honor, 1730
Blessing of Zebulon, 2018
Brief dissertation, 3887
Brief enquiry, 1801
Case of Satan's fiery, 5366
Character of his excellency, 3147
Charge, 3723
Christ standing, 4231
Credibility of the Christian, 3148
David's dying, 2419
Death and the grave, 3009
Death of God's saints, 2420
Declaration of a number, 4917
Devout and humble, 1731
Devout contemplation, 1671
Discourse, (1713) 1600, (1722) 2324
Dissertation, 4001
Divine compassions, 1764
Doctrine and law, 2620
Duty and honour, 1497
Duty of young, 3010
Dying in peace, 3261
Early piety, 2102
Faith victorious, 1042
Faithful ministers, 3149
Faitful pastors, 4351
Faithful servant, 4488
Fast which God, 3759
Fidelity, 2852
Four sermons, 1872
Friend of Christ, 3404
Glory of God, 5155
God deals with us, 2421
God is a great, 3645
God's concern, 2425
Gospel ministry, 1732, 1802
Gospel order, 966-67
Government and improvement, 1293
Government the pillar, 3262
Great duty, 4130
Great God, 4916
Hainous nature, 1601, 1626
Holy & useful, 1733
Holy walk and glorious, 3011
Holy walk with God, 1873
Honour and happiness, 1803
Hope of the righteous, 2210
Humble discourse, 1734-35, 4489
Imprecation, 1294
Industry and diligence, 1874
It is a fearful, 2737
It is of the Lord's, 4131
Jacob's vow, 2325
Jesus weeping, 5367
Judgments, 2853
Letter (to Williams), 5368
Lord shall rejoice, 4695
Master taken, 2514
Merchandise, 4002
Ministers and people, 3520
Nature of early piety, 2256
One chosen, 5753
Ossa Josephi, 2103
Parents and grown children, 2854
Peaceful end, 4003
Piety and duty, 1346
Plain and familiar, 1736
Poem, 1295, 1329
Practical discourses, 1602, 5921
Prayer, 2855
Prophet's death, 2422

Religious regards, 1949
Reliquiae turellae, 3888
Rending of the vail, 1875
Righteousness, 4004
Sermon, (1708) 1347, (1716) 1804-806
Some observations, 2211
Some of the honours, 1737
Some reasons, 2019
Souls flying, 4490
Testimony, 2051
Three letters, 4354
Unspeakable gift, 4352
Vanity of man, 5754
Vindication, 2104
Warnings, 1807
Wither'd hand, 4353, 4491
    appendix by, 2112
    death, 5937
    favors Croswell, 4926
    letter, (from Edwards) 4137, (from Osborn)
        5265, (from Sergeant) 5288
    life of, 6434
    preface by, 3091, 4600-601, 4808, 10165
    reply to, 2163, 2190
Colman, George, 1733-1794
    Clandestine marriage, (1766) 10263, (1774)
        13203, (1777) 15255
    Jealous wife, 8818
    Man of business, 13202
Colman, George, 1762-1836
    Days of old, 28446, 30240
    Epilogue, 38001
    Happy tawny, 30242
    Inkle & Yarico, 24200, 26558, 26782
    Mountaineers, 28447-48, 30241
    Negro boy, 30243
    Pauvre Madelon, 25314, 33536
    Way worn traveller, 26783
    When pensive, 33537
    When the hollow, 31954
Colman, John. Distressed state, 2105-106
Col. Choate's reasons, 8617
Colonel Hamilton's second letter, 18367
Colonel reconnoitred, 9612
Colonel Tilghman, 17309
Colony of Connecticut, court of vice-admiralty,
    6832
        of Massachusetts Bay; in Council, a proclama-
            tion see Mass. Proclamation
        of Massachusetts Bay, 1776; we the subscrib-
            ers, 14840
        of New Hampshire; by the Council . . . see
            New Hampshire. Proclamation
        of New Hampshire; in committee of safety,
            14904
        of Rhode Island, &c., 13498
        of the Massachusetts-Bay, 14201
Cololvo, an Indian tale, 28977
Colquhoun, Patrick, 1745-1820. Treatise, 33538
Colson, Adam, satirized, 28726
Colton, Benjamin, d. 1749. Danger of apostasie,
    4232
Colton, Benjamin, 1690-1759
    Danger of apostasie, 4232?
    Two sermons, 3889
Columbanus, 2354
Columbia, S.C. Address to the people, 26784
Columbia, an ode, 26923
        and Britannia, 19922
        and liberty, 33602
Columbia college

VOL.	ITEMS	VOL.	ITEMS
1	1-3244	8	22298-25074
2	3245-6623	9	25075-28145
3	6624-9891	10	28146-30832
4	9892-13091	11	30833-33261
5	13092-16176	12	33262-25854
6	16177-19448	13	35855-39162
7	19449-22297		

14327, (May 12, 1775) 14328, (Aug. 22, 1775)
14334, (Nov. 3, 1775) 14335, (Jan. 10, 1776)
14924, (Apr. 9, 1776) 14926, (Apr. 13, 1776)
14927
chamber, Philadelphia, May 18, 1776, 15014
consisting of Mr. Beresford, Mr. Jefferson,
18830
    Mr. Carrington, Mr. Varnum, 20766
    Mr. Dane, Mr. Clarke, 20767
    Mr. Dane, Mr. Hawkins, 20768
    Mr. Duane, Mr. Peters, 18262-63
    Mr. Gerry, Mr. Williamson, 19293
    Mr. Hardy, Mr. Houston, 19294
    Mr. Howell, Mr. Monroe, 19295
    Mr. Johnson, Mr. King, 20057
    Mr. Johnson, Mr. Pinckney, 20058, 20769
    Mr. Kearney, Mr. Carrington, 20770
    Mr. King, Mr. Howell, 19296
    Mr. King, Mr. Pinckney, 20085
    Mr. M'Henry, Mr. Dick, 18831, 19297
    Mr. M'Henry, Mr. Read, 19298
    Mr. Mercer, Mr. Lee, 18832
    Mr. Pinckney, Mr. Dane, 20059
    Mr. Pinckney, Mr. Monroe, 20060
    Mr. St. Clair, Mr. Lee, 20061
    Mr. Smith, Mr. Long, 20062
    Mr. Spaight, Mr. Gerry, 18833
    Mr. Wadsworth, Mr. Irvine, 21521
    Mr. Williamson, Mr. Stewart, 19299
consisting of   to whom was referred the
    memorial, 20765
consisting of.   to whom was referred the
    motion, 19301
consisting of   to whom was referred the
    report, 21519
consisting of   to whom were referred,
    19300
Committee for improving the condition of the
    free blacks. Address, 38247
Committee for tarring and feathering, 12941
    for the city and liberties, 16464
    for the city of Philadelphia, 14385
    from the several, 13096
    of both houses appointed, 14864
    of both houses on the letter, 14857
Committee of correspondence in New York. Ad-
    vertisement, 13094
Committee of mechanicks. Advertisement, 13093
Committee of Presbyterian ministers. Substance
    of a council, 9848
Committee of safety, New York, Jan. 27, 1776,
    14925
Committee of the First society in Danbury. Vindi-
    cation, 9846
Committee of twenty-five, 13474
Committee on tarring and feathering. To the
    Delaware pilots, 12943
Committee or the faithful Irishman, 8883
    room, (May 28, 1779) 16465, (May 31, 1779)
    16466, (June 10, 1779) 16467, (June 18, 1779)
    16468, (June 26, 1779) 16469
    to which was referred, 27897
    to whom the subject, 24871
    to whom was recommended, 18834-35
    to whom was referred a motion of Mr. R. R.
        Livingston, 19303
        a motion of the delegates, 20063
        sundry letters, 18836
        that part, 27901
        the bill authorizing, 36505, 38724
        the letter, 19304

    the memorial of Mr. P. Landais, 19305
    the memorial of the directors, 24872
    the report, 38725
    the several petitions, 26532
to whom were referred a letter, 19302
to whom were referred the act, 18264
Common safety the cause, 12773
Common sense, pseud. see Paine, Thomas, 1736-
    1809; Sherman, Josiah, 1734-1789
Common sense (Paine), (1776) 14954-62, 14964,
    14966, (1791) 23657-58, 24658, 27466
Common sense in dishabille, 35454
Common sense, or natural, 29820-21
Common sense, with the whole appendix, 14966
Commonwealth of Massachusetts; Alexander
    Hodgdon, 23557
    of Massachusetts; by his excellency . . . see
        under person named, or under Mass. Gov-
        ernor
    of Massachusetts; general orders, 23551-52
    of Massachusetts; in Senate . . . see In Senate
    . . .
    of Massachusetts; in the House of represen-
        tatives . . . see In the House of representa-
        tives . . .
    of Massachusetts. [Resolve, 1788], 21241
    of Massachusetts; tax no. 4, 18597
    of Massachusetts; the honorable Henry Gard-
        ner, 17218, 17595
    of Massachusetts; this twenty fourth, 37916
    of Massachusetts; Thomas Davis, (1793)
        25786, (1794) 27293, (1795) 29048
    of Massachusetts; Thomas Ivers, 19795
    of Massachusetts; to the high, 17940
    of Massachusetts; to the hon. Senate, 32446
    of Massachusetts; to the honorable the Sen-
        ate, 30769
    of Mass. To the selectmen, 25781
    of Massachusetts; to the selectmen, 27285
    of Utopia, 7068
Communicant's companion, (1716) 1813, (1723)
    2433, (1731) 3429, (1792) 24386, (1798) 33868
Communicant's spiritual companion, 19706, 27103
Communication from the joint committee, 34348
Communications from several, 38952
    from the secretary, 26343
    interesting, 22177
    of the several, 36639
Communion of churches, 101
    of faith, 11797
    -office, or order, 19982
Companion, being a selection, 35333
    for communicants, (1690) 535, (1730) 3367,
        (1735) 3970
    for prayer, 6452, 10539
    for the afflicted, 992
    for the young, 10921
    for young ladies, 27020
Company of printers, Philadelphia
    Catalogue of books, 27506
    Constitution, 27505
Comparative views, 31209
Comparison of the institutions, 36160
Compass, a poetical, 29591
Compassionate address, 3345
Compassionate call, 7016-19, 35580
Compassions called for, 1506-507
Compend of English grammar, (1779) 16249,
    (1783) 17901, (1784) 18431, (1785) 18980
Compend of military, 27370
Compendious American grammar, 24415
    and plain, 27702

VOL.	ITEMS	VOL.	ITEMS
1	1-3244	8	22298-25074
2	3245-6623	9	25075-28145
3	6624-9891	10	28146-30832
4	9892-13091	11	30833-33261
5	13092-16176	12	33262-25854
6	16177-19448	13	35855-39162
7	19449-22297		

VOL.	ITEMS	VOL.	ITEMS
1	1-3244	8	22298-25074
2	3245-6623	9	25075-28145
3	6624-9891	10	28146-30832
4	9892-13091	11	30833-33261
5	13092-16176	12	33262-25854
6	16177-19448	13	35855-39162
7	19449-22297		

bank, 23723
Boston Tontine, 23215
Carpenters society, 28393
Ciceronian society, 38246
Columbianum, 29311
commonwealth of Mass., 29041
commonwealth of Pennsylvania, (1776)
14979, (1777) 15512, (1781) 17285, (1784)
18680, (1786) 19883, (1790) 22759-60
Company of printers, 27505
Connecticut academy, 35344
Connecticut society, 24220
Democratic society, 27405
Dutch church, 27602
Essex musical, 33699
Federal Tontine, 24315
Franklin society, 24687
French, 28694
general Grand, 32165, 35504
Germantown society, 22534
Grand royal arch, 27013
Hibernian society, 37615
Humane society, 29202
Independent, 20266
Ladies society, 35952, 38101
Magdalen society, 38249
Maryland society, 21940
Missionary society, 37232
New Jersey society, 25890-91
New York friars, 24607
New York lying-in, 35954
New York society for promoting Christian knowledge, 27409
New York society for promoting the manumission, 30885
Northern missionary society, 32601
Pennsylvania society for promoting, 20636, 21381
Philological society, 21320
Presbyterian church, (1789) 22079, (1792) 24711, (1797) 32711
Protestant Episcopal, 23722, 27579
Reformed Dutch, 26065
Reliance property, 36195
republic, 25495
Royal arch, 33761
Scots thistle, 36108
Social society, 38368
Society for the attainment, 27513
state of Delaware, 24259
state of Georgia, (1777) 15308, (1785)
19024, (1787) 20387, (1789) 21850, (1796)
30482, (1798) 33790, (1799) 35541
state of Kentucky, 35682
state of Massachusetts, 34076
state of New York, (1777) 15472-74,
(1783) 18059, (1785) 19130
state of Tennessee, 31278-79
state of Vermont, 16151, 19343
U.S., (1787) 20795-98, 20802, (1788) 21523,
(1790) 22976-77, (1791) 23888, (1793)
26331, (1795) 29729, (1798) 34794-96,
(1799) 36404, 36507-511
Virginia society, 29803
Washington society, 36795
of Vermont, (1786) 20096, (1792) 24956, (1793)
26378
or deed of settlement, 38343
or form of government, (Kentucky) 24443,
35681, (North Carolina) 16419
or frame of government (Mass.), (1780)

16844-45, (1781) 17229, (1784) 18598, (1787)
20512
or frame of government (U.S.), 20799-801
proposed, 20803
public, 22019
rules, regulations, 22324
shown to be consistent, 24225
subscribers names, 27430
together with the by-laws, 33762
Constitutional articles, 35431
courant, 9941-42
rules, 31003
Constitutional society, Philadelphia
Principles, 16948
To the citizens, 16949
Constitutional society, Richmond. Minutes, 18756
Constitutionalist, or an enquiry, 26987
Constitutions and government of Harvard, 5041-
42
des treize, 18265
of the Ancient and hono(u)rable, (1782) 17536,
(1785) 18910, (1789) 21837, (1791) 23388,
(1792) 24052, (1794) 27012, (1798) 33303
Freemasons, 3744, 6454
Publick academy, 6405
several, (1781) 17390, (1785) 19306, (1786)
20064
sixteen, 33044, 37244
thirteen, 20065
U.S., (1791) 23887, (1796) 31403, (1800)
37245
Consummation, or an end, 26490
Contemner of licentiousness. Answer to a pamph-
let, 6809
Contemplations of the state, 2295, 2471
Contemplations on mortality, 517, 820
Contes du tems, 29300
Contested election, 32312
Conti, Armand de Bourbon, prince de, 1629-1666
Extracts of several, 7175
Continental Congress
An die einwohner, 14574
Articles of association, 13299-300, 13705
Auszüge, 13735
Extract from the journal, 15125
Extracts from the proceedings, 14573
Extracts from the votes and proceedings, (1774)
13713-33, 13736, 14551, 14553, (1775) 14572
Following extract, 13710
Following extracts, 13708-709, 31711-12
For the benefit of those, 14554
In Congress, May 17, 1775, 14561
In Congress, Dec. 6, 1775, 14567-68
In Congress, Friday, June 9, 1775, 14562
In Congress, Friday, Nov. 3, 1775, 14566
In Congress, Monday, June 12, 1775, 14563, 14565
Journal of the proceedings, (1774) 13737-39,
(1775) 14569-71, 15144, (1776) 15145
Lettre addressée, 13740
9th article of the association, 13706
Petition, (1774) 13741, (1775) 14554-55

VOL.	ITEMS	VOL.	ITEMS
1	1-3244	8	22298-25074
2	3245-6623	9	25075-28145
3	6624-9891	10	28146-30832
4	9892-13091	11	30833-33261
5	13092-16176	12	33262-25854
6	16177-19448	13	35855-39162
7	19449-22297		

Proceedings of the general Congress, 13701
Second Norwich edition, 13734
Whole proceedings, 14552
Continental harmony, 26673
    impost, 23890
    key, 14720
    naval board, 15637-41
Continuance of peace, 29830
Continuatio supplementi, 2641
Continuation of an essay, 6999, 7190-91
    of exercises, 10016-21
    of the abridgment, 4441
        account, 8972
        answers, 11261
        calm, 6637
        children's, 21677
        essay, 6313, 6666
        history, 34118
        letters, 27558, 29352
        narrative of the Indian, (1771) 12284,
          (1773) 13077, (1775) 14623
        narrative of the missions, (1795) 28464,
          (1796) 30259, (1797) 31968
        narrative of the state, 10207
        New York, 23618
        proceedings of the House, 11733
        proceedings of the Humane, 21895
        Reverend, 4453, 4633-36, 4846-55
Contract; being a concise, 11611
    for erecting, 23626
    for the purchase, 35111
    of the Ohio company, 20604
Contrast, 30803
Contrast, a comedy, 22948, 23336
    a novel, 30497-98
    between the effects, 36737
    or striking, 30604-605
    read, my fellow, 11223
    to the reverend, 15805
Contrivances, or more, 9082
Controversia oder disputations-schreiben, 25345
Controversial letters, 33745
Controversy between Great Britain, 11305
    between the four, 13890
    between the Rev. John Thayer, 26250-51,
      29620
Convention at Concord, 16230
    between his most Christian majesty, 21525
    between the French, 38726
Convention of ministers. Observations upon the
    congregational, 12857
Convention of said presbyteries. Brief account,
    31040
Convention of the Prostestant Episcopal, 27569
Conversation and conduct, 32133
Conversation cards, 27027, 35351
Converse, Abigail, d. 1788, death, 20955
Conversion and death, 24226, 24390
    exemplified, 1175
    of a Mahometan, (1795) 28721, (1796) 30467,
      (1797) 32169-70
    of a Mehometan, (1773) 12778, (1775) 14056,
      (1792) 24335
    of a young, 4698
    of Juvenis, 27734
Converted sinner, 2551
Convict's visitor, 23776
Conway, Henry Seymour, 1721-1795
    (tr.) False appearances, 28312
    Speeches, 10463

motion by, 17461
Conway, Thomas, 1735-1800, treatment of, 15867
Cook, David
    American arithmetic, 35352, 37246
    American ready reckoner, 33567
Cook, David, relief of, 23884
Cook, Ebenezer
    Maryland muse, 3407
    Sotweed redivivus, 3266
Cook, James, 1728-1779
    New journal, 13218
    Third and last voyage, (1793) 25346, (1795)
      28476-77, (1796) 30275-76
    Three voyages, 31982-83
    Voyage to the Pacific, 30274
    discoveries mapped, 21213
    portrait, 31664
    voyages by, 13224, 17921, 17998
Cook, Jesse, memorial from, 20090
Cook Jesse, d. 1790, death, 22626
Cook, John. Proclamation, 17519
Cook, Joseph Platt, 1730-1816
    reports on sundry motions, 19307
    reports on supplies, 19308
Cook, Moses, d. 1771, murdered, 12493-96, 12907-
    911, 13508
Cook, Orchard, petition by, 33015, 34753
Cook, Rozel, 1755-1798. Sermon, 18422
Cook, Solomon, d. 1737, death, 4314
Cook, William. Plain truths, 7879
Cook, William, 1696-1760. Sermon, 3408
Cooke, Rev. ——, reply to, 6010
Cooke, Elisha, 1678-1737
    Just and seasonable, 2109-110
    Letter (to Burrill), 2022
    Reflections, 2111
Cooke, George. Complete English farmer, 11612
Cooke, Nicholas, express to, 14027
Cooke, Samuel, 1687-1747
    Divine sovereignty, 4699
    Letter, 5591
    Necessarius, 3409
    Solemn charge, 6116
    ordained, 4614
    reply to, 6010
Cooke, Samuel, d. 1783
    Charge of St. Paul, 8329
    Christ holding, 6654
    Sermon, 11613
    Violent destroyed, 15279
Cooke, William, 1696-1760
    Great duty, 6922
    Sermon, 3408?
Cook's American arithmetic, 35352
Cool thoughts on the present, 9663-64
Cool thoughts on the subject, 19583
Cooley, Simeon
    To the public, 11224
    contemptible, 11380
Cooley, Timothy Mather, 1772-1859
    Sermon, 37247
    ordained, 30009
Coolidge, Samuel, 1703-1767. Sermon, 4235
Coombe, Thomas, 1758-1822
    Edwin, or the emigrant, 13891
    Exercise containing, 10594
    Harmony, 13219
    Peasant of Auburn, 18423, 19584-85
    Sermon, 13892-94
Coombs, Isaac, d. 1786
    Last words, 20299

Sketch of the life, 20300
adventures, 22443
execution, 20721
Cooper, ———, appendix, 3851
Cooper, ———, favors Croswell, 4926
Cooper, ———, hypocrisy of 13840
Cooper, ———, preface by, 10165
Cooper, ———, remarks on, 4947-49
Cooper, ———, requests troops, 14028
Cooper, Elizabeth, 1704?-1726, death, 2774
Cooper, Ezekiel, 1763-1847. Funeral discourse, 35353
Cooper, J., tr. Oriental moralist, 31743
Cooper, Jane, 1738-1762. Letters, 28478
Cooper, John, 1766-1845. Oration, 26818
Cooper, Myles, 1735-1785
    Address from the clergy, 12021
    American querist, 13220-22
    Ethices compendium, 13223
    Friendly address, 13224-26
    hypocrisy of, 13840?
    preface by, 10165?
    reply to, 13372-73, 13824, 14151-55
Cooper, Samuel, clerk Mass. Senate, 27281-82
Cooper, Samuel
    Blossoms of morality, (1795) 28479, (1796) 30277, (1798) 33568
    History of North America, (1793) 25347, (1795) 28489, (1796) 30278, (1797) 31984, (1800) 37251
    History of South America, 25348
    (tr.) Looking-glass, (1792) 24095, (1793) 25165, (1794) 26645, (1795) 28267, (1800) 36947
    New history of England, 21766
    New history of France, 21767
    New history of the Grecian, 21768, 26819
    New Roman history, 21769
    Youth's library, 37248
Cooper, Samuel, 1725-1783
    Crisis, 7176
    Discourse, 13227-28
    Sermon, (1751) 6655, (1753) 6984, (1756) 7642, (1759) 8330, (1760) 8573, (1761) 8828, (1780) 16753
    Two letters, 7400
    death, 18399
    dedication to, 14255
    elegy on, 18726
    ordained, 5753
    sermon before his congregation, 6592, 7094, 18887
Cooper, Samuel, 1772-1798
    Dissertation, 31985
    eulogy of, 35262
Cooper, Thomas, 1759-1840
    Account of the trial, 37249
    Political arithmetic, 33569
    Political essays, 35354, 37250
Cooper, W. D. History of North America, 37251
Cooper, William, of Boston. Anthem, 24227
Cooper, William, 1694-1743
    Beatifick vision, 3762
    Blessedness, 2859
    Compendium evangelicum, 4357
    Concio hyemalis, 4134
    Confession of faith, 1806
    Danger of people's loosing, 2860
    Divine teaching, 3523
    Doctrine of predestination, 4497
    Early piety, 3014
    God's concern, 2425, 3267
    Honours of Christ, 4498
    How and why, 1810
    Jabez's character, 1811

Man humbled, 3524
Objections, 2256
One shall be, 4700
Reply to the objections, 3268-70
Rules of advice, 3869
Serious exhortations, 3525
Sermon, 2112
Service of God, 2740
Sin and danger, 4701
Three discourses, 3526
Work of ministers, 4007
appendix, 3851?
death, 5367
examined, 5150
favors Croswell, 4947-49?
letter (from Ashley), 5120
letter (from J. F.), 4950
letters (from Smith), 5292
preface by, 2872, 4486, 4600-601, 4711, 4808, 4937
remarks on, 4926?
Cooper, William, fl. 1767-1784
    At a meeting of the freeholders, 10564
    Boston, Mar. 30, 1773, 12688
    Gentlemen, the inhabitants, 17105
    Notification, (1767) 15063, (1784) 18374
    clerk Comm. of correspondence, 14193
    speaker Mass. House, 14839, 14851, 14859, 14865-66
    town clerk Boston, 9350, 11133, 13159-60, 13162, 17480, 18937
Cooper, William, 1776-1796. Promised seed, (1796) 30279-80, (1797) 31986-92, (1798) 33570-71
Coote, Richard see Bellomont, Richard Coote, earl, 1636-1701
Cope, Thomas P. To the Society for promoting, 31687
Copernicus. Almanac see Almanacs (Gale)
Copie eines brief, 8645
Copies of letters and articles, 16788
    of letters from Gov. Bernard, 11178
    of letters from Sir Francis, 11179
    of original letters from the army, 35496
        letters from the French, 37252
        letters recently, 34606
    of some original, 3084
    of sundry petitions, 18335
    of the communications, 36512
    of the two letters, 5581
    of two bills, 16292
Copley, John Singleton, 1737-1815, portrait of Adams, 31689
Copperplate copies, 28481
Copy of a case, 3893
Copy of a letter, (Banneker to secy. of state), 24073-74, (Jackson to friend), 3782, (Kirkland to Gates) 15642, (Lawrence to Archdickne) 4983, (Read to Ladd) 9809-811
    of a letter found, 30049, 36937
        from a gentleman, 10867
        from a merchant, 3763
        from a young man, 37254
        from Quebeck, 5925

VOL.	ITEMS	VOL.	ITEMS
1	1-3244	8	22298-25074
2	3245-6623	9	25075-28145
3	6624-9891	10	28146-30832
4	9892-13091	11	30833-33261
5	13092-16176	12	33262-25854
6	16177-19448	13	35855-39162
7	19449-22297		

VOL.	ITEMS	VOL.	ITEMS
1	1-3244	8	22298-25074
2	3245-6623	9	25075-28145
3	6624-9891	10	28146-30832
4	9892-13091	11	30833-33261
5	13092-16176	12	33262-25854
6	16177-19448	13	35855-39162
7	19449-22297		

Cow chace, 16697, 21655
Cowell, Ebenezer. Concise view, 18976
Cowles, Giles Hooker, 1766-1835. Jewish and Christian, 37263
Cowley, Abraham, 1618-1667
  Cutter of Coleman street, 28493
  excerpts from, 23246
  life of, 18543
Cowley, Hannah Parkhouse, 1743-1809
  Belle's stratagem, 26559, 26824
  Bold stroke, 26825
  Day in Turkey, 28494-95
  Town before you, 28496
Cowper, Frances Maria. Original poems, 25353
Cowper, James. Narrative, 15775
Cowper, William, 1731-1800
  African's complaint, 27699
  Facetious history, 25354, 26826
  History of John Gilpin, 26827
  Journey of John Gilpin, 23126
  (ed.) Original poems, 25353
  Poems, 24229
  (tr.) Power of grace, 30194
  Task, (1787) 20303-304, (1791) 23293, (1795) 28497, (1796) 30290-92
  Tirocinium, 19590
  Verses, 32501, 37168
  excerpts from, 23246
Cowpland, Jonathan, reply to, 11476
Cox, ——, inventor, 12703
Cox, ——, travels of, 31692
Cox, Francis, trial, 34040
Cox, James, cancels subscription, 13677
Cox, John. Rewards and punishments, 28498
Cox, Sir Richard, 1650-1733. Letter (to Prior), 2113, 6481
Cox, T. Bibliotheca curiosa, 3765
Cox, Zachariah. Estimate, 35360
Coxe, John Redman, 1773-1864
  Inaugural essay, 26828
  Short view, 37264
Coxe, Tench, 1755-1824
  Address to an assembly, 20305
  Address to the Republicans, 36070
  Authentic view, 35361
  Brief examination, 23294-95
  Enquiry into the principles, 20306
  Examination of the constitution, 21028
  Federalist, 30293-94
  Observations on the agriculture, 21774
  Plan for encouraging, 25355
  Reflexions on the state, 24230
  Strictures upon the letter, 37265
  Thoughts concerning the bank, 19591, 20307
  To the public, 37266
  View of the U.S., 26829
Cozens, Dr. ——. Fables, 21029
Cozens, William R. Inaugural dissertation, 23296
Crabbe, George, 1754-1832. The village, 22433, 23297
Cradock, Thomas, 1718-1770
  New version, 7619
  Two sermons, 5928
Cradock, Thomas, fl. 1784, reply to, 18757
Craft, Gershom. New Jersey justice, 30295
Crafton, William Bell
  Address, 24231-33
  Short sketch, 24233, 24292
Crafts, Thomas, 1767-1798. Oration, 23298
Craftsman, a sermon, 2615, 7007
Craghead, Robert see **Craighead, Robert**
Craighead, Robert. Advice to communicants, 24234

Craik, James, 1730-1818, account of Washington's illness, 39139
Craik, William, 1761-1814, message referred to, 34807
Crakelet, William. Catalogue of words, 37375
Cranch, Robert G. Robert G. Cranch, sadlers ironmonger, 13233
Crane, Isaac Watts. Oration, (1795) 28499, (1797) 32000
Crane, John, 1756-1836
  Baptism of Jesus, 22502, 23374-75
  Sermon, 37267
  reply to, 22540
Crane, John, d. 1795, death, 28200
Crane, William
  Dissertation, 30296
  Observations, 28500
Crary, ——, colonel RI brigade, 34455
Crashaw, William, ed. Italian convert, 6633
Crasshold, Krishtian. Modern poemander, 5758
Crawford, Col. ——, execution, 17993, 35689
Crawford, A. Curious and authentick, 8829
Crawford, Adair, 1748-1795. Experiments, 20308
Crawford, Charles
  The Christian, a poem, 17893, 26830
  Dying prostitute, 32001
  Essay upon the eleventh, 37268
  Essay upon the propagation, 35362
  Liberty, 17894-95
  Observations upon Negro-slavery, 18425, 22434
  Observations upon the downfall, 21030
  Observations upon the fall, 18977
  Observations upon the revolution, 25356
  (tr.) Oration delivered at Paris, 21738
  (tr.) Oration upon the necessity, 21001
  Poem on the death, 17896
  Poems on various, 18426
  Poetical paraphrase, 17897, 30087
  Progress of liberty, 30297
Crawford, John. John Crawford of said city, 11226
Crawford, William, 1676-1742. Dying thoughts, 8331
Crazy Jane, 37269
Creaghead, Alexander
  Discourse, 4924
  animadversions on, 4895
Creation, fall, 25758
Credibility of the Christian, 3148
Creek Indian. Speech, 7321
Creek Indians
  account of, 22329, 23159-60
  treaty with, 22989
Crell, J., tr. Lautere wahrheit, 5950
Cressin, ——
  Exhibitions comic, 30398
  Innocent amusement, 30299
Creuzé-Dufresne, Michel Pascal. Conspiration, 28501-502
Crèvecoeur, Michel Guillaume St. Jean de, 1735-1813
  Letters from an American farmer, 25357, 33582
  extracts from, 20605
Cries of London, 19592
  of Philadelphia, 19593
  of the oppressed, 6117
Crisis, (I) 13896-905, (II) 13906-915, (III) 13916-25, (IV) 13926-34, (V) 13935-43, (VI) 13944-52, (VII) 13953-59, (VIII) 13960-66, (IX) 13967-69, (X) 13970-71, (XI) 13972-73, (XII) 13974-75, (XIII) 13976-77, (XIV) 13978-79, (XV) 13980-81, (XVI-XXVIII) 13982-94

Crisis, vol. I (no. 1-28), 14721
Crisis (Cooper), 7176
Crisis (Paine), 24658, 27466
Crisis (Paine), (I) 14953, (II-IV) 15493-95, (V)
    15951-53, (VI-VII) 15954-55, (VIII-IX) 16916-17,
    (X-XII) 17648-50, (XII) 18077
Crisis (Steele), 2703
Crisis; Centinel office, 30249
Crisis extraordinary; it is impossible, 16918-19
Crisis extraordinary, Wed., Aug. 9, 1775, 13995-96
Crisis; to the people, 33277
Crisp, Gertrude Niessen. Paper first printed, 946
Crisp, Samuel, 1670-1704. Two letters, (1722) 2330,
    (1762) 9098, (1799) 35518
Crisp, Stephen, 1628-1692
    Epistle of tender, 591
    Epistle to Friends, 16754
    Faithful warning, 592
    Kur(t)ze beschreibung, (1748) 6118, (1755) 7401,
        (1791) 23299, (1792) 24235
    Reise nach Jerusalem, 25358
    Scripture truths, 20309
    Sermons, or declarations, (1768) 10868, (1773)
        12740, (1774) 13145
    Short history of a long travel, (1724) 2518, (1751)
        6656, (1753) 6986, (1754) 7177, (1765) 9944,
        (1770) 11616, (1788) 21031, (1794) 26831, (1797)
        32002
    defended, 1578
Crispianus. The every thing, or an history, 18427
Crispin, William, accounts, 18709
Criterion of natural, 30166
Critic, or a tragedy, 20703, 29499
Critical commentary, 11995
    disquisitions, 37649
    dissertation, 22633
    examination, 20981
    remarks, 9922
Crocker, Joseph, signs circular, 24135
Croes, John, 1763-1832. Discourse, 37270
Crogan, George, conference with Indians, 11301
Cronin, Laurence, tr. American herbal, 29472
Crook in the lot, 24130
Crop the conjuror, wisdom of, 20153, 28117
Crosby, Joseph. Copy of a case, 3893
Crosby, Joshua, ordained, 23381
Crosby, Thomas, 1635-1702. Work of a Christian,
    1044, 4008
Crosley, David. Samson a type, 30300
Cross, John C.
    The purse, or benevolent, 32003
    Songs in The purse, 26832
    Way to get married, 33583
    When seated, 28503-504
Cross, Ralph, d. 1788, death, 21276
Cross, Robert. Protestation, 4704
Cross of Christ, 8368, 27116
Croswell, Andrew, 1709-1785
    Answer to the Rev. Mr. Garden, 4705
    Apostle's advice, 5371
    Brief remarks, 12022
    Carmina lugubria, 11617
    Comfort in Christ, 10595
    Discourse, 18428
    Free forgiveness, 10274
    Free justification, 9945
    Heaven shut, 5929
    Heavenly doctrine, 8110
    Letter (to Cumming), 9099
    Letter (to Turell), 4925

Mr. Murray unmask'd, 13997-98
Narrative of the founding, 6302
Observations on several, 10869
Part of an exposition, 10870-71
Remarks on an absurd, 9946
Reply to a book, 4926
Reply to the declaration, 4927-28
Second defence, 5930
Testimony against the prophaness, 8574
What is Christ, 5568
letter (from Blanchard), 4897
letter (from Garden), 4957-58
letter (from Moorhead), 5011
letter (from Prentice), 12205
preface by, 7578
remarks on, 9340, 9371, 9903
reply to, 5161, 5893
Croswell, Joseph. Ode to liberty, 26102
Croswell, Rebecca, d. 1770?, poem on, 11617
Croswell, William, d. 1834. Tables, 23300
Crotchet, Timothy. Modest proposal, 5931
Crouch, Nathaniel, 1632-1725
    Journey to Jerusalem, (1794) 26833, (1795) 28505,
        (1796) 30301
    (tr.) Memorable accidents, 16321, 28506
    Travels of fourteen, 32004
    Vanity of the life, 11227
Croucher, Richard D., trial, 38373
Crowley, Ann, 1757-1774. Some expressions, 13999,
    14722
Crowley, Mary, daughter's death, 13999, 14722
Crowley, Thomas
    Dissertations, 13234
    (ed.) Some expressions, 13999
    daughter's death, 14722
Crown and glory, 358
Crown of eternal life, 11161
Croxall, Samuel, d. 1752
    (ed.) Fables of Aesop, (1777) 15230, (1783) 17810,
        (1787) 20185
    Fair Circassian, 7178, 28507
Cruger, Henry, 1737-1827, speech in Parliament,
    14092
Cruger, John, 1710-1792
    From the Bristol gazette, 17506
    Managers on the part, 11372
    To the freeholders, 11228-29, 11234
    To the honourable, 11371
    Whereas a paper, 11230
    candidate, 11263, 11389-90, 11529
    election favored, 11495
    letter (from Aristides), 11968, 13121
    mayor of N.Y., 9463
    song in favor of, 11472
    speaker NY assembly, 14295
Cruse, Englehart. Projector detected, 21032
Cruttenden, Robert. Experience of Mr. R., 5372
Cry against oppression, 753
    of oppression, 6090
    of Sodom, 186

VOL.	ITEMS	VOL.	ITEMS
1	1-3244	8	22298-25074
2	3245-6623	9	25075-28145
3	6624-9891	10	28146-30832
4	9892-13091	11	30833-33261
5	13092-16176	12	33262-25854
6	16177-19448	13	35855-39162
7	19449-22297		

Curtis, John
  New collection, 32008
  Twelve cents worth, 28520-21
Curtis, Philip, hand of fellowship, 25573
Curtis, Samuel, 1747-1822. Almanac see **Almanacs (Curtis)**
Curtius. Letters, 34657
Curwen, George, d. 1717?
  Catalogue of library, 1953
  death, 1865, 1924
Curzon, Sir Nathaniel, letter (from Bohun), 9916-17
Cushing, Rev. ——. Charge, 35630
Cushing, Caleb. Letter, 5569
Cushing, Henry. Catalogue, 38341
Cushing, Jacob, 1730-1809
  Christian ministers, 25367
  Discourse, 32010
  Divine judgments, 15776
  Sermon, (1765) 10275, (1770) 12023, (1772) 12370, (1788) 21035
  (ed.) Submission, 18315
Cushing, John, trial judge, 11683
Cushing, John, d. 1772
  Gospel-ministers, 8332
  at Salisbury, 6792
Cushing, John, d. 1823
  Christians mourn, 22438
  Discourse, 30306
Cushing, Matthew, d. 1734, execution, 3851
Cushing, Thomas, d. 1746, death, 5855
Cushing, Thomas, 1725-1788
  Proclamation, 19084
  dedication to, 17183, 17557, 17970, 18521, 19035, 19703, 20408
  delegate to Congress, 13425
  sermon before, 17114, 17450, 17899, 18526, 19269, 20142, 20469
Cushing, Thomas C. Discourse, 37276
Cushing, William, daily record, 24490
Cushing and Cushing. Proposal for printing, 38453
Cushman, Joshua. ordained. 31629

Cushman, Robert, 1580-1625. Sin and danger, (1724) 2519, (1785) 18981, (1788) 21036
Customs of primitive, 10891
Cutbush, Edward. Inaugural dissertation, 26838
Cuthbertson, John, errors, 7300
Cutler, Manasseh, 1742-1823
  Boston, Nov. 10, 1785, 18901
  Charge, 34609
  Explanation of the map, 20312, 21037
  Sermon, 35367
  To the honorable, 26369
  agent of Ohio co., 20604
  report from, 20602
Cutler, Timothy, 1683-1765
  Depth of the divine, 2115
  Final peace, 3894
  Firm union, 1878
  Good and faithful, 5932
  death, 9923
Cutter, R., petition of, 34754
Cutter of Coleman street, 28493
Cutting, Asa. Letter (to Foster), 26839
Cutting, John Browne
  Facts and observations, 28522
  claim by, 24893, 36531
Cuttss, John, commission of, 12146
Cyd-Gordiad, 3323
Cyder-maker's instructor, 9084-85
Cynthia, 32011, 33592-93
Cyril, St., prophecies, 9318
Cyrus, travels of, 26052, 29383
Cyrus the Great, a tragedy, 8791

VOL.	ITEMS	VOL.	ITEMS
1	1-3244	8	22298-25074
2	3245-6623	9	25075-28145
3	6624-9891	10	28146-30832
4	9892-13091	11	30833-33261
5	13092-16176	12	33262-25854
6	16177-19448	13	35855-39162
7	19449-22297		

D

Reflection and prospect, 20316
Sermon, (1779) 16252, (1794) **26846**
Two discourses, 10598
ordained, 8363, 8838
questions relative to, 8540, 8794
remarks on, 9061
reply to, 28070
settlement in Wallingford, 8342
vindication, 8504
Dana, Joseph, 1742-1827
  Discourse, 37288
  Duty and reward, 35378
  New American selection, (1792) 24245, (1794) 26847, (1799) 35379
  Sacrifice, 17508
  Sermon, (1794) 28531, (1795) 28532-33
  ordained, 10439
Dana, Josiah. Discourse, 28534
Dana, Samuel, d. 1798
  Address, 31798
  death, 33419
Dana, Samuel Whittlesey, 1760-1830
  Essay, 37381
  Yale College subject, 18434
  message referred to, 33054-55
Danbury. Vindication of the proceedings, 9846
Danbury association. Minutes, (1790) 22447, 23309, (1791) 23310, (1792) 24246
Danbury Baptist association. Minutes, (1793) 25375, (1800) 37289
Dance, James, 1722-1774. Village wedding, 30311
Dance for waltzing, 28535
Dance of Herodias, 35125
Dance assembly, Savannah. Rules, 22873
Dancing exploded, 15848
Danck-predigt, 8129
Dandridge, ——, secy. to Washington, 31365
Dane, Nathan, 1752-1835
  Beverly, Jan. 19, 1799, 35380
  Motion, 20069
  On motion by Mr. Dane, 20070
  reports on accounts, 20059, 21534
  reports on civil department, 20767
  reports on emoluments, 20090
  reports on Illinois tract, 21514
  reports on Indian affairs, 20768, 20770
  reports on invalid establishment, 21512
  reports on new states, 20058, 20769
  reports on treasury report, 21516
Danforth, John, 1660-1730
  Blackness of sins, 1450
  Cases of conscience, 2485
  Elegy, (Belcher) 2454, (Foxcroft) 2218
  Holy striving, 2454
  Judgment begun, 1812
  King Hezekiah's bitterness, 1451
  Kneeling to God, 780
  Poem, 1673
  Right Christian temper, 1046
  Sermon, 3016
  Vile prophanations, 1154
  preface by, 2862
Danforth, Samuel, 1626-1674
  Almanac see **Almanacs (Danforth)**
  Astronomical description, 99
  Brief recognition, 160
  Catechism, 34
  Cry of Sodom, 186
Danforth, Samuel, 1666-1727
  Bridgwater's monitor, 1888, 10940
  Cases of conscience, 2485
  Duty of believers, 1348
  Elegy, 1605

Exhortation, 1674
Piety encouraged, 1204
Woful effects, 1452
death, 3016
Danforth, Thomas, daughter's death, 2218
Danger of America delineated, 35756
  of an unconverted ministry, 4609-10, 5070-71
  of an unqualified ministry, 5198
  of apostasie, 4232
  of breaking, 4135
  of disregarding, 7391
  of excessive drinking, 25376
  of forgetting, 3964
  of hypocrisy, 1533
  of neutrality, 7893
  of not reforming, 1341
  of people's loosing, 2860
  of schisms, 4358
  of sinners hardening, 7806
  of speedy, 1234
  of spiritual pride, 5696
  of taking, 582
  of the unconverted, 11640
Dangerous vice, 21736
Dangers of our national, 19359
Dangers which threaten, 29020
Daniel, selections from, 30489, 32189-90
Daniel, Thomas, d. 1683, death, 802
Daniel catcher, 1650
Daniel in the den, 35297
Daniel Leeds justly rebuked, 1094
Danielson, Timothy, speaker Mass. House, 14862-64
Danse; article extrait, 30816
Daranzel, 37386
Darbe, Esther, d. 1757, death, 7858
Darbe, John, 1725-1805
  Last enemy, 7402
  wife's death, 7858
Darbie, John, ordained, 8244
Darby, Ann, accessory, 10919
Darby and Joan, 28875
Darby's return, 21804, 23338
D'Arcy, 31198
Dardin, Amey, petition, 38833
Darley, John, sings song, 25627, 27647-48, 27789, 30370
Darling, Thomas, 1720-1789. Some remarks, 7881
Darnell, Henry. Just and impartial, 3017
Darragh, William, ed. Discourse, 11241, 26895
Dartmouth, William Legge, earl of, 1731-1801
  dedication to, 13015-18, 14635-36, 14457
  letter (from English American), 14964-66
  sums issued to, 13677
Dartmouth college
  Catalogue (catalogus), (1779) 16253, (1789) 21784, (1792) 24247, (1795) 28536, (1798) **33599,** (1799) 35381
  Charter, 11231
Dartmouth (ship), loaded with tea, 12913
D'Artois, ——, comte. Voyage to the moon, 20117
Darton, William. Little truths, (1789) 21785, (1794) 26848-49, (1800) 37291

VOL.	ITEMS	VOL.	ITEMS
1	1-3244	8	22298-25074
2	3245-6623	9	25075-28145
3	6624-9891	10	28146-30832
4	9892-13091	11	30833-33261
5	13092-16176	12	33262-25854
6	16177-19448	13	35855-39162
7	19449-22297		

Darwin, Erasmus, 1731-1802
  Botanic garden, 33600
  Plan for conduct, 33601
  Zoonomia, 30312, 32017
Dass das evangelium, 23334, 25416
Daughter of America. Women invited to war, 20895
Davenport family, history of, 34505
Davenport, ——, tavern keeper, 11793, 11876-80
Davenport, Barnett, 1760-1780. Brief narrative, 16756
Davenport, Ebenezer. Oration, 37292
Davenport, James, 1717-1757
  Confession, 5374
  Faithful minister, 7643
  Letter (to Barber), 5373
  Song of praise, 4929
  comments on, 5368
  declaration relating to, 4917
  letter (from Chauncy), 4912
  letter (from Moorhead), 5011
  letter (from Pickering), 5037
  letters (from Williams), 5523
  reply to, 5414
Davenport, James, fl. 1798. Columbia and liberty, 33602
Davenport, John, 1597-1670
  Another essay, 78
  Catechism printed, 136
  Discourse, 79
  Gods call, 137
  life of, 724
  reply to, 89
Davenport, John, d. 1731, death, 3409
David, King
  commentary on, 24408
  military character, 8383
  poem on, 6667, 7000, 7192, 8591, 9110, 9966, 19001, 24297, 30575, 32079
David, Enoch. Offers of Christ, 11624
David, William, blasphemous assertions, 1111
David Hall, at the new, 11282
David serving, 185, 831
David West's catalogue, 26468
Davideis, (1751) 6667, (1753) 7000, (1754) 7192, (1760) 8591, (1762) 9110, (1765) 9966, (1785) 19001, (1792) 24297, (1797) 32079
Davidge, John Beale, 1768-1829. Treatise on the autumnal, 33603
David's dying charge, 2419
David's lamentation, 23710
Davidson, ——, tr. Metamorphoses, 22753
Davidson, J., ed. Selectae e Veteri Testamento, 21683
Davidson, James, 1732-1809
  Easy and practical, 33604
  Short introduction, 36309, 38501
Davidson, John, relief, 22961
Davidson, Robert. Address of the Presbyterian, 14411
Davidson, Robert, 1750-1812
  Geography epitomized, (1784) 18435, (1790) 22448, (1791) 23311, (1794) 26850
  Oration, 20317
  Sermon, 26851
Davidson, Robert G. W. Inaugural dissertation, 26852
Davie, William Richard, 1756-1820
  Address, 21041
  Instructions, 35383
Davies, Benjamin
  American repository, (1795) 28537, (1796) 30313, (1797) 32018, (1798) 33605, (1799) 35384

Map of Philadelphia, 35385
Some account, 26853
Tit for tat, 30314
reply to, 30160
Davies, Nathan. Catholic liturgy, 31819
Davies, Richard, 1635-1708. Account of the convincement, 6833, 11625
Davies, Samuel, 1724-1761
  Curse of cowardice, 8333-36
  Little children invited, (1759) 8337, (1764) 9629, (1766) 10276, (1770) 11626, (1791) 23312, (1798) 33606
  Method of salvation, 25377
  Miscellaneous poems, 6834
  Ode on the prospect, 8831
  Religion and patriotism, 7403
  Religion and public, 8832-33, 9101
  Sermon, (1748) 6121, (1752) 6987, (1761) 8834-36
  Sermons, (1766) 10277, (1792) 24248, (1794) 26854
  State of religion, 6657
  Virginia's danger, 7644
  death, 8864
  pres. Princeton, 8684
Davies, Thomas, 1736-1766. Sermon, 9948
Davis, ——, revises N.C. laws, 15488
Davis, Adjutant ——. Treatise on the military, 14729
Davis, Col. ——, battalion accounts, 18109
Davis, Mrs. ——, sings song, 33583
Davis, Caleb, speaker Mass. House, 16863-64, 16866, 17219
Davis, Catherine, d. 1759, death, 8559
Davis, Daniel, 1762-1835
  Address, 23313
  Oration, 30315
  death, 35811
Davis, Hugh, d. 1755. Last speech, 7404
Davis, Ignatius
  Ten dollars reward, 25378
  Thirty dollars, 23314
Davis, Isaac, depositions before, 14110
Davis, James. Almanac see **Almanacs (Davis)**
Davis, James, 1721-1785. Office and authority, 13236
Davis, John, 1721-1809. Baltimore circular, 28233?
Davis, John, fl. 1759, wife's death, 8559
Davis, John, 1761-1847
  Address, 35386
  Eulogy, 37293, 37383
  sketches life of Cushman, 18981, 21036
Davis, John, 1774-1854
  (tr.) Campaign of General, 34393
  Farmer of New Jersey, 37294
  Lettres originales, 33608
  Original letters, 33607
  Poems, 35387
  Tribute to the U.S., 33609
  (tr.) Wieland, 35247
Davis, Jonathan. Some queries, 6303
Davis, Joseph. Gospel ministers, 25379
Davis, Joseph, storekeeper, 30299
Davis, Matthew Livingston, 1773-1850
  Brief account, 28538
  Oration, 37295
Davis, Polly, recovery, 24162-66, 25241-45, 26721
Davis, Richard, 1658-1714. Hymns, 4706
Davis, Thomas
  Commonwealth of Massachusetts, 25786
  Report, 27292
  Specie tax no. 11, 27293
  Tax no. 12, 29048

VOL.	ITEMS	VOL.	ITEMS
1	1-3244	8	22298-25074
2	3245-6623	9	25075-28145
3	6624-9891	10	28146-30832
4	9892-13091	11	30833-33261
5	13092-16176	12	33262-25854
6	16177-19448	13	35855-39162
7	19449-22297		

VOL.	ITEMS	VOL.	ITEMS
1	1-3244	8	22298-25074
2	3245-6623	9	25075-28145
3	6624-9891	10	28146-30832
4	9892-13091	11	30833-33261
5	13092-16176	12	33262-25854
6	16177-19448	13	35855-39162
7	19449-22297		

Descant of sinful, 13501
Descant on the command, 14007
Descartes, René. Compendium, 3878, 8092
Descending of Christ, 26872, 27990
Description and history, 33894
    and use, 7012
    of a good, 19699
        new, 24713
          plantation, 31158
          wonderful, 30337
    of counterfeit, 16562
    of Kentucky, 26268
    of Occacock inlet, 29351
    of Pennsbury, 10724
    of the American yellow, 7040, 35733
        anatomical, 27510
        attack, 15284
        Genesee, 35033
        last, 12919
        malignant, 25366
        monument, 28403
        most remarkable, 33629
        principles, 33729
        river, 30338
        settlement, 36727
        situation, 25720
        soil, 32510
        vibrating, 35388
    topographique et politique, 30817
    topographique, physique, 32504, 34137
    with instructions, 21568
Descriptions, virtues, 6783
Desengano del hombre, 27584
Deserted daughter, 28847, 30572
    infant, 34525
    village, (1771) 12060, (1782) 17550, (1783)
      17958, (1786) 19689, (1789) 21723, (1791)
      23235, (1793) 25552-53, (1799) 35557
Deserter, a comic opera, (1787) 20331-32, (1795)
    29482-83, (1796) 31171
Desiderius, 2037
Design and blessedness, 24746
    and nature, 19948
    of the institution, 4724
Desires of the repenting, 1402
Desires that Joshua's resolution, 1854
Deperantius. Dialogue, 5177
Desponding Negro, 25313, 33535
Dessert to the True American, 33630, 35402
D'Estaing, comte see Estaing, Charles Hector
    Théodat, comte d', 1729-1796
Destouches, Philippe Néricault, 1680-1754
    Know your own, 28563
    Libertine, 8837
    Married man, 28564, 30339
Desultory extracts, 30574
Desultory reflections, 37417-19
Detection detected, 8040
    of Bache, 33524
    of injurious, 7671
    of the conduct, 10152
Detector, Daniel see Henderson, A.
Determination of the case, 2502
Detur digniori, 2139
Detweiler, Leonard, acrostic on, 16815
Deus nobiscum, 2667
Deus visibilis, 1157
Deutsche gesellschaft (N.Y.)
    Gesetze, 35943
    Grundregeln, 18993
Deutsche gesellschaft (Phila.)
    Acte zur incorporirung, 17676

Regeln, 25994, 27507
Deutsche schrift, 5933
De Valcourt, 30056
Devastation by the king, 35386
Develope, Titus. Partymaker's assistant, 30340
Devens, Richard, 1749-1835
    Comment on some, 12749
    Discourse, 32035
    Paraphrase, 28273
    Witness of the spirit, 35404
Devereux, James, commands ship, 34695
Devereux, John, petition, 31372
Devèze, Jean, 1753-1829. Enquiry, 26873, 36287
Device devised against, 26874
Devienne, François, 1759-1803
    Battle of Gemappe, 30341
    selections from, 34516
Devil and a ghost, 20351
    and George III, 20330
    let loose, 36020
    upon crutches, 12358
    upon two sticks, 28965
Devonshire wonder, 29671
Devotion, Ebenezer, 1714-1771
    Answer of the pastor, 5934
    Civil ruler, 6989
    Examiner examined, 10280-81
    Fortitude, 9104
    Half-way covenant, 11236
    Letter (to Bellamy), 11630
    Mourning piece, 7406
    Mutual oligation, 6482
    Parishioner, 11237
    Second letter, 11631
    Work of the gospel, 6990
Devotion, John, 1730-1802
    Duty and interest, 15285
    God the dwelling, 18994
    Necessity of a constant, 10282
    Sermon, 21054
Devotional exercises, 27072
    harmony, 39140
    papers written, 12790
    papers wrote, 35547
Devotions of God's people, 12054
Devout and humble, 1731
    Christian's vade mecum, 21794, 24264
    companion, 8339
    contemplation, 1671
    exercises, (1742) 5048, (1743) 5282, (1745)
      5684, (1754) 7311, (1790) 22860, (1791)
      23743-44, (1792) 24758, (1794) 27644-45,
      (1796) 31125, (1798) 34487-88, (1800) 38424
    thoughts, 29936
    wish, 17442
Dewees, Samuel, accounts. 18119
Dewees, William, sheriff, 14970-71
Dewey, Israel. Letter (to Hopkins), 13375, 25390
Dewey, Joseph, patron of literature, 2722
Dewey, Sherman, 1772-1813
    Account of a hail storm, 35405
    Oration, 37319

VOL.	ITEMS	VOL.	ITEMS
1	1-3244	8	22298-25074
2	3245-6623	9	25075-28145
3	6624-9891	10	28146-30832
4	9892-13091	11	30833-33261
5	13092-16176	12	33262-25854
6	16177-19448	13	35855-39162
7	19449-22297		

Dewey, Solomon. Short and easy, 35406
DeWitt, Benjamin, 1774-1819
  Chemico-medical essay, 32036
  Memoir on the Onondaga, 33632
DeWitt, Charles, 1727-1787
  reports on Conn. expenses, 18838
  reports on Penobscot expedition, 19312
DeWitt, Simeon, 1756-1834. Map of the state, 24265
Dewsbury, William, d. 1688
  Sermon, 4501, 10874
  Sermon or declaration, 10868
Dexter, Andrew, d. 1816. Oration, 33633
Dexter, Samuel, 1700-1755
  Call from the dead, 3020
  Our father's God, 4236, 30342
Dexter, Samuel, 1761-1816
  Progress of science, 16759, 22621
  Thoughts upon several, 23324
Dexter, Timothy
  congratulations to, 26010
  ode to, 32695
Daye, Thomas C., letter (from Martin), 21220
D'Happart, Jh. Leger. Appeal, 32037
Diable boiteux, 23497-98, 28965
Dialogue, &c., 10131
Dialogue between A and B, 18445
  between a believer, 30343
        a blind man, (1736) 4027, (1738) 4255,
          (1751) 6520, (1790) 22902, (1793) 26199-
          200, (1794) 27733, (1797) 32869
        a Boston, 21055
        a minister and Billy, 26875
        a minister and his, (1724) 2590, (1742)
          5076-77, (1772) 12597
        a predestinarian, 11931, 31611
        a separate, 16227
        a southern, 13245-46
        a young, 28133
        an uncle, 9636
        Andrew Trueman, 9634-35, 9837
        Evangelist, 5177
        Freeman and Trusty, 3021, 3049
        George the Third, 17681
        Philagathus, 28336
        Poimen, 24637
        Robert Rich, 2624
        Sam. Sword, 27657
        the devil, 17520, 20330
        the ghost, 14966
        the giant, 9637, 10022
        the governor, 9105
        the pulpit, 26177-78
        two countrymen, 5160
        two gentlemen, 5376
    betwixt a burgomaster, 2523
    betwixt a learned divine, 2524
    concerning the slavery, 14804, 19044
    containing questions, 9189, 10979
    containing some reflections, 9638
    curieux, 22607
    of courtship, 11632
    on peace, 9386
    on the Christian, 9063
    or discourse, 26172, 32844
    or representation, 4065
    shewing, 2652
    spoken, 12750
Dialogues between a minister, 4690
    between Common sense, 30710
    for schools, 37320
    of the dead, 32396
    on the nature, 26774

Diana's shrines, 12965
Diazius, John, history of, 30012, 33357
Dibdin, Charles, 1745-1814
  Ben Backstay, 26877
  Collection of songs, 35407
  Deserter, 20331-32, 29482-83
  Harvest-home, 28566
  Jack at the windlass, 25392
  Lucky escape, 26878
  Museum, 32039
  Nancy, 32040
  Poor Tom Bowling, 26879
  Poor Vulcan, 28567
  Quaker, 26558, 26880, 27449
  Soldier's adieu, 26881
  Songs in The deserter, 26882
  Sweet passion, 32041
  Token, 26883
  'Twas in the good ship, 26884
  Veterans, 30345
  Waggoner, 26885
  selections from, 32901, 34516
Dibdin's museum, 32039
Dick, Elisha Cullen, 1762-1825
  Doctor Dick's instructions, 33635
  account of Washington's illness, 39139
Dick, Samuel, 1740-1812
  reports on Conn. expenses, 18838
  reports on invalids, 18831, 19297
  reports on Penobscot expedition, 19312
Dickdock leshon, 3931
Dickins, Asbury, 1780-1861
  Claims of Thomas Jefferson, 37187
  Eulogium, 37321
Dickins, John, d. 1799?, death, 35353
Dickinson, ——, actor, 31853
Dickinson, James, 1658-1741. Memorable instance,
  25394, 26886
Dickinson, John, 1732-1808
  address to the committee, 10283
  Declaration by the representatives, 14544-50
  Essay, 13247
  Farmer's and monitor's letters, 11239
  Friends and countrymen, 9949
  Last Tuesday, 9639
  Late regulations, 9950
  Letter from the country, 12751
  Letters from a farmer, 10875-79, 11238
  Letters of Fabius, 32042
  Liberty song, 10881
  New song, 10880
  Proclamation, (1781) 17134-35, (1782) 17516-18,
    17664, (1783) 18084-91, (1784) 18685-86, 18688
  Rede gehalten, 9643
  Remarks on a late, 14735
  Reply to a piece, 9640
  Speech, 9641-42
  defeat of, 10341
  gives annual medal, 18956
  imitated, 10014
  letter (from Macpherson), 11712
  opposed, 10433
  portrait, 16765
  reply to, 9671-74
Dickinson, Jonathan, 1663-1722
  God's protecting, (1699) 863, (1735) 3896, (1751)
    6658
  Göttliche veschützung, 7646
  Remarkable deliverance, 25393
Dickinson, Jonathan, 1688-1747
  Brief discourse, 4294
  Brief illustration, (1746) 5759-60, (1763) 9376,

(1781) 17136, (1793) 25395
Call to the weary, 4502
Danger of schisms, 4358
Defence of a sermon, 4136
Defence of Presbyterian, 2525
Defence of the dialogue, 5161
Display of God's, 4931, 5162
Familiar letters, (1745) 5572, (1792) 24267, (1797) 32043
Nature and necessity, 5163-64
Observations, 4503
Protestation presented, 4932
Reasonableness of Christianity, 3527
Reasonableness of nonconformity, 4237
Reflections, 5377
Remarks upon a discourse, 3156
Remarks upon a pamphlet, 3897
Remarks upon Mr. Gales, 2215
Remarks upon the postscript, 2526
Scripture-bishop, 3528, 3651
Second vindication, 6123
Sermon, (1722) 2428, (1733) 3652
True scripture-doctrine, (1741) 4710, (1793) 25396, (1800) 37322
Vanity of human, 4010
Vindication, 5761
Witness of the spirit, 4504, 5165-66
death, 6221
letter, (from Checkley) 2619, (from Johnson) 5978-79
ordained, 1573
remarks by, 5513-14
reply to, 3984, 4113, 5513-14, 5906, 6094, 6506
strictures on, 2510
vindicated, 6829
Dickinson, Moses, 1695-1778
Answer, in the form, 11633
Answer to a letter, 8838
Discourse shewing, 4933
Inquiry, 6483
Letter (to Wetmore), 6693
Second vindication, 6123
Sermon, (1732) 3653, (1755) 7407, (1774) 13248
Dickinson, Samuel. Vindication of the proceedings, 9846
Dickinson, Samuel Fowler, 1775-1838. Oration, 32044
Dickinson, Timothy, 1761-1813
Sermon, 37323
ordained, 22175
Dickson, Joseph, 1745-1825
Philadelphia, May 1st, 1800, 37324
defended, 36841
reply to, 37637
Dickson, William. Almanac see **Almanacs (Dickson)**
Dictates of right, 30597
Dictionary of love, 33637
of the Bible, 33638
of the Holy Bible, 33463
Diegel, Jacob. Account of the births, (1771) 12524, (1773) 12950, (1774) 13541, (1775) 14388
Diejenigen anmerkungen, 5103
Diese neue, 8579
Dietrich, prinz von Anhalt-Dessau. Letzte wylle, 6991
Dietrick, ——, tobacconist, 8579
Difference between a legal, 6278
Difference briefly stated, 21679
Difficulties and discouragements, 6329

Difficulties, duties, 8450
Difinitive friedens-tractat, 18254
Digby, ——, letter (from Washington), 30392
Digest of the law of actions, 23354
of the laws of Maryland, 35617
laws of the state, 37505
laws of the U.S., 37613
Dignity and duty, 6793
and glory, 32082
and importance of the gospel, 7444
and importance of the military, 12044
of human, 26719
of man, 20344, 33673
Dignum, Charles, composes song, 32104
Diligence in the work, 8259
Diligent servant, 23584
Dillwyn, George. Sermon, 32807
Diluvium ignis, 2765, 3317
Dilworth, Thomas, d. 1780
Dilworth's Assistant, 33639
New guide to the English, (1754) 7183, (1755) 7408, (1757) 7883, (1761) 8839, (1765) 9951, (1766) 10284, (1767) 10602, (1769) 11240, (1770) 11634, (1771) 12027, (1772) 12374, (1774) 13249, (1778) 15782-83, (1779) 16258-60, (1780) 16760-63, 19403, (1781) 17137, (1782) 17521-22, (1783) 17916-17, (1784) 18446, (1786) 19607-608, (1787) 20333-34, (1788) 21056-57, (1789) 21795, 21797, (1790) 22462-63, (1791) 23325, (1792) 24268, 24271, (1793) 25397-99, (1794) 26887-88, (1795) 28568, (1796) 30349, (1797) 32046-47, (1799) 35409, (1800) 37326
Practical English grammar, 7082
Schoolmaster's assistant, (1773) 12752, (1781) 17138, 19404, (1784) 18447-48, (1785) 18995, (1787) 20335, (1790) 22461, (1791) 23326, (1792) 24269-70, (1793) 25400-402, (1796) 30350-52, (1797) 32048, (1799) 35410-11, (1800) 37327
Spelling book improved, 30346-48
Spelling-book, or a new, 21796
Young bookkeeper's assistant, 26889, 33640
tables by, 38206
Dilworth, W. H.
Complete letter-writer, (1761) 8840, (1763) 9377, (1786) 19609, (1790) 22464, (1793) 25403, (1794) 26890-91, (1795) 28569-70, (1797) 32049
Leben und heroische, 8841
Life and heroic, 8580
Lord Anson's voyage, 8534
New and complete letter writer, 23327
New complete letter writer, 23326
Diman, James, 1707-1788
Sermon, 12375
colleague ordained, 17995
ordained, 4145
Dimension proper, 30353
Dimsdale, Thomas, baron, 1712-1800
Present method, 12028
inoculation method discussed, 14891
Dinarbas, a tale, (1791) 23473, (1792) 24446, (1795)

VOL.	ITEMS	VOL.	ITEMS
1	1-3244	8	22298-25074
2	3245-6623	9	25075-28145
3	6624-9891	10	28146-30832
4	9892-13091	11	30833-33261
5	13092-16176	12	33262-25854
6	16177-19448	13	35855-39162
7	19449-22297		

Haverhill, 28333
Hebron, 36379
Kensington, 14002
Litchfield, 33825
Malden, 37538
Medfield, 36154
New-Ark, 7373
New Braintree, 28534
New Haven, 37339
New London, 8779
North Coventry, 35070
Northampton, 22181
Peterborough, 38621
Plymouth, 37722
Portsmouth, 21718
Providence, 26772
Reading, (1799) 36373, (1800) 38564
Salem, 34414-16
South parish, 36897
the anniversary, 13049
the dedication, 28839
the Episcopal, 18669
the First church, 20273
the funeral, (Breck) 18552, (Howard) 18920, (Kendall) 24567
the new chapel, 23999-24000
the North church, 27730
the ordination, (Chapin) 27491, (Flint) 23442, (Gould) 25608, (Harris) 21809, (Howe) 23218, (Miller) 24678, (Thomas) 26134, (Wilson) 26135, (Wood) 33244
the public consecration, 33845
the request, 34683
the Roman Catholic, 34646-47
the third parish, (1783) 18203, (1795) 29617
the West church, 10248
Wardsborough, 32084
Wells, 37605
Wethersfield, 18572
Wilton, 35484
Windsor, 22325
Woodbury, 37270
Worcester, 14030
delivered before a special, 30636
an assembly, 29480
his excellency, (1794) 28093, (1795) 28378
his honor, 33220
St. John's, 21798
the Ancient, 29908
the association, 24282
the Aurora, 33826
the Grand lodge, 23777
the Humane society, (1793) 25303, (1794) 26620, (1795) 28351, (1796) 31110, (1798) 34953
the Roxbury, (1794) 29342, (1796) 30035, (1800) 37367
the triennial, 24774
delivered by the particular, 28127
delivered by Timothy Upham, 27986
delivered in Chelsea, 37734
Chester, 31207
Chesterfield, 24034
Christ church, 34042
Christ's church, 23778, 32723
Dover, 33812
Harvard, 26940
New London, 30182
New York, 17927
Newmarket, 26893, 27322

Newport, 37308
presence of, 24788
Providence, 10886
Roxbury, 31799
St. James', 29481
St. John's, 23755, 26175
St. Paul's, (1790) 22338, (1791) 23173, (1792) 24091
the chapel of Harvard, (1794) 27773-74, (1795) 29605, (1798) 34629
the chapel of Rhode Island, 35814
the church, 35648
the city, 36463
the court-house, 29556
the First church, (1783) 18385, (1795) 30199
the first parish, 33470
the First Presbyterian, 33427
the meeting house, 35021, 36464
the new Dutch, 26921
the new Presbyterian, 29081
the Presbyterian, 36802
the 2d Congregational, 38196-97
the South, 37061
the synagogue, 34524
delivered near York, 17531
delivered on . . . Dec. 27, 1799, 38577
. . . Feb. 22, 1800, 37353
Saturday, (1769) 11534-35, (1792) 25047
Thanksgiving-Day, 35815
the 18th day of December, 15791
the 18th of October, (1797) 34561, (1798) 33361
the 22d of February, 32851
the 26th of November, 28974
the anniversary, 32582
the day of annual, 29250
the day of the annual, 12001
the national fast, 35444
the public, 33664-65
delivered to the First church, 11940
the religious, 34627-28
the students, 31267
the young people, 35436
designed to explain, 30778
from the 1st Epistle, 18428
had in College-hall, 2324
in order to confute, 7911
in two parts, 24342
intended, 24085
introductory, 38203
Jan. 28, 1750, 6625
occasioned by the death, (Checkley) 11584, (M. Clap) 11530, (N. Clap) 5751, (Fowler) 37354, (Foxcroft) 11207, (George II) 8925, (Hamlin) 23458, (Howard) 15367, (Jackson) 32010, (Kendall) 24326, (Loring) 2119, (Mayhew) 10254, (Parsons) 17855, (Richards) 11681, (J. Sewall) 11206, (S. Sewall) 8666, (Stiles) 29280
occasioned by the death (Washington),

VOL.	ITEMS	VOL.	ITEMS
1	1-3244	8	22298-25074
2	3245-6623	9	25075-28145
3	6624-9891	10	28146-30832
4	9892-13091	11	30833-33261
5	13092-16176	12	33262-25854
6	16177-19448	13	35855-39162
7	19449-22297		

VOL.	ITEMS	VOL.	ITEMS
1	1-3244	8	22298-25074
2	3245-6623	9	25075-28145
3	6624-9891	10	28146-30832
4	9892-13091	11	30833-33261
5	13092-16176	12	33262-25854
6	16177-19448	13	35855-39162
7	19449-22297		

of predestination, or what, 29096
of predestination unto life, 4497
of regeneration, 23573, 24552
of reprobation, 9541
of singular, 1320
of sovereign, 11971
of the covenant, 684
    covenants, 17990
    cross, 19096
    holy, 1052
    last judgment, 1676
    law, 4905
    New Jerusalem, 29595-96
    particular, 21663
    passions, 29843
of universal free, 6124
of universal salvation, 17464
of water baptism, 8937
Doctrines and discipline, (1792) 24543, (1797)
32472, (1798) 34102
    of glorious, 5356
    of predestination, 4896
    of the church, 25405
Documents and dispatches, 34816
    referred to, 32966
    relative to, 28886
Dod, John, 1547-1645. Old Mr. Dod's sayings, (1673)
174, (1731) 3412, (1760) 8583, (1768) 10884,
(1793) 25406
Dodd, Bethuel. Singular goodness, 30354
Dodd, William, 1729-1777
    Beauties of history, 20336, 30355
    Futurity, 25149
    Reflections on death, (1773) 12754, (1793) 25407,
      (1796) 30356
    Thoughts in prison, (1779) 16261, (1786) 19610,
      (1794) 26898
Doddington (ship), lost, 9058
Doddridge, Philip, 1702-1751
    Care of the soul, 8842, 25408
    Christ formed, 24272
    Four sermons, 26904, 30359
    Plain and serious address, (1756) 7647, (1764)
      9644, (1766) 10287, (1767) 10604, (1777) 15287,
      (1790) 22465, (1791) 23328-29, (1795) 28573,
      (1798) 33644, (1799) 35414, (1800) 37329
    Practical discoveries, 26899-900
    Principles of the Christian, (1754) 7184, (1788)
      21059, (1793) 26437, (1795) 28574, (1796) 30357-
      58, (1797) 33163, (1798) 33645, (1799) 35415-16,
      (1800) 37330
    Rise and progress, (1749) 6305, (1772) 12376,
      (1788) 21060, (1790) 22466, (1791) 23330, (1793)
      25409, (1794) 26901-902, (1795) 28575-76
    Sermon preached at Maidwell, 35417
    Sermon urging, 24273, 26903
    Sermons on the religious education, (1763) 9378,
      (1790) 22467-68, (1793) 25410-11, (1794) 26905,
      (1797) 32057
    Sermons to young, 26906
    Some remarkable passages, (1748) 6125, (1765)
      9952, (1789) 21799, (1792) 24274, (1795) 28577-
      78
    Three sermons, 21800
    commentary on Bible, 21680, 22347
    life of, 13511, 25154
    paraphrase by, 9246
    preface by, 5600, 5774-75, 6323, 6503, 11660
    reflections on Bible, 20960
Dodge, Amos. City of New-York, 10885
Dodge, John

Narrative of his sufferings, 16765
Narrative of the capture, 16262
Dodge, Oliver
    decision concerning, 26240
    ordained, 25491
Dodge, Paul, 1777-1836. Poem, 32058
Dodsley, Robert, 1703-1764
    Auserlesene fabeln, 26538
    Blind beggar, 15288
    Chronicle of the kings, (1744) 5378, (1758) 8112,
      (1759) 8340, (1773) 12755, (1774) 13253, (1775)
      14008-9, (1791) 23331, (1795) 28579, (1797)
      32059
    Economy of human life, (1787) 20338, (1795)
      28582, 28584, (1797) 32060, (1798) 33646, (1800)
      37331
    Family companion, 8113
    King and the miller, (1750) 6486, (1794) 26558,
      26907
    Oeconomy of human life, (1752) 6836-38, (1765)
      9953, (1772) 12377, (1781) 17139-42, (1784)
      18449, (1786) 19611, (1787) 20337, (1788) 21061-
      62, (1790) 22469-70, (1791) 23332-33, (1792)
      24275-78, (1793) 25412-15, (1794) 26908-910,
      (1785) 28580-81, 28583, (1797) 32061
    Original fables, 22300, 33274
    Rhetoric, 30360
    Select fables, (1777) 15232, (1786) 19455, (1791)
      24027, (1794) 26539
    Toy shop, 6487, 26911
Doehling, John Jacob, b. 1715. Beschriebung, 5379
Döring, August Salomon, life of, 23334, 24279, 25416
Döring, Friedrich Christlieb
    Dass das evangelium, 23334, 25416
    That the gospel, 24279
Doggett, Simeon, 1765-1852
    Concerning the way, 30361
    Discourse, 32062
    Oration, 35418
Doing righteousness, 5025
Dolby, Joseph. Account of the baptisms, 29309
Domestic happiness, 37062
    medicine, a treatise, (1784) 18384, (1798) 33469
    medicine, or a treatise, (1789) 21715, (1793)
      25235-36, (1795) 28365-66, (1797) 31886-88,
      (1799) 35252
    medicine, or the family physician, (1772)
      12338, (1774) 13181, (1778) 15751, (1790)
      22376, (1792) 24151
Dominion of providence, 15224
Don Juan, 24564, 29494
Don Juan Ventura, 35741
Donagan, Patrick, trial, 34040
Donaldson, Arthur. To the tories, 14739
Donance, Phelim, letter (from Taylor) 21487
Donelson, ———, defendant, 31669
Dongan, Thomas, lieutenant-governor N.Y., 2161
Donkin, Robert. Military collections, 15289
Donna, Donna, 32271
Donnison, William. General orders, (1795) 29042,
    (1797) 32447-48, (1798) 34081, (1799) 35791,

VOL.	ITEMS	VOL.	ITEMS
1	1-3244	8	22298-25074
2	3245-6623	9	25075-28145
3	6624-9891	10	28146-30832
4	9892-13091	11	30833-33261
5	13092-16176	12	33262-25854
6	16177-19448	13	35855-39162
7	19449-22297		

VOL.	ITEMS	VOL.	ITEMS
1	1-3244	8	22298-25074
2	3245-6623	9	25075-28145
3	6624-9891	10	28146-30832
4	9892-13091	11	30833-33261
5	13092-16176	12	33262-25854
6	16177-19448	13	35855-39162
7	19449-22297		

VOL.	ITEMS	VOL.	ITEMS
1	1-3244	8	22298-25074
2	3245-6623	9	25075-28145
3	6624-9891	10	28146-30832
4	9892-13091	11	30833-33261
5	13092-16176	12	33262-25854
6	16177-19448	13	35855-39162
7	19449-22297		

E

E., J. see **Eliot, John,** 1604-1690; **Eliot, Joseph,** 1630-1694; **Ellis, Jonathan,** d. 1785
E . . ., O . . .   On the death, 5947
E., S. Further queries, 507
E.W.A.M., preface by, 19985
E. . .g, J. .n see **Ewing, John**
E tenebris, 20360
Eacker, George I. Observations, 33658
The Eagle. New Year's address, 28612
Eagle (ship), captain murdered, 32308
Eames, Jonathan, 1730-1800
   Walking with God, 24285
   ordained, 8450
Earl of Essex, a tragedy, 22592, 24049
Earle, Jabez, 1676-1768
   Christian at the table, 3367, 3970
   Sacramental exercises, (1715) 1739, (1725) 2628, (1729) 3158, (1756) 7649
Earle, John, defended, 3352
Early offerings, 1583
      piety, a sermon, 16998
         again, 2102
         encouraged, 4243
         exemplified, (1690) 536, (1718) 1973, (1719) 2038, (1742) 5008
         joyful, 3014
         recommended, (Bellamy) 6095, (Chauncy) 3518, (Everett) 16268
         the duty, 2988
      religion urged, 698
      seeking, 1786, 3132
Earnest address, 14019
   call, 25427
   desire, 19700
   exhortation, to seek, 4703
      to the children, 1515
      to the inhabitants, 221
   persuasive, 22133
Earth delivered, 7634
Earth devoured, 2853
Earthquake a divine, 7665
Earthquake Naples, 715
Earthquakes a token, 7380
   explained, 634
   improved, 7518
   the effects, 7374
   the works of God, 2945-46, 7549
   tokens of God, 5383-84
   under the divine, 2840
East, Edward, d. 1770?, death, 12200
East India company of North America. Constitutional articles, 35431

East India marine society. By-laws, 38454
East Indian, a comedy, (Kotzebue) 37748, (Lewis) 37825
Eastburn, Benjamin. Doctrine of absolute, 2430, 3532
Eastburn, Robert. Faithful narrative, 8116-17
Easter anthem, 2831
Easter gift, 19614
Easterbrooks, Rev. ──
   Authentic account, 25244
   Faithful narrative, (1792) 24162-64, 24166, (1793) 25243, 25245, (1794) 26721
Eastern association
   Brief narrative, 9871
   Vindication of the proceedings, 26958
Eastern consociation. Invitations, 5591
Eastern herald. Carrier of the Eastern herald, 30378
Eastern Indians. Journal of the proceedings, 6336
Eastern lands, 21244
Eastern stage road, 25429
Eastham, Mass.
   Church of Christ, 2528
   Copy of the result, 2217
Easy and compendious system, (1789) 21869, (1792) 24370, (1799) 35578
   and pleasant guide, 29443
   and practical introduction, 33604
   guide, 9247
   instructor, 34004
   introduction to the art, 30380
      to the attainment, 29987
      to the knowledge, 31316
      to the Latin, 22736
   plan, 14404
   way to prolong, 30381
Eaton, ──, defendant, 32223
Eaton, Daniel Isaac, d. 1814. Trial, 26930-31
Eaton, Edward, d. 1709. Almanac see **Almanacs (Eaton)**
Eaton, Isaac, d. 1772?
   Qualifications, 7409

VOL.	ITEMS	VOL.	ITEMS
1	1-3244	8	22298-25074
2	3245-6623	9	25075-28145
3	6624-9891	10	28146-30832
4	9892-13091	11	30833-33261
5	13092-16176	12	33262-25854
6	16177-19448	13	35855-39162
7	19449-22297		

death, 12422
Eaton, Joshua, d. 1772
  Some short account, 12756
  ordained, 5604
Eaton, Peter, 1765-1848. Sermon, 35433
Eaton, Samuel. Charge, 28749
Eaton, Sarah, d. 1770, death, 12756
Eaton, William, 1764-1811
  Address, 33662
  reply to, 34439
Ebenezer, a memorial, 29214, 32580-81
Ebenezer, or a faithful, 3117
Eberhard Ludwig Grubers grundforschende, 13392, 35475
Ebsworth, Daniel. Republican harmonist, 37343
Ecclesiae monilia, 2766
Ecclesiastes, the life, 790, 2553
Ecclesiastic council, 28465
Ecclesiastical characteristics, 10804
  establishments, 25430
  history, 32513, 34154, 38009
  researches, 29424
Eccleston, Theodore, 1651-1726. Epistle, 3533
Echantillon, 504
Echo (Russel), 36259
Echo from the temple, 16254
  or a satyrical, 28855
  or Columbian songster, 37344
  or federal songster, 33663
Echo's of devotion, 1822
Eckerlin, Israel
  Kurtzer bericht, 5171
  Richtschnur, 5578
  Wandel, 5579
Eckley, Joseph, 1750-1811
  Discourse, 33664-65
  Divine glory, 17524
  Prayer, (Jan. 9, 1800) 36999, (Feb. 11, 1800) 37453
  Sermon, 21806, 24287
  hand of fellowship, 22275
  letter to, 19420
Eclipse, 6491, 7186
Eclogue occasioned, 9338
Eclogue sacred, 10325
Economy of human life, (1787) 20338, (1795) 28582, 28584, (1797) 32060, (1798) 33646, (1800) 37331
Economy of love, 28210
Eddy, John. Almanac see **Almanacs (Eddy)**
Eddy, Samuel, 1769-1839
  Address, 35434
  secy. Rhode Island, 34449
Eddy, Zechariah, 1780-1860. Philandrianism, 37346
Eden, Robert. Proclamation, 12110
Eden, William
  Letters and other papers, 15826
  Manifesto, 15832-34
  address to, 15954
Edes, Peter, 1756-1840. Orations, 18997
Edewakenk, Indian sachem, 3554
Edgar, John, deposition, 17633
Edgar, William, memorial of, 34732
Edgar and Emmeline, 9134
  and Matilda, 30831
  Huntl(e)y, 35244, 37054
Egerton, Elisha. Impartial relation, 35650
Edinburgh new dispensatory, 23504, 30692-93
Edmond, David, 1778-1824. Oration, 35435
Edmundson, W., dispute with Roger Williams, 228
Edridge, John, dispute with Fenwick, 9970
Edson, Jesse, 1773-1805
  Discourse, 35436

ordained, 32083
Education (caption title), 3380
Education, a poem, 35204
Edulcorator, 2668
Edward IV, concubine of, 27121, 30563
Edward and Emily, 33666
  and Emma, 9649
  and Matilda, 34417
  various views, 34129
Edwards, Dr. ——, remarks on, 26169, 29526
Edwards, Bryan, 1743-1800. Thoughts on the late, 18452
Edwards, Daniel, d. 1765, death, 9954
Edwards, Edward, capt. Narcissus, 17552
Edwards, George, d. 1704, suicide, 30012, 33357
Edwards, John, 1637-1716
  Fruits of the spirit, 4936
  Short account, 5580
Edwards, Jonathan, of Pennsylvania, runs snuff mill, 29286
Edwards, Jonathan, 1703-1758
  Account of the life, 6311, 25431-32
  Careful and strict, (1754) 7187, (1766) 10289, (1790) 22476
  Christ the great, 6492
  Church's marriage, 5766
  Copies of the two, 5581
  Danger of the unconverted, 11640
  Discourses, 4239
  Distinguishing marks, (1741) 4711, (1742) 4937, (1791) 23342
  Divine and supernatural, 3768, 28616
  Essay on the nature, 19615
  Expostulatory letter, 5582
  Faithful narrative, (1737) 4137, (1738) 4240, (1790) 22477
  Farewel-sermon, 6665, 10887
  God glorified, 3415
  Great Christian doctrine, (1758) 8118, (1771) 12032, (1780) 16768
  Great concern, 5172
  History of redemption, 25433
  History of the work, (1782) 17525, (1786) 19616, (1792) 24288
  Humble attempt, 5938, 26594
  Humble inquiry, 6312, 24289
  Inquiry into the modern, 19617
  Justice of God, 12757, 35437
  Letter, 4103
  Life and character, 9961
  Misrepresentations corrected, 6839
  Resort and remedy, 4712
  Result of a council, 6577
  Ruth's resolution, 8589
  Sermons, 16767
  Sinners in the hands, (1741) 4713, (1742) 4938, (1769) 11244, (1786) 19618, (1796) 30382, (1797) 32072
  Some thoughts, (1742) 4939, (1768) 10888-89, (1784) 18453
  Strong rod, 6130
  Treatise concerning religious affections, (1746) 5767, (1768) 10890, (1784) 18454, (1787) 20339, (1794) 26932-33
  True excellency, 5385
  True grace, 6996, 23343-44
  True saints, 5939
  Two dissertations, 9962, 23345
  Waere genade, 7188
  defended, 12615, 12811, 28070
  dismissal, 6471, 6694, 9063
  examination of, 12746

extracts from, 4103, 33515
letter (from Clap), 5561
life of, 10008
preface by, 6462
remarks on, 11826, 12067
reply to, 5150, 5561, 6798, 11623
views on Whitefield, 5560
Edwards, Jonathan, 1745-1801
  All divine truth, 24290
  Brief observations, 18455, 28617
  Dissertation, 32073
  Duty of ministers, 28618
  Faith, 24291
  Faithful manifestation, 17919
  Farewell sermon, 35438
  Future state, 32820
  Injustice and impolicy, 23346, 24292
  Marriage of a wife's sister, 24293
  Necessity of atonement, 18998
  Necessity of the belief, 26934
  Observations, 21068
  Salvation of all, 22478
  Sermon, 25434
  approves pamphlet, 26595
  dismissal, 28465
  remarks on, 26169?, 29526?
  reply to, 31201-202
Edwards, Morgan, 1722-1795
  Customs of primitive, 10891
  Materials towards a history, 11641, 24294
  New-Year's-gift, 11642-43
  Res sacrae, 21069
  Sermon, 9383
  Two academical, 21070
Edwards, Pierrepont, 1750-1826
  love affairs, 32142
  opinion of, 24421
  reports on ratification, 21520
Edwards, Thomas, d. 1795
  death, 29515
  satirized, 28726, 35400
  signs circular, 24135
Edwards, Timothy, 1670-1758. All the living, 3534
Edwin, ——, selections from, 32901
Edwin, D., engraver, 37194, 38990
Edwin and Angelina, 32843
  and Angeline, 19694
  or the emigrant, 13891
Edwy and Edilda, 39085
Edy, Samuel, petition, 33005
Eel-River Indians, treaty with, 29742
Eells, Edward, d. 1776
  Charge, 13781
  Christ the foundation, 10605
  Some serious remarks, 8342
  ordained, 4359
  reply to, 8749
Eells, Nathaniel, 1678-1750
  Evangelical bishop, 3769
  Letter (to Second church), 5583
  Ministers of God's word, 2629
  Ministers of the gospel, 3159
  Pastor's introduction, 4359
  Religion is the life, 5173
  Wise ruler, 6131
  letter, (from Gee) 5191-92, 5392, (from Hancock) 5202, (from Prescott) 5278
Eells, Nathaniel, d. 1786
  death, 19700
  ordained, 3769
Een der voorrechten, 11644
Effect of the nitrous, 36328

Effects of slavery, 26448
Effects of the stage, 24371
Efficacy of Dr. Church's, 35305
Effigy burning, 28619
Effusions of female fancy, 22479
Egbert, king of England, 10781
Eglise protestante
  Confession, 28408
  Trois hymnes, 28409
Egremont association. Minutes, 25436-38
Egron, Peter. Level of Europe, 28970
Ehe das zuchthaus, 3251
Ehmals verdorrete, 4466
Eight dollars, 11484
Eight propositions, 13263
Eighteen sermons, 33217
Eikoon, 37309
Eine dem hochedlen, 9631
Eines Christen reise, 7162-63, 30137
Einfältige lehr-betrachtungen, 11657
  und gründlich, 11636-37
  warnungs- und waechter-stimme, 4725
Einfältiges reim-gedichte, 17367
Einige gedichte, 15860
  glaubens-bekenntnisse, 18296, 34972
  vermischte gedanken, 28629
Ela, or the delusions, 21723, 23235
Elder, Joshua, accounts of, 19177
Elders and messengers from the various, 33106
Elders and messengers of the several, 15728, 16200
Eldridge, Enoch. Charge, 29657
Election, a medly, 9650
  ball, 15724
  humbly inscribed, 9963
  of president, 37348
  sermon, (Belknap) 18927, (Foster) 22505, (Moss) 1769, (Worcester) 39145
Electioneering for office, 30655
Elector
  To the citizens, 36421
  To the freemen, 34671
  To the public, 26265
Elector of Herkimer. To the committee, 34668
Electuarium novum, 3549
Elegant collection, 33594
  extracts, a collection, 30383, 33667
    for the German flute, 26936
    or useful, 20340
Elegia de originali, 28620
Elegiac poem on the death, (Branch) 21712, (Washington) 36453, 37077-80, (Whitefield) 11812-15
  poem sacred to the memory, 11645
  sonnets, 20711, 29522-23
Elegiack tribute, 420
Elegie sur la mort, 37776
Elegie upon the death, 240
Elegies and other, 37350
Elegy address'd, 3597
  in a country churchyard, 30395
  occasioned by the death, 12758
  on the death, (Belding) 13264, (Broadwell) 3276-77, (Mayhew) 10259, (Murray) 26008,

VOL.	ITEMS	VOL.	ITEMS
1	1-3244	8	22298-25074
2	3245-6623	9	25075-28145
3	6624-9891	10	28146-30832
4	9892-13091	11	30833-33261
5	13092-16176	12	33262-25854
6	16177-19448	13	35855-39162
7	19449-22297		

VOL.	ITEMS	VOL.	ITEMS
1	1-3244	8	22298-25074
2	3245-6623	9	25075-28145
3	6624-9891	10	28146-30832
4	9892-13091	11	30833-33261
5	13092-16176	12	33262-25854
6	16177-19448	13	35855-39162
7	19449-22297		

moral and religious, 35296-98, 37374
   novelist, 28632
   passages, 1800
Entertainment for a winter's evening, 6510-11, 28766
Enthusiasm described, 4912
   detected, 6675
   of Methodists, 6525
Enthusiastic patriot, 11250
Enthusiastical errors, 17856
Entick, John, 1703?-1773. New English spelling, 37375
Envy wishes, 31654
Epaminondas, history of, 34412
Ephemeris see **Almanacs**
Ephemeron, 2562
Ephrata. Theosophischen lectionen, 6840
Epicedium, 6580
Epictetus
   Enchiridion, 24302, 25452
   Morals, 3160
Episcopal charitable society. Articles, 5137
Episcopalian
   Address, 24025
   see also **Purcell, Henry**
Epistle (Burlington yearly meeting), (1724) 2534, (1726) 2875, (1734) 3771, (1746) 5776
Epistle (Carey to Oswald), 19539
Epistle (London meeting for sufferings), 14050
Epistle (London yearly meeting), (1771) 12050, (1775) 14051, (1776) 14768, (1777) 15301, (1778) 15800, (1779) 16280, (1780) 19412, (1781) 19413, (1782) 17540, (1786) 19659-60, (1787) 20378, (1788) 21099, (1789) 21842, (1790) 22515, (1791) 23392, (1792) 24332, (1793) 25517, (1794) 27022, (1796) 30456, (1797) 32161, (1798) 33767, (1799) 35520, (1800) 37471-72
Epistle (Philadelphia meeting for sufferings), 14049
Epistle (Phila. yearly meeting), (1704) 1158, (1709) 1387, (1748) 6145, (1749) 6324, (1754) 7200, (1760) 8603, (1761) 8859, (1774) 13285, (1776) 14769
Epistle (Wesley to Whitefield), 23064, 26459
Epistle by way of encouragement, 3533
   for general service, 549
   from John Burnyeat, 401
      our general spring meeting, 7422
      the three, 35519
      Titus, 17146
      Yarico, 24822, 27748
   in true love, 2434, 35660
   of caution and advice, 7201
   of caution to Friends, 2338
   of tender caution, 21100
   of tender love, 591
   sent from God, 8028
   to Friends concerning, 16754
   to Friends in Great Britain, 9221
   to Peter Pindar, 37514
   to the Christian, 936, 1266
      churches, 1232
      Ephesians, 30088
      national meeting, (1757) 8008, (1770) 11661, (1783) 18083
      quarterly, 974, 12630
   to Zenas, 19662
Epistles domestic, 30392
Epistolae familiares, 9912
Epistolary correspondence between S.P., 9469
Epistolary correspondence between the Rev., 23519
Epitaph (George III), 17528

Epitaph, &c., 13268
Epithalamium, 11504
Epitome of English, 782
Epitome of the life, 36921
Equal rights, 39067
Equal to Hutchins, 35166
Equality of rich, 25424
Equiano, Olaudah. Interesting narrative, 23353
Er. ehrw. Hrn. Philip, 9874
Erasmus, Desiderius, 1465-1536
   Collection of the wise, 22487
   Collection of wise, 18459
   Colloquia selecta, (1782) 17529, (1786) 19626, (1793) 25453
   Familiaria colloquia, 21771
Erbauliche lieder, 19628, 28641
Erdmann, Carl
   Gelbe fieber, 35449
   (tr.) Kurze nachricht von Algier, 26734
   (tr.) Kurze nachricht von dem bösartigen, 26739-40
   (tr.) Short account, 27108
Erfahrene Americanische, 18460
Erklärung und vorstellung, 9631
Erläuterude bemerkungen, 38209
Erlaubte klage, 21139
Ernst, John Frederic
   Oration, 37378
   Poems, 32287
   Sermon, 37379
Ernst Christoph Hochmanns von Hochenau glaubens-beckanntniss, 37631
Ernsthaf(f)te Christenpflicht, (1745) 5585, (1770) 11648, (1785) 19002
Ernstliche ermahnung, 4292
Ernstliche erweckungs-stimm, 5586
Ernstlicher ruf an die deutschen, 35450
Ernstlicher ruff in Christlicher, 5971
Erra pater
   Book of knowledge, (1790) 22488-89, (1793) 25454, (1794) 26948-49, (1795) 28633-34, (1796) 30393, (1797) 32089-90, (1798) 33696, (1799) 35451
   Fortune teller, 26950
   Signification, 30394
   Universal interpreter, 28635
Errata, or the art, 9407-408
Errinnerung an die Englische, 7633
Errington, Capt. ———, arrival in Annapolis, 11720
Erskine, David Stewart see **Buchan, David Stewart Erskine, earl, 1742-1829**
Erskine, Ebenezer, 1680-1754
   (ed.) Assembly's shorter catechism, 10611, 21600
   Assurance of faith, 8346
   Collection of sermons, 5388, 5587
   Sermon, 37380
   Sermons on sacramental, 8850
   Sermons upon the most, 24303
   (ed.) Westminster assembly's shorter, 28077
Erskine, Ralph, 1685-1752

VOL.	ITEMS	VOL.	ITEMS
1	1-3244	8	22298-25074
2	3245-6623	9	25075-28145
3	6624-9891	10	28146-30832
4	9892-13091	11	30833-33261
5	13092-16176	12	33262-25854
6	16177-19448	13	35855-39162
7	19449-22297		

(ed.) Assembly's shorter catechism, 10611, 21600
Collection of sermons, 5388, 5587
Gospel sonnets, (1740) 4506, (1742) 4945, (1743)
    5174, (1749) 6315, (1760) 8593, (1772) 12383,
    (1790) 22490, (1793) 25455, (1798) 33697
Letter (to Whitefield), 4714
Paraphrase, 5130
Sermons on sacramental, 8850
Sermons upon the most, 32091
(ed.) Westminster assembly's shorter, 28077
doctrine of justification, 6302
Erskine, Thomas, 1750-1823
Celebrated speech, 25456-58
Christianity vindicated, 32092
Speeches, 32093, 33698
View of the causes, 32094-99
attacked by Paine, 33947
letter (from Paine), 32632
speech by, 26280
Erskine, William. Proclamation, 15820
Erste frucht, 10138
Erste oder theoretische, 20938
Ersten früchte, 19630
Erwin, ———, address by, 21695
Erzählungen von Maria, 8347
Erzehlung derer durch, 13269
Erzehlung von den, 7663
Es ist noch, 9112
Es werden verteigert, 18481
Esau, thoughts upon, 23324
Eschol, 12500
Eshcol, 5468
Espinasse, Isaac
Cases argued, 28636
Digest of the law, 23354
Espousals, or a passionate, 3965, 4819
Esquisse interessant, 17925
Essai raisonné, 32410
    sur la manière, 29108
    sur la ville, 28637
Essay concerning gratitude, 3573
    concerning silver, 4238
        the restoration, 3985
        the true, 12834
    delivered, 18956
    for reviving, 3735
        the charitable, 2005
        the recording, 372-3
    of a Delaware-Indian, 15228
    of a frame, 14748
    on a declaration, 14984
    on agriculture, 22805
        baptism (Rice), 22115
        baptism which solves, 21075
        building, 32642
        canon and feudal, 17975-76
        cantharides, 37536
        comets, 5389, 12498
        conduct, (1752) 6846, (1753) 7004, (1754)
            7203
        conversion, (1794) 26951, (1795) 28638-39,
            (1798) 33990, (1799) 35720
        credit, 20129
        crimes, (1773) 12665, (1778) 15730, (1793)
            25150
        education, 12384
        faith, 10759
        fevers, (1732) 3614, (1767) 10575, (1796)
            30167
        free trade, 16670
        hereditary, 34022

honour, 23441
infant baptism, 10933, 28640
man, (1747) 6055, (1748) 6224, (1760) 8718,
    (1778) 16018, (1780) 16955-56, (1785)
    19197, (1786) 19931, (1787) 20657, (1789)
    22075, (1790) 22809-810, (1791) 23707,
    (1792) 24702-703, (1793) 26017-18, (1794)
    27535, (1795) 29337-39, (1796) 31023-26,
    (1797) 32701-702, (1798) 34398, (1800)
    38299-300
marriage, 21076
matter, 18554
money, 20154-55, 20894
moral agency, 28070, 36750
Negro slavery, 18668
outward, 20991
pleurisy, 5074
political, 37381
primitive, 19746
punctuation, 22119
quick-lime, 35770
religion, 23030
religious subjects, 9652
remarkables, 2451
scripture-prophecy, 2509
slavery, 13005
on the administration, 3536
    African slave trade, 22337
    agitations, 8851
    beauties, 13765
    best system, 35690
    causes, nature, 17607
    causes of the decline, 18461
    causes of the variety, 20712
    character, 13650
    constitutional, 13247
    culture and management, 14022
    culture of silk, 22491, 24306
    decalogue, 2080, 2298
    domestic, 20470
    eclipse, 7232
    education, 29135
    end, 29838
    excellency, 25459
    expediency, 7701
    fall of angels, (1793) 26169, (1795) 29526,
        (1796) 31201-202
    faults, 21433
    good impressions, 2923
    gospel ministry, 9387
    happiness, 30813
    history, 12766
    iliac, 4693
    impolicy, 21001, 21738
    influence, 21418
    invention, 9109
    kingdom, 23213
    law of bailments, 30646
    law of God, 23788
    liberty, 35605
    life of the honorable, (1788) 21160, (1794)
        27144, (1798) 33914
    life of the late, 28868
    malignant, 35302
    manner, 29109
    medicinal, 31031
    merchandize, 3413
    natural, 25234
    nature and cure, 19216
    nature and foundation, 9931
    nature and glory, (1762) 9064) (1797)
        31796, (1798) 33397

nature of true, 19615
new birth, 29077
origin, 37445
pleurisy, 4085
real deity, 23110
seat, 22262
signs, 26952
slavery and commerce, 19561, 20274
ten, 16298
theory, 28137
trade, 9653
use and advantages, 11901
use of the celestial, 36757
uterine, 19964
West-India, 5553
on toleration, 19156
on universal redemption, 10770
poems and letters, 32774
tending to promote, 1289, 1369
to defend, 9364
discover, 510
do good, 1491
excite, 4798
prove that when, 2495
prove the interest, 2978
revive, 3589
silence, 2627
solve, 3830
towards an easy, 30130, 31879
towards propagating, 6494, 7651
II; on the nature, 18490
upon field-husbandry, (1748) 6132-33, (1753)
6998, (1754) 7190-91
government, 14023
nursing, 12344, 12705
oeconomy, 10196-99
that paradox, 2592
the eleventh chapter, 37268
the propagation, 35362
Essays and notes, 35216
civil, moral, 31748
in prose, 28653
literary, moral, 34495
moral and literary, 24447, 25696
on liberty, 26469, 29873-74
on physiognomy, 27203
on rhetoric, (1789) 21693, (1797) 31833
on rhetorick, (1788) 20971, (1793) 25198-99,
(1798) 33426
on the following, 35068
intellectual, 24731, 26066
nature, 21694
spirit of legislation, (1798) 33407, (1799)
35186, (1800) 37382
on various subjects, 19810, 30814
political, economical, 34656, 36251
relating to yellow fever, 35452
the nature, uses, 11997
to do good, 1460
towards the most easy, 16202
upon field-husbandry, (1760) 8590, (1761)
8847-48
upon the making, 14929-30
Essential requisites, 21601
Essential rights, 5520
Essex, Arthur Capel, earl of, 1631-1683. Speech,
3005
Essex, Robert Devereux, earl of, 1566-1601
Extract of a letter, 13832?
secret history, 36286
Essex county. County of Essex; colony of Massa-

chusetts, 14749
Essex gazette. John Nurse, carrier, 13271
Essex harmony, (1770) 11560, (1771) 11979, (1772)
12319, (1780) 16709, (1785) 18925, (1800) 37732
Essex musical association. Constitution, 33699
Essex, ss. To either of the constables, 23751
Estabrook, Hobart, 1716-1766
Blameless bishop, 6841
Praying warrior, 8121
hand of fellowship, 6994
Estabrook, Joseph, 1640-1711. Abraham the pas-
senger, 1205
Estabrook, Joseph, fl. 1787, ordained, 20999
Estabrook, Samuel, 1675-1727. Sermon, 1955
Estaing, Charles Hector Théodat, comte d', 1729-
1794
Declaration, 16265
arrival, 16370
at Newport, 17111
grant to, 19677
in San Domingo, 10032
Estaugh, John, 1675-1742. Call to the unfaithful,
5390
Esten, Cornelius. To the public, 9654
Esterbrook, Nehemiah. Address of the inhabitants,
14908
Esterbrooks, ———. Faithful narrative, 25243
Estimate for an appropriation, 31444
of commercial, 35360
of state debt, 21221
of the average, 16563
expenditures, 23895, 24908
manners, 8094
religion, 25845, 29103
Et sicut illud, 37653
Eternal damnation, 25749-50
Eternal salvation, 19245
Eternity of God, 3497
Ethelgar, a Saxon, 28977
Ethica, or the first, 6859-60
Ethices compendium, 13223
Ethices elementa, 5794, 6172
Etliche anmerkungen, 19501
Christliche, 22493
merkwürdige, 9655
schöne, 4884, 6632
zu dieser zeit, 5104
Etwas aus der schatzlade, 9967
für kleine, 20348
vom rechten, 17199
Eugenius see Stevenson, John Hall
Eugenius and Selima, 33700
Eulogeum in honor, 22863
Eulogical poem, 37358
Eulogies and orations, 37383
Eulogium and vindication, 24305
delivered, 38946-47
in honor, 22862-63
intended, 31143
of the brave, 16213
on Benjamin Franklin, 24799, 27009

VOL.	ITEMS	VOL.	ITEMS
1	1-3244	8	22298-25074
2	3245-6623	9	25075-28145
3	6624-9891	10	28146-30832
4	9892-13091	11	30833-33261
5	13092-16176	12	33262-25854
6	16177-19448	13	35855-39162
7	19449-22297		

Everett, Moses, d. 1813
Early piety, 16268
Sermon, 17532
ordained, 14111
Everett, Oliver, 1752-1802
Eulogy, 37332, 37387
ordained, 17532
Everlasting gospel commanded, 7033
gospel; the gospel, 923
punishment, 19737
Everndon, Thomas, reproved, 611
Evertson, Nicholas. Certificate, 37388
Every friend, 13488
man his own brewer, 30189
his own doctor, (1734) 3743-44, (1736) 4086, (1737) 4204
his own lawyer, 10935
his own physician, (1767) 10783, (1794) 27790, (1800) 38626
man's right, 5323
one has, 27154
thing, or an history, 18427
Evidence and import, 32053
for the truth, 12428
in a cause, 36396
of personal Christianity, 25043
Evidences for the truth, 19059, 22612
of Christianity, 32398
of revealed, 32465, 34094
of the Christian religion, 20223, 28150
of the efficacy, 32667-70
Evident tokens, 2910
Evil and adulterous, 6997
Evil designs, 17807
Evolutions of the foot, 7153, 7621
Ewer, John, d. 1774
Apology for the Bible, 30204
Sermon, 10895
letter (from Livingston), 10948-49
letter (from Snape), 1886
remarks on, 10579
vindicated, 10934
Ewing, James, 1744-1824. Columbian alphabet, 33703
Ewing, John, 1732-1802
Address, 9560
Fidelity, 20350
Sermon, 23359
To the citizens, 17743
address to, 9892
passes on medical candidate, 21716, 21964, 23449, 24534, 25055, 25664, 26140, 26153, 27193, 28161, 28645, 30014, 30643, 30934, 31644, 31716, 31832, 31935, 32131, 32289, 32319, 32324, 32407, 32592, 32883, 33233, 33518, 33641, 33831, 33908, 34418, 34619, 34974, 35042, 35177, 35291, 35494, 35687, 35807
imitated, 10014
Exact abridgment, 4204
Exact table, 6495
Examen sommaire, 27198
Examination and refutation, 4946
into the leading principles, 20865
into the principles, 10571
of a catechism, 640
of and some answer, 3996
of Baron Messeres, 13626
of Benjamin Franklin, 10618
of certain, 3954
of Doctor Benjamin, 10300-303
of Mr. Randolph's Vindication, 31311
of the Age of reason, 27464, 28016-19

conduct, 32172
Connecticut claim, 13629
constitution, 21028
Examiners examined, 29929
executive, 36673
figurative, 26663
late president, 12746
late proceedings, 26245
late Rev. president, 11623
opinion, 37389
passages, 29269
principles, 29127
Reverend, 24116
treaty, 28980
of usury, 6786
Examinations relative, 25905
Examiner examin'd, (1736) 3997, (1743) 5297-98, (1766) 10280-81, (1771) 12042
Examiner, No. I-III, 11252-54
Examiner, or Gilbert, 5200-201
Examiners examined, 26954
Example of Christ, 6792
Excellence and importance, 8808
of scripture, 14099
of the gospel, 34306
Excellency of a good, 10872
of a publick, 1076
of the Christian ministry, 26780
Christian religion, 4227
gospel, 2976
word, 7694
Excellent new song, 11429
priviledge, 433
sermon preached, 14952
sermon upon salvation, 3424
spirit, 13512
Excelling election, 32102
Excessive wickedness, 10926
Exchange catalogue (Carey), 33497
Excise law, 23896
Excursion into Bethlehem, 38149
Execution of La Croix, 37391, 37781
Execution sermon (Bascom), 20955
Exemplary pastor, 23787
Exercise containing a dialogue, (1761) 8882, (1762) 9108, (1763) 9484, (1766) 10336, (1767) 10594, (1775) 14396
Exercise of the musket, 1047
Exercises adapted, 38020
Exercitatio med. inaug., 22328
Exeter, N. H.
At a convention, 16269
Constitution and rules, 33705
Result of a council, 5391
Exeter, for thanksgiving, 33893
Exhibition, 5 December, 34459
in College chapel, 34458
of Tom Thumb, 20749, 29632
Exhibitions comic, 30298
Exhortation & caution, 636
or call, 3224

VOL.	ITEMS	VOL.	ITEMS
1	1-3244	8	22298-25074
2	3245-6623	9	25075-28145
3	6624-9891	10	28146-30832
4	9892-13091	11	30833-33261
5	13092-16176	12	33262-25854
6	16177-19448	13	35855-39162
7	19449-22297		

F

VOL.	ITEMS	VOL.	ITEMS
1	1-3244	8	22298-25074
2	3245-6623	9	25075-28145
3	6624-9891	10	28146-30832
4	9892-13091	11	30833-33261
5	13092-16176	12	33262-25854
6	16177-19448	13	35855-39162
7	19449-22297		

Rosamond, 32255
Rosanna, 25465
solitary, (1790) 22605, (1795) 28942, (1797) 32347
weather, 560-561, 699
Fairbank, Drury, ordained, 37323
Fairfax, Bryan, 8th baron, 1727-1802. Strictures, 32105
Fairfield, John, brings intelligence, 36272
Fairfield, Josiah. Price act, 15704
Fairfield county
Invitations to the Reverend, 5591
Vindication of the proceedings, 26958
The fairing, (1786) 19634, (1788) 21079, (1799) 35457
Fairland, May 28th, 38629
Fairservice, James. Plain dealing, 6497
Fairy tales, or the histories, 29299
Faith absolutely necessary, 4499
and a good, 24291
and prayer, 4599
and profession, 22665
at work, 791
encouraged, 1974
in divine, 16873
of the fathers, 874
victorious, 1042
Faithful advice, 881
and approved, 2894, 6867
and wise, 9905
evangelist, 2618
hint, 30781
man abounding, 4562
man described, 1212-13
manifestation, 17919
minister, a funeral, 6221
minister encouraged, 7643
minister the glory, 5209
ministers of Christ, 3149, 5118
of Jesus, 23141
the fathers, 6843
minister's trials, 6784
minister's work, 29650
monitor, 1174
narrative of Elizabeth, 19635-39
of God's gracious, 4166
of the conversion, 12874
of the dealings, 25241
of the many, 8116-17
of the proceedings of the ecclesiastical, 3958
of the proceedings of the First, 8504
of the remarkable, 10250
of the surprising, 22477
of the surprizing, 4137, 4240
of the wicked, 4245
of the wonderful, (1792) 24162-66, (1793) 25243-45, (1794) 26721
pastors, 4351
reprover, 1534
ruler, 3757
servant approv'd, 3597
in the joy, 4488
of Christ call'd, 18168
of Christ described, 4209
of Christ honoured, 15233
of God, 6154
rewarded, 3517, 29425
serving, 10597
steward, 4940, 25741
warning, 592

warnings against bad, 2398
warnings to prevent, 1175
watchman, 22926
Faithfulness in the ministry, 2489
in the service, 14685
of a minister, 23219
Faith's victory, 13688
Falckner, Justus. Grondlycke onderricht, 1350
Falcon (sloop), at Gloucester, 28689
Falconar, Magnus
Choice collection, 4361
Dialogue, 5177
Free grace, 4715
Vindication, 4508
Falconer, William, 1732-1769. The shipwreck, (1774) 13257, (1788) 21080-81, (1796) 30399, (1800) 37393
Falgate, Israel. Dealer's companion, 8596
Fall of Adam, 37155
Babylon, 1309
British tyranny, 14823-25
Lucifer, 17152
man, 34566
Saguntum, 8852
the mighty, 4276
Fallacy detected, 22496
Fallen cottage, 26089
Fallen sinners, 15795
Falmouth (brig), murder on board, 26534
False and seducing, 7842
appearances, 28312
confidences, 5122
dealer, 1215
hopes, 4262
judgments, 611
news, 1192
shame, 37749-50
Falseness of the hopes, 1371
Falses on all sides, 3040
Fame, let thy trumpet, 16523
Familiar conference, 9601
dialogue between Cephas, 26502
dialogues for the instruction, 26959
dialogues on dancing, 26959
discourse, 30677
guide, 1954
illustration, 27553
letters (Mather), 24532
letters to a gentleman, (1745) 5572, (1792) 24267, (1797) 32043
Family adviser, 26482, 29891
book, 35458
companion, 6659-61, 8113
devotion, 4519
exercises, 29356
female physician, 25580
instructor, (1740) 4500, (1792) 24252, (1795) 28550
party, 28646
physician, 20251
prayer book, 10610
prayer not to be, 10232
religion excited, (1707) 1310, (1714) 1689, (1720) 2140, (1727) 2911, (1740) 4559
recommended, 26576
urged, 1403, 6007
sacrifice, 1122
tablet, 30577
well-ordered, 875
worship, 36406
Famous history of Doctor Faustus, 33719

history of Sir Richard, 31633
history of Whittington, (1788) 21602, (1790) 23083, (1800) 37395
Tommy Thumb's, 12040
Fan for fanning, 12081
Faneuil, Peter, d. 1742, death, 5231-32
Faniel, Benjamin, refugee in N.Y., 1352
Fanny, or the happy, (1785) 18917, (1787) 20205, (1791) 23131, (1795) 28211-12, (1797) 31752, (1799) 35117
Farewel hymn, 25466
    life, 10163
    orders, 33148
    sermon (1750), 6665, 10887
    address to his pupils, 34140
Farewell address of George Washington, 38989
    discourse delivered, 36313
    discourse to the First, 25565
    exhortation, 47
    sermon, (Edwards) 35438, (Fowler) 35495, (Hovey) 11687, (Lee) 7695, (Smith) 38515, (Welton) 2826
Farm house, 28919
Farmer, ———. Two very circumstantial, 7653-54
Farmer, A. W. Friendly address, 13224-26
Farmer, Dick. Whereas great quantities, 5178
Farmer, Ferdinand, d. 1786, death, 19806
Farmer, Hugh, reply to, 11874
A farmer
    Essay on the culture, 14022
    Letter to the inhabitants, 12833
    Letters of a farmer, 30689
    Sentiments on what, 18347, 18352
    Some remarks, 16993
    To D . . . . r R . g . .s, 12575
    To the public, 34674
      see also **Benezet, Anthony, 1713-1784; Logan, George, 1753-1821; Seabury, Samuel, 1729-1796**
The farmer, a comic opera, (1792) 24644, (1794) 26558, 27439
Farmer and citizen, 24307
Farmer of Massachusetts. Complete guide, 24207
Farmer of New Jersey see **Livingston, William, 1723-1790**
Farmer of New Jersey, or a picture, 37294
Farmer of Orange county. To the General assembly, 12576
Farmer refuted, 14096
Farmer's and monitor's letters, 11239
    catechism, 29855
    catechizm, 23056
    companion, 8929
    daughter, 32107-108, 34320
    dispensatory, 2535
    friend, 25609, 26524
Farnham, Benjamin. Dissertations, 37404
Farnsworth, H. Oration on music, 28650
Farquhar, George, 1678-1707
    Inconstant, 8853
    Twin rivals, 8854
Farrago, John, adventures, 31862
Farrand, Daniel, 1722-1803. Redemption, 10295
Farrar, Stephen, 1738-1809
    Charge, (1782) 18080, (1799) 38621
    Sermon, 33716, 35465
    ordained, 8899
Farriery abridged, 30117
Farriery improved, (1794) 26696, (1796) 30118, (1798) 33449

Farther continuation of the catalogue, 24610-11
Farther proceedings, 3845
Fasciculus viventium, 2767
Fashion, or the art, 37690
Fashionable lover, (1770) 11619, (1772) 12368, (1773) 12741-42
Faslosus, dialogue with Impiator, 28786
Fast day sermon, 37905
Fast friend. To the free electors, 22936
Fast of God's chusing, 258
Fast sermon pointing, 16296
Fast which God, 3750
Fatal consequences of the unscriptural, 7032
    consequences of youthful, 25108
    effects of parental, 33700
    effects of seduction, 21815
Fate of blood-thirsty, 14679
Father Ab--y's will, 3474-75
    Abraham's speech, (1758) 8131, (1764) 9665, (1767) 10619, (1770) 11929
    departing, 2453
    Nicholas, 24312
    or American, 21805
Father's advice, 24310
    charge, 7011
    gift, (1786) 19641, (1788) 21082, (1795) 28651, (1799) 35466
    instructions, (1788) 21382, (1797) 32666, (1800) 38232
    legacy, (1775) 14093, (1778) 15842, (1779) 16297, (1780) 16792, (1781) 17177, (1782) 19415, (1785) 19030, (1786) 19694, (1787) 20399, (1788) 21120, (1789) 21866, (1791) 23422, (1793) 25567, (1795) 28771, (1796) 30514-15, (1798) 34595
Fathers, or the good, 28670
Fauchet, Claude. Eulogium, 27009
Fauchet, Jean Antoine Joseph, 1761-1834
    Sketch of the present, 32115
    dispatch intercepted, 28698-99
Faugeres, Margaretta V. Bleecker, 1771-1801
    Collection of essays, 25208
    Belisarius, 28652
    Essays in prose, 28653
    Ghost of John Young, 32116
    Ode, 33522, 33717
Faugeres, Peter, d. 1798. Treatise on febris, 23364
Faulder, ———, bookseller, 37514
Faulks, ———. Mr. Faulks, the noted performer, 12041
Faults on all sides, 3039
Fauquier, Francis. Speech, 8277
Faust, Bernhard Christoph, 1755-1842. Catechism of health, 28654, 33718
Faust(us)
    history of, 3668, 28655, 33719
    statue, 26252
Favorite ballad, 27126
    new federal, 33896
    rondo, 35606

VOL.	ITEMS	VOL.	ITEMS
1	1-3244	8	22298-25074
2	3245-6623	9	25075-28145
3	6624-9891	10	28146-30832
4	9892-13091	11	30833-33261
5	13092-16176	12	33262-25854
6	16177-19448	13	35855-39162
7	19449-22297		

sonata, 30904
song of Nancy, 34166
song translated, 35467
songs, 25307
Favour of God, 4526
Fawcett, Benjamin, ed. Saint's everlasting rest, (1763) 9335, (1794) 26626, (1796) 30040
Fay, Dr. ———, sings song, 34683, 37453
Fay, Jonas
  Concise refutation, 16694
  on committee, 17842
  secy. Vt. Council, 16651, 16652?, 16653
Fay, Joseph, secy. Vt., 16651, 16694, 17405, 20829-30, 23014, 26377, 27994
Fay, Lewis. Advertisement; I born a Parisian, 11652
Fay, Samuel, secy. Vt., 23935-36
Fayerweather, Hannah, d. 1755, death, 7548
Fayette county. Resolutions, 35468
Fe del Christiano, 876
Fear God, 23467
  of an oath, 1034
  of God an antidote, 8119
  of God restraining, 2188
Fearon, Jane, divine guidance of, 25394, 26886
Feast of merriment, 28656
Feast of reason, 35279
Features of Mr. Jay's treaty, 28527, 31172
Febrifugium, 1898
23d February, 1796; read, 31381
25th February, 1796; referred, 31382
4th February, 1800; read the first, 38732
11th February, 1800; read the first, 38730
13th February, 1800; read first, 38909
Federal arithmetic, 32605
  arithmetician, 22870, 26137
  catechizm, 23056
  constitution and liberty, 27321, 34113
  constitution for the U.S., 20804
  constitution with the amendments, 31405
Federal convention. Proceedings, 20809
Federal elector see **Broome, John, 1738-1810**
Federal farmer see **Lee, Richard Henry, 1732-1794**
Federal gazette
  Address of the carriers, 22500
  Friday, Jan. 24, 1800, 37411
  New Year's wish, 21817
Federal gazette office, Friday, 37411
  harmony, (1785) 19268, (1788) 21485, (1790) 22340, 22919, (1792) 24092, 24831, (1793) 25159, (1794) 26640, 27762, (1795) 28261, (1796) 30054
  march, 21421
  money, 32603
  museum, 35108
  or new ready, 25475
Federal orrery. Carrier of the Federal orrery, (1795) 28661, (1796) 30409
Federal politician, 29373
  primer, 32120
  ready reckoner, 28666
Federal republican
  Reply, 38370
  Review of the constitution, 20678
Federal republicanism, 36023
Federal republicans. Address, 36766
Federal society of cabinet and chairmakers. Philadelphia cabinet, 27508
Federal songster, 37413
  system, 34701
Federal Tontine association. Constitution, 24315

Federalist see **Webster, Noah, 1758-1843**
Federalist, a collection, 21127, 35581
Federalist, containing some, 30293-94
Fee bill, (1794) 27396, (1796) 30762
Feeble attempt, 39080
Felbinger, Jeremiah, 1616-1690. Christliches hand-büchlein, 35475
Felicity of the times, 9329
Fellow citizen. Political establishment, 18735
Fellow citizen of Virginia see **Evans, Thomas**
Fellow citizens and brother farmers, 32348
  citizens and countrymen, 12387
  citizens, friends, 12765
  citizens, remember, 16270
  citizens; the approach, 28156
  citizens; the first, 30411
  citizens; the 2d, 33727
  craft hymn, 22624
Fellow-freeholder and inhabitant. Address, 11135
Fellow of Harvard college see **Prince, Nathan, 1698-1748**
Fellows, John. Fellows's circulating library, 30412
Fellowship society, Charleston, S.C. Rules, (1762) 9086, (1769) 11205, (1774) 13195
Female American, 39123
  character, 28664, 30413
  fortitude, 18465
Female Friend
  Discourse, 11241, 26895
  see also **Moorhead, Sarah Parsons**
Female friendship, 32122
  guide, 25938
Female hand
  Christian pattern, 6342
  see also **Rowe, Elizabeth Singer, 1674-1737**
Female hermit, 22605, 22876
Female humane association. Plan, 36884
Female jockey club, 27523
  patriot, a farce, 27300
  patriot, no. 1, 11653
  patriotism, 33475
  piety, 1217
  policy detected, (1742) 5086, (1786) 20119, (1793) 26416, (1794) 28022, (1795) 29828-29, (1798) 34954, (1800) 38975
  review, 32417
  whig, 16271
Fénelon, François de Salignac de La Mothe, 1651-1715
  Adventures of Telemachus, (1796) 30414, (1797) 32124-26, (1800) 37416
  Aventures de Télémaque, (1784) 18466, (1791) 23366, (1797) 32123
  Dissertation on pure love, (1738) 4246, (1750) 6498
  Pattern of Christian education, 7655
  Some advice, 35476
  Uncertainty of a deathbed, (1756) 7656, (1760) 8597, (1766) 10296
Fenn, Lady Eleanor Frere, 1743-1813
  Fables, 33728
  Tom Thumb's song book, 28987
  Tommy Thumb's song book, 21089
Fenn, Nathan, d. 1799. Sermon, 23367
Fennell, James, 1766-1816
  Description of the principles, 33729
  Mr. Fennell respectfully, 30415
Fenner, Arthur, 1745-1805
  Proclamation, (1790) 22844, (1793) 26076, (1795) 29404, (1797) 32758, (1798) 34449, (1799) 36216, (1800) 38382

To the town-clerk, 31096
candidate for governor, 36222
governor, 27616
supported, 22937
Fenning, Daniel
American youth's instructor, 28665, 30416
Federal or new, 25475
Federal ready reckoner, 28666
Geschwinde rechner, (1774) 13275, (1793) 25476, (1794) 26969
New ready reckoner, 19642
Ready reckoner, (1774) 13274, (1789) 21822, (1792) 24316, (1794) 26967-68, (1797) 32127, (1798) 33730, (1799) 35477
Universal spelling book, (1769) 11255, (1772) 12388, (1786) 19643, (1787) 20354, (1788) 21090, (1799) 35478
Fenno, Jenny. Original compositions, 23368
Fenno, John Ward, 1778-1802
Desultory reflections, 37417-19
Supplementary catalogue, 38098
controversy with Carey, 35274
Fentham, ———, excerpts from, 23246, 31959
Fenton, Elijah. Rhode Island register, 28066
Fenton & Lyon. Church bells, 38058
Fenwick, Mrs. E. Secrecy, 28667-68
Fenwick, John
(tr.) Memoirs of General Dumourier, 26918
True state, 9970
Ferguson, Adam, 1724-1816
Essay on the history, 12766
proposals for printing, 12671
proposals for reprinting, 11983
Ferguson, Elizabeth Graeme. Postscript, 9888
Ferguson, Hugh Henry, ed. Military instructions, 14475
Ferguson, James, astronomer, 25574
Ferguson, Robert see **Fergusson, Robert, 1750-1774**
Ferguson, Samuel. Almanac see **Almanacs (Ferguson)**
Fergusson, Robert, 1750-1774. Scots poems, 20992
Ferme de Pensylvanie, 14029
Fernandez, Felipe. New practical grammar, 33731
Ferne, Charles. Trial of the honourable, 7890-92
Ferree, John
By virtue of a certain, 13366
sheriff, 14819
Ferries; hogs, 38388, 38390
Ferriss, Benjamin, books sold by, 11661
Fervent zeal, 2006
Fessenden, Benjamin. Gospel order, 4362
Fessenden, Caleb Page. Oration, 33732
Fessenden, Thomas, 1739-1813
Luminous shining, 21823
Remarks on the doings, 17533
Sermon, 25477, 28669
Fessenden, Thomas Green, 1771-1837
Country lovers, 30417-18
Oration, 33733
Poem, 35479
Fest-psalm, 14529
Festival discourse, 25753
of mirth, 37420
of the sons, 38284
Festive companion, 29328
Fever, an elegiac poem, 35480
Few breif remarks on Mr. Graham, 8604
brief remarks on a late, 11838
drops, 26970
lines, 7415
notices, 33846

observations on some, 32168
on the conduct, 11039
upon the new, 25478
particulars, 31885
political reflections, 13760
psalmes, 50
reasons, 12389
remarks on Mr. Hamilton, 38271
on the remarker, 8608
upon Quaker politicks, 9875-78
upon some, 14074
upon the ordination, 8363
salutary hints, 19644-45
words in favour, 3023
words respecting, 2606
Ffirth, John. Truth vindicated, 26971
Fidelity approved, 38976
in the gospel, 20350
of ministers, 4963
rewarded, 33734
to Christ, 2852
Field, ———, case in court, 31667
Field, Miss ———. Glory of the heavenly, (1787) 20355, (1789) 21824, (1793) 25479
Field, Henry, case of, 36389
Field, John, 1648-1723
Christianity, 910, 1048, 1880
postscript, 2588
Field, Martin. Oration, 37422
Fielding, Henry, 1707-1754
Beauties of Fielding, 24317
Fathers, 28670
History of the adventures, 19646, 23369-70
History of Tom Jones, (1791) 23371, (1792) 24318, (1794) 26972, (1795) 28671, (1797) 32128
Remarkable history of Tom Jones, (1786) 19647, (1787) 20356, (1795) 28672, (1799) 35481-82, 36198
Fielding, John
Account of the discovery, 19527, 20252
Wonderful discovery, 19532
Fielding, Sir John, d. 1780. True example, 35297-98
Fielding, Phoebe see **Catherines, Phoebe Fielding**
Fielding, Sarah, 1714-1768. Governess, 23372
Fields, R. Practical treatise, 37423
Fiery tryal, 336
15 boxes, 38254
Fifteen comforts, 28948
discourses for the liberties, 10070
on the marvellous, 23729
upon doctrinal, 10071
sermons, 28078-79
Fifth Congress of the U. S. . . . An act see under **U. S. Laws (separates)**
Congress; third session. A list, 36516
essay, 17065
letter, 3551
supplement to the catalogue, 36100
Fighting sailor, 2654

VOL.	ITEMS	VOL.	ITEMS
1	1-3244	8	22298-25074
2	3245-6623	9	25075-28145
3	6624-9891	10	28146-30832
4	9892-13091	11	30833-33261
5	13092-16176	12	33262-25854
6	16177-19448	13	35855-39162
7	19449-22297		

VOL.	ITEMS	VOL.	ITEMS
1	1-3244	8	22298-25074
2	3245-6623	9	25075-28145
3	6624-9891	10	28146-30832
4	9892-13091	11	30833-33261
5	13092-16176	12	33262-25854
6	16177-19448	13	35855-39162
7	19449-22297		

VOL.	ITEMS	VOL.	ITEMS
1	1-3244	8	22298-25074
2	3245-6623	9	25075-28145
3	6624-9891	10	28146-30832
4	9892-13091	11	30833-33261
5	13092-16176	12	33262-25854
6	16177-19448	13	35855-39162
7	19449-22297		

of prayer . . . to be used, 7888
of presbyterial, 5709
of publick, 3022
Forma sacra, 13155
Forms and directions, 35922
   of daily prayer, 5490
   of prayer, 20990
Forrest, Andrew, accounts, 22772
Forrest, Michael
   Political reformer, 32140
   Travels through America, 25490
Forrest, Thomas. Disappointment, 10554, 30036
Forrester, James. Polite philosopher, (1758) 8124-
   25, (1762) 9115, (1781) 17155, (1786) 20002,
   (1787) 20363, (1789) 22158, (1795) 29560
Forsey, Thomas. Report of an action, 9660
Forsyth, Fanny, petition, 33062
Forsyth, Robert, d. 1794?
   murdered, 26695
   provision for widow, 27865
   widow's petition, 33062
Forsyth, William
   Palida mors, 35491
   Sermon, 33743
Fortitude, love, 9104
Fortunate discovery, 33744
Fortune (Negro). Dying confession, 9116
Fortune, Michael
   (tr.) General view, 32505
   (tr.) Treatise, 30594
Fortune teller, 34133
Fortune teller and experienced, 26950
Fortune-teller, by which, 33918
Fortune's foot-ball, 31902, 33481
Fortunes of the house, 27101
Forty dollars, 15316
Forward, Justus, 1730-1814
   Controversial letters, 33745
   Duty of Christ's ministers, 12045
   True God, 35583
Foss, John. Journal, 33746-47
Foster, ——, additions from, 10935
Foster, ——, observations on, 18403
Foster, ——, reply to, 16215
Foster, Abiel
   Motion, (1799) 36559, (1800) 38786
   reports on sundry motions, 19307
   reports on supplies, 19308
Foster, Abigail, d. 1711, death, 1497, 1510, 1513
Foster, Benjamin, of Philadelphia. Circular letter,
   22792
Foster, Benjamin, 1750-1798
   God dwelling, 14035
   Primitive baptism, 18474
   Washing of regeneration, 16275
   observations on, 18403?
   reply to, 16215?, 16272
Foster, Dan, 1748-1810
   Election sermon, 22505
   Funeral sermon, 21832
   Sermon, 12394, 37435
   Short essay, 14036
   Twenty biographical, 32141
   ordained, 13280?
Foster, Daniel, 1751-1795
   Duty of gospel ministers, 25491
   Sermon, 22506, 23381
   death, 28534
   ordained, 15795, 16276
Foster, Dwight. Motion, 34721
Foster, Edmund, 1752-1826
   Husbandry, 37436

Ministry of reconciliation, 24325
   Sermon, 25492
   letter (from Cutting), 26839
Foster, Francis, d. 1727, death, 2986
Foster, Hannah Webster, 1759-1840
   Boarding school, 33748
   Coquette, 32142
Foster, Isaac, 1740-1781
   Brief reply, 16276
   Christ Jesus, 16277
   Defence of religious, 16775
   Fallen sinners, 15795
   Holiness of infants, 10298
   Letter (to Buckminster), 16776
   Sermon, 13280
Foster, Isaac, 1755-1794
   Misrepresentation, 17156
   heresy, 17357
Foster, Isaac, d. 1807. Divine righteousness, 26990
Foster, Jacob. Two short discourses, 19409
Foster, James, extracts from, 9067, 9341-42
Foster, James, 1697-1753
   Account of the apparition, 5943-45
   Account of behaviour, 5946
Foster, Jedediah, d. 1779, death, 16273
Foster, Joel, 1755-1812
   Christ the lord, 19007
   Discourse, 24326
   Duties of a conjugal, 37437
   Literary correspondence, 35146, 35492
   Office of the high, 33749
   Oration, 32143
   ordained, 16277
Foster, John, 1648-1681
   Almanac see **Almanacs (Foster)**
   verses to, 308
Foster, John, d. 1711, death, 1510, 1513
Foster, John, 1763?-1829
   Discourse, 37438
   Sermon, 35493
   installation, 24023
   ordained, 19007
Foster, Sir Michael, 1689-1763, arguments of, 12328,
   12684, 13154
Foster, Nathaniel. Young Freemason's guide, 32144
Foster, Theodore
   To the free, 29948
   gives books, 19410
Foster, William, d. 1780. True fortitude, 14758
Foster, R. I. Providence, Nov. 24, 1781, 19410
Fothergill, John, 1675-1744. Account of the life,
   7194
Fothergill, John, fl. 1773-1777, employs Bartram,
   22329
Fothergill, Samuel, 1715-1772
   Discourses, 37439
   Grace of our Lord, (1771) 12046, (1772) 12395,
      (1773) 12768, (1784) 18475
   Necessity and divine, 16777, 24327
   Necessity of divine, 17932
   Prayer of Agur, 10899, 12769
   Repent, 15796, 18476
   Sermon, 12770
   Two discourses, 10615-16
Foundation of Christian, 328
Foundations, effects, 5029
Foundling, a comedy, (1794) 26559, 27339
Foundling, or the history, 33750, 35732
Fountain opened, (1700) 960, (1722) 2406, (1726)
   2959, 2977
Four discourses delivered, 25223
   discourses entitled, 20152

VOL.	ITEMS	VOL.	ITEMS
1	1-3244	8	22298-25074
2	3245-6623	9	25075-28145
3	6624-9891	10	28146-30832
4	9892-13091	11	30833-33261
5	13092-16176	12	33262-25854
6	16177-19448	13	35855-39162
7	19449-22297		

draws up proclamation, 6043
election of successor, 14970-71
eulogy of, 24799
hoax by, 15633
instructions to deputies, 15127
introduction by, 7916
minister abroad, 20789
ode to, 22798
opposed, 9578, 9713, 9799, 9803, 9853, 9865, 9915
paper read at home of, 20306, 20689, 20870
portrait, 32690
recommends book, 29099
reply to, 9841-42, 9904
satire on, 16697
tribute to, 23879
unmasked, 9586
verses on, 9581
views on spelling, 22259
writes commendatory letter, 20526
Franklin, W., ed. Compilation of the laws, 30977
Franklin, William, 1729-1813
    Answer of his excellency, 9973
    Letter, 14915
    Proclamation, 10997
    address to, 14286-87
Franklin, Mass. Commonwealth of Massachusetts;
    to the hon., 32446
Franklin college, charter, 20445
Franklin library company. Constitution, 27430
Franklin (ship), instructions to, 34695
Franklin society. Constitution, 24687
Franklin's legacy, 34376
Franks, David
    Catalogue of a collection, 16711, 16779
    New-York directory, 19655, 20369
Franks, David S., secy. to Arnold, 16108
Franks, William. Man in iron, 32152
Fraser, Donald
    Collection of select, 33760
    Columbian monitor, 27010
    Essay, 37445
    Mental flower-garden, 37446
    Party-spirit, 35501
    Recantation, 32153-54
    Young gentleman, (1793) 23387, (1794) 27011, (1796) 30447
Frasier [Frazier], Isaac, d. 1768, thief, 10926, 10808
Fraternal affection, 33533
Fraternal society. Rules and articles, 25914
Fraternal tribute, 37582
Fraud and injustice, 1590
Fraunces, Andrew G. Appeal, 25504
Frazer, William Clark. Funeral oration, 37448
Freame, John, d. 1745. Scripture-instruction, 7198
Frederick Augustus, duke of York, 1763-1827,
    captured, 27055, 27156
Frederick Louis, prince of Wales, 1707-1751, death,
    6648, 6716-17, 6766
Frederick county, Sept. 30, 1796, 30448
Fredericksburg academy. At a meeting, 20370
Frederickton library company. Catalogue, 32155
Free, John, 1711-1791
    Common safety, 12773
    England's warning, 12772
Free, Timothy, secy. fire company, 11597
Free and calm, 13553
Free and independent elector. Sentiments, 12224
Free and natural, 31679
Free citizen. Petition, 14384
Free citizens. To the public, 13668
Free examination, 13193
    forgiveness, 10274

gift, 2597
grace, a sermon, 4838-40
    in truth, 4723
    indeed, 4857
    maintained, 1256
    of God, 7860
    with a witness, 4715
inquiry, 28896
justification, 9945
Mason sermon, 34567
Masons pocket book, 17537
Masons pocket companion, 27014
Free suffrage. Constitution shown, 24225
Free thoughts on the inconsistency, 20613
    thoughts on the proceedings, 13602
    universal magazine, 25505-507, 27015
Freedom and love, 6474
    from civil, 13513
    the first, 7233
    triumphant, 25508
Freeholder
    Answers, 11260
    Conclusion of the answers, 11262
    Continuation of the answers, 11261
    Querist, 11432
    To the freeholders, freemen, 14497
    To the freeholders, merchants, 11884
    To the inhabitants, 17744
    To the public; as it is, 11499
    To the public: I was sorry, 20025
    To the respectable, 14515
Freeholder of Jamaica. To the freeholders, 14499
Freeholder of Liliput. Letter, 12433-35
Freeholder of South Carolina see **Zubly, John Joachim, 1724-1761**
Freeholder's address, 21838
Freeholders and freemen of the city and county, 11263
    freemen of the city of New-York, 11264
    freemen of this city, 11377
    inhabitants, 14819
    other electors, 13537
    other inhabitants, 30106, 35218
Freeholder's political catechism, 8030, 11450
Freelove (snow), wrecked, 27863
Freeman, ——, observations on, 4088-89
Freeman, A. Cumberland, colony of Rhode Island, 9370
Freeman, Bernard, 1660-1743
    Spiegel, 2120
    Verdeediging, 2745
    Morning and evening, 9835
    Weegshale, 2219
Freeman, Frank. Almanac see **Almanacs (Freeman)**
Freeman, James. Boston, 15th May, 1794, 26687
Freeman, James, 1759-1835
    Extracts from a liturgy, 25509
    Liturgy, 18938
    Remarks, 25510
    Sermon, 30451
Freeman, Jonathan, 1765-1822. Sermon, 35512

VOL.	ITEMS	VOL.	ITEMS
1	1-3244	8	22298-25074
2	3245-6623	9	25075-28145
3	6624-9891	10	28146-30832
4	9892-13091	11	30833-33261
5	13092-16176	12	33262-25854
6	16177-19448	13	35855-39162
7	19449-22297		

Voyage to Boston, 14043-44
  excerpts from, 23246, 31959
Freret, ———. Letter (to Ramsay), 31070
Fresenius, Johann Philipp, 1705-1761
  Beyspiele, 25515
  pastor in Frankfurt, 6437
Fresh advices, 14045
  important intelligence, 15300
  intelligence; Baltimore, 14046
  intelligence; Monday, 14047
  news from Boston, 14763
Fresneau, Andrew, executors of, 3019
Freund in der noth, 25604
Frey, Andreas. Declaration, 6144
Freylinghausen, Johann Anastasius, 1670-1739
  Ordnung, 14764
Freymüthige gedanken, 18485
Friar and the boy, 6550
Friars Tontine. Constitution, 24607
Friday, Jan. 24, 1800, 37410
  morning's conversation, 11387
  the fourth day, 30983-84
Friedrich II, the Great
  Relaxation of war, 8133-34
  imprisons Trenck, 26277-79
  life of, 8580, 8841
A friend. Nature and importance, 6015
Friend and well-wisher to vital religion. Poem, 21398
Friend in London. Reading no preaching, 8015
Friend of American liberty see **Green, Jacob, 1722-1790**
Friend of Christ, 3404
Friend of college, the church and his country see **Trumbull, Benjamin, 1735-1820**
Friend of democracy. Zion besieged, 20908
Friend of religion and his country. American independent, 21641
Friend of the churches. Plea for the ministers, 1276
Friend of theirs see **March, Edmund, 1703-1791**
Friend of truth
  Account of a meeting, 36745
  see also **Cleveland, John, 1722-1799; Pickering, Theophilus, 1700-1747**
Friend to America see **Hamilton, Alexander, 1757-1804**
Friend to church and common-wealth. Essay, 7651
Friend to fair play, 37731
Friend to good government see **Bouchard de La Poterie, Claude Florent**
Friend to harmony. Candid considerations, 21725
Friend to his country see **Gale, Benjamin, 1715-1790**
Friend to justice see **Martin, Luther, 1748-1826**
Friend to justice and humanity. Following is a copy, 14032
Friend to literature. Fatal effects, 21815
Friend to Maryland
  Answer to the queries, 9582
  Remarks upon a message, 9497
Friend to merit. Defence, 12025
Friend to native simplicity see **Leonard, David Augustus, 1771-1818**
Friend to order. To the public, 14513
Friend to peace and good order
  Two Congresses, 13697-98
  see also **Gray, Harrison**
Friend to political equality see **Carey, James**
Friend to pure scriptural orthodoxy. Letter, 19420
Friend to rational liberty. Jacobin looking-glass,

28894
Friend to real religion see **Knox, Samuel, 1756-1832**
Friend to regular government see **Swanwick, John, 1760-1798**
Friend to the Congress. To the freeholders, 14494
Friend to the country. Abstract from Dr. Berkley, 5539
Friend to the education of children. Child's reading, 35301
Friend to the liberty of his country see **Church, Benjamin, 1734-1776**
Friend to the public. Remarks on the report, 22833
Friend to the sex see **Adams, ———**
Friend to the truth see **Austin, David, 1759-1831**
Friend to the useful arts. Philadelphia, Jan. 31, 1797, 32684
Friend to the youth of Columbia see **Haswell, Anthony**
Friend to trade. To the merchants, 12246
Friend to truth see **Eckley, Joseph, 1750-1811; Thomas, Moses**
Friend to truth and lover of mankind see **Tucker, John, d. 1792**
Friend of youth. Love triumphant, 32390
Friendly address to all, 13224-26
  address to the inhabitants, 27580
  address to the Jews, 28290
  advice, 1483, 3078
Friendly association, Philadelphia see under **Philadelphia**
Friendly brothers of St. Patrick
  Appendix, 14048
  Fundamental laws, 13284
Friendly check, 2310
  debate, 2339, 2386
  dialogue, 18792
  epistle, 8069
  expostulation, 9336
Friendly fire society, Boston
  Boston, Dec. 4, 1783, 17847
  Rules, 18376
Friendly fire society, Cambridge. Rules, 31908
Friendly influence, 21911
  instructor, (1745) 5600, (1746) 5774-75, (1749) 6323, (1750) 6503, (1770) 11660, (1794) 27020, (1797) 32160
  letter (Robbins to Cumings), 31112
  letter (Worcester to Baldwin), 24011
  letter from a minister, 35517
  monitor, 34402
  remarks, 36005
  visit, 30173, 31924-25
Friends and countrymen (Dickinson), 9949
Friends and countrymen, three years, 16097-104
  and fellow citizens, 33769
  brethren, and countrymen, 10306
  brethren, countrymen, 12774-75
  countrymen and fellow-electors, 13286
Friends' library. Catalogue, 29312

VOL.	ITEMS	VOL.	ITEMS
1	1-3244	8	22298-25074
2	3245-6623	9	25075-28145
3	6624-9891	10	28146-30832
4	9892-13091	11	30833-33261
5	13092-16176	12	33262-25854
6	16177-19448	13	35855-39162
7	19449-22297		

Mercury office, 33060
monthly meeting, 17162
New York journal, 15078
office of the Daily advertiser, 37285, 38097
Pennsylvania journal, 15339
Virginia gazette, 13287
yearly meeting, 28713
thee, Eliza, 35524
Fromme mägdelein, 30459
Frommen lotterie, 5501, 6791
Front view of Yale, 20165
Frontiers well-defended, 1311
Frost, Amariah, d. 1792
Charge, 22175
Five sermons, 10307
Frost, Charles, d. 1724, death, 2720
Frost, George P., memorials of, 34731
Frost, Samuel, d. 1793
Confession, 25521-22
execution, 25137, 26013
Frothingham, Ebenezer
Articles of faith, 6504
Key to unlock, 10621
Letter treating upon, 11267
answer to, 11557
remarks on, 7849
Frothingham, Thomas, petition, 38848
Froward, Francis, history of, 29509
Frühauf, Daniel. Beschreibung, 12776
Fruehling ist herbey, 4248
Frugal housewife, (1772) 12348, (1774) 13186,
(1792) 24180, (1796) 30168
Fruits of a father's love, (1727) 2941, (1787) 20617,
(1792) 24662, (1794) 27473
of retirement, (1729) 3191, (1730) 3322, (1783)
18035
of solitude, 24663, 27473
of the spirit, 4936
Fry, Benjamin. Almanac see Almanacs (Fry)
Fry, John, 1699-1775
Essay on conduct, (1752) 6846, (1753) 7004,
(1754) 7203
Select poems, 20381, 37479
Fryer and Brown, publishers
Chesterfield's impenetrable, 27026
Conversation cards, 27027
Jeu de carte, 27028
Fünff schöne, 6847
Fürbilde der heilsamen, 21422
Fuessli, Johann Heinrich, tr. Aphorisms, 21194
Fugitive, a comedy, 29412
Fugitive and miscellaneous, 33651
Fulfilling of the scripture, 5185
Full and authentick, 7661
and clear, 4373
& just, 1352
and true relation, 9974
answer, 10624
clear, and familiar, 23510
relation, 8861
statement, 9392
strong, and clear, 9975
vindication, 13313
Fuller, Andrew, 1754-1815
Calvinistic and Socinian, 30462
Gospel . . . contrasted, 37480
Sermon, 30463
Fuller, Jeremiah, d. 1798, death, 34304
Fuller, John. Funeral sermon, 13288
Fuller, Samuel, d. 1736. Some principles, (1753)

7005, (1765) 9976, (1769) 11268, (1783) 17939
Fuller, Sylvester. New Ohio lands, 35526
Fuller, Thomas, 1608-1661, excerpts from, 5991
Fuller, Timothy, d. 1805. Remarks, 18488
Fuller, William, 1670-1717. True mother, 5777
Fulling, Thomas. Almanac see Almanacs (Fulling)
Fulness of joy, 3550
Fulness of life, 6228
Fulton, David, sale at tavern of, 36882-83
Funck, Heinrich
Restitution, 9393
Spiegel, 5400
Fundament und klare, 27310
Fundamental laws, 13284
Fundamental truths, 603-604
Funeral address, 38526
dirge (1793), 26009
dirge; adopted for, 37302
dirge on the death, 37009
discourse see under author, or name of person
deceased
elegy composed, 14771
occasioned, 12777
on the death, 39131
on the Reverend, 11662
or an elegiac, 31763
elogium (Burr), 7933
eulogium pronounced, 37549
eulogy and oration, 37666
occasioned, 37834
sacred, 9657
or grief, 9014
oration commemorative, 37742
delivered in the Brick, 37902-903
delivered in the chapel, 30576
in honor, 37798-802
. . . in memory, 37448
in remembrance, 38421
occasioned by the death (Washington),
36911, 38680
on Brother George Washington, 37124
on General George Washington, 38435
on Gen. Washington, 37903
on George Washington, 37334
on the death (Washington), 37797, 37803-
808, 38415
upon the death, 36922
procession, 35937
sermon see under author, or name of person
deceased
sermon on Michael Morin, 6146
tribute, 224
Funereal address, 38023
Funk, Christian. Aufsatz, 19015
Funny companion, 32166
Funny stories, 28720
Furbush, Charles, d. 1795?, murdered, 29329
Furlong, Lawrence, 1734-1806. American coast pilot, (1796) 30464, (1797) 32167, (1798) 33882,
(1800) 37483

VOL.	ITEMS	VOL.	ITEMS
1	1-3244	8	22298-25074
2	3245-6623	9	25075-28145
3	6624-9891	10	28146-30832
4	9892-13091	11	30833-33261
5	13092-16176	12	33262-25854
6	16177-19448	13	35855-39162
7	19449-22297		

Furman, Moore
An das publicum, 12052
To the public, 12053
controversy, 12170
Furman, Richard, 1755-1825
Humble submission, 37484
Oration, 30465
Rewards of grace, 30466
Unity and peace, 27029
Furneaux, Philip, 1726-1783. Letters (to Blackstone), (1772) 12328, (1773) 12684, (1774) 13154
Furtado, Emanuel, account of, 27818
Further account, 5886-87
quaeries, 507
report from the committee appointed, 34793
from the committee of impeachment, 34787

in part of the committee of privileges, 38733
in part of the committe of revisal, 38734
in part of the committee to whom, 38735
of the committee appointed, 34792
of the committee of revisal, (1798) 34762, (1799) 36518, (1800) 38736
of the committee of ways and means, 34766
of the managers, 34790
salutation, 28714
testimony against, 2148
testimony to theses, 13132
Furtherance of the gospel, 27199
Future inheritance, 10826

G

G., E. Brief account, 5401
G., F. see **Gregory, Francis, 1625-1707**
G Fox digg'd out, 228
G., G.
Almanac see **Almanacs (G. G.)**
Divinity and humanity, 7204
G., J.
poem by, 23400
see also **Galloway, Joseph, 1730-1803; Graham, John, 1694-1773**
G., L. Journal of the taking, 5601
G., N. Scriptural comment, 23396
G., W. Brief narrative, 13289
Gabrielis, Petrus. Kurzer bericht, 25524
Gadsden, Christopher, 1723-1805. Few observations, 32168
Gage, Thomas, 1597-1655. Traveller, 8136
Gage, Thomas, 1720-1787
Account of the late battle, 14192
Cambridge, June 14, 1775, 14185
Instructions of 22d February, 16293
Letter (to Randolph), 13738, 13741
Letters (to Hillsborough), 11331-32
Letters to the ministry, 11176
New proclamation, 14526
Proclamation, (1774) 13412-14, (1775) 14184-86, 14188-89
Proclamation versified, 14527
Whereas, complaints, 11277
address to, 13379, 13701, 13736
arrival in Boston, 16797
at point of death, 14046
besought, 15095
conduct, 14225

confession, 14039
correspondence with Washington, 14558-59
expedition to Concord, 14269
letter (from Brattle), 13175-76
occupancy of Boston, 14403
parodied, 13444
plans of, 14028
ravages by, 16380
releases Boston dwellers, 14224
remarks on, 13995-96
reply to, 11133-34
sermon before, 13330
soliloquy, 14040
supplies not sent to, 14336
supplies received from N. Y., 14505
supplies seized, 15073
Gager, William, ordained, 2599
Gaifer
Account of the conversion, 23397
Conversion of a Mahometan, (1795) 28721, (1796) 30467, (1797) 32169-70
Conversion of a Mehometan, (1773) 12778, (1775) 14056, (1792) 24335
Gaine, Hugh, 1726-1807
Almanac see **Almanacs (Gaine)**
Catalogue of books, 24336
New memorandum book, 12779
Universal register, 17168, 19661
broadside by, 10347
reply to, 11137
publishes handbill, 14519
Gaining of souls, 6153
Gair, Thomas, d. 1790. Sermon, 18489
Galatea, 33741

VOL.	ITEMS	VOL.	ITEMS
1	1-3244	8	22298-25074
2	3245-6623	9	25075-28145
3	6624-9891	10	28146-30832
4	9892-13091	11	30833-33261
5	13092-16176	12	33262-25854
6	16177-19448	13	35855-39162
7	19449-22297		

sends orders to selectmen, 16852
  treasurer Mass., 17218, 17595
Gardner, Hezekiah, demandant, 11614
Gardner, John. Brief consideration, 30472
Gardner, Jonathan, demandant, 11614
Gardner, Jonathan, d. 1791, death, 23177
Gardner, Joseph, 1752-1794, reports on secy. of
  Congress, 19295
Gardner, Thomas, demandant, 11614
Gardner, Urian, demandant, 11614
Garner, ——, letter to, 10264
Garnier, ——, extracts from, 30489, 32189-90
Garran-Coulon, ——, observations by, 24426
Garrard, James
  approves resolve, 33952
  petitions to, 36389
Garret, Katherine, d. 1738, execution, 4215
Garrettson, Freeborn, 1752-1827. Experience and
  travels, 23401-402, 25527
Garrick, David, 1716-1779
  Bon ton, 26558, 27031
  Bucks have at ye, 30569
  Catharine and Petruchio, 9270
  Clandestine marriage, (1776) 10263, (1774) 13203,
    (1777) 15255
  Irish widow, 12780-83
  Lilliput, 9121
  Lying valet, (1778) 15804, (1794) 26558, 27032
  excerpts from, 23246, 34112
Garrigues, Samuel
  Catalogue of the sale, 20884
  Philadelphia, May 19, 1766, 10308
Garth, Charles, agent for S. Carolina, 10748
Gascoign, ——, surveys by, 13240
Gass, George, constable, 36092
Gass, Jacob. Chronicon, 19558
Gatchel, Elisha. Honest man's interest, 2482
Gatchel, Samuel
  Constrast, 15805
  Signs of the times, 17169
Gatchell, Increase, 1699- . Young American
  ephemeris *see* **Almanacs (Gatchell)**
Gates, Hezekiah. King George's right, 12400
Gates, Horatio
  Instructions for the officers, 14243
  convention with Burgoyne, 15274
  dedication to, 16185
  express from, 15438
  letter (from Kirkland), 15642
  letter (to Congress) considered, 15675
  portrait, 15705, 26771
  reinforcements for, 15437
  victor at Saratoga, 16529
Gates, Thomas, petition by, 25444
Gaudet, ——, reads observations, 24426
Gauvain, ——, d. 1799, death, 37126
Gavin, Antonio. Master-key, 12784
Gay, Abigail, d. 1792, death, 24342
Gay, Anthelme
  French prosodical, 28727
  New French pronouncing, 32174
Gay, Bunker, d. 1815
  Accomplished judge, 12785
  Discourse, 24342
  Genuine and correct, 24343
  Sermon, 15806
  To sing of mercy, 25528
  ordained, 9394
Gay, Ebenezer, 1696-1787
  Alienation of affections, 5956
  Beloved disciple, 10309
  Call from Macedonia, 10910

Character and work, 5602
  Devotions, 12054
  Discourse, 3029
  Duty of people, 3282
  Evangelical preacher, 9394
  Jesus Christ, 7006
  Levite not to be forsaken, 7670, 25529
  Ministers are men, 2638
  Ministers insufficiency, 4960
  Mystery, 6848
  Natural religion, 8354
  Old man's calendar, (1781) 17170, (1793) 25530,
    (1794) 27033
  St. John's vision, 10310
  Sovereignty in God, 10628
  True spirit, 5779
  Untimely death, 5403
  Well-accomplish'd soldiers, 4249
  Work of a gospel minister, 7425
  Zechariah's vision, 3030
  death, 20708
  hand of fellowship, 8332
Gay, Ebenezer, d. 1796
  colleague ordained, 25374
  death, 30678
  wife's death, 32359
Gay, Ebenezer, 1766-1837
  Oration, 22518, 37493
  ordained, 25374?
Gay, John, 1688-1732
  Beggar's opera, 6673
  Fables, 27034
  excerpts from, 34112
Gay, Mary, d. 1796, death, 32359
Gayot de Pitaval, adapted, 36316
Gazette of the U. S., (1790) 22520, (1791) 23404,
    (1792) 24345
Gearing, Henry, d. 1694, death, 1194, 2175
Gebahnte pilgerstrasse, 7683
Gedanken über die rechtmässigkeit, 30476
Gedichte dem andenken, 37495
Gee, Joshua, 1698-1748
  Catalogus librorum, 2432
  Israel's mourning, 3031
  Letter (to Eells), 5191-92
  Strait gate, 3167
  favors Croswell, 4926
  letter (from Prescott), 5278
  remarks on, 5392
  reply to, 5202
  wife's death, 3362
Gee, Sarah, d. 1730, death, 3362
Geestelyk-lied, 4516
Gefahr bey unbekehrten, 4611
Geheiligten wissenschaften, 9978
Geheime unt offentliche, 6285
Geistiges wetter-glöcklein, 24147
Geistlich lied, 12499
Geistliche fama, (1730) 3273, (1731) 3410, (1732)
    3529
Geistliche lieder, 36276
Geistlichen brief, 27037
Geistlicher irrgarten, 9122
Geistliches blumen-gärtlein, (1747) 6073, (1769)
    11492, (1773) 13036, (1791) 23823, (1800) 38615
Geistliches magazien, 9676
Geistreiche lieder, 6917, 9495
Gekruicigde Christus, 6776
Gelbe fieber, 35449
Gellatly, Alexander

Detection of injurious, 7671
Some observations, 8137
charges against Delap, 8040
Gelston, David, candidacy, 21350
Gemein-litaney, 9859
Gemeinnützige Philadelphische correspondenz
Neujahrs-verse, (1782) 17546, (1783) 17944, (1784) 18494
Gemeinnützige sammlung, 30561
Geminiani, ———, examples for violin, 16016
Gemmil, John. Sermon, 28731
Genealogy of Jesus, 9057
Genealogy of the family, 12236
General account, 20066
General Allen's memorial, 26549
General association of Connecticut
Address, 31967
At a meeting, 37224
General atlas (Carey), 37097
atlas for the present, 26741, 30162
attacked, 13823-24
Burgoyne's defeat, 16284
cause, 4755-56
General committee. Minutes, 26397-400
General committee, May 1, 1775, 14325
General compendium, 19337
General court see Mass.   General court
General courts answer, 412
directions, 9289
election, 19631
epistle, 405
Gage's account, 14192
confession, 14039
instructions, 16293
soliloquy, 14040
heads, 15994
idea, 7121
instructor, 37034
introduction, 16023-24
Lee's letter, 14148
list, 38930
magazine, and historical, 4722
magazine, and impartial, 33782
map, 7411-13
militia orders, 16438
General officer
Rules, maxims, 15588
see also Cavan, Richard Lambart, 6th earl of;
Pommereul, François René Jean de, 1745-1823
General orders, (Dec. 14, 1776) 15182; (Jan. 22, 1777) 15644; (Apr. 11, 1777) 15514; (Apr. 14, 1777) 15646; (Apr. 16, 1777) 15515; (Jan. 28, 1791) 23551; (April 1791) 23552; (Mar. 1, 1794) 27286; (June 6, 1794) 27287; (July 7, 1794) 27288; (Feb. 28, 1795) 29042; (Feb. 20, 1796) 30763; (June 13, 1797) 32447; (Aug. 22, 1797) 32448; (May 1, 1798) 34081; (Mar. 30, 1799) 35791; (July 7, 1800) 37917
peace, 17965
post office, Oct. 24, 1782, 17764
post office, New York, Jan. 20, 1790, 22978
post office, Philadelphia, May 1, 1776, 15127
practice of the churches, 12367, 12739
regulations, 22510
remarks, 33783
return, 15516
rules and regulations, 28707
rules for country schools, 37429
General society of mechanics and tradesmen

Charter, 34224
General state of the revenue, 26344
statement of appropriations, 26345
statement of the foreign, 22206
Gen. Sullivan's address, 19266
General tables, 24251
view of receipts, 17765
of the arguments, (1784) 18741, (1794) 27554, (1796) 31053
or abstract, 32505
General Washington (brig), at Philadelphia, 18400
General Washington's letter (to Adams), 34829
Gen. Washington's resignation, 18258
General Wolfe, a song, 16285
General Wolfe's instructions, 16174
Generation of light, 30284
Generosity of an injured, 33533
Generous lady, 34525
Genesis, chapter III, 21682
Genêt, Edmond Charles, 1763-1834
correspondence with Federal government, 25496, 26334, 26993-94, 27925
express from, 27055, 27156
Genethlia pia, 2039
Genevieve of Brabant. Historie, 22524
Genin, ———. Freemasons march, 33649
Genius of liberty (Morristown)
Address to the citizens, 36770
At a meeting, 36854
Memorial, 37500
Genlis, Stéphanie Félicité Ducrest de St. Aubin, comtesse de, 1746-1830
Alphonso and Dalinda, 20385, 35537
Alphonso and Delinda, 21106
Beauties of Madam Genlis, 23406
Beauty and the monster, 19021
Castle of truth, 28733
Child of nature, 22525, 22619
Sacred dramas, 32179
Sylvan, 33786
Genovefa, history of, 13297
Genoveva, history of, 22524
Genteel & surprizing, 23263
Gentiles inheritance, 35287-88, 37111
Gentle shepherd, (1750) 6599, (1771) 12209, (1795) 29382, (1798) 34432
Gentleman
Account of the French, 5725
County and town officer, 10967
Essay on the merchandize, 3413
Letter (to friend), 7227
Letter (to friend in England), 29236
Letter from a gentleman, 2163
Gentleman and ladies musical, 13642, 18197
and lady's Angloamerican, 32332
& lady's companion, 33823
pocket memorandum, 15808, 16784
town and country magazine, 18495
Gentleman at Elizabeth-Town. Letter (to friend

VOL.	ITEMS	VOL.	ITEMS
1	1-3244	8	22298-25074
2	3245-6623	9	25075-28145
3	6624-9891	10	28146-30832
4	9892-13091	11	30833-33261
5	13092-16176	12	33262-25854
6	16177-19448	13	35855-39162
7	19449-22297		

letter, 14061
principles, 14734
speech, 4830
works of Flavius, 27173
Geodaesia, 25731, 30704
Geographic, historical summary, 10911
Geographical and hydrographical, 23104
cards, (1787) 20386, (1791) 23407, (1793) 25937
catechism, 30963
clock, 24347
historical, political, 7411-13, 7652
ledger, 26781
view, 31132-33
Geography epitomized, (1784) 18435, (1790) 22448, (1791) 23311, (1794) 26850
Geography made easy, (1784) 18615, (1790) 22681, (1791) 23579, (1794) 27351, (1796) 30827, (1798) 34146, (1800) 38004
George I
Proclamation, 2223
Speech, 1741
death, 2846-47, 2873, 2909, 2949, 2957
George II
His majesty's royal commission, 4020
Letters patent, 3454
Proclamation, (1733) 3661, (1748) 6150
Speech, 3909
accession, 2846, 2873, 2909, 2949
authorizes primer, 12989
death, 8784. 8801, 8811, 8828, 8834-36, 8879, 8925, 8958, 9015, 9023
poem on, 8882
portrait, 32854
George III
Dialogue, (1792) 17520, 17681, (1787) 20330
Proclamation, (1764) 9680, (1775) 14077, (1783) 17964
Speech, (1770) 11673, (1774) 14079, 14081-83, (1775) 14784-88, (1778) 16294, (1781) 17552
character, 9023
coronation, 9107
epitaph, 17528
ode on, 9108
petition to, 10451
portrait, 12141, 32854
George, Daniel, 1758-1804. Almanac see **Almanacs (George)**
George Alexander Stevens' celebrated, 27742
George Barnwell, a new novel, 38596
George Christoph Reinholdt, buchbinder, 12971
George Fox digg'd out, 228
George Keith once more, 1143
George Town on Arrowsick, 1894
George Washington, President of the U. S. of A.; to all, 29742, 31409
George Washington to the people, 38990
George Washington's resignation, 31552
Georgia
Account showing, 4961
Address and remonstrance, 37504, 38705
Amendments made, 30483
Constitution, (1777) 15308, (1785) 19024, (1787) 20387, (1789) 21850, (1796) 30482, (1798) 33790, (1799) 35541
Directions for the officers, 12055
Journal of the convention, 28738
Opinions of the judges, 24353
Ordinance for ascertaining, 19683
Representation and remonstrance, 32183

State of Georgia; by his excellency, 27040
To the honorable, 28739
Georgia. General assembly
Journal, (1769) 11663, (1792) 24351
Votes, (1755-56) 7672, (1756-60), 8605, (1760) 8863, (1764) 9677
Georgia. Governor
Proclamation, (1773) 12786, (1777) 15291, 15309, (1800) 37506
Georgia. House of representatives
Journal, (1796) 30484, (1799) 37507
Georgia. Laws (collective)
Acts (1783-89), 22529
Digest of the laws, 37505
Land laws, 27042, 28737
Georgia. Laws (session)
Acts, (1773) 13292, (1788) 21107, (1792) 24352, (1793) 25536, (1794) 27043, (1795) 28735, (1796) 30481, (1797) 32182, (1798) 33789, (1799) 35540, 37503
Georgia. Laws (separates)
Act, 1777, (intestate estates) 15307
Act, 1782, (confiscation) 17548
Act, 1783, (arrears of taxes) 17947, (confiscation) 17949, (courts) 17950-51, (depreciation) 27041, (immigration) 17953, (land office) 17952, (recovery of property) 17955, (relief) 17954, (taxes) 17948
Act, 1784, (Indian trade) 18496
Act, 1786, (amercing) 19666, (Bourbon county) 19671, (citizenship) 19667, 19674, (confiscation) 19676, (conveying lands) 19680, (courts) 19669, (foreigners) 19673, (grant to d'Estaing) 19677, (imports) 19681-82, (intestate estates) 19679, (land acts) 19675, (religion) 19672, (Savannah) 19668, (taxes) 19670, (tobacco) 19678
Act, 1792, (patrols) 24349, (slaves) 24350
Act, 1795, (unlocated territory) 28736-37
Act, 1796, (annulling act) 30479, (judiciary) 30480
Duty act, 13293
Militia law, 17173
Toll act, 13294
Georgia. Senate
Journal, (1792) 24351, (1796) 30485, (1799) 37508
Georgia association. Minutes, (1790-93) 25537-40, (1794) 27044
Georgia, by his honour John Adam Treutlen, 15309
Georgia Mississippi company
Grant to the Georgia, 28742-44
State of facts, 28745
Georgia Orphan House destroyed, 24436
Georgia spec, 32946
Georgia speculation unveiled, 31830, 33425
Gerard, ——, dispute with Greene, 18219
Gerard, C. A.
Chaplain's sermon, 16198
credentials, 16279
minister plenipotentiary, 15798

VOL.	ITEMS	VOL.	ITEMS
1	1-3244	8	22298-25074
2	3245-6623	9	25075-28145
3	6624-9891	10	28146-30832
4	9892-13091	11	30833-33261
5	13092-16176	12	33262-25854
6	16177-19448	13	35855-39162
7	19449-22297		

Gerhard, Johann, 1582-1637. Free grace, 4723
Gerhard Tersteegens lebens, 26247
Geringen bericht, 5195
Geringen schein, 5957
Germaine, George, viscount Sackville
    Rights of Great Britain, (1776) 14727-28, (1794)
        27328, (1795) 29484
    correspondence with Clinton, 17876, 18208
    despatch from, 15827
    letter (from Clinton), 15284
German charitable society's lottery, 12939
    freeholder, 11665
    grammar, 20937
German Lutheran church. Arrangement of the
    music, 36111
German psalmody, 7772
German theatre, 37335
Germanicus, 27597
Germantauner zeitung, 9980
Germantown, Pa. Certain agreements, 8606
Germantown society for promoting domestic manu-
    factures. Constitution, 22534
Gerrald, Joseph, trial, 27591
Gerrish, Benjamin, wife's death, 1824, 3983
Gerrish, Joseph, d. 1719, death, 2139
Gerrish, Martha, d. 1736, death, 3983
Gerrish, Mehitable, d. 1716, death, 1824
Gerrish, Paul, white pine cutter, 3715
Gerrish, William. New Year verses, 38346
Gerry, Elbridge, 1744-1814
    Circular letter, 16558-61
    Observations, 21111-12
    instructions to, 34837, 34839
    reports on accounts, 18833, 19293
    reports on Conn. expenses, 18838
    reoprts on frontier posts, 18832
    reports on Penobscot expedition, 19312
    reports on representation, 18827
    reports on sundry motions, 19307
Gesäng der einsamen, 5958-59
Geschichte der tage, 11273
    des Isaac, 23257
    Florentius, 32326
    von der marterwoche, 35201
    von der pfaltz-gräfin, 13297
Geschwinde rechner, (1774) 13275, (1793) 25476,
    (1794) 26969
Gesetze und verfassung, 35943
Gesner, Salomon, 1730-1788
    Death of Abel, (1762) 9125-26, (1765) 9981, (1766)
        10313, (1770) 11667, (1787) 20390, (1790) 22535,
        (1791) 23412, (1793) 25545, (1794) 27049, (1795)
        28747, (1797) 32187-88
    Tod Abels, 14775, 29989
Gespräch betreffend, 37511
    im reich, 25546
    zwischen dem kleinen, 22536
        Doctor Beale, 15811
        einem flüchtigen, 4507
        einem jüngling, 7210
        einem pilger, 15311, 24493
        einem Protestanten, 32464
Gesunde vernunft, 14963
Getchell, Dennis, 1724-1791. Testimony, 27050,
    37512
Getreue warnung gegen, 9865
Getreuer warnungs brief, 4898
Gewissenhaffte vorstellung, 4517
Geyer, Andreas. Andreas Geyer, buchbinder, 12789
Ghost of John Young, 32116

Ghost-seer, 31163-64
Gib, Adam, 1713-1788. Kaina kaipalaia, 21114
Gibbon, Edward, dedication to, 23470, 25712
Gibbons, J., petition of, 32992
Gibbons, James, ed. Dilworth's assistant, 33639
Gibbons, Thomas, of Georgia
    To the freemen, 21855
    election apposed, 21732
Gibbons, Thomas, 1720-1785. Divine conduct, (1761)
    8864, (1792) 24248, (1794) 26854
Gibbs, George, obtains drawback, 29705
Gibbs, Henry, 1668-1723
    Bethany, 1677
    Certain blessedness, 2221
    Godly children, 2876
    Right method, 1159
Gibson, ———, veterinarian, 27771
Gibson, Edmund, 1669-1748
    Last pastoral letter, 4518
    Pastoral letter, 3283
    Sacrament, 4519
    charges to, 3638
    letter (from Campbell), 3513
    remarks on, 4594
    reply to, 4457
Gibson, George, compensated for services, 24902
Gibson, J. Commonwealth of Massachusetts, 17595
Gibson, James. Atlas minimus, 33794
Gibson, John
    Description of counterfeit, 16562
    auditor general, 15657
Gibson, Robert. Treatise, (1785) 19026, (1789)
    21856, (1792) 24357, (1798) 33795
Gibson, William. Farrier's dispensatory, 2535
Giddings, Eliphalet, collects beef, 16880
Gifford, Andrew, ed. Eighteen sermons, 33217
Gifford, John, 1758-1818
    History of France, 30489, 32189-90, 33796
    Letter (to Erskine), 32191
    Residence in France, 33797, 35030
Gifford, William, 1756-1826
    Baviad, 35546, 37513
    Epistle, 37514
    Works, 37515
Gilbert, George, petition, 38763
Gift for children, 30490
Gifts of the spirit, 4013
Gignoux, John. Child's best plaything, 10314-15
Gil Blas, (1790) 22619, (1791) 23499, (1796) 30686,
    (1797) 32372
Gilbert, Benjamin, of Penna. Narrative, 18497
Gilbert, Benjamin, 1711-1780
    Discourse, 11274
    Truth vindicated, 6148
Gilbert, Francis, appointed warden, 15340
Gilbert, Sir Geoffrey, 1674-1726. Law of evidence,
    21113
Gilbert, Jacob, petition, 38673
Gilbert, Mary. Extract of Miss Mary, 11275
Gilby, Antony, tr. Testament of the twelve, (1709)
    1426, (1714) 1710, (1716) 1849
Gilchrist, Robert, plaintiff, 38083
Gildersleeve, Cyrus, 1769-1838. Century sermon,
    32192, 33798
Giles Gingerbread, 19949, 20675
Gill, John, 1697-1771
    Argument from apostolic, 9982
    Divine right, 6506
    Doctrine of justification, 5404
    Glorious state, 7673

Reply to A defence, 10316
Reply to Mr. Clark, 7205
Three sermons, (1756) 7674, (1777) 15312, (1797) 32193
commentary by, 20960?, 21680?, 22347?
extracts from, 27564-66?
pastor in London, 24481
proposals for printing book of, 16704
reply to, 6829
Gill, John, fl. 1783, accounts of, 18101
Gill, Moses
Proclamation, 35790, 37914
approves law, 37919
dedication to, 27098, 28809, 30545, 32234, 33853, 35598
petition of, 38836
sermon before, 28686, 30454, 33675, 35317
wife's death, (Rebecca) 34501, 34641, (Sarah) 12080
Gill, Obadiah. Some few remarks, 975
Gill, Rebecca, 1727?-1798, death, 34501, 34641
Gill, Sarah Prince, d. 1771?
Devotional papers, 12790, 35547
death, 12080
meditations, 22082
Gillam, Benjamin. Boston ephemeris see **Almanacs (Gillam)**
Gillaspie, Hugh, execution, 8356
Gillespie, George
Letter (to brethren), 4520
Remarks, 5405
Sermon, 4521
Treatise, 3906
Gillet, Alexander
True Christianity, 32820
ordained, 14478, 26287
Gillet, Ashbel, reply to, 25568-69
Gillet, Eliphalet, 1768-1848
Discourse, 35548-49
Oration, 37516
Sermon, 28748-49
ordained, 29423
Gillies, John, 1712-1796. Memoirs of the life, 13298, 33799
Gillis, ———. Collection of hymns, 10202
Gilman, J. W., music engraver, 10829
Gilman, John Taylor
Proclamation, 29164, 30854-55
To the selectmen, 27377
sermon before, 28124, 31126
Gilman, Nicholas, fl. 1740-1783, treasurer N. H., 17257
Gilman, Nicholas, 1755-1814, letter referred to, 31429
Gilman, Samuel. Sermon, 3032
Gilman, Tristram, 1735-1809. Death of the righteous, 30491
Gilpin, John
imitated, 20035
story of, 22591, 25354, 26826-27, 30803
Gilpin, Johnny. Toddy-mill, 37519
Gilpin, William, 1724-1804
Account of a new, 32194
Life of William Baker, 35297, 37156
Girardin, Louis Hue, 1771-1825. Education, 33800
Giraud, Jean Jacques, 1750-1825. Sel specifique, 32195
Girl with a cast, 35551
Gisborne, Thomas, 1758-1846. Enquiry into the duties, 33801, 35552
Give Caesar his due, 4241

ear, 27051
us but light, 5187
Glad tidings, 31844
Glas, John, 1695-1773. Christian songs, 20391
Glasgow, J., petition, 32967
Glass, Samuel, petition, 38893
Glass, or speculation, 23413
Glasse, Hannah. Servants' directory, 8607
Glasse, Samuel, tr. Advice from a lady, (1786) 19454, (1789) 21630, (1796) 29954
Glaubens-bekenntniss, 5213
Gleaner, a miscellaneous, 34162
Gleason, Benjamin, 1777-1847. Oration, 37520
Gleason, Ezra. Almanac see **Almanacs (Gleason)**
Gleason, James, 1723-1803. Exposition, 32196
Glebe house, 35553
Glen, James. Proclamation, 5492
Glendinning, William
Lamentations of Mary, 25549
Life, 28750
Short account, 27054
Glendy, John, 1755-1832. Oration, 37521
Glezen, Levi, 1774?-1842. Oration, 37522
Gloria Britannorum, 2438
Glories of the Lord, 4482, 1196
Glorious authentic intelligence, 15313
espousal, 2040
news; a brief, 36876, 37523-24
news, Boston, 10317
news from France, 27055
news; just received, 10318
rest, 5550
resurrection, 28057
reward, 3381
state, 7673
throne, 1077, 1690
union, 2915
victory, 36241
Glory of America, 17978
of Christ, 12082, 29844
of God, 5155
of goodness, 1123
of the church, 7674
heavenly city, (1787) 20355, (1789) 21824, (1793) 25479
redeemer, 35738
Gloucester, Samuel, bp. of see **Hallifax, Samuel**
Gloucester, Mass.
Appeal to the impartial publick, 19028
Letters from the First church, 5406
Rules and orders agreed, 21858
Gloucester, N. J. At a meeting of the inhabitants, 37525
Gloucester county, N. J. Address, 36767
Gloucester county, state of New Jersey, 37526
Gloucester united library. Catalogue, 30492
Glover, Henry
Brief explications, 468
Essay to discover, 510
Glover, John, 1732-1797

VOL.	ITEMS	VOL.	ITEMS
1	1-3244	8	22298-25074
2	3245-6623	9	25075-28145
3	6624-9891	10	28146-30832
4	9892-13091	11	30833-33261
5	13092-16176	12	33262-25854
6	16177-19448	13	35855-39162
7	19449-22297		

escorts Burgoyne, 15438
officers of, 16360
soldier under, 17197
Glover, Joseph, 1770- . Attempt to prove, 37527
Glover, Richard, 1712-1785. Substance of the evidence, 14067
Gluck, Christopher Willibald von, 1714-1787. Ouverture d'Iphigénie, 28751
Glückliche genügsamkeit, 6074
Glynn, Robert. Day of judgment, 31953
Goad, Benjamin, villainy of, 186
God acknowledged, 4257
  admonishing, 19547, 20264
  and not ministers, 4669
  arising, 15378
  brings about, 13333
  brings to the desired, 1925
  by his power, 3026
  deals with us, 2421
  destroyeth, 6766
  dwelling, 14035
  giveth, 2316
  glorified, (1731) 3415, (1743) 5228-29, (1744) 5425, (1771) 12098, (1795) 28982, (1798) 34013-14
  glorious, 5354
  in no sense, 18781
  in the camp, 1339
  is a great, 3645
  is to be praised, 18812-13
  our protector, 32358
  ruling, 18530
  shakes the earth, 2945-46
  sometimes answers, 3861
  the author of human, 38547
      of promotion, 27255
      of spiritual, 28082
  the dwelling, 18994
  the judge, 2873
  the only, 6648
  the pious soldier's, 7874
  the poor man's, 32295
  the strength and portion, 6826
      and salvation, 8855
      of rulers, 4871
  visiting, 8962
  will trouble, 8356
Goddard, Edward. Brief account, 6507
Goddard, Josiah. New and beautiful collection, 33802, 35554
Goddard, William, 1739-1817
  Advertisement (1770), 11668
  Andrew Marvell's second, 12793
  Baltimore, April 18, 15391
  General post-office, Philadelphia, 15127
  Mr. David Rusk, 15314
  New York, May 2, 1775, 14068
  No. 1; Philadelphia, 12792
  Partnership: or the history, 11669-71
  Philadelphia, Dec. 23, 1766, 10319
  Proposals for printing, 19029
  Prowess of the Whig, 15315
Godfrey, Thomas, d. 1749. Almanac see **Almanacs** (Godfrey)
Godfrey, Thomas, 1736-1763
  Court of fancy, 9127
  Juvenile poems, 9983
Godian, ——. The tear, 30585
Godliness excludes, 18921
Godly and faithful, 5922
  children, 2876
  fathers, 12713

  sorrow, 4904
God's awful determination, 3015
  awful warnings, 28354
  call to his people, 137, 7880
  care, 15606
  challenge, 32360
  concern, 2425, 3267
  conduct, 1780
  eye, 381
  face, 2530
  fatherly care, 4155
  frown, 1146
  goodness, 8049
  hand, 8665
  help, 2507
  joyful welcome, 25835
  love, 23233
  marvellous kindness, 5584
  mercy shewed, 40
  mercy surmounting, (1728) 2996, (1754) 7160, (1780) 16721
  people, 5055
  promise to an obedient, 7594
  promise to his plantations, 402
  protecting providence, (1699) 863, (1735) 3896, (1751) 6658
  providence, 2323
  sovereign, 1541
  sovereignty, 5906, 10182
  special care, 7806
  tender mercy, 21487
  terrible voice, (1668) 132, (1770) 11908, (1791) 23942, (1795) 29795
  thoughts, 16717
  voice, 6849
  way, 2015
  wonderful goodness, 8769
  wonders, 6458-59
Godwin, Mary Wollstonecraft see **Wollstonecraft, Mary, 1759-1797**
Godwin, William, 1756-1836
  Enquirer, 32197
  Enquiry, 30493
  (ed.) Maria, 35555
  Memoirs of Mary, 35556
  Things as they are, 28752
Görgel, ——. Gespräch, 22536
Goethe, Johann Wolfgang von, 1749-1832
  Sorrow and sympathetic, 18501
  Sorrows of Werter, (1786) 19688, (1789) 21859, (1794) 27056, (1795) 28753, (1796) 30494-95
  Werter and Charlotte, 33803
Goetschius, Johannes Hendricus, 1718-1800. Onbekende God, 5193
Göttliche liebes-andacht, 6508
  liebes und lobesgethöne, 3253
  offenbahrungen, 5387
  veschützung, 7646
  wunderschrift, 21860
Goetz, Gustav Friedrich
  (tr.) Akten, 29797
  (tr.) Auserlesene fabeln, 26538
  (tr.) McPherson's Vorlesungen, 24496
Goetz, Johann Nepomuck
  Lied der freude, 32198
  Moralphilosophische rede, 33804
  Predight, 30496
Goffe, William, 1605?-1679, regicide, 25998, 27743
Goix, ——, plaintiff, 38079
Gold, Hezekiah, 1731-1790
  True state, 17957
  wife's death, 10295

Gold, Sarah, d. 1766, death, 10295
Gold, Thomas Ruggles, 1764-1827. To the people, 37528
Golden balls, 32199
    bull, 25550
    cabinet, 25551
    chain, 2887
    curb, 1404
    dust, 7220
    plaything, 22188, 29658
    toy, 21078, 35457
    treasure, 24359
    treasury abridged, 25209
    treasury for the children, 30102, 31843
Goldsborough, Charles Washington, 1779-1843
    Original and correct, 37529
Goldsmith, Oliver, 1728-1774
    Abridgment of the history, 28754
    Beauties of Goldsmith, 32200
    Citizen of the world, 27057
    Deserted village, (1771) 12060, (1782) 17550, (1783) 17958, (1786) 19689, (1789) 21723, (1791) 23235, (1793) 25149, 25552-53, (1799) 35557
    Edwin and Angelina, (1795) 28977, (1797) 32843, (1798) 33880
    Edwin and Angeline, 19694
    Grecian history, 37531
    History of the earth, 28756
    Miscellaneous works, (1793) 25554, (1794) 27058, (1795) 28757
    Poems, 23416, 37530
    Roman history, 28755, 33805
    She stoops to conquer, (1773) 12794-95, (1794) 26559, 27059
    Traveller, 10914, 19690
    Vicar of Wakefield, (1772) 12405, (1773) 12796, (1780) 16787, (1791) 23417, (1792) 24360-61, (1794) 27060, (1795) 28758-59
    (comp.) World displayed, 31664
    excerpts from, 23246, 26014, 29926
Goldthwait, Ezekiel. Proposals for carrying on, 10828
Golgotha, 1621
Gooch, Elizabeth Sarah Villa-Real. The contrast, 30497-98
Gooch, Sir William, 1681-1751
    Charge, 3370
    dedication to, 3298
Good advice, 1025
    and faithful, 5932
    character, 2454
    child's delight, 25555, 28760
    conversation, 1298
    evening, 1362
    fetch'd out, 1257, 19426
    government, 5972
    impressions, 2908
Good Intent (brigantine), goods imported by, 11720
Good lessons, 1258, 2455
    linguist, 924
    man making, 828
    man useful, 17378
    man's character, 7797
    master, 754
    men, 11014
    minister, a sermon, 3676, 8856
    minister of Jesus, 11861, 32882
    mother-in-law, 23336
    mother's legacy, 35297
    natured men, 28670
    news for America, 10320
        for the French, 27327

    from a far country, 7746, 10503
    from the Netherlands, 6674
  of the community, 7312
  old age, 2768
    genuine, 25865
    way, 1259
    ways, 13432
  order, 386
  public roads, 12797
  rulers, 2662, 6175
  Samaritan, 31087
  soldiers, 2182
  souldiers, 562, 958
  subject's wish, 2741
  wife, 30499
  works, 6103
Goodell, ——, plaintiff, 31668
Goodere, Sir John Dinely, murdered, 4681, 4809
Goodere, Samuel
    murderer, 4681
    trial, 4809
Goodhue, Joseph, wife's death, 302, 11672
Goodhue, Josiah, d. 1797, death, 33196, 34999
Goodhue, Sarah Whipple. Valedictory, 302, 11672
Goodlet, John. Vindication of the associate, 10631
Goodness consider'd, 6815
Goodness of God, 36356
Goodrich, Chauncey, 1759-1815, letter referred to, 33068
Goodrich, Elizur, 1734-1797
    Duty of gospel-ministers, 9128
    Principles of civil, 20393
    Sermon, (1784) 18502, (1786) 20394, (1790) 22538
    Three letters, 37281-83
    death, 32069
Goodrich, John, 1753-1800. Civil and executive, 25556, 33807
Goodwin, Mrs. Abiel, d. 1727, death, 2914, 3060
Goodwin, Daniel, d. 1772?, death, 12503
Goodwin, Hezekiah, 1740-1767
    Remarkable vision, 37533
    Vision, (1769) 11276, (1774) 13301, (1775) 14069, (1776) 14778-79, (1793) 25557, (1795) 28762, (1800) 37534
Goodwin, Solomon, d. 1773?, execution, 12725
Goodwin, T., preface by, 30235, 33532
Goodwin, Thomas, 1600-1680
    abridgment of, 29844
    extract from, 21670, 27564-66
Goodwin, William. Forty dollars reward, 15316
Goody Two-shoes, (1775) 14117, (1776) 14799, (1785) 19039, (1786) 19710, (1787) 20412, (1795) 28833, (1797) 32256-57, (1799) 35621
Gookin, Daniel, 1612-1687
    Catalogue of rare, 1984
    Historical collections, 24362, 24530
Gookin, Nathaniel, 1687-1735
    Day of trouble, 3033, 30501
    colleague ordained, 3764
Gookin, Nathaniel, fl. 1739, ordained, 4423

VOL.	ITEMS	VOL.	ITEMS
1	1-3244	8	22298-25074
2	3245-6623	9	25075-28145
3	6624-9891	10	28146-30832
4	9892-13091	11	30833-33261
5	13092-16176	12	33262-25854
6	16177-19448	13	35855-39162
7	19449-22297		

VOL.	ITEMS	VOL.	ITEMS
1	1-3244	8	22298-25074
2	3245-6623	9	25075-28145
3	6624-9891	10	28146-30832
4	9892-13091	11	30833-33261
5	13092-16176	12	33262-25854
6	16177-19448	13	35855-39162
7	19449-22297		

VOL.	ITEMS	VOL.	ITEMS
1	1-3244	8	22298-25074
2	3245-6623	9	25075-28145
3	6624-9891	10	28146-30832
4	9892-13091	11	30833-33261
5	13092-16176	12	33262-25854
6	16177-19448	13	35855-39162
7	19449-22297		

Grey cap, 29372, 34426
Gridley, Richard, 1711-1796. Plan of the city, 5783
Griendlief, Thomas see Carey, James
Grier, James, d. 1791, death, 25654
Grievous, Peter see Hopkinson, Francis, 1737-1791
Griffin, ———, made adjutant general, 15182
Griffin, Cyrus, 1740-1810
   Copy of a letter, 30516
   Proclamation, 21517
Griffin, John, petition, 31375
Griffinbury, Elizabeth, accessory, 10919
Griffith, Mrs. ———
   (tr.) Shipwreck, 35425
   (tr.) Surprizing yet real, 13257
Griffith, Benjamin. Short treatise, 5124, 5194, 33370
Griffith, David, 1742-1789
   Passive obedience, 14793
   death, 22149
Griffith, Dennis. Map of the state, 27070, 28772
Griffith, Elizabeth Griffith, 1720-1793. Letters, 30517
Griffith, John. Gentleman & lady's companion, 33823
Griffith, John, 1713-1776
   Journal, 16793
   Some brief remarks, 10917, 17178
Griffith, John, fl. 1768, preface by, 11044
Griffith, William, 1766-1826
   Address from the council, 28773
   Eumenes, 35570
   Oration, 37548
   Scrivener's guide, 32212
   Treatise, 30518, 32211
Griffiths, John
   Collection of the newest, (1788) 21121-22, (1795) 28774, (1797) 32213
   Gentleman & lady's companion, 33823?
Griffitts, Samuel Powel, ed. Domestic medicine, 28366, 31886
Grimes, John, execution, 10036
Grimké, John Faucherand, 1752-1819
   Charge, 33824
   Duty of executors, 32214
   Proposals for printing, 21867
   Public laws, 22897
   South Carolina justice, 30519
Griswold, Alexander Viets, 1766-1843
   Discourse . . . at Harwinton, 32215
   Discourse delivered at Litchfield, 33825
   Discourse delivered before the Aurora, 33826
   Sermon, 30520
   Short sketch, 33827
Griswold, Benjamin, d. 1772, death, 12394
Griswold, Elijah. Connecticut harmony, 30521
Griswold, Ezra
   Answer to Mr. Ashbel, 25568-69
   Letter in answer, 30522
Griswold, Matthew
   Proclamation, 18417, 18970
   dedication to, 17445, 18892, 19393
   wife's death, 21054
Griswold, Michael, d. 1771, death, 12558
Griswold, Roger, fracas with Lyon, 33586, 34757, 34760
Griswold, Stanley, 1763-1815
   Funeral eulogium, 37549
   Statement of the singular, 33828
   Truth its own, 37550
   ordained, 22628
Griswold, Ursula, d. 1788, death, 21054

Grondlycke onderricht, 1350
Gronow, Lewis, accounts, 18108
Groote gelukzaligheid, 8149
Gros, Johann Daniel, 1737-1812. Natural principles, 28775
Gros mousqueton, 30208
Grosch, C. Allerneuste harfenspiel, 28623
Gross, ———. Historick recital, 24368
Grosse gebet-buch, 7014
Grosthed, Robert, tr. Testament, 1426, 1710, 1849
Grosvenor, Benjamin, 1675-1758
   Health, 8869
   Mourner, (1781) 17179, (1791) 23423, (1794) 27071
Grosvenor, Daniel, 1750-1834
   Sermon, 19031
   ordained, 13310
Grosvenor, Ebenezer, 1739-1788
   Sermon, 13310
   death, 21464
   ordained, 9381
Grosvenor, Lady Harriet, adultery, 11898
Grotius
   Pills for the delegates, 14094
   see also Clinton, DeWitt, 1769-1828
Grotius, Hugo, 1583-1645, lectures on, 36260
Groton, Conn. Proceedings of a meeting, 15846
Groton union conference. Minutes, 37551
Ground and nature, 10918, 37552
Ground plan of the city, 26853
Grounds and reason, 23993
   and reasons, 4734, 14146
   and rules, (1721) 2303, (1723) 2490, (1740) 4622, (1746) 5878, (1760) 8760
   of a holy, (1753) 7130, (1772) 12586, (1782) 17753, (1788) 21509, (1800) 38682
Grouniosaw, James Albert Ukuwsau
   Life and adventures, 17180
   Narrative, 13311
Group, a farce, 14611-13
Group, or an elegrant, 30202
Grout, Jonathan
   Young child's accidence, 35571
   installation, 25736
Grove, Henry, 1684-1738. Discourse, (1793) 25570, (1794) 27072, (1800) 37553
Grove plantation, 37994
Grovenor, Benjamin see Grosvenor, Benjamin, 1675-1758
Grubb, Sarah Tuke, 1756-1790. Some account, 28776-77
Grube, Bernhard Adam, 1715-1805
   Dellawaerisches gesang-büchlein, 9400
   (tr.) Harmony of the gospels, 9348
Gruber, Eberhard Ludwig
   Grundforschende fragen, 35475
   reply to, 13392
Gruber, Johann Adam
   Einfaeltige warnungs- und, 4725, 5082

VOL.	ITEMS	VOL.	ITEMS
1	1-3244	8	22298-25074
2	3245-6623	9	25075-28145
3	6624-9891	10	28146-30832
4	9892-13091	11	30833-33261
5	13092-16176	12	33262-25854
6	16177-19448	13	35855-39162
7	19449-22297		

Geringen bericht, 5195
Gründliche an- und aufforderung, 4964, 5082
Kurtzer doch nöthiger, 4965
Gründe für die nothwendigkeit, 19523
Gründe und ursachen, 4735
Gründliche an- und aufforderung, 4964, 5082
Gruendliche anweisung, 6151
Gründlicher unterricht, 5784, 9333
Gruendliches zeugnüss, 6152
Grumbo, giant, 32931
Grundforschende fragen, 35475
Grundlegung zum thätigen, 29965
Grundregeln der deutschen, 18993
Grundregeln der gesellschaft, 28642
Guaging epitomized, 21618
Gualdo, J. Philadelphia, Nov. 21, 1769, 11280
Guard, Theodoredela see **Ward, Nathaniel, 1570-1653**
Guard against extremes, 10640
Guardian of freedom. New Year's verse, 28780
Gubernatocial collection, 19416
Güldene A.B.C., 6513
Gueldene aepffel, 5603
Gueldenstaedt, Johann Anton, 1745-1781. Short account, 21123
Güldin, Samuel. Unpartheyisches zeugnüss, 5196
Guénée, Antoine, 1717-1803. Letters of certain Jews, 28781
Guenin, ————. Freemasons march, 33649
Guerard, Benjamin
   Message, 19252
   dispute with Greene, 18219?
Guide for the doubting, 1787-88, 2191
   or counsellor, 27075
      to Christ, (1714) 1716, (1735) 3962, (1742) 5067
      to eternal glory, (1702) 1101, (1757) 8065, (1759) 8521
      to heaven, (1679) 269, (1683) 342, (1689) 469, (1707) 1296, (1717) 1881, (1796) 30528
      to prayer, (1739) 4443, (1746) 5879, (1797) 33165
      to reason, 27744
      to the English, 6995
      to the health, 35576
      to vestrymen, 5960
Guild, Benjamin
   Boston, Nov. 10, 1785, 18901
   Catalogue, 22545
   New select catalogue, 21868
Guild, Ebenezer. Advertisement, 30524
Guildhall, Bristol, 13847
Guilford, Frederick North, 2d earl see **North, Frederick, 2d earl of Guilford, 1732-1792**

Guillotina, (1796) 30269, 30590-91, 31173, (1797) 31978-79, (1798) 33562
Guillow, Francis, petition, 33005
Guilt of innocent blood, 15872-73
Guion, Jeanne Marie see **Guyon, Jeanne Marie Bouvières de La Mothe, 1648-1717**
Guirey, William
   Funeral sermon, 37558
   History of episcopacy, 35577
Gulliver revived, (1787) 20670-72, (1792) 24727, (1795) 29387, (1797) 32740
Gulliver's travels, 26239, 29599
Gulston, Ralph, licence to, 3715
Gunter, Edmund, 1581-1626, line described, 20709, 24790, 27706, 32840, 35734
Gurley, John Ward. Address, 37560
Gurnall, William, 1617-1679. Christian in compleat armour, 12062
Gurney, David. Sermon, 25573
Gurney, John, 1715-1770. Two epistles, 17968
Gurney, Joseph, 1744-1815.
   Trial of Frederick Calvert, 10919
   Whole proceedings, 27076
   transcribes sermons, 33217
Gurney, Thomas, 1705-1770. Easy and compendious system, (1789) 21869, (1792) 24370, (1799) 35578
Gurney's brachygraphy, 24370
Gustavus Vasa, a tragedy, 26559, 26704
Gustavus Vasa the deliverer, (1778) 15749, (1791) 23224, (1792) 24049
Gustavus Vassa see **Equiano, Flaudah**
Gustine, Dr. ————, chairman of meeting, 25263
Gute kind, 30525
Guthrey, William. Sermon, 5197
Guthrie, William, 1620-1665
   Christian's great interest, (1701) 977, (1796) 30526-27, (1797) 32217
   Sermon, 5197?
   Short treatise, 3034
Guthrie, William, 1708-1770. New system, (1793) 25574, (1794) 27077, (1795) 28782
Guy, Pierre, signs capitulation, 14540
Guyon, Jeanne Marie Bouvières de La Mothe, 1648-1717
   Worship of God, 21870
   life, 6498
Guyse, ————, preface by, 4240, 22477
Gwatkin, Thomas. Letter (to clergy), 12408
Gwinett, Ambrose, adventures, (1784) 18505-507, (1786) 19695, (1795) 28294, (1798) 33418, (1800) 37561
Gyles, John. Memoirs, 4021-22
Gymnast, Christopher. Paxtoniade, 9685-86

H

H. see **Hockley,** ——
H., A. Deplorable state, 2214
H., C. see **Hall, Clement**
H., E.
Great love, 2747
Letter (to Rogers), 16326
H., E., M.A. Present way, 6328
H., F. see **Harrison, Francis**
H., G. I saw the other day, 11281
H., I. Faction, a sketch, 15356
H., J., letter to, 12978
H., J. N. Country man's help, 5961
H., N. Almanac see **Almanacs (Hobart)**
H., P.
Sermon, 25575
Small sketch, 25576
H., S.
Guide to heaven, 30528
see also **Hume, Sophia, 1701-1774**
H., S. J. see **Honeywood, St. John, 1763-1798**
Habermann, Johann, 1516-1590
Christlich gebät-buch, 27078
Christliche morgen- und abend-gebäter, (1759)
8360, (1764) 9687, (1776) 14794, (1788) 21124,
(1790) 22546, (1795) 28783, (1796) **30529**
Grosse gebet-buch, 7014
Kleines Christlich, 8870, 9131
Habitant des Kaskaskia. Invitation, 12421
Hackett, Elizabeth, d. 1781, death, 17281
Hackley, Levi. Almanacs see **Almanacs (Hackley)**
Hades look'd into, 1899
H . . ds . . n's speech, 9144
Haeghoort, Gerard. Keten der goddelyke, 4250
Händel, Georg Friedrich, 1685-1759
Anthem for Christmas, 27087
Te deum, 21130
Water music, 33837
discourses on, 32580
oratorio by, 29215
Hagar in the desert, 19032, 22547
Hagen, P. A. von. Funeral dirge, 37009
Haggar, Henry. Order of causes, 3171
Hahn, John. Observations, 33831
Hail Columbia!, 33899
Hail patriots all, 33832
Hainous nature, 1601, 1626
Hair powder, 29915
Hairbrain, Dick, character of, 13051
Hake, Samuel
To the publick, 14095
letter (from Leigh), 12830

Halbert, Henry. Last speech, 9996
Hale, Alexander. Account of the births, 13542
Hale, David. Almanac see **Almanacs (Hale)**
Hale, David, of Phila. U. S. register, 27983
Hale, David, 1765-1837. Oration, 37562
Hale, Enoch, 1753-1837
Essential divinity, 35583
Spelling book, 35579
ordained, 16803
Hale, James, ed. Sermon, 19149
Hale, John, 1636-1700
Mass. election sermon, 360
Modest enquiry, 1050, 12063
Hale, John, fl. 1795. Statement, 28788
Hale, Jonathan, letter (from Balch), 5735
Hale, Sir Matthew, 1609-1676
Affectionate epistles, 22548
Great audit, 6327
Some necessary, (1728) 3035, (1733) 3663, (1736)
4023, (1759) 8361
Sum of religion, 4524
extracts from, 6478
Hale, Moses, d. 1779. Sermon, 12409
Hale, Thomas. To the friends, 17181
Hales, Mathew see **Hale, Sir Matthew, 1609-1676**
Half Town, speech by, 28886
Half-way covenant, 11171-72, 11236
Halhed, Nathaniel Brassey, 1751-1836
Calculation, 28789, 31877
Testimony of the authenticity, (1795) 28790-91,
(1796) 30126, 30530, (1797) 31877
letter (from Williams), 31639
Haliburton, William. Effects of the stage, 24371
Halket, Sir Peter, regiment of, 7630
Hall, ——, captain of teaship, 12696, 12913
Hall, Aaron, 1751-1814
Oration, 21125
Sermon, 22549
Hall, Alexander. Account of the births, 12526
Hall, Clement. Collection of many, 7015
Hall, Daniel, ordained, 33960

VOL.	ITEMS	VOL.	ITEMS
1	1-3244	8	22298-25074
2	3245-6623	9	25075-28145
3	6624-9891	10	28146-30832
4	9892-13091	11	30833-33261
5	13092-16176	12	33262-25854
6	16177-19448	13	35855-39162
7	19449-22297		

Hamilton, Sir W., travels of, 31692
Hamiltons versus Eaton, 32223
Hamlet, prince of Denmark, 26559, 27692
Hamlin, Amos. Republic of reason, 32224
Hamlin, Jabez, d. 1791, death, 23458
Hamlin, William, engraver, 37951
Hammer, ———,
  Card, 10849, 11198
  reply to, 11199
Hammet, William
  Appeal to the truth, 24377
  Rejoinder, 24378
  connection with Phillips, 31007
Hammett, John, 1679-1773
  Printed sheet, 4365
  Promiscuous singing, 4366
  Vindication, 2877
Hammon, Briton. Narrative, 8611
Hammon, Jupiter
  Address to the Negroes, 20400
  Essay, 16298
  Evening's improvement, 17969
  Winter piece, 17554
Hammond, George
  correspondence with Jefferson, 27924, 27927, 29754-55
  letter (from Randolph), 27892
Hammond, John, 1663-1749, death, 6333
Hammond, William. Advice, 11676
Hamond, Sir Andrew Snape, 1738-1828. Map of the bay, 25581
Hampden. The alarm, no. I-V, 12799-803
Hampshire county, Mass. Sermons on various, 35583
Hampton, Samuel. Longitude, or the art, 22554
Hampton, Wade. To the citizen, 27092
Hancock, Capt. ———, oration before, 34587
Hancock, Rev. ———, hand of fellowship, 5902
Hancock, Ebenezer, ordained, 3913
Hancock, John, 1671-1752
  Continuatio supplementi, 2641
  Gaining of souls, 6153
  Lord's ministers, 3913
  Prophet Jeremiah, 3778
  Rulers should be, 2340
  Sermon, 2748
  death, 6810, 6956
  hand of fellowship, 5902?
Hancock, John, 1702-1744
  Danger of an unqualified, 5198
  Discourse, 5199
  Examiner, 5200-201
  Instability, 4251
  Memorial, 4367
  ordained, 2748
Hancock, John, 1737-1793
  Discours, 14736
  Oration, 13230, 13314-17, 14097
  Proclamation, (1780) 16855, (1781) 17217, (1782) 17593-94, (1783) 18024-25, (1784) 18591-93, (1787) 20507, (1788) 21336-39, (1789) 21946-47, (1790) 22652-54, (1791) 23549-50, (1792) 24519-20, (1793) 25778-80
  Several assemblies, 14583
  Speech, 25790
  address to, 24540
  absent from Congress, 20088
  approves law, 19424
  approves resolve, 16863-66, 17219-23, 17596
  approves Thanksgiving proclamation, 17386
  death, 25563, 26248
  dedication to, 14444, 17183, 17557, 17970, 18521,

  20408, 21136, 21879, 22560, 23431, 24384, 24962, 25589, 26084, 26104
  denied pardon, 14184-86
  funeral, 25214, 25280
  ignorance of, 13840
  letter to, 15636
  life, 21886, 26234-35
  owner of brig, 10317
  portrait, 15450, 17070
  pres. Congress, 14532, 14534, 14545, 14548, 14550, 14562-66, 14578, 14583, 15123, 15132-34, 15137, 15151, 15155-58, 15161-64, 15166-67, 15169, 15173, 15178, 15648, 15650, 15662, 15664, 15675, 15686
  pres. Provincial congress, 13415, 13417-19, 13421-22, 14216-20
  satire on, 16697, 35400
  sermon before, 16753, 17114, 17450, 18526, 21360, 21713, 22506, 23741, 24841
  speaker Mass. House, 16364-68, 16370, 16856-61
Hand, Edward, 1744-1802
  Address, 32348
  reports on Conn. expenses, 18838
  reports on Penobscot expedition, 19312
Hand-in-hand fire company. Rules, 17634
Handbuch für meine freunde, 27189
Handel, Georg Friedrich see **Händel, Georg Friedrich, 1685-1759**
Handleidinge, 27988
Handschuh, Johann Fr., tr. Todt als eine seligkeit, 7604
Handwercksmann see **Franklin, Benjamin, 1706-1790**
Handwercksmann in Philadelphia. Kurtze verteidigung, 6174
Handwerksmann in Germanton see **Saur, Christoph**
Handy, Hast. Inaugural dissertation, 23427
Hanger, Gabriel, marriage, 6856
Hanly, Thomas, letters patent, 3454
Hanmer, John. Observations, 39082
Hannah, Robert. Catalogue of the books, 31068
Hannum, John, accounts, 19171,
Hansford, ———. Letters (to Webster), 31593
Hansford, Theodosius. Debates, 34935
Hanson, Alexander Contee, 1749-1806
  Considerations, 19698
  (ed.) Laws of Maryland, 20483
  Political schemes, 18517
  Remarks on the proposed, 20403, 21131
  To the General assembly, 18518
  To the members, 18519
  claim presented to, 32385
Hanson, Elizabeth, captivity, 2996, 7160, 16721
Hanson, John, fl. 1724, wife's captivity, 2996, 7160, 16721
Hanson, John, fl. 1782
  Proclamation, 17762-63
  pres. Congress, 17393, 17769-70
Hanson, Thomas. Prussian evolutions, 14098
Hanway, Jonas, 1712-1786. Travels, 35585
Hapless orphan, 25584

Happiness, a characteristic poem, 13652
    and pleasure, 12297
    of a free, 27200
    of a people, 214, 8151
    of rewarding, 7798-99
    of the blessed, 8559
Happy child, 28798
    effects, 14805
    family, 37752
    man, 15847, 18520
    ship-carpenter, 28799
    tawny Moor, 30242
    voyage, 19106
    waterman, 35297
Hard, Isaac M., clerk of meeting, 13817
Hard way, 156
Harden, Richard, reply to, 3352
Hardenbergh, Jacob R., d. 1791?, death, 23811
Hardenbrook, Abel. To the independent, 11677
Hardie, James, 1760 (ca.)-1826
    Account of the malignant, 35586
    American remembrancer, 28800
    Impartial account, 37576
    (ed.) New and complete, 34316
    Philadelphia directory, (1793) 25585, (1794) 27089
    Principles of the Latin, 21132, 27088
    (ed.) Selectae e Veteri, (1787) 20226, (1795) 28272, (1796) 30069
    Short account, 27090
Harding, Elisha, ordained, 6293
Harding, Robert, supplies Gen. Gage, 14505
Harding, Seth, authorized to locate lands, 38877
Harding(e), John
    claim, 26314-15
    relief for widow of, 38823
Hardwicke, Philip Yorke, earl of, 1720-1790
    Speech, 7676
Hardy, Sir Charles
    Proclamation, 7974-75
    Speech, (1755) 7512, (1756) 7739, (1757) 7976
    You are hereby, 7737
    address to, (1755) 7451, 7513-14, (1756) 7740, (1757) 7977
Hardy, Samuel, 1636-1691. Guide to heaven, (1679) 269, (1683) 342, (1689) 469, (1707) 1296, (1717) 1881
Hardy, Samuel, 1758-1785
    reports on accounts, 19293
    reports on Conn. expenses, 18838
    reports on Denning's letter, 19299
    reports on Indian affairs, 19294
    reports on Penobscot expedition, 19312
    reports on sundry motions, 19307
    reports on supplies, 19308
Hare, Francis, 1671-1740
    Difficulties, 6329
    sketches Hebrew poetry, 9514
Hargrave, Francis, 1741-1821. Argument, 13318
Hargrove, John
    Sermon, 37577
    letter to, 35657
Harington, Henry, 1727-1816. Damon & Clora, 27091
Harison, Francis see **Harrison, Francis**
Harison, George. City of New-York, ss., 11284
Hark, from the tombs, 37642
Harker, Ahimaaz. Companion for the young, 10921
Harker, Samuel
    Appeal from the synod, 9491
    Predestination, 8874

    reply to, 7151, 9073, 9849
Harlequin (schooner), at Baltimore, 18076
Harlow, Lawrence
    Account of the conversion, 26971, 28801
    Bericht von der bekehrung, 30536
Hamar, Josiah, 1753-1813
    court of enquiry, 23905
    expedition, 23474, 25665-71, 28907
Harmon, Martin, d. 1798, death, 34512
Harmon, Nathaniel. Poetical sketches, 30537
Harmonia Americana, 23446
    coelestis, 35179
    selecta, 21893
Harmonie der evangelium, 14021
Harmonist's companion, 28255, 31792
Harmony between the Old, 13219
    of Maine, 26636
    of the divine, 11978
    of the gospels, 246, 9348
Harper, J. A. United States repository, 37578
Harper, Robert Goodloe, 1765-1825
    Address from Robert Goodloe Harper, 28802, 30538-40
    Address to the people, 27092
    Bystander, 37074
    Case of the Georgia, 35587-88
    Motion, (Dec. 31, 1795) 31359, (Feb. 9, 1797) 32978, (June 5, 1798) 34722, (July 3, 1798) 34723, (July 6, 1798) 34724, (Dec. 12, 1798) 34725, (Mar. 10, 1800) 38788
    Observations, 32226-27, 33841-43
    Report of the secretary, 23783
    Short account, 33838
    Speech, (1797) 33844, (1798) 33839-40, (1799) 35589, (1800) 37579
    correspondence with Nicholas, 35972
Harpur, Robert, secy. N.Y., 21308
Harrington, Timothy, d. 1795
    Century-sermon, 7020
    Peaceable temper, 8612
    Prevailing wickedness, 7680
    colleague ordained, 25952
    death, 31287
    hand of fellowship, 9593
    installation, 6153
    pastor in Lancaster, 17143
    preface by, 29555
Harris, ——, judge, 29646
Harris, Benjamin, case against, 31671
Harris, Caleb. Map of the state, 28803
Harris, Harding, engraver of maps, 28803
Harris, Henry. Sermon, 1544, 1608
Harris, James. Account of the births, 12526, 13542
Harris, Matthias. Sermon, 7909
Harris, Raymund. Scriptural researches, 22555
Harris, Thaddeus Mason, 1768-1842
    Anniversary ode, 37543
    (ed.) Beauties of nature, 38583
    Charge, 28804
    Clear and practical, 24751, 31113
    Constitutions of the ancient, 33303
    Dirge, 31283
    Discourse addressed to the religious, 35590
    Discourse delivered at Bridgewater, 32228
    Discourse delivered at Dorchester, 37332, 37581
    Discourse delivered at the public, 33845
    Few notices, 33846
    Fraternal tribute, 37582
    Hymn sung, 32914
    Ignorance, 32229
    Masonic emblems, 30541-42

Masonick eulogy, 27093
Massachusetts magazine, 30774
Natural history, 25586
New Year's wish, 30543
Selected catalogue, 25587
Sermon, (1797) 32230, (May 9, 1798) 33847, (Sept. 13, 1798) 35592, (Oct. 10, 1798) 35591
Triumphs of superstition, 22556
hand of fellowship, 32078
ordained, 27180
writes on Masonry, 24052
Harris, Walter, 1761-1843
Discourse, 35593
ordained, 21809
Harris, William, d. 1791, death, 2210
Harris, William, 1765-1829. Sermon, 28805, 35594
Harris, William Wager, case against, 31671
Harrison, ———, case in court, 31667
Harrison, Benjamin
Proclamation, 18242
War office, Nov. 14, 1776, 15192
letter (from Washington), 30392
Harrison, Francis
To Mr. A. C., 3547
To the right worshipful, 3779, 3848
case against, 3848
letter (from Campbell), 3512
Harrison, P., draws map, 5063
Harrison, R. Introduction to the art, 22615
Harrison, Ralph, 1748-1810
New edition, with corrections, 33849
Rudiments of English grammar, (1787) 20404, (1795) 28806, (1798) 33848-49, (1800) 37585
Harrison, Richard. Reasons in support, 24730
Harrison, Robert H., secy. to Washington, 15633
Harrison, W., engraver, 38995
Harrison, William, fl. 1785-1841. Circular; Philadelphia, 14th May, 37586
Harrison (brig), arrival at Boston, 10317
Harry Heedless, history of, 20851, 31514
Hart, ———, sheriff in London, 14164
Hart, ———, conversion, 19457
Hart, Benjamin. Pastoral letter, 14410
Hart, John, d. 1731, death, 3517
Hart, Joseph, of Bucks co., accounts, 18103, 19167
Hart, Joseph, 1712-1768
Divine songs, 21877
Hymns, &c., (1782) 17555, (1787) 20405-406, (1799) 35595
conversion, 19457?
Hart, Levi, 1738-1808
Christian minister, 12065, 20407
Description of a good, 19699
Duty and importance, 12411
Earnest desire, 19700
Excellence of scripture, 14099
God the unfailing, 24382
Importance of parental, 24381
Important objects, 21133
Liberty described, 14100
Perfection of saints, 19701
Religious improvement, 33850, 37587
Resurrection, 19702
Sermon, 21876
War between Michael, 22558
ordained, 9418
Hart, Oliver, 1723-1795
America's remembrancer, 23428
Dancing, 15848
Gospel church, 23429

Humble attempt, 19033
Sermon, 15357
death, 30466, 31115
Hart, Sarah, d. 1788, death, 22480
Hart, Thomas, d. 1727, death, 2974
Hart, William, 1713-1784
Brief remarks, 11285
Discourse, 4966
Faithful servant, 6154
Few remarks, 8363
Holy scriptures, 5203
Letter (to a friend), 7876
Letter (to Hopkins), 11678
Letter (to Paulinus), 8613
Letter (to Whitaker), 12066
Remarks on a late, 8614
Remarks on President, 12067
Scriptural answer, 12412
Sermon, 11286
daughter's death, 22480
death, 18994
letter (from Bellamy), 8540
reply to, 8880, 11686, 11938, 12811
vindicates Dana, 8504
Hart, William, fl. 1794. One hundred dollars, 27094
Hartegan, James, trial, 11683
Hartford
At a numerous meeting, 36857
By-laws of the city, 21134, 32231
Having received, 35596
Hartford and New Haven turnpike company. We the subscribers, 37588
Hartford county. Testimony of the North, 5605
Hartford library company. Constitution, 32232
Hartford selection, 36382
Hartley, ———, speaks in Parliament, 14092
Hartley, Thomas, 1707-1784
Auszug aus einer rede, 10637
Discourse on mistakes, (1759) 8309, 8364, (1765) 9998
extracts from, 10505
Hartley, Thomas, 1748-1800
Observations, 21878
Treatise, 27765
letter referred to, 31429
Hartmann, Henrich. Wahre brantewein-brennerey, 33851
Hartwell, Jonas, ordained, 26063
Hartwell, Josiah, d. 1791, death, 25492
Hartwick, Johann Christopher, dedication to, 6285
Harvard college
Catalog, (1674) 188, (1683) 343, (1697) 783, (1700) 912, (1727) 2878, (1730) 3286, (1733) 3665, (1736) 4024, (1739) 4368, (1742) 4967, (1745) 5606, (1748) 6155, (1751) 6690, (1758) 8147, (1761) 8875, (1764) 9689, (1767) 10638, (1770) 11679, (1773) 12804, (1776) 14795, (1779) 16299, (1782) 17556, (1785) 19034, (1788) 21135, (1791) 23430, (1794) 27096, (1797) 32233, (1800) 37589

VOL.	ITEMS	VOL.	ITEMS
1	1-3244	8	22298-25074
2	3245-6623	9	25075-28145
3	6624-9891	10	28146-30832
4	9892-13091	11	30833-33261
5	13092-16176	12	33262-25854
6	16177-19448	13	35855-39162
7	19449-22297		

Catalogus bibliothecae, 22559
Catalogus librorum, 2432, 12805
Continuatio supplementi, 2641
Extracts from the laws, 37590
Following pages, 37591
Harvard university in Cambridge, 32235, 37592
Humble proposal, 55
Laws of Harvard, 22561, 33854
Order of the exercises, (1791) 23432, (1792)
    24383, (1793) 25588, (1794) 27097, (1795)
    28808, (1796) 30544, (1797) 32235, (1798) 33852,
    (1799) 35597, (1800) 37592
Pietas et gratulatio, 8877
Proposals made, 689
Quaestiones, (1655) 41, (1660) 59, (1664) 92,
    (1665) 102, (1666) 108, (1668) 123, (1669) 140,
    (1674) 189, (1675) 199, (1676) 213, (1678) 248,
    (1679) 270, (1680) 285, (1681) 303, (1682) 315,
    (1684) 361, (1687) 428, (1688) 443, (1689) 470,
    (1690) 511, (1692) 596, (1781) 17184, (1782)
    17558, (1783) 17971, (1784) 18522, (1785) 19036,
    (1786) 19704, (1787) 20409, (1788) 21137, (1789)
    21880, (1790) 22562, (1791) 23433
Testimony of the president, 5409
Theses, (1642) 9, (1643) 12, (1647) 22, (1670)
    148, (1686) 406, (1693) 638, (1730) 3287,
    (1731?) 3428, (1732) 3548, (1733) 3428, 3666,
    (1734) 3780, (1735) 3914, (1736) 4025,
    (1737) 4143, (1738) 4252, (1739) 4369,
    (1740) 4525, (1741) 4726, (1742) 4968,
    (1743) 5204, (1744) 5408, (1745) 5607,
    (1746) 5786, (1747) 5963, (1748) 6156, (1749)
    6330, (1750) 6514, (1751) 6691, (1752) 6852,
    (1753) 7021, (1754) 7208, (1755) 7429, (1756)
    7681, (1757) 7910, (1758) 8148, (1759) 8365,
    (1760) 8615, (1761) 8876, (1762) 9133, (1763)
    9402, (1764) 9690, (1765) 9999, (1766) 10329,
    (1767) 10639, (1768) 10922, (1769) 11287, (1770)
    11680, (1771) 12068, (1772) 12413, (1773) 12806,
    (1776) 14796, (1777) 15358, (1778) 15849, (1779)
    16300, (1780) 16794, (1781) 17183, (1782)
    17557, (1783) 17970, (1784) 18521, (1785) 19035,
    (1786) 19703, (1787) 20408, (1788) 21136, (1789)
    21879, (1790) 22560, (1791) 23431, (1792) 24384,
    (1793) 25589, (1794) 27098, (1795) 28809, (1796)
    30545, (1797) 32234, (1798) 33853, (1799) 35598,
    (1800) 37593
Harvard university in Cambridge, commonwealth
    of Massachusetts, (1794) 27097, (1795) 28808,
    (1796) 30544, (1797) 32235, (1800) 37592
Harvard university in Cambridge; the order, (1792)
    24383, (1793) 25588
Harvest home, (1795) 28566, (1799) 35297, (1800)
    37149
Harvey, Miss ———, selections from, 32741, 36191
Harvey, Ann, accessory, 10919
Harvey, Edward
    Manual exercise, (1766) 10330, (1774) 13319-23,
    (1775) 14101-107, 14109, (1776) 14797, 15083,
    (1777) 15359, (1780) 16795, (1794) 27099
    New manual, (1769) 11288, (1773) 12807, (1775)
    14108, 14594
Harvey, James. Letter (to his brother), 23434
Harward, Thomas
    Electuarium, 3549
    Fulness of joy, 3550
Harwood, John Edmund, 1771-1809
    Ellen, arise, 33855
    sings in duet, 30242
    sings sea song, 28503-504
Harwood, W., clerk Md. House, 30747

Haselden, Thomas, d. 1740. Seaman's daily assist-
    ant, 15360, 16301
Hasell, William Soranzo, 1780-1815. Alfred, an his-
    torical, 37594
Haseltine, Ebenezer. Warning to young, 25590
Hasenclever, Francis. Francis Hasenclever in dem,
    12808
Haskell, Jonathan, petition, 34740
Haslewood, Francis. Sermon, 3172
Hassan, dey of Algiers, treaty with U.S., 31409-410
Hastings, Elizabeth, life of, 10609, 11275, 11654,
    18355
Hastings, Jonathan. Post-days, 28323
Hasty pudding, (1796) 30022-24, (1797) 31771-73,
    (1798) 33373-74, (1799) 35152
Haswell, Anthony, 1756-1816
    Almanacs see Almanacs (Haswell)
    Interesting stories, 30546
    Little scholar's pretty, 28810
    Oration, (Aug. 16, 1799) 35599, (Dec. 27, 1799)
    37595
    Patriotic exultation, 35601
    School lessons, 28811
    family records, 35602
    meridian of printing office, 19000
Haswell, Lydia Baldwin, 1759-1799. Record of the
    family, 35602
Haswell's Federal and Vermont register, 32236
Hatborough, Penna. Charter, laws, and catalogue
    of books, 21138
Hatchets to hew, 1214
Hatchway, Jack. Card, 11199
Hatchway, Tom
    Card, 10848
    reply to, 10849
Hatfield, Mass.
    Covenant for reformation, 1390
    Regulations ascertaining, 30547, 32237
Hatterfly, Josiah. Robbery, 16796
Hatton, Aly ben see Aly ben Hatton
Hatton, Ann Julia Kemble. Songs of Tammany,
    27100
Hatzar-Maveth, 2769
Hauer, Elizabeth, trial, 34040
Hauer, John, trial, 34040
Haunted cavern, 30953-54
    priory, 27101
    tower, 26776
Hausam, Anthony. Depositions, 14110
Hautereve, ———, receives express, 27156
Haven, Elias, 1714-1754
    Christ's agony, 4969
    Youthful pleasures, 4727
Haven, Jason, 1733-1803
    Charge, 32078
    Discourse, 11681
    Duty of thanksgiving, 8366
    Sermon, (1761) 8878, (1764) 9691, (1769) 11289,
    (1771) 12069, (1774) 14111-12, (1783) 17972,
    25592, (1796) 30548
    hand of fellowship, 27180
    reprints sermon, 35417
Haven, Samuel, 1727-1806
    Disinterested benevolence, 37597
    Election sermon, 19705
    Funeral discourse (Stevens), 23435, 24385
    Guard against, 10640
    Joy and salvation, 9403
    Oration, 35603
    Poetic miscellany, 33856
    Preaching Christ, 8616

VOL.	ITEMS	VOL.	ITEMS
1	1-3244	8	22298-25074
2	3245-6623	9	25075-28145
3	6624-9891	10	28146-30832
4	9892-13091	11	30833-33261
5	13092-16176	12	33262-25854
6	16177-19448	13	35855-39162
7	19449-22297		

Henderson, Joseph, claim, 26308, 26311
Henderson, Matthew, received into communion, 21662
Henderson, Richard. Bladensburgh, 2 August, 1775, 14113
Hendrickson, Daniel. Groote geluksaligheid, 8149
Henfrey, Benjamin
   Philadelphia, Feb. 1795, 28822
   Plan with proposals, 32245
Hening, William Waller, 1768-1828. New Virginia justice, 28823, 35611-12
Henley, David, court martial, 15752, 16139, 16626
Henley, Samuel, 1740-1815
   Candid refutation, 13326
   Sermon, 12072, 13327
Henly, ——. Speech, 7676
Henrich Miller, buchdrucker, 10690
Henrich Millers des buchdruckers, 15911
Henry II, mistress of, 30563
Henry Frederick, duke of Cumberland, 1745-1790
   adultery, 11898
   letters (from Brutus), 11587
Henry, George. All the male, 15508
Henry, John, of N. Y.
   actor, 25941?
   manages theatrical company, 19986
Henry, John, 1750-1798
   reports on accounts, 20062?
   reports on commerce, 20053?
   reports on Indians, 20052?
   reports on new states, 20058?, 20769?
   reports on supplies, 19308?
Henry, Matthew, 1662-1714
   Church in the house, 22564
   Communicant's companion, (1716) 1813, (1723) 2433, (1731) 3429, (1798) 33868
   Directions for daily, 1882, 3037
   Extracts, 13328
   Method for prayer, 4527
   Plain catechism, 1883
   Two prayers, 24842
   commentary on Bible, 17843, 20960, 21680, 22347
   commentary on Psalms, 26659, 31810
Henry, Patrick, 1736-1799
   Sir, as the committee, 14600
   express to, 15836
Henry, William, accounts, 19183
Henry, William, chairman committee, 16470
Henry and Emma, 21723, 23235
Henry Bernhard Koster, 811
Henry (sloop), given to city, 14589
Henry Villars, 36127
Henry's cottage maid, 31017
Henshaw, Benjamin, condolences with, 21162
Henshaw, Samuel. Articles of impost, 19476
Hepburn, John. American defence, 1678
Herb bill, 22280
Herbert, ——, reply to, 33834
Herbeson, Massey, deposition of, 25080, 26540, 36779
Hercules (ship), wrecked, 32886, 38570-71
Herderen wachter-stem, 2991
Here's the pretty girl, 32273
Heresie and hatred, 641
Heresy detected, 17357
Hermes see **Rodney, Caesar Augustus, 1772-1824**
Hermit, a poem, (1753) 7084, (1767) 10760, (1784) 18673, 18767, (1786) 19881
Hermit of New-Jersey, 11297
Hermit of the forest, (1789) 21884, (1795) 28827, (1798) 33871, (1800) 37610-11
Hermit; or the justice, 25601
Hermit, or the unparalled, 28297-98, 31823

Herodias, 12440
Hero's philosophy, 8133-34
Herr, Franz
   Kurze erklärung, 22566
   reply to, 22648, 23545
Herrliche erscheinung, 9518
Herrn Pyrlaei, 4879
Heron, P., petition, 34756
Heron, Robert, tr. Widow of the village, (1797) 32421, (1798) 34045, (1799) 35769
Herrick, Claudius, 1775-1831. Oration, 37612
Herschel, Sir William, 1738-1822, discoveries of, 25574, 27077, 28782
Herty, Thomas. Digest of the laws, 35617, 37613
Herumträgers der Pennsylvanische, 11946
Hervey, James, 1714-1758
   Aspasio vindicated, 27114
   Beauties of Hervey, (1794) 27115, (1796) 30558, (1797) 32249
   Collection of the letters, 9136
   Considerations, 9695
   Cross of Christ, 8368, 27116
   Letter (to brother), 23440?
   Meditations among the tombs, 27117, 28828
   Meditations and contemplations, (1750) 6515-16, (1778) 15851, (1789) 21885, (1791) 23440, (1792) 24394, (1794) 27118, (1795) 28829, (1797) 32250, (1798) 33872
   Ministry of reconciliation, 8618
   Remarks, 6854
   Time of danger, 8150
   Treatise, 9137
   death, 8484-85
   defended, 9100, 12635?
   letters (from Sandeman), 9825
   life, 9711
   remarks on, 8469, 10075
   sentiments of, 8297
Herzlicher gruss, 30559
Heskith, Thomas. Divine providence, 1455
Heston, Edward. To the public, 36433
Het, René, defendant, 3019
Heth, William, 1750-1807, ed. Infallible cure, 33271, 33873-74
Heusch, A. Henry de. The teacher, 30560
Hewes, Joseph. Collection of occurrences, 14115
Hewitt, James, 1770-1827
   Book of songs, 27542
   Federal constitution, 34113
   How happy, 35618
   Songs, &c., 32482
   When the old, 34115
   Wounded hussar, 37614
   adapts music, 27321
   arranges Cherubini, 28412
   composes music for Ode, 29444
Hey, ——, examination of, 13626
Hey, John. Fulness of times, 32384
Hey dance to the fiddle, 32261
Heydelbergische catechismus, 10924

VOL.	ITEMS	VOL.	ITEMS
1	1-3244	8	22298-25074
2	3245-6623	9	25075-28145
3	6624-9891	10	28146-30832
4	9892-13091	11	30833-33261
5	13092-16176	12	33262-25854
6	16177-19448	13	35855-39162
7	19449-22297		

Heyliger, William, d. 1794, death, 26843
Heylsaame onderwysinge, 7240
Heylyn, Peter. Pocket commentary, 8369
Heysham, William, lottery drawing under inspection of, 12192
Heywood, Joshua, b. 1761. Oration, 32251
Hezekiah, a Christian, 1622
Hibbard, John. Letter (to Seaver), 28830
Hibernia (brig), lawsuit, 19164, 22053
Hibernia fire company. Articles, 19918
Hibernian society. Constitution, 37615
Hichborn, Benjamin, d. 1817. Oration, (1777) 15363, (1784) 18527
Hickok, David, d. 1800, death, 37862
Hicks, John. British and American register, (1773) 12869-70, (1775) 13440-41, (1776) 14889, (1777) 15442, (1778) 15912, (1779) 16374, (1780) 16869
Hicks, John B. Inaugural dissertation, 25602
Hicks, Whitehead
  Copy of the address, 14296
  Mayor, New-York, 12486
  To the inhabitants, 11776
  affidavit before, 14624
  letter (from Tryon), 14298
  letter to, 14297
  mayor N. Y., 13473
Higginson, ———. Speech to the House, 15073
Higginson, John, 1616-1708
  Cause of God, (1663) 80, (1722) 2363, (1774) 13445
  Deplorable state, 2214
  Our dying, 407
  Testimony to the order, (1701) 978, (1717) 1941, (1772) 12626
  death, 1405
  preface by, 656
Higginson, Nathaniel, address to Queen, 1332
Higginson, Stephen, 1743-1828. Writings of Laco, 21886
High attainment, 1125
  esteem, 356
  importance, 35133
  value, 16315
Highest dwelling, 1535
Highland reel, 27441-42, 32611
Highwayman's soliloquy, 19584-85
Hildebrand, Johannes, 1679-1765
  Gespräch, 7210
  Mistisches und kirchliches, 5205
  Ruffende wächter stimme, 5965
  Schrifftmässiges, 5206
  Wohlgegründetes, 5207, 5966
  letter (from synod), 5284
Hildrop, John, 1725-1756. Essay, 23441
Hill, Capt. ———, arrival in Marblehead, 14163
Hill, Abraham, ordained, 5044
Hill, Ebenezer, ordained, 23666
Hill, Hannah. Legacy for children, (1714) 1679, (1715) 1743, (1717) 1884
Hill, Henry, petition of, 32990-91, 34741
Hill, Jeremiah. Trial, 25603
Hill, John. Young secretary's guide, (1708) 1354, (1713) 1609, (1717) 1885, (1718) 1957, (1727) 2879, (1730) 3288, (1750) 6517
Hill, John, d. 1732. De par son excellence, 1498
Hill, John, 1716-1775. Old man's guide, 14116
Hill, Sir Richard, 1733-1808. Address to persons, 10644
Hill, Rowland
  Glorious displays, 32384

recommends Bible, 26651, 30068
Hill, Samuel
  Complete set, 22567
  engraver, 22663, 23166, 23186, 27203, 28428, 29426, 30392, 33188, 36052, 38583
Hill, Thomas. Young secretary's guide, 3288
Hill, Timothy, d. 1781, death, 17378
Hill, William, petition, 38867
Hillard, Isaac. To the public, 32252
Hillary, ———, medical practice of, 30574
Hiller, Joseph
  Charge, (1780) 19417, (1781) 17188
  inducts officers, 35180
Hillhouse, James, fl. 1716-1737
  Sermon, 2225
  defended, 4188
  remarks on, 4190
Hillhouse, James, 1754-1832
  report by, 32967
  witnesses contract, 34849
Hillhouse, Rachel, d. 1716, death, 2225
Hillhouse, William, 1757-1833. Dissertation, 21887
Hilliard, Joseph, d. 1843. Reciprocal duties, 33875
Hilliard, Timothy, 1746-1790
  Duty of a people, 13329
  Paradise promised, 19037
  Sermon, (1785) 19038, (1787) 21143, (1788) 21142, 21888
  death, 23085
  ordained, 12289
Hilliard Magna, 10002
Hillier, Richard. Liberty, 37616
Hills, John. Plan of the city, 32253
Hills, Joseph. Supplement to the book, 30
Hills, William, preface by, 26571
Hillsborough, Wills Hill, viscount, 1718-1793
  letter to, 10968, 11310
  letters (from Bernard), 11178-79, 11331-32
Hindman, William, 1743-1822
  Address, 35619
  message referred to, 33054-55, 34799
  reports on sundry motions, 19307
  reports on supplies, 19308
Hindmarsh, Robert, 1759-1835. Short account, 24395
Hine, Homer, 1776-1856. Oration, 27119
Hinsdale, Theodore
  Heresy detected, 17357
  reply to, 17156
Hinsdell, Ebenezer, ordained, 3723
Hint to Freemasons, 35620
Hints and instructions, 15518
Hippocrates, rules of, 30574
Hippocrates Mithridate. Some serious thoughts, 6366
Hiram: or the grand, 10925
Hirst, Elizabeth, d. 1716, death, 1803
Hirst, Grove, d. 1717
  Catalogue of books, 1958
  death, 1873
  wife's death, 1803
Hirst, Samuel, d. 1727, death, 2913, 2947-48, 2956
Hirte, Tobias
  Freund in der noth, 25604
  Gemeinnützige sammlung, 30561
  Neues auserlesenes, 24396
  Prophetische muthmassungen, 27566
Hirten-lieder, 4971
Hirzel, Hans Kasper, 1725-1803. Rural Socrates, (1776) 15226, (1792) 25061, (1800) 38923
His Britannic majesty's speech, 17552

VOL.	ITEMS	VOL.	ITEMS
1	1-3244	8	22298-25074
2	3245-6623	9	25075-28145
3	6624-9891	10	28146-30832
4	9892-13091	11	30833-33261
5	13092-16176	12	33262-25854
6	16177-19448	13	35855-39162
7	19449-22297		

Hoare, Prince, 1755-1834
  Favorite ballad, 27126
  Hey dance, 32261
  No song, no supper, (1792) 24400, (1793) 25611-
    12, (1794) 27125
  Sailor boy, 25613
  Sighs, 37760
  Spoil'd child, 30568-69
Hobart, ——, trial judge, 32712
Hobart, Nehemiah, 1648-1712
  Absence of the comforter, 1887
  Almanac see **Almanacs (Hobart)**
Hobart, Noah, 1706-1773
  Attempt to illustrate, 10003
  Civil government, 6692
  Congratulatory letter, 7430
  Excessive wickedness, 10926
  Ministers of the gospel, 5968
  Principles of congregational, 8342, 8370
  Second address, 6693
  Serious address, 5208, 6158
  Vindication of the piece, 8880
  death, 13759
  letter (from Wolcott), 9041
  remarks on, 8614, 10621
  reply to, 6081, 6283, 6637, 8749, 11826
Hobbies, a favorite song, 33231
Hobbs, Josiah, d. 1784, death, 18468
Hobby, John, memorial, 33061
Hobby, William, 1708-1765
  Faithful minister, 5209
  Happiness of a people, 8151
  Inquiry into the itinerancy, 5610
  Self-examination, 5787
  Soldier caution'd, 5969
  Vindication of the protest, 6694
  letter, (from Breck) 6645, (from Cleaveland)
    5563, (from Henchman) 5608, (from J. F.)
    5590
Hobby, William J., d. 1841
  Contract, 35111
  Oration, 33884, 35625
Hobson, Elizabeth, case of, 25012
Hobson, John. Prospectus, 35626
Hoch-deutsch Americanische calender see **Alma-
  nacs (Hoch-deutsch)**
Hoch-deutsches A.B.C., 28843
Hoch-deutsches Lutherisches A.B.C., (1775) 14171,
  (1789) 21812, (1790) 22494, (1794) 27128
Hoch-deutsches reformirtes A.B.C., (1794) 27129,
  (1795) 28844, (1798) 33886, (1800) 37630
Hochedlen herrn guvernör, 9631
Hoch-edler grafen, 14407
**Hochmann von Hochenau, Ernest Christoph, 1661-
  1721**
  Glaubens-beckanntniss, 37631
  Glaubens-bekenntniss, 5213
Hochreutiner, Johann Jacob, d. 1748. Schwanen
  gesang, 6160
Hockley, Richard
  Advertisement, 7828, 8780
  proprietary officer, 9799
Hocus pocus, 28540
Hodder, James. Arithmetic, 2026
Hodgdon, Alexander. Commonwealth of Massachu-
  setts, 23557
Hodge, Allen & Campbell. New York, Mar. 1, 1790,
  22573
Hodges, Benjamin, inducts officers, 35180
Hodges, John. Brief apology, 2016

Hodgkinson, Mrs. ——, sings song, 25630, 30931,
  32261
Hodgkinson, John, 1767?-1805
  Let Washington be, 37633
  Narrative of his connections, 32263
  delivers address, 34301
  introduces song, 25613
  portrait, 37747-48, 37757, 37766
  sings song, 32261, 33855, 34489, 35762, 36248
  speaks Ode, 28444
Hodgson, ——, defendant, 31669
Hodgson, Edward. Trial of Renwick, 23445
Hodgson, John, d. 1781. Trial of William Wemms,
  11683
Hodson, James
  Divinity of the redeemer, 27130
  Young Christian's introduction, 27131
Höchstmerkwürdige prophezeyung, 8620
Hoell, David, dedication to, 15060
Hölty, ——. Invitation, 33892
Hoffman, Christian. Longevity, 33887
Hoffman, Josiah Ogden. Oration, 21147
Hoffmeister, ——, selections from, 31182
Hog, James, preface by, 33834
Hogan, Edmund
  Pennylvania state trials, 27132
  Prospect of Philadelphia, 28845, 30571
Hohburg, Christian, 1607-1675. Kurtzer und erbau-
  licher, 6161
Hoisington, Joab, application for pay, 14932
Holbach, Paul Henri Dietrich, baron d', 1723-1789
  Christianity unveiled, 28846
Holcombe, Henry, 1762-1824
  Discourse, 25615
  Sermon, (1791) 25616, (1793) 25617, (1800) 37634
Holcroft, Thomas, 1745-1809
  (tr.) Alphonso and Dalinda, (1787) 20385, (1788)
    21106, (1799) 35537
  (tr.) Caroline, 34126
  Deserted daughter, 28847, 30572
  Dying prostitute, 28977
  (tr.) Essays on physiognomy, 27203
  (tr.) Life of baron Frederic, (1789) 22187, (1792)
    24861
  (tr.) Life of baron Frederick, (1793) 26278,
    (1796) 31313, (1799) 36446-47
  Love's frailties, 27133
  Road to ruin, 24402
  (tr.) Sacred dramas, 32179
Holden, A. Deposition, 34787
Holden, Oliver, 1765-1831
  American harmony, 24403
  Dedicatory poem, 27134
  (ed.) Laus deo, 32363
  Massachusetts compiler, 28848
  Massachusetts musical magazine, 25618
  Modern collection, 37980
  Plain psalmody, 38276
  Sacred dirges, 37635
  Union harmony, 25619, 30573

VOL.	ITEMS	VOL.	ITEMS
1	1-3244	8	22298-25074
2	3245-6623	9	25075-28145
3	6624-9891	10	28146-30832
4	9892-13091	11	30833-33261
5	13092-16176	12	33262-25854
6	16177-19448	13	35855-39162
7	19449-22297		

Mourner's friend, 25625
Succession of generations, 24406
Homes, John. Catalogue of books, 32268
Homes, William, 1663-1746
Brief and plain, 2881
Discourse, 2122
Good government, 5972
Proposals, 3553, 13336
Homeward bound, 32926
Honest American. To the respectable public, 13679
Honest and solid, 35631
Honest farmer; a drama, 26644
Honest freeholder of King's county. No placemen, 14401
Honest freeholder of Westchester. No placemen, 14400
Honest man's interest, 2482, 2749
Honesta parsimonia, 2245
Honestus
Anecdote of a certain, 11293
Seventeenth jewel, 32269
see also **Austin, Benjamin, 1752-1820**
Honesty, Obadiah. Remonstrance, 7914-15
Honesty shewed, 19716
Honeycomb, William. The bee, 10006
Honeycomb, with choicest, 35632
Honeyman, James, d. 1750
Falses on all sides, 3040
Faults on all sides, 3039
Sermon, 2750, 3669
Honeywood, St. John, 1763-1798
Address, 19043
Poem, 30579-80, 37644
Honorable Henry Gardner, esq., treasurer, (1780) 16852, (1782) 17595
Honoribus laureatus, 37659
Honourable Mr. Sedgwick's political, 37645
Honour and happiness, 1803
of Christ, 3124
of the gout, 3574, 3690
Honouring God, 2017
Honours due, 10937
Honours of Christ, 4498
Hood, Samuel Hood, viscount, 1724-1816
Letters to the ministry, 11176
reply to, 11133-34
Hoofmaster, ———, selections from, 34516
Hook, James, 1746-1827
Alone by the light, 30581, 32270
Cottage in the grove, 30582
Donna Donna Donna Della, 32271
He loves his winsome, 32272
Here's the pretty girl, 32273
Hither Mary, 25626
Hoot awa, 32274
Hours of love, 35633
If a body, 32276
I'm in haste, 32275
Indigent peasant, 25627
Linnet, 32277
Listen, listen, 30583
Lucy, 27136
Ma belle coquette, 25628
Sweet lilies, 25629
Sweet little girl, 30584
The tear, 30585
Wedding-day, 25630
What can a lassy do, 32278
When Lucy was kind, 30586
Where Liffey rolls, 32279
Where's the harm, 32280
William of the ferry, 30587

selections from, 34516
Hooke, Ellis. Instructions for right spelling, 5186
Hooker, Asahel. Divine sincerity, 32820
Hooker, John, 1729-1777
Christ's ministers, 9700
Vindication of divine, 14802
Hooker, Nathaniel, 1737-1770
Invalid instructed, 11294
Religious improvement, 10334
Six discourses, 12077
death, 11811
Hooker, Samuel, 1635-1697
Connecticut election sermon, 979
Righteousness rained, 230
Hooker, Thomas, 1586-1647
Poor doubting Christian, 5214-15
life, 724, 727
Hookey, Betsy, d. 1782, death, 19443
Hookey, Lydia, d. 1782, death, 19443
Hoole, Charles, tr. Sententiae, 1045, 2427
Hoop petticoats, 2341
Hooper, Hezekiah, ordained, 29468
Hooper, M. Lamentations, 690
Hooper, Robert, petition, 33015, 34753, 38852
Hooper, Robert, recants, 14194
Hooper, Thomas Woodbridge, d. 1816. Oration, 30588
Hooper, William, tr. Memoirs, 29068, 35813
Hooper, William, 1674-1767
Apostles, 4974
Christ the life, 4731
Jesus Christ, 4975
On the truth, 5973
Sermon, 9405
Hoornbeek, Jacob. Waare deught, 7432
Hoot awa, 32274
Hope, Adam. Account of the burials, 10739
Hope (brig), proceedings concerning, 38328
Hope, a poem, 37834
a rhapsody, 13337
for the heathen, 32438
in death, 24486
of immortality, (Welch) 22263, (Wigglesworth) 16681
of the righteous, 2210
Hopkins, ———, excerpts from, 31959
Hopkins, ———, memorial of, 31370
Hopkins, Rev. ———, remarks on, 13325
Hopkins, Rev. ———, **of Springfield.** Charge, 5172
Hopkins, Benjamin. Catalogue, 27137
Hopkins, Daniel, engraver of music, 17997, 19753
Hopkins, Daniel, 1734-1814. Sermon, 37646
Hopkins, Lemuel, 1750-1801
Democratiad, (1795) 28853-54, (1796) 30589, 31173
Echo, 28855
Guillotina, (1796) 30269, 30590-91, (1797) 31978-79, (1798) 33562
New Year's verses, 28472
Political green-house, 35634, 36133
excerpts from, 31959?
Hopkins, Roswell, secy. Vermont, 33115

VOL.	ITEMS	VOL.	ITEMS
1	1-3244	8	22298-25074
2	3245-6623	9	25075-28145
3	6624-9891	10	28146-30832
4	9892-13091	11	30833-33261
5	13092-16176	12	33262-25854
6	16177-19448	13	35855-39162
7	19449-22297		

Frailty of man, 25637
Hotchkiss, Frederick William, 1762-1844
On a merciful, 28859
On national, 25638
Oration, 37651
Sermon, 37652
Houdet, René. Treatise, 30594
Houdin, Michael Gabriel. Et sicut illud, 37653
Hough, Simon
Alarm to the world, 24410
Letter to anybody, 28860
Sign of the present, 35641
Houghton, Asa. Almanac see **Almanacs (Houghton)**
Hours of love, 35633
Housatonic Indians
conference, 3916
desire gospel, 3867
gospel among, 7916-17
influence of Hollis, 5288
House, George, petition, 31453
House lots for sale, 19390
of delegates on a report, 19552
of mourning, 1127
of representatives apprehending, 20513
of wisdom, 33490-92
that Jack built, (1786) 19718-20, (1795) 28861, (1796) 30596, (1800) 37655-56
Houseal, B. M., tr. Manifesto, 15834
Housman, Hannah Pearsall. Power and pleasure, 7524
Houston, ——, portrait of Washington, 35365
Houston, Elizabeth, robbed, 18687
Houston, William Churchill, 1745-1788
reports on Indian affairs, 19294
reports on sundry motions, 19307
reports on supplies, 19308
Hovey, Ebenezer, b. 1726. True ministers, 30597
Hovey, Ivory, 1714-1803
Duty and privilege, 6333
Farewell sermon, 11687
Sermon, 27139, 28862
Hovey, James, wife's death, 12215
Hovey, John, ordained, 5316
Hovey, Lydia, d. 1771, death, 12215
How, James, tr. Narrative, 36608
How, Nehemiah, 1693-1747. Narrative, 6162
How, Samuel
Simplicity, 12418
Sufficiency, 9410
How and why, 1810
can I forget, 29502
Christ, 5870
God wills, 6955
happy, 35618
to grow rich, 27606, 28863
to live, 1695
Howard, Rev. ——
Charge, 24023
hand of fellowship, 35630
Howard, Bezaleel, 1753-1837
Sermon, (1790) 23451, (1793) 27140, (1799) 37657
ordained, 19038
Howard, Elizabeth, d. 1777, death, 15367
Howard, Henry, history, 22876
Howard, John, 1726?-1790, ode to, 21905, 26542-43
Howard, John, d. 1785, death, 18920
Howard, John, d. 1789, death, 21899
Howard, Martin, d. 1781
Defence of the Letter, 10012

Letter from a gentleman, 10011
Howard, Sir Robert, 1626-1698. Committee, or the faithful, 8883
Howard, Simeon, 1733-1804
Charge, 24023?
Christians no cause, 16306
Discourse, 15367
Sermon, (1773) 12813, (1778) 16307, (1780) 16800, (1791) 23452
moderator convention, 22417
ordained, 10580
Howard, Thomas. History of the seven, 31176, 32285-86
Howe, ——
address to, 15493
besought, 15095
head of Cerberus, 13985
ode to, 29997
reply to proclamation of, 15632-33
sermon before, 14952
Howe, Abraham, d. 1779, death, 19429
Howe, Jasper, ordained, 12745
Howe, Jemima, captivity, 24343
Howe, John, ed. Substances of General, 15752
Howe, John, preface by, 19587
Howe, Nathaniel, ordained, 23218
Howe, Perley, ordained, 30935
Howe, Richard, viscount, 1726-1799
Declaration, 14782
Proclamation, 14783
letter (from Drayton), 14742
on the Delaware, 15839
Howe, Robert, court martial, 17772
Howe, Solomon, 1750-1835
Comprehensive abridgment, 34964
Divine law, 37658
Honoribus laureatus, 37659
Worshipper's assistant, 35643
Howe, Sir William, 1729-1814
As linnen and wolen, 14781
Declaration, 14782
Letter, 15168
Orders to be observed, 14084
Proclamation, (1775) 14085-87, 14089, (1776) 14783, (1777) 15324-34, (1778) 15816-23
address to, 15493?, 15951-53
association proposed by, 14088
besought, 15095?
commands Phila. Loyalist battalion, 15352
destroys prisoners, 16180-82, 16692
head of Cerberus, 13985?
invades Pennsylvania, 15510
letter (from Drayton), 14742
ode to, 29997?
officers commanded by, 15335, 15824, 15835
provision for prisoners, 16112
regulations issued by, 15349
reply to, 20382
reply to proclamation of, 15632-33?

VOL.	ITEMS	VOL.	ITEMS
1	1-3244	8	22298-25074
2	3245-6623	9	25075-28145
3	6624-9891	10	28146-30832
4	9892-13091	11	30833-33261
5	13092-16176	12	33262-25854
6	16177-19448	13	35855-39162
7	19449-22297		

into the rules, 6312, 24289
into the scripture, 7650
petition, 61
proposal, 55
representation, 1477
submission, 37484
Humdrum, Humphrey see **Lewis, Joseph**
Hume, David, 1711-1776
History of England, 28867, 30602
Life, 15853, 15914
history continued, 31214, 32854, 34564-65
proposals for reprinting his History, 11984
reply to, 22387
Hume, Sophia, 1701-1774
Caution to such, 12079
Exhortation, 5974, 6165-66
Extracts from divers antient, 10337
Humilis confessio, 6500
Humming bird, or collection, 23456
Humming bird, or new, 33913
Humours of Phelim, 9106
Humphreys, Daniel. Philadelphia, Jan. 14, 1775, 14476
Humphreys, Daniel, 1740-1827
Appeal to the Bible, 32290
Bible needs, 30603
Compendious American, 24415
The contrast, 30604-605
Observations, 30606
Plain attempt, 37661
Humphreys, David, 1752-1818
Aristocracy, 28171-72
Essay on the life, (1788) 21160, (1794) 27144, (1795) 28868, (1798) 33914
Glory of America, 17978
Miscellaneous works, 22578
Oration, 21896
Poem addressed, 16801
Poem on industry, 27145, 31173
Poem on the happiness, (1786) 19723, (1788) 21161, (1790) 22579
Poems, 21897, 28869
Remarkable story, 25261
Select poems, 20420
dedication to, 32945
excerpts from, 23246?, 31959
mistakes, 244343
Humphreys, James. Philadelphia, Jan. 2, 1775, 14122
Humphreys, Thomas. Marriage, 6856
Humphreys, Whitehead, encounter with Matlack, 17146
Humphreys, William, ed. Songs, 29120
Hundert und neunzehnte, 23198
Hundertjährige calendar, 37662
Hunn, Nathanael, 1708-1749. Welfare, 5975
Hunt, Asa, ordained, 12316
Hunt, Holloway Whitfield. Sermon, 30607
Hunt, Isaac, 1751-1809
Advertisement, 10338
Birth, parentage, 10339-40
Continuation of exercises, 10016-21
Dialogue, 10022
Humble attempt, 10014
Letter from a gentleman, 9701
Looking-glass, 9702-703
Political family, 14123
Substance of an exercise, 10015
lampoon on, 10143
Hunt, John, d. 1775

Bill in the chancery, 10654
Following remonstrance, 15498
Sermon, 12080, 12419
death, 14802
ordained, 12318
Hunt, Joseph, d. 1786, death, 19874
Hunt, Richard, constable, 36092
Hunter, ———, collector of excise, 19900
Hunter, Andrew, ordained, 5872
Hunter, Henry, 1741-1802
(tr.) Botanical harmony, 32795
(tr.) Paul and Virginia, 31148, 31150, 36267
Sacred biography, 27146, 28870
(tr.) Vindication of divine, 32797
Hunter, John, 1728-1793
Treatise on the blood, 30608
Treatise on the venereal, 20421, 23457
Hunter, N., letters from, 38463
Hunter, Robert, d. 1734
Androboros, 1681
Ordinance for altering, 1772
Ordinance for regulating, 1481-82, 1848
Proclamation, 1523, 1990
Speech, (1712) 1575, (1713) 1639, (1715) 1773, (1716) 1846
address to, 1642
Hunter, Samuel, accounts, 18706
Hunter, Thomas, 1712-1777. Reflections, 16802
Hunter, William, M.D., letter (from Bayley), 17092
Hunter, William, of Kentucky. Ohio navigator, 33915-16
Hunter, William, of Williamsburg. Catalogue of books, 13252
Hunter, William, 1774-1849. Oration, 28871
Hunting of Chevy Chace, 35300
Huntingdon, Selina Hastings, countess, 1707-1791
Letters (to Wesley), 12821
chaplain's death, 11662, 11812
letter (from Milton), 25825
selections from, 32741, 36191
Huntington, Dr. ———, reply to, 27632
Huntington, Asahel, 1761-1813. Sermon, 37663
Huntington, Benjamin, introduces copyright bill, 22192
Huntington, Bethiah, d. 1799, death, 35442
Huntington, David, 1745-1812
Conferences on baptism, 20422
Infant baptism, 21898
Two conferences, 27147
ordained, 14806
installation, 34613
Huntington, Eliphalet, 1737-1777. Freeman's directory, 10930
Huntington, Enoch, 1739-1809
Discourse, 23458
Happy effects, 14805
Life and character, 32293
Oration, 37664

VOL.	ITEMS	VOL.	ITEMS
1	1-3244	8	22298-25074
2	3245-6623	9	25075-28145
3	6624-9891	10	28146-30832
4	9892-13091	11	30833-33261
5	13092-16176	12	33262-25854
6	16177-19448	13	35855-39162
7	19449-22297		

epitaph, 13268
signers of address to, 13767, 14194
secret correspondence, 12690
sermon before, 10569, 11071, 11289, 11613, 12256, 12502, 13053
Hutchinson, William, 1732-1814. Spirit of Masonry, 37671
Hutton, Charles, 1737-1823. Course of bookkeeping, 22582
Hutton, J., engraver, 26819
Huyman, ———, withdraws credit, 19109
Huzza for the Constellation, 36246
Hyde, Alvan, 1768-1833
  Purpose of God, 32820
  Sermon, 32299
Hyde, Dana, petition, 37255
Hyde, Elijah. Impartial relation, 35650
Hyde, Ephraim, ordained, 10766
Hyde, Samuel, d. 1763, death, 9608
Hyder Aly (ship), at Philadelphia, 17849
Hylton, ———, defendant, 29888
Hymen's recruiting, 39064
Hymn and prayer-book, 28939
  composed by the late, 23079
  composed by the reverend, 22146
  ode and dirge, 38041
  on the death, 37673
  on Washington, 37674
  to be sung, 38100
  to Jesus, 5335
  book for the children, 9527
Hymne des marseillais, 26106
Hymns and divine songs, 23632
  and odes, 37675
  and poems, 22473
  and sacred poems, 4624
  &c. composed, (1782) 17555, (1787) 20405-406, (1799) 35595
  and spiritual songs (Alline), 28169, 31714
  and spiritual songs (Baptists), 10233, 12660
  and spiritual songs (Dixon), 26767
  and spiritual songs (Proud), 24599
  and spiritual songs (Watts), (1742) 5087, (1743) 5307, (1752) 6945, (1761) 9036, (1767) 10797, (1769) 11520, (1771) 12273-74, (1772)

12605-606, (1773) 13068, (1775) 13835-36, (1778) 16165, (1781) 17099, 17423, 19399, (1782) 17475, 17791, 19444, (1785) 18930, (1787) 20231-32, 20858, 20963, (1789) 21687, 22245, (1790) 23042, (1791) 23193, (1792) 24105-106, 24990-91, (1793) 25181, 25184-85, (1794) 26656-58, 28036, (1795) 28279, 28281, (1796) 30072, (1797) 31811, (1798) 33413, (1799) 35192-94, (1800) 39027-29
  and spiritual songs (Wesley), 17426
  being a selection, 24748
  composed on several, 4706
  composed on the death, 38400
  for the amusement, 23765
    instruction, 29519
    use of the Society, 32946
  for those, 17425
  for youth, 24812
  illustrated, 19726
  in prose, (1786) 19493, (1788) 20945, (1797) 31770, (1798) 33372
  on different spiritual, (1786) 19562, (1788) 21002, (1792) 24195
  on different subjects, 25304
  on various occasions, 25493
  on various subjects, (Allen) 28167, (Beeman) 24082
  particularly designed, 31899
  performed at the anniverary, (1794) 28108, (1795) 29053, (1796) 30145
  suited, 20229-30
  to be sung, 37961
  used, 23730
Hypocrite, a comedy, 28293
Hypocrite unmask'd, 33360

VOL.	ITEMS	VOL.	ITEMS
1	1-3244	8	22298-25074
2	3245-6623	9	25075-28145
3	6624-9891	10	28146-30832
4	9892-13091	11	30833-33261
5	13092-16176	12	33262-25854
6	16177-19448	13	35855-39162
7	19449-22297		

I

of ministers, 3027
of parental, 24381
of religion, 16170
of righteousness, 13278
of salvation, 12709
of the colonies, 10471
    divine presence, 8299, 8473
    early and proper, 28362
    rising generation, 28687-88
Important advices, 27152
  case, 4008
  connection, 11316
  documents, 34817
  doubts, 12335
  duties, 23994
  duty, 2867
  examination, 10035
  intelligence from St. John's, 14127
    just received, 16111
    Providence, 4 o'clock, 19418
    received, 17087
  objects, 21133
  state paper, 27003
  state papers, 29760
Imported in the last, 11190
Imposition of inoculation, 2222
Impositions on the sixth, 35944
Impossibility of sinners' coming, 34258
Impostor detected, 30119-20
Impotency of sinners, 12616
Imprecation against the enemies, 1294
Improved method, 19763
Improvement of the doctrine, 7550
Improvement of the mind, 26440
Imrie, David
  Letter (to a gentleman in Edinburgh), 7685-86, 9147
  Schreiben an seinen freund, 7687
In Assembly, Dec. 12, 1776, 14986
  Dec. 24, 1776, 14988
  Thursday, Dec. 5, 1776, 14985
  Tuesday, Dec. 2, 1783, 18092
In committee, Dec. 14, 1774, 13539
  July 14, 1779, 16470
  Albany, 28157
  chamber, May 16, 1776, 15013
  Lancaster, 14817
  of inspection and observation, 14316, 15011
  of inspection, observation, 14820
  of safety, Apr. 12, 1776, 14904
    Mar. 27, 1778, 16118
    Apr. 10, 1779, 16553
    Apr. 14, 1781, 17387
    Apr. 16, 1783, 18044
    Cambridge, 14194-95
    Exeter, (Apr. 14, 1780) 17014, (Nov. 1, 1782) 17763, (Nov. 14, 1783) 18248
    for the state of New York, (Nov. 7, 1776) 14928, (Mar. 1, 1777) 15476
  of supplies, 14196
In Congress, May 17, 1775, 14561
  June 12, 1775, 14564
  Oct. 12, 1775, 15676
  Dec. 6, 1775, 14567-68
  Jan. 17, 1776, 15128
  Mar. 6, 1776, 15131
  Mar. 23, 1776, 15135-36
  Apr. 3, 1776, 15138-39
  May 6, 1776, 15140
  May 15, 1776, 15141, 15649

May 21, 1776, 15143
July 4, 1776, 15155-57, 15159-64, 15650
July 19, 1776, 15165
Aug. 26, 1776, 16128
Aug. 28, 1776, 15166
Sept. 16, 1776, 15167
Oct. 3, 1776, 15169-70
Oct. 29, 1776, 15171
Nov. 23, 1776, 15172
Dec. 11, 1776, 15175-76
Dec. 17, 1776, 15651
Dec. 23, 1776, 15177
Dec. 30, 1776, 15178
Dec. 31, 1776, 15179
Feb. 15, 1777, 15653
Feb. 24, 1777, 15654
Feb. 25, 1777, 15655
Mar. 25, 1777, 15657
Apr. 1, 1777, 15658
Apr. 4, 1777, 15659
Apr. 7, 1777, 15660, 16574
Apr. 11, 1777, 15661
Apr. 29, 1777, 15668
May 12, 1777, 15669
May 14, 1777, 15670-71, 16123
June 10, 1777, 15672
Aug. 6, 1777, 15674
Sept. 6, 1777, 15675
Oct. 8, 1777, 15677
Nov. 1, 1777, 15678-79
Dec. 19, 1777, 16112
Feb. 3, 1778, 16113
Feb. 5, 1778, 16115
Mar. 2, 1778, 16116
Apr. 23, 1778, 16119
May 2, 1778, 16120
May 18, 1778, 16124
May 22, 1778, 16125
May 27, 1778, 16126
June 6, 1778, 16127
Aug. 14, 1778, 16580
Sept. 26, 1778, 16130
Oct. 8, 1778, 16131, 16581
Nov. 9, 1778, 16122
Nov. 24, 1778, 16136
Jan. 2, 1779, 16564
Jan. 9, 1779, 16565
Jan. 13, 1779, 16566
Mar. 2, 1779, 16567
Mar. 5, 1779, 16568
Mar. 6, 1779, 16569
Mar. 15, 1779, 16570
Mar. 23, 1779, 16571-73
Apr. 12, 1779, 16647
Apr. 14, 1779, 16575
May 22, 1779, 16576
June 29, 1779, 16577-78
July 30, 1779, 16579
Oct. 28, 1779, 16582
Nov. 25, 1779, 16583

VOL.	ITEMS	VOL.	ITEMS
1	1-3244	8	22298-25074
2	3245-6623	9	25075-28145
3	6624-9891	10	28146-30832
4	9892-13091	11	30833-33261
5	13092-16176	12	33262-25854
6	16177-19448	13	35855-39162
7	19449-22297		

Feb. 25, 1780, 17020
May 2, 1780, 17021
June 28, 1780, 17022
Oct. 3, 1780, 17023
Oct. 30, 1780, 17024
at Exeter, 14901
at New York, 22979
Baltimore, (Jan. 14, 1777) 15652, (Feb. 26, 1777) 15656
Friday, (June 9, 1775) 14562, (Nov. 3, 1775) 14566
Monday, (June 12, 1775) 14563, 14565, (June 30, 1777) 15673
Saturday, Mar. 16, 1776, 15132-34
the delegates of the United Colonies, 15129
the delegates of the United States, 15180, 15681
Wednesday, Apr. 3, 1776, 15137
In consequence of a conference, 12693
In convention, (June 5, 1779) 16386, (June 16, 1780) 16846
In convention at Newcastle, 14732
at Poughkeepsie, 21312
for the state of Pennsylvania, 14980-83
of the representatives, 14931-32
present, 112 members, 15200
Saturday, Mar. 25, 1775, 15201
In Council, Nov. 7, 1775, 14198
Dec. 1, 1775, 14200
June 16, 1779, 16657
Jan. 3, 1780, 16928
Jan. 19, 1781, 17410
Mar. 26, 1781, 17411
May 4, 1781, 17288
29th Dec., 1788, 21554
January the 16th, 1797, 33127
8th of January, 1798, 34938
a proclamation, 14199
In Council of safety, Nov. 27, 1776, 15022
Dec. 3, 1776, 15024
Mar. 11, 1777, 15524
Lancaster, (Oct. 21, 1777) 15529, (Nov. 7, 1777) 15530-31
Philadelphia, Oct. 14, 1776, 15017
Nov. 14, 1776, 15021
Dec. 2, 1776, 15023
Dec. 8, 1776, 15025
Dec. 13, 1776, 15026
Dec. 23, 1776, 15027
Jan. 1, 1777, 15520, 15651
Jan. 22, 1777, 15522
In Council of war, June 4, 1778, 16044
June 9, 1778, 16045
Aug. 2, 1778, 16046
Aug. 17, 1778, 16047
Mar. 11, 1779, 16497
Mar. 12, 1779, 16498
Oct. 2, 1779, 16499
June 16, 1781, 17342
East-Greenwich, 17343-44
In Council, Philadelphia, Apr. 9, 1777, 15525
July 9, 1777, 15526
July 28, 1777, 15527
Sept. 4, 1777, 15528
Feb. 3, 1779, 16439
May 28, 1779, 16440
July 8, 1779, 16441
Oct. 13, 1779, 16442
Oct. 26, 1779, 16443
June 1, 1780, 16929
Feb. 15, 1781, 17286

Mar. 10, 1781, 17287
In Council, Watertown, 14197
In Council, Windsor, 16653
In der Assembly, 15966
In General assembly (Pennsylvania) see under Pennsylvania. Laws; or under Pennsylvania. General assembly. Resolve
In General assembly, June session, 27612-14
September session, 22843
Windsor, 36617
In obitum magnae, 7845
In Provincial congress, Apr. 15, 1775, 14220
Aug. 8, 1775, 14308
at Trenton, 14283
at Watertown, 14221
Cambridge, Oct. 22, 1774, 13415
Oct. 26, 1774, 13416
Dec. 5, 1774, 13417
Dec. 6, 1774, 13418-19
Dec. 10, 1774, 13421-22
Feb. 14, 1775, 14216
Feb. 16, 1775, 14217
Wednesday, Dec. 7, 1774, 13420
Concord, Mar. 31, 1775, 14218
Concord, Apr. 12, 1775, 14219
Exeter, 14275-77
New York, May 29, 1775, 14299
May 31, 1775, 14300
June 2, 1775, 14301
June 3, 1775, 14303
June 7, 1775, 14304
July 7, 1775, 14306
Aug. 29, 1775, 14310
Sept. 1, 1775, 14311
October 1775, 14312
Dec. 12, 1775, 14313
Mar. 4, 1776, 14933
May 31, 1776, 14934
June 7, 1776, 14935
June 13, 1776, 14936
June 20, 1776, 14937
Watertown, Apr. 23, 1775, 14222
May 1, 1775, 14224
May 5, 1775, 14225-26
May 8, 1775, 14227
May 9, 1775, 14228
May 15, 1775, 14229
June 8, 1775, 14230
June 12, 1775, 14231
June 16, 1775, 14232
June 17, 1775, 14233-34
June 27, 1775, 14235
June 29, 1775, 14236
June 30, 1775, 14237-38
July 9, 1775, 14240
In pursuance of a writ, 14970, 15537
In pursuance of an act, 15484
In seinem leben, 9154
In Senate, Feb. 26, 1781, 17219
July 4, 1782, 17596
Feb. 17, 1787, 20508
Nov. 19, 1788, 21240
Feb. 24, 1790, 22655
June 13, 1791, 23602
Apr. 4, 1792, 24943
Jan. 20, 1794, 27281-82
March the 26th, 1794, 27890
Apr. 4, 1794, 27891
May 12, 1794, 27892
May 23, 1794, 27893
May 29, 1794, 27894

Feb. 9, 1795, 29038
Feb. 10, 1796, 31622
June 4, 1796, 30761
Jan. the 20th, 1797, 33050
March 15th, 1800, 38091
Mar. 22, 1800, 38092
In Senate of the U. S., Dec. 5, 1794, 27895
Jan. 9, 1795, 29722
Mar. 1, 1797, 32967
Mar. 2, 1797, 32968
Apr. 5, 1798, 34813
July 9th, 1798, 34718
Jan. 16, 1800, 38738
Jan. 23, 1800, 38739
Feb. 7, 1800, 38740
Feb. 26, 1800, 38741-42
Mar. 5, 1800, 38743
Mar. 6, 1800, 38744
Mar. 14, 1800, 38745
Apr. 29, 1800, 38746
May 8, 1800, 38747
In Senate of the U. S.; a bill, 38737
In suis non fallitur, 28314
In the committee for Lancaster, 14818
committee of safety, 14315
court, 38083
dead of the night, 30829
House of delegates, Nov. 14, 1785, 19352
Friday, Jan. 11, 1799, 36641
Saturday, Dec. 12, 1795, 29798
Thursday, (Oct. 25, 1787) 20839, (Nov. 28, 1793) 26391
Tuesday, (Nov. 1, 1786) 20105, (Dec. 13, 1796) 31501
House of representatives, Nov. 2, 1775, 14209
Dec. 2, 1775, 14211
Dec. 16, 1775, 14212
Jan. 25, 1777, 15425
Jan. 26, 1777, 15426
May 5, 1777, 15433
Jan. 2, 1778, 15922
Feb. 3, 1778, 15900
Mar. 13, 1778, 15901
Apr. 20, 1778, 15902
June 16, 1778, 15904
June 20, 1778, 15903
Sept. 19, 1778, 15905
Feb. 4, 1779, 16360
Feb. 16, 1779, 16361
Feb. 19, 1779, 16362
Apr. 30, 1779, 16363
June 8, 1779, 16364-65
June 17, 1779, 16638
June 21, 1779, 16366
Sept. 14, 1779, 16367
Sept. 30, 1779, 16368
Oct. 8, 1779, 16369
Oct. 9, 1779, 16370
Nov. 16, 1779, 16389
Dec. 28, 1779, 16390
Jan. 13, 1780, 16856
June 5, 1780, 16857
June 22, 1780, 16858
June 23, 1780, 16859-60
Sept. 25, 1780, 16861
Sept. 29, 1780, 16862
Nov. 13, 1780, 16863
Nov. 27, 1780, 16864-65
Dec. 2, 1780, 16866
Apr. 5, 1781, 17250
June 16, 1781, 17220

June 22, 1781, 17221
June 30, 1781, 17222
Oct. 20, 1781, 17223
Feb. 27, 1783, 18045
June 20, 1783, 18046-47
June 21, 1783, 18048
Feb. 18, 1791, 23553
Dec. 29, 1791, 23603
Dec. 11, 1792, 25878
Mar. 12, 1794, 27896
June 18, 1794, 27283
June 18, 1796, 31095
June 12, 1798, 34065
June 28, 1798, 34066
Dec. 26th, 1798, 35885
Nov. 29, 1799, 36337
Dec. 10, 1799, 35886
In the House of representatives; for the encouragement, 14870
Friday, the 10th, 22199
Monday, 24th August, 22201
of the U. S., Monday, 31365
Thursday, 23883
Tuesday, (July 28, 1789) 22200, (May 8, 1792) 24909
Watertown, Aug. 10, 1775, 14206
In the land of Hibernia, 27153
life of the lady, 18355
name and by the authority, 17657
Senate, Dec. 21, 1793, 26184
In vain, 31129
In what sense, 7161
Inability of the sinner, 12560
Inaugural address of Thomas M'Kean, 38210
botanico-medical dissertation, 29510
dissertation, being an attempt to disprove, 26153
being an attempt to prove, 38514
containing an enquiry, 26140
dissertation on absorption, (Rousseau) 38423, (Wilson) 33233
apoplexy, 34680
camphor, 31935
cataract, 38481
cholera, (Disborough) 33641, (Hosack) 23449
chronic mania, 29990
chronic pneumony, 35177
compression, 25602
cynanche, 33307
digitalis, 37990
dysentery, 26530
fractures, 31832
gangrene, 32289
general dropsy, 25922
hydrocele, 32324
insanity, 26838
intermeittent fevers, 27238
opium, (Handy) 23427, (Seaman) 24775
perspiration, 36780

VOL.	ITEMS	VOL.	ITEMS
1	1-3244	8	22298-25074
2	3245-6623	9	25075-28145
3	6624-9891	10	28146-30832
4	9892-13091	11	30833-33261
5	13092-16176	12	33262-25854
6	16177-19448	13	35855-39162
7	19449-22297		

Indians. Ottawa
    Minutes of debates, 25653
Indians. Pennsylvania
    Inhalt von der verschiedenen conferentzen,
        (1756) 7924, (1757) 7992
    Minutes of a treaty, 8157
    Minutes of conferences, (1756) 7923, (1757) 7920-
        21, (1758) 8156
    Proceedings and treaty, 7925-26
Indians. Six Nations see **Six Nations**
Indians. Southern
    Journal of the congress, 9706
    Treaty held with the Catawba, 7689
Indictment & trial, 27656, 31140
Indigence and nobleness, 37754
Indigent peasant, 25627
Indigorier, 15040
Inducement to right, 8623
Industry and diligence, 1874
        & frugality, 7027
        and sloth, 33926
Indwelling of the spirit, (1739) 4451, (1740) 4641,
        (1741) 4858
Inexcusableness of neglecting, 1372
Infallible cure, 33270-71, 33873-74
Infant baptism, an answer, 3237
        baptism from heaven, (1765) 10119, (1767)
            10722, (1784) 18403
        baptism vindicated, 21898
        seed, 11561
Infants of the faithful, 2907
Infernal conference, (1794) 27249, (1795) 29005,
        (1797) 32403
Infidelity, or the victims, 32746
Infinite importance, 23140
Inflexible captive, 29104
Influence of Christianity, 17073
Influence of civil, 33864
Information and defence, 1841
        for Europeans, 22390
        for immigrants, 28321
        to those, 28411
Ingenieur de campagne, 14678
Ingenious hand
    New and complete guide, 4566
    New complete guide, 5648
Ingenious poet. Real beauty, 12061
Ingersoll, Jared, 1722-1781. Letters, 10342
Ingersoll, Jared, 1749-1822. Act of the legislature,
        30975
Ingersoll, Jonathan, 1714-1778. Sermon, 8888
Ingles, Charles, claim, 36504
Inglis, Charles, 1734-1816
    Christian soldier's duty, 15372
    (ed.) Discourse concerning the evidences, 11618
    Duty of honouring, 16810
    Essay on infant, 10933
    Letters of Papinian, 16311
    Plain truth, 15088-89
    Sermon, 13349, 15373
    True interest, 14809-810
    Vindication of the bishop, 10934
    remarks on, 11437
Inglis, John. Advertisement, 14128
Inglis, John. By the way, 9413
Inhabitant of Baltimore county. Investigation,
        35657
Inhabitant of Boston
    Master and scholar, 20520
        see also **Tompson, Benjamin, 1642-1714**
Inhabitant of Richmond see **Villiers, R.**
Inhabitant of said parish. Short account, 12658

Inhabitant of the state of Maryland see **Wharton,
    Charles Henry, 1748-1833**
Inhabitants of Pennsylvania, 12940
        of the city of New York, 11817
        of the town, 15610
Inhalt von der verschiedenen, 7922, 7924
Iniquity purged, 11299
Injustice and impolicy, 23346, 24292
Inkle
    epistle to, 24822
    poetical letters by, 15724
Inkle & Yarico, (1792) 24200, (1794) 26558, 26782
Innes, Col. ———, brings news, 15323
Innes, Thomas, 1662-1744. Catechism, 23466
Innocency's complaint, 232
Innocent amusement, 30299
        blood, 12094
        victim, 25584
Inoculation of the small-pox, 2332
Inoffensive ministry, 35490
Inordinate love, 5386
Inquiries by the Agricultural, 37935
Inquiry concerning the future, 17977
        concerning the state, 10691
        into the causes and nature, 36678
            causes of suspended, 24409
            causes of the insurrection, 24426
            consequences, 6483
            constitution, 10915
            effects of light, 38666
            effects of spirituous, 20690, 22864-65
            ground and import, 28071
            itinerancy, 5610
            modern, 19617
            modus operandi, 36942
            natural history, 22122
            nature and causes, 22148, 31196
            nature and uses, 4533
            nature, cause, 25526
            nature, obligation, 6337
            nature of true, 12811, 23448
            rights, 10244
            state, 5217
        relating to the extent, 30421
        herein the end, 26228
        whether the scriptures, 11096
Inquisitor, or invisible, 26108, 27653
Ins wasser, 10601
Insanabilia, 1691
Inspected store, 22611
Inspired scripture, 27180
Instability of humane, 4251
Installment law (South Carolina), 20717
Institutes of natural law, 36260
Institution of the Boston, 31851
Institution of the Society, 18788
Institutions of medicine, 21033
Institutions of the Humane, 21157-58
Instruction fetch'd, 2913
Instructions by the commissioners, 10634, 11278
        for assistant, 34452

VOL.	ITEMS	VOL.	ITEMS
1	1-3244	8	22298-25074
2	3245-6623	9	25075-28145
3	6624-9891	10	28146-30832
4	9892-13091	11	30833-33261
5	13092-16176	12	33262-25854
6	16177-19448	13	35855-39162
7	19449-22297		

Irwin, Nathaniel, d. 1812. Sermon, 25654
Irwin, Thomas
   To the public, 12084
   controversy, 12170
Is there not, 13944-52
Isaacks, Jacob, petition, 23919
Isaiah, a new translation, 26662
Isaiah's mission, 2985, 32083
Iscariot, Judas see Judas Iscariot
Isham, Jirah, 1778-1842. Oration, 37691
Ishmael, emperor of Morocco, tyranny of, 905
Isle of man, 2012
Isles of Pines, 127
Israel ben Ader. Chronicle, 7927
Israel, Frederick. Fear God, 23467
Israel, Israel, election opposed, 34672-73
Israel, Samuel
   15 boxes, 38254
   Valuable library, 36107
Israelite indeed, 13391
Israel's mourning, 3031
    triumph, 8871
    true safety, 1198
It being expedient, 15821
It is a disagreeable, 11466
    a fearful, 2737
    agreed between the master, 29503
    agreed between the masters, 18539

   of the Lord's, 4131
   proposed, 14443
Italian convert, 6633, 26601
   lover, 28898
   or the confessional, 32734-38
It's honourable, 2715
Ivernois, Sir Francis d', 1757-1842
   Account of the late, 33927
   Authentic history, 27159
   On the downfal, 33929
   Reflexions, 33928
Ivers, Thomas, d. 1787?
   Commonwealth of Massachusetts, tax no. 4, 18597
   Tax no. 5, 19093, 19795
   death, 20506
Ives, John H. Twenty-four figures, 35658
Ivins, Samuel. Almanac see Almanacs (Ivins)

VOL.	ITEMS	VOL.	ITEMS
1	1-3244	8	22298-25074
2	3245-6623	9	25075-28145
3	6624-9891	10	28146-30832
4	9892-13091	11	30833-33261
5	13092-16176	12	33262-25854
6	16177-19448	13	35855-39162
7	19449-22297		

J

Three practical discourses, 1746, 2887
Token for children, (1700) 914, (1718) 1959, (1728) 3042, (1749) 6339, (1771) 12085-87, (1781) 17196, (1786) 19734, (1792) 24428, (1793) 25655, (1795) 28895, 33931, (1797) 32315, (1799) 35662
Token for youth, 2886
Janeway, John, life, 24427
Jansen, Gen. ——, negotiates with Indians, 7924
Janua coelestis, 6461
January, Peter. Advertisement, 17987
Jan. 7, 1778; when the chimneys, 15831
January 17, 1774; supplement, 13533
Janus, 2758
Janvrin, Elizabeth, d. 1729, death, 3246
Japheth dwelling, 12390, 12767
Japheth yet dwelling, 16272
Jaquelot, Isaac, 1647-1708. Abstract of the history, 1611
Jarossay, R., d. 1800, death, 37126
Jarratt, Devereux, 1733-1801
  Nature of love, 24429
  Sermon, 24430-31
  Sermons, (v.1-2) 25656, (v.3-4) 27161
  Solemn call, 24432
  Thoughts on some, 23468
Jaudon, Daniel, 1767-1826
  English orthographical, 37698
  Short system, 32316
Jarvis, Abraham, 1739-1813
  Charge, 33932
  Discourse, 30636
  consecrated, 33430, 34561
Jarvis, Peter
  Peter Jarvis at the commencement, 35663
  Supplications, 33933
Jauncey, James
  Mr. Jauncey heartily thanks, 11302
  To the freeholders, 11234
  Whereas a paper, 11230
  candidacy, 11228-29, 11263-64, 11293, 11390, 11429, 11447-48
  conduct of, 11223
  letter (from Aristides), 11968, 13121
  present at delivery of note, 13335
Javotte, 35569
Jay, John, 1745-1829
  Address to the people, 21175
  Charge delivered, (1777) 15376, (1793) 25657
  Charge of chief justice, 22587
  Extract of a letter, 14813
  Gentlemen of the Senate, 37699, 38082a
  Gentlemen, I herewith, 38082
  Gentlemen, I now lay, 35923
  Letter (to Harper), 30539-40
  Letters (to Littlepage), 19735-36
  Message, 35928
  Office for foreign affairs, 13th May, 1785, 19318
      July 4, 1785, 19319
      Sept. 19, 1785, 19320
      29th Sept. 1785, 19321
      7th Oct., 1785, 19322
      Oct. 13, 1785, 19324
      20th Oct. 1785, 19325
      6th April, 1787, 20775
  Proclamation, 38076
  Secretary of the U. S. for the Department, 19323
  Speech, 34217
  State of the duties, 19331
  To the independent, 21501

To the inhabitants, 19442
To the respectable, 13680-81
Whole correspondence, 20430
candidacy, 13661, 14756, 15105, 15110, 33275, 33277-78
charge against Clinton, 24859
defended, 34674
delegate to Congress, 13093-94
effigy, 28619
election favored, 28156-57, 29641-42
falsehoods against, 34668
loses election, 24856-57
nominated, 14654, 14927
on committee of correspondence, 13478
praised, 13653
pres. Congress, 16552-53, 16636-39
proclamations on epidemic, 28538
reply to, 16545, 19926, 20462-63, 21465
satirized, 16697
treaty examined, 28527, 28624, 29520, 29535, 29559, 29757, 30255, 31172, 31948
Jealous wife, 8818
Jean Gray, 8889
Jeanne de la Nativité
  Blessed effects, 16811
  Daily conversation, (1741) 4732, (1754) 7218, (1762) 9149, (1767) 10659
  life, 10455
Jeder sein eigener, 6340
Jedidiah, 1126
Jefferies, Capt. ——, arrival in N. Y., 14082
Jefferies, G. Citizen and countryman's, 9718, 32419
Jefferies, George see **Jeffreys, George, 1648-1689**
Jefferson, Thomas
  Act for establishing, 20102
  Appendix to the Notes, 37700-701
  Bill for establishing, 19350
  Correspondence, 27925
  Extract of a letter, 30637
  In Council, Jan. 19, 1781, 17410
  In Council, Mar. 26, 1781, 17411
  Letter (to Hammond), 29754-55
  Notes on the establishment, 18541, 19328
  Notes on the state of Virginia, (1788) 21176, (1794) 27162, (1800) 37702-703
  Rules for conducting, 33043
  Secretary of state to whom was referred . . . the letter, 23001
  Secretary of state to whom was referred . . . the petition, 23919
  Several assemblies of N. J., 14583
  Summary view, 13350-52
  Supplementary notes, 33934
  Test of the religious, 37704-706
  War office, Williamsburg, 16663
  annotates report, 18834
  approves law, 23849
  candidate for president, 37187
  correspondence with Hammond, 27924, 27927

VOL.	ITEMS	VOL.	ITEMS
1	1-3244	8	22298-25074
2	3245-6623	9	25075-28145
3	6624-9891	10	28146-30832
4	9892-13091	11	30833-33261
5	13092-16176	12	33262-25854
6	16177-19448	13	35855-39162
7	19449-22297		

John Nurse, carrier, 13271
John Peter (Indian), murdered, 2782
John Rhea desires, 12536
John Rogers, a servant, 7310, 15068
John Street theatre. By the Old American, 27407
John Wright Stanley's reply, 11476
John and Mary, 34539
Johnson, ———, excerpts from poetry, 23246
Johnson, ———, extracts from, 29926, 31664
Johnson, ———
  reports on accounts, 20059, 20062
  reports on governor's letter, 20057
  reports on new states, 20058, 20769
Johnson, Adjutant ———, letters brought by, 14113
Johnson, Mrs. ———, benefit for, 22722
Johnson, Alfred. Fellowship of the churches, 28749
Johnson, B., engraver, 16205
Johnson, Ebenezer. Short account, 33936
Johnson, Gordon. Introduction to arithmetic, (1792)
  24435, (1793) 25661, (1794) 27163, (1795) 28902
Johnson, Isaac, d. 1750, death, 6799
Johnson, Israel, d. 1787, death, 20892
Johnson, Jacob, 1722-1797
  Animadversions, 7622
  Golden dust, 7220
  Honours due, 10937
  Zion's memorial, 10024
Johnson, Lieut. John. Reward of $10, 38902
Johnson, John, of Charleston. Rape of Bethesda,
  24436
Johnson, John, of Philadelphia. Short account,
  27168
Johnson, John, 1706-1791
  Advantages and disadvantages, (1761) 8891,
    (1764) 9707, (1766) 10345, (1783) 17989, (1790)
    22589, (1793) 25662, (1794) 27164-65, (1795)
    28903, (1796) 30639
  Mathematical question, (1762) 1951, (1789) 21906,
    (1790) 22590, (1794) 27166-67, (1797) 32317
Johnson, John, d. 1765, execution, 10036
Johnson, John Barent, 1769-1803
  Dealings of God, 33937
  Eulogy, 37709
  Oration, 27169
  Sermon, 32318
Johnson, John I. Reflections, [32318a]
Johnson, Joseph. Experimental inquiry, 32319
Johnson, Richard, 1573-1659. Illustrious and re-
  nowned, 36291
Johnson, Samuel, captain Commerce (ship), 27671,
  32804
Johnson, Samuel, 1696-1772
  Christian indeed, 10938
  Demonstration, 8627
  Elementa philosophica, 6859-60
  Eleutherius, 3731
  Ethices elementa, 5794, 6172
  First easy rudiments, 10025
  Introduction to the study, 5220
  Letter (to Dickinson), 5978-79
  Letter from a minister, 3672
  Letter from Aristocles, 5614
  Second letter, 3784
  Sermon, (1744) 5795, (1761?) 8892
  Short catechism, (1753) 7030, (1761) 8893, (1765)
    10026
  Third letter, 4148
  death, 12320, 12429
  letter (from Mills), 6010
  preface by, 6094

reflections on, 6123
reply to, 6693
Johnson, Samuel, 1709-1784
  Abridgement, 18543
  Beauties of Johnson, 20433
  History of Rasselas, 10939
  Obidiah, 28977
  (ed.) Plays and poems, 29496, 31180
  Prince of Abissinia, 23473
  Rambler, 37710
  Rasselas, 28904
  Thoughts on the late, 12088
  School dictionary, 30640
  Selected pronouncing, 37355-56
  extracts from, 29926?, 31664?
  life of Thomson, 22931, 23827, 29628, 38634
  travels of, 31692
Johnson, Simon. Life and experience, 17197
Johnson, Stephen, 1724-1786
  Everlasting punishment, 19737
  Integrity, 11691
  Some important observations, 10346
Johnson, Susanna Willard, 1730-1810
  Narrative, 30641
  captivity, 30180
Johnson, Thomas. Inaugural dissertation, 25663
Johnson, Thomas. Kentucky miscellany, 28905
Johnson, Thomas. Remarks, 35671
Johnson, Thomas, petition, 38839
Johnson, Thomas, 1732-1819? To the freemen, 37711
Johnson, W. M., tr. Christianity unveiled, 28846
Johnson, William. Course of experiments, 10027
Johnson, Sir William, 1715-1774
  Camp on Lake George, 7441
  Proceedings and treaty, 7924?, 7925-26
Johnson, William Samuel, 1727-1819
  dedication to, 28193
  pres. Columbia, 25213, 25602, 26028, 26246, 26520,
    26530, 27158, 27238, 27303, 29431, 29881, 29990,
    31155, 31780, 32283
  reports on accounts, 20059?, 20062?
  reports on governor's letter, 20057?
  reports on new states, 20058?, 20769?
Johnston, ———, publisher, 21970
Johnston, Andrew, orders minutes printed, 5253
Johnston, Francis, case of, 36065
Johnston, P., letter (from Pickering), 34378
Johnston, Robert. Inaugural dissertation, 25664
Johnston, Samuel, pres. NC convention, 22039
Johnston, Thomas. Rules for singing, 7442
Johnston, Thomas, engraver of maps, 7363
Johnstone, Commodore ———, captures ship, 17566
Johnstone, Abraham, d. 1797. Address, 32320
Johnstone, Benjamin, d. 1797. Address, 32320
Johnstone, George, 1730-1787
  Letters and other papers, 15826
  reply to, 16483
  speech in Parliament, 14092
Johonnet, Jackson

VOL.	ITEMS	VOL.	ITEMS
1	1-3244	8	22298-25074
2	3245-6623	9	25075-28145
3	6624-9891	10	28146-30832
4	9892-13091	11	30833-33261
5	13092-16176	12	33262-25854
6	16177-19448	13	35855-39162
7	19449-22297		

Remarkable adventures, (1791) 23474, (1793)
   25665-71, (1795) 28907, (1797) 32322
adventures, 25080, 26540, 36779
Jolly Hibernian, 22591
Jonah, or the dove, 2562
Jonathan the Jew. Conversion, 9824
Jones, ——, correspondence with Jay, 19324-25
Jones, ——, of N. Y., partner of Stewart, 26213
Jones, Mrs. ——, of Mecklenburg, life, 35072
Jones, Rev. ——, reply to, 12846, 13403
Jones, Rev. ——, vindicated, 4605
Jones, Rev. ——, of Titbury, sees apparition,
   21620, 26512
Jones, Absalom. Narrative, 27170
Jones, Andrew
   Black book, (1732) 3556, (1742) 4980-81, (1771)
      12089
   Dooms-day, 363
Jones, Archibald. Oration, 35673
Jones, B., engraver, 36393
Jones, Benjamin. Letter (to J. Jones), 7221
Jones, Calvin. Treatise, 27171
Jones, Charles. History of Charles, 37168
Jones, Daniel, advertisement by, 11961
Jones, David
   memorial of, 38763, 38831
   petition, 38849
Jones, David, 1663-1724. Discourse, 8628
Jones, David, 1736-1820
   Declaration, 35674
   Defensive war, 14133
   Doctrine, 19738
   Journal of two, 13356
Jones, Edward. Inaugural dissertation, 30643
Jones, Edward Thomas. English system, 30644,
   32323
Jones, Epaphras, relief of, 29684
Jones, Giles
   Lilliputian auction, 19739
   Lilliputian masquerade, (1786) 19740, (1787)
      20434, (1795) 28908
   Natural history, 20435
   Renowned history, 19949, 20675
Jones, Griffith, petition, 38849
Jones, Henry, 1721-1770. Earl of Essex, 22592, 24049
Jones, Hugh, 1669-1760. Protest, 5615
Jones, Ira. New treatise, 30645
Jones, Jenkin
   letter (from Kinnersley), 4538
   vindicated, 4605?
Jones, Jesse, accounts, 18705
Jones, John, of Penna., letter (from B. Jones),
   7221
Jones, John, 1729-1791
   Plain, concise, 14134, 14814
   Surgical works, 28909
Jones, John Paul, 1747-1792
   Charges and proofs, 20436
   on Ranger, 15648
Jones, Pearson, describes Falmouth fire, 14027
Jones, Samuel, 1735-1814
   Circular letter, 22792
   Doctrine, 17990
   Resignation, 12422
   Selection of psalms, 22593, 33939
   Treatise, 33940
   letter (from Evans), 23356-57
   ordained, 9383?
   reply to, 12846?, 13403?
Jones, Samuel, fl. 1772-1797. Inaugural dissertation,

32324
Jones, Thomas, of Boston. Teas at auction, 37020
Jones, Thomas, of Reading. Triumph, 33941
Jones, Thomas, of Southwark
   Beauties of spring, 8379
   Religious remembrancer, 8380
   Sermon, 7691
   preface by, 8984, 10142
Jones, Sir William, 1746-1794. Essay on the law,
   30646
Jones, William, d. 1791. Wonderful and surprising,
   23475
Jones, William, d. 1813. Oration, 27172
Jones's English system, 30644, 32323
Jonson, Ben, 1573-1637. Volpone, 8894
Jorck, J. M., tr. Einige glaubens-bekenntnisse,
   34972
Jordan, Mrs. ——, sings, 30622
Jordan, Robert, letter (from Logan), 4740
Joseph II. Briefwechsel, 17568
Joseph, story of, 36377
Joseph (Indian), d. 1709, executed, 1452
Joseph (Negro), behavior toward, 1022
Joseph, of Arimathea, life, 9140
Joseph, of Israel
   life, 22629, 23522-25, 25742-43, 27250-53, 29006-9,
      30718-21, 32404-405, 34037, 36377?, 37870-71
   poem on, 21438, 32613
Joseph Alleins grundlegung, 29965
Joseph Andrews, 19646, 23369-70
Joseph embalmed, 7031
Joseph Nancrede's catalogue, 30833
Joseph Reed, defendant, 11053
Joseph Scott, Jun.; at his shop, 31168
Joseph Whittemore presents, 31632, 35025
Josephus, Flavius
   Genuine works, 27173
   Wars of the Jews, 2226
   Whole genuine and complete, (1792) 24437,
      (1793) 25672, (1794) 27174, (1795) 28910, (1799)
      35675
   Works, (v.1) 12822, (v.2) 13357, (v.3-4) 14135
   extracts from, 29927
   proposal to print, 23340
Josiah Flagg, surgeon dentist, 30427
Josias (Indian), d. 1709, executed, 1452
Jotham. To my respected, 2889
Jouet, Cavalier. Letter (to Beech), 28911
Journal des Senates, 38211
   durant un séjour, 27343
   during a residence, (1793) 25838-39, (1794)
      27340-42
   for lunar observations, 23954
   from London, 4845
   of a convention of the Prot. Epis. church,
      (1785) 19209, (1786) 19941-42, (1789) 22084
      Prot. Epis. church (Maryland), (1799)
        36171, (1800) 38331
      Prot. Epis. church (Virginia), 36178
   of a gaming lady, 8265
   of a voyage from Gibraltar, 4453, 4632
      from London, 4454, 4630-31
      from Savannah, 4598
   of Capt. Cook, 17998
   of Congress (p. 241), 19317
   of conventions, 29358
   of Lieut. Simon, 8741-42
   of Major George Washington, 7531
   of my forty-fifth, 25207
   of occurrences in the tower, 35314

of occurrences which happened, 14888
of the adventures, 30135-36
    captivity and sufferings, 33746-47
    captivity of Jean Lowry, 8642
    committee of the states, 18841
    congress of the four southern, 9706
    convention met in Newbern, 13497
    convention of North Carolina, 21337
    convention of the state, (Georgia) 28738, (New York) 21313, (North Carolina) 22738
    convention of Virginia, 21555
    Council, 18093
    expedition, 8381
    fifteenth convention, 36174
    House . . . see under issuing body, e.g. New York. House of repr. Journal
    landing, 8076
    Legislative council, 27726, 29552
    life and travels, 12914-15
    life, gospel labo(u)rs, (1774) 13782, (1775) 14631, (1790) 23090
    life, travels and gospel labours, (1772) 12565, (1797) 32810-11, (1798) 34518
    life, travels and labours, 16793
    meetings, 22819
    proceedings at two conferences, 7222
    proceedings in the detection, 5413
    procedings in the late, 513
    proceedings of a convention begun and held, 31280
    proceedings of a convention of the Protestant Episcopal church . . . see under Protestant Episcopal church. Maryland [etc.]
    proceedings of Jacob Wendell, 6861
    proceedings of the bishops, (1789) 24722, (1791) 22822, (1795) 29364
    proceedings of the commissioners, 6336
    proceedings of the Congress, (1774) 13737-39, (1775-76) 15144-45
    proceedings of the Continental, 14569-71
    proceedings of the convention, 14594
    proceedings of the Prot. Episc. church, (N.Y.) 31058, (U.S.) 36177
    proceedings of the Provincial congress, (1775) 14354, (1776) 14948, 15489
    taking of Cape Breton, 5601
    transactions, 23086
    travels, 27671, 32804
    votes and proceedings, 14914
of travels, 5616
of two visits, 13356
of votes . . . see under state, e.g. **Mass. General court.** Journal
of what passed, 743
of William Scudder, 27681
or historical account of the life, (Chalkley) 6297, 22397, (Fox) 37441
Journals of Congress, (1774-77) 15683-85, (1774-84) 38750
    of Congress, Wednesday, 15185
    of five conventions, 29360
    of the lives, 8308
Journée du chretien, 31118
Journey from Philadelphia 20375
    over land to India, 31911
    to Jerusalem, (1794) 26833, (1795) 28505, (1796) 30301
    to London, 26559

Journeymen cabinet and chair-makers, 29308, 30880
Journeys of the children, 8309
Jovial crew, 9079
Jovial songster, (1793) 25675, (1798) 33943, (1800) 38110
Joy, George. Innocency's complaint, 232
Joy and gladness, 10612
    and gratitude, 8632
    and salvation, 9403
    of children, 2440
    of faith, 429
    of duty, 4687
    to America, 10347
Joyce, Jr. Brethren and fellow citizens, 13358
Joyce & Snowdon. American ink powder, 22594
Joyful news for America, 10464
Joyful news to America, 10465
Joyfulness and consideration, 8811
Jubeart, John, d. 1769. Confession, 11303
Jubilee, an half-century discourse, 10950
Jubilee jester, 13608
Judas Iscariot, character, 10183, 10784, 11493, 11877, 22929, 27222, 30647, 32325, 32924
Judas the traitor, 1704, 8931
Judd, Eben W. Almanac see **Almanacs (Judd)**
Judd, Jonathan, 1719-1803
    On what constitutes, 35583
    Soldiers directed, 8382
    ordained, 5172
Judge Wolcott, a funeral poem, 8629
Judgements in the admiralty, 22053
Judgment and mercy, 11895
    begun, 1812
    of several, 660
    of the rector, 5720-21
    of the renowned, 5574
    of whole kingdoms, 13023, 13631-33
Judgments of Providence, 2853
Judson, David, 1715-1776
    Letters (to a friend), 10348
    On church discipline, 11692
    Remarks, 10028
    Sermons, 13360
    Timely warning, 6862
    hand of fellowship, 6818
    reply to, 9910, 10237, 12987
Judson, Ephraim, 1737-1813
    Advantages of going, 37712
    Ambassadors appointed, 21908
    Duty of the ministers, 37713
    On preaching, 30648
    On the first, 32820
Jüngers Nicodemi evangelium, 9863
Juga jucunda, 2914, 3060
Juhan, Alexander. Set of six songs, 27176
Julia and the illuminated, 39134
    de Roubigné, (1782) 17578, (1786) 19764, (1793) 25747
    or the adventures, (1792) 24440, (1794) 25751, (1799) 35759

VOL.	ITEMS	VOL.	ITEMS
1	1-3244	8	22298-25074
2	3245-6623	9	25075-28145
3	6624-9891	10	28146-30832
4	9892-13091	11	30833-33261
5	13092-16176	12	33262-25854
6	16177-19448	13	35855-39162
7	19449-22297		

or the Italian, 28898
Julian the Apostate, life, 30012, 33357
Juliana library company. Charter, 10034, 10350
Juliet Grenville, 13178
Julius. Translation of a passage, 10660
Julius Africanus. Historia, 9863
Jung-Stilling, Johann Heinrich, 1740-1817. Geschichte Florentius, 32326
Junior sophister see **Dexter, Samuel, 1761-1816**
Junius
    Crisis, no. X, 13970-71
    Letter (to Wesley), 16017
    Letter addressed to two, 8584-85
    Letters, (1791) 23477-78, (1795) 28912
    Remarkable plan, 11693
Junius, Jr. see **Parkes, J.**
Jupiter Hammon
    Address to the Negroes, 20400
    Essay, 16298
    Evening's improvement, 17969
    Winter piece, 17554
Jurieu, Pierre, 1637-1713
    Dialogue, 2523
    extracts from, 27564-66
Jurisdiction of the court, 4088
Just and impartial account, 3017
        and impartial narrative, 3899
        and plain vindication, 2753-54
        and seasonable vindication, 2109-110
        arrived from London, 5419
        commemorations, 1757
        expectations, 4682
        imported and to be sold, 18504

in time, 28872
    man's prerogative, 1286
    published and now selling, 17830
    rebuke to a dialogue, 2807
    rebuke to several, 590
    vengeance, 5980
Justice and policy of taxing, 10076
    and policy of the act, 13364
    of God in the damnation, 12757, 35437
    of God in the mortality, 8389
    of the present, 7410
    progressive, 29326
Justification by the free grace, 10204
    not by works, 6347
    of believers, 21980
    of Lewis Tousard, 26269
    through the merits, 19245
Justinian. Letter to the legislative, 11694
Justitius. Remarks, 36201
Juvenal, Horatio
    Address, 22598
    Second address, 22599
Juvenile biographer, 20440
    correspondence, 23479
    entertainment, 37693
    essays, 34341
    poems (Hazard), 21882
    poems designed, 25678
    poems on various, 9983
    trials, 31700
Juvenis
    Algerine slaves, 33747
    see also **Bostwick, S.**

K

K., J. see **Kearsley, John**
K., L. Letter (to Whitefield), 5420-21, 5617
K., M. Fatal consequences, 7032
K., R. see **Kitchen, Robert**
K., S. Plan for establishing, 33944
K's answer, 12090
Kachline, Andrew, accounts, 18102, 19168
Kaims, Lord see **Kames, Henry Home, lord, 1696-1792**
Kaina kaipalaia, 21114
Kalendarium Nov-Anglicanum, 1203
Kalendarium Pennsilvaniense, 382
Kalkoen, Johannes, 1709-1778. Brief, 10029
Kames, Henry Home, lord, 1696-1792
  Blacksmith's letter, 22574
  Culture of the heart, 32267
  Elements of criticism, 30578
  Letter from a blacksmith, 20417, 37819
  Six sketches, 14801
  reply to, 20712
Kamper, Peter, plaintiff, 27777
Karigal, Haijm Isaac. Sermon, 12823
Kaskaskia Indians, treaty, 29742
Kawanio che keeteru, 7788-89
Keach, Benjamin, 1640-1704
  God acknowledged, 4257
  Progress of sin, 5422
  Protestant tutor, 387
  Sion in distress, 344-45
  Travels of True Godliness, (1793) 25679, (1795) 28913-14, (1796) 30649, (1797) 32327, (1799) 35677
  War with the devil, 1207, 1682
  refuted, 516?
Kean, John, 1756-1795
  Advertisement, (1781) 17198, (1783) 17991, (1784) 18546
  motion by, 20763
  reports on accounts, 20062
  reports on apportioning taxes, 20069
  reports on Indian affairs, 20768
  reports on prisoners, 17383
  reports on revenue, 20085-85
Kearney, Dyre, d. 1791
  reports on Illinois tract, 21514
  reports on Indian affairs, 20770
Kearsley, John, Jr. Narrative, 11695
Kearsley, John, 1684-1772
  Case of Mr. T. L., 8630
  Letter (to friend), 6697
  remarks on smallpox, 6689

Keate, George, 1729-1797
  Account of the Pelew Islands, (1789) 21909, (1792) 24441, (1794) 27177, (1796) 30650-51, (1797) 32328-29
  Sketches from nature, 25680
Keatinge, George
  Maryland Ahiman Rezon, 32330
  Sale catalogue, 30652
Kedzie, James. Catalogue of books, 28915
Keech, B., refuted, 516
Keech, Joseph, ordained, 6229
Keep, John, ordained, 12618
Keep your heart, 26695
Keeping of the commandments, 22146-47
Keeping the heart, 2117, 2868
Keete, George see **Keate, George, 1729-1797**
Kehukee association. Minutes, (1789) 21910, (1790) 25681-82, (1791) 23152, 25683, (1792) 25684, 26292, (1793) 25685, (1794) 27178, (1796) 31329
Keimer, Samuel
  Advertisement, 3044
  Compleat ephemeris see **Almanacs (Keimer)**
  Elegy, 2436
  Parable, 2437
  Prospectus of a lottery, 3045
  Touch of the times, 3174
Keir, Susanna Harvey, 1747-1802. Interesting memoirs, 24442
Keith, George, 1639-1716
  Account of a national, 980
  Answer to Mr. Samuel, 1160
  Appeal from the twenty-eight, 597-99
  Christian faith, 600
  Counter testimonial, 601
  Discovery of the mystery, 602
  Doctrine of the holy, 1052
  Examination, 640
  False judgments, 611
  Fundamental truths, 603-4
  Great necessity, 1161
  Heresie, 641

VOL.	ITEMS	VOL.	ITEMS
1	1-3244	8	22298-25074
2	3245-6623	9	25075-28145
3	6624-9891	10	28146-30832
4	9892-13091	11	30833-33261
5	13092-16176	12	33262-25854
6	16177-19448	13	35855-39162
7	19449-22297		

VOL.	ITEMS	VOL.	ITEMS
1	1-3244	8	22298-25074
2	3245-6623	9	25075-28145
3	6624-9891	10	28146-30832
4	9892-13091	11	30833-33261
5	13092-16176	12	33262-25854
6	16177-19448	13	35855-39162
7	19449-22297		

Kingsbury, Samuel, d. 1737, death, 4314
Kingsbury, Samuel, fl. 1761, ordained, 9048
Kingston, R. By permission of his excellency, 15336
Kinloch, Francis, 1755-1826. Eulogy, 27735
Kinnan, Mary. True narrative, 28931
Kinne, Aaron, 1744-1824
  Alamoth, 33962
  New-Year's gift, 21189
Kinnnersley, Ebenezer, 1711-1778
  Course of experiments, 9708
  Letter (to Baptist ministers), 5981
  Letter (to friend), 4536
  Letter (to Jones), 4538
  Second letter, 4537
  letter to, 4542
  remarks on, 4605
Kinsey, John, 1693-1750
  Collection of all the laws, 5033
  notes on laws, 14364
Kippis, Andrew, 1725-1795. Life of Dr. Doddridge, 25154
Kirby, Ephraim, 1757-1804. Reports of cases, 21914
Kirchen-agende, 19629
Kirchen formularien, 33701
Kirk, ———. Letter (to Howe), 20382
Kirk of Scotland. Confession of faith, 5709
Kirkbridge, Joseph, accounts, 19169
Kirke, Samuel. Account of the births, (1751) 6755, (1752) 6914, (1753) 7092, (1754) 7293, (1755) 7539, (1756) 7763, (1757) 8004, (1758) 8236, (1759) 8467, (1760) 8714
Kirkland, ———, correspondence with Congress, 19335
Kirkland, John Thornton, 1770-1840
  Discourse, 37383, 37736-37
  Oration, 33963
  Sermon, (1795) 28932, (1798) 33964-65, (1800) 37738
  ordained, 27775
Kirkland, Moses, letters intercepted, 15126
Kirkland, Samuel. Copy of a letter, 15642
Kirkpatrick, J., tr. Advice to the people, 12243
Kirtland, Daniel, ordained, 2663
Kissam, Benjamin
  Argument, 11373
  Managers on the part, 11372
  To the honourable, 11371
Kissam, Samuel. Inaugural essay, 12091
Kisses sued for, 28933
Kissin, William, ed. Baptist discovered, 6039
Kitchell, Aaron, 1744-1820
  Motion, 31360
  letter (from Hornblower), 37648, 38754
Kitchen, Robert, d. 1716, memoirs of, 1912
Kittera, John Wilkes, 1752-1801, memorial referred to, 32976-77
Kittle, Marie, history of, 25208, 31837
Kittletas, William see Keteltas, William
Klagen über den tod, 37603, 38260
Klagte van eenige, 2605
Klare und gewisse, 5982
Klaugen eines theils, 9153
Klein-Nicolai, Georg
  Das von Jesu Christo, 10942, 11304
  Everlasting gospel, 7033
Kleine A.B.C., 4982
  catechismus, (1744) 5426, (1749) 6349, (1752) 6869, (1765) 10045, (1766) 10359, (1767) 10665, (1770) 11705, (1774) 13385, (1777) 15382, (1782) 17576, (1784) 18563-64, (1786) 19761-62, (1787) 20468, (1791) 23514, (1793) 25735, (1795) 28992-93, (1798) 34024, (1800)

37740
Darmstädtische catechismus, 9423
Davidische psalterspiel, (1744) 5340, (1760) 8548, (1764) 9602, (1777) 15242, (1781) 17100, (1791) 23197, (1795) 28283, (1797) 31815-16
geistliche harfe, 7034
harfe, 24445, 31815
  Kempis, (1750) 6523, (1751) 6698, (1773) 12824, (1788) 21183, (1795) 28920
Kleines Christlich gebätbuch, 8870, 9131
Klopstock, Friedrich Gottlieb, 1724-1803. Messiah, 21190, 28935
Knapp, Francis, b. 1672. Gloria Britannorum, 2438
Knapp, Joshua, ordained, 12543
Kneeling to God, 780
Knight, Ellis Cornelia, 1757-1837. Dinarbas, (1791) 23473, (1792) 24446, (1795) 28904
Knight, John, d. 1838. Narrative, 17993, 35689
Knight, Sir William Phipps, commander-in-chief, 513
Knight and friars, 20035
Knights, a farce, 26986
Knolton, ———, reply to, 28500
Know all men, 28075
Know your own, 28563
Knowledge of Christ, 2288
  of God, 1202
  of Jesus, 26477
  of our end, 11585
  of salvation, 8484-85
  of the chief, 17877
  or well grounded, 17277
Knowlege of Christ, 4779
Knowles, Sir Charles, d. 1777
  character, 6307
  expedition, 8138-39
Knox, Henry, 1750-1806
  Catalogue of books, 12424
  Causes of the existing, 24944
  For sale, lots, 33967
  Plan for the general arrangement, 20076, 22987-88
  Secretary of the U.S. for the Dept. of war, 20786
  War department, Aug. 6, 1792, 24946
  War-office, Apr. 25, 1785, 19334, 20090
  approves pension form, 22197
  claims Waldo land, 31477
  offers books for sale, 11962
  reference to, 37916
Knox, Hugh, 1733-1790
  Dignity and importance, 7444
  Letter (to Green), 12425
  Moral and religious, 14137, 22603
  New-Year's discourse, 10943
  Sermon, 14138
Knox, John, 1505-1572
  First blast, 10349
  at meeting in N.Y.?, 13126
  extracts from, 27564-66
Knox, Samuel, 1756-1723
  Essay, 35690
  Funeral oration, 37742
  Scriptural doctrine, 32342
  Vindication of the religion, 37702-703
Knox, Vicesimus, 1752-1821
  Complete library, 33968
  Essays, 24447, 25696
  Spirit of despotism, 28936, 35691
Knox, William, 1732-1810
  Controversy, 11305
  Justice and policy, 13364

VOL.	ITEMS	VOL.	ITEMS
1	1-3244	8	22298-25074
2	3245-6623	9	25075-28145
3	6624-9891	10	28146-30832
4	9892-13091	11	30833-33261
5	13092-16176	12	33262-25854
6	16177-19448	13	35855-39162
7	19449-22297		

L

Lake, Sir Byby, claims land, 7098
Lake, John Neal, tr. Principles, 32455
Lamb, John, circular addressed to, 24135
Lamb, John, Jr. Inaugural dissertation, 27193
Lamb, Joshua, d. 1722, death, 2360
Lamb slain, 5685
Lambart, Richard, earl of Cavan see **Cavan, Richard Lambart, 6th earl of**
Lambert, Anne Thérèse, marquise de, 1647-1733
   Advice of a mother, (1792) 24452, 25067-69, (1794) 27192
   Advice to her son, 25064-65
   Fair solitary, (1790) 22605, (1795) 28942, (1797) 32347
   Polite lady, 24453
Lambert, John. Short and practical, 33974
Lambert, Nathaniel, ordained, 23220
Lamboll, William. Lamentation, 10030
Lambrecht Myseras, 35854
Lamech. Chronicon, 19558
Lamenspraak, 7445
Lamentable state, 12392
Lamentation and farewell, 20701
   for Gen. Washington, 37771-72
   of Penna., 10031
   of the distressing, 2617
   on the death, 37846
   over Zion, 10030
Lamentations of a sow, 15862
   of Charles, 6061
   of Mary, 25549
   for her sons, 690
Lamont, —— de
   Art of war, 14816
   excerpts from, 26054
La Montagne (flagship), cruise, 27664
La Montaigne, ——, widow, meeting at house of, 14500, 14502
La Motte, ——, countess, accused, 21724
La Motte, Douin de. Mémoire apologétique, 10032
Lampadarius, 2771
Lampe, Friedrich Adolph, 1683-1729. In seinem leben, 9154
Lampoon on modern, 10033
La Musse, Marguerite de, 1665-1681. Triumphs of grace, 1933, 28944
Lancashire collier girl, 35297
Lancaster, Thomas, ordained, 14676
Lancaster, Pa.
   Charter, laws, catalogue, 10350
   Charter of the Juliana, 10034
   Freiheitsbrief, 20445
   Ordnung, 20446
Lancaster county
   Address; fellow citizens, 32348
   An die hochgeehrten, 15379
   At a meeting of the committee of inspection, 14141
   At a meeting of the committee of observation, 14140
   At a meeting of the committee of the county, 14821
   Be liberty thine, 14819
   By virtue of a certain, 13366
   Extarcts from the minutes, 14143-44
   Extracts from the votes, 14142
   In committee, Lancaster, 14817
   In committee of inspection, 14820
   In the committee for Lancaster, 14818
   Lancaster county, to wit, 12828

   To the [MUTILATED], 37775
Lancaster county, to wit, 12828
Lancaster, Jan. 6, 1800, 38360
Land for sale, 31560
   in the moon, 32946
   laws of the state, 27042
   laws passed, 28737
   office, 17th of June, 1765, 10123
      of Pennsylvania, 38216
      Philadelphia, 9476
   we live in, 32350
Landaff, John, bp. of see **Ewer, John**
Landais, Pierre de, 1734-1820
   Memorial, 18549
   Second part, 19056
   conduct of, 20436
   memorial considered, 19305
Landholder. Reflections on taxes, 27601
Landmanns advocat, 8897
Landon, Benjamin, d. 1747, death, 5922
Lands; for sale two hundred, 21957
   in New-Connecticut, 33565
   to be sold, 20447
Lane, Ebenezer, d. 1790, death, 23084
Lane, Isaac. Anthem, 33977
Lane, Jeremiah
   (ed.) Few drops, 26970
   Memorial and tear, 10351
Lane, Job, d. 1768, death, 10872
Lane, Oliver W. Psalms, hymns, 24952
Lane, Phebe, d. 1781, death, 17242
La Neuville, J. Elégie sur la mort, 37776
Lang, Edward. Medicine chests, 38455
Lang, J. Very important, 34363
Lang, William. Remainder of a large, 36270
Langdon, Chauncey, 1763-1830
   Beauties of psalmody, 19749
   Oration, 37777
   Select songster, 19750
Langdon, John, of New York. Catalogue of English, 33978
Langdon, John, 1741-1819
   Proclamation, 19116, 19824, 19826
   pres. convention, 16230, 16269, 16386
   speaker NH House, 16135, 17018, 17389, 19823
   pres. NH Senate, 19822
Langdon, Samuel, 1723-1797
   Coincidence of natural, 14822
   Correction of some, 24454
   Discourse, 24455
   Duty and honor, 9415
   Excellency of the word, 7694
   Government corrupted, 14145
   High value, 16315
   Impartial examination, 10035, 11306
   Joy and gratitude, 8632
   Map of the province, 8898
   Observations, 23486
   Rational explanation, 13368
   Remarks on the leading, 27195

VOL.	ITEMS	VOL.	ITEMS
1	1-3244	8	22298-25074
2	3245-6623	9	25075-28145
3	6624-9891	10	28146-30832
4	9892-13091	11	30833-33261
5	13092-16176	12	33262-25854
6	16177-19448	13	35855-39162
7	19449-22297		

Lathrop, Joseph, Joseph, 1731-1820
Christ's warning, (1789) 21916, (1790) 22606, (1791) 23488, (1792) 24459, (1793) 25704
Church of God, 24460
Discourse, 18552
Familiar discourse, 30677
Funeral sermon, 30678, 32359
Furthermore of the gospel, 27199
God's challenge, 32360
Letter from the elders, 11587
Miscellaneous collection, 19751
National happiness, 28952
Sermon, (1787) 20451, (1794) 27200, (1797) 32361, (1798) 33986, (1800) 37783
Sermons on the mode, 25705
Sermons on various subjects, 25706, 30679
Sprinkling, 12829, 21917
Stedfastness, 32362
reply to, 25131?
Lathrop, Mary, d. 1778, death, 16316
Lathrop, Samuel, d. 1846. Oration, 23489
Lathy, Thomas Pike. Reparation, 37784
Latin epitaph, 1871
Latin grammar, 4071
Latrobe, Benjamin Henry, 1764-1826
American copper-mines, 33987, 37785
Answer to the joint, 36086
Remarks, 35714
View of the practicability, 35715
remarks on, 35399, 36200
Latta, James, 1732-1801. Discourse on psalmody, 27201, 33988
Latter part, 3711
Latter sign, 321, 352
Laudable character, 8165
Lauderdale, James Maitland, 8th earl of, attacks Burke, 30142-43
Laugh and be fat, 35716
Laughing philosopher, 21956
Launy, David Frederick. Sir; conscious of your, 28953
Laurance, John, 1750-1810
candidacy, 20983?, 21329?
election urged, 22936?
reports on courts-martial, 20061?
reports on sundry motions, 19307?
Laurens, Henry, 1724-1792
Extracts from the proceedings, 10945, 11307
corresponds with Lux, 16111
papers of, 20382
parole, 17757
petition to, 38594
pres. Congress, 15678-79, 15975, 16097-98, 16103-104, 16117-18, 16121-22, 16134-35
reports on sundry motions, 19307?
satirized, 16697
Laus Deo; the New England, 35667, 37707
Laus Deo; the Worcester, (1786) 19752, (1787) 20452, (1788) 21193, (1791) 23490, (1792) 24461, (1794) 27202, (1797) 32363, (1800) 37786
Lautere wahrheit, 5950
La Valière, ——, chevalier de. Art of war, 14816
La Valinière, Pierre Huet de
Curious and interesting, 22607
Vraie histoire, 24462
Lavater, Johann Caspar, 1741-1801
Aphorisms on man, (1788) 21194, (1790) 22608-610, (1791) 23326, (1793) 25707, (1794) 27039, (1795) 28954
Essays on physiognomy, 27203

Nachdenken, 21195
Remonstrance, 35717
Lavington, George, 1684-1762. Enthusiasm of Methodists, 6525
Lavinia, a pastoral, 28978
Lavoisier, Antoine Laurent, 1743-1794
Elements of chemistry, 35718
chemical doctrines, 30692-93
proposes nomenclature, 36347
Law, Andrew, 1748-1821
Art of singing, 27204, 37787
Christian harmony, 27205, 30680
Collection of hymn tunes, 19753, 24463
Collection of hymns, 17571, 17996
Collection of the best, (1779) 16317, (1781) 17201, (1782) 17572
Musical magazine, (1792) 24464, (1793) 25708, (1794) 27206, (1795) 28955, (1799) 35719
Musical primer, 16816, 25709
Rudiments of music, (1783) 17997, (1785) 19057, (1791) 23491, (1792) 24465-66, (1794) 27207
Select harmony, (1779) 16318, (1784) 18553, (1786) 19754, (1791) 23492, (1792) 24467
Select number, (1767) 10662, (1772) 12427, (1781) 17097-98, (1782) 17475, (1785) 18930, (1794) 27208
Law, Jonathan, 1672-1750
character, 7298
death, 6651, 6789
dedication to, 5098, 5321, 5525, 5722, 5895, 6085, 6272, 6447, 6622
Law, Lyman, 1770-1842. Oration, 37666
Law, Richard, witnesses contract, 34849
Law, William, 1686-1761
Extract from a treatise, (1760) 8633, (1766) 10352, (1780) 16817
Extract from Mr. Law's, 25710
Grounds and reasons, 4734, 14146
Gründe und ursachen, 4735
Humble, earnest and affectionate, 19755, 30681
Instructions for ministers, 30682
True grounds, 23493
extracts from, 10505
Law and gospel, 6135
and the gospel, 36118
established, 712
for regulating carts, 7278
given at Sinai, 15282
in all respects, 19991
is a bottomless, 26574
of evidence, 21113
of liberty, 14635-36
of nations, 31483
of nature, 31516, 33141
of the United States, 36522
our school master, 7618
Lawer's pedigree, 7446
Lawfulness, excellency, 9424-25
of defensive, 7697
of swearing, 439

VOL.	ITEMS	VOL.	ITEMS
1	1-3244	8	22298-25074
2	3245-6623	9	25075-28145
3	6624-9891	10	28146-30832
4	9892-13091	11	30833-33261
5	13092-16176	12	33262-25854
6	16177-19448	13	35855-39162
7	19449-22297		

Le Compte, Lewis. Voyage to China, 20444
Lecture containing, 28154
   on earthquakes, 7597
   on the excellence, 23789
   on the prodigal, 5089
   read, 35644
   sermon, asserting, 2179
   sermon preached, 2538
Lectures delivered, 23470
   on diet, 39111-12
   on female education, (1794) 26722-23, (1796)
      30147, (1798) 33580, (1799) 35261
   on moral philosophy, 23529, 34041
   on rhetoric(k), (1784) 18369, (1793) 25200-201,
      (1800) 36982
   on the materia medica, 14000
   supposed to have been, 25712
Ledyard, ———. Eulogy on women, 28875
Ledyard, Isaac, 1754-1803
   Essay on matter, 18554
   Mentor's reply, 18367, 18555
   Oration, 37790
Ledyard, John, d. 1771?, death, 12286
Ledyard, John, 1751-1789. Journal, 17998
Lee, ———
   arrogance of, 13840
   reports on accounts, 18833
   reports on civil department, 20767
   reports on courts-martial, 20061
   reports on emoluments, 20090
   reports on frontier posts, 18832
   reports on Indians, 20052
   reports on representation, 18827
Lee, Capt. ———, arrival in New York, 14164
Lee, Andrew, 1745-1832
   Blessedness, 19756
   Declensions, 27210
   Duty of gospel, 22614
   Origin and ends, 28957
   Sermon, 37791
   Sin, 14826
   Words of Moses, 20453
Lee, Arthur, 1740-1792
   Appeal to the justice, 14147
   Board of treasury, June 22, 1786, 20043
   Board of treasury to whom, 20044
   Copy of a letter, 16111
   Extracts from a letter, 16319, 16818
   Farmer's and monitor's letters, 11239
   Observations, 16819
   Ordinance for the establishment, 20073
   True state, 13282
   concludes treaty, 18817
   reports on accounts, 18833?
   reports on frontier posts, 18832?
   reports on Indian affairs, 18262-63
   reports on representation, 18827?
Lee, Charles, 1731-1782
   Account of the treatment, 15867
   Letter (to Burgoyne), 14148-49
   Letters (to Percy), 14150
   Strictures on a pamphlet, (1774) 13372-73, (1775)
      13824, 14151-55
   arrogance of, 13840?
   article in Maryland journal, 15315
   correspondence with Burgoyne, 14559
   court martial, 16140
   life, 24456, 25701
   proposal to print papers, 19029
Lee, Charles, 1758-1815. Defence of the alien, 33991
Lee, Chauncey, 1763-1842
   American accomptant, 32366

Divine architecture, 28958
Duty and importance, 27211
Ode, 36436
Oration, 32367
Spiritual temple, 28959
Tree of knowledge, 37792-93
Lee, Elias
   Christmas dispute, 37794
   Dissolution, 27212
   letter (from Smith), 36323
Lee, Elisha, 1757-1835
   Oration delivered at Lenox, 25713
   Oration delivered in Sheffield, 37795
Lee, Francis Lightfoot. War office, Nov. 14, 1776,
   15192
Lee, Harriet, 1756-1851
   Arundel, 37796
   Constantia de Valmont, 35722
Lee, Henry, 1756-1818
   Circular; Richmond, 28000
   Council chamber; Jan. 25, 1794, 28001
   Funeral oration, 36859, 37383, 37797-808
   National eulogy, 37809
   Plain truth, 35723
   To the inhabitants, 27978
   motion by, 38789
Lee, John
   Remarks on a passage, 4984
   reply to, 5076-77
Lee, Jonathan, 1718-1788
   Farewell sermon, 7695
   Funeral sermon, 21198
   Sermon, (1754) 7447, (1758) 8384, (1766) 10354
   preface by, 9984
Lee, Joseph, 1742-1819
   Four sermons, 17573
   Resurrection, 37810
   hand of fellowship, 20999
   ordained, 11486
Lee, Matthew, 1732-1752. Some account, 28960
Lee, Nathaniel, 1655-1691
   Nero, 8901
   Theodosius, 8902
Lee, Richard, b. 1747
   Flowers from Sharon, 30683
   Lines on the last, 24468
   Melancholy end, 28961
   Songs, 32368
Lee, Richard E. Letter, 37811
Lee, Richard Henry, 1732-1794
   Additional number, 21197
   Observations, 20454-55
   Proclamation, 19327
   Twelve united, 14532-34
   arrogance of, 13840?
   pres. Congress, 19283
   reports on civil department, 20767?
   reports on courts-martial, 20061?
   reports on emoluments, 20090?
   reports on Indians, 20052?
Lee, Samuel, 1625-1691

VOL.	ITEMS	VOL.	ITEMS
1	1-3244	8	22298-25074
2	3245-6623	9	25075-28145
3	6624-9891	10	28146-30832
4	9892-13091	11	30833-33261
5	13092-16176	12	33262-25854
6	16177-19448	13	35855-39162
7	19449-22297		

Young misses' magazine, 24472, 38324
Le Roy, Marie, captivity, 8347
Le Roy, Pierre Louis. Narrative, 19058
Le Sage, Alain René, 1668-1747
  Adventures of Gil Blas, 30686
  Comical adventures, 22619
  Comical and entertaining, 32372
  Diable boiteux, 23497-98, 28965
  History and adventures, 23499
  Point of honor, 29428
  imitated, 12358
Lesebuch für deutsche, 29258
Lesley, ———, reply to, 2581
Leslie, Charles, 1650-1722
  Extract of a short, 38496
  Religion of Jesus, 2029
  Short and easie method, 3675, 5619
  Short and easy method, (1783) 17999, (1797)
    32373, (1798) 33993
  Short method, 29237
Lessing, Gotthold Ephraim, 1729-1781
  Lucy Sampson, 21922
Lesslie, George, d. 1800
  Nature and tendancy, 16322
  Sermon, 10037
  controversy with Thayer, 26250-51, 29620
Lessons adapted, 26615
    for children, (1788) 20946-49, (1795) 28234,
      (1800) 36890-91
    for lovers, 18671
    for youth, 35725
    in elocution, (1786) 19980, (1788) 21451, (1790)
      22879, (1794) 27680, (1795) 29477, (1797)
      32814, (1798) 34521, (1799) 36283-85, (1800)
      38475
    of caution, 3655
    of godliness, 2052
    of the Protestant, 33752
    to a young, 24001-2, 31172
L'Estrange, Sir Roger, 1616-1704
  Afterthought, 24778
  Discourse, 27682-83
  History of the life, 33273
  (tr.) Seneca's Morals, 37818
  (tr.) Wars of the Jews, 2226
  (tr.) Works of Flavius, 12822, 13357
Lesueur, Jean François, 1763-1837. Wretched
  slave, 32374
Let the will, 1702
Let Washington, 37633
Letchworth, John. Address of the committee, 38247
Letchworth, Thomas, 1738-1784
  Morning and evening's meditation, 10355
  Twelve discourses, 27217
Letter (J. Adams to Barnard), 5110-11
    (Allen to friend), 4467
    (Angeloni to Manzoni), 9838-39
    (Ashley to Cooper), 5120
    (Auchmuty to Montresor), 13818
    (Backus to Lord), 9587
    (Bacon to Huntington), 17465
    (Bard to author), 23156
    (Barlow to National convention), 25143-44
    (Bass to Miles), 6960
    (Bayley to Bard), 23162
    (Bellamy to author), 8080
    (Bellamy to Scripturista), 8540, 8794
    (Bland to clergy), 8551
    (Bourk to Chamberlaine), 15747
    (Bowden to Stiles), 20979

(Bray to contributors), 903
(Breck to Hobby), 6645
(Buchan to patentee), 26707, 28367
(Bull to Penn), 4480
(Burke to Duke of Portland), 31894
(Burke to member), 23237
(Burke to noble lord), 30142-43
(Candidus to Philo-Africanus), 20993
(Canonicus to Whitefield), 5152-53
(Carroll to reader), 16216
(Chalkley to friend), 2416
(Chamberlaine to Bourk), 15757
(Chauncy to friend), 10579, 13197
(Chauncy to Whitefield), 5152, 5557
(Checkley to Dickinson), 2619
(Clap to Edwards), 5561
(Clap to friend), 5560
(Clarke to Mather), 17492
(Clarke to student), 30200
(Cleveland to Foxcroft), 5551
(Coade to clergyman), 12728
(Cobbett to Paine), 30211
(Cole to gentleman), 7392
(Colman to Williams), 5368
(Conant to friend), 7876
(Conant to Huntington), 8322
(Condorcet to magistrate), 25327
(Cooke to Burrill), 2022
(Cox to Prior), 2113, 6481
(Croswell to Cumming), 9099
(Croswell to Turell), 4925
(Cutting to Foster), 26839
(Davenport to Barber), 5373
(Devotion to Bellamy), 11630
(Dewey to Hopkins), 13375, 25390
(Dummer to gentleman), 3157
(Dummer to noble lord), 1542, 5764
(Dutton to Whitefield), 5169
(Dwight to Washington), 31314-15, 32940
(Eliphaz to preacher), 24475
(Erskine to Whitefield), 4714
(Evans to Jones), 23356-57
(J.F. to Foxcroft), 5589
(J.F. to Hobby), 5590
(Finley to friend), 4509, 5592
(Finley to Smith), 8040
(Foster to Buckminister), 16776
(B. Franklin to friend), 3902
(W. Franklin to council), 14915
(Gale to J.W.), 11269
(Gee to Eells), 5191-92
(Gifford to Erskine), 32191
(Gillespie to brethren), 4520
(Green to preacher), 24365
(Griswold to Perry), 30522
(A. Hamilton), 37566-70
(Harper to constituent), 33838
(Hart to Hopkins), 11678
(Hart to Whitaker), 12066
(Harvey to brother), 23434

VOL.	ITEMS	VOL.	ITEMS
1	1-3244	8	22298-25074
2	3245-6623	9	25075-28145
3	6624-9891	10	28146-30832
4	9892-13091	11	30833-33261
5	13092-16176	12	33262-25854
6	16177-19448	13	35855-39162
7	19449-22297		

clergy-man in the country, 1055
clergyman in town, 9716
country gentleman, 4541
countryman, 3912
father, 33994
freeholder, 2893
friend, 14003
gentleman at Elizabeth-Town, 9774
gentleman at Halifax, 10011
gentleman containing, 2163
gentleman in Boston, 5424
gentleman in Connecticut, 10356
gentleman in England, 9156
gentleman in Mount Hope, 2228
gentleman in New York, (1733) 3707,
    (1750) 6526, (1769) 11309, (1772) 12432
gentleman in Philadelphia, (1728) 3048,
    (1742) 4987, (1757) 7929
gentleman in Richmond, 19757
gentleman in Scotland, 5224
gentleman in the country to his friend in
    Boston, 7930
gentleman in the country to his friend in
    town, 3530, 7931
gentleman in Transilvania, 9701
gentleman of New Brunswick, 6864
gentleman of the city, 823
gentleman on Long-Island, 25718
gentleman to his friend in England, 29236
gentleman to his friend upon the excise,
    7227
gentleman travelling, 11699
meeting, 8860
merchant, 7932
Romish priest, 3216
tradesman, 8631
veteran, 13554
Virginian, 13167-70
weaver, 21710
from Alexander Hamilton, 37566-70
from an American, 18367
    eminent minister, (1743) 5225, (1773)
    12832, (1785) 19060, (1791) 23500, (1799)
    35726
    Irish emigrant, 33424, 35210
from Aristocles, 5614
    Baptista, 9838-39
    Christ, 30687
    Common Honesty, 7696
    Connecticut, 36323
    Father La Chaise, 438
    Freeman of South Carolina, 13256
    * * * * * * * in London, 18557
    Lewis Thurenstein, 5324
    Manlius, 37820
    Miss S——a, 23501
    one in Boston, 1663
    one in the country to his friend in Boston,
    2128
    one in the country to his friend in the city,
    2229, 2476
    one of the Society, 28967
    Phocion, 18508-515
    Quebeck, 7225
    Scots Sawney, 9489
    some aged, 1571
    some of the representatives, 5984
from the assistant postmaster, 34903
    Asociate reformed, 20209
    associated ministers, 5717

association, 11900
attorney general accompanying his report,
    (Forsyth petition) 33062, (petition of
    sundry) 31429, (resolution) 31430
attorney general inclosing, 33061
commissioners, 36525
country, 12652, 12751
director, 33091
elders, 11586
First church, 5406
French minister, 17934
lord bishop, 6607
minister, 28696
postmaster general, 36526
Presbyterian, 2503
secretary at war accompanying a report,
    34891, 38755
secretary at war accompanying his report,
    34886
secretary at war to the chairman of the
    committee appointed, 34892
secretary at war to the chairman of the
    committee on so much, 34888
secretary at war to the chairman of the
    committee on the naval, 33094
secretary at war transmitting, 33095
secretary inclosing, 36527
secretary of state accompanying a report,
    34841
secretary of state accompanying an ad-
    dress, 27926
secretary of state accompanying his report,
    36531
secretary of state enclosing, 31433
secretary of state inclosing a report, 33068
secretary of state inclosing abstracts,
    36532, 38756
secretary of state inclosing his report,
    38757
secretary of state inclosing the estimates,
    31432
secretary of state to Charles C. Pinckney,
    33063
secretary of the commonwealth, 34332
secretary of the navy accompanying, 36528
secretary of the navy to the chairman,
    36529-30
secretary of the navy transmitting, 38758
secretary of the treasury accompanied,
    (with a report) 36533, 38759, (with his
    report) 33075
secretary of the treasury accompanying,
    (a letter) 34860, (a plan) 33076, (a re-
    port and estimate) 34861, (a report and
    estimates) 31446, (a report and state-
    ment) 34862, (a report and statements)
    31448, (a report and sundry) 33077, (a
    report from the commissioners) 33078,
    (a report of the commissioners) 38760,

VOL.	ITEMS	VOL.	ITEMS
1	1-3244	8	22298-25074
2	3245-6623	9	25075-28145
3	6624-9891	10	28146-30832
4	9892-13091	11	30833-33261
5	13092-16176	12	33262-25854
6	16177-19448	13	35855-39162
7	19449-22297		

Prince of Wales, 28968
Protestant-dissenters, 12135, 12470
publisher, 7820
Roman Catholics, 18883
right honourable, 11310
Second church, 5583
Rev. Mr. Hobby, 6645
unconverted (Philanthropos), 11041
to Thomas Paine, 32375, 33996
to those towns, 1440
treating, 11267
written, 23502
Letters (Aikin to his son), 26541
(Bennet to young lady), (1791) 23176, (1792) 24093, (1793) 25160, (1796) 30055
(Chesterfield to Stanhope), 14471, 16534-36
(Clark to friend), 24194
(Cogan to Wilberforce), 35318
(Furneaux to Blackstone), 12328, 12684, 13154
(Jay to Littlepage), 19735-36
(Judson to friend), 10348
(Lee to Percy), 14150
(Orton to clergyman), 27455
(Pintard to Pickering), 38272
(Priestley to Burke), 23716, (Priestley to inhabitants of Northumberland), 36161-62, (Priestley to Jews), 27555, (Priestley to philosophers), 26035, 27556-57, (Priestley to Volney), 32718
(Smith to Buel), 31593
(Smyth to Preston), 32855
(Sterne to friends), 16082
(Taylor to Webster), 31593
(Washington to friends), 15868
(Werden to friend), 31610
(Williams to Baptist church), 26486
(Yorick to Eliza), 13025
Letters addressed to the electors, 39135
addressed to the philosophers, 27557
to the yeomanry, 23507, 25724
to young married, 30517
and conversations, 32027, 35392
observations, 21471
other papers, 15826
remarks, 29921
sermons, (1792) 24622, (1795) 29213-15, (1796) 30899, (1797) 32580
&c., 11713
between Theophilus, 5985
by the author of Common sense, 27466
containing a sketch, 31634-35
from a farmer in Pennsylvania, 10875-79, 11238
a father to his son, (1794) 26541, (1796) 29957-58, (1800) 36783
an American farmer, 25357, 33582
France, (1792) 25039, (1793) 26484, (1794) 28090
General Washington, 28969
Sylvius, 20887
the dead, 6591
the Health-office, 35161
occasioned, 23650
of a farmer, 30689
of Abelard, 13787, 29945
of an Italian nun, 27642, 31123-24
of certain Jews, 28781
of Charlotte, 32313-14, 33803
of chev. d'Yrujo, 34788
of Curtius, 34657
of Fabius, 32042

of Franklin, 29256
of friendship, 16804
of gratitude, 17085
of Helvidius, 30734
of Junius, 23477-78, 28912
of Pacificus, 30533
of Papinian, 16311
of Sicilius, 28889
of the late Thomas, 17577
Right hon., 10393
two commanders-in-chief, 14559
of Verus, 33259
on appreciation, 16820, 18614
on frequent communion, 33997, 34062
on liberty, 34442
on missions, 32281
on the existence, 35413
French Revolution, 24003
improvement, (1783) 17869, (1786) 19548, (1793) 25277
questions, 28562
spirit, 6412, 7786
on various subjects, 35516
originally published, (1788) 21332, (1792) 24621, (1795) 29213
patent, 3454
relatng to the Stamp Act, 10342
relating to the transit, 7038
suited to children, 23479
supposed to have been, 20281, 25325
to a philosophical, 29354
wife, (1794) 27415, (1795) 29214, (1797) 32580-81
young lady, 33402-403
to married women, 24796, 31204
to the high and mighty, 15374
inhabitants, 38322
late incorporated, 26486
merchants committee, 11658
ministry, 11176
upon the overtures, 18329
written by Jane Cooper, 28478
during a short residence, 31653
during a tour, 26912
Lettre adressée aux habitans de la province, 13740
adressée aux habitans opprimés, 14575
aux espagnols, 36658
Lettres de Verus, 33260
Lettres originales, 33608
Letts, Ezekiel. Advertisement, 13376
Lettsom, ——, medical practice of, 30574
Letzte privat-erklärung, 5105
Letzte wylle, 6991
Level of Europe, 27218, 28970
Leveret, John, 1616-1679
death, 277
wife's death, 1217
Leveret, John, 1662-1724 see Leverett, John, 1662-1724
Leveret, Sarah, d. 1704, death, 1217

VOL.	ITEMS	VOL.	ITEMS
1	1-3244	8	22298-25074
2	3245-6623	9	25075-28145
3	6624-9891	10	28146-30832
4	9892-13091	11	30833-33261
5	13092-16176	12	33262-25854
6	16177-19448	13	35855-39162
7	19449-22297		

VOL.	ITEMS	VOL.	ITEMS
1	1-3244	8	22298-25074
2	3245-6623	9	25075-28145
3	6624-9891	10	28146-30832
4	9892-13091	11	30833-33261
5	13092-16176	12	33262-25854
6	16177-19448	13	35855-39162
7	19449-22297		

VOL.	ITEMS	VOL.	ITEMS
1	1-3244	8	22298-25074
2	3245-6623	9	25075-28145
3	6624-9891	10	28146-30832
4	9892-13091	11	30833-33261
5	13092-16176	12	33262-25854
6	16177-19448	13	35855-39162
7	19449-22297		

Looking-glass for changelings, 5295
  for children, 1425
  for Elder Clarke, 2209
  for Presbyterians, 9702-703
  for the Americans, 15041
    Jews, 18477
    mind, (1792) 24095, (1793) 25165, (1794) 26645, (1795) 28267, (1800) 36947
    modern, 3051
    Presbyterians, 10756
    times, 211, 9388
Looking to Jesus, 5319
Loomis, Abdiel, d. 1800, death, 38978
Loomis, Amasa, d. 1793, death, 27243
Loose were her tresses, 30239
Lord, Anne, d. 1748, death, 6701
Lord, Benjamin, 1694-1784
  Aged minister's solemn, 18003
  Believers, 4989
  Christian's comfort, 13383
  Christ's embassadors, 9418
  Civil rulers, 12835
  Faithful and approved, 2894, 6867
  God glorified, (1743) 5228-29, (1744) 5425, (1771) 12098, (1795) 28982, (1798) 34013-14
  Great importance, 8387
  Great preparations, 9419
  Heaven a glorious, 6701
  Humble importunity, 5230
  Important connection, 11316
  Jubilee, 10950
  Love to Jesus, 8905
  Ministers of the gospel, 9420
  Necessity of regeneration, 4261
  Parable, 12836
  Religion and government, 6868
  Sobermindedness, 9421
  True Christianity, 2895
  colleague ordained, 16086
  death, 18405
  hand of fellowship, 3769
  letter (from Backus), 9587
Lord, Hezekiah, d. 1761, death, 9419
Lord, Joseph, d. 1748
  Great priviledge, 3435
  Letter to the general, 3839
  Postscript, 3840
  Reason why, 2030
  Two letters, 4377
Lord, Samuel. Price act, 15375
Lord Anson's voyage, 8534
  Camden's opinion, 11427
  Chesterfield's advice, (1781) 17372, (1786) 20002, (1789) 22158, (1794) 27735, (1795) 29560
  Chesterfield's letters, 16536
  Chesterfield's principles, 22159
  -High-Admiral, 2456
Lord Hyde (packet), at New York, 14082, 18252-53
Lord is to be praised, 15726
  Jesus Christ, 4219
  Jesus his legacie, 165
  Jesus walking, 2251-52, 2300
Lord mayor of London see **Barnard, Sir John, 1685-1764**
Lord of the manor, 22382, 23234
  our righteousness, 5090
  save us, 34015
  shall rejoice, 4695
Lord's day, 2193

  ministers, 3913
  prayer, 10387
  protest, 3285
  trumpet, 34318
  voice crying, 1729
  voice in the earthquake, 3068
Lorenzo. Dialogue, 11297
Loring, Israel, 1682-1772
  Duty of an apostatizing, 4153
  Duty which ministers, 7231
  False hopes, 4262
  Justification, 6347
  Ministers insufficient, 4990
  Ministers must, 3436
  Nature & necessity, 3052
  Private Christians, 3920
  Scriptural light, 4264
  Serious thoughts, 3559
  Sermon, 1963
  Service of the Lord, 4263
  Two sermons, 2545
Loring, Israel, fl. 1796, petition, 31380
Loring, John, d. 1720?, death, 2119
Loring, Nicholas. Letter (to T. Smith), 5621
Loring, Samuel. Three discourses, 3437
Loron, Indian chief, 3554
Loss of Christian friends, 32704
Loss of the soul, 3515
Lost and undone, (1765) 10183, (1767) 10784, (1769) 11493, (1770) 11877, (1790) 22929, (1797) 32924
Lot Merkel, no. 31, Hanover square, 23563
Lothrop, Col. ——, d. 1750?, death, 6605
Lothrop, Elijah see **Lathrop, Elijah, 1724-1797**
Lott, Abraham, ed. Journal of the votes, 9756, 10418
Lottery, a dialogue, 8114
Loudoun, John, earl of
  dedication to, 8239
  issues treaty, 7925-26
Loughby, Dennis, of Pittsburgh
  Lamentation, 37846
  New song, 37847
Louis XVI
  anecdotes of reign, 20601
  death, 26271-74, 27549-50
  defence of, 24783
  eulogy, 18385
  funeral service, 27685
  imprisonment, 35314
  tragedy, 22943
  trial, 25499
Louis XVII. Ronde chanté, 27228
Louis, by the grace of God, 15798, 16279
Louis the Sixteenth, 27550
Louisa, a poetical, 22137
Louisiana
  Bando de buen, 34016
  Circulaire, 28983
  Don Juan Ventura, 35741
  Official account, 32387
  Ordre du roi, 34017

VOL.	ITEMS	VOL.	ITEMS
1	1-3244	8	22298-25074
2	3245-6623	9	25075-28145
3	6624-9891	10	28146-30832
4	9892-13091	11	30833-33261
5	13092-16176	12	33262-25854
6	16177-19448	13	35855-39162
7	19449-22297		

Powers of the governor, 30703
Lounger, a periodical, 21929
Lousiad, 20156, 22286
Louvet de Couvray, Jean Baptiste, 1760-1797
Amelia Vermont, 34018
Emilia de Varmont, 35743
Interesting history, 37849
Love and patriotism, (1797) 32388, (1799) 35744, (1800) 37850
Lovat, Lord Simon, death, 5917-18
Love, ———, plaintiff, 31669
Love, Charles. Poem on the death, 37851
Love, Christopher, 1618-1651
Prophecies, (1791) 23508, (1793) 25725-30, (1794) 27229-33, (1795) 28984-85, (1797) 32389, (1798) 34019
Sixteen sermons, 24482
Strange and wonderful, 8499-501, 23509
extracts from, 27564-66
Love, James see **Dance, Thomas, 1722-1774**
Love, John. Geodaesia, 25731, 30704
Love à la mode, 22630
   an essential attribute, 28921
   and patriotism, (1797) 32388, (1799) 35744, (1800) 37850
   and unity, 1587
   his own rival, 9163
   in a village, 26672, 31175
   in Mexico, 28986
   of Christ constraining, 8965
   of Christ the source, 27234
   of our country, a sermon, 15368
      recommended, 13643
      represented, 25044
   of the world, 10294
   to Christ a leading, 23515
   to Christ a necessary, 5497, 5942
   to Jesus, 8905
   to our neighbour, 6372-73, 38410
   to our neighbours, 2925
   triumphant, a sermon, 2356
   triumphant, or constancy, 32390
Lovechild, Nurse see **Fenn, Lady Eleanor Frere, 1714-1813**
Lovelace, John, baron of Hurley see **Hurley, John Lovelace, 4th baron, d. 1709**
Lovelass, Peter. Full clear, and familiar, 23510
Lovell, James, 1738-1814
Essay on the eclipse, 7232
Oratio in funere, 8640
Oration, 12099
Lovell, Capt. John, fight by, 36392
Lovell, John, 1708-1778
Freedom, 7233
Funeral oration, 5231-32
The seasons; an interlocutory, 10043
Lovell, Shubael, ordained, 29657
Lover and friend of mankind. Affectionate address, 14641
Lover of architecture. Town and country, 27810
Lover of astronomy. Almanac see **Almanacs (Clough)**
Lover of constitutional liberty. Appendix, or some observations, 12651
Lover of good men. Vindication, 5704
Lover of harmony see **Billings, William, 1746-1800**
Lover of his country
Address to the inhabitants, 5900
Money the sinews, 3450
   see also **Mather, Cotton, 1662-1728; Morgan,**

Joseph, 1672-1740; Smith, William, 1728-1793
Lover of his king and country. Christian's duty, 7635, 9362
Lover of his memory
Fruits of a father's love, 2941
   see also **Rhodes, John**
Lover of internal devotion see **Kelpius, Johannes, 1673-1708**
Lover of liberty. Letter to the freemen, 6865
Lover of liberty and a mechanic's friend. To the free and patriotic, 11882
Lover of liberty and property. Queries humbly offered, 6597
Lover of mankind
Zeal for the truth, 24021
   see also **Benezet, Anthony, 1713-1784**
Lover of Pennsylvania see **Rush, Benjamin, 1745-1813**
Lover of the mathematics see **Travis, Daniel**
Lover of the same see **Mayhew, Experience, 1673-1758**
Lover of the truth
Short direction, 4421
   see also **Haynes, J.**
Lover of their precious souls. History of the holy Jesus, (1747) 5967, (1748) 6157, (1749) 6331, (1754) 7211, (1762) 9138, (1771) 12073, (1786) 19712, (1790) 22568-69, (1792) 24398-99, (1793) 25607, (1794) 27122, (1795) 28835-36, (1796) 30564
Lover of this country see **Rawle, Francis, 1660-1727**
Lover of true English liberty. Note-maker, 5263
Lover of true piety. Methodism anatomiz'd, 9444
Lover of truth. Address to the Rev. Dr. Alison, 9892
Lover of truth and decency see **Inglis, Charles, 1734-1816**
Lover of truth and his country see **Gale, Benjamin, 1715-1790**
Lover of truth and liberty see **Williams, Elisha, 1694-1755**
Lover of truth and peace
Copy of the letter, 91
   see also **Chauncy, Charles, 1705-1787**
Lover of truth in America. Impartial view, 12821
Lover's almnaac, 34996
   instructor, 30705
   secretary, 29145
   vows, 35696-97
Love's frailties, 27133
   ingenuity, 35114
   pilgrimage, 35745
Lovett, Anna, d. 1739, death, 4338
Lovett, John, 1761-1818. Tribute to Washington, 37852
Lovett, Joseph, wife's death, 4338
Lovewell, John, d. 1725?, death, 2705-706
Lovewell lamented, 2705
Lovigny, Joh. Berniers. Verborgenes leben, 5987
Lovzinski, Baron see **Louvet de Couvray, Jean Baptiste, 1769-1797**
Low, ———, defendant, 38079
Low, Cornelius P. Committee chamber, New York, 14924
Low, Isaac
Respectable public, 14318
To the respectable public(k), 13680-81, 14167
candidate, 13661
chairman committee of 51, 14314
      committee of correspondence, 13477-79
      committee of observation, 14319-20, 14322-

26, 14329
chairman of meeting, 14125
charges against, 14519
delegate to Congress, 13093-94
praised, 13653
Low, John. New York directory, 30706
Low, John, d. 1796, death, 32139
Low, Nathaniel, 1740-1808
Address to the inhabitants, 13384
Address to the soldiers, 14168
Almanac see **Almanacs (Low)**
Low, Samuel, b. 1765
Anthem, 25734
Fellow-craft, 22624
Ode, (1790) 22625, (1800) 37295, 37855
Poems, 37856
Politician outwitted, 21926
Winter displayed, 18562
Lowater, Stephen, arrival in Salem, 14449
Lowder, Jonathan, messenger from Boston, 10318
Lowell, John, 1704-1767
Advantages of God's presence, 7452
Laudable character, 8165
Ministers of the gospel, 4378
Sermon, 8641
death, 10791
ordained, 2744
Lowell, John, 1743-1802
Boston, Nov. 1, 1796, 30772
Eulogy, 23513, 25092
secy. Mass. Council, 14854-55, 14862-64
Lowell, John, 1769-1840
Antigallican, 32393
Essay on hereditary, 34022
Oration, 35747
Lowman, ——, commentary on Revelation, 23486
Lownes, Caleb. Account of the alteration, 25225, 35748
Lowry, Jean. Journal, 8642
Lowth, Robert, 1710-1787
(tr.) Isaiah, 26662
Short introduction to English, (1775) 14169, (1780) 16822, (1783) 18005, (1795) 28990, (1799) 35749, (1800) 37857
grammarian, 13123, 16194, 18918, 19477, 20936
extracts from, 29080
introduction to his grammar, 24059, 26578, 28214, 35118, 36851
Loyal address, 1057
Loyal American. To the disunited, 16545
Loyal and humorous, 16326
Loyal layman. Blessings, 30101
Loyal patriot. Some observations, 11073
Loyalty vindicated, 824
Lozano, Pedro, 1697-1759. True and particular, (1749) 6348, (1750) 6531, (1755) 7453
Lucas, Charles, 1769-1854. History of Jack Smith, 34023
Lucas, Margaret Brindley, 1701-1769. Account of the convincement, 37858
Lucas, Richard, 1648-1715. Rules relating, 8643
Lucca, Gaudentio di, adventures, 30059, 35183, 36945-46
Lucianus Samosatensis. Select dialogues, 21927, 28991
Lucifer's decree, 1004
Lucius
To the freemen, 14170
To the inhabitants, 14924
Lucius, Samuel see **Lutz, Samuel, 1674-1750**

Lucky escape, 26878
Lucky idiot, 32798
Lucy, or Selim's complaint, 27136
Lucy Sampson, 21922
Ludger, C., tr. Peevish man, 37756
Ludlow, ——, plaintiff, 38079
Ludlow, Edmund. Inaugural dissertation, 27238
Ludlow, Roger. Book of the general laws, 173
Ludovici a Thurenstein in antiquissima, 5106
Ludwig, Nikolaus, 1700-1760 see **Zinzendorff, Nikolaus Ludwig, graf von, 1700-1760**
Lukins, George. Narrative, 24485, 27239
Lullaby; a favorite, 25308
Luminous shining character, 21823
Lunar hermit see **Dewey, Israel**
Lunsford, Lewis, d. 1793, death, 29650
Lurting, Robert, mayor, 3458
Lurting, Thomas. Fighting sailor, 2654
Lush, Stephen, nominated, 36853
Lustige-aria, 9715
Luther, Martin, of New York. Card, 10850
Luther, Martin, of Rhode Island, manages lottery, 28026
Luther, Martin, 1483-1546
(tr.) Biblia, (1763) 9343, (1775) 13834, (1776) 14663
(tr.) Gantze psalter, 10556
Kleine catechismus, (1744) 5426, (1749) 6349, (1752) 6869, (1765) 10045, (1766) 10359, (1767) 10665, (1770) 11705, (1774) 13385, (1777) 15382, (1782) 17576, (1784) 18563-64, (1786) 19761-62, (1787) 20468, (1791) 23514, (1793) 25735, (1795) 28992-93, (1798) 34024, (1800) 37740
Kleine Darmstädtische catechismus, 9423
(tr.) Neue Testament, (1745) 5542, (1755) 7359, (1761) 8799, (1763) 9347, (1769) 11181, (1775) 13837, (1783) 17846, (1787) 20236, (1788) 20969, (1791) 23202, (1794) 26667, (1795) 28286-87, (1796) 30081-82, (1800) 36956
(tr.) Psalter des königs, (1760) 8549, (1762) 9071-72, (1768) 10837-38, (1773) 12682, (1783) 17845, (1784) 18361, (1791) 23357, (1793) 25189-90, (1796) 30074-77, (1797) 31814
Shorter catechism, 19055
Small catechism, 8907
Vollständiges Marburger, (1759) 8390, (1762) 9166, (1770) 11714
articles of belief, 13122, 30000
commentary recommended, 38354
hymns by, 15387
life, 35737
psalms by, 36660
Lutherans. Hoch-deutsche lutherisches A.B.C., 14171
Lutherische und reformirte A.B.C., 16028, 18565
Lutterell, Henry Temple, speech in Parliament, 14092
Lutz, Samuel, 1674-1750. Paradiesische, 11706
Lux, Willliam
clerk of meeting, 13130

VOL.	ITEMS	VOL.	ITEMS
1	1-3244	8	22298-25074
2	3245-6623	9	25075-28145
3	6624-9891	10	28146-30832
4	9892-13091	11	30833-33261
5	13092-16176	12	33262-25854
6	16177-19448	13	35855-39162
7	19449-22297		

letter (from Laurens), 16111
Lydekker, Gerrit. Discourse, 10493
Lydius, John Henry
 dispute with, 9889
 indenture with, 9212
 proclamation concerning, 8953
Lying-in hospital
 Act to incorporate, 35953
 Constitution, 35954
Lying valet, (1778) 15804, (1794) 26558, 27032
Lyk-reden op wylen, 27989
Lyman, Caleb, 1678-1742, death, 5318
Lyman, David, son's death, 39138
Lyman, Eliphalet, 1754-1836
 Two discourses, 27240
 ordained, 16823
Lyman, Gershom Clark, 1753-1813. Sermon, 18566,
 22626
Lyman, Isaac, colleague ordained, 34471, 35816
Lyman, Jonathan, d. 1766, death, 10550
Lyman, Joseph, 1749-1828
 Administrations, 27241
 Advantages, 35750
 Approbation, 16823
 Belief of the peculiar, 35583
 Grace of the redeemed, 25736
 Love to Christ, 23515
 Sermon, (1774) 14172, (1787) 20469, (1794) 28994
 Settled ministry, 32394
 proposals for printing sermon by, 36169
Lyman, Moses, d. 1768, death, 11014
Lyman, Phineas, d. 1799, death, 39138
Lyme dispute, 3484
Lynch, Jane, petition, 38841
Lynch, Samuel. Table of excitement, 28364
Lynde, Benjamin, trial judge, 11683
Lynde, Samuel. Vindication, 1685
Lyne, James. Plan of the city, 3438
Lynn, A., engraver, 37302

Lynzey, ——, captain of sloop, 28689
Lyon, Abigail Blodget Stickney, 1751-1808. Ob-
 servations, 34027
Lyon, Asa, 1763-1841
 Dialogues, 30710
 Mourner's hope, 37862
Lyon, Elisha, d. 1767, death, 11080
Lyon, James, of Richmond, ed. National magazine,
 35857, 38027
Lyon, James, of Vermont. Republican magazine,
 34028
Lyon, James, 1735-1794
 Lawfulness, excellency, 9424-25
 Proposals for printing, 22627
 Saint's daily assistant, (1791) 23516, (1793) 25737,
 (1796) 30711
 Urania, (1761) 8908, (1767) 10666, (1773) 12839
 music by, 21578
Lyon, Joseph, remarks on, 35266
Lyon, Matthew, 1746-1822
 Capt. John Wood's lottery, 34029
 Copy of a memorial, 28997
 associated with lottery, 35048
 election, 32102
 fracas with Griswold, 33586, 34757-60
 petition, 31377, 31397
 released from jail, 35601
Lyon, Patrick. Narrative, 35752
Lyons, Israel, teacher of Hebrew, 9514
Lyric works of Horace, 19717
Lyttelton, George, baron, 1709-1773
 Dialogues of the dead, 32396
 Observations on the conversion, (1749) 6442,
 (1761) 8909, (1785) 19064, (1800) 37863
Lyttelton, Thomas, baron, 1744-1779
 Letter (to Chatham), 13386-87
 Letters, 17577
Lyttleton, William Henry, baron, 1724-1808, trav-
 els, 31692?

M

M., A. State of religion, 5344
M., C.
  Account of the sufferings, 30149
  Masonic hymn by, 38399
M. Carey's catalogue, (1792) 24174-76, (1793) 25253
M., I. Original rights, 2346
M., L., dirge by, 38399
M. Martel's literal translation, 33125
M. S. see Menno Simons
M., T. see Maule, Thomas
M., W. see Masters, William
Ma belle conquette, 25628
Maas, Johannes Theodorus Wilhelmus, death, 14138
Mably, Gabriel Bonnot, 1709-1785. Remarks, 19065
M'Adam, ——, present at delivery of note, 13335
Macanulty, Barnard B. Salem, December, 34030
Macaroni, a comedy, 13331
Macartney, Lord ——, ambassador to China, 31648
Macaulay, Catharine Sawbridge, 1733-1791
  Address, 14173
  Observations, 23517
MacBride, David, 1726-1778
  Improved method, 19763
  Principles of virtue, 30813
McCall, George, recants, 14194
McCalla, Daniel, 1748-1800
  Acceptable year, 37864
  Mystery, 35753
MacCarty, Thaddeus, 1722-1785
  Advice of Joab, 8388
  Guilt, 15872-73
  Letter, 5693
  Most heinous, 11707
  Power and grace, 10952
  Praise, 14830
  Reformation, 13388
  Success, 5988
  ordained, 4963
M'Cauley, William, trial, 11683
McClallen, Robert, treasurer N.Y., 38081
McClanachan, William. Letter from a clergyman, 9716
MacClanechan, ——, letter (from Secker), 13191-92
M'Clary family, case in court, 28788
M'Clelin, Daniel, d. 1773?, death, 12758
M'Clenachan, Blair
  To the citizens, 17743
  chairman committee, 16474
  suspected of importing, 14386

McClenachan, William. Christian warrior, 5622
MacClintock, Samuel, 1732-1804
  Advantages, 11708
  Agur's choice, 32397
  Artifices, 11709
  The choice, 34031
  Discourse, 23518
  Epistolary correspondence, 23519
  Evidences, 32398
  Herodias, 12440
  Justice, 8389
  Oration, 37865
  Sermon, (1774) 14174, (1784) 18567
  correspondence with Ogden, 23650
  ordained, 7694
  strictures on, 32290
M'Cloud, Alexander. Surprising account, 32401
M'Clung, J., address by, 30830
McClure, David, 1748-1820
  Discourse, 37866
  New Year, a sermon, 35754
  Oration, 18006
  Pleasures of early, 27242
  Sermon, (1784) 24486, (1790) 22628, (1791) 24487, (1793) 27243, 27245, (1794) 27244, 28998
  Sermons, 28999
  abstract of journal, 13077
M'Clurg, James, 1746-1823. Experimental treatise, 12840
McConkey, Mary, meeting at house of, 37525
M'Connell, Matthew. Essay, 20470
McCord, William, settlement in Pennsylvania, 8642
M'Corkle, Samuel Eusebius, 1746-1811
  Charity sermon, 29000
  Discourse, 34032
  Sermon, (1792) 24488, 27246, (1795) 29001
  True greatness, 37867
  Work of God, 34033
M'Cormick, James. Almanac see Almanacs (M'Cormick)

VOL.	ITEMS	VOL.	ITEMS
1	1-3244	8	22298-25074
2	3245-6623	9	25075-28145
3	6624-9891	10	28146-30832
4	9892-13091	11	30833-33261
5	13092-16176	12	33262-25854
6	16177-19448	13	35855-39162
7	19449-22297		

(ed.) The mirror, 24494, 25748
Rights of Great Britain, 14727-28
Mackenzie, Robert, secy. to Howe, 15340
Mackenzie, Roderick. Reading no preaching, 32408
MacKercher, Daniel. Memorial, 4154
M'Kesson, John, secy. Provincial congress, 14304
Mackey, James, petition, 31428
M'Kinley, John, chairman of committee, 13820
M'Kinney, James. View of the rights, 32409
McKinstry, Elizabeth, d. 1763?, murdered, 9355, 9616
Mackintosh, Duncan
   Essai raisonné, 32410
   Plain, rational essay, 32411
Mackintosh, Sir James, 1765-1832
   Rights of Great Britain, 14727-28
   Vindiciae, 24495
Macklin, Charles, 1699-1797
   Love à la mode, 22630
   True-born Irishman, (1784) 18568, (1787) 20474-75, (1792) 24049
M'Knight, John, 1754-1823
   Divine goodness, 29014
   God the author, 27255
   Life to the dead, 35738
   Six sermons, 22631
Mackrill, Joseph
   History of the yellow, 30729
   reply to, 30922
MacLaine, Archibald
   Address, 20594
   (tr.) Ecclesiastical history, 32513, 34154
M'Lane, ——. Eternal damnation, 25749-50
McLaurin, John, 1693-1754. Sermons, 19765
Maclay, Samuel, 1741-1811. Motion, 14th April, 1796, 31361
M'Lean, Angus, relief of, 29709
Maclean, Charles. View of the science, 33254
Maclean, John, 1771-1814. Two lectures, 32412
MacLeane, Lauchlin. Essay, 7701
M'Leod, Alexander. Surprising account, (1787) 20472, (1788) 21210, (1794) 27248, (1796) 30713
Maclin, William, secy. Tennessee, 34637
McMahon, Simon Crea. Life and adventures, 22632
M'Mains, John, tr. Compendium, 21354
M'Manus, Charles. Correct account, 34040
McMasters, James, conduct, 11576
McMasters, Patrick, conduct, 11576
McMillan, ——. Julia, 25751, 35759
M'Murray, William. Map of the U.S., (1786) 19766, (1787) 20476, (1788) 21212, (1793) 25752
MacNally, Leonard, 1752-1820. Songs, 27256
M'Neal, Archibald, petition, 31372
M'Neal, William, petition, 31372
Macnemara, M., reply to, 10253
M'Nutt, Alexander
   Considerations, 16825
   Constitution and frame, 16824
   To the inhabitants, 16826
Macomb, Alexander, memorial, 34732
MacOneil, Marcus, cheat, 35355
Macpherson, ——. Directory for the city, 19067
MacPherson, Capt. James. History of the present rebellion, 5623
Macpherson, James, 1736-1796
   Oscar and Malvina, 30730-31
   Poems of Ossian, 22633
   Rights of Great Britain, 14727-28
Macpherson, John, broker, 18729
Macpherson, John, of Philadelphia

History of the life, 21930
Introduction to the study, 17580
Lectures, 23529, 34041
Letter (to Dickinson), 11712
Letters, &c., 11713
Mount-Pleasant, May 5, 1766, 10360
Pennsylvania sailor's letters, 12107
To be published and sold, 12106
Vorlesungen, 24496
reply to, 10308
Macready, William, 1755-1829. The bank-note, 30732
McRee, James, 1752-1840. Eulogium, 37874
M'Shane, Capt. ——, letter from, 26733
MacSparran, James, 1680-1757
   Answer to a printed, 4379
   Sacred dignity, 6870
   Sermon, 4741, 5990
   attacked, 6954
M'Whorter, Alexander, 1734-1807
   Blessedness, 30733
   Festival discourse, 25753
   Funeral sermon, 37875
MacWhorter, Alexander Cumming, 1771-1808
   Oration, 27257
   reads Declaration, 25753
M'William, Rebecca. Notice; to be sold, 19873
M'William, Richard, d. 1786?, goods auctioned, 19873
Macy, Joseph, respondent, 11614
Mad house scene, 28978
Madam Willis's letters, 21608
Madan, Martin, 1726-1790
   Account of the triumphant, (1764) 9717, (1765) 10047, (1772) 12442, (1795) 29015
   Collection of hymns, 10361
   Scriptural comment, 12443
Maddox, Isaac, 1697-1759. Sermon, 6871
Made the 4th of January, 1796, 31371
   4th of February, 1796, 31379
   8th of February, 1796, 31380
   11th of December, 1795, 31366
   11th of January, 1796, 31372
   13th of January, 1796, 31373
   14th of December, 1795, 31368
   26th January, 1796, 31428
   26th of January, 1796, 31374-76
   29th of December, 1795, 31370
   29th of January, 1796, 31378
Madison, George. Account of receipts, 35679
Madison, James, 1749-1812
   Address to the convention, 24497
   Address to the members, 35761
   Discourse, 37876-77
   Letter (to Morse), 29662
   Manifestations, 29016
   Oration, 12444
   Sermon, 17203, 19767
Madison, James, 1751-1836
   Address and recommendations, 18223-28

VOL.	ITEMS	VOL.	ITEMS
1	1-3244	8	22298-25074
2	3245-6623	9	25075-28145
3	6624-9891	10	28146-30832
4	9892-13091	11	30833-33261
5	13092-16176	12	33262-25854
6	16177-19448	13	35855-39162
7	19449-22297		

Letter (to member of Congress), 35760
Letters of Helvidius, 30734
Political observations, 29017
Speech, 27258
To the honorable, 20108
  address to, 29559
  proposes commercial regulations, 27714
  reports on Northwest Territory, 18264
Madness of mankind, 7193, 8122
Madness of the Jacobite, 2546
Magaw, Jacob, 1778-1867. Eulogy, 37878
Magaw, Lucia, d. 1790, death, 22338, 22634
Magaw, Samuel, 1740-1812
  Discourse, (1775) 14176, (1794) 27259, (1797)
    32413, 34042
  Notes on the last, 22634
  Oration, 37879-80
  Prayer, (1786) 20647, (July 28, 1787) 20477,
    20691-92, (Oct. 31, 1787) 20736
  Sermon, (1779) 16327, (1780) 17204, (1783)
    18569, (1786) 19768, (1787) 20478
  Substance of an address, 24498
  Things lovely, 27260
  wife's death, 22338
Magazine containing, 31963
Magdalen society. Constitution, 38249
Magellan, I. H. de, donation by, 29977
Magens, Jochum Melchior
  (tr.) Articles of faith, 7262
  Heylsaame onderwysinge, 7240
Maginnis, ———. To the curious, 29018
Magistracy an institution, 5326
Magistrate acting for the counties see **Colquhoun,**
    Patrick, 1745-1820
Magna Britannia, 10048
Magnetic atlas, 37183
Magruder, William B. Address, 37881
Mahomet, life, 31048, 34412
Mahony, Matthew, murderer, 4681
Maid of the mill, 22360
  of the oaks, 15252
  the mistress, 9022
  with a bosom, 35762
Maiden's best, 24310
Maillet, Benoit de, 1656-1738. Telliamed, 32414
Main point, 9895
Maine spelling book, 36156-57
Mair, John. Introduction to Latin, 35763
Maiss, J. M. Circular, 6828
Maitland, David, joins commercial firm, 26151
Maitland, Thomas. De juri regni, 10249
Majesty and mortality, 38679
Major Andre's complaint, 27261
Major est veritas, 22923
Makemie, Francis, 1658?-1708
  Answer to George Keith, 693
  Catechism, 553
  Good conversation, 1298
  Letter (to Cornbury), 1299
  Narrative, 1300, 7455
  reply to, 640
Malachi, or the everlasting, 1902, 10686
Malcom, James Peller, d. 1815. Liberty, 20479
Malcom, John, punished, 13358
Malcomson, James. Sermon, 29019
Malden, Mass.
  Articles drawn up, 2896
  Subscribers to Malden bridge, 20480
Malham, John, 1747-1821. Naval gazetteer, 32415
Mall, Thomas

History of the martyrs, 5991
Short collection, 35764
Mallet, David, 1700-1765
  William and Margaret, 28977
  excerpts from, 26014
Mallet du Pan, Jacques François, 1750-1800
  Dangers which threaten, 29020
  History of the destruction, 35765-66
  proposals for printing his History, 35855
Mamusse, 72-73, 385
Man, Samuel, d. 1719, death, 2076
Man, Spencer, relief of, 29695
Man as he is, 28224
  eating, 1466
  humbled, 3524
  in iron, 32152
  like grass, 6309
  mortal, 7700
  of business, 13202
  of feeling, (1782) 17579, (1791) 23527-28, (1794)
    27254, (1795) 29012
  of God furnished, 1363
  of God thoroughly furnished, 8098
  of his word, 1623
  of real sensibility, 20696, 38474
  of reason, 1976
  of sensibility, 32812
  of the times, 31790
  of the world, (1783) 18007, (1795) 29013, (1799)
    35758
Man of truth. To the worthy, 14519
Man of war, 899-900
  on probation, 32606
  unmasked, 11308
  worth forty, 16161
Manadus, Willem Johonas van Dore. New Jersey,
    Feb. 19, 1768, 11040
Management of the tongue, 18008, 19769
Managers of the Delaware lottery, 13242
Managers on the part, 11372
Manhattan committee. Report, 35950
Manhattan company, incorporated, 35917
Manheim, Frederic, captivity of family, 25080,
    26540, 31616, 32520, 35639, 36391, 36779
Manifestations of the beneficence, 29016
Manifesto and proclamation, 15832-33
    or declaration, 859
    und feyerliche, 15834
Manitowompae, 95, 383
Manliffe, Richard, dying words, 950
Manlius. Letter (to Marshall), 37820
Manlius, with notes, 27062-63
Mann, Elias, 1750-1825. Northampton collection,
    32416
Mann, Herman, 1772-1833. Female review, 32417
Mann, James, 1759-1832
  Address, 37883
  Oration, 34043
Mann, John, suit by, 12159
Mann, Mercy, suit by, 12159
Mann, Nancy, d. 1799, death, 35785
Manna gathered, 6743
Manner in which, 23136
Manner of receiving, 6532
Manners, Nicholas
  Confutation of many, 25755
  Creation, 25758
  Preachers described, 25756
  Seventeen discourses, 25757
  Two sermons, 27262
Manners of the ancient, 28684

Manners of the times, 9240
Manning, James, 1738-1791
    death, 23380, 23559, 30779
    dedication to, 15060
    pres. Brown university, 11444, 21432, 22113, 22850
Manning, John, meeting at house of, 25818
Man's chief end, 456
    dignity, 9363
    extremity, 739
    frailty, 3362
    liableness, 5050
    life, 3402
    mortality, 26599
    self reflection, 278, 858
    whole duty, 1964
Mansergh, J. W., testimonials by, 38531
Mansfield, Achilles, 1751-1814. Christianity, 23531
Mansfield, Isaac, 1750-1826. Sermon, 14831
Mansfield, Sir James, 1733-1821
    conduct of, 13992
    letter (from Casca), 13983
    letter (from Williamson), 15713
Mansfield, Jared, approves manuscript, 22910
Mansfield, John, d. 1783. Last words, 17994
Mansfield, Joseph, d. 1830. Hope, a poem, 37884
Mansfield, Richard, 1723-1820
    Discourse, 22635
    Funeral sermon, 17581
Mansfield, William Murray, earl of, 1705-1793
    Case relating, 7261
    Speech, 12328, 12684, 13154
Manson, David. New primer, 16328, 18570
Manson's primer, 23532-33
Mantissa, 1757
Manton, Thomas. Sacramental sermon, 21670
Manual exercise (1798), 34895-96
Manual exercise and evolutions, (1787) 20774, (1788) 21528, (1789) 22209-210, (1792) 24915, (1793) 26355, (1795) 29777
    exercise as ordered, (1766) 10330, (1774) 13319-23, (1775) 14101-107, 14109, (1776) 14797, (1777) 15359, (1780) 16795, (1794) 27099
    for self-examination, 2047
    of a free man, 35767
    of Catholic, 13588, 16058
    of exercises, 36543
    of religious, 10668
    of the theophilanthropes, 37885
Manuductio ad ministerium, 2772
Manuduction to blessedness, 2667
Manufactory sermon, 8078
Manufacture of potash, 7940
Many members, 12194
    of the electors, 4380
    respectable, 11879
Manzoni, ——, letter (from Angeloni), 9838-39
Map and description, 34310
    of Barbary, 26732
    of General Dumourier's, 32493
    of Kentucke, 18467
    of Kentucky, 26616
    of man's misery, (1692) 615, (1732) 3560, (1772) 12423
    of Messrs. Gorham, 29341
    of part, 30691
    of Pennsylvania, (1749) 6316, (1791) 23454, (1792) 24412
    of Philadelphia, 35385
    of South Carolina and part, 13240
    of South Carolina and parts, 19847

    of that part, 29183
    of the bay, 25581
        Cayuga, 30735
        Connecticut, 34317
        country between Albemarle, 21277
        country of the Five Nations, 2513
        county of Philadelphia, 27141
        county of Worcester, 26481
        district, 29589
        federal territory, 20312, 21037
        Five Nations, 3921
        French, Austrian, 25258
        harbour, 3922
        improved part, 8489
        north west parts, 19648
        peninsula, 20272
        province of New Hampshire, 8893
        province of Nova Scotia, 15121
        state of Connecticut, 15585
        state of Delaware, 35768
        state of Kentucky, 28191
        state of Maryland, 27070, 28772
        state of New York, 24265
        state of North Carolina, 31047
        state of Pennsylvania, 23453, 24411
        state of Rhode Island, 28803
        state of Vermont, 26478, 28094
        states of Maryland and Delaware, 30334
        states of Virginia, North Carolina, 21412
        Tennessee, 26168
        three northern, 25259
        U. S., (Bradley) 30122-23, (Carleton) 23250, (Howell) 27142, (Lewis) 32378
        U. S. (M'Murray), (1786) 19766, (1787) 20476, (1788) 21212, (1793) 25752
        U. S. (Norman), 23638
        world, 21213
    those parts, 29589
Maps of Carey's, 27077
Maqua Indians, propositions by, 545
Marah spoken to, (1716) 1825, (1718) 1977, (1721) 2248
Marat, ——, dialogue with Porcupine, 30593
Marblehead, Mass.
    Laws and regulations, 34044
    Price act, 15386
Marburg hymn book, (1759) 8390, (1762) 9166, (1770) 11714, (1774) 13394, (1777) 15387
Marcandier, ——. Published for the general, 10362
Marcellus, published, 27263
March, Edmund, 1703-1791
    Divine providence, 9167
    Fair play, 8166
    Great difficulty, 9168
    Necessity, 9169
Mar. 18, 1783; resolved, 18268
Marchant, William. Oration, 32418
Marcus see Iredell, James
Marcus Brutus. Serious facts, 38486

VOL.	ITEMS	VOL.	ITEMS
1	1-3244	8	22298-25074
2	3245-6623	9	25075-28145
3	6624-9891	10	28146-30832
4	9892-13091	11	30833-33261
5	13092-16176	12	33262-25854
6	16177-19448	13	35855-39162
7	19449-22297		

Mare, J., news from, 16702
Mare pacificum, 1216
Margarot, Maurice, trial, 27592-96, 31173
Margery Two-Shoes see Goody Two-shoes
Maria Cecilia, 22636
    Feodorovna, 34525
    or the generous, 19502-503
    or the triumph, 29264
    or the wrongs, 35555
Marie Antoinette
    memoirs of, 27308-309
    sings ballad, 26218
Marie de Bordes, J. Défense des colons, 30736
Marin ben Jesse, David
    Letter, 7043
    Remark, 7456
    Remonstrance, 7457
Marine Anti-Britannic society. Rules, 18395
Marine insurance company, Boston, incorporated,
    35221
Marine insurance office, Baltimore, established,
    35147
Marine list, 23668
Marine rules, 34893, 36544
Marine society, Boston. Directions for sailing, 10882
Marine society, Marblehead. Laws and regulations,
    34044
Marine society, New York. Charter, 17270, 21319,
    30882
Marine society, Newport. Laws, 19142, 35968
Marine society, Portland. Laws, 34403
Marine society, Providence. Charter, 36183
Marine society, Salem. Laws, 18775, 22868
Mariner's divine mate, 1749
Mariner's guide, 35066
Marius, John. Advice, 22637
Mark, St., life of, 9863
Mark (slave), execution, 7415
Mark, Jacob. Papers relative, 31473
Markham, Bernard, case against, 31671
Markham, Gervase, 1568-1637. Citizen and country-
    man's, 9718, 32419
Markland, J. Typographia, 3298
Markoe, Peter, 1753-1792
    Algerine spy, 20481
    Miscellaneous poems, 20482
    Patriot chief, 18571
    Reconciliation, 22638
    Storm, 21081
    The times, 21214-15
    excerpts from, 23246
Marks of the new, 4456
Marlborough, John Churchill, duke of, 1650-1722
    elegy on, 2438
Marlborough, Mass.
    At a council, 3788
    Testimony of an association, 5678
Marmajou, Anthony. Five hundred, 15877
Marmontel, Jean François, 1723-1799
    Amitié, 15377
    Belisarius, 30737
    History of Belisarius, 11715
    Palaemon, 27667
    Romance of an hour, 28918
    Selima, 24049, 24500
    Shepherdess, 29021, 32420
    Widow of the village, (1790) 32421, (1798) 34045,
        (1799) 35769
Marolles, Louis de, martyr, 1611
Marple, Richard, murderers rewarded, 18686
Marrant, John. Sermon, 21931

Marriage, an epic, 32422
    an honourable, 6856
    of a deceased, 32423, 32009
    of a wife's sister, 24293
    of Cana, 5091
Married man, 28564, 30339
Marriot, Dr. ——, examination of, 13626
Marriott, ——, play adapted for, 29471
Marriott, Mrs. ——. Chimera, 29022-23
Marrow of modern, 5182, 25485
Marrow of the gospel, 2915
Marschalk, Andrew
    Liberty, 11322
    reply to, 11458
Marseilles—march, 26107
Marsequunt, Indian chief, 3916
Marsh, Christopher Bridge. Two practical, 29265
Marsh, Ebenezer Grant, 1777-1803. Oration, (1797)
    34046, (1798) 34047, (1800) 37886
Marsh, Elisha, ordained, 4922
Marsh, John, 1743-1821
    Discourse, 18572
    Great sin, 18009, 21216
    Sermon, 30738, 32424
    extracts from, 17828, 26629
    ordained, 13781
Marsh, Jonathan, 1684-1747
    Great care, 2231
    God's fatherly care, 4155
    Sermon, 2232
Marsh, Jonathan, 1714-1794. Sermon, 21217
Marsh, Joseph. Ordinance for the suppression,
    27502
Marshall, ——, remarks on, 8297?, 9339
Marshall, Charles. Introduction, 35770
Marshall, Humphrey, 1722-1801. Arbustrum Amer-
    icanum, 19068
Marshall, Humphrey, 1756-1841
    Address, 30739
    Aliens, 34048
    Reply to the address, 29024
    extracts from, 29952
Marshall, Jane. Sir Harry Gaylove, 15388
Marshall, John, 1755-1835
    Speech, 37887
    amendments by, 38794
    arrives in Paris, 34363
    dedication to, 34657?
    instructions to, 34837, 34839
    letter (from Manlius), 37820
    motion by, 38792
Marshall, Walter, 1628-1680. Gospel-mystery, 21218
Marshall, William, 1735-1808
    Catechism for youth, 18010
    Child's catechism, 34049
    Propriety of singing, 13395
    Religious instruction, 18573
    Vindication of the Associate, 23534
Marshall, William, 1740-1802
    Some remarkable, 35771
    Theological dissertation, 35772
Martel, Michel
    Elements, 30740, 32425
    Proposals for printing, 30741
    (tr.) Works of Virgil, 33125
Martens, George Friedrich, 1756-1821. Summary
    of the law, 29025
Martial, Martin. Milkiad, 21932
Martial wisdom, 4210
Martin, ——. Copie eines brief, 8645
Martin, Alexander, 1740-1807

America, a poem, 11323
New scene, 34050-51
Proclamation, 18821
dedication to, 12904
Martin, Daniel. Some meditations, 11716
Martin, François Xavier, 1762-1846
(tr.) Cases determined, 25702
Chart of the law, 30742
Collection of the statutes, 24627
Funeral oration, 22639
Notes of a few, 32426
Office and authority, 23535
Report of a case, 30743
Treatise, 30744
Martin, Georg Adam. Christliche bibliothek, 24501
Martin, Hugh. Narrative, 17582, 18574
Martin, James. Oration, 30745
Martin John. New invented friction, 21219
Martin, John Paul see **Bishop, Abraham, 1763-1844**
Martin, Joseph, concludes treaty, 19279
Martin, Josiah. Proclamation, 14949
Martin, Luther, 1748-1826
Genuine information, 21220
Queries, 16331
To Robert Lemmon, 16330
To the inhabitants, 15389
To the public, 16329
letter (from Cineas), 16225
remarks on, 16513
reply to, 16320
Martin, William Thomas, d. 1754, death, 7318
Martin and James, 32258
Martinet, Joannes Florentius, 1729-1795. Catechism
of nature, (1791) 23536, (1792) 24502, (1793)
25759, (1795) 29026, 34052-53, (1797) 32427-28,
(1799) 35773, (1800) 37888
Martin, Count ——, transformation, 9974
Martis, 29 die Octobris, 10065
Martyn, Mary, d. 1725, death, 2631
Martyrology, 4032
Marvell, Andrew. Second address, 12793
Marvellous things, 5558
Marvellous works, 9391
Marvin, Deacon ——, punishment, 35007
Marxly, Theodosia, d. 1793, death, 27054
Mary II, queen of England
grant to, 678
life of, 726
Mary, queen of Scots, beheading, 36286
Mary Magdalene, lamentations, 25549
Mary, John
(tr.) Anecdotes, 19153, 20601
New French, 18575
Mary Somerville, 12108
Maryland
Account of the gross, 18576
Annapolis, Jan. 20, 1785, 19069
Annapolis, June 1, 1785, 19070
Articles of agreement, 3710, 4182
Association of the freemen, 14179
At a council, Aug. 1, 1739, 4544
At a meeting of the committee, 13396
At a meeting of the delegates, 14178
Baltimore, Apr. 18; the following, 15391
By his excellency the governor, 8910
By the House of delegates, (Dec. 13, 1796) 30747,
(Jan. 1, 1799) 35776, (Dec. 9, 1800) 37892
Charter, 2655, 8168
Council proceedings, 10367
Declaration of rights, 14836
Estimate of state debt, 21221

November session 1784, 18579
Proceedings of several, 16334
Proceedings of the committee, 11720
Preceedings of the convention(s), (1774) 14177,
(1775) 14832, (1776) 14833-35
Proceedings upon the conference, 12446
Report of the committee appointed, 19771
Report of the intendant, 18580
Summary and comparative, 18581
Testamentary system, 32431
To his excellency Benedict, 3302-303
To his excellency Horatio Sharpe, 7044
To his excellency Samuel Ogle, 4382
To his excellency the governor, 18582
To the honourable Benedict, 3301
To the honourable Benjamin, 6872
Maryland. General assembly
Proceedings, 2655, 16830
Maryland. Governor
Proclamation, (1771) 12110, (1783) 18239, (1784)
18820, (1796) 30746, (1799) 35774
Speech, 3300, 3561
Maryland. House of delegates
Journal, (1739) 4381, (1740) 4545-46, (1741)
4742, (1742) 4994, (1745) 5624
Votes and proceedings, (1731) 3439, (1732) 3562,
(1733) 3677, (1747) 5992-93, (1748) 6178, (1749)
6350-51, (1750) 6533, (1751) 6702-703, (1752)
6873, (1753) 7045, (1754) 7236-38, (1755) 7459-
61, (1756) 7936-38, (1757-58) 8169-72, (1759)
8392-93, (1760) 8646-47, (1761) 8911, (1762)
9171, (1763) 9719, (1765) 10365-66, (1766)
10670, (1768) 10955, (1769) 11719, (1770) 12111-
12, (1772) 12447, (1773) 12843, (1774) 13400,
(1777) 15397, 16335, (1778) 16336, (1779) 16831,
(1780) 17207, (1781) 17585, (1782) 18013, (1783)
18014, 18583, (1784) 19072, (1785) 19772, (1786)
20487-88, (1787) 21224-25, (1788) 21934, (1789)
22641, (1790) 23538, (1791) 24505-506, (1792)
25762, (1793) 27269, (1794) 29027, (1795) 30749,
(1796) 32432, (1797) 34055, (1798) 35779, (1799)
37895
Votes and resolves, 3180, 3304
Maryland. Laws (collective)
Abridgment and collection, 8391
Acts . . . for the regulation, 37889-90
Acts of Assembly, 10953
Acts passed at different sessions, 32429
Compleat collection, 2897
Digest of the laws, 35617
Laws, from 1754 to 1758, 8168
Laws of Maryland at large, 10049
Laws of Maryland made since 1763, 20483
Laws of Maryland, to which, 35775, 37894
Laws of the province, 1965
Maryland. Laws (session)
Acts, (1725) 2656, (1726) 2760, (1727) 2898,
(1737) 4156, (1740) 4543, (1753) 7235, (1755)
7458, (1756) 7934, (1757) 7935, (1765) 10050,
(1766) 10363-64, 10669, (1768) 10954, (1769)

VOL.	ITEMS	VOL.	ITEMS
1	1-3244	8	22298-25074
2	3245-6623	9	25075-28145
3	6624-9891	10	28146-30832
4	9892-13091	11	30833-33261
5	13092-16176	12	33262-25854
6	16177-19448	13	35855-39162
7	19449-22297		

VOL.	ITEMS	VOL.	ITEMS
1	1-3244	8	22298-25074
2	3245-6623	9	25075-28145
3	6624-9891	10	28146-30832
4	9892-13091	11	30833-33261
5	13092-16176	12	33262-25854
6	16177-19448	13	35855-39162
7	19449-22297		

In the House of representatives; for the encouragement, 14870

In the House of representatives . . . Whereas . . . see **Mass. House of representatives.** Resolve

Instructions for the officers, 14243

Instrument agreed upon, 20575

Journal of the proceedings of Jacob Wendell, 6861

Journal of the proceedings of the commissaries, 10706

Letter (to Rockingham), 10969

Martis, 29 die Octobris, 10065

Massachusetts-Bay, Jan. 11, 1736, 4165

Massachusetts district, 34079

Narrative of the progress, 206

Notice to assessors, 34078

Notification to persons, 14187

Oath of a freeman, 1

Observations upon the congregational, 12857

Order . . . see **Mass. Laws (separates)**   Order . .

Order of procession, 35793

Order of the day, 37920

Petition and representation, 10970

Proceedings of his majesty's council, 11737

Proceedings of the council, 11732

Proclamation, (1669) 141, (1670) 149, (1676) 216, (1678) 250, 252, (1679) 273, (1680) 287, (1681) 304, (1683) 348, (1686) 409, 411, (1688) 449, (1690) 529, (1691) 554, (1699) 870-71, (1702) 1061, (1723) 2448, (1757) 7951, (1775) 14199, 14205, (1776) 14839, 14841-44, (1777) 15419-23, (1778) 15897-99, (1779) 16358-59, 16555, (1780) 16853-54

see also **Mass. Governor.** Proclamation

Proclamation by the President, 37921

Proposal, Aug. 9, 1667, 115

Propositions concerning the subject, 68

Province of Massachusetts-Bay; the honorable, 12122, 12459

Province of the Massachusetts-Bay; by the honorable, 751

Province of the Massachusetts-Bay; in the House, 4042

Report of a constitution, 16352
    of the committee for the sale, 29043-44
    of the committee on the judicial, 34071
    of Thomas Davis, 27292
    on the Virginia resolutions, 35795

[Resolve], (bounties) 21241, (commissioners) 32451, (disorders) 8414, (districting) 24524-26, (firearms) 14857, (grant of land) 19088

Resolves and orders, 15892

Resolves of the General court see **Mass. General court.** Resolves

Results of three, 2661

Rules and regulations for the Massachusetts army, 14244-45

Salem, June 17, 1774, 13425

Scale of depreciation, 17235

Some reasons given, 5643

State of Massachusetts-Bay. In Council . . . see **Mass. Proclamation**

State of Massachusetts-Bay; in the House of representatives . . . see **Mass. In the House of representatives . . .**

State of Massachusetts from the best, 35800

State of Massachusetts; the board, 34077

Statement of the Kennebeck, 19794

Suffolk, ss. At the Superior court, 13426

Table of the weight, 18604

Tax for the year, (1798) 34074-75, (1799) 35798-99

Tax no. (4) 18597, (5) 19093, 19795, (6) 21249, (7) 21950, (8) 22660, (9) 23556, (10) 25787, (11) 27294, (12) 29047, (13) 30767-68, (14) 32452

Thirty dollars reward, 15440

To . . . constable or collector, 4039

To his excellency, Richard, 872

To the hon. the Senate, 37926

To the inhabitants, 15439

To the military, 14241

Treasury-office, Boston, 25788-89

Watertown, July 6th, 1775, 14239

We the subscribers do hereby severally, 14247, 14882
    do hereby solemnly, 14246
    inhabitants of the town, 13427

We whose names, 14883

Massachusetts. Council

Proclamation see **Mass.** Proclamation

Resolve see **Mass.** Resolve

Massachusetts. General assembly

Proceedings, 16847

Resolves, (1776) 14879-81, 15412-17, (1778) 15893-96, 16353-57, (1779) 16848-49

Massachusetts. General court

Collection of proceedings, 3184

Proclamation see **Mass.** Proclamation

Resolves, (1780) 16850, 17230-34, (1782) 17598-601, 18026-28, (1784) 18601-603, (1785) 19089-92, (1786) 19791-93, (1787) 20514-17, 21246-48, (1788) 21951-52, (1789) 22656-59, (1791) 23554-55, 24527-29, (1793) 25782-85, 27289-90, (1794) 29045-46, (1795) 30764-66, (1797) 32449-50, (1798) 34072-73, (1799) 35796-97, (1800) 37922-24

Massachusetts. Governor

Proclamation, (1668) 126, (1685) 390-91, (1689) 482-85, (1690) 530-32, (1691) 557-58, (1692) 619-20, (1696) 751, (1699) 869, (1701) 987, (1721) 2240, (1730) 3309, (1731) 3444, (1732) 3567-68, (1733) 3684, (1734) 3793, (1735) 3926, (1737) 4160, (1738) 4269, (1740) 4553-54, (1741) 4746-47, (1742) 5005, (1743) 5245, (1744) 5434-35, (1745) 5632-37, (1746) 5805-809, (1747) 6001, (1748) 6002, 6185-88, (1749) 6358-61, (1750) 6542-43, (1751) 6712, (1752) 6881-83, (1753) 7056-57, (1754) 7251-52, (1755) 7476-79, (1756) 7480, 7710-13, (1757) 7950, 7952, (1758) 8185-87, (1759) 8406-409, (1760) 8658-59, (1761) 8919, (1762) 9181-83, (1763) 9434-36, (1764) 9729-30, (1765) 10060-61, (1766) 10379-81, (1767) 10681-82, (1768) 10963-64, (1769) 11329-30, (1770) 11728-29, (1771) 12118-19, (1772) 12454-55, (1773) 12852-53, (1774) 13412-14, (1775) 14184-86, 14188-89, (1780) 16855, (1781) 17217, (1782) 17593-94, (1783) 18024-25, (1784) 18591-93, (1785) 19084-86, (1786) 19787-90, (1787) 20501-507, (1788) 21236-39, (1789) 21946-47, (1790) 22652-54, (1791) 23549-50, (1792) 24519-20, (1793) 25778-80, (1794) 27279-80, (1795) 29036-37, (1796) 30759-60, (1797) 32442-43, (1798) 34069-70, (1799) 35789-90, (1800) 37913-14

see also **Mass.** Proclamation

Speech, (1700) 907, (1702) 1062, (1716) 1818, (1773) 12856, (1793) 25790

Mass. House of representatives

Continuation of the proceedings, 11733

Extract from the journal, 7481
House of representatives apprehending, 20513
Journal, (1715) 1753, (1717) 1817, 1893, (1718) 1971, (1719) 2034-35, (1720) 2132-33, (1721) 2238-39, (1722) 2350, (1723) 2447, (1724) 2549, (1725) 2660, (1727) 2763, 2903-904, (1728) 3058, (1729) 3185-86, (1730) 3311-14, (1731) 3445-48, (1732) 3569-71, (1733) 3685-89, (1734) 3794-97, (1735) 3927-30, (1736) 4040-41, (1737) 4161-64, (1738) 4271-73, (1739) 4385-88, (1740) 4555-58, (1741) 4748-50, (1742) 5006-7, (1743) 5246-48, (1744) 5436-38, (1745) 5638-42, (1746) 5810, (1747) 6004-6, (1748) 6190-91, (1749) 6362-64, (1750) 6544-46, (1751) 6713-15, (1752) 6884-85, (1753) 7058-60, (1754) 7253-55, (1755) 7482-85, (1756) 7714-18, (1757) 7953-56, (1758) 8188-91, (1759) 8410-13, (1760) 8660-63, (1761) 8921-24, (1762) 9184-86, (1763) 9437-38, (1764) 9732-34, (1765) 10062-64, (1766) 10383-85, (1767) 10683-84, (1768) 10968, (1769) 11331-32, (1770) 11734-36, (1771) 12120-21, (1772) 12456-58, (1773) 12855, 13423-24, (1775) 14213-14, 14874-77, (1776) 15407-411, (1777) 15887-91, (1778) 16348-51, (1784) 18599-600, (1785) 19087
Martis, 29 die Octobris, 10065
Petition and representation, 10970
Proclamation see **Mass.** Proclamation
Resolve (1775), (army absentees) 14207, (firearms) 14210, (hay) 14212, (poor of Boston) 14209, (prohibiting sailing) 14206, (raising troops) 14211, (salt petre) 14208
Resolve (1776), (axes) 14872, (blankets) 14851, (enlistment) 14854-55, (estates of refugees) 14861, (hard money) 14863, (male inhabitants) 14873, (militia) 14852, 14862, 14866, (new levies) 14850, (officers and seamen) 14860, (powder) 14853, (reconsidering advance pay) 14856, (silver and gold) 14859, (tax receipts) 14858, (three-year enlistment) 14869, (two-months service) 14867, (two regiments) 14865
Resolve (1777), (blankets) 15424, 15429, (draft) 15432, 15434, 15436, (firearms) 15430, (militia to march) 15437, (plantations) 15431, (powder) 15435, (rum export) 15427
Votes see **Mass. House of representatives.** Journal
Massachusetts. Laws (collective)
Acts and laws, 867, 1686, 2762, 5003, 8399, 17211
Acts contained in this book, 9432
Book of the general lawes, 28, 37, 60
Book of the general laws (Plymouth), 171
Capital lawes, 10
County and town officer, 10967
General laws (to 1672), 168, 200
Laws for regulating, 37918
Liberties of the Massachusetts, 6
Perpetual laws, (1780-88) 21245, (1789-89) 21948-49, (1788-99) 35794
Supplement to Book of the general lawes, 30
Temporary acts, (1742) 5004, (1755) 7467, (1763) 9430-31
Third supplement, 46
Massachusetts. Laws (session)
Acts, (1661-63) 81, (1661-64) 88, (1665) 103, (1666) 109, (1668) 124-25, (1669) 142, (1672) 169, (1673) 177-78, (1674) 190-91, (1675) 201-204, (1676) 219, (1677) 235-36, (1678) 253, (1679) 271-72, (1680) 289-91, (1681) 305, (1682) 318, (1683) 349-50, (1684) 366, 368-69, (1685) 389, (1692) 617-18, 647-48, (1693) 649-51, 694,

(1694) 695-97, 718, (1695) 719-21, 747, (1696) 748-50, (1697) 788-89, (1698) 825-26, (1699) 917, (1700) 918, 984, (1701) 985, (1702) 1058-59, (1703) 1114-17, 1166, (1704) 1167-69, 1209, (1705) 1210-11, (1706) 1249-53, 1301, (1707) 1302-305, (1708) 1357-59, 1395, (1709) 1396-97, 1458, (1710) 1459, (1711) 1502, (1715) 1750-52, (1716) 1815-16, (1717) 1891-92, (1718) 1966-68, (1719) 2031-32, (1720) 2130-31, 2233, (1721) 2234-37, (1722) 2347-49, 2442, (1723) 2443-45, (1724) 2657, (1725) 2658, (1726) 2761, 2900, (1727) 2901-902, 3054-55, (1728) 3056-57, 3182, (1729) 3306, (1730) 3307, (1731) 3440-42, 3564, (1732) 3565, 3679-80, (1733) 3681-82, 3790-91, (1734) 3792, 3923-24, (1735) 3925, 4034-35, (1736) 4036, 4157, (1737) 4158, 4265, (1738) 4266-67, 4383, (1739) 4384, 4547-48, (1740) 4549-51, 4743, (1741) 4744, 4998-5000, (1742) 5001, 5236, 5240, (1743) 5237-39, 5241-44, 5427, 5430, (1744) 5428-29, 5431-33, 5626, 5628, (1745) 5627, 5629-31, 5799, (1746) 5798, 5800-804, 5996, (1747) 5995, 5997-99, 6180-81, (1748) 6182-84, 6353, 6355, (1749) 6354, 6356-57, 6535, 6537, (1750) 6536, 6538-40, 6705-711, (1751) 6875, 6878, (1752) 6876-77, 6879-80, 7047-48, 7051, (1753) 7049-50, 7052-53, 7241-42, 7245-46, (1754) 7243-44, 7247-50, 7463, 7466, (1755) 7464-65, 7468-73, 7705-706, (1756) 7703, 7707-709, 7941-42, 7944-45, 8915, (1757) 7943, 7946-47, 8175-77, 8179-81, (1758) 8178, 8182-83, 8395-96, (1759) 8397-98, 8401-405, 8649-50, 8652-54, (1760) 8651, 8655-56, 8913, 8917, (1761) 8914, 8916, 8918, 9173-74, 9177-78, (1762) 9175-76, 9179, 9428, (1763) 9429, 9431, 9721, 9725, (1764) 9722-24, 9726-27, 10052, 10055, (1765) 10053-54, 10056-58, 10370, 10374, 10678, (1766) 10371-73, 10375-77, (1767) 10675-77, 10679, 10959, 10961, (1768) 10960, 10962, (1769) 11327, 11723, 11725, (1770) 11724, 11726-27, 12115, (1771) 12116-17, 12450, 12452, (1772) 12451, 12453, 12847, 12849, (1773) 12848, 12850, 13404, 13407, (1774) 13405-406, 13408-410, (1775) 14202-203, (1766) 14845-46, (1777) 15400-401, 15883, (1778) 15884-85, 16343-44, (1779) 16345-46, 16837, (1780) 17212-13, (1781) 17214-15, 17589-90, (1782) 17591-92, (1783) 18021-22, 18588, (1784) 18589-90, 19078, (1785) 19079-80, 19778, (1786) 19779-80, 20496-97, (1787) 20498-99, 21233, (1788) 21234-35, 21943, (1789) 21944-45, 21949, 22650, (1790) 22651, 23548, (1791) 23547, (1792) 24516-18, 25775, (1793) 25776-77, 27277, (1794) 27278, 29034, (1795) 29035, 30756, (1796) 30757-58, (1797) 32440-41, (1798) 34063-64, (1799) 35786-87, (1800) 37909-910
Massachusetts. Laws (separates)
Act, (1676) 217-18, (1677) 233-34, 237, (1680) 288, (1683) 346-47, (1684) 365, 367, (1689) 476-81, (1690) 522-25, (1700) 919-20, (1701) 986, (1702) 1060, (1708) 1306, (1709) 1398, (1711)

VOL.	ITEMS	VOL.	ITEMS
1	1-3244	8	22298-25074
2	3245-6623	9	25075-28145
3	6624-9891	10	28146-30832
4	9892-13091	11	30833-33261
5	13092-16176	12	33262-25854
6	16177-19448	13	35855-39162
7	19449-22297		

VOL.	ITEMS	VOL.	ITEMS
1	1-3244	8	22298-25074
2	3245-6623	9	25075-28145
3	6624-9891	10	28146-30832
4	9892-13091	11	30833-33261
5	13092-16176	12	33262-25854
6	16177-19448	13	35855-39162
7	19449-22297		

VOL.	ITEMS	VOL.	ITEMS
1	1-3244	8	22298-25074
2	3245-6623	9	25075-28145
3	6624-9891	10	28146-30832
4	9892-13091	11	30833-33261
5	13092-16176	12	33262-25854
6	16177-19448	13	35855-39162
7	19449-22297		

Plain discourse, (1712) 1568, (1713) 1634, (1721) 2257
Practical truths plainly, 1981
Practical truths tending, 322-23, 1182
Pray for the rising, 255, 275, 393
Present state, 492
Prevalency of prayer, 6452
Private letter, 2780
Relation of the troubles, 238
Renewal of covenant, 239
Returning unto God, 293
Seasonable testimony, 2149
Sermon, (1674) 394, (1682) 324, (1684) 375, (1686) 417, 432, (1713) 1634, (1718) 1982
Sermons wherein, 1983, 2054
Several reasons, 2258, 2781
Several sermons, 1767
Solemn advice, 728
Some further account, 2259
     important truths, 374, 2260
     remarks, 1078
Soul-saving gospel truths, (1703) 1134, (1712) 1569, (1743) 5249
Surest way, 880
Testimony against, 451
Testimony finished, 2363
Times of men, 209
Two discourses, 1838
Vindication of New England, 452, 542
Voice of God, 1183
Wicked man's portion, 210
Wo to drunkards, 179, 1570
attestation by, 2241
death, 2422, 2453, 2557, 4753
defended, 516
denies authorship, 975
life, 4753
praises Boyd, 2105
preface by, 78, 681, 991, 1155, 1428, 1581, 1645, 1716, 1870, 1888, 1925, 1963, 1972, 1977, 2074, 2086, 2142-43, 2248, 2256, 2262-63, 2324, 2962, 4790, 10940
pres. Harvard, 303, 315, 406, 428, 596
recommends son's book, 2450
recommends White's book, 2716
refuted, 516
reply to, 89, 472, 957, 966-67, 1109, 1433, 2307
wife's death, 1673, 1693, 1702
Mather, Katharin, d. 1717?, death, 1911, 2922
Mather, Marie, d. 1714
death, 1693, 1702
poem on, 1673
Mather, Moses, 1719-1806
America's appeal, 14253
Brief view, 12463
Divine sovereignty, 9439
Sermon, 17236
Visible church, 8415, 11742
remarks on, 12811
reply to, 8539, 11174, 11565
Mather Nathanael, 1630-1697
Boston ephemeris see **Almanacs (Mather)**
Discussion, 3318
Sermon, 375
Mather, Nathanael, 1669?-1688, death, 536
Mather, Ralph. Familiar letters, 24532
Mather, Richard, 1596-1699
Catechism, 31
Defence, 89
Farewell exhortation, 47
Mass. election sermon, (1644) 15, (1660) 62

Summe of certain, 35
death, 150
Mather, Samuel, 1626-1671. Testimony, 151, 2676
Mather, Samuel, 1651-1728
Dead faith, 800, 4560
Essay, 2923
Funeral sermon, 1518
Self-justiciary, 1322, 4561
Vita B. Augusti, 3656?
Mather, Samuel, 1706-1785
All men, 17603, 18031
Apology for the liberties, 4275
Attempt to show, 12861
Christ sent to heal, 12862-63
Departure and character, 3063
Dissertation, 8664
Dying legacy, 18032
Essay, 3573
Faithful man, 4562
Fall of the mighty, 4276
Funeral discourse, 6716
Life of Cotton Mather, 3188
Lord's prayer, 10387
Of the pastoral care, 9187
Sacred minister, 12864
Serious letter, 18033
Thoughts produced, 2774
To the author, 18034
Walk of the upright, 7061
War is lawful, 4389
     letter (from Clarke), 17492
     reply to, 18215
Mather, Warham, 1666-1745. Short discourse, 1839
Mathetees Archaios see **Mather, Samuel, 1706-1785**
Mathew Carey, no. 118 Market Street, 25253
Mathew Carey's catalogue, 24173, 26730
Mathew Carey's exchange catalogue, 33497
Mathews, ——, murdered, 8829
Mathews, David, appointed mayor, 15106
Mathews, George
State of Georgia; by his excellency, 27040
dedication to, 26695
Mathews, Thomas, 1676-1751, battle in Mediterranean, 5499
Mathias, Thomas James, 1754?-1835
Imperial epistle, 37937
Pursuits of literature, 37938-40
Shade of Alexander Pope, 37941
Mathiot, François, signs capitulation, 14540
Matilda, a favorite ballad, 35805
Matlack, Timothy, 1730-1829
Oration, 16867
encounter with Humphreys, 17146
secy. Pennsylvania, 16925-26, 17283-84, 17286-87, 17664, 18084
Matlack, White. To the representatives, 17165
Matson, Nathaniel
Case of Nathaniel Matson, 2151
To the honorable, 2150
Matthew, St., life, 9863

VOL.	ITEMS	VOL.	ITEMS
1	1-3244	8	22298-25074
2	3245-6623	9	25075-28145
3	6624-9891	10	28146-30832
4	9892-13091	11	30833-33261
5	13092-16176	12	33262-25854
6	16177-19448	13	35855-39162
7	19449-22297		

Mechanics in union, 14940-41
Mechanics lecture, 21627
Mecom, Benjamin. Philadelphia, Sept. 11, 1770, 11743
Medaganesset, Indian sachem, 3554
Mede, ———, commentary on Revelation, 23486
Medical and philosophical commentaries, (v.1-3) 25798, (v.7) 27305
    commentaries, (v.4-6, 8-10) 29057-62, (v.11) 32459
    discourse, 11338
Medical gentleman. Easy way, 30381
Medical inquiries, (1789) 22123, (1793) 26112, (1794) 27660, (1796) 31144, (1797) 32784, (1798) 34496
    papers, 22661
    pocket-book, (1784) 18456, (1791) 23348, (1795) 28621
    repository, (1797) 32460, (1798) 34089, (1799) 35808, (1800) 37946-47
    sketch, 26747
    sketches, 27344
Medical society (New Haven). Cases, 21296
Medical society (N.Y.). Report of the committee, 35933
Medical society (Phila.) Act of incorporation, 25996
Medical vade mecum, 29063, 37948
Medicina Britannica, 6783
Medicine boxes, 30511
    chests with particular, 37604
    chests with suitable, 38455
Medico-chemical dissertations, 30960
Medina, Solomon de. Decree, 3019
Meditation on the weaver's, 1824
Meditations among the tombs, 27117, 28828
    and contemplations, (1750) 6515-16, (1778) 15851, (1789) 21885, (1791) 23440, (1792) 24394, (1794) 27118, (1795) 28829, (1797) 32250, (1798) 33872
    and spiritual experiences, 6067
    of a silent, 29064
    on Abraham's conduct, 26434
    on death, 1321, 14887
    on divine subjects, 5620, 6529-30
    on several divine, 6193
    on the glory, 1222-23, 1516
        incomprehensibility, 9313
        sanctification, 1566-67
    representing, 5510
Meeker, Joseph, letters (from Campbell), 35266
Meers, ———, memorial of, 31370
Meet help, 862
Meeting of the freeholders, 3748
Megara, 32159
Meier, Georg Friedrich, 1718-1777. Laughing philosopher, 21956
Meigs, Janna, d. 1739, death, 5303
Meigs, Josiah, 1757-1822. Oration, 17604
Meigs, Return Jonathan, 1740-1823. Journal of occurrences, 14888
Meigs, Return Jonathan, 1764-1825. Poem spoken, 18608
Meigs & Dana. To the public, 19830
Mein, John
    Catalogue of Mein's Circulating library, 10069
    Controversy between Great Britain, 11305
    Mein and Fleeming's register, (1766) 10390, (1767) 10687, (1768) 10973
    Sagittarius's letters, 14255
    State of the importations, 11336, 11744

    conduct, 11576
Mein herr, 36064
Mein heyland, 4279
Melancholy case, 12596
    end, 28961
    narrative, 13436
Melcher, Col. ———, directions to, 15522
Melcher, Adam. To the public, 16990
Melcher, Isaac. To the public, 16990
Melcher, John, 1759-1850. Almanac see Almanacs (Melcher)
Melchior, Leonhard, predecessor of Hasenclever, 12808
Melchizedek, history of, 19987
Mellen, Henry, 1757-1809. Sketches of Masonic history, 34091
Mellen, John, 1722-1807
    Discourse, 7957
    Doctrine of the cross, 19096
    Duty of all, 7719
    Duty of ministers, 7062
    Faith and profession, 22665
    Fifteen discourses for the liberties, 10070
    Fifteen discourses upon doctrinal, 10071
    Great and happy, 29066
    Merit of doing good, 10072
    Non-conformity, 25801
    Religion productive, 12867
    Sermon, 8669
Mellen, John, 1752-1828
    Affection for the house, 29067
    Discourse, 35810
    Sermon, (1791) 23562, (1794) 27307, (1796) 32463, (1797) 32462, (1799) 35811
Melmoth, Courtney see Pratt, Samuel Jackson, 1749-1814
Melmoth, William, 1666-1743. Great importance, 3189
Melsheimer, Friedrich Valentine, 1749-1814
    Brief, 30782
    Gespräche, 32464
    reply to, 30125
Melville, Daniel C. Miscellaneous extracts, 34092
A member
    Doctrines of the church, 25405
    Serious address, 24779
Member dissenting. Speech, 7573
Member of said Council see Edwards, Jonathan, 1703-1758
Member of said presbytery. Justification, 32709
Member of that community. Dialogue containing, 9638
Member of the Agricultural society. Treatise, 26276
Member of the Belles-lettres society. Observations, 24639
Member of the Calcannon club. Wits of Westminster, 13085
Member of the Church of England. Observations, 11394
Member of the Church of England and a Son of

VOL.	ITEMS	VOL.	ITEMS
1	1-3244	8	22298-25074
2	3245-6623	9	25075-28145
3	6624-9891	10	28146-30832
4	9892-13091	11	30833-33261
5	13092-16176	12	33262-25854
6	16177-19448	13	35855-39162
7	19449-22297		

liberty, 11594
Member of the Congress on the Stamp Act see
Gadsden, Christopher, 1723-1805
Member of the consociation see Todd, Jonathan,
1713-1791
Member of the convention. Observations, 24638
Member of the Episcopal church see Seabury,
Samuel, 1729-1796
Member of the Holy Catholic church. Caveat,
23252
Member of the House of representatives
Notes on the finances, 35997
see also Dennis, John, 1771-1807
Member of the Musical society see Langdon,
Chauncey, 1763-1830
Member of the old Congress see Beresford, Richard
Member of the Protestant Episcopal association in
South Carolina see Purcell, Henry
Member of the Protestant Episcopal church see
Duke, William, 1757-1840
Member of the Protestant Episcopal church of
Maryland see Bissett, John, 1762-1810
Member of the Royal arch. Hiram, 10925
Member of the synod
Synod of New York, 9849
see also Blair, John, 1720-1771
Member of their body see Lee, Andrew, 1745-1832
Members composing the Senate, 35927, 38088
of the association, 12637
of the House of assembly, 38089
Memento mori, 3324
Memoir concerning the disease, 36903
concerning the fascinating, 30037
on the analysis, 37110
extraneous, 36459
Onondaga salt, 33632
use of the thermometer, 25040
Mémoire apologetique, 10032
pour Rodolphe, 38637
relatif, 26415
Memoirs by James Wilmer, 25045
illustrating, 35153-56
of . . . a native, 38422
a peg top, 21188
an antiquated, 34667
Capt. Clap, 3403
Capt. Roger Clap, 10261, 13199
General Dumourier, 26918
James Lackington, 30668
Major general Heath, 33865
Marie Antoinette, 27308-309
Mary Wollstonecraft, 35556
Mrs. Coghlan, 28442
Mons. and Madame, 28090-91
odd adventures, 4021-22
Stephen Burroughs, 33478
of the American academy, 18900, 25092
Bloomsgrove family, 22570
life, (Doddridge) 13511, (Gough) 17961,
18146, (Guthrie) 30526-27, (Lee) 24456,
25701, (Osborn) 35636, (Phillips) 34371,
(Turell) 3969, (Whitefield) 13298, 33799
lives, 25154
principal transactions, 8258
remarkable life, 6456
reverend, 30532
year 2000, 29068
year 2500, 35813
yellow fever, 33589
of Tom, Moses, and John, 29326

Memorable accidents, 16321, 28506
account, 3205-206
instance of divine, 25394
instance of the divine, 26886
passages, 700
providences, 486
Memorandum; the more, 13141
Memorandums for a report, 13770
Memoria Wilsoniana, 725
Memorial (New Eng. Mississippi land co.), 34179
Memorial and remonstrance of the public, 22983
and remonstrance presented, 20109
&c. (Sackett), 19232
and tear, 10351
between jest, 569
containing, 7895-97
from the envoys, 34820
humbly shewing, 2261
of divine, 33262
of Evan Drummond, 2564
of God's goodness, 4367
of Lexington, 17655
of some, 7978
of the council, 7508
Illinois, 32976-77
merchants, 10101
present, 1331
Providence association, 36181
publick, 22984
respect, 37500
of William Moore, 7958
on the practicability, 34093
relating to the Kennebeck, 2292
relating to the tobacco, 4154
to justify, 18549
to the inhabitants, 13707
to United States, 31151
vouchers, 26549
Memorials of early, 1508
of godliness, 1643
presented, 24536
Memory of God's great goodness, 10946
Memory of Washington, 37951
Men have freedom, 8561
Men self-condemned, 1283
Menachem, 1826
Mendenhall, Thomas. Traverse tables, 18609
Mendicamens et précis, 30755
Mendon association. Evidences, 32465, 34094
Menno Simons, 1492-1559. Fundament, 27310
Mennonites
Bericht, 10688
Christian confession, 2924
Kurze und aufrichtige, 14257
Short and sincere, 14256
Mennye, J. English grammar, 19799
Mens sana, 829
Men's sins, 17903
Mental flower-garden, 37446
Mental improvement, 36664
Mentelle, Mme. ———. Voyages, 38971
Mentor, or the American, 29917
Mentoria, 27654, 29130
Mentor's reply, 18555
Mercantile laws, 21317
Mercatorius, Causidicus. Dissertation, 12868
Mercenary match, 18365
Mercer, George, estate sold, 21957
Mercer, Hugh, education, 26326
Mercer, James, 1747-1793

At a meeting of the trustees, 20370
Lands; for sale, 21957
Mercer, John, 1704-1768
Continuation of the abridgment, 4441
Exact abridgment, 4204
Mercer, John, fl. 1792. Oration, 24537
Mercer, John Francis, 1759-1821
Introductory discourse, 21958
Mr. Mercer considers, 24538
election opposed, 24756
reports on frontier posts, 18832
Mercer, Thomas, b. 1709. Sentimental sailor, 17605
Merchandise of a people, 4002
Merchant, John. Genuine and impartial, 6009
Merchant
Letter to certain, 30688
Times, mankind is highly, 11881
Merchant freighters, 9354
Merchant in Boston. Some observations, 4308
Merchant in Halifax. Letter (to merchant in Boston), 7932
Merchant in Philadelphia, letter (from gentleman in Virginia), 10867
Merchant resident, 7602
Merchants and all others, 11575
and traders in this town, 11184
and traders of this town, 13156
and traders security, 8928
Merchants'-Hall; the sincere, 10974
Merchants of Boston. Observations, 11392-93
Merchants of this city, 11337
Merchant's vade mecum, 34097
Mercier, J. B., tr. Solitude considered, (1793) 26528, (1796) 31684-85, (1797) 33261
Mercier, Louis Sébastien, 1740-1814
Memoirs, 29068, 35813
Night cap, 21959, 27311
Seraphina, 32467
Mercutio, adventures, 31902
Mercy exemplified, (1767) 10585, (1769) 11213-14, (1799) 35337
magnified, 379
of God, 8312
remembered, 29033
with God, 3641
Meredith, John. Short discourse, 3190
Meredith, Samuel, militia for, 8333-36
Meredith, Samuel. Treasury of the U.S., (Dec. 5, 1791) 23928, (Feb. 28, 1792) 24938, (Dec. 20, 1798) 34885, (Feb. 11, 1799) 36595
Meredith, Samuel C., certifies subscriptions, 28403
Meredith, Sir William. Letter (to Chatham), 13386-87
Meredith association. Minutes, (1790) 25803, (1791) 25804, (1792) 24539, (1793) 25805, (1794) 27313
Meriam, Jonas, d. 1780. Sermon, 10073
Meriden, Conn. Transactions of the council, 10975
Merit of doing, 10072
Merkel, Lot. Lot Merkel, no. 31, 23563
Merkwürdige geschichte, 5765, 22877
Indianer-predigt, 19501
leben, 34098
lebenslauf, 33404
nachricht, 9585
prophezeyung, (1792) 24772, (1793) 26145, (1794) 27676, (1796) 31165, (1797) 32808
Merkwürdigen traum, 10976
Merlinus liberatus, 3588
Merriam, Matthew, 1739-1797
Sermons, 24540
ordained, 10328

Merrick, ——, excerpts from, 34112
Merrick, Nathan, d. 1788, death, 21357
Merrick, Pliny, 1755-1814. Eulogy, 37953
Merril, Daniel, ordained, 27731
Merill, ——, of Plaistow, hand of fellowship, 28711
Merrill, Gyles
Charge, 32087
ordained, 9909
Merrill, John, d. 1798?, death, 34624
Merrill, Phinehas. Scholar's guide, (1793) 25806, (1795) 29070, (1798) 34099
Merrill, R. Musical practitioner, 32468
Merrill, Thomas, letter (from Balch), 5735
Merrimack humane society
By-laws, 24541
Laws, 24542
Merritt, Nicholas, adventures, 2602, 2839
Merry, Robert, 1755-1798
British album, 25807
Pains of memory, 30785, 32469
excerpts from, 23246
Merry companion, 34100
-fellow's companion, (1789) 21643, (1795) 29574, (1797) 32470, (1798) 34101
fellow's pocket companion, 35241
piper, 6550
piping lad, 29608
Merwin, Noah, ordained, 15253
Mesnard, Thomas. To the public, 13666
Message concerning the dispatches, 34810
confidential, 33055
from Governor Jay, 35928
from the governor, 19252
from the President, (1794) 27913, 27915, 27918, (Jan. 8, 1796) 31406, (Jan. 13, 1796) 31407, (Mar. 1, 1796) 31411, (Mar. 8, 1796) 31408, (Mar. 25, 1796) 31421, (Mar. 29, 1796) 31418, (Mar. 30, 1796) 31417, (Jan. 19, 1797) 33048, (Feb. 15, 1797) 33051, (June 12, 1797) 33052, (June 22, 1797) 33053, (Jan. 1, 1798) 34799, (Jan. 18, 1799) 34800, (Jan. 23, 1798) 34801, (Feb. 2, 1798) 34802, (Feb. 5, 1798) 34803, (Feb. 12, 1798) 34804, (Feb. 19, 1798) 34805, (Feb. 20, 1798) 34806, (Feb. 23,1798) 34807-808, (June 5, 1798) 34822, (June 18, 1798) 34823-24, (June 27, 1798) 34826, (Dec. 31, 1798) 36549, (Jan. 8, 1799) 36550-51, 36553, (Jan. 21, 1799) 36546-48, (Jan. 22, 1799) 36552, (Jan. 28, 1799) 36545, (Jan. 31, 1799) 36555, (Feb. 15, 1799) 36554, (Mar. 1, 1799) 36556, (Dec. 5, 1799) 36557, (Jan. 8, 1800) 38780, 38784, (Jan. 13, 1800) 38783, (Jan. 20, 1800) 38778, (Jan. 23, 1800) 38779, (Feb. 7, 1800) 38782, (Apr. 17, 1800) 38781, [1800] 38785
from the Senate communicating, 34791, 36558
of Gov. Bernard, 8155
of the President, (1793) 26334, 29735-36, (1794) 27914, 27916-17, (1797) 34798, (Mar. 5, 1798) 24809, (Apr. 3, 1798) 34812, 34814, (May 4,

VOL.	ITEMS	VOL.	ITEMS
1	1-3244	8	22298-25074
2	3245-6623	9	25075-28145
3	6624-9891	10	28146-30832
4	9892-13091	11	30833-33261
5	13092-16176	12	33262-25854
6	16177-19448	13	35855-39162
7	19449-22297		

law (Penna.), 25970
law (Va.), 36645
laws now in force, 35985
Milk and honey, 1378
Milkiad, 21932
Mill, John, ed. Novum Testamentum, 36952
Millen, John see **Mellen, John, 1722-1807**
Millenial door, 35128
Millen(n)ium, (1758) 8081, (1794) 26594, (1795) 28220
Miller, Alexander
  Concise grammar, 29080
  Sermon, 14259, 37963
Miller, Edward, 1760-1812
  Dissertatio medica, 21964
  Medical repository, 32460, 37946-47
Miller, Henry. Account of the Conewago, 33551
Miller, Johann Peter. Chronicon, 19558
Miller, John, address to, 15724
Miller, John, letter (from Latrobe), 35715
Miller, John Henry, 1702-1782
  Catalogus von mehr als 700, 11339
  Henrich Miller, buchdrucker, 10690
  Henrich Millers des buchdruckers, 15911
Miller, Jonathan, 1761-1831. Appendix on the mode, 37263
Miller, Margaret, raped, 38373
Miller, Robert Johnston. Introduction to the knowledge, 36714
Miller, Samuel, 1769-1850
  Discourse, 29081, 32477
  New York, Feb. 10, 1798, 34110
  Sermon, (1793) 25823, (1795) 29082, (1798) 34109, (Feb. 5, 1799) 35821, (Dec. 29, 1799) 37964
Miller, William F., ordained, 24678
Milligan, Jacob
  Charleston directory, (1786) 19802, (1788) 21258, (1790) 22670
  Directory of the city of Charleston, 27320
Millot, Claude François Xavier, 1726-1785
  Elements of ancient, 32478
  Elements of general, 21965-66, 30796
Mills, Gideon, d. 1772, death, 12570
Mills, Jedidiah, 1697-1776
  Inquiry concerning the state, 10691
  Vindication of gospel-truth, 6010
  defended, 12416
  letter (from Beach), 6093
  reply to, 11295
Mills, John, d. 1784
  Modern system, 30797
  Treatise on cattle, 29083
Mills, Nathaniel. British and American register, (1773) 12869-70, (1775) 13440-41, (1776) 14889, (1777) 15442, (1778) 15912, (1779) 16374, (1780) 16869
Mills, Samuel John, 1743-1833
  Nature and importance, 14260
  Religious sentiments, 32820
Mills, Thomas. Compendium of Latin, 29084
Millstones to be sold, 13201
Milman, ——, opinions refuted, 26283
Milner, ——, reply to, 25755
Milns, William, 1761-1801
  All in a bustle, 34111
  American accountant, 32479
  Columbian library, 30798, 34112
  Federal constitution, 27321, 34113
  Penman's repository, 32481
  Songs &c., 32482
  Well-bred scholar, 32480

When the old heathen, 34114-15
Miltimore, James, 1755-1836
  Discourse, 27322
  Sermon, (1793) 25824, (1794) 27323, (1800) 37965
  Terrors of death, 29085
  hand of fellowship, 28531
Milton, Abraham. Farmer's companion, 8929
Milton, Charles William. Narrative, 25825
Milton, John, 1608-1674
  Old looking-glass, 11745, 13442
  Paradise lost, (1777) 15443, (1787) 20525, (1791) 23569
  Paradise regain'd, 22671, 23570
  Poetical works, (1791) 23571-72, (1794) 27324, (1796) 30799
  anecdotes of, 29846, 29865
  excerpts from, 23246
  imitated, 35400
  life, 18543
Milton, John Gardiner. Brief consideration, 34116
Milton, William, petition, 38774
Mind at ease, 1540
Miner, John. Defence, 17237
Minerva, a literary weekly, 35822
Minerva, or rural, 27325
Minisink Indians
  At a conference, 8154
  conferences, 8156
  message to, 8155
  treaty, 8157
Minister, a sermon, 2357
Minister in Boston
  Letter (to Sandeman), 10357
  see also **Cooper, William, 1694-1743**
Minister in the country. Pastoral letter, 36043
Minister of Christ, 3538
Minister of God, 5316
Minister of the Church of Christ. First day Sabbath, 11256
Minister of the Church of England
  Serious address, 7765
  see also **Johnson, Samuel, 1696-1772**
Minister of the Church of Scotland. Letter, 5225
Minister of the gospel
  Poor orphan, 3828
  Serious reflections, 8036
  see also **Parkman, Ebenezer, 1703-1789**
Minister preaching his own funeral, (1790) 22398, (1791) 23254, (1792) 24185, (1793) 25274
Ministerial affection, 11131
  authority, 9382
  catechism, 12128
  faithfulness, 6065
  necessity, 15071
  office, 8900, 9155
  -ordnung, 25462
  work, 10328
Ministers and other, 8270
  and people excited, 6279
  and people under special, 3520

VOL.	ITEMS	VOL.	ITEMS
1	1-3244	8	22298-25074
2	3245-6623	9	25075-28145
3	6624-9891	10	28146-30832
4	9892-13091	11	30833-33261
5	13092-16176	12	33262-25854
6	16177-19448	13	35855-39162
7	19449-22297		

27220, (1800) 37826
meetings, 18756
Meredith association, (1790-91) 25803-804, (1792) 24539, (1793) 25805, (1794) 27313
Methodist conferences, 29071
Middle district association, 25817, 27317
Neuse association, 29144
New association, 25863
New Hampshire association, (1790) 25879, (1792-93) 25880-81, (1794) 27378, (1797) 32538, (1799) 35889
New-York association, (1792-93) 25910-12
New York Baptist association, (1794) 27402, (1795) 29197, (1796) 30879, (1797) 32565, (1798) 34223, (1800) 38102
North Carolina Neuse Baptist, 35987
Orange district association, (1790-91) 25946-48
Otsego Baptist association, 30932
Philadelphia Baptist association, (1790) 22792, (1792) 24685, (1793) 25990, (1794) 27503, (1795) 29307, (1796) 30997, (1797) 32677, (1798) 34353, (1799) 36096, (1800) 38244
Philadelphia association, (1769) 11415, (1770) 11821, (1771) 12195, (1773) 12951, (1775) 14393
Philadelphian Baptist association, (1781) 17312, (1791) 23695
proceedings of a convention, (Abolition society) 26533, (Baptist churches) 23151, (Prot. Epis. church) 27574
proceedings of delegates, 33264
proceedings of the Baptist, 14614
proceedings of the committee, 27501
proceedings of the convention, 14977
proceedings of the fourth, 31686
proceedings of the second, 28146
proceedings of the sixth, 37969
proceedings of the third, 29947
proceedings of the Warren association, (1773) 13064, (1774) 13756, (1776) 15214
proceedings of Warren association, (1772) 12602
Redstone association, (1790-93) 26058-61
Rensselaer-ville association, (1799) 36204, (1800) 38369
Reusselaer-ville conference, (1798) 36203
Roanoke district association, (1790-93) 26094-101, (1794) 27628
Salem association, (1790-93) 26121-24
Salisbury association, (1790-93) 26127-30
Sandy-Creek association, (1792-93) 26132-33
second general, 15973
second session of the convention, 22765
second session of the ninth, 19162
second sitting, 17292-94
Shaftsbury association, (1786) 19984, (1788) 21459, (1789) 22138, (1790) 22889, (1791) 23760, (1792) 24784, (1793) 26154, (1794) 27691, (1795) 29495, (1796) 31179, (1797) 32824, (1798) 34534, (1799) 36295
South Kentucky district, (1790) 26187, (1791) 26188-89, (1792) 26190-91, (1793) 26192-93
Stonington association, (1789) 22167, (1790) 22911, (1791) 23803, (1792) 24821, (1793) 26216, (1794) 27747, (1795) 29570, (1796) 31241, (1797) 32885, (1798) 34607,

(1799) 36374, (1800) 38565
Strawberry district, (1790) 26219-20, (1791) 26221-22, (1792) 26223-24, (1793) 26225-26
third general, 15974
United Baptist association, (1791) 23152, (1792) 26292, (1795) 29225, (1796) 31329
Vermont association, (1790) 23153, 26381, (1791-93) 26382-84, (1795) 29791, (1800) 38931
Virginia Portsmouth, (1791-93) 26025-27
Warren association, (1771) 12270, (1777) 15701, (1778) 16164, (1779) 16669, (1780) 17063, (1781) 17420, (1782) 17790, (1783) 18293, (1784) 18869, (1785) 19360, (1786) 20122, (1787) 20856, (1788) 21573, (1789) 22243, (1790) 23036, (1791) 23959, (1792) 24985, (1793) 26423, (1794) 28027, (1795) 29831, (1796) 31523, (1797) 33146, (1798) 34956, (1799) 36669, (1800) 38979
Warwick Baptist association, (1791-93) 26424-29, (1794) 28028, (1795) 29832, (1796) 31524, (1797) 33147, (1798) 34957
Western-shore association, 26471-72
Woodstock association, (1790-93) 26498-501, (1794) 28129, (1796) 31656, (1797) 33247
Yadkin association, (1790-93) 26514-17
taken at the several, (1791) 23565, (1792) 24544, (1793) 25808, (1794) 27314, (1795) 29072, (1796) 30787, (1797) 32473, (1798) 34103, (1799) 35818, (1800) 37959
Mirabeau, Honoré Gabriel Riquette, comte de, 1749-1791
Considerations on the Order, 19803
Observations on the Society, 29484
Reflections on the Observations, 19804
Reflexions on Price's Observations, 27328
Mirabilia Dei, (1719) 2043, (1746) 5748, (1793) 25228
Miraculous power of clothes, 8930, 12466
Miranda, ———. Letters, 28090
Miranda, or the discovery, 37970
Mirror. Newsboy's New Year's address, 35824
Mirror, 24494
Mirror for a printer, 13444
    for the female, 36117
    of divine, 2678
    representing, 19471
Mirrour. Good news, 27327
Miscellaneous collection, 19751
    essays, 24407
    extracts in prose, 34092
    extracts of pious, 26970
    observations, 31054
    pamphlets, 27328
    poems, (Davies) 6834, (M'Grath) 30725, (Markoe) 20482
    poems (Tilden), (1756) 7802, (1757) 8045,

VOL.	ITEMS	VOL.	ITEMS
1	1-3244	8	22298-25074
2	3245-6623	9	25075-28145
3	6624-9891	10	28146-30832
4	9892-13091	11	30833-33261
5	13092-16176	12	33262-25854
6	16177-19448	13	35855-39162
7	19449-22297		

(1758) 8268
poems (Whitcomb), 29884
reflections, 24547
remarks, 15235
sketches, 31069
thoughts in prose, 31580-81
    on the doctrine, 33618, 35393
    or some occasional, 4563, 5440
trifles, 30158
works (Freneau), 21097
works (Goldsmith), (1793) 25554, (1794) 27058, (1795) 28757
works (Humphereys), 22578
works (Linn), 28973
Miscellanies by M. de Voltaire, 16162
for sentimentalists, 15914
in prose and verse, 27030
moral and instructive, (1787) 20526, (1792) 24548, (1793) 25827, (1794) 27329, (1795) 29099, (1796) 30809
the time-piece, 22827
Miscellany containing, 21261
Misery and duty, 13758
Misfortunes of a week, 28837
Misiatrus, Philander. Honour of the gout, 3574, 3690
Misrepresentation and falsehood, 17156
Misrepresentation corrected, 6839
Miss Ashmore's choice collection, 13124
Miss Harriet, history of, 21144
Missionary-encouragement, 34599
Missionary from the honorable society see **Wetmore, James**, 1695-1760
Missionary society, Connecticut. Constitution, 37232
Missionary society, London. Sermons preached, 32384
Mississippi Territory
By Winthrop Sargent, 37973
Grove planation, M. T., 37974
Mississippi Territory. Governor
Proclamation, 37976
Mississippi Territory. Laws (session)
Laws, (1799) 35828, (1800) 37975
Mistake in the contents, 29894
Mr. Abiel Foster's motion, (Feb. 16, 1799) 36559, (Feb. 4, 1800) 38786
Mr. & Mrs. Solomon, 27717
Mr. Bascom's execution sermon, 20955
Mr. Bayard's motion, 38787
Mr. Belcher's celebrated, 31791
Mr. Blount's motion, 31358
Mr. Bradley's Thanksgiving sermon, 35228
Mr. Burke's speech, 18388
Mr. Carleton, professor, 20261
Mr. Charles Pinckney's speech, 19926
Mr. Cook's just, 2109-110
Mr. Croswell's reply, 4926
Mr. David Rusk, 15314
Mr. Dodge's narrative, 16765
Mr. Dutch's discourse, 28605
Mr. Dwight Foster's motion, 34721
Mr. Emerson's exhortation, 4942
Mr. Faulks, the noted, 12041
Mr. Fennell respectfully, 30415
Mr. Fiske's discourse, 33736
Mr. Foster's sermon, 24326
Mr. Franklin, the absolute, 6194
Mr. George Keith's account, 980
Mr. Harper's motion, (Dec. 31, 1795) 31359, (Feb.

9, 1797) 32978, (June 5, 1798) 34722, (July 3, 1798) 34723, (July 6, 1798) 34724-25, (Mar. 10, 1800) 38788
Mr. Harper's speech, (1798) 33839-40, (1799) 35589
Mr. Hart's anniversary sermon, 24381
Mr. Hart's sermon occasioned, 24382
Mr. Henry Lee's motion, 38789
Mr. Hobby chastised, 5670
Mr. Hutchinson's sermon, 15370
Mr. Ingersoll's letters, 10342
Mr. Jauncey heartily, 11302
Mr. Kitchell's motion, 31360
Mr. Leland's circular, 23494
Mr. Livingston's motion, (Feb. 13, 1800) 38790, (Feb. 20, 1800) 38791
Mr. Maclay's motion, 31361
Mr. Marshall's motion, 38972
Mr. Mercer considers, 24538
Mr. Mitchel's letter, (1732) 3575, (1750) 6551, (1764) 9739
Mr. Moody's discourse, 11746
Mr. Morris's farewell, 34140
Mr. Murray unmask'd, 13997-98
Mr. Murray's opinion, 3799
Mr. Nash's sermon, 24567
Mr. Nicholas's motion, (Mar. 13, 1800) 38796, (Apr. 2, 1800) 38793-94, (Nov. 21, 1800) 38795
Mr. Noxon's observations, 3585
Mr. Nugent's vindication, 35999
Mr. Occom's address, 12911
Mr. O'Leary's plea, 19156
Mr. Parker, a bill was sent, 11470
Mr. Parsons corrected, 5250
Mr. Patten's sermon, 19702
Mr. Payne's game, 36048
Mr. Pickering's letter, 5676
Mr. Pike's present thoughts, 11044
Mr. Pitt's speech, 10462
Mr. Prescott's examination, 3954
Mr. Prime's two ordination, 8244
Mr. printer, in order that, 20380
Mr. printer, this is certainly, 20379
Mr. Punch's silver toy, 19805
Mr. Ripley's sermon, 24747
Mr. Rivington, Friday, 13335
Mr. Sandeman refuted, 10075
Mr. Samuel Smith's motion, (Jan. 4, 1796) 31362, (May 7, 1796) 31363
Mr. Sitgreave's motion, 34726
Mr. Smith's opinion, 3834
Mr. Stone's and Mr. Underwood's sermon, 31240
Mr. Story's two sermons, 29571
Mr. Tennent's speech, 15612
Mr. Thomas Paine's trial, 28338
Mr. Truman's observations, 4089
Mr. Trumbull's sermon, 23840
Mr. Turell's brief and plain, 6255
Mr. Turell's dialogue, 5076-77
Mr. Turell's directions, 5078-81
Mr. W———d's soliloquy, 5644
Mr. Whitbread's brewhouse, 21615
Mr. Wilder's sermon, 35027
Mr. William Smith's motion, 32979
Mr. Worcester's letter, 20158
Mistisches und kirchliches, 5205
Mrs. Barbauld's Lessons, 20946-49
Mrs. Judith Hull, 738
Mrs. Pleasants' story book, 34386
Mrs. Pownall's address, 26032
Mitchel, John. Epistle in verse, 6796

Mitchel, Jonathan, 1624-1668
  Defence of the answer, 89
  Discourse, 2262-63
  Elijah's mantle, 2363, 13445
  Letter (to his brother), (1719) 2055, (1732) 3575,
    (1750) 6551, (1764) 9739
  Nehemiah, 163
  death, 790
  life of, 2553
Mitchel, Justus, ordained, 18558
Mitchell, ——, reports on apportioning taxes,
  20069
Mitchell, Ammi Ruhami, 1762-1824. Eulogy, 37977
Mitchell, David, d. 1796, death, 30491
Mitchell, Euphemia, death, 24811
Mitchell, John
  American youths museum, 21262
  Elementary principles, 25828
Mitchell, John H., proposals on coinage, 23001
Mitchell, Nathaniel, 1753-1814, reports on appro-
  tioning taxes, 20069?
Mitchell, Stephen Mix, marriage, 11504
Mitchell, William. New and complete, 30802
Mitchelson, David, witnesses confession, 15874
Mitchill, Samuel Latham, 1764-1831
  Address to the citizens, 37978
  Life, exploits, 29088
  Medical repository, 32460, 37946-47
  Nomenclature, 27330
  Observations, 20527
  Oration, 25829
  Outline of the doctrines, 24549
  Present state of learning, 27331
  Present state of medical, 32488
  Remarks, 29089
  (ed.) Zoonomia, 30312
Mitchinar, Robert, dispute with Crawford, 11226
Mite cast into the treasury, 12322-23, 18928
  into the treasury, 8146
  of praise, 37979
Mithridate, Hippocrate. Some serious thoughts,
  6366
Mix, Stephen, 1672-1738. Extraordinary displays,
  3064
Moale, John, address to, 14520
Mocking-bird: a collection, 25830
Mode of elections, 11517
Mode of partition, 30273
Model for erecting, 1703
Models of letters, 29377
Moderate man. To the freeborn, 13655
Moderate Whig. Some seasonable observations,
  14462
Modern author's instructor, 9797
  chivalry, (1792) 24142-43, (1793) 25224, (1797)
    31862
  collection, 37980
  infidelity, 37564
  poemander, 5758
  priest, 29332
  primer, 37981
  Quaker, 37982
  riding-master, 14653
  story teller, 30803
  system, 30797
  vindication, 22923
Modes of Presbyterian, 10392, 21967
Modest account, 11060
  and impartial narrative, 570
  apology for Parson, 2536

apology for the eight, 3065
enquiry into the nature, (1702) 1050, (1729)
  3165, (1771) 12063
enquiry into the state, 7355
proof, 2417
proposal, 5931
reply to a letter, 8490
reply to the speech, 2890
vindication, 5645
Moffatt, Tabitha, marriage, 37437
Mohawk Indians
  Minutes of conferences, 8377
  books for, 1740
  conferences, 8156
  missionary to, 9088
  proposals by, 632?, 819?
  translation into language of, 11248
  treaty, (1694) 702?, 743?, (1758) 8157
Mohican Indians
  conference, 3916?
  conferences, 8156, 8887
  language of, 21068?
  translation into language of, 29879?
  treaty, (1757) 7925-26, (1758) 8157
Molière, Jean-Baptiste Poquelin, 1622-1673, plagi-
  arized, 28293
Molineaux, ——, fl. 1769. State of the embarrass-
  ments, 11478
Molineux, Frederic. Plan of the town, 30805
Moller, John Christopher, ed. First number, 25831
Mollineux, Mary Southworth, 1651-1695. Fruits of
  retirement, (1729) 3191, (1730) 3322, (1783) 18035
Molyneux, Robert. Funeral sermon, 19806
Monarchy, 29091
Monckton, Robert. Speech, 9214
Monday morning, Dec. 27, 1773, 12944
Money the sinews, 3450
Money toss'd, 26511
Monica Americana, 1217
Monis, Judah, 1683-1764
  Dickdock leshon, 3931
  Dissertation, 3932
  Proposals, 3798
  Truth, 2324
Monitor. To the Provincial congress, 13446
Monitor for communicants, (1714) 1694, (1715)
  1758-59, (1716) 1827, (1727) 2916, (1732) 3572,
  (1750) 6547
  for delaying, 2074
  for gospel ministers, 6293
  or a poem, 22672
Monitory and hortatory, 928
  letter about the maintenance, 927
  letter to them, (1702) 1070, (1712) 1553, (1738)
    4274
Monk, Christopher, wounded, 12094
Monk, a romance, 35729
Monmouth, James Fitzroy, duke of, 1649-1685
  Abridgment of the English, 508
Monody, 28978

VOL.	ITEMS	VOL.	ITEMS
1	1-3244	8	22298-25074
2	3245-6623	9	25075-28145
3	6624-9891	10	28146-30832
4	9892-13091	11	30833-33261
5	13092-16176	12	33262-25854
6	16177-19448	13	35855-39162
7	19449-22297		

Monody in honor, 18610
   inscribed, 10855
     on Major André, (1781) 17368, (1782) 17719,
      (1788) 21457-58, (1790) 22888, (1798) 33290,
      34533
     on the unfortunate, 24782, 27690
Monro, John. Collection of about fifty, 22673
Monroe, James, 1758-1831
   Address and recommendations, 18223-28
   Letter (to General assembly), 38956
   Letter (1800), 38957
   Observations, 21264
   Some observations, 21263
   View of the conduct, 32491
   motion on cession of territory, 20067
   motion on commerce, 19301
   motion on western posts, 19303
   motion to repeal acts, 19313
   reports on accounts, 20059
   reports on apportioning taxes, 20069
   reports on governor's letter, 20057
   reports on Indian department, 20060
   reports on revenue, 20084-85
   reports on secy. of Congress, 19295
   reports on supplies, 19308
   views on foreign affairs, 34676
Monster of monsters, 7532
Monstrous good songs, 24551
Montagu, Edward Wortley, 1713-1776. Life, travels,
   18611, 27335
Montagu, Lady Mary Pierrepont Wortley, 1690-
   1762
   Additional volume, 10978
   Letters, 10393
   Poetical works, 11340
   son's travels, 18611, 27335
   travels, 31692
Montague, ———. New systematical, 22674
Montague, John. Arguments offer'd, 1000
Montaigne, Michel Eyquem de, 1533-1592, imitated,
   31748
Montalbert, a novel, 29524, 38512
Monteath, Walter. Brotherly-love, 21968
Montfort, Robert
   To the planters, 21969
   To the public, 21970
   election opposed, 21732
Montgomerie, John, d. 1731, grants charter, 14939
Montgomery, Hugh, trial of, 11683
Montgomery, James. Decius's letters, 21971
Montgomery, Joseph, 1733-1794. Sermon, 14261
Montgomery, Richard, 1738-1775
   captures Montreal, 14540
   death, 15084-87, 15248-50, 22946
   ghost of, 14966
   letter from, 14541
   life, 27221
   poem on, 17896
Montgomery county, N.Y. Twenty dollars, 37986
Montgomery county, Penna. Advertisement, 29093
Monthly magazine, 35831, 37988
   meeting of Friends, 17163
   military repository, 30807, 32492
   mirror, 25833
   miscellany, 27336
   observations, 627
   review, 27711
Montolieu, Isabelle, 1751-1832. Caroline of Litchfield, 34126
Montresor, Capt. ———, letter (from Auchmuty),

13818
Monument to the praise, (1795) 29214, (1796)
   30900, (1797) 32580-81
Monumental gratitude, 2882
Monumental memorial, 377
Moodey, Eleazar see **Moody, Eleazar**
Moodey, Joshua, 1633-1697
   Believers happy change, 802
   Catalogue of rare, 1984
   Exhortation, 413, 432
   Great sin, 571
   People of New England, 625
   Practical discourse, 396, 5811
   Principles, 502
   Souldiery spiritualized, 193
   death, 797
   reply to, 515
Moodey, Samuel, 1676-1747
   Children of the covenant, 1840
   Debtor's monitor, 1768
   Dialogue containing, 9189, 10979
   Discourse to little, 11746, 20528
   Discourse to the little, 2264, 6367-68
   Faithful narrative, 4166
   Gospel way, 1475, 4390
   Judas the traitor, 1704, 8931
   Sermon, 2265
   Summary account, 2782
   Vain youth, 1323-24, 8670
   death, 6136
   preface by, 4245
Moodey, Samuel, d. 1795. Attempt to point out,
   8418
Moody, Amos, ordained, 10512
Moody, Eleazar. School of good manners, (1786)
   19807, (1787) 20528, (1793) 25834, (1794) 27337,
   (1795) 29094, (1796) 30808, (1799) 35832
Moody, Joseph, d. 1753
   death, 7031
   preface by, 4245
Moody, Joseph, d. 1766?, death, 10497
Moody, Samuel see **Moodey, Samuel, 1676-1747**
Moody, Silas, 1742-1816
   Sermon, 37989
   ordained, 12167
Moody, Thomas. Compendium, 12129
Mooney, Nicholas, d. 1752. Life, 6886, 7063
Moor, Abraham
   God's joyful, 25835
   ordained, 30726
Moor, Walter, d. 1798, death, 35130
Moore, ———, excerpts from, 23246
Moore, ———, travels of, 31692
Moore, Alpheus. Oration, 34127
Moore, Benjamin, 1748-1816
   Address, 25836
   Doctrine of baptismal, 25837
   Doctrine of regeneration, 23573, 24552
   Sermon, 15444, 20529
   remarks on, 25722
   reply to, 26502
Moore, Daniel
   System of exchange, 37696
   conduct, 10748
Moore, Edward, 1712-1757
   Fables for the female sex, (1792) 24452, (1794)
     27192, (1797) 32345, (1798) 34128
   Fables for the ladies, 20530, 27338
   Foundling, (1793) 26559, (1794) 27339
   Gamester, (1790) 22675, (1792) 24049, (1795)

29095
excerpts from, 23246?, 34112
Moore, George. Grasville Abbey, 35833
Moore, Sir Henry, 1713-1769
Proclamation, (1765) 10094-95, (1766) 10416-17, (1768) 11002
Speech, (1765) 10097, (1766) 10420-21, (1767) 10707-708, (1768) 11003, (1769) 11367
address to, 10098, 10422-23, 10709-711, 11004-5
dedication to, 11434
elegy on, 11245
Stamp Act dispute, 10096
Moore, Henry, 1751-1844. Life of the Rev. John, 25311
Moore, James, of Ky., trials, 31039
Moore, James, of Phila. Letter (to Stancliff), 21265
Moore, John, of N. Y. To the respectable, 13681
Moore, John, of Penna. Inaugural dissertation, 37990
Moore, John, V.D.M. Doctrine of predestination, 29096
Moore, John, 1646-1714. Of religious melancholy, 4043
Moore, John, 1729-1802
Edward; various views, 34129
Essays on the causes, 17607
Journal, (1793) 25838-39, (1794) 27340-43, (1797) 32493
Medical sketches, 27344
View of society, 18036, 24553-54
Zeluco, 24555, 25840
travels of, 31692?
Moore, John Hamilton, d. 1807
New and practical, 37991
New practical navigator, 35834
Young gentleman and lady's monitor, (1789) 21972, (1790) 22676-77, (1792) 24556, (1793) 25841, (1794) 27345, (1795) 29097-98, (1797) 32494-95, (1798) 34130, (1799) 35835, (1800) 37992
Young gentlemen and lady's, 20531
Moore, Jonathan, ordained, 10809
Moore, Maurice, d. 1777. Justice, 10076
Moore, Milcah Martha Hill, d. 1829. Miscellanies, 29099, 30809
Moore, Richard. Almanac see **Almanacs (Moore)**
Moore, Samuel. Accurate system, 30810
Moore, Thomas. Almanac see **Almanacs (Moore)**
Moore, Thomas. Oration, 32496
Moore, Thomas Lambert. Sermon, 21975, 24558
Moore, William, of Gt. Brit. The crisis, 13896-996
Moore, William, 1699-1783, charges against, 14110
Moore, William, 1735-1793
Preface to a memorial, 7958
satirized, 8160
vice-pres. Penna. Council, 16928
Moore, Zephaniah Swift, 1770-1823
Sketches of the reciprocal, 34232
Thanksgiving sermon, 32498
ordained, 33353
Moorhead, John, d. 1774
Fair narrative, 7720
death, 13391
letter (from Abercrombie), 7826
letter (from Murray), 9745
member of presbytery, 7142
Moorhead, Sarah Parsons. To the Reverend, 5011
Moor's Indian charity school, 12051, 12284
Moral and entertaining, 21268
  and historical, 34435
  & instructive, 32499

and literary, 34342
and religious, 14137, 22603
character, 31922
disquisitions, 22156
distiches, 3884
instructions, (1786) 19613, (1796) 30365, (1797) 32064
library, 30813
ode, 12131
sketches, 37994
story teller, 32500
Morales, Juan Ventura, intendant, 35741
Moralist, or young, 24559, 25844
Morality not to be, 962
  of the Bible, 10251
  of the Sans-Culottes, 26764
Moralphilosophische rede, 33804
Morals, by way of abstract, 24778, 27682-83
Morals to a set, 33728
Moravians see **United Brethren**
Morbid anatomy, 28226
Mordaunt, Gen. ——, expedition, 8138-39
More, H., extracts from, 27564-66
More, Hannah, 1745-1833
Armine and Elvira, 29102
Arminie and Elvira, 28978
Bear ye, 36163
Betty Brown, 37165
Black Giles, 27142-43
Consideration on religion, 27347
Dan and Jane, 37165
Day of judgment, 37164
Essays, (1786) 19810, (1792) 24452, (1794) 27192, (1796) 30814, (1797) 32345
Estimate of the religion, 25845, 29103
Fortune teller, 34133
History of Mr. Fantom, 37161
History of Tawny Rachel, 37144
History of the two shoemakers, 37145-48
History of Tom White, 34134, 37138
Hymn of praise, 37149
Inflexible captive, 29104
Lady and the pye, 37162
Moses in the bulrushes, 37995
Sacred dramas, 20534
Search after happiness, (1773) 12872, (1774) 13449, (1775) 14263, (1786) 19811-12, (1787) 20535, (1791) 23575-76, (1793) 25846, (1795) 29105, (1796) 30815, (1797) 32502
Sensibility, 19102
Shepherd of Salisbury, 37128-29
Shopkeeper, 37158
Slavery, 21269-70
Sorrowful Sam, 37137
Strictures on the modern, 37996-97
Tawny Rachel, 35298
Thoughts on the importance, (1788) 21271, (1795) 29106, (1797) 31503
Two shoemakers, 32501
Two wealthy farmers, 37132-36

VOL.	ITEMS	VOL.	ITEMS
1	1-3244	8	22298-25074
2	3245-6623	9	25075-28145
3	6624-9891	10	28146-30832
4	9892-13091	11	30833-33261
5	13092-16176	12	33262-25854
6	16177-19448	13	35855-39162
7	19449-22297		

Way to plenty, 37139
More, Roger. Almanac see **Almanacs (Poor Roger)**
More, Sarah, d. 1817
　　Cheapside apprentice, 34135
　　Good mother's legacy, 35297
　　Hubbub, 34136
　　Hubub, 37162
More, Thomas. Almanac see **Almanacs (More)**
More, Sir Thomas, 1480-1535. Common-weath, 7068
More excellent, 5093
More fresh news, 14264
More impartial pen. Poem, 7298
More just vindication, 2759
　　last words, 5815
　　wonders, 30149
Moreau de St. Méry, Médéric Louis Elie, 1750-1819
　　Catalogue of books, 29107
　　Danse, 30816
　　Description topographique, (1796) 30817, (1797)
　　　32504, (1798) 34137
　　Essai sur la manière, 29109
　　Essay on the manner, 29109
　　General view, 32505
　　Idée generale, 30819
　　Philadelphia, 1st November, 1794, 27348
　　Porcupine, a print, 30820
　　Topographical and political, 30818, 34138
　　(ed.) Voyage de l'Ambassade, 31860
Morehouse, Abraham see **Morhouse, Abraham**
Moreland, Henry, earl of, history, 26703
Morgan, ———. Indian narrative, 31616
Morgan, Capt. ———, sermon preached before,
　13828
Morgan, Abel, 1637-1722. Cyd-Gordiad, 3323
Morgan, Abel, 1713-1785
　　Anti-paedo-rantism, 6013, 6555
　　answer to, 6137
　　remarks on, 6419
Morgan, Benjamin R., election favored, 33769,
　34672-73
Morgan, Evan, d. 1763, death, 9379
Morgan, George, memorial of, 21513-14
Morgan, Jacob, accounts, 18099
Morgan, James. Life and death, 24560
Morgan, John, fl. 1735. Myfyrdodau, 1333
Morgan, John, 1735-1789
　　Conclusion, 17240
　　Discourse, 10082
　　Four dissertations, 10400
　　Recommendation, 14891
　　To his excellency, 15446
　　To the citizens, 15917
　　Vindication of his public, 15447
Morgan, Joseph, d. 1725, death, 2679
Morgan, Joseph, 1674-1740
　　Brief history, 3066
　　Duty and a mark, 2679
　　General cause, 4755-56
　　Great concernment, 1573
　　Letter to the authors, 2565
　　Love to our neighbour, 6372-73
　　Love to our neighbours, 2925
　　Nature and origin, 2926
　　Nature of riches, 3576
　　Only effectual, 2680
　　Portsmouth disputation, 1635
　　Sin its own punishment, 3067
　　Temporal interest, 3691
Morgen- und abend-gebet, 32100
Morhouse, Abraham
　　First trial, 21976

Writings, 30821, 32506
Morin, Michael, death, 6146
Morison, William, 1748-1818
　　Charge, 28531
　　Sermon, (1792) 24563, (1796) 30822, (1797) 34139,
　　　(1800) 37999
Morning and evening prayer, (1715) 1740, (1763)
　9385, (1795) 29365
　　and evening's meditation, 10355
　　health, 2947-48
　　is up, 34540
　　prayer, 4596, 16935
　　star, 1076
Morphy, Diego, letter (from Clarke), 34786
Morrell, Thomas. Sermon, 38000
Morrill, Isaac, 1718-1793
　　Charge, 12985?
　　Faith in divine, 16873
　　Soldier exhorted, 7493
　　death, 27745
Morrill, Nathaniel, 1698-1730
　　Lord's voice, 3068
　　Memento mori, 3324
　　ordained, 2961
Morris, ———, actor, 10573
Morris, ———, encounter at house of, 17849
Morris, ———, satire on, 16697
Morris, Dr. ———, sells tickets, 13841
Morris, Charles, 1745-1838. Prologue, 38001
Morris, Edward, d. 1815. Secret, 38001
Morris, Frederick. Account stated, 3803
Morris, Governeur, 1752-1816
　　Letters on appreciation, 18614
　　Observations, 16625, 17039
　　Oration, 37383, 38002
　　Plan, 19328
　　satirized, 16697?
Morris, Jacob. Gentlemen, the interest, 19136
Morris, James, 1752-1820
　　Farewell address, 34140
　　Oration, 38003
Morris, John
　　By the Council, 15511
　　secy. convention, 14980
Morris, Lewis, 1726-1798
　　At a court, 6832
　　Speech, (1738) 4282, (1739) 4393, (1742) 5254
　　Speeches, 5442
　　address to, 4394-95
　　candidate, 12335
　　demands seals, 4057
　　representation to, 5443
Morris, Morris
　　Reasons for his conduct, 3069
　　conduct of, 3111
Morris, Robert, 1734-1806
　　Articles of agreement, 26586
　　Historical account, 29474
　　Plan, 17395, 19328
　　Statement of the account, 19333
　　To the citizens, 16377
　　accounts, 22993, 23922
　　correspondence with Yates, 20080
　　land titles, 23376
　　lands sold, 36080
　　letter (from Deane), 18439-40
Morris, Robert Hunter. Proclamation, 7754-55
Morris, Thomas, 1732-180-
　　At a meeting, 30455
　　Quashy, 32507, 34141
　　Rules for the good, 29305

Morris county, N.J. Petition, 27350
Morrison, John, robber, 6624
Morrison, William see Morison, William, 1748-1818
Morris-Town ghosts, 34482
Mors, Obadiah, counterfeiter, 5045
Morse, Benjamin, town clerk Sutton, 15610
Morse, Ebenezer, d. 1802
  Antient promise, 11345
  ordained, 5145
Morse, James. Narrative, 19103
Morse, Jedidiah, 1761-1826
  Abridgment of the American, 34143
  Address to the students, 35837
  America, 22486
  American gazetteer, 32509
  American geography, 21978
  American universal geography, (1793) 25847,
    (1795) 29110, (1796) 30823-24
  Boston, Apr. 15, 1799, 35340
  Character and reward, 34144
  Description of the soil, 32510
  Duty of resignation, 30825
  Elements of geography, (1795) 29112, (1796)
    30826, (1798) 34145
  Geography made easy, (1784) 18615, (1790)
    22681, (1791) 23579, (1794) 27351, (1796) 30827,
    (1798) 34146, (1800) 38004
  History of America, (1790) 22682, (1795) 29111,
    (1798) 34147
  Information for immigrants, 28321
  New system, 27077
  New York, June 23, 1788, 21272
  Prayer, (1797) 31776, (1799) 37120-21
  Present situation, 29113
  Proposals for printing, 30828
  Sermon, (1790) 22683, (May 9, 1798) 34148-49,
    (June 25, 1798) 34150, (Nov. 29, 1798) 34151-
    52, 35841-43, (1799) 35838-40
  installation, 21673
  letter (from Tucker), 29662
  sketch of Washington, 38999
Morse, Samuel Benjamin, d. 1798. School dia-
  logues, 32511
Mortal man, 7226
Mortality; an account, 29309, 36097
Mortimer, Charles, history of, 33615
Morton, Charles, 1626-1698. Spirit of man, 661
Morton, Ebenezer. More last words, 5813
Morton, John P., dedication to, 33627
Morton, Nathaniel, 1612-1685. New England's me-
  morial, (1669) 144, (1721) 2266-67, (1772) 12469
Morton, Perez, 1751-1837
  Oration, 14892-95, 18997
  To all people, 26690
  secy. Council, 14198, 14200, 14206-212, 14839,
    14850-53, 14856-61, 15133
Morton, Sarah Wentworth Apthorp, 1759-1846
  Beacon Hill, 32512
  Death song, 25848
  Ouabi, 22684
  Power of sympathy, 21979
  Virtues of society, 35844
Morton, Thomas, 1764-1838
  Children in the wood, 29114-17
  Columbus, 27352
  Cure for the heart-ache, 34153
  Dear Walter, 29118
  In the dead, 30829
  Secrets, 35845
  See brother, 29119
  Songs, duets, 29120

Speed the plough, 38006-7
Young Simon, 29121
Morveau, ———, proposes nomenclature, 36347
Mose, Henry, ed. Hodder's Arithmetic, 2026
Moseley, Jonathan Ogden, 1762-1839. Oration,
  38008
Mosely, John, sermon before, 7615
Mosely, Samuel, d. 1791, death, 24197
Moses, institutions of, 36160
Moses Paul, d. 1772
  execution, 12493-96, 12907-911, 13508
  letter (from Z—n), 12634
Moses, Isaac, & sons. Extensive and valuable, 35949
Moses a witness, 2324
    and Aaron, 3141
    in the bulrushes, 37995
Mosheim, Johann Lorenz von, 1694-1755. Eccle-
  siastical history, (1797) 32513, (1798) 34154,
  (1800) 38009
Moss, Charles, 1711-1802. Sermon, 11346
Moss, Joseph. Election sermon, 1769
Moss, Reuben, ordained, 26286
Most bloody, 25849
    heinous, 11707
    honourable, 2666
    illustrious, 27686
    important, 8872
    promising, 26596
    remarkable, 8676
    surprising adventures, 21788, 28552
    tragical, 29862
Mote point, 16224
Mother Goose, 29300
Mother Goose's melody, (1785) 19105, (1795) 29122,
  (1799) 35847
Mother Midnight's comical, 9416
Mother's catechism, (1729) 3192, (1783) 18313,
  (1787) 20888, (1788) 21611-12, (1789) 22281,
  (1791) 24005, (1794) 28102-103, (1795) 29901-902,
  (1798) 35034
Mother's gift, (1775) 14265, (1785) 19104, (1786)
  19813, (1787) 20536, (1791) 23580, (1797) 32514,
  (1799) 35846
Motion made in the committee, 38797
Motion of Mr. Dane, 20069
Motley assembly, 16668
Mott, J., pamphlet by, 3378
Mott, Samuel. Almanac see Almanacs (Mott)
Moulton, William. Oration, 30830
Moultrie, Alexander. Appeal to the people, 27354
Mounier, ———, extracts from, 35307
Mounseer Nong, 35848
Mount, Thomas, confession, 23773-75
Mount Pleasant, May 5, 1766, 10360
Mount Vernon, a poem, 38479
Mountain, Joseph, d. 1790, execution, 22441-43,
  22446
Mountain cottager, 38544
Mountain piper, 30831
Mountaineers, 28447-48, 30241

VOL.	ITEMS	VOL.	ITEMS
1	1-3244	8	22298-25074
2	3245-6623	9	25075-28145
3	6624-9891	10	28146-30832
4	9892-13091	11	30833-33261
5	13092-16176	12	33262-25854
6	16177-19448	13	35855-39162
7	19449-22297		

VOL.	ITEMS	VOL.	ITEMS
1	1-3244	8	22298-25074
2	3245-6623	9	25075-28145
3	6624-9891	10	28146-30832
4	9892-13091	11	30833-33261
5	13092-16176	12	33262-25854
6	16177-19448	13	35855-39162
7	19449-22297		

N

N., I. see **Norris, Isaac, 1671-1735**
N., N.
  From a gentleman, 493
  Some reflections, 7495
N., S. see **Nowell, Samuel, 1634-1688**
N., W. English liberties, 2208
N. . . . . .s, J. .n D see **Noailles, John de**
Naboth's vineyard, 15380
Nachdenken über mich, 21195
Nachdrückliche buss-stimme, 13189-90
Nachklang, 7496
Nachricht seiner von Gott, 24755
Nachrichters, oder nützliches, 11627, 12026
Nadere trouwhartige, 9451
Nadir, William. Almanac see **Almanacs (Douglass)**
Nails fastened, 2773
Naimbanna, memoirs, 36310, 37164
Nalton, James, 1600-1662. Nature and necessity, 4757
Name of God, 28689
Names and places of abode, 32656
      of the streets, 1342, 36997
      of the subscribers, 29417
Nancrede, Paul Joseph Guérard de, 1760-1841
    Abeille, 24566
    (ed.) Adventures of Telemachus, 32124-25
    (ed.) Aventures de Télémaque, 32123
    Books; importation of May, 34165
    Boston, Feb. 5, 1799, 35855
    Catalogue of books, 30833
    (tr.) Discourse, 23222
    (tr.) Plan of constitution, 28695
Nancy, or the sailor's journal, 32040, 34166
Nanfan, John. Proclamation, (1699) 886-87, (1701) 1002-1012, (1702) 1081-82
Nanticoke Indians
    conferences, 8156, 8887
    treaty, (1757) 7925-26, (1758) 8157
Napoleon I see **Buonaparte, Napoleon**
Narborough, Sir John, additions to, 7859
Narcissus (ship), at New York, 17552
Narragansett Indians. Declaration, 17
Narrative and confession, 31036-37
      &c., 33447
      concerning, 18738
      containing, 34405
      of a discovery, 17582, 18574
          late expedition, 17993, 35689
          new and unusual, 1300, 7455
      of an attempt, 632
      of Colonel Ethan, 16692-93

  of Colonel Ethen, 16180-82
  of his connection, 32263
  of his sufferings, 16765
  of his travels, 13062
  of Lieutenant-general, 17876
  of many facts, 11695
  of Mr. Adam, 27545
  of Mr. John, 38531
  of Mrs. Elizabeth, 36837
  of Mrs. Scott, 19979
  of part, 11151
  of Patrick, 35752
  of remarkable, 20972, 26679
  of some sufferings, 38519
  of the British embassy, 29189-90
      captivity and sufferings, (Fletcher) 33740, (Gilbert) 18497
      captivity of John Vandike, 36608
      captivity of Mrs. Johnson, 30180, 30641
      captivity of Nehemiah, 6162
      captivity, sufferings, (1770) 11841, (1771) 12217, (1773) 12988, (1774) 13589, (1791) 23745, (1794) 27646, (1795) 29436, (1796) 31127, (1800) 38425
      capture and treatment, 16262
      capture of certain, 18273, 18850
      effects, 15775
      excursion, 14269, 16380
      expedition, 22176
      extraordinary adventures, (1785) 19058, (1798) 33487, (1799) 35265
      extraordinary case, 24485, 27239
      extraordinary sufferings, (1791) 23221, (1792) 24144, (1793) 25226-27, (1794) 26698, (1797) 31864
      founding, 6302
      gracious dealings, 25825
      horrid murder, 39087
      Indian wars, 14120, 35646
      late massacres, 9667
      life, (Beadle) 17828, 26629, 28246, (Bly) 20974, (Lewis) 8638, 9157, (Ryer) 26118, (Venture) 34560, (White) 18886, (Young) 33255
      loss, 32886, 38570-71
      miseries, 450, 14252
      missions, 26803
      most remarkable, 13311
      mutiny, 22367
      planting, 709
      proceedings of Sir Edmond, 572

proceedings of the Baptist, 19103
proceedings of the black, 27170
proceedings of those, 4044
proceedings subsequent, 12889
progress, 206
revival, 5698
rise and progress, 17823
rise, progress, 28622
shipwreck, (1727) 2863, (1728) 3018, (1762) 9102
strange principles, 17735
success, 3263
sufferings and surprising, 7658-62
sufferings of James, 30336
sufferings underwent, 37309
treatment, 1079
trial, 26820
troubles, 231
uncommon, 8611
unhappy life, 9197
wicked life, 7796
two excommunications, 30124
Whiting Sweeting, (1791) 23814-15, (1792) 24836-38, (1793) 26237, (1794) 27767, (1797) 32899
relating, 194
shewing, 31007
Nash, Judah, 1728-1905
Charge, 33368
Discourse, 24567
Nash, Melatiah
(tr.) Amelia Vermont, 34018
(tr.) Emilia, 35743
Nash, Thomas, resolutions concerning, 37887
Nashauanittue, 550
Naskov, Peder Z., 1635-1695. Articles of faith, 7262
Nassy, David de Isaac Cohen
Observations on the cause, 25855, 31172
Observations sur la cause, 25854
Nathan ben Saddi
Fragment of the chronicles, 8130, 9662
see also Dodsley, Robert, 1703-1764
Nathan, John. Almanac see Almanacs (Nathan)
Nathanael's character, 3640
National affliction, 37715
arithmetick, 20016
bankrupt law, 38798
convention; collection of the heroic, 26999
report on the means, 27000
report on the organization, 27001
report upon the principles, 27002
eulogy, 37809
happiness, 28952
ingratitude, 5588
magazine, 35857 38027
monument, 26752
peace, 32086, 33673
Native and member of the House of burgesses see Jefferson, Thomas, 1743-1826
Native citizen and servant of the state see Hanson, Alexander Contee, 1749-1806
Native of America see Parke, John
Native of Boston see Jackson, Jonathan, 1743-1810
Native of Donegall. Paxton boys, 9776-78
Native of New England
Almanac see Almanacs (Bowen)
see Alpin, John; Leonard, Daniel, 1740-1829
Native of Pennsylvania see Grey, Isaac; Williamson, Hugh, 1735-1819
Native of that colony see Braxton, Carter, 1736-1797

Native of the province see Andrews, Samuel, 1737-1818
Native of this state. Treatise of gardening. 26275
Native of Virginia see Monroe, James, 1758-1831
Nativity of Christ, 21783
Natstock, Joshua, clerk, 513
Natural and civil history, 28094
and moral government, 6408, 6596
history of beasts, 26797
of four-footed, 20435, 29656
of the Bible, 25586
of the slug, 36052
ideas, 29820-21
Natural man. Sermon on natural religion, 12225
Natural principles of liberty, 17559
principles of rectitude, 28775
religion aided, 16303
as distinguished, 8354
insufficient, 33834
son, a comedy, 26559, 26834
son, a domestic tale, 26988
teacher, 35053
Naturalisationsform, 8936
Nature and art, 30623
and cause, 12517
and danger of infidel, 33657
and danger of sinful, 2889
and design of Christianity, (1744) 5511, (1756) 7814, (1792) 25013
of the baptism, 39092
of the evangelical, 29578
and effects of Christian, 27786
of drunkenness, 13128
of the works, 35523
and evil, 16084-85
and extent of Christ's, 7126
of parliamentary power, 10985-86
of the redemption, 8245
and happiness, 22321
and importance of a pure, 23172
of Christian, 37789
of oaths, 6015
of rightly, 18793
of the duty, 14260
and mnaner of giving, 28339
and manner of man's, 1865
and necessity of a growth, 20278, 21742
of an habitual, 8099
of an internal, 24062
of humiliation, 4757
of regeneration, (1743) 5163-64, (1753) 6969, (1765) 10164
of repentance, 3100
of society, 4648
of spiritual, 8029
of the new-birth, 3052
and origin, 2926
and subjects, 28518
and tendancy, 16322
and treatment, 15100
certainty and evidence, 7523, 25949-50

VOL.	ITEMS	VOL.	ITEMS
1	1-3244	8	22298-25074
2	3245-6623	9	25075-28145
3	6624-9891	10	28146-30832
4	9892-13091	11	30833-33261
5	13092-16176	12	33262-25854
6	16177-19448	13	35855-39162
7	19449-22297		

extent and importance, 33342
folly and evil, 4909
obligation and importance, 30653
of early piety, 2256
of humiliation, 28340
of justification, 5697
of love, 24429
of moral agency, 20705
of ordination, 7371
of regeneration, 3968
of religious fasting, 3756
of religious thanksgiving, 3883
of riches, 3576
of saving conversion, 11873
of that faith, 12635
pleasure and advantages, 11955
power, deceit, 25953
Naudowessie Indians, vocabulary, 31920
Naughty boy reformed, (1786) 19989, (1789) 22145,
   (1797) 23764, (1795) 29516
Naughty girl reformed, (1794) 26705, (1795) 28352-
   53, (1799) 35242, (1800) 37051-52
Naumann, D., prayers, 8360
Naunautooghijau, Indian chief, 3916
Nautical songster, 34167
Naval engagements, 17611
Naval gazetteer, 32415
Navigation (snow), at Philadelphia, 34352
Navigation spiritualized, 2472, 30428
Nazro, John. Public auction, 39148
Ne kesukod Jehovah, 1313
Ne orhoengene, 1740
Ne sutor, 309
Neal, James Armstrong, 1774-1808. Essay, 29135
Neal, Moses Leavitt, d. 1829. Presbyteriad, 32516-17
Neale, Mary, life, 30834
Neale, Samuel, 1729-1792. Some account, 30834
Neander, Joachim. Bundes-lieder, 6917
Near prospect, 13598
Necessaries, 14896
Necessarius, 3409
Necessary admonitions, 1072
   directions, 4565
   truth, 6241
Necessity and divine excellence, 24327
   and divine excellency, 16777
   and importance, 11132
   of a constant, 10282
      speedy, 1429
      well experienced, 276, 307
   of acknowledgment, 1026
   of an early, 904
   of an established, 15448
   of atonement, 18998
   of brotherly, 9169
   of contending, 4477
   of divine, 17932
   of God's drawing, 7094
   of good works, 4979
   of holding, 5299
   of keeping, 5699
   of piety, 7875
   of praising, 5700
   of reformation, 263, 7857
   of regeneration, 4261
   of religion, 1598
   of religious violence, 3966
   of repealing, 10402
   of repentance, 17878
   of sincerity, 335

of studying, 5498
of thankfulness, 5499
of the belief, 26934
of the pouring, 259
Necker, Jacques, 1732-1804
   Of the importance, 23588, 30835
   account of administration, 19153, 20601
Neederlander. Een der voorrechten, 11644
Needful caution against, 1270
Needful caution in a critical, 5027
Neele, S. J. Map of the country, 21277
Neglect of supporting, 425
Negociator's magazine, 9693
Negotio, James, wife's sufferings, 34207
Negro boy, 30243
   Christianized, 1262
   girl, 28977
   slavery defended, 34370
Nehemiah, a brief essay, 1467
   on the wall, 163
   or the struggle, 16379
Neighbour
   Elegy, 12758
   see also Chaplin, Ebenezer, 1733-1822
Neighbour's tears, 1489
Neill, Hugh. Doctrine of water baptism, 8937
Neilson, James H., case of, 38156
Neilson, William
   To the public, 11350
   transaction with M'Donald, 11318
Neisser, Georg. Aufrichtige nachricht, 5013
Nelson, David, 1752-1829. Investigation, 38028
Nelson, Horatio, 1758-1805
   intercepts letters, 35496
   victory, 33814
Nelson, J., petition of, 34743
Nelson, John. Extract, 24560
Nelson, John, 1707-1774. Case of John Nelson,
   12134
Nelson, John, d. 1734, death, 3894
Nelson, John, 1738-1766. Letter to the Protestant-
   dissenters, (1771) 12135, (1772) 12470, (1797)
   32518, (1798) 34168
Nelson, Seth, petition, 38827
Nelson, Stephen Smith, ordained, 32882
Nelson, Thomas. Headquarters, York, 15517
Nelson, William, of Gt. Brit. English liberties,
   13185
Nelson's Charleston directory, 38029
Nepenthes evangelicum, 1624
Neptune (warship), courtmartial on, 32837
Nero, a tragedy, 8901
Nestor. To the militia, 15919
Netley Abbey, 30836
Nets of salvation, 1176
Neu-eingerichtetes gesang-buch, 9266
   -eingerichtetes schul-büchlein, 21982
   trauer-lied, 18041
   -vermehrt und vollständiges gesang-buch,
      (1753) 7102, (1763) 9495, (1772) 12534,
      (1774) 13565
   -vermehrtes gesäng, 9062
Neue acte enthaltend, 7070
   anrede, 9747
   charte, 29136
   charter, 5271
   deutsche A.B.C., 29137
   Testament, (1745) 5542, (1755) 7359, (1761)
      8799, (1763) 9347, (1769) 11181, (1775) 13837,
      (1776) 14663, (1783) 17846, (1787) 20236,

(1788) 20969, (1791) 23202, (1794) 26667,
(1795) 28286-87, (1796) 30081-82, (1800)
36956
und verbesserte, (1797) 32100, (1799) 35453,
36193
Neuer erfahrner, 27362, 30842
Neues auserlesenes, 24396
   lied, 16815
   schauspiel, 29163
Neuffville, John. Letters, 11658
Neufville, Anna de, memorial, 33033
Neufville, John de
   Boston, Sept. 5, 1783, 19109
   widow's memorial, 33033
Neujahrs verse (Philadephische correspondenz),
   (1782) 17546, (1783) 17944, (1784) 18494
Neujahrs-verse (Philadelphische s t a a t s b o t e),
   10218, 10525
Neuman, Henry, tr. Self immolation, 35702, 37759
Neumann, ———. Kern aller gebäter, (1776) 14794,
   (1788) 21124, (1796) 30529
Neun und neunzig, 2991
Neuse association. Minutes, (1795) 29144, (1799)
   35987
Never performed, 33439
Nevil, Thomas. To the several, 15115
Nevile, Henry, 1620-1694. Isle of Pines, 127
Nevill, Samuel, 1697?-1764
   (ed.) Acts of the General assembly, 8947
   History of North America, 8939
   New American magazine, (1758) 8199, (1759)
     8426, (1760) 8678
   observations on his speech, 5901?
New academy of compliments, 29145
   Ahimon Rezon, 23727
   American Latin grammar, (1784) 18758, (1788)
     21434, (1790) 22853, (1797) 32766
      magazine, (1758) 8199, (1759) 8426, (1760)
       8678
      melody, 21841
      mock-bird, 8940
      selection of lessons, (1792) 24245, (1794)
       26847, (1799) 35379
      songster, 33913
      spelling-book (Peirce), (1795) 29282,
       (1796) 30970, (1797) 32644, (1799) 36054,
       (1800) 38205-206
      spelling book (Ross), 19227, 19968
      spelling book (Thomas), 19271
   and accurate index, 19484
   and beautiful collection of hymns, 33802
   and beautiful collection of select, 35554
   and complete book, 26991
     guide, 4566
     introduction, (1764) 9598 - 600, (1766)
      10236, (1768) 10829
     letter writer, 23327
     life, 29927-28
     system of arithmetic, 21394, 32692
     system of bookkeeping, 30802
     system of federal, 34644
     system of introductions, 23335
     system of universal, (1798) 34316, (1799)
      36047, (1800) 38199
   and concise history, 27364
     correct map, 24124-25
     correct table, 20973
     easy plan, 28956
     old principles, 21281
     practical, 37991

   select collection, 16874
   true Aegyptian, 7101
   universal gazetteer, 34519, 36282, 38473
   valuable, 37022
  art of cookery, 24145, 33458-59
  assistant, 30695
New association. Minutes, 25863
New Baltimore directory, 38040
New Bedford, Mass.
   Hymn, ode, 38041
   Regulation for the government, 35866
New book of knowledge, (1762) 9200, (1767) 10699,
   (1772) 12472
New book of poems, 13084
New Castle county. Ordinances, 23594
New-Castle, Feb. 6, 1772, 12473
New-Castle, June 15, 1771, 12139
New-Castle lottery
   Christiana bridge, 12140
   New-Castle, June 15, 1771, 12139
New-Castle upon Delaware, 2542
New chart, 24713
   collection of country dances, 35867
     of hymns, 25965, 32008
     of sacred, 31884
     of verses, 10085
   complete American, 21985
     guide, 5648
     letter writer, (1791) 23326, (1794) 27365,
      (1798) 34177, (1800) 38042
     system, 34380
   Constitution march, 21462
   constitution with buttermilk, 17813
   converts, 4486
   creature delineated, 10562
   creature describ'd, 4688
   display, 35868
   drawing book, 30844
   duty, 17243
   edition; Farriery improved, 30118
     of Two discourses, 25632
     with corrections, 33849
   England astrology, 20343
New England diary see **Almanacs (New England**
   diary)
New England farmer see **Lowell, John, 1769-1840**
New England farmer, or georgical, 22450, 32020
   farrier, 28901
   freemen, 181
   harmonist, 35667, 37707
   magazine, 8200
New England man
   Letter to the freeholders, 6344
   Letter to the inhabitants, 6700
New England memorandum book, 10086
New England Mississippi land co.
   Memorial, 34179
   XXIII articles, 34178
New-England pesecutors, 801
   pleaded with, 180

VOL.	ITEMS	VOL.	ITEMS
1	1-3244	8	22298-25074
2	3245-6623	9	25075-28145
3	6624-9891	10	28146-30832
4	9892-13091	11	30833-33261
5	13092-16176	12	33262-25854
6	16177-19448	13	35855-39162
7	19449-22297		

Journal, (1745) 5649, (1768) 10991, (1784) 18624, (1786) 19818-20, (1787) 20550-52, (1788) 21283-86, (1789) 21994-95, (1790) 22699-700, (1791) 23599, (1792) 24581-82, (1793) 25872-73, (1794) 27371, 27373, (1795) 29165, (1796) 30851, (1797) 32533-34, 34193, (1798) 34195, 35879, (1799) 35880, 38048, (1800) 38051

New Hampshire. Laws (collective)
Acts and laws, (1706) 1271, (1716) 1842, (1726) 2784, (1761) 8943, 8945, (1766) 10408, (1771) 12146, (1780) 16877
Laws of the state, (1792) 24585, (1797) 32536
Perpetual laws, (1776-89), 21997
Temporary acts, 10994
Temporary laws, 12880

New Hampshire. Laws (session)
Acts, (1699) 882, (1718) 1985, (1719) 2057, (1721) 2269, (1765) 10408-409, (1776) 14899-900 (1784) 18622-23, (1785) 19111-13, 19817, (1786) 20548, (1787) 20549, (1788) 21282, 21991, (1789) 21996, 22703, (1792) 24586, 25876, (1793) 25877, 27375, (1794) 27376, (1795) 29168-69, (1796) 30852-53, (1797) 32535, 32537, (1799) 35883-84, (1800) 38052-53

New Hampshire. Laws (separates)
Act (1759), (1000 men) 8427
Act (1776), (armed vessels) 14900
Act (1778), (loyalists) 15923
Act (1780), (beef) 16880, (600 men) 16879
Act (1781), (army quota) 17254-55, (Continental bills) 17256, (£120,000) 17252, (sheriff of Cheshire) 17251, (West India rum) 17253
Act (1787), (militia) 20547
Act (1790), (representatives) 22704
Act (1792), (balloting) 25869, (bank incorporation) 24587, (militia) 25870
Act (1799), (S. Blodget) 35887, (turnpike road) 35888
Additions to the militia laws, 25870

New Hampshire. President see **New Hampshire. Governor**

New Hampshire. Senate
Journal, (1784) 18625, (1785) 19114, (1786) 19821, (1787) 20553-57, (1788) 21287-90, (1789) 21992-93, (1790) 22701-702, (1791) 23600-601, (1792) 24583-84, (1793) 25874-75, (1794) 27372, 27374, (1795) 29166-67, (1796) 32532, (1797) 34194, (1798) 34196, 35881, (1799) 35882, (1800) 38049-50

New Hampshire and Vermont magazine, 32540
New Hampshire association. Minutes, (1790-93) 25879-81, (1794) 27378, (1797) 32538, (1799) 35889
New Hampshire grants. Public defence, 16391
New Hampshire magazine, 25885
New Hampshire medical society
Charter, 24588
Laws, 35891
New-Hampshire register, (1786) 19879, (1787) 20609, (1788) 21352, (1794) 25934, (1796) 29286
New harmony, 9021, 20956
New Haven, Conn.
Bye laws, 22708
Caution against contagion, 27383
Charter, 18630
Church bells, 38058
New Haven county
Cases and observations by the Medical society, 21296
Declaration of the Association, 5690
New Haven gazette. To the public, 19830
New Haven, Jan. 1, 1800, 37233

New help, 2408
hieroglyphical, 26651, 30068
highland laddie, 27443
history of a true, 32543
of Blue Beard, 38059
of England, 21766
of France, 21767
of the Grecian states, 21768, 26819
of the Trojan, 27384
holiday present, 34198
husbandry, 626
hymns, 18924, 31766
instructions, 15925
instructive history, 38060-61
introduction to book keeping, 27824
to reading, (1793) 26119, (1794) 27663, (1795) 29455-56, (1796) 31146
to the Latin, 28163
invented friction roller, 21219
New Jersey
Answer of his excellency, 9973
At a conference held, 8154
Bill in the chancery, 6021
Brief of the claim, 11356
Burlington, Nov. 1776, 14916
Cases adjudged, 27391
Catalogue of fees, 1186
Constitution, 14912
Copy of the petition, 4046
Division orders, 27388
Evidence in a cause, 36396
Extracts from the journal, 14282
First publication of the council, 6022
Grants, concessions, 8205
Humble representation of the General assembly, 1477
In Provincial congress at Trenton, 14283
Journal of the votes and proceedings as well, 14913
of the votes and proceedings of the contion, 14914
of the votes and proceedings of the Provincial, 14284
Letter from his excellency, 14915
Memorial of the Council of proprietors, 7508
Minutes and proceedings of the Council, 16890
of a treaty, 8157
of the convention, 21302
Ordinance . . . see under **New Jersey. Laws (separates)**
Petitions and memorials, 18640, 19126
Plea and answer, 11765
Proclamation, 10997, 11766
Publication of the Council of proprietors. 6024
Remonstrance of the General assembly, 1325
Reply of the General assembly, 1326
Second publication of the Council, 6023
Short state of the proceedings, 14285
Speeches and addresses, 2270
Speeches in the General assembly, 2366
To his excellency, (Lewis Morris) 4394-95, 5443,

VOL.	ITEMS	VOL.	ITEMS
1	1-3244	8	22298-25074
2	3245-6623	9	25075-28145
3	6624-9891	10	28146-30832
4	9892-13091	11	30833-33261
5	13092-16176	12	33262-25854
6	16177-19448	13	35855-39162
7	19449-22297		

President's march, 35638
primer (Manson), 16328, 18570
primer (Ross), 21437, 22859
primmer, 851
principle, 32838
proclamation, 14526
Pygmalion, 33533
ready reckoner, 19642
recruit, 16405
road law, 32558
Robinson Crusoe, (1790) 22389, (1792) 24171, (1800) 38071
Roman history, 21769
rules, 8142
scene, 34050-51
select catalogue, 21868
sentiments, 19452
sermons, 13450
set of copies, 9522
song about Miss Ketty, 10092
song book, 11969
song; hail Columbia, 33900
song in high vogue, 12153
   in praise, 37847
   on the repeal, 10415
   suitable, 10093
   sung, 27648
song, to the tune of Hearts of oak, 10880
song, to the tune of The British grenadiers, 14918
songs on different, 36909
star, 30869, 32550
system of chemistry, 38072
   of husbandry, 19338
   of military discipline, 14815
   of modern geography, (1793) 25574, (1794) 27077, (1795) 28782
   of philosophy, 18058
   of stenography, 38364
systematical, 22674
Testament see **Bible. New Testament**
-Testament interpretation, 12076
New Theatre, Phila.
At a meeting of the subscribers, 29315
For the benefit of Miss Hallam, 7294
Last night Mr. Reinagle's benefit, 36101
On Wednesday evening, 36102
Playbill of Richard III, 31002
Playbill of The dramatist, 29316
Resolutions and articles, 36103
New Theatre, Providence; on Wednesday, 29370
New theoretic, 33433
   three penny plaything, 29633-34
   tobacco-law, 3299
   trade directory, (for New York) 35913, (for Phila.) 35914
   travels in the U. S., 24146, 31871
      through North America, 18167, 18765
      to the westward, (1788) 21044, (1789) 21786, (1796) 30321-23, (1797) 32024, (1798) 33615, (1799) 35391
treatise on large noses, 9223
treatise on the consumption, 30645
union, 29185
universal harmony, 12664
universal letter-writer, 38074
vade mecum, 27728
version of the Psalms, (1710) 1444, (1713) 1594-95, (1720) 2094, (1725) 2603, (1733) 3625, (1737) 4114, (1740) 4471, (1752) 6820, (1754) 7149, (1755) 7358, (1756) 7619, (1757)

7846, (1760) 8544, (1762) 9068-69, (1763) 9344-45, (1765) 9913-14, (1766) 10241, (1767) 10557-58, (1769) 11180, (1770) 11569-70, (1771) 11988-91, (1773) 12673-77, (1774) 13149-51, (1775) 13835, (1787) 20228, (1788) 20962, (1790) 22351, (1791) 23187, (1793) 25176, (1795) 28274
views of the origin, 31777
views on the origin, 33378
Virginia justice, 28823, 35611-12
Virginia tobacco-law, 3371
voyage, 13324
weeks preparation, 26946
work; George Barnwell, 38596
Yankee Doodle, 35064
Year, a sermon, 35754
   from the carrier, 35965
   gift, 22437
   sermon, 33798
   verses (American weekly mercury), (1741) 4666, (1742) 4877, (1743) 5115, (1744) 5329, (1745) 5530, (1746) 5730
   verses (Baltimore daily repository), 24068
   verses (Freeman's journal), (1782) 17539, (1783) 17937, (1784) 18484, (1785) 19013
   verses (Independent gazetteer), 18536
   verses (New York gazette), 6575
   verses (New York weekly post-boy), 5467
   verses (Pennsylvania chronicle), (1768) 11029, (1769) 11405, (1770) 11805, (1771) 12181, (1772) 12509, (1773) 12926, (1774) 13527
   verses (Pennsylvania evening post), (1776) 15002, (1779) 16452, (1782) 17666, (1783) 18127
   verses (Pennsylvania gazette), (1743) 5274, (1744) 5476, (1745) 5673, (1746) 5850, (1747) 6046, (1748) 6216, (1749) 6400, (1750) 6585, (1751) 6750, (1752) 6910, (1753) 7088, (1754) 7289, (1755) 7534, (1756) 7759, (1757) 8000, (1758) 8232, (1759) 8462, (1760) 8709, (1761) 8974, (1762) 9234, (1763) 9479, (1764) 9789, (1765) 10126, (1766) 10447, (1767) 10732, (1769) 11407, (1770) 11807, (1771) 12183, (1772) 12511, (1779) 12928, (1774) 13529, (1775) 14376, (1776) 15004, (1779) 16454, (1780) 16939, (1781) 17302, (1782) 17668, (1783) 18129, (1784) 18717
   verses (Pennsylvania journal), (1745) 5675, (1747) 6048, (1748) 6218, (1749) 6402, (1750) 6587, (1751) 6752, (1752) 6912, (1753) 7090, (1754) 7291, (1755) 7536, (1756) 7761, (1757) 8002, (1758) 8231, (1759) 8464, (1760) 8711, (1761) 8976, (1762) 9236, (1763) 9481, (1764) 9791, (1765) 10128, (1766) 10449, (1767) 10734, (1768) 11033, (1769) 11409, (1770) 11809, (1771) 12185, (1772) 12513, (1773) 12930, (1775) 14378, (1776) 15006, (1779)

VOL.	ITEMS	VOL.	ITEMS
1	1-3244	8	22298-25074
2	3245-6623	9	25075-28145
3	6624-9891	10	28146-30832
4	9892-13091	11	30833-33261
5	13092-16176	12	33262-25854
6	16177-19448	13	35855-39162
7	19449-22297		

VOL.	ITEMS	VOL.	ITEMS
1	1-3244	8	22298-25074
2	3245-6623	9	25075-28145
3	6624-9891	10	28146-30832
4	9892-13091	11	30833-33261
5	13092-16176	12	33262-25854
6	16177-19448	13	35855-39162
7	19449-22297		

New York. House of representatives see New York.
General assembly
New York. Laws (collective)
Collection of acts, 38078
Collection of penal laws, 35921
Laws, (1691-94) 703-705, (1691-1709) 1480, (1691-
1713) 1636, (1691-1719) 2065, (1691-1725) 2785,
(1691-1751) 6897, (1691-1773) 13467
Laws (1726-30), 3328
Laws (1752-62), 9213
Laws (1754-58), 8209
Laws (1777-80), 17630
Laws (1777-83), 18645
Laws (1777-88), 22012
Laws (1777-1800), (v.1) 24602, 34214, (v.2) 24602,
(v.3) 32555, 38086
Mercantile laws, 21317
New York. Laws (session)
Acts, (1695) 731-32, (1696) 757-58, (1697) 803,
(1699) 883, (1700) 940-41, (1701) 1001, (1702)
1080, (1703) 1137, (1704) 1187, (1705) 1225,
(1706) 1272-73, (1708) 1367, (1709) 1413, (1710)
1478, (1711) 1521, (1712) 1574, (1713) 1637-38,
(1714) 1706, (1715) 1770, (1716) 1845, (1717)
1918, (1718) 1988-89, (1719) 2060-61, (1720)
2154, (1721) 2271, (1722) 2371-72, (1723) 2466,
(1724) 2569, (1726) 2786-87, (1727) 2931, (1728)
3072, (1729) 3194, (1730) 3329, 3331, (1731)
3453, (1732) 3581, (1733) 3694-95, (1734) 3804-
808, (1735) 3937, (1736) 4048, (1737) 4170,
4284, (1739) 4397-99, (1740) 4570, 4761, (1741)
4762, (1742) 5017, (1743) 5255, (1744) 5447,
(1745) 5652, 5823, (1746) 5824, (1747) 6202,
(1748) 6203, (1751) 6732-33, (1754) 7268, 7510,
(1755) 7735, (1757) 8431, (1759) 8432, (1760)
8687, (1767-68) 11001, 11359, (1769) 11360,
(1770) 11772, 12154, (1772) 12481, (1773) 12886,
(1774) 13460, (1775) 14292, (1782) 17631, (1783)
18060, (1784) 18645-47, (1785) 19133, (1786)
19854, (1787) 20578, (1788) 21316, (1789) 22013-
14, 22720, (1791) 23617, (1792) 24603, 25902-903,
30872, (1794) 27399, 30873, (1795) 29189-90,
30874, (1796) 30875-76, (1797) 32556, (1798)
34215-16, (1799) 35926, (1800) 38087
New York. Laws (separates)
Act, (1693) 663-67, (1703) 1138-39, (1705) 1226,
(1709) 1414-23, (1711) 1522, (1715) 1771, (1721)
2272-73, (1722) 2370, 2373-75, (1725) 2684,
(1730) 3330, (1734) 3805, (1738) 4288, (1739)
4399-400, (1740) 4570, (1742) 5016, (1744) 5448-
49
Act (1745), (£5000) 5653, (liquors) 5654, (repay-
ing £270) 5652
Act (1746), (liquors) 5827, (provisions) 5825,
(raising £40000) 5826
Act (1750), 6564-65
Act (1754), (carts) 7278, (justices) 7270, (liquors)
7271, (paying £5000) 7272, (militia) 7269
Act, (1755) 7509, (1756) 7736, (1759) 8432, (1760)
8686, (1769) 11358, (1772) 12482-83, (1774)
13472
Act (1778), (battalions) 15935, (forage) 15936,
(militia) 15937
Act, (1779) 16407, (1780) 16905-906, (1782) 17632,
(1784) 18642-43, (1785) 19128-29, (1786) 19850-
51
Act (1787), (debts) 20573, (elections) 20572,
(militia) 20574
Act (1788), (flax-seed) 21308, (impost) 21311,
(insolvency) 21306, (militia) 21318, (poor)
21307
Act, (1789) 22015, (1792) 24608
Act (1793), (militia) 25896-98, (roads) 25899
Act, (1794) 27396, 29192, (1795) 29191, (1796)
30877
Act (1798), (debtors) 34205-206, (highways)
34207, (Mutual assurance co. incorporated)
34225, (N. Y. insurance co. incorporated) 34226,
(Schenectady incorporated) 34208
Act (1799), (elections) 35918, (Lying-in hospital
incorporated) 35953, (Manhattan co. incorpor-
ated) 35917, (militia) 35919, (raising money)
35920, (taxes) 35916
Act, (1800) 38075
Extract of an act, (1758) 8211, (1759) 8435
Fee bill, 27396
Militia act, (1758) 8212, (1799) 35929
Ordinance see New York. Ordinance
Road act, 32557-60
Ten pound act, (1782) 19134, (1789) 22017, (1795)
29193-95, (1796) 30878
New York. Lieutenant governor see New York.
Governor
New York. Senate
Journal, (1784) 18644, (1785) 19132, (1786) 19853,
(1787) 20577, (1788) 21315, (1789) 22010-11,
(1790) 22719, (1791) 23616, (1792) 24601, (1793)
25901, (1794) 27398, (1795) 29188, (1796) 30871,
(1797) 32554, (1798) 34211, 34213, (1799) 35925,
(1800) 38085
Votes and proceedings, (1777) 15479-80, (1784)
18650
New York, November 26; last Sunday, 18252-53
New York, (March 24, 1736) 3980, (Apr. 20, 1748)
6207, (Nov. 12, 1753) 7077, (Oct. 8, 1759) 8373,
(Feb. 2, 1768) 11009, (Jan. 4, 1769) 11375, (Jan.
6, 1769) 11376, (Jan. 9, 1769) 11377, (Jan. 17,
1769) 11378, (Jan. 20, 1769) 11448, (June 23,
1769) 11445, (July 7, 1769) 11379, (July 20, 1769)
11380, (Sept. 18, 1769) 11381, (Jan. 5, 1770) 11778,
(Jan. 8, 1770) 11779, (May 17, 1770) 11780, (May
30, 1770) 11781, (May 31, 1770) 11782, (June 12,
1770) 11783-84, (July 7, 1770) 11785, (Jan. 18,
1772) 12486, (Feb. 15, 1773) 12982, (Sept. 15,
1773) 12893, (Nov. 5, 1773) 12711, (Jan. 1, 1774)
13487, (May 11, 1774) 13490, (June 22, 1774)
13492, (July 25, 1774) 13493, (Sept. 9,
1774) 13184, (Oct. 1, 1774) 13484, (Apr.
27, 1775) 14435, (Apr. 29, 1775) 14339, (May
1, 1775) 14340, (May 2, 1775) 14068, (May 8,
1775) 14341, (June 21, 1775) 14332, (June 24,
1775) 14342, (Aug. 29, 1775) 14343, (Sept. 5, 1775)
14164, (Sept. 8, 1775) 14165, (Dec. 6, 1775) 14297,
(Apr. 16, 1776) 14941, (July 1, 1776) 14942, (Oct.
8, 1777) 15323, (Mar. 27, 1783) 18236-37, (June
23, 1788) 21272, (Feb. 18, 1789) 21871, (Mar. 1,
1790) 22573, (May 18, 1790) 22722, (July 5, 1790)
22920, (May 1, 1791) 23340, (Dec. 17, 1791) 23620,
(1792) 24033, (May 17, 1793) 26241, (June 1,
1793) 26151, (June 13, 1793) 25916, (Aug. 2,

VOL.	ITEMS	VOL.	ITEMS
1	1-3244	8	22298-25074
2	3245-6623	9	25075-28145
3	6624-9891	10	28146-30832
4	9892-13091	11	30833-33261
5	13092-16176	12	33262-25854
6	16177-19448	13	35855-39162
7	19449-22297		

1793) 25917, (Nov. 1793) 25295, (Feb. 10, 1798)
34110, (Apr. 9, 1799) 35934
New York Baptist association
    Minutes, (April 1791) 25909, (Oct. 1791) 23151,
      (1792) 25910, (1793) 25911-12, (1794) 27402,
      (1795) 29197, (1796) 30879, (1797) 32565, (1798)
      34223, (1800) 38102
New York collection, 28216
New York, College of see **College of New York**
New York, committee-chamber, (29th May) 14330,
    14330, (5th June) 14331
      committee chamber; the following, 13475
      committee chamber, Wednesday, 14322
      directory, (1786) 19655, (1787) 20369, (1789)
        22021, (1790) 22724, (1791) 23337, (1792)
        24281, (1793) 25422, (1794) 26919, (1795)
        28598, (1796) 30706
New York dispensary
    Charter, 29200, 32566
    Rules, 29201
New York; every friend, 13488
New York gazette
    Jem-mi-bul-le-ro, 10426
    New Year verses, 6575
    News-boy's verses, 9217
New York; in Senate, Feb. 10, 1796, 31622
New York insurance co.
    Act to incorporate the stockholders, 34226
    Articles of association, 30884
New-York journal &c., no. 1424, 11918
New York lottery. New York, Apr. 20, 1748, 6207
New York magazine, (1790) 22728, (1791) 23624,
    (1792) 24615, (1793) 25920, (1794) 27412, (1795)
    29206, (1796) 30889, (1797) 32571
New York military society. Constitution, 30887
New York missionary magazine, 38104
New York missionary society. Address and consti-
    tution, 30883
New York museum, 21325
New York packet. Anniversary address, 22730
New York poor lottery. List of the fortunate, 17642
New York preserved, 21329
    primmer, (1746) 5838, (1747) 6033, (1750) 6572
    register, 35740
    reviewers, 29209
New York; sir, 13494
New York society for promoting Christian know-
    ledge. Constitution, 27409
New York society for promoting manumission
    Constitution, 30885
New York society library
    Additional catalogue, 32569
    Catalogue, 8217
    Charter, (1773) 12895, (1789) 22018, (1793) 25915
    Continuation of the catalogue, 23618
    Farther continuation, 24610-11
    Supplementary catalogue, 38099
New York, Sunday, 14337
New York; the following, 13489
New York, Theatre, 1782, 17635
New York, Tuesday, 14338
New York Washington military society. Constitu-
    tion, 34227
New York, Wednesday, 13491
    weekly magazine, (1795) 29208, (1796) 30891-
      92, (1797) 32573
    weekly museum, (1789) 22025, (1790) 22731
New York weekly post-boy. New Year verses, 5467
Newark, N. J. Contract for erecting, 23626
Newark fire association. Articles, 32574

New-ark lottery
    Christiana bridge, Mar. 23, 1771, 12137
    New-ark land and cash, 12138
Newark stocking manufactory. Number of jour-
    neymen, 24617
Newbern, N. C. Journal of the convention, 13497
Newbern, October 6th, 1794, 28089
Newberry, John, 1713-1767. History of the world,
    19863
Newbury, Mass. In pursuance of an act, 15484
Newburyport, Mass.
    Articles and regulations of the Relief fire so-
      ciety, 14347
    Sacred concert, 38108
Newburyport herald
    New Year; from the carrier, 35965
    To the patrons, 32432
Newburyport herald-office, Dec. 17, 1798, 34834
Newburyport, July 23, 1794, 27530
Newburyport; notice of a meeting, 32577
Newcastle, Thomas Pelham-Holles, duke of, 1693-
    1768
    letter (from Douglas), 8584-85
    letter (from council members), 3847
Newcomb, Richard English, 1770-1849. Oration,
    35966
Newell, Abel, 1730-1813. Good men, 11014
Newell, Jonathan, 1749-1830
    Sermon, 18658
    ordained, 14621
Newell, Samuel, d. 1789, death, 22801
Newest fashion; the jovial, 38110
Newfield, Conn. Act of incorporation, 38111
Newland, Jeremiah. Earthquakes improved, 7518
Newman, Henry, 1670-1748
    Non cessant, 544
    Ut fluctus, 574
Newman, John, philom. Almanac see **Almanacs**
    (Newman)
Newman, John, fl. 1747, ordained, 5902
Newman, John, fl. 1784-93
    Inaugural dissertation, 25922
    (ed.) Narrative of a discovery, 18574
    Treatise on schirrus, 23627
Newport, R. I.
    Articles of the Star, 30896
    At a town meeting, 10716
    Colony of Rhode Island, &c., 13498
    First Congregational meeting-house, 38112
    Laws of the Marine society, (1785) 19142, (1799)
      35968
    Newport, Jan. 1, 1800, 38113
    Newport engine company, number V, 35967
    Resolved, that the followng, 30895
    Short confession, 3476
    Theatre, Newport, 38114
    Town tax, 23628
Newport, R. I. Redwood library see **Redwood li-**
    brary
Newport, June 19th, 1751, 6773
Newport, Jan. 1, 1800, 38113
Newport association of mechanics. Charter, 24618
Newport engine company, number V, 35967
Newport in 1795, 28930
Newport insurance company, incorporated, 36215
News; Nov. 1, 1777, 15486
News-boy's address, (Albany centinel, 1799) 35089,
    (American mercury, 1795) 28177, (Conn. cou-
    rant, 1790) 22429, (Middlesex gazette, 1795)
    29079, (New Jersey state gazette, 1799) 35909,

(State gazette of North Carolina, 1799) 36361
News-boys; an eclogue, 20295
Newsboys annual address, 35996
Newsboy's New Year's address, 35824
Newsboy's verses, (Maryland gazette, 1788) 21331,
    (New York gazette, 1763) 9216
News carriers' address, (Burlington advertiser)
    23240, (Centinel of freedom) 37114
News from the liberty-pole, 11387
News from the moon, 2281, 12491
News lad's address, 24222
News of a trumpet, 786

NEWSPAPERS

Adams centinel, (1800) 36758
Albany centinel, (1797) 31702, (1798) 33279, (1799)
    35088, (1800) 36787
Albany chronicle, (1796) 29959, (1797) 31703,
    (1798) 33280
Albany gazette, (1771) 11958, (1772) 12300, (1773)
    12640, (1774) 13101, (1775) 13793, (1784) 18323,
    (1785) 18898, (1788) 19456, (1787) 20187, (1788)
    20917, (1789) 21633, (1790) 22301, (1791) 23108,
    (1792) 24028, (1793) 25082, (1794) 26545, (1795)
    28158, (1796) 29960, (1797) 31704, (1798) 33281,
    (1799) 35090, (1800) 36788
Albany journal, (1788) 20918, (1789) 21634
Albany register, (1788) 20919, (1789) 21635, (1790)
    22302, (1791) 23109, (1792) 24029, (1793) 25083,
    (1794) 26546, (1795) 28159, (1796) 29961, (1797)
    31705, (1798) 33282, (1799) 35091, (1800) 36788
Alexandria advertiser, (1800) 36796
American (Baltimore), (1799) 35100, (1800) 36809
American apollo, (1793) 25093, (1794) 26552
American chronicle, (1761) 8785, (1762) 9052
American citizen, (1800) 36810
American constellation, (1800) 26811
American daily advertiser, (1791) 23339, (1792)
    24282, (1793) 25423, (1794) 26920, (1795) 28604,
    (1796) 30201, (1797) 31942, (1798) 33521, (1799)
    35313, (1800) 37190, 38314
American eagle, (1799) 35101, (1800) 36813
American farmer, (1798) 33291, (1799) 35102,
    (1800) 36814
American gazette, (1776) 14645, (1792) 24038,
    (1793) 25094, (1794) 26553-54, (1795) 28173,
    (1796) 29968, (1797) 31719
American herald, (1784) 18325, (1785) 18902-903,
    (1786) 19461-62, (1787) 20190, (1788) 20923-24,
    (1789) 21640, (1790) 22304, (1791) 23113
American herald of liberty, (1793) 25095, (1794)
    26555, (1795) 28174
American intelligencer, (1795) 28175, (1796) 29969,
    (1797) 31721
American journal, (1779) 16186, (1780) 16695,
    (1781) 17077, (1786) 19463
American mercury, (1784) 18326, (1785) 18904,
    (1786) 19464, (1787) 20192, (1788) 20926, (1789)
    21644, (1790) 22305, (1791) 23115, (1792) 24039,
    (1793) 25098, (1794) 26556, (1795) 28176, (1796)
    29974, (1797) 31723, (1798) 33292, (1799) 35104,
    (1800) 36817
American minerva, (1793) 25099, (1794) 26657,
    (1795) 28178, (1796) 29975
American naval and commercial register, (1795)
    28181, (1796) 30420, (1797) 32129, (1798) 33735
American price-current, (1786) 19466
American recorder, (1785) 18905, (1786) 19467,

(1787) 20196
American spy, (1791) 23118, (1792) 24048, (1793)
    25105, (1794) 26560, (1795) 28183, (1796) 29978,
    (1797) 31726, (1798) 33296
American star, (1794) 26561
American telegraphe, (1795) 28184, (1796) 29979,
    (1797) 31727, (1798) 33297, (1799) 35109, (1800)
    36823
American USA recorder, (1787) 20196
American weekly mercury, (1719) 2011, (1720)
    2091, (1721) 2199, (1722) 2313, (1723) 2410, (1724)
    2499, (1725) 2600, (1726) 2724, (1727) 2837,
    (1728) 2983, (1729) 3127, (1730) 3247, (1731)
    3385, (1732) 3498, (1733) 3621, (1734) 3742, (1735)
    3865, (1736) 3981, (1737) 4108, (1738) 4216, (1739)
    4333, (1740) 4468, (1741) 4665, (1742) 4876, (1743)
    5114, (1744) 5328, (1745) 5529, (1746) 5729
Americanische staatsbothe, (1800) 36825
Amherst journal, (1795) 28187, (1796) 29986
Andrews's Western star, (1794) 26570, (1795) 28199,
    (1796) 29992, (1797) 31738
Apollo, or Chestertown spy, (1793) 25116
Argus (Boston), (1791) 23129, (1792) 24056, (1793)
    25119
Argus (Bridgetown), (1795) 28207, (1796) 29998,
    (1797) 31750
Argus (New York), (1795) 28208, (1796) 29999,
    (1797), 31751, (1798) 33310, (1799) 35115, (1800)
    36847
Argus (Putney), (1797) 31749, (1798) 33309
Arnett's New Jersey federalist, (1793) 25121,
    (1794) 26575, (1795) 28213
Augusta chronicle, (1789) 21853, (1790) 22530,
    (1791) 23410, (1792) 24355, (1793) 25541, (1794)
    27045, (1795) 28740, (1796) 30486, (1797) 32184,
    (1798) 33791, (1799) 35542, (1800) 37510
Augusta herald, (1799) 35123, (1800) 36862
Aurora for the country, (1800) 36864
Aurora. General advertiser, (1794) 26592, (1795)
    28219, (1796) 30005, (1797) 31756, (1798) 33339,
    (1799) 35124, (1800) 36865
Bache's Philadelphia aurora, (1797) 31760, (1798)
    33347, (1799) 35132, (1800) 36871
Baltimore daily advertiser, (1793) 25435, (1794)
    26935
Baltimore daily intelligencer, (1793) 25135, (1794)
    26605
Baltimore daily repository, (1791) 23144, (1792)
    24067, (1793) 25134
Baltimore evening post, (1792) 24069, (1793) 25136
Baltimore intelligencer, (1798) 33365, (1799) 35149
Baltimore postbote, (1800) 36885
Baltimore telegraphe, (1795) 28230, (1796) 30018
Bartgis's federal gazette, (1794) 26624, (1795)
    28241, (1796) 30033, (1797) 31775, (1798) 33376,
    (1799) 35157, (1800) 36900
Bartgis's Maryland gazette, (1792) 24077, (1793)
    25146, (1794) 26623
Bartgis's republican gazette, (1800) 36901

VOL.	ITEMS	VOL.	ITEMS
1	1-3244	8	22298-25074
2	3245-6623	9	25075-28145
3	6624-9891	10	28146-30832
4	9892-13091	11	30833-33261
5	13092-16176	12	33262-25854
6	16177-19448	13	35855-39162
7	19449-22297		

Columbian centinel, (1790) 22413, (1791) 23266, (1792) 24203, (1793) 25317, (1794) 26787, (1795) 28451, (1796) 30247, (1797) 31957, (1798) 33540, (1799) 35322, (1800) 37207

Columbian chronicle, (1793) 25319, (1794) 26788, (1795) 28452, (1796) 30250

Columbian courier, (1794) 26789, (1798) 33542, (1799) 35324, (1800) 37209

Columbian gazette, (1799) 35325

Columbian gazetteer, (1793) 25320, (1794) 26790

Columbian herald, (1784) 18407, (1785) 18963, (1786) 19564, (1787) 20279, (1788) 21006, (1789) 21744, (1790) 22414, (1791) 23267, (1792) 24204, (1793) 25321, (1794) 26791, (1795) 28453, (1796) 30251

Columbian informer, (1793) 25322, (1794) 26792, (1795) 28454

Columbian mercury, (1794) 26793, (1795) 28455

Columbian minerva, (1799) 35326, (1800) 37210

Columbian mirror, (1792) 24205, (1793) 25323, (1794) 26794, (1795) 28456, (1796) 30252, (1797) 31958, (1798) 33543, (1799) 35327, (1800) 37211

Columbian museum, (1796) 30253, (1797) 31960, (1798) 33544, (1799) 35328, (1800) 37212

Columbian patriotic gazette, (1799) 35329, (1800) 37213

Commercial advertiser, (1797) 31964, (1798) 33547, (1799) 35332, (1800) 37216

Companion; and Commercial centinel, (1798) 33548

Complete counting house companion, 19567

Concord herald, (1790) 22416, (1791) 23269, 23450, (1792) 24208, (1793) 25639, (1794) 27138, (1795) 28462

Concord mirrour, (1792) 24209

Connecticut courant, (1764) 9623, (1765) 9939, (1766) 10271, (1767) 10591, (1768) 10865, (1769) 11221, (1770) 11608, (1771) 12019, (1772) 12365, (1773) 12735, (1774) 13215, (1775) 13885, (1776) 14714, (1777) 15275, (1778) 15771, (1779) 16242, (1780) 16749, (1781) 17125, (1782) 17502, (1783) 17889, (1784) 18418, (1785) 18972, (1786) 19579, (1787) 20295, (1788) 21020, (1789) 21763, (1790) 22428, (1791) 23286, (1792) 24221, (1793) 25341, (1794) 26813, (1795) 28471, (1796) 30268, (1797) 31977, (1798) 33561, (1799) 35346, (1800) 37234

Connecticut gazette, (1755) 7399, (1756) 7640, (1757) 7878, (1758) 8109, (1759) 8328, (1760) 8572, (1761) 8826, (1762) 9096, (1764) 9624, (1765) 9940, (1766) 10272, (1767) 10592, (1774) 13216, (1775) 13886, (1776) 14715, (1777) 15276, (1778) 15772, (1779) 16243, (1780) 16750, (1781) 17126, (1782) 17503, (1783) 17890, (1784) 18419, (1785) 18973, (1786) 19580, (1787) 20296, (1788) 21022, (1789) 21764, (1790) 22430, (1791) 23288, (1792) 24223, (1793) 25342, (1794) 26814, (1795) 28473, (1796) 30270, (1797) 31980, (1798) 33563, (1799) 35347, (1800) 37238

Connecticut journal, (1767) 10593, (1768) 10866, (1769) 11222, (1770) 11609, (1771) 12020, (1772) 12366, (1773) 12736, (1774) 13217, (1775) 13887, (1776) 14716, (1777) 15277-78, (1778) 15773, (1779) 16244, (1780) 16751, (1781) 17127, (1782) 17504, (1783) 17891, (1784) 18420, (1785) 18974, (1786) 19581, (1787) 20297, (1788) 21023, (1789) 21765, (1790) 22431, (1791) 23289, (1792) 24224, (1793) 25343, (1794) 26815, (1795) 28474, (1796) 30271, (1797) 31981, (1798) 33564, (1799) 35348, (1800) 37239

Constitutional diary, (1799) 35349, (1800) 37242

Constitutional gazette, (1775) 13889, (1776) 14718

Constitutional telegraphe, (1799) 35350, (1800) 37243

Continental journal, (1776) 14719, (1778) 15774, (1779) 16248, (1780) 16752, (1781) 17128, (1782) 17505, (1783) 17892, (1784) 18421, (1785) 18975, (1786) 19582, (1787) 20298

Country journal, (1785-86) 19589, (1787) 20302, (1788) 21027, (1789) 21772

Country porcupine, (1798) 33576, (1799) 35356

Courier (Boston), (1795) 28487, (1796) 30285

Courier (Brooklyn), (1799) 35358, (1800) 37261

Courier (Fredericksburg), (1800) 37259

Courier (Norwich), (1798) 33577, (1799) 35357, (1800) 37260

Courier and general advertiser, (1796) 30286

Courier de Boston, (1789) 21773

Courier of New Hampshire, (1794) 26821, (1795) 28489, (1796) 30287, (1797) 31996, (1798) 33578, (1799) 35359, (1800) 37262

Courier politique, (1793) 25351

Courrier de l'Amérique, (1784) 18424

Courrier de la France, (1795) 28490, (1796) 30288

Courrier français, (1794) 26822, (1795) 28492, (1796) 30289, (1797) 31997, (1798) 33579

Courrier politique, (1793) 25352, (1794) 26823

Cumberland gazette, (1786) 19594, (1787) 20311, (1788) 21034, (1789) 21778, (1790) 22436, (1791) 23302

Daily advertiser (New York), (1786) 19597, (1787) 20315, (1788) 21040, (1789) 21781, (1790) 22444, (1791) 23307, (1792) 24243, (1793) 25369, (1794) 26844, (1795) 28525, (1796) 30310, (1797) 32015, (1798) 33597, (1799) 35373, (1800) 37284

Daily advertiser (Phila.), 31915, 32016

Daily evening gazette, (1795) 28526

Dartmouth gazette, (1799) 35382, (1800) 37290

Delaware and Eastern-Shore advertiser, (1794) 26869, (1795) 28560, (1796) 30331, (1797) 32032, (1798) 33623, (1799) 35397

Delaware courant, (1786) 19605, (1787) 20327

Delaware gazette, (1785) 18992, (1786) 19606, (1787) 20328, (1788) 21053, (1789) 21793, (1790) 22458, (1791) 23323, (1792) 24260, (1793) 25389, (1794) 26870, (1795) 28561, (1796) 30332, (1797) 32033, (1798) 33624, (1799) 35398

Dessert to the True American, 35402

Deutsche bauer's register, 37318

Deutsche porcupein, (1798) 33631, (1799) 35403

Deutsche Washington correspondent, (1797) 32034

Deutsche wöchentliche zeitung, (1748) 6122

Diary (New York), (1792) 24266, (1793) 25391, (1794) 26876, (1795) 28565, (1796) 30344, (1797, Van Alen) 32038, (1798, Crookes) 33634

Dixon's observatory, 33643

Dover gazette, (1796) 31252, (1797) 32895

Dresden mercury, (1779) 16263

Dunlap and Claypoole's American daily advertiser, (1794) 26920, (1795) 28604

Dunlap's American daily advertiser, (1791) 23339, (1792) 24282, (1793) 25423

Dunlap's Maryland gazette, (1775) 14016, (1776) 14743, (1777) 15293, (1778) 15787

VOL.	ITEMS	VOL.	ITEMS
1	1-3244	8	22298-25074
2	3245-6623	9	25075-28145
3	6624-9891	10	28146-30832
4	9892-13091	11	30833-33261
5	13092-16176	12	33262-25854
6	16177-19448	13	35855-39162
7	19449-22297		

Gazette United States, (1796) 30475
Gemeinnützige   Philadelphische   correspondenz,
    (1781) 17171, (1782) 17545, (1783) 17943, (1784)
    18493, (1785) 19020, (1786) 19664, (1787) 20384,
    (1788) 21105, (1789) 21847, (1790) 22521
General advertiser, (1790) 22522, (1791) 23405,
    (1792) 24346, (1793) 25533, (1794) 27038
General-postbothe, (1789) 21848, (1790) 22523,
    (1793) 25534
Genius of liberty (Fredericksburg), (1797) 32178,
    (1798) 33785, (1799) 35536, (1800) 37498
Genius of liberty (Knoxville), (1798) 33969
Genius of liberty (Morristown), (1798) 33784,
    (1799) 35535, (1800) 37499
Genius of liberty (New Brunswick), (1795) 28732,
    (1796) 30477
Georgetown chronicle, (1795) 28734, (1796) 30478,
    (1797) 32181
Georgetown gazette, (1798) 33788, (1799) 35539,
    (1800) 37502
Georgetown times, (1785) 19023
Georgetown weekly ledger, (1790) 22528, (1791)
    23408, (1792) 24348, (1793) 25535
Georgia. Augusta chronicle see Augusta chronicle
Georgia gazette, (1763) 9395, (1764) 9678, (1765)
    9979, (1766) 10311, (1767) 10629, (1768) 10912,
    (1769) 11271, (1770) 11664, (1771) 12056, (1772)
    12401, (1773) 12787, (1774) 13295, (1775) 14064,
    (1788) 21108, (1789) 21851, (1790) 22531, (1791)
    23409, (1792) 24354, (1793) 25542, (1794) 27046,
    (1795) 28741, (1796) 30487, (1797) 32185, (1798)
    33792, (1799) 35543, (1800) 37509
Georgia journal, (1793) 25543, (1794) 27047
Georgia state gazette, (1786) 19684, (1787) 20388,
    (1788) 21109, (1789) 21852-53
Germantauner zeitung, (1761) 8978, (1762) 9124,
    (1763) 9396, (1764) 9679, (1765) 9980, (1766)
    10312, (1767) 10630, (1768) 10913, (1769) 11272,
    (1770) 11666, (1771) 12057, (1772) 12402, (1773)
    12788, (1774) 13296, (1775) 14065, (1776) 14774,
    (1777) 15310, (1785) 19025, (1786) 19685, (1787)
    20389, (1788) 21110, (1789) 21854, (1790) 22533,
    (1791) 23411, (1792) 24356, (1793) 25544, (1794)
    27048, (1795) 28746, (1796) 30488, (1797) 32186,
    (1798) 33793, (1799) 35544
Gilmanton gazette, 37517
Gilmanton rural museum, (1799) 35550, (1800)
    37518
Goshen repository, (1789) 21862, (1790) 22539,
    (1791) 23418, (1792) 24363, (1793) 25560, (1794)
    27064, (1795) 28763, (1796) 30502, (1797) 32201,
    (1798) 33808, (1799) 35558
Grafton minerva, (1796) 30506, (1797) 32202
Green & Russell's Boston post-boy, (1760) 8609,
    (1761) 8867, (1762) 9129, (1763) 9398, (1764)
    9683, (1765) 9994, (1766) 10326, (1767) 10636,
    (1768) 10916
Green Mountain patriot, (1798) 33819, (1799) 35565,
    (1800) 37539
Greenfield gazette, (1792) 24367, (1793) 25566,
    (1794) 27067, (1795) 28768, (1796) 30512, (1797)
    32208, (1798) 33820, (1799) 35567, (1800) 37542
Greenleaf's New daily advertiser, (1799) 35115
Greenleaf's New York journal, (1794) 20769, (1795)
    28769, (1796) 30513, (1797) 32210, (1798) 33821,
    (1799) 35568, (1800) 37544
Green's Impartial observer, 37546
Guardian (New Brunswick), (1792) 24369, (1793)
    25571, (1794) 27073, (1795) 28778, (1796) 30523,
    (1797) 32216, (1798) 33829, (1799) 35572, (1800)
    37557

Guardian of freedom, (1793) 25572, (1794) 27074,
    (1795)   28779,   (1798)   33830,   (1799) 35573-74,
    (1800) 37554
Guardian of liberty (Huntingdon), (1799) 35575,
    (1800) 37556
Guardian of liberty (Newport), (1800) 37555
Hall's Wilmington gazette, (1797) 32219, (1798)
    33833
Hampshire and Berkshire chronicle, (1792) 24379,
    (1793) 25582, (1794) 27085, (1795) 28796, (1796)
    30534
Hampshire chronicle, (1787) 20401, (1788) 21128,
    (1789) 21873, (1790) 22552, (1791) 23425
Hampshire gazette, (1786) 19696, (1787) 20402,
    (1788) 21129, (1789) 21874, (1790) 22553, (1791)
    23426, (1792) 24380, (1793) 25583, (1794) 27086,
    (1795) 28797, (1796) 30535, (1797) 32225, (1798)
    33836, (1799) 35584, (1800) 37575
Hampshire herald, (1786) 19697
Harrisburgh journal, (1789) 21875, (1790) 22557
Harrisonburg morgenröthe zeitung, 38918
Hartford gazette, (1794) 27095, (1795) 28807
Haswell's Massachusetts spy, (1777) 15361
Haverhill federal gazette, (1798) 33858, (1799)
    35604
Henrich Millers Pennsylvanischer staatsbote,
    (1775) 14114, (1776) 14798, (1777) 15362, (1778)
    15850, (1779) 16302
Herald, a gazette for the country, (1794) 27111,
    (1795) 28824, (1796) 30554, (1797) 32246
Herald and Eastern Shore intelligencer, (1799)
    35613, (1800) 37606
Herald, and Norfolk and Portsmouth advertiser,
    (1794) 27112, (1795) 28825
Herald of freedom, (1788) 21141, (1789) 21883,
    (1790) 22565, (1791) 23439, (1799) 35614
Herald of liberty, (1793) 25599, (1796) 30555, (1798)
    33869, (1799) 35615, (1800) 37607
Herald of the times, (1796) 30556, (1797) 32247
Herald of the United States, (1792) 24392, (1793)
    25600, (1794) 27113, (1795) 28826, (1796) 30557,
    (1797) 32248, (1798) 33870, (1799) 35616, (1800)
    37608
Herald of Vermont, (1792) 24393
Herald of Virginia, 37609
Hive, (1797) 32260
Hoch-deutsch Pensylvanische geschicht-schreiber,
    (1739) 4371, (1740) 4529, (1741) 4729, (1742)
    4973, (1744) 5412, (1745) 5612
Hochdeutsche Pennsylvanische journal, (1743) 5212
Hoch-deutsche Pensylvanische berichte, (1746)
    5789
Hough's Concord herald, (1791) 23450, (1793) 25639,
    (1794) 27138
Hudson gazette, (1785) 19045, (1792) 24413, (1793)
    25640, (1794) 27143, (1795) 28866, (1796) 30601,
    (1797) 32288, (1798) 33911, (1799) 35647, (1800)
    37660
Hudson weekly gazette, (1786) 19722, (1787) 20419,
    (1788) 21154, (1789) 21894, (1790) 22577, (1791)

VOL.	ITEMS	VOL.	ITEMS
1	1-3244	8	22298-25074
2	3245-6623	9	25075-28145
3	6624-9891	10	28146-30832
4	9892-13091	11	30833-33261
5	13092-16176	12	33262-25854
6	16177-19448	13	35855-39162
7	19449-22297		

34059, (1799) 35781
Maryland herald (Elizabethtown [Hagerstown]), (1797) 32436, (1798) 34060, (1799) 35782, (1800) 37899
Maryland journal, (1773) 12845, (1774) 13402, (1775) 14182, (1776) 14838, (1777) 15399, (1778) 15881, (1779) 16341, (1780) 16834, (1781) 17210, (1782) 17588, (1783) 18018, (1784) 18587, (1785) 19076, (1786) 19777, (1787) 20494, (1788) 21332, (1789) 21939, (1790) 22647, (1791) 23544, (1792) 24514, (1793) 25767, (1794) 27273, (1795) 29031, (1796) 30753, (1797) 32437
Massachusetts centinel, (1784) 18605, (1785) 19094, (1786) 19796, (1787) 20518, (1788) 21250, (1789) 21953, (1790) 22662
Massachusetts gazette, (1764) 9735, (1765) 10066, (1766) 10386, (1767) 10685, (1768) 10971-72, (1769) 11333-34, (1770) 11739-40, (1771) 12123-24, (1772) 12460-61, (1773) 12858-59, (1774) 13428-29, (1775) 14248-49, (1776) 14884, (1782) 17602, (1783) 18029, (1784) 18606, (1785) 19095, (1786) 19797, (1787) 20519, (1788) 21251
Massachusetts herald, (1783) 18030
Massachusetts mercury, (1793) 25795, (1795) 29051, (1796) 30775, (1797) 32454, (1798) 34083, (1799) 35804, (1800) 37932
Massachusetts spy, (1770) 11741, (1771) 12125-26, (1772) 12462, (1773) 12860, (1774) 13430, (1775) 14250-51, 24483, (1776) 14885, 15102, (1777) 15361, 15441, (1778) 15910, 16091, (1779) 16542, (1780) 17005, (1782) 17741, (1783) 18209, (1784) 18806, (1785) 19273, (1786) 20019, (1788) 21494, (1789) 22178, (1790) 22927, (1791) 23826, (1792) 24846, (1793) 26253, (1794) 27791, (1795) 29625, (1796) 31292, (1797) 32921, (1798) 34653, (1799) 36417, (1800) 38632
Medley, (1792) 24535, (1793) 25799, (1794) 27306, (1795) 29065, (1796) 30782, (1797) 32461, (1798) 34090, (1799) 35809
Mercantile advertiser, (1798) 34095, (1799) 35812, (1800) 37952
Merchants' daily advertiser, (1797) 32466, (1798) 34096
Mercury, (1793) 25802, (1794) 27312, (1795) 29069, (1796) 30784
Messenger, 37954
Middlesex gazette, (1785) 19099, (1786) 19801, (1787) 20524, (1788) 21257, (1789) 21963, (1790) 22669, (1791) 23568, (1792) 24546, (1793) 25819, (1794) 27318, (1795) 29078, (1796) 30791, (1797) 32476, (1798) 34107, (1799) 35820, (1800) 37960
Mifflin gazette, (1796) 30794
Minerva (Dedham), (1796) 30800, (1797) 32483
Minerva (New York), (1796) 30801, (1797) 32484, (1798) 34117
Mirror (Edinburgh), 25748
Mirror (Newburgh), (1797) 32486, (1798) 34120, (1799) 35825
Mirror (Washington, Ky.), (1797) 32487, (1798) 34121, (1799) 35826
Mirro(u)r (Concord, N.H.) (1793) 25826, (1794) 27326, (1795) 28658, 29087, (1796) 30407, (1797) 32485, (1798) 34119
Mirror of the times, (1799) 35827, (1800) 37971
Mississippi gazette, 37972
Mohawk mercury, (1794) 27332, (1795) 29090, (1796) 30804, (1797) 32489, (1798) 34122
Moniteur de la Louisiane, (1794) 27333, (1795) 29092, (1796) 30806, (1797) 32490, (1798) 34123, (1799) 35829, (1800) 37983
Monitor (Litchfield), (1792) 24550, (1793) 25832,

(1794) 27334, (1798) 34124, (1799) 35830, (1800) 37984
Monitor (Wilmington), 37985
Monitor of Mifflin and Huntington, (1798) 34125
Monthly herald, 37987
Moral and political telegraphe, (1795) 29101, (1796) 30812
Morning chronicle, (1780) 16872
Morning post, (1789) 21977, (1790) 22680, (1791) 23577, (1792) 24561
Morning ray, (1791) 23578, (1792) 24562
Morning star, (1794) 27349
Morris county gazette, (1797) 32508, (1798) 34142
Mott and Hurtin's New York chronicle, (1795) 29125
Mount Pleasant courier, (1799) 35849
Mount Pleasant register, (1798) 34156, (1800) 38010
Museum (Georgetown), 38021
Nashville intelligencer, (1799) 35856
National gazette, (1791) 23587, (1792) 24568, (1793) 25856
National intelligencer, 38026
Neue Philadelphische correspondenz, (1790) 22689, (1791) 23591, (1792) 24571, (1800) 38034
Neue unpartheyische Baltimore bote, (1795) 29140, (1796) 30829, (1797) 32522, (1798) 34172, (1800) 38035
Neue unpartheyische Lancäster zeitung, (1787) 20540, (1788) 21280, (1789) 21983, (1790) 22690, (1791) 23592, (1792) 24572, (1793) 25859, (1794) 27360, (1795) 29141, (1796) 30840, (1797) 32523
Neue unpartheyische Readinger zeitung, (1789) 21984, (1790) 22691, (1791) 23593, (1792) 25860, (1793) 25861, (1794) 27361, (1795) 29142, (1796) 30841, (1797) 32524, (1798) 34173, (1799) 35862, (1800) 38036
Neuer unpartheyischer Eastoner bothe, (1793) 25862, (1794) 27363, (1795) 29141, (1796) 30843, (1797) 32526, (1798) 34176, (1799) 35865, (1800) 38039
New Bedford marine journal, (1792) 24535, (1795) 29065
New daily advertiser, (1799) 35115
New England chronicle, (1775) 14271, (1776) 14808, 14898
New England courant, (1721) 2268, (1722) 2364, (1723) 2462, (1724) 2566, (1725) 2681, (1726) 2783
New England weekly journal, (1727) 2928, (1728) 3070, (1729) 3193, (1730) 3325, (1731) 3451, (1732) 3577, (1733) 3692, (1734) 3800, (1735) 3935, (1736) 4045, (1737) 4168,(1738) 4281, (1739) 4391, (1740) 4567, (1741) 4759
New Hampshire and Vermont journal, (1795) 29170, (1796) 30856, (1797) 32539
New Hampshire gazette, (1756) 7726, (1757) 7965, (1758) 8202, (1759) 8428, (1760) 8679, (1761) 8946, (1762) 9204, (1763) 9455, (1764) 9749, (1765) 10087, (1766) 10411, (1767) 10702, (1768) 10995, (1769) 11355, (1770) 11761, (1771) 12149,

VOL.	ITEMS	VOL.	ITEMS
1	1-3244	8	22298-25074
2	3245-6623	9	25075-28145
3	6624-9891	10	28146-30832
4	9892-13091	11	30833-33261
5	13092-16176	12	33262-25854
6	16177-19448	13	35855-39162
7	19449-22297		

VOL.	ITEMS	VOL.	ITEMS
1	1-3244	8	22298-25074
2	3245-6623	9	25075-28145
3	6624-9891	10	28146-30832
4	9892-13091	11	30833-33261
5	13092-16176	12	33262-25854
6	16177-19448	13	35855-39162
7	19449-22297		

Recorder, (1791) 23832, (1792) 24855, (1793) 26263, (1794) 27803, (1795) 29394, (1796) 31074

Republican, (1799) 36206, (1800) 38375

Republican citizen, (1796) 31081, (1797) 32748

Republican gazette, 36901

Republican gazetteer, (1796) 31082, (1797) 32749

Republican journal (Danbury), (1793) 26069, (1796) 31084, (1797) 32750

Republican journal (Dumfries), (1795) 29398, (1796) 31085

Republican journal (Poughkeepsie), (1795) 29397, (1796) 31083, (1798) 34440, (1799) 36208, (1800) 38376

Republican ledger, (1799) 36209, (1800) 38377

Republican rush-light, 38378

Republican star, (1799) 36210, (1800) 38379

Republican watchtower, 38380

Rhode Island gazette, (1732) 3602, (1733) 3721

Rhode Island museum, (1794) 27619

Richmond and Manchester advertiser, (1795) 29418, (1796) 31102

Richmond chronicle, (1795) 29419, (1796) 31103

Rights of man (Frederick), (1794) 27626, (1795) 29420, (1796) 31104, (1797) 32768, (1798) 34468, (1799) 36233, (1800) 38408

Rights of man (Nashville), (1799) 36234

Rights of man (Newburgh), (1799) 36235, (1800) 38409

Rights of man (Paris, Ky.), (1797) 32769, (1798) 34469

Rind's Virginia gazette, (1766) 10481

Rising sun (Keene), (1795) 29422, (1796) 31109, (1797) 32771, (1798) 34474

Rising sun (Kingston), (1793) 26093, (1794) 27627, (1795) 29421, (1796) 31108, (1797) 32770, (1798) 34473

Rivington's New York gazette, (1783) 18165

Rivington's New York gazetteer, (1773) 12983, (1774) 13580, (1775) 14437, (1777) 15582

Rivington's New York loyal gazette, (1777) 15583

Roulstone's Knoxville gazette, (1796) 31120, (1797) 32779

Royal American gazette, (1777) 15586, (1778) 16060, (1779) 16510, (1780) 16984, (1781) 17358, (1782) 17710, (1783) 18169

Royal gazette, (1777) 15587, (1778) 16061, (1779) 16511, (1780) 16985, (1781) 17359-60, (1782) 17711-12, (1783) 18170

Royal Georgia gazette, (1779) 16512, (1780) 16986, (1781) 17361, (1782) 17713

Royal Pennsylvania gazette, (1778) 16062

Rural gazette, 38431

Rural repository, (1795) 29451, (1796) 31142, (1797) 32783

Russel & Davis' Republican gazetteer, (1797) 32789

Russell & George's Eastern hearald, 38442

Russell's Gazette, (1798) 34503, (1799) 36258, (1800) 38440

Russel's Echo, (1798) 34502, (1799) 36259

Rutland herald, (1794) 27662, (1795) 29453, (1796) 31145, (1797) 32792, (1798) 34504, (1799) 36262, (1800) 38443

Salem chronicle, (1786) 19975

Salem gazette, (1774) 13594, (1781) 17363-64, (1782) 17714, (1783) 18175, (1784) 18776, (1785) 19233, (1790) 22869, (1791) 23752, (1792) 24767, (1793) 26126, (1794) 27668, (1795) 29463, (1796) 31153, (1797) 32801, (1798) 34510, (1799) 36271, (1800) 38457

Salem impartial register, 38458

Salem mercury, (1786) 19976, (1787) 20693, (1788) 21444, (1789) 22126

Saratoga register, (1798) 34515, (1799) 36275, (1800) 38462

Saturday evening herald, (1790) 22871

Schenectady gazette, (1799) 36280, (1800) 38469

Scioto gazette, 38471

Shippensburgh messenger, (1797) 32830

South Carolina and American general gazette, (1758) 8261, (1759) 8496, (1760) 8740, (1761) 9013, (1762) 9277, (1763) 9517, (1764) 9845, (1765) 10172, (1766) 10500, (1767) 10773, (1768) 11076, (1769) 11474, (1770) 11865, (1771) 12232, (1772) 12564, (1773) 13027, (1774) 13636, (1775) 14469, (1776) 15093, (1777) 15600, (1778) 16074, (1779) 16533, (1780) 16994

South Carolina gazette (Charleston, Childs), (1786) 19999

South Carolina gazette (Charleston, Constable), (1792) 24805, (1793) 26185

South Carolina gazette (Charleston, Crouch), (1765) 10173, (1766) 10501, (1767) 10774, (1768) 11077, (1769) 11475, (1770) 11866, (1771) 12233, (1772) 12564, (1773) 13027, (1774) 13636, (1775) 14470, (1776) 15094, (1777) 15601, (1778) 16075, (1779) 16532

South Carolina gazette (Charleston, Miller), (1783) 18191, (1784) 18790, (1790) 22899, (1791) 23782, (1792) 24806

South Carolina gazette (Charleston, Powell), (1772) 12562, (1773) 13025, (1774) 13635, (1775) 14468

South Carolina gazette (Charleston, Timothy), (1734) 3837, (1735) 3961, (1736) 4083, (1737) 4200, (1738) 4310, (1739) 4427, (1740) 4606, (1741) 4813, (1742) 5064, (1743) 5293, (1744) 5494, (1745) 5689, (1746) 5868, (1747) 6070, (1748) 6242, (1749) 6420, (1750) 6614, (1751) 6788, (1752) 6936, (1753) 7123, (1754) 7320, (1755) 7572, (1756) 7794, (1757) 8043, (1758) 8260, (1759) 8495, (1760) 8739, (1761) 9012, (1762) 9276, (1763) 9516, (1764) 9844, (1765) 10171, (1766) 10499, (1767) 10772, (1768) 11075, (1769) 11473, (1770) 11864, (1771) 12231, (1777) 15305

South Carolina gazette (Charleston, Whitmarsh), (1732) 3606, (1733) 3724

South Carolina gazette (Columbia), (1799) 36342, (1800) 38537

South Carolina independent gazette, (1795) 29546

South Carolina state gazette (Charleston, Miller), (1785) 19255, (1786) 20000, (1787) 20718, (1788) 21473, (1789) 22154

South Carolina state gazette (Charleston, Timothy), (1793) 26186, (1794) 27722, (1795) 29548, (1796) 31223, (1797) 32859, (1798) 34579, (1799) 36343, (1800) 38538

South Carolina state gazette (Columbia), (1795) 29547, (1796) 31222, (1797) 32858, (1798) 34580, (1799) 36342

South Carolina weekly advertiser, (1783) 18192

VOL.	ITEMS	VOL.	ITEMS
1	1-3244	8	22298-25074
2	3245-6623	9	25075-28145
3	6624-9891	10	28146-30832
4	9892-13091	11	30833-33261
5	13092-16176	12	33262-25854
6	16177-19448	13	35855-39162
7	19449-22297		

VOL.	ITEMS	VOL.	ITEMS
1	1-3244	8	22298-25074
2	3245-6623	9	25075-28145
3	6624-9891	10	28146-30832
4	9892-13091	11	30833-33261
5	13092-16176	12	33262-25854
6	16177-19448	13	35855-39162
7	19449-22297		

END OF NEWSPAPERS

of liberty, 32584
or a melange, 30906
or charms, 34237
or songster's, 23634
Niles, Ann, d. 1732, death, 3586
Niles, Elisha. Narrative, 34560
Niles, Nathaniel, 1741-1828
American hero, 14349
Descant, 13501
Perfection of God, 15941, 23635
Remembrance of Christ, 12900
Secret prayer, 12901
Substance of two sermons, 16414
Two discourses on I. John, 12902
Two discourses on liberty, 13502
Niles, Samuel, 1674-1762
Brief and plain essay, 5666, 6037
Charge, 7116
Sentiments, 5668
Tristitiae, 5667
True scripture-doctrine, 7984
Vindication, 6902
wife's death, 3586
Niles, Samuel, 1743-1814
Vanity of man, 38117
ordained, 12610
Niles, Sands. Some short, 21334
Nimble-chops, Aquiline see **Livingston, Henry Brockholst, 1757-1823**
Nine sermons (Whitefield), 5311
19th June, 1797, committed, 33098
9th article of the association, 13706
Ninth edition; the minister, 22398
Nineveh's repentance, 4597
Nips, Jack see **Leland, John, 1754-1841**
Nisbet, Charles, 1736-1804
Address to the students, 19865
Natural religion, 33834
Usefulness and importance, 19866
Nisbet, Richard
Capacity of Negroes, 24623
Numbers of poetry, 35975-76
Slavery not forbidden, 12903
Source of virtue, 24624
Nishmath Chajim, 2352
Niveau de l'Europe, 27218, 28970
Nixon, Gen. ——, officers under, 16360
Nixon, John, accounts of, 19891
Nixon, William
Analogical vocabulary, 24625
Easy introduction, 22736
Prosody made easy, 19867
Specimen of a plan, 22029
No cause nor need, 28092
No cross, no crown, (1747) 6041, (1751) 6744, (1789) 22050, (1796) 30972, (1797) 32645
No new thing, 3356
No placemen, 14399-401
No provincial convention, 14350
No song, no supper, (1792) 24400, (1793) 25611-12, (1794) 26558, 27125
No stamped paper, 10106
No standing army, 14351
Noah's flood, 31481, 33109
Norristown library company. Act of incorporation, 35982
North, ——, of Charleston, petition, 33013-14
North, Major ——, correspondence with Congress, 19303
North, Edward. Inaugural dissertation, 32592
North, Frederick, earl of Guilford, 1732-1792

Recantation, 16017
Speech, 15942
address to, 13944-52
conduct of, 13670
damnable advice of, 15095
dedication to, 13599-600, 18039
designs of, 14028
inducement offered by, 13493
introduces bills into Commons, 15354
letter (from Casca), 13984, 13987
motion for reconciliation, 14539
observations on, 14964-66
policies considered, 13582-87
rebuked, 13757
North American see **Cooper, Myles, 1735-1785; Dickinson, John, 1732-1808**
North American land company. Plan of association, 29220
North association. Testimony, 5605
North Briton, 11119, 11532
North Briton extraordinary, 11471
North Briton no. 45, 9542-45
North Carolina
Abstract of the proceedings of the Grand lodge, 35986
Account of monies, 21336
Constitution, 16419
Declaration of rights, 20593
Index to the appendix, 38122
Journal of the convention, 21337, 22738
Journal of the proceedings of the Provincial congress, (1775) 14354, (1776) 14948, 15489
Minutes of the North Carolina Neuse Baptist, 35987
Minutes of the United Baptist, 29225
Proceedings and debates of the convention, 22037
Regulations for the exercise, 22038
State of North Carolina; in convention, (Aug. 1, 1788) 21341, (Nov. 23, 1789) 22039
Statement of the taxes, 19871
True and faithful narrative of the proceedings, 4582
North Carolina. Assembly
Journals, (1762) 9470, (1764) 9768-69, (1785) 19869
North Carolina. Governor
Message, 7284
Proclamation, (1776) 14949, (1784) 18821
North Carolina. House of commons
Journal, (1786) 20594, (1787) 21338, (1788) 22034, (1789) 22739, (1790) 23639, (1791) 24628, (1792) 25926, (1793) 27420-21, (1794) 29222, (1795) 20910, (1796) 32593, 34240, (1797) 34242, (1798) 34244, (1799-1800) 38123
North Carolina. Laws (collective)
Acts, (1751) 6742, (1795) 29221
Collection of all the public acts, 6903
Collection of all the acts of Assembly, 9767
Collection of the private, 27419
Collection of the statutes, 24627, 30909

VOL.	ITEMS	VOL.	ITEMS
1	1-3244	8	22298-25074
2	3245-6623	9	25075-28145
3	6624-9891	10	28146-30832
4	9892-13091	11	30833-33261
5	13092-16176	12	33262-25854
6	16177-19448	13	35855-39162
7	19449-22297		

Complete revisal of all the acts, 12904, 15488
Laws (1715-1790), 23641
Militia laws now in force, 35985
North Carolina. Laws (session)
Acts, (1753) 7080, (1754) 7283, (1755) 7520-21,
(1756) 7743, (1757) 7985-86, (1758) 8221-22,
(1759) 8448, 8695, (1760) 8696-99, (1762) 9470,
(1764) 9768-69, (1765) 10107, (1774) 13504,
(1777) 15487, 15943, (1778) 15944, 15946, (1779)
16416-18, (1780) 16913-14, (1781) 17278-79,
(1782) 17644, (1783) 18069, (1784) 18660-61,
(1785) 19870, (1786) 20596, (1787) 21340,
(1788) 22036, (1789) 22741, (1790) 23642,
(1791) 24630, (1792) 25928, (1793) 27424,
(1794) 27425, 29224, (1795) 30912, (1796)
32595-96, (1797) 34246, (1798) 34247, 35984,
(1799) 38125-26
North Carolina. Laws (separates)
Act, (1763) 9469, (1778) 15945
North Carolina. Senate
Journal, (1786) 20595, (1787) 21339, (1788)
22035, (1789) 22740, (1790) 23640, (1791)
24629, (1792) 25927, (1793) 27422-23, (1794)
29223, (1795) 30911, (1796) 32594, 34241, (1797)
34243, (1798) 34245, (1799-1800) 38124
North Carolina planter. Petition, 23692, 27496
North Carolina. University
Laws, 38130
North Kingstown academy. Charter, 38383
Northampton, Mass. Result of a council, 6577
Northampton collection, 32416
Northcote, William
Extract from the marine practice, 15100
Preventatives of the scurvy, 15611
Northern inland-lock navigation co. Report, 24635
**Northern inland-lock navigation company will
purchase,** 24634
Northern light, 36775-76
Northern missionary society. Constitution, 32601
Northern raps, 31830
Northrop, Lydia, d. 1794, death, 27214
Northrop, Stephen, wife's death, 27214
Northup, William, ed. Divine hymns, 32850, 36319-
20
Northwest Territory
Plat of the seven, 30918
Table of the variations, 30917
Northwest Territory. House of representatives
Journal, 38134-35
Northwest Territory. Laws (collective)
Laws passed (to 1791), 24633
Northwest Territory. Laws (session)
Acts, (1792) 27428, (1795) 30916, (1798) 34257,
(1799) 38137
Northwest Territory. Laws (separates)
Militia law, 38138
Northwest Territory. Legislative assembly
Journal, (1799) 35994, (1800) 38136
Norton, ———, cautions colonists, 709
Norton, Elijah
Fools in their folly, 19147
Impossibility of sinners, 34258
Methodism examined, 23645
Salvation for all, 27429
Norton, John, 1606-1663
Brief catechisme, 63, 110
Heart of N. England, 56
Three choice and profitable, 90
memoir of, 724
Norton, John, 1651-1716. Essay tending, 1369
Norton, John, 1716-1778. Redeemed captive, 6211

Norton, John, fl. 1741, ordained, 4883
Norton, Noah U. Oration, 23646
Norton, Samuel
answer to, 472
cautions colonists, 709?
Norwich, George Horne, bp. of see **Horne, George,
1730-1792**
Norwich, John Moore, bp. of see **Moore, John,
1646-1714**
Norwich, Conn.
At an adjourned, 16420
Charter, 18663
Constitution, 27430
First principles, 267
Norwich mutual assurance co. Insurance policy,
34259
Norwich packet. Newsboys annual address, 35996
Norwood, E., court martial, 16334
Nosegay for the young, 33494-95
Nosum nosorum, 9223
Note-maker noted, 5263
Notes addressées, 30440
Notes and observations, 5264
from citizen Adet, 30440
of a few, 32426
of the true, 1162
on farming, 20599, 28144
on the establishment, 18541, 19328
finances, 35997
last illness, 22634
slave trade, 17095, 17838
state of Virginia, (1788) 21176, (1794)
27162, (1800) 37702-703
two reports, 27432
upon Luke XVII, 38140
upon scripture, 34261
Noth und hülfsbüchlein, 30920
Notice is hereby, 4783, 6816
of a town meeting, 9350
of meeting, 33764
of the ferry lease, 890
Notice; the subscriber, 23142
to assessors, 34078
to be sold, 19873
to postmasters, 10633
Notices (Clarkson), 15254
Notification; freeholders and other, 21700
[of a meeting of the freeholders], 11998
of a meeting to be held, 18937
of a town meeting, 18936
Notification; the freeholders, (1767) 10563, (1784)
18374, (1796) 30106, (1797) 31848, (1799) 35218,
(1800) 36998
Notification to persons, 14187
Nott, Abraham, hand of fellowship, 3316
Nott, Eliphalet, 1773-1866. Federal money, 32603
Nott, Samuel, 1754-1852
Funeral oration, 15949
Sermon, (1786) 19874, (1793) 25932
Nottingham (galley), shipwrecked, 2863, 3018, 9102
Nourse, G. History of the Independents, 35998
Nourse, Joseph
Accounts of the United States, 20037
General abstract, 23926
General account, 20066
General view, 17765
Report of the register, 22993
Schedule of requisitions, 20081, 20785
State of the receipts, 18270
Treasury department, 29775
successor to, 19070

Nouvelles étrennes, 32777
Nova Scotia
   Extract from the votes, 14357
Novelty of novelties, 17740
November 18th, 1793, 25924
November session, 1784, 18579
Novion, citoyen de see Sullivan, James, 1744-1808
Novum Testamentum, 36952
Now in the press and speedily will be, 12379
   in the press and will be speedily, 10433
   in the press; the true art, 12170
   or never, 1633
Nowell, Alexander, 1645-1672. Almanac see Almanacs (Nowell)
Nowell, Samuel, 1634-1688. Abraham in arms, 256
Noxon, Thomas
   Observations, 3585
   reply to, 3514
Noyes, Rev. ———, examined, 7876
Noyes, Rev. ———, sermon in his meeting-house, 7576
Noyes, Abigail, d. 1768, death, 11118
Noyes, Belcher, d. 1785. Rudiments of Latin, 18072
Noyes, Edmund, ordained, 6792
Noyes, James, 1608-1656. Short catechism, (1641) 7, (1661) 67, (1676) 222, (1694) 707, (1714) 1708, (1797) 32604
Noyes, James, d. 1720?, death, 2090
Noyes, James, fl. 1797. Federal arithmetic, 32605
Noyes, Joseph
   examined, 7876?
   sermon in his meeting-house, 7576?
   wife's death, 11118
Noyes, Matthew, ordained, 22538
Noyes, Moses, 1643-1729
   Sermon, 19149
   death, 3449
Noyes, Moses, fl. 1800. To industry, 37346
Noyes, Nathaniel, 1735-1810
   Charge, (1795) 28533, (1797) 32625, (1799) 36019
   Dialogue, 24637
   Man on probation, 32606
   Sermon, 19150
Noyes, Nicholas, 1647-1717
   Elegy upon the death, 1405
   Elegy upon the much lamented, 1870
   New Englands duty, 850
   elegy upon, 1924
Noyes, Oliver. Letter from a gentleman, 2163
Noyes, Thomas, of Needham, ordained, 35076
Noyes, Thomas, of Westerly, candidate, 38374

Noyes, Thomas, 1769-1837. Discourse, 32607
Nützliche anweisung, (1751) 6777, (1762) 9224, 9264, (1772) 12552, (1792) 24771
Nützliche gegen nachricht, 11390
Nugae Canorae, 26641, 31802
Nugent, ———. Epistle to a lady, 34527
Nugent, ———. Speeches, 10463
Nugent, Henry Paul
   Mr. Nugent's vindication, 35999
   (tr.) National convention, 26999
   (tr.) Summary journal, 27664
Nugent, Thomas, 1700?-1772, tr. Principles of natural, 24158
Nullum tempus, 3608
Number 1: female fortitude, 18465
No. 1; in Senate, 34718
Number 1; of the Christian, 29235
No. 1; Philadelphia, June 10, 1773, 12792
Number I; poems written, 35387
No. 2; statement of the monies, 33084
Number II; the saint's daily assistant, 25737
No. 3; statement by the accountant, 33084
No. 3; the Dougliad, 11638
No. 33, Smith-street, 22857
No. XLV; in General assembly, 32650
Number of journeymen, 24617
   of the beast, 14425
   of the inhabitants, 10134
   of the subscribers, 11793
Numbers of poetry, 35975-76
Nun will ich, 11389
Nunc dimit(t)is, 1405, 7632
Nuncia bona, 1760
Nuptial dialogues, 7133
Nurse, John. John Nurse, carrier, 13271
Nurse, a poem, 38604
Nurse Truelove's Christmas box, (1786) 20029-30, (1789) 22188, (1795) 29658, (1796) 31317
Nurse Truelove's New-Year's gift, (1786) 20031-33, (1793) 26284, (1794) 27820

VOL.	ITEMS	VOL.	ITEMS
1	1-3244	8	22298-25074
2	3245-6623	9	25075-28145
3	6624-9891	10	28146-30832
4	9892-13091	11	30833-33261
5	13092-16176	12	33262-25854
6	16177-19448	13	35855-39162
7	19449-22297		

O

O., J. see Oxenbridge, John, 1609-1674
O come away, 34262
O! dear, 25936
O had it been, 34263
O Justitia, 10110
O Liberty, 3595
O tempora, 13599-600
Oakes, Urian, 1631-1681
    Almanac see Almanacs (Oakes)
    Elegie, 240
    New-England pleaded with, 180
    Seasonable discourse, 325
    Soveraign efficacy, 326
    Unconquerable, 195
    poem on, 319
    pres. Harvard, 199, 213, 248
Oath of a freeman, 1, 10
        of fidelity, 15838
        to be administered, 7756
Obedience and submission, 4145
        to the divine law, 2596
        to the law, 33816
Obedient sufferer, 1978
O'Beirne, Thomas Lewis, 1748-1823. Excellent sermon, 14952
Oberdam, Hans von. Ernsthaffte, 5585
Objections to early piety, 2256
Objections to the bank, 1675
Obligation of ministers, 33241
Obligations of a grateful, 30663
        of baptism, 2309
        of the confederate states, 17722, 18188
        upon all, 4806
        which the profession, 2639
O'Brien, Matthew. Charity sermon, 38141
O'Brien, William, dedication to, 21707
O'Bryan, Blany. Irishmen's petition, 11485
Obscure individual. Observations on a late pamphlet, (1783) 18073, (1784) 18665, (1796) 31173
Observable things, 873
Observanda, 726
Observation of the Lord's day, 24842
Observations anatomical, 20527
        and experiments, 33831
        and remarks, 19732
        by the committee, 21369
        concerning the funding, 22042
        concerning the increase, 7389
        historical, 3280
        in defence, 20614

leading to a fair, 20454-56
made, 3911
moral, 7768
occasioned, 24638
of a person, 893
of that terrible, 4503
on a late epitaph, 9772
        late pamphlet, (1783) 18073, (1784) 18665, (1796) 31173
        letter, 36000
        pamphlet, 11270
        variety of subjects, 13258-59
on accidental fires, 32608
on African slavery, 18666
on, and a reply to, 28500
on animal electricity, 33112
on certain commercial, 16819
on certain documents, 32222, 37571-73
on conventions, 26176
on Dr. Mackrill's, 30922
on Doctor Priestley's, 32732
on Dr. Rush's, 25254, 31172
on 1st. the chronology, 29230
on Free Masonry, 34027
on government, 20465
on Masonary, 39082
on Mr. Buckminster's, 30606
on Mr. Freeman's, 4089
on Mr. Justice, 11391
on novel-reading, 24639, 27696
on Samuel Shepard, 25233
on several acts, 11392-93
on several passages, 10869
on slave-keeping, 12322-23, 18928
on some fatal, 9539, 9872-73
on the act for granting, 2164
        act of Parliament, 13561-62
        agriculture, 21774
        alien, 36001
        American Revolution, 16625, 17039
        angina, 11449
        Articles of Confederation, 20600
        cause of nature, 25854-55, 31172
        causes, 33590
        charter, 9441
        combination, 26496
        commerce of Spain, 38142
        commerce of the American, 17975-76
        conversion, (1761) 8909, (1785) 19064, (1800) 37863

culture, 35427
decision, 22089
dispatch, 32905
dispute, 32226-27, 33841-43
divine, 26267
doctrine, 32719
doctrines, 8050
emigration, (1794) 26777-78, (1795) 28439-
    40, (1796) 30217-18, 30234, (1797) 31948,
    (1798) 33528
fall of Antichrist, 19875
importance of the American, (1784) 18739,
    (1785) 19201-204, (1786) 19937
importance of the northern, 6524
increase of infidelity, 29355, 32721
influence of the moon, 34264
inslaving, 8298, 8542
justicative, 17039
language, 21068
late and present, 7389
late law, 12171
late popular, 13179
minutes, 23463
national character, 33658
nature and cure, 31782
nature and use, 17091
nature of civil, 15030-34
new constitution, 21111-12
part, 34906
peculiar, 19151
pernicious, 19481
plan, 20649-50
present situation, 24640
present state, 28594
progress, 23158
proposed bill, 27433
proposed constitution, 21344
proposed state road, 39109
propriety, 21878
public fast, 10434
reasons, 4057, 11394
reconciliation, 14790-91
Reflections, 23517
religious education, 32938
Revelation, 23486
Rev. pastor, 14358
right, 15950
river Potomack, 25711, 27209
scarlatina, 31194
scurvy, 26283
slaves, 15239
speech, 33268
superior, 18178
whale-fishery, 21345
on two campaigns, 9242
on universal, 22746
relative, 12668
sur l'origine, 16713
    la cause, 25854
    la depeche, 32904
upon beauty, 6040
upon Negro slavery, 18425, 22434
upon parson Campbell, 3585
upon the cause, 19231
    congregational, 12857
    downfall, 21030
    effects, 17419
    fall, 18977
    government, 23812
    new divinity, 25935

origin, 36253
present government, 15589, 18172
present state, 18206
proposed plan, 21264
revolution, 25356
Observator. Thoughts on Christian, 30923
Observator observed, 3705
Observator's trip, 2794
Observer observed, 3706
Observer of Europe, 28970
Observer of the dispute. Rules of trial, 11842
Occasional essays, 38145
    observations, 33835
    ode for February 22, 38146
    ode for 17th of June, 19875
    reflections, 35582
    reverberator, 7081
    Salem gazette, 15073
Occasionalist. To the freeholders, 11017
Occom, Samson, 1723-1792
    Address, 12911
    Choice collection, (1774) 13507, (1784) 18667,
        (1785) 19152, (1792) 24641
    Sermon, (Sept. 2, 1772) 12493-86, 12907-910,
        13508
    ordained, 8808
Occurences of the times, 22043
Ocean spectre, 29231
Ockamickon, Indian king, 4660
O'Conner, Patrick. Irishmen's petition, 11485
O'Connor, Arthur, 1763-1852. Address, 32610, 34290
O'Connor, John, tr. Anecdotes of the reign, 19153,
    20601
O'Connor's geographical cards, 25937
Oct. 13, 1775; resolved, 14208
Ocuish, Hannah, 1774-1786, execution, 19547, 20264
Ode, anniversary, June 2, 1794, 27434
Ode composed, 28599-600
    for St. John's, 22625
    for the 4th of July, (1788) 21346, (1798) 33717,
        (1799) 36436, (1800) 37855
        23rd of October, 24647
        Thanksgiving, 6277
    in honor, 37031
    inscribed, 21905, 26542-43
Ode; oh for a muse, 21151
Ode on ends, 36004
    on St. Cecelia's, 21495
    on the birthday, 30924
        late glorious, 9113
        passions, 28444
        prospect, 8831
    sudden death, 34528
    performed at the celebration, 30366
    performed at the First church, 37008
    set to music, 11794
    sung at the feast, 29232-34
    sung at the lecture, 29590

VOL.	ITEMS	VOL.	ITEMS
1	1-3244	8	22298-25074
2	3245-6623	9	25075-28145
3	6624-9891	10	28146-30832
4	9892-13091	11	30833-33261
5	13092-16176	12	33262-25854
6	16177-19448	13	35855-39162
7	19449-22297		

(1792) 24049, (1793) 26558, (1794) 27445
Prisoner at large, 22750, 23653
Quaker, 27449
Songs, duets, 22748
Songs in The castle, 27438
Songs in The highland reel, 27444
Songs in The son-in-law, 27446
Songs of The farmer, 27440
Wild oats, 25940-42, 31175
World in a village, 27447
Young Quaker, 27448
O'Kelly, James, 1735-1826. Essay, 18668
O'Kelly, John. Preceptor's guide, 34270
O Kely, Francis, 1719-1794. Disjointed watch, 29240
Olcott, Bulkley, 1733-1793
Brotherly love, 17647
Righteousness, 18075
death, 25477
pastor in Charlestown, N. H., 19437
Olcott, Peter, discourse before, 24788
Old and experienced trader see **Cluny, Alexander**
Old bachelor's masterpiece, 32612
Old bachelor's reasons, 27450
Old covenanting and true Presbyterian layman
Bridle, 8807
Second letter, 9003
True copy, 9027, 9288
Old divinity, 16799, 28849
Old Dutchman. To the freeholders, 11495
Old English baron, 32742
Old fire club. Articles, 22125
Old Ireland's misery, 6904
looking-glass, 11745, 13442
maid, 9195
man's calendar, (1793) 25530, (1794) 27033
calender, (1781) 17170
guide, 14116
honour, 534, 564
Old member of Parliament see **Lee, Arthur, 1740-1782**
Old men's tears, (1691) 576, (1715) 1779, (1732) 3604, (1749) 6413, (1769) 11457
Mr. Dod's sayings, (1673) 174, (1731) 3412, (1760) 8583, (1768) 10884, (1793) 25406
path, 10111
pathes, 1509
principles, 929
Old statesman see **Williams, David, 1738-1816**
Old trusty see **Donaldson, Arthur**
Old Whig. From the Independent, 20379-80
Oldden, John
letter to, 30231-33
threatened, 31948
Oldmixon, Mr. ——, sings song, 33855, 34489
Oldmixon, Mrs. ——, sings song, 30242, 35618
Oldys, Francis. Life of Thomas Paine, 30178
O'Leary, Arthur, 1729-1802. Essay, 19156
Olevianus, C. Catechismus, 9135
Oliphant, James, 1734-1818. Sacramental catechism, 23654
Olive-branch, Simon see **Roberts, William**
Olive-branch; Baltimore, 18076
Oliver, Andrew, 1731-1799
The censor, 12006
Copy of letters, 12818-19
Essay, 12498
dedication to, 12806
deposition, 11737
secret correspondence, 12690
sermon before, 12256, 12502

Oliver, Daniel, 1663?-1732
death, 3597
wife's death, 3955
Oliver, Daniel, d. 1727, death, 3599
Oliver, Daniel, d. 1768, death, 10858
Oliver, Daniel, fl. 1787, ordained, 20374
Oliver, Elizabeth, d. 1735, death, 3955
Oliver, Jerusha, life, 1508
Oliver, John. Present for teeming women, 708
Oliver, Peter, 1713-1791
Poem, 7988
Speech, 6578
Charged with misdemeanors, 13426
daughter's death, 10755
son's death, 10858
trial judge, 11683
Oliver, Peter, fl. 1798. Adopted son, 34271
Oliver, Robert. To the honorable, 26369
Oliver, Thomas Fitch, 1749-1797. Discourse, 18669
Olney, Jeremiah. Extract from the act, 31338
Olney hymns, (1787) 20588, (1790) 22734, (1791) 23631, (1795) 29216, (1797) 32580
Omar Khayyam, 1025-1123. Consolation, 22046, 29241
On a merciful disposition, 28859
soul pleading, 14409
vertuous woman, 1121
On account of pleas, 4429
On account of the indisposition, 16006
On board the prize, 36241
On church discipline, 11692
On dying very suddenly, 2452
On equality, 25943
On female excellence, 24187
On Friday evening, 39009
On Friday next, the 1st of May, 16010
the 10th day, 16005
the 24th of April, 16009
On General Wayne's taking, 16424
On Joseph's making, 32613
On Monday next, the 13th, 16007
the 19th, 15995
the 30th, 16004
On Monday, the 2d day, 15998
the 9th day, 16000
the 16th day of February, 15997
the 16th day of March, 16001
the 23d day, 16002
the 26th day, 15996
On monies, 21698
On motion of Mr. Dane, 20070
On national greatness, 25638
On preaching, 30648
On reading, 31617
On Saturday next, 13841
On Saturday the 24th, 27219
On taking an affectionate, 36711
On the advantages, 27135
alien act, 35077
conqueror, 14042

VOL.	ITEMS	VOL.	ITEMS
1	1-3244	8	22298-25074
2	3245-6623	9	25075-28145
3	6624-9891	10	28146-30832
4	9892-13091	11	30833-33261
5	13092-16176	12	33262-25854
6	16177-19448	13	35855-39162
7	19449-22297		

24, 1775) 14432, (Mar. 6, 1775) 14608-610,
(Mar. 15, 1775) 13840, (Mar. 5, 1777) 15363,
(Mar. 5, 1778) 15725, (Mar. 5, 1779) 16550,
(May 8, 1779) 16521, (Mar. 6, 1780) 16836,
(Mar. 16, 1780) 16867, (Mar. 2, 1781) 17103,
(Mar. 5, 1781) 17132, (Mar. 5, 1782) 17606,
(Mar. 5, 1783) 18302, (July 4, 1783) 18292,
(July 5, 1784) 18527, (July 4, 1785) 19017,
(July 4, 1786) 19482, (July 4, 1787) 20318,
(July 4, 1788) 21145, 21355, (July 4, 1789)
22120, 22165, (July 5, 1790) 22541, (Nov. 10,
1791) 26435, (July 4, 1796) 30384, (Nov. 3,
1797) 32228, (July 4, 1798) 34536, (Jan. 8,
1800) 37516, (Feb. 22, 1800) 36906
delivered at a public exhibition, 35673
  at Amherst, 33419, **(Bedford)** 38169, **(Ben-**
    nington) 35599, **(Bozrah)** 39023, **(Brook-**
    field) 17153, **(Buckston)** 34587
  at Byfield, (1799) 36037-38, (1800) 38184
  at Canterbury, 35136, **(Castine)** 30959,
    (Charlestown) 19496, **(Chesterfield)**
    38192, **(Christ church)** 21393, **(Concord)**
    32121, **(Conway)** 33732, **(Deerfield)**
    37612, **(Dighton)** 35112, **(Dover)** 23133
  at East Haddam, (Blakslee) 36986, (Mose-
    ley) 38008
  at Elizabethtown, 25219, **(Flemington)**
    35561, **(Greenville)** 29399, **(Hackinsack)**
    17150
  at Hanover, (1796) 30367, (1798) 35051
  at Hartford, 37319, **(Hingham)** 37837, **(Ip-**
    swich) 17938, **(Lanesborough)** 33909,
    (Lansingburgh) 32367, **(Lavana)** 31863
  at Lenox, (1793) 25713, (1800) 38522
  at Machias, 26818, **(Manchester)** 29649
  at Marietta, (1788) 21538, (1789) 21802
  at Mason's hall, 33385, **(Mendon)** 31192,
    (Middletown) 37664, **(Mt. Pleasant)**
    35065, **(New Salem)** 32143, **(Newburgh)**
    34282, **(Old York)** 37955, **(Paris)** 21738,
    (Plymouth) 37440, **(Portland)** 30315,
    (Portsmouth) 21456, **(Pownalborough)**
    36717, **(Ridgfield)** 35435, **(Rochester)**
    26769, **(Roxbury)** 35163, **(St. Paul's)**
    33884, **(Salisbury)** 35054, **(Saybrook)**
    37651, **(Southington)** 23646, **(Suffield)**
    37493, **(Taunton)** 35418
  at the Beneficent, 35094
  at the Benevolent, 33285
  at the celebration, (1795) 28299, (1796)
    31628, (1797) 32775
  at the chapel, 17960
  at the Charleston, 30465
  at the college chapel, 29922
  at the interment, (Northrop) 27214,
    (Parsons) 18487
  at the King's chapel, 14892-95, 18997
  at the meeting-house, 28242
  at the North church, 20219
  at the North meeting-house, 37047
  at the Orphan-house, 28369
  at the request of P B K, 33963, (the inhab-
    itants) 21125, (the . . . militia) 37999
  at the Rev. Mr. Olcott's, 19437
  at the Reverend T. Harrington's, 17143
  at the town, 21463
  at Thomaston, 33225, **(Washington)** 34278,
    (Watertown) 15101, **(Wethersfield)**
    37886, **(Whitestown)** 32496, **(Williams-**
    town) 35137, **(Wiscasset)** 35724, **(Wor-**
    cester) 23145

before Nova Caesaria, 37069
before St. John's, 22550
before the American philosophical, 19972-
  73
before the citizens, (1797) 32900, (1799)
  36370
before the General society, 33145
before the . . . Masons, 24479
before the members, (Hudson lodge)
  37490, (Livingston lodge) 37491
before the Mosheimian society, 29511
before the most ancient, (Sumner) 22918,
  (Todd) 22941
before the Phi Beta Kappa, 34046
before the Providence association, (1794)
  28108-109, (1795) 29053, (1796) 30145
before the Republican, 28815
before the right worshipful, (1796) 30588,
  (1797) 32205, (1798) 33930
before the Society of black friars, (1788)
  21147, (1789) 22182, (1797) 33482
before the Society of Cincinnati, 28031
before the Society of the Cincinnati, 20464
before the Society of the Phi Beta Kappa,
  31932
before the Uranian, 27758
by request, 37595
in Christ's church, 18001
in Free Masons hall, 17375
in Middleborough, 32265, **(Portland)** 25381
in public, 17749
in Richmond, 39124, **(Rutland)** 36021
in St. Michael's, 29663
in St. Paul's, 35625, 37295
in St. Philip's, 31210-11, 38326
in Sheffield, 37795, **(South Farms)** 38003,
  (Taunton) 35023
in the Baptist, (Hunter) 28871, (Maxcy)
  29054, (Whiting) 35022
in the Benevolent, (1796) 29967, (1797)
  31901, (1798) 33452
in the College-hall, 21357
in the First Congregational, 35806
in the meeting house, Colchester, 18868
in the meeting house of the First, 31262,
  36371
in the Presbyterian, 28499, 32000
on Saturday, 37790
on the anniversary, (1793) 27697, (1794)
  27590, (1796) 31274
on the 4th July, (Burnham) 33476, (Mac-
  Whorter) 27257
on the 4th of July, (Burnet) 35259, (Clinton) 33522, (Mercer) 24537, (Ogden)
  34266, (Parkhurst) 34308, (Wells) 34998,
  (Williams) 31638
on the late public, 13153
on the twenty-second anniversary, 34520
. . . Petersburgh, 37057
the 22nd of February, 37565

VOL.	ITEMS	VOL.	ITEMS
1	1-3244	8	22298-25074
2	3245-6623	9	25075-28145
3	6624-9891	10	28146-30832
4	9892-13091	11	30833-33261
5	13092-16176	12	33262-25854
6	16177-19448	13	35855-39162
7	19449-22297		

VOL.	ITEMS	VOL.	ITEMS
1	1-3244	8	22298-25074
2	3245-6623	9	25075-28145
3	6624-9891	10	28146-30832
4	9892-13091	11	30833-33261
5	13092-16176	12	33262-25854
6	16177-19448	13	35855-39162
7	19449-22297		

Osborn, Sarah Haggar, 1714-1796
Nature, certainty, 7523, 25949-50
death, 35636
Osborn, Selleck, 1783-1826. Oration, 34282
Osborne, Judge ——, impeachment, 24917
Osborne, George Jerry. New Hampshire register, (1786) 19879, (1787) 20609, (1788) 21352
Oscar and Malvina, 30730-31
Osgood, David, 1747-1822
Conclusive argument, 36019
Devil let loose, 36020
Discourse delivered Feb. 19, 1795, 29246-49
Discourse delivered Dec. 29, 1799, 38170
Discourse delivered on the day, 29250
Reflections, 18670
St. Paul's example, 25952
Sermon, 21353
Signal advantages, 34283
Some facts, 34284
Uncertainty of life, 32621
Unsearchable riches, 19157
Wonderful works, (1794) 27456-57, (1795) 29251-55
reply to, 29585-88
Osgood, John, d. 1773
Letter of prudent, 10115
death, 13090
Osgood, Jonathan, ordained. 24325
Osgood, Nathan. Oration, 36021
Osgood, Phineas, sermon before, 7493
Osgood, Samuel, 1748-1813
Board of treasury, (Aug. 27, 1785) 19280, (Apr. 8, 1786) 20042, (June 22, 1786) 20043
Board of treasury to whom, 20044
General post-office, 22978
Ordinance for the establishment, 20073
Remarks on the book, 26663
reports ordinance, 20755
Osmer, ——, veterinarian, 27771
Ossa Josephi, 2103
Ossian
adaptation from, 30730-31
imitated, 37832
Ossory, Lord ——, history of, 18142
Osterwald, Jean Frédéric, 1663-1747
Compendium, 21354
Practical observations, 23184, 23656
commentary on Bible, 20960, 21680, 22347
Ostrander, ——, jailer, 32899
Oswald, Eleazar, 1755-1795
Letters of Franklin, 29256
case against, 21363
dedication to, 19540
letter (from Carey), 19539
Oswald, James. One kind kiss, 30931
Other side, 13381
Otis, Cushing, 1768-1837. Oration, 38172
Otis, Harrison Gray, 1765-1848
Letter (to Heath), 34285
Oration, 21355
proposes amendments, 34714
Otis, James, 1725-1784
Brief remarks, 10116
Colony of Massachusetts-Bay, 14840
Rights of the British colonies, 9773
Rudiments of Latin, 8701
Vindication of the British, 10117
Vindication of the conduct, 9225
consents to resolve, 14207-208, 14210, 15133
preface by, 9884
satire on, 10519

Otis, Samuel Allyne, 1740-1814
reports on ratification, 21520
secy. Congress, 22201
secy. Senate, 27890-94, 29722
Otsego Baptist association. Minutes, 30932
Ottawa Indians
Debates in council, 24647
treaty, (1785) 19278, (1795) 29742
Otterbein, Georg Gottfried. Lesebuch, 29258
Otterbein, Johann Daniel. Jesus und die kraft, 22752
Otterbein, William, 1726-1813. Heilbringende menschwerdung, 9471
Otto, Johann Heinrich. Geistlich lied, 12499
Otto, John C., 1775-1845. Inaugural essay, 30934
Ottolenghe, Joseph. Directions for breeding, 12172
Ouabi, 22684
Oudenaarde, Hendrick
Expostulatory letter, 10437
Seven letters, 10438
Oulton, Walley Chamberlain, 1770-1820. Wonderful story-teller, 32623
Ountaussogoe, Indian chief, 3916
Our country, 34287
dying Saviour's, 407
father's God, 4236, 30342
great king, 3140
lapse, 23103
Outcasts comforted, 17803
Outline of the doctrines, 24549
Outline of the evidences, 32722
Outlines of a plan, 26682, 27512
of an historical, 30257
of the theory, (1790) 22551, (1794) 27084, (1797) 32220-21
Outlines; say, great, 11795
Outpouring, 4914
Ouverture d'Iphigenie, 28751
Ouvière, Felix Pascalis see **Pascalis-Ouvière, Alexandre Felix, 1750-1833**
Overthrow of the papal, 28291-92
Overture, by Haydn, 32241
de Démophon, 28412
La buona figliuola, 31009
La schiava, 22069
presented, 3223
to the new opera, 22142
Ovid Americanus. Lessons, 18671
Ovidius Naso. Metamorphoseon libri X, 22753
Owen, ——
Dull o fedyddio, 3336
extracts from, 33515
preface by, 30235, 33532
prognosticks, 709
Owen, John. Youth's instructor, 7082
Owen, John, grammarian, 4012, 5762, 6485, 7884, 10603?
Owen, John, 1616-1683
Death of death, 24648
Eschol, 12500
Eshcol, 5468
Nature, power, 25953
ordained, 3245
Owen of Carron, 28978
Oxenbridge, John, 1609-1674
New England freemen, 181
Quickening word, 152
Oxenstierna, Count ——, extracts from, 13832
Oxford county. Petition, 32624
Oxfordshire tragedy, 20610

P

P. see **Pugh,** ——
P., A. see **Mifflin, Thomas, 1744-1800**
P., C.
  Letter (to George III), 10118
    see also **Pusey, Caleb, 1650-1727**
P., D. R. Reflections, 38365
P., E. see **Parkman, Ebenezer, 1703-1789**
P., F. D. see **Pastorius, Francis Daniel**
P., G.
  Methodism, 29259
    see also **Petyt, George**
P., H. Looking-glass, 1425
P., J.
  Cantata-quartetto, 20611
  Concerning the number, 15492
P., P. Letter, 3707
P., S. see **Pike, Samuel, 1717-1773**
P., S. T., tr. Algerine spy, 20481
P., W.
  Letter, 9774
  To the public, 20481
P., W. D., illustrator, 36052
P**, J****.** Life of General James Wolfe, 8702-703
Paaneah, Zaphnath. Two covenants, 18672
Paca, William
  Proclamation, 18239, 18820
  letter (from Washington), 18257
  letter concerning bribery, 29646
Pache, ——, correspondence with Dumouriez, 28090
Pacheco, Roderigo. Decree, 3019
Pacificatory letter, 2457
Pacificus
  To the public, 11018-19
    see also **Hamilton, Alexander, 1757-1804; Walker, Timothy, 1737-1822**
Pack of cards changed, (1761) 8942, (1785) 19110, 19158, (1800) 38174
Packard, Asa, d. 1843. Sermon, 30935
Packard, Hezekiah, 1761-1849
  Catechism, 30936, 34288
  Federal republicanism, 36023
  Plea, 29260
  Rational method, 32625
  Sermon, 34289, 36024
  ordained, 28088
  preface by, 29555
Packer, Joseph Bill. Journal, 12914-15
Pacsiello, ——, composes song, 26720
Paddock, Mercy, 1720?-1729, death, 3126

Paddy, from Cork. Comical sayings, 25326, 26798-99
Paddy's resource, 30937, 34290
Padlin, B. Ernstliche ermahnung, 4292
Padlock, 28295-96
Page, John, of N.H., ordained, 9597
Page, John, 1744-1808
  Address to the citizens, (1794) 32626, (1796) 30938, 36026
  Address to the freeholders, 36027
  To the citizens, 34291
  letter referred to, 33068
Page, Reed
  Sermon, 30939
  ordained, 24405
Page, Sarah, character of, 21608
Page, Thomas. Sermon, 25954
Page, William. To the public, 17779
Paige, Reed see **Page, Reed**
Paige, Winslow, ordained, 22386
Pain, Philip. Daily meditations, (1668) 128, (1670) 153, (1682) 327
Pain, William, 1730-1790
  Builder's pocket treasure, 25955
  Carpenter's pocket dictionary, 32627
  Practical builder, 25956
  Practical house carpenter, 30940, 32628
Paine, Clement, 1769-1849. Oration, 36028
Paine, Ephraim, 1730-1785, reports on frontier posts, 18832
Paine, Joshua, 1762?-1788, death, 21489
Paine, Robert Treat, 1731-1814
  delegate to Continental Congress, 13425
  speaker Mass. House, 15437
Paine, Robert Treat, 1773-1811
  Adams and liberty, (1798) 33437, 33903, 34293-99, 34394, 34683, (1800) 38177
  Adams and Washington, 34300
  Dedicatory address, 34301
  Eulogy, 36859, 37383, 38178-79
  Green Mountain farmer, 34302

VOL.	ITEMS	VOL.	ITEMS
1	1-3244	8	22298-25074
2	3245-6623	9	25075-28145
3	6624-9891	10	28146-30832
4	9892-13091	11	30833-33261
5	13092-16176	12	33262-25854
6	16177-19448	13	35855-39162
7	19449-22297		

Invention of letters, 29270-71
Masonic ode, 37491
On custom, 30409
Oration, 36030-32
Prize prologue, 27467
Ruling passion, 32634
Thomas Paine, to the friends, 27468
To arms, 36033
song by, 26688?
Paine, Seth. Eulogy, 38176
Paine, Thomas, 1697-1757
Discourse, 2283
Doctrine of earthquakes, 3079
Doctrine of original sin, 2574
Gospel-light, 3460
Of the evidence, 3586
Pastoral charge, 2165
Temporal safety, 3587
Paine, Thomas, 1737-1809
Age of reason, (1794) 27458-64, (1795) 29261-67, (1796) 30941-42
Agrarian justice, 32629-30
Common sense, (1776) 14954-62, 14964, 14966, (1791) 23657-58
Crisis, (no. I) 14953, (no. II) 15493, (no. III-IV) 15494-95, (no. V) 15951-53, (no. VI) 15954, (no. VII) 15955, (no. VIII) 16916, (no. IX) 16917, (no. X-XI) 17648-49, (no. XII) 17650, (no. XIII) 18077
Crisis extraordinary, 16918-19
Decline and fall, 30943-48
Dissertation on first principles, 29268, 30949
Dissertations on government, 19880
Examination, 29269
First principles, 30950
Gesunde vernunft, 14963
Letter (to Dundas), 24649, 25960
Letter (to Erskine), 32632
Letter (to Raynal), 17651-54
Letter (to Washington), 30951, 32631
Letter addressed, 25957-58
Letter to the people, 25327, 34292
Pennsylvania magazine, 15009
Prospects on the war, 27465
Public good, 16920
Rights of man, (1791) 23659-65, (1792) 24650-57, (1793) 25959-61, (1796) 31174
Supernumary crisis, no. XIV-XV, 18078-79
Thoughts on the present, 14965
To the public, 14967
Works, 32633
Writings, 24658, 27466
animadversions on, 28344
burlesque on, 29613
clerk Penn. Assembly, 16923
defended, 26050
examined, 28338
extract from, 30983
imaginary address by, 32153-54
letter (from American citizen), 32375
letter (from Cobbett), 30211, 30227-28, 30233, 31948
letters (from Fraser), 33760
letters (from Levi), 32376
letters (from Watson), 31564-73, 32373, 33154-58
letters (from Winchester), 28112, 29909
life, 30178
portrait, 30221-23
publication causes trial, 32092-93, 33698
reply to, 26983, 27558, 27744, 28016-19, 28096-100, 28107, 29237, 29352, 29354, 29883, 30131, 30204,

30423, 30603, 30710, 30727, 31328, 32633, 32813, 32871, 33947, 33996, 35423, 38028
trial, 25456-58, 26280
Paine, Thomas, 1773-1811 see **Paine, Robert Treat, 1773-1811**
Paine, Timothy. House lots, 19390
Paine, Tom, pseud. Tom Paine's jests, 27469, 30952
Paine's second part, 31328
Painful ministry, 1940
Pains of memory, 30785, 32469
Painting in general, 24979
Pakington, Dorothy Coventry, lady, d. 1679. Art of contentment, 7083
Palacha, Augustus, account of, 27818
Paley, William
Authenticity, 33158
Principles of moral, (1788) 21356, (1794) 27470, (1795) 29272
View of the evidences, 29273-74
Palida mors, 35491
Palladio delineated, 25955
Palladium, a literary, 36034, 38180
Palladium of conscience, 13154
Palm-bearers, 2670
Palmer, David, ordained, 37791
Palmer, Edward, d. 1797, death, 33197, 35000
Palmer, Elihu, 1764-1806
Enquiry, 32635
Political happiness, 38181
extracts from, 26015
Palmer, Herbert, 1601-1647. Memorials of godliness, 1643
Palmer, John, Jr. Haunted cavern, 30953-54
Palmer, John, 1650-1700
Present state, 495
reply to, 575, 12973
Palmer, John, 1729-1790
Free thoughts, 20613
Observations, 20614
Palmer, Joseph
moderator of meeting, 14353
ordained, 7062
orders issued to, 13420
Palmer, Obadiah. Obadiah Palmer and others, 2940
Palmer, Robert F. Prodigal reformed, 30955
Palmer, Samuel, account of Watts, 25154
Palmer, Stephen, 1766-1821
Sermon, (1795) 29275, (1797) 32636, (1798) 34304
hand of fellowship, 35076
ordained, 25592
Palmer, Thomas. Serious address, 6579
Palmerston, ——, excerpts from poetry, 23246
Pamela, (1744) 5485-87, (1786) 19963, (1792) 24744, (1793) 26088, (1794) 27622, (1796) 31101, (1797) 32763, (1799) 36230-31
Pandomicus, 33451
Panegyrick, 9280
Panet, Pierre, signs capitulation, 14540
Panther, Abraham
Account of a beautiful, 20615
Extraordinary account, 27471
Surprising account, 20875
Surprising narrative, (1787) 20616, (1795) 29276, (1797) 32638, (1799) 36035-36
Very surprising narrative, (1796) 30956-57, (1797) 32637, (1798) 34305, (1800) 38182-83
Papendick, George, tr. The stranger, 35703-704
Paper concerning some, 5669
Paper containing, 6056
Papers on agriculture, 35802

relating, 2512
relative to an application, 31473
relative to certain, 30038
relative to Great Britain, 26334
respecting, 30958
Papinian. Letters, 16311
Papist's curses, 5266
Par son excellence George Washington, 14543
Parable (Keimer), 2437
Parable of the labo(u)rers, 35297, 37130
of the merchant-man, 12836
of the unclean, 24115
Paracelsus. Pill for the committee, 11395
Paradiesische aloe, 11706
Paradigm of inflections, 21446
Paradise lost, (1777) 15443, (1787) 20525, (1791)
23569
of God, 19407
promised, 19037
regain'd, (1777) 15443, (1790) 22671, (1791)
23570
regain'd; to all the great, 11849
Paradisisches wunder-spiel, 7147, 10239
Paranque, Stephen, relief of, 27843
Paraphrase on eight, 28284
on part, 8307
on some, 28273
or large, 5130
Paraphrastical exposition, 680
Parental duty, 25660, 28899
Parental wishes, 1219
Parentalia, 1761
Parentator, 2557, 4753
Parent's advice, 24659
Parents and children, 3250
Parents and grown children, 2854
Parent's assistant, 30565
gift, 4775
monitor, 26771
Paris papers, 17509
Pariset, Nicholas. American trooper, 25962
Parish, Ariel, ordained, 24660
Parish, Daniel, d. 1795, elegy on, 29653
Parish, Elijah, 1762-1825
Charge, 36152
Excellence of the gospel, 34306
Oration, 36037-38, 38184
Sermon, 24660, 36039
Parishioner see **Devotion, Ebenezer, 1714-1771**
Parishioner having studied, 11237
Parismas, Thomas. History, 34307
Park, Sir James Alan, 1763-1838
Appendix to a system, 38185
System of the law, (1789) 22048, (1799) 36040,
(1800) 38186-87
Park, Joseph, d. 1777
God visiting, 8962
Sermon, 8963
Park, Mungo, 1771-1806. Travels, 38188-89
Park, Thomas. Oration, 21357
Park, John, 1754-1789
Battle of Bunker's-Hill, 14668
Death of General Montgomery, 15248-50
(tr.) Lyric works of Horace, 19717
reply to Duché, 15868
Parker, ——, of Georgia, memorial of, 31370
Parker, ——, of N.Y., letter (from Smith), 11470
Parker, Capt. ——, on Phoenix, 14298
Parker, Alexander, defended, 1578
Parker, Benjamin, 1694-1790
Difficulties, 8450

Excellent spirit, 13512
Vindication of an association, 8272
ordained, 5332
Parker, Daniel, 1669-1728
Persuasive to make, 3334
Perswasive to make, 11796
Parker, Hyde. Proclamation, 16290
Parker, Isaac, 1768-1830. Oration, (1796) 30959,
(1800) 37383, 38190
Parker, Isaiah, 1752-1848. Funeral discourse, 38191
Parker, James, 1714-1770
Brief of the claim, 11356
Conductor generalis, (1764) 9775, (1767) 10721,
(1788) 21358-59, (1790) 22754, (1792) 24661,
(1794) 27472
Notice to postmasters, 10633
Parker, Jonathan, d. 1776, death, 15075
Parker, Nathaniel, secy. NH Senate, 35774
Parker, Sir Peter. Description of the attack, 15284
Parker, Richard, trial, 32837
Parker, Samuel, 1744-1804
Sermon, 25963
suggests edition of Common prayer, 26045
Parker, Stephen, ordained, 3723
Parker's New York gazette. On the cry, 10908
Parkes, J. Spirit of liberty, 12501
Parkhurst, Jabez. Oration, 34308
Parkinson, Richard, 1748-1815. Experienced farmer,
36041
Parkinson, Sydney. Vocabulary, 13218
Parkman, Ebenezer, 1693-1782. Reformers, 7989
Parkman, Ebenezer, 1703-1789
Love of Christ, 8965
Zebulun advised, 4293
Parks, William, letter (from a gentleman), 2806
Parlour preacher, 34309
Parmerlee, Reuben, ordained, 23437
Parnassian sprig, 20268-70
Parnell, Thomas, 1679-1718
Hermit, a poem, (1753) 7084, (1784) 18673, 18767,
(1786) 19881, (1793) 25149, (1797) 31953
excerpts from, 23246, 26014
Parody on a late, 13287
Parrington, John Rivington. Map and description,
34310
Parsons, Benjamin, 1769-1857. Oration, 38192
Parson, David, fl. 1739-1781
death, 17855
ordained, 4415
Parsons, David, 1749-1823
Duty of a people, 29277
Sermon, 21360
ordained, 17855
Parsons, Eli, rebel, 20829
Parsons, Elijah, ordained, 12814
Parsons, Jesse. Almanac see **Almanacs (Parsons)**
Parsons, Jonathan, 1705-1776
Communion of faith, 11797
Connection between true, 8451
Consideration, 18674
Doctrine of justification, 6213

VOL.	ITEMS	VOL.	ITEMS
1	1-3244	8	22298-25074
2	3245-6623	9	25075-28145
3	6624-9891	10	28146-30832
4	9892-13091	11	30833-33261
5	13092-16176	12	33262-25854
6	16177-19448	13	35855-39162
7	19449-22297		

VOL.	ITEMS	VOL.	ITEMS
1	1-3244	8	22298-25074
2	3245-6623	9	25075-28145
3	6624-9891	10	28146-30832
4	9892-13091	11	30833-33261
5	13092-16176	12	33262-25854
6	16177-19448	13	35855-39162
7	19449-22297		

Facts and calculations, 36051
Poem, 26012
extracts from, 26200
Peck, William Dandridge, 1763-1822. Natural history, 36052
Peculiar advantages, 2256
Pedantic pedagogue, 16513
Peddle, Mrs. ——. Rudiments of taste, (1790) 22756, (1797) 32345, 32643, (1798) 33601, (1799) 36053
Pede, ——. Door of salvation, 3335, 4778
Peden, Alexander, 1626-1686
  Lord's trumpet, 34318
  life of, 8279
Pedrick, John, recants, 14194
Peep into the Anti-federal, 25968
Peevish man, 37756
Pegasus (ship), arrives in Baltimore, 27677
Peggy (snow), in Cape-Fear River, 14949
Peggy Stewart (brig), arrives in Annapolis, 13120
Peirce, Charles. Valuable medicines, 38310
Peirce, James, 1673-1726
  Caveat, 2575
  Curse causeless, 3081-82
  Y dull o fedyddio, 3336
Peirce, John, Jr. New American spelling book, (1795) 29282, (1796) 30970, (1797) 32644, (1799) 36054, (1800) 38205-206
Peirce, Nathanael. Account of the gerat, 7747
Peirce, Proctor, 1768-1821. Eulogy, 38207
Peirson, Abraham, 1608-1678. Some helps, 52-53
Peisley, Mary, life, 30834
Pelham, William. At Pelham's book store, 30971
Pelissier, Victor. Edwin and Angelina, 32843
Pell, ——, candidacy, 20983, 21329
Pelopidas, history of, 34412
Pelosi, Vincent M. Marine list, 23668
Pemberton, Ebenezer, 1671-1717
  Advice to a son, 1229
  Catalogue of books, 1921
  Christian fixed, 1190
  Discourse, 1996
  Divine original, 1484
  Funeral sermon, 1329
  Ill-boding symptoms, 1275
  Massachusetts artillery election, 1427
  Souldier defended, 1016
  True servant, 1577
  death, 1874, 1928
  epitaph, 1871
  hand of fellowship, 8830
  letter (from March), 8166
  ordained, 2855
  preface by, 1734
Pemberton, Ebenezer, 1704-1777
  Account of her life, 6530
  All power, 7748
  Duty of committing, 5267
  Exhortation, 5549
  Heaven the residence, 11799
  Knowledge of Christ, 4779
  Practical discourses, 4780
  Salvation by grace, 13514
  Sermon, (1735) 3945, (1738) 4294, (1743) 5268, (1744) 5471, (1746) 5842, (1756) 7749, (1757) 7991, (1771) 12174
  Sermons on several, 4295
  preface by, 4489, 5620
Pemberton, Israel
  Address, 15496-97
  Following remonstrance, 15498

To the Congress, 15499
To the inhabitants, 15501
To the president, 15500
Pemberton, James
  Apology for the people, 7900, 14767
  Epistle from our yearly meeting, 13285
  Epistle from the three, 35519
Pemberton, John
  Ancient testimony, 14765
  Philadephia, 27th tenth month, 14053
  To our friends, 14770
  testimony concerning, 33768
Pemberton, Samuel. Short narrative, 11580-81
Pemberton, Thomas, 1728-1807
  Historical journal, 25791, 29283
  Topographical and historical, 27297
Pembroke, N.H. Plan of union, 34319
Penacook Indians, declaration against, 1106?
Pender, Thomas. Divinity, 3083
Pendleton, Edmund, 1721-1803
  Address, 36055
  pres. Virginia convention, 15200
  revisor, 18863
Pendleton, J. List of pensioners, 26393-95, 29801
Penhallow, John. Report of the opinions, 29284
Penhallow, Samuel, 1665-1726. History of the wars, 2796
Penicooke Indians, declaration against, 1106
Penington, Isaac, 1617-1679
  Select pieces, 18081
  extracts from, 15844
Penington, John, 1768-1793
  Chemical and economical, 22757
  Inaugural dissertation, 22758
Penman's repository, 32481
Penn, Ann, attorney for, 10724
Penn, Hannah
  Letter (to Keith), 2797
  Letter of instructions, 2576
Penn, James, 1727-1800. Farmer's daughter, 34320
Penn, John, 1759-1834
  Philadelphia, 15th May, 1783, 21362
  Proclamation, (1764) 9783-84, (1766) 10444, (1768) 11024-26, (1769) 11402, (1771) 12178, (1773) 12922, (1774) 13518-22, (1775) 14365
  acta passed by, 10278, 10600
  address to, 9670
  dedication to, 11850
  governor Delaware, 12748
Penn, Richard, d. 1771
  death, 12030
  dedication to, 8489, 8981, 9239, 9485, 11850
  governor Delaware, 12747
Penn, Thomas
  dedication to, 8489, 8981, 9239, 9485, 11850
  letter (from Bull), 4480
Penn, William, 1644-1718
  Argumentum ad hominem, 14360
  Brief account, 11661
  Charter of privileges, 2690
  Epistle, 405
  Excellent priviledge, 433
  Extract from the writings, 10723
  Forderung der Christenheit, 23669
  Fruits of a father's love, (1727) 2941, (1787) 20617, (1792) 24662
  Fruits of solitude, 24663, 27473
  Gospel-times, 1578
  Governor's speech, 1017
  Key opening, 1922
  Letter (to La Chaise), 438

VOL.	ITEMS	VOL.	ITEMS
1	1-3244	8	22298-25074
2	3245-6623	9	25075-28145
3	6624-9891	10	28146-30832
4	9892-13091	11	30833-33261
5	13092-16176	12	33262-25854
6	16177-19448	13	35855-39162
7	19449-22297		

VOL.	ITEMS	VOL.	ITEMS
1	1-3244	8	22298-25074
2	3245-6623	9	25075-28145
3	6624-9891	10	28146-30832
4	9892-13091	11	30833-33261
5	13092-16176	12	33262-25854
6	16177-19448	13	35855-39162
7	19449-22297		

VOL.	ITEMS	VOL.	ITEMS
1	1-3244	8	22298-25074
2	3245-6623	9	25075-28145
3	6624-9891	10	28146-30832
4	9892-13091	11	30833-33261
5	13092-16176	12	33262-25854
6	16177-19448	13	35855-39162
7	19449-22297		

Petyt, George. Lex parliamentaria, 1850
Peyton, V. J.
Elemens de la langue, 27498
Elements of the English, 24680
Pfeiffer, George
Eulogium, 38240
Inaugural dissertation, 23693
Phaenomena quaedam, 813, 2959
Pharmacopoeia Londinensis, 2114
Pharmacopoeia simpliciorum, 15750, 17108
Phelps, ——, land purchase, 29341
Phelps, Charles, 1715-1789. Vermonters unmasked, 17674
Phelps, M. Controversial letters, 33745
Philadelphia
Account of the baptisms, 14391
Act to incorporate the subscribers, 25989
Acte zur incorporirung, (1782) 17676, (1793) 25994
Additional charter of the college, 7540
Address and petition, 25986
Address from the Philadelphia society, 19193
Address of the committee for improving, 38247
Address of the committee of the city, 16462
Amicable fire company are requested, 15992
Answer to the joint, 36086
Arrangement of the music, 36111
Articles and bye laws, 38248
    of agreement, 34359
    of association of the African, 36095
    of the Friendship fire, 31000
    of the Hibernia fire, 19918
    of the Reliance fire, 19919
    or by-laws for the government of the Associated, 34351
    of by-laws for the government of the Second Philadelphia, 36109
Artikel der Patriotischen, 12525
At a general meeting of the citizens, 16463
At a general meeting of the merchants, 10133
At a meeting at the Philosophical, 13534
    held at the Philosophical, 15018
    of a number, 15019-20
    of the subscribers, 29315
Auction of very select, 38256
By the mayor, aldermen, 30995
By the mayor, recorder, 10132
Bye-laws and regulations for the government, 29317
Bye-laws of the Friendship, 29313
Calculation shewing in what, 34360
Calculation shewing that, 34361
Catalogue of books (Company of printers) 27506, (Friends' library) 29312, (Medical library) 22795, (Union library co.) 10139
Catalogue of the books (Loganian library) 29314, (Medical library) 27510
Catalogus Bibliothecae Loganianae, 8715
Charter, articles, 32678
Charter, constitution, 22794
City of Philadelphia in the state, 38259
Committee appointed to confer, 18135
    appointed to examine, 32675
    appointed to prepare, 38250
    chamber, Dec. 6, 1774, 13538
    chamber, Philadelphia, 15014
    for tarring, 12941
    for the city and liberties, 16464
    for the city of Philadelphia, 14385
    on tarring, 12943
Committee-room, (May 28, 1779) 16465, (May

31, 1779) 16466, (June 10, 1779) 16467, (June 18, 1779) 16468, (June 26, 1779) 16469
Communication from the joint, 34348
Constitution and ordinances, 22791
    and rules, 11416, 23698
    of the Academy, 36093
    of the Ciceronian, 38246
    of the Columbianum, 29311
    of the Company of printers, 27505
    of the Franklin society, 24687
    of the Magdalen, 38249
    of the Society for the attainment, 27513
Constitutional rules, 31003
Constitutions of the Publick, 6405
Copy of a petition, 25988
Declaration and constitution, 32676
Deed of settlement of the Society, 6757
Directions for the inspectors, 24683
Drugs & medicine, 38255
Erste frucht der Teutschen, 10138
Examination and refutation, 4946
Extract of the minutes, 3951
Extracts and remarks, 22796
Facts and observations, 34355
15 boxes, 38254
First Uranian concert, 20646
For the benefit of Miss Storer, 11867
For the benefit of the widows, 15995
For very particular reasons, 15999
Freeholders and other, 13537
From the merchants, 11816
Gentlemen merchants, 15991
Health office, port of Philadelphia, 29304
Illumination; Colonel Tilghman, 17309
In committee, (Dec. 14, 1774) 13539, (July 14, 1779) 16470
In committee chamber, 15013
In committee of inspection, 15011
In council of safety, (Nov. 27, 1776) 15022, (Dec. 3, 1776) 15024
In council of safety, Philadelphia, (Oct. 14, 1776) 15017, (Nov. 14, 1776) 15021, (Dec. 2, 1776) 15023, (Dec. 8, 1776) 15025, (Dec. 13, 1776) 15026, (Dec. 20, 1776) 15027
Independent & constitutional, 16471
Inhabitants of Pennsylvania, 12940
Introductory lessons, 19194, 19920
Journeymen cabinet, 29308
Klagen über den tod, 38260
Last night Mr. Reinagle's benefit, 36101
Laws of the Academy, 36094
List of articles, 29310
List of the sub-committees, 15012
Lob und anbetung, 22797
Minutes of the Philadelphian association, (1769) 11415, (1770) 11821, (1771) 12195, (1773) 12951, (1775) 14393, (1781) 17312
Minutes of the proceedings, 27501
Monday morning, 12944
Mortality; an account of the baptisms, 29309
Number of the inhabitants, 10134
On account of the indisposition, 16006
On Friday next, (the first of May) 16010, (the tenth) 16005, (the twenty-fourth) 16009
On Monday next the thirteenth, 16007
On Monday next the thirtieth, 16004
On Monday the second, 15998
On Monday, (the 9th) 16000, (the 16th of February) 15997, (the 16th day of March) 16001, (the 23d) 16002, (the 26th) 15996
On Wednesday evening, 36102

VOL.	ITEMS	VOL.	ITEMS
1	1-3244	8	22298-25074
2	3245-6623	9	25075-28145
3	6624-9891	10	28146-30832
4	9892-13091	11	30833-33261
5	13092-16176	12	33262-25854
6	16177-19448	13	35855-39162
7	19449-22297		

Philadelphia academy. Prayer for the use, 7093
Philadelphia Baptist association. Minutes, (1798) 34353, 36096, (1800) 38244
Philadelphia cabinet and chairmakers, 27508, 30999
Philadelphia den 19ten May, 10454
Philadelphia directory, (1785) 19385, (1791) 23205, (1793) 25585, (1794) 27089, (1795) 26680, (1796) 31235, (1797) 32868, (1798) 34593, (1799) 36353, (1800) 38549
Philadelphia fire company. Articles, 38252
Philadelphia (galley), at Philadelphia, 15815
Philadelphia gazette
    Brown's gazette extra, 32686
    Very important, 34363
Philadelphia harmony, (1789) 21629, (1796) 29953, (1799) 35083
Philadelphia hospital. Committee appointed, 32680
Philadelphia; in Congress, (May 21, 1776) 15142, (Monday, May 15, 1775) 14560, (Thursday, Sept. 22, 1774) 13702
Philadelphia jest book, 22799
Philadelphia Jockey club, 29638
Philadelphia magazine, (1789) 22068, (1799) 36114
Philadelphia medical society, incorporated, 25996, 38253
Philadelphia militia legion. Legionary orders, 36105-106
Philadelphia; Monday, 12945
    monthly magazine, 34365-66
    pocket companion, (German flute) 27516, (guittar) 27517
    price current, 18729
    reformed, 33464
    register, 36238
Philadelphia society for alleviating the miseries
    At a quarterly meeting, 21388
    On Tuesday, 20644
Philadelphia society for promoting agriculture
    Laws, 21389, 22067
Philadelphia songster, 21628
    spelling book, 26622
    27th tenth month, 14053
    vocabulary, 20398, 28770
    Wednesday, June 2, 22986
    Wednesday evening, 17176
Philadelphiad, 18730
Philadelphian
    Age of error, 31697
    Essays, 35452
    Occasional essays, 38145
    To the freemen, 12946-47
Philadelphian association. Minutes, (1769) 11415, (1770) 11821, (1771) 12195, (1773) 12951, (1775) 14393, (1781) 17312
Philadelphian Baptist association see Philadelphian association; Baptist association, Philadelphia
Philadelphiensis. Manners of the times, 9240
Philadelphische correspondez. Neujahrs verse, 17944
Philadelphisches magazin, 34369
Philadelphos. Letter, 2476
Philadephus. To the public, 11823
Philaeni. Strictures on the landed, 18821
Philagathos. Poem, 25998
Philagathus, dialogue with, 28336
Philalethes
    Christian piety, 10455, 16952
    (tr.) De juri regni, 10249
        see also Hancock, John, 1702-1744; Montfort, Robert; Maule, Thomas, 1645-1724; Williams, Elisha, 1694-1755

Philander Misiatrus. Honour of the gout, 3574, 3690
Philandrianism, 37346
Philanthropic lottery. List of all, 38266
Philanthropic lottery by act, 33861
Philanthropist, or a good twelve, 36694-96
Philanthropist, or a good twenty-five, 36997-98
Philanthropos
    Few observations, 11039
    Letter to the unconverted, 11041
    Negro slavery, 34370
    Serious address, 7765
    To the freeholders, 11040
    Universal peace-maker, 9797
    Valedic(t)ion, 9487
        see also Rhees, Morgan John, 1760-1804
Philaretes. Letters from the dead, 6591
Phileleutheros
    Address, 6758
    No placemen, 14399
Phileluth. Bangor see Foxcroft, Thomas, 1697-1769
Philenia see Morton, Sarah Wentworth Apthorp, 1759-1816
Phileunomos see Sherman, Roger, 1721-1793
Philip, King
    portrait, 12352
    war with, 220, 1800
Philips, A., tr. Distrest mother, 8986
Philipse, Adolph
    defendant, 2940
    justice N.Y., 3846?
    letter to, 3112
Philipse, David, meeting at his house, 13490
Philirenaeus. To the free, 15028
Phillipps, ——, grammarian, 6928, 8728, 10758, 27639-40
Phillips, Catherine Payton, 1727-1794. Memoirs, 34371
Phillips, John, of Charlestown, Mass., father-in-law of C. Mather, 566
Phillips, John, of Philadelpha. Paraphrastical exposition, 680
Phillips, John, of South Carolina
    Appeal to matter of fact, 34372
    Familiar dialogue, 34373
    Narrative, 31007
    Short treatise, 34374
Phillips, John, 1770-1823. Oration, 27520
Phillips, Nathaniel. Almanac see Almanacs (Phillips)
Phillips, Samuel, runaway, 15316
Phillips, Samuel, 1690-1771
    Advice, 3207
    Children well imployed, 4413
    Elegy, 1924
    Gospel doctrine, 10456
    Gospel ministers, 6915
    History of our Lord, 4301
    Living water, 6592
    Necessity, 7094
    Orthodox Christian, 4302
    Political rulers, 6593
    Preaching peace, 7095
    Seasonable advice, 8982
    Serious address, 9488
    Sin of suicide, 10740
    Sinner's refusal, 7096
    Soldiers counselled, 4788
    Three plain, 3091
    Wisdom, 8468
    Word in season, 2944

Speech, 22800
Pinneo, Bezaleel, ordained, 31872
Pintard, John
   (tr.) Decree, 19009
   (tr.) Scheme of a convention, 19330
Pintard, John Marsden. Letters (to Pickering),
  38272
Pinto, Isaac, tr. Prayers, 10343-44
Pious advice, 14637
   Christian, 37600
   cry, 5855
   guide, 24695
   heart-elations, 3080
   man's directions, 3208
   remains, 9610
   soul, 24786, 35412
Piozzi, Hester. Letter (to young gentleman), 34527
Pipon, John, ordained, 37738
Piracy and robbery, 30635
Piscataqua association. Prayer book, 36125
Piscator evangelicus, 727
Pitcher, Nathaniel, d. 1723, poem on, 2579
Pitcherio-threnodia, 2579
Pitkin, Timothy, 1727-1812
   Sermon, 11045, 22801
   wife's death, 12518
Pitkin, William, 1694-1769
   Proclamation, (1766) 10269-70, (1768) 10863-64,
     (1769) 11219
   Their majesties colony, 686
   death, 11943
   dedication to, 10528, 10807, 11128, 11541, 11951,
     12295, 12633, 13088
Pitnam, Thomas. Vision, 38627
Pitt, C. I. Poor blind girl, 34383
Pitt, William, earl of Chatham, 1708-1778
   Rede, 14407
   Speech (Jan. 20, 1775), 14405-406
   Speech (repeal of Stamp act), 10462
   Speech of the statue, 11868
   Speeches, 10463
   anecdotes of, 29846, 29865
   defeated, 13916-25
   letter (from Douglas), 8584-85
   letter (from Lyttelton), 13386-87
   letter (from Massachusetts), 10970
   letters (from Amherst), 8076
   ode to, 29997?
   portrait, 12281
   proposes bill, 14076
   remarks upon, 10985-86
Pitt, William, 1759-1806. Speech, 38273
Pitts, J., speaker Mass. House, 15902
Pity the sorrows, 26006
Pizarro, a tragedy, 35698-701
   in Peru, 37757
   or the Spaniards, 37758
Placket-Hole, Moll, adventures of, 10002
Plagi-scurriliad, 19540
Plain account of Christian, 21961
   account of the ordinance, (1771) 12199, (1793)
     26412, (1798) 34385
   address, 9261
   and brief, 4595
      concise grammar, 39136
      concise table, 36146
      concise view, 36736
      earnest, 11980
      easy catechisms, 23961, 24992
      easy introduction, 12704
      faithful narrative, 9537

   faithful testimony, 9906
   familiar, 1736
   full, 10461, 31012
   modern, 26482
   serious address, (1756) 7647, (1764) 9644,
     (1765) 10287, (1767) 10604., (1777)
     15287, (1790) 22465, (1791) 23328-29,
     (1795) 28573, (1798) 33644, (1799) 35414,
     (1800) 37329
   attempt, 37661
   case stated, 453
   catechism, 1883
   concise, practical, 14134, 14814
   dealer, 9875-78
Plain-dealing, Thomas. Dialogue, 4065
Plain dealing, or the proud, 6497
   discourse for little, 10142
     on vain, 2302
     shewing, (1712) 1568, (1713) 1634, (1721)
      2257
Plain English. To the inhabitants, 13658
Plain facts, 17437
   instructions, 8367
   narrative of the proceedings of the reverend,
     5281, 6063
     of the proceedings which, 5920
     of the uncommon, 8557-58
   path to Christian, (1772) 12530, (1774) 13145,
     (1780) 16953
   path-way, 21620
   planter, 21397
   political, 31645-46
Plain politician. Honesty shewed, 19716
Plain psalmody, 38276
   rational essay, 32411
   reasons for dissenting, 2721
   reasons why, 17873
   road, 11620
   sense, 36127
   sermon, 8984
   short catechism, 514
   short, comprehensive, 34486
Plain singular man. Scripture warning, 34522
Plain spelling book, 39137
Plain truth. To the independent, 24859
Plain-truth, Tom. To the freemen, 22071
Plain truth, addressed to the inhabitants, 15088-89
   truth, addressed to the people, 35723
   truth, or serious, 5948-49
   truths in few words, 11046
   truths of the gospel, 7879
Plainness and innocent, 17472, 25158
Plaisted, John, daughter's death, 1824
Plan de vente, 27527
   for a school, 22361
   for conducting the hospital, 17040
     the inspector's department, 17041
     the quartermaster-general's department,
      17042
   for correspondence, 38277
   for encouraging, 25355

VOL.	ITEMS	VOL.	ITEMS
1	1-3244	8	22298-25074
2	3245-6623	9	25075-28145
3	6624-9891	10	28146-30832
4	9892-13091	11	30833-33261
5	13092-16176	12	33262-25854
6	16177-19448	13	35855-39162
7	19449-22297		

for establishing a general, 33944
for establishing a national, 17395
for liquidating, 16954
for the conduct, 33601
    establishment of a company, 32682
    establishment of public, 19974
    general arrangement, 20076, 22987-88
    maintenance, 2580
    more effectual, 38278
    payment, 20653-54
more effectual, 38279
of a proposed, 13866
    report, 19163
    review, 30017
    society, 12406
of an African ship's, 21807
of an American, 14790-91
of association of the Asylum, 28215
    of the North American, 29220
    of the Pennsylvania land co., 32660
    of the Pennsylvania property co., 29296,
      32661
    of the territorial, 29550
of Boston, 35005
of consocation, 39121
of constitution, 28695
of exercise for the militia of Massachusetts,
  11121, 12290
    for the militia of the colony, 12623-24
    for the militia of the province, 12622,
      13777
of Philadelphia, 27679
of Sierra Leone, 29513
of the battle, 7390
    book auction, 23702
    city and environs, 15593
    city and fortress, 5783
    city intended, 24471
    city of New York, 3438, 30504
    city of Philadelphia, (1754) 7209, (1796)
      30505, 32253
    city of Washington (Ellicott), 24296,
      27209
    city of Washington (Freeman), 30452
    Female humane, 36884
    foedereal constitution, 20806
    improved part, 9267
    invasion, 33753
    New York, 24612
    Pennsylvania society, 20637
    Philadelphia dispensary, 19917
    plantation, 31158
    review, 30015
    town, (Baltimore) 24323, 26984, (Boston)
      30164, (Erie) 30805
of union, 34319
to render, 37363
wherein the power, 21092, 21440
with proposals, 32245
Plant, Thomas. Joyful news, 10464-65
Planter see Chandler, Samuel
Plat of the seven, 30918
Platform of church discipline, (1649) 25, (1761)
  159, (1680) 282, (1701) 969, (1711) 1496, (1713)
  1599, (1717) 1869, (1731) 3400-401, (1749) 6295,
  (1757) 7866, (1772) 12625-26
Platt, Jonas
  To the people, 38281
  reply to, 38461, 37528
Platt, Zephaniah, 1735-1807, reports on supplies,
  19308

Plattes, Gabriel
  Discovery of subterranean, (1784) 18732, (1792)
    24697, (1796) 31174
  Discovery of subterraneous, 27328
Playbill of Hamlet, 20217
    Isabella, 19474
    Richard III, 31002
    Rickett's circus, 27625
    The dramatist, 29316
    The jealous wife, 19491
    the Old American, 20943
    The rivals, 19490
    The wonder, 19492
Playfair, William, 1759-1823. History of Jacobinsm,
  31016
Plays and poems (Shakespeare), 29496, 31180
Plea and answer, 11765
  before the ecclesiastical, 17561
  before the venerable, 16805-806
  for God, 2088
  for literature, 25162, 26642
  for peace, 34312
  for pure, 5038
  for the life, 353
    ministers, 1276, 2529
    nonconformists, 9374, 37309
    poor and distressed, 7296
    poor soldiers, 23060-61
    righteousness, 1193
  for truth, 4414
  in vindication, 13691-92
  of patriotism, 29260
  of the colonies, 15713
  of the innocent, 612
Pleasant art, 7097
Pleasant history, 26007
Pleasants, Mrs. ———. Story book, 34386
Pleasants, John, son's case, 38963
Pleasants, Robert, case of, 38963
Pleasants, Samuel. Following remonstrance, 15498
Pleasing history of Pamela, 26088
  incitements, 38282
  instructions, 32056
  instructor, 29518
  songster, 29328
Pleasure and advantages of church, 32351
Pleasures and advantages of friendly, 24768
  of a country, 26242
  of early piety, 27242
  of hope, 37087-92
  of imagination, 26544, 28155
  of memory, 29426, 38418
  of religion, 3120
  of true piety, 1828
  peculiar, 10809
Plebeian
  Answer to the citizen's address, 11159
  see also Smith, Melancthon, 1724-1798
Pleyel, Ignaz Joseph, 1757-1831
  Henry's cottage maid, 31017
  Twelve duets, 27528
  selections from, 31182, 34516
Plot, by way of a burlesk, 9799
Plot discovered, 14408
Ploughjogger, Richard. Brief inquiry, 8238
Plowden, Charles, 1743-1821. Short account, 23703
Plowden, Francis Peter, 1749-1829. Short history,
  27529
Plower, ———, sheriff in London, 14164
Plowman's complaint, 10570
Plumb pudding, 35272-73

Plumer, Jonathan, Jr. see Plummer, Jonathan, Jr.
Plumer, William, speaker NH House, 24587
Plummer, Jonathan, Jr.
  Address, 24698
  Awful malignant, 31018
  Declaration of war, 26010
  Dying confession, 29329
  Elegy, 26008
  Funeral dirge, 26009
  Newburyport, July 23, 1794, 27530
  Sketch of the history, 29330
  To Sir Timothy, 32695
  To the inhabitants, 26011
Plumptre, Anne
  Antoinette Percival, 38283
  (tr.) Force of calumny, 37751
  (tr.) Virgin of the sun, 37763-64
  (tr.) Widow, 37765
Plumstead, Clement, d. 1745, death, 5702
Plumstead, W., election, 7929
Plymouth, Mass. Festival of the sons, 38284
Plymouth colony
  Address presented, 543
  Book of the general laws, 171, 397
  Declaration, 12885
  Patent, 6761
  Remarks on the plan, 7098
Pocket Bible, 24101
  book for the German flute, 16014
    for the guitar, 16015
    for the violin, 16016
  commentary, 8369
  companion, 34516
  gazetteer, 29331
  hymn book, (1786) 20271?, (1788) 21254,
    (1790) 22667, (1791) 23566-67, (1792) 24545,
    (1793) 25809-810, (1794) 27315-16, (1795)
    29073-74, (1796) 30788, (1797) 32474, (1798)
    34104, (1800) 38285
  map of the state, 22804
  memorandum, 18734
  miscellany, 34387
Pocock, Sir George, Havana taken by, 9091, 9933
Pöllnitz, F. C. H. B. Essay on agriculture, 22805
Poem addressed to a young, 11688
  addressed to the armies, 16801
  commemorative, 25998
  containing, 35422
  dedicated, 319
  delivered at the commencement, 32058
  delivered in the chapel, 34659
  in seven parts, 13549
  in two cantos, 35479
  in two letters, 28587-88, 35421
  occasioned by a funeral essay, 7298
    by hearing, 13548
    by the death, (Alden) 426, (Law) 6651
    by the spreading, 5039
  on death, 26012
  on divine, 13172
  on Elijah's translation, 1295
  on industry, 27145, 31173
  on reading President, 30579
  on reading the President's, 30580
  on religious, 29332
  on the bloody, 14426
    day of judgment, 7141
    death, (Barns) 11422, (Brown) 27531,
      (George I) 2846, (Howe) 19429, (Mont-
      gomery) 17896, (Washington) 37851
    destruction, 22788

execution, (Frost) 26013, (Shaw) 12200
Fourth of July, 34500
happiness of America, (1786) 19723,
  (1788) 21161, (1790) 22579
last day, (1753) 7140-41, (1777) 15714,
  (1793) 26521, (1795) 29937
last distress, 15061
President's, 37644
prospects, 20521, 23561
rebuke, 8595
rise and progress, 12051, 12284
rising glory, 12398, 22514
on visiting, 7122
or an hymn, 21398
presented, 3004, 3092
sacred to the memory, (Conant) 8323, (Washington) 36806, (Willard) 7988, (Wolfe) 8471
spoken at the public, 17090
spoken in the chapel, 18608
to the blessed memory, 780
upon the death, 4187
  much honoured, 1673
  present, 14403
which the committee, 12301, 18899
wrote by a clergyman, 12251
Poems, (Arnold) 31753, (Arouet) 19747, (Cowper)
  24229, (Freneau) 19658, (Goldsmith) 23416,
  37530, (Humphreys) 21897, 28869, (Hurdis)
  30613, (Jerningham) 21905, (Low) 37856, (Ossian) 22633, (Southey) 36345
Poems and compositions, 34159
  chiefly in the Scottish, 20991-92, 33477
  chiefly occasional, 37194
  dramatic and miscellaneous, 23035
Poems; first on a soul, 14409
Poems occasioned, 15754-56
  on divers subjects, 7855, 8093
  on several occasions, (Adams) 5527, 6275,
    (Beattie) 20224, (Belknap) 18343, (Byles)
    5355, (Evans) 12386, (Freneau) 21098, (gen-
    tleman of Virginia) 4066, (Rose) 4593,
    (Smith) 19994, (Swanwick) 32898
  on several occurrencies, 16217-19
  on several subjects, (Anketell) 28202, (Duck)
    3531, 25421
  on the most, 22928
  on the rising glory, 17737
  on various subjects, (Crawford) 18426, (Sear-
    son) 32817, (Wheatley) 19913, 25983, (a
    youth) 17314
Poems; philosophic solitude, 22621
Poems; the conflagration, 7376
Poems upon several occasions, (anon.) 16479,
  (Pomfret) 6762, 19195, 23705, 24700, 27532
  upon several sermons, 12031
  written at Coosahatchie, 35387
  written between the years, 28712
Poetic essays, 31949
Poetic miscellany, 33856, 34388
Poetical and miscellaneous works, 33669
  description of song birds, 21399

VOL.	ITEMS	VOL.	ITEMS
1	1-3244	8	22298-25074
2	3245-6623	9	25075-28145
3	6624-9891	10	28146-30832
4	9892-13091	11	30833-33261
5	13092-16176	12	33262-25854
6	16177-19448	13	35855-39162
7	19449-22297		

planter's physician, 3843-44
Poor Richard. Father Abraham's speech, 8131
Poor Richard; sung at the principal, 25265
    soldier, (1787) 20606-608, (1790) 22748, (1794)
      26558, 27445
    Tom Bowling, 26879
    Vulcan, 28567
Pope, Alexander, 1688-1744
    Eloisa to Abelard, 13787
    Essay on man, (1747) 6055, (1748) 6224, (1760)
      8718, (1778) 16018, (1780) 16955-56, (1785)
      19197, (1786) 19931, (1787) 20657, (1789) 22075,
      (1790) 22809-810, (1791) 23707, (1792) 24702-
      703, (1793) 26017-18, (1794) 27535, (1795)
      29337-39, (1796) 31023-26, (1797) 32701-702,
      (1798) 34398, (1800) 38299-300
    (tr.) Iliad, 28852
    Journal of a gaming, 8265
    Messiah, 8242
    Ode, 21495
    Select collection, 31027
    anecdotes of, 29846, 29865
    excerpts from, 23246, 26014, 29945, 34964
Pope, Amos, 1771-1837. Almanac see **Almanacs**
    (Pope)
Pope, John, of Boston. Cancers, 26021
Pope, John, of Providence. Certificates of cures,
    38342
Pope, John, 1770-1845
    To the citizens, 38301
    Tour through the southern, 24705
Pope, Joseph, 1745-1826. Loss of Christian, 32703
Pope, Nathaniel, d. 1809. Speech, 38302
Popish cruelty, 7100
    hierarchy, 33462
    idolatry, 10068
Popkin, John Snelling, 1771-1852, ed. Grammar,
    37085
Poplicola
    To the worthy, 12955-57
    answered, 13040, 13042
Porcupine, Peter
    confession, 32353-56
    see also **Cobbett, William, 1762-1835**
Porcupine, a print, 30820
Porcupine, alias the hedgehog, 18774
Porcupine's Gazette. Carrier of Porcupine's, 34400
Porcupine's Political censor, (1796) 30226-28,
    30233, (1797) 31946-48
Porcupine's works, 30233, 31948
Porcupiniad, 35275-77
Porny, Marc Antoine see **Pyron de Martre, An-**
    toine
Port-Royal, messieurs de. Royal convert, (1793)
    26022, (1794) 27537, (1796) 31029
Porter, Rev. ——, of Bridgewater, remarks on,
    6472
Porter, Ann, assaulted, 23445
Porter, Augustus, 1769-1864. Map, 29341
Porter, David, ed. The shipwreck, 30399
Porter, David, 1761-1851
    On the endless, 32820
    Two discourses, 38304
Porter, Eliphalet, 1758-1833
    Discourse, (1794) 29342, (1798) 34401
    Eulogy, 38305
    Sermon, (1783) 18736, (1799) 36142
Porter, Ethel, d. 1797, death, 32723
Porter, Huntington, 1755-1844
    Discourse, 27538
    Funeral discourse, 38306

wife's death, 26708
Porter, John, ed. Journal of the transactions,
    23086
Porter, John, 1716-1802
    Absurdity, 6595
    Evangelical plan, 11421
    Superlative love, 6225
    Vindication, 6764
    remarks on, 6472?, 6646
Porter, Joseph, d. 1794, murdered, 26534, 31995
Porter, Nathaniel, 1745-1837
    Discourse, 38307
    Friendly monitor, 34402
    Oration, 23709
Porter, Samuel, 1709-1758. Sermon, (1747) 6226,
    (1755) 7544
Porter, Samuel, 1760-1825. Discourse, 26023
Porter, Sarah. Royal penitent, 23710, 26024
Porter, Susannah, d. 1794, death, 26708, 27538
Porterfield, James, criticism of, 6611
Porteus, Beilby, 1731-1808
    Death, (1773) 12958-59, (1780) 16957, (1793)
      25149, (1797) 31953
    Life of Archbishop Secker, 13191-92
    Review of the life, 12960
    Summary of the principal, 38308
Porteus, John, signs capitulation, 14540
Portia. Polite lady, 34389
Portius. O Liberty, 3595
Portlack, Nathaniel. Description of the natives,
    28989
Portland, ——, duke of
    letter (from Burke), 31894
    protests, 14090
Portland
    Address of the Portland convention, 29343
    Address to the people, 27539
    Laws of the Marine society, 34403
Portrait; behold, 11048
Portsmouth
    By-laws of the town, 29344
    Ça ira, 29345
    Resolves of a meeting, 12961
    State of Newhampshire, 38309
    Valuable medicines, 38310
Portsmouth association. Minutes, (1791-93) 26025-
    27
Portsmouth disputation, 1635
Portsmouth, in New Hampshire, 8052
Portsmouth, N. H., Dec. 27, 1733, 3715
Posie out of Mr. Dod's, 10884
Possibility of God's, 330
Post, Jotham. Inaugural dissertation, 26028
Post-days at Boston, 28323
Post office law, 34904, 38801
Post-office, Philadelphia, 34358
Posthumous pieces of the late, 26980
    pieces of the reverend, 25489
    publication, 36366
    works, 25208
Postscript, being a short, 2333

VOL.	ITEMS	VOL.	ITEMS
1	1-3244	8	22298-25074
2	3245-6623	9	25075-28145
3	6624-9891	10	28146-30832
4	9892-13091	11	30833-33261
5	13092-16176	12	33262-25854
6	16177-19448	13	35855-39162
7	19449-22297		

VOL.	ITEMS	VOL.	ITEMS
1	1-3244	8	22298-25074
2	3245-6623	9	25075-28145
3	6624-9891	10	28146-30832
4	9892-13091	11	30833-33261
5	13092-16176	12	33262-25854
6	16177-19448	13	35855-39162
7	19449-22297		

answer to, 3997
hand of fellowship, 4111
Prescott, Robert, 1725-1816. Letter from a veteran, 13554
Presence of Christ, 1999
    of God, 8586
    of the great God, 5737
Present for a servant-maid, 5964
    for an apprentice, (1747) 5904, (1749) 6282,
        (1774) 13133, (1788) 20953, (1794) 26619,
        (1798) 33375, (1800) 36895
    for children, 9246
    for misses, 27548
    for teeming women, 708
    melancholy, 2067
    method, 12028
    necessary defensive, 13978
    of summer-fruit, 1625
    political state, 14158
    scope, 3729
    situation of affairs, 14412
    situation of other, 29113
    state of America, 22080
        Ireland, 32204
        learning, 27331
        literature, 37337
        medical learning, 32488
        New-England, 495, 538
        North America, 7434
        the colony, 7423
        the controversy, 17452
        the New-English, 492
    thoughts, 11044
    times, 35364
    to children, 23715
    to the unprejudiced, 29350
    way, 6328
Presented to the House, (Jan. 4, 1796) 31447, (Jan. 19, 1796) 31459
Preservation, or the hovel, 39110
Preservative against the doctrine, 11826
    from damnable errors, 3279
    from the sins, (1774) 5509, (1745) 5707, (1748)
        6264, (1755) 7589, (1765) 10201, (1789)
        22247
President and commander-in-chief, 4054
President II, 31042-43
President Washington's resignation, 31537, 38996
President's address to the people, 31526, 31531, 31542-44, 31546-48
    answer, 34836
    march, (1795) 29609, (1796) 31044, 31554,
        (1798) 33901-902
    message on the treaty, 31415-16
    message: Philadelphia, 31420
    speech; American Congress, 31427
    speech; on Saturday, 38802
    speech; Providence, 34833
    speech to both, 34835
    speech to the Congress, 31545
Preston, Capt. ——, troops commanded by, 12094
Preston, Charles, proposes capitulation, 14541
Preston, Francis
    Address, 31045
    letter (from Smyth), 29538, 31215
    letters (from Smyth), 32855
Preston, John B., ordained, 34625
Preston, Samuel. Charge, 38321
Preston, William, 1753-1807
    Death of Louis, 27549

Louis the Sixteenth, 27550
Presumer detected, 3967, 4612
Pretended antidote, 515
Pretended plain narrative, 6170
Pretensions of Thomas Jefferson, 31212-13, 32853
Pretty book, 9247
    New-Year's gift, 19995, 31218
    plaything, (1775) 14413, (1785) 19200, (1786) 19936
    story, 13338-40
Prevailing wickedness, 7680
Prevost, Augustin
    Proclamation, 16290
    attacks Charleston, 19418
Prey taken, 2696
Price, Capt. ——, sermon preached before, 13828
Price, Dr. ——, letter (from Turgot), 31689-91
Price, Elisabeth, d. 1732, death, 3518
Price, Isaac. Jersey man's common, 34411
Price, Jonathan
    Chart of the sea coasts, 31046
    Description of Occacock, 29351
    Map of the state, 31047
Price, Laurence, 1628-1680. Key to open, 20659
Price, Nathaniel. Trial, 32712
Price, Richard, 1723-1791
    Additional observations, 16022
    Discourse, 22814
    General introduction, 16023-24
    Observations on the importance, (1784) 18739, (1785) 19201-204, (1786) 19937
    Observations on the nature, 15030-34
    Sermons, 21404, 27551
    reply to, 19804, 27328
Price, Roger, 1696-1762
    Funeral sermon, 3716
    Sermon, 4305
Price act, (Ipswich) 15375, (Marblehead) 15386, (Massachusetts) 15406, (Newbury, Mass.) 15484, (Salem) 15590, (Wenham) 15704
Price-book, 24064
Prices current, (Rogers & Barker) 29427, (Somerville & Noble) 14464
Prichard, ——, excerpts from poetry, 23246, 31959
Prichard, William
    Auction room, 20663-64
    Catalogue of a collection, 20661
        of a gentleman's, 22081
        of a large, 21406
        of a sale, 22815
        of a scarce, 19205
        of a very valuable, 18740
        of ancient and modern, 20660, 21405
        of books by auction, 19938
        of the circulating, 18143
        of two extensive, 20662
    Literature, 24712
Prichard's auction room; December 8th, 20663
Prichard's auction room, next door, 20664
Pride, Kitty, history of, 35622
Pride humbled, 5670
Prideaux, Humphrey, 1648-1724
    History of the life, 31048
    True nature, 34412
Priest, ——. Twelve duets, 27528
Priestcraft defended, (1769) 11320-21, (1770) 11711, (1771) 12104-105, (1791) 23526, (1792) 24492, (1793) 25744
Priestley, Joseph, 1733-1804

Address to Protestant, 13555-57
Address to the Unitarian, 32713
Answer to Dr. Blackstone, 12328, 13154
Appeal to the serious, 18741, 27552
Case of poor, 32714
Comparison of the institutions, 36160
Considerations, 31049
Continuation of the letters, 27558, 29352
Description of a new, 24713
Discourses on the evidence, 29353
Discourses relating, 31050-51, 32715
Dr. Priestley having continued, 32716
Extracts from a catechism, 34413
Extracts from Doctor Priestley, 19206, 31052
Familiar illustration, 27553
General view, 27554, 31053
History of the corruptions, 32717
Letters (to Burke), 23716
Letters (to inhabitants of Northumberland),
    36161-62, 38322
Letters (to Jews), 27555
Letters (to philosophers), (1793) 26035, (1794)
    27556-57
Letters (to philosophical unbeliever), 29354
Letters (to Volney), 32718
Miscellaneous observations, 31054
Observations on the doctrine, 32719
Observations on the increase, 29355, 32721
Outline of the evidences, 32722
Reflexions, 32720
Remarks on some paragraphs, (1772) 12328,
    (1773) 12684, (1774) 13154
Two sermons, 27559
Unitarianism, 31055
arrival in New York, 28439-40
defended, 28290, 29665
emigration, 30217-18, 30234, 31948, 33528
letters (from Webster), 39056
letters to, 34606
observations on, 26777-78, 32732
remarks on, 31625, 32412
reply to, 20614, 25031, 28203, 33140
trial, 18794
Priestley, Timothy, 1734-1814
    Christian's looking-glass, 26036, 27560-61
    Family exercises, 29356
Priests lips, 8617
Prima morum, 15035
Primative physic, 21589
Prime, Benjamin Young, 1733-1791
    Columbia's glory, 23717
    Excellent new song, 11429
Prime, Ebenezer, 1700-1779
    Importance of the divine, 8473
    Nature of ordination, 7371
    Sermon, 5480
    Two ordination sermons, 8244
Primer (Church of England), (1746) 5768, (1749)
    6314, (1786) 19624
Primer (Franklin, printer), 9802, 10147
Primer (Indian), 36, 70
Primer (Manson), 23532-33
Primer, adorned, 16480
Primer for the colony, 1776
Primitive baptism, 18474
    Christianity, 18081
    physic(k), (1764) 9867, (1769) 11524, (1770)
        11932, (1773) 13073, (1788) 21588-89, (1789)
        22265, (1791) 23977, (1793) 26482, (1795)
        29892

religion, 505
Primrose's deck, 27562, 29357
Prince of Orange see **William III**
Prince, Deborah, 1724?-1744
    Dying exercises, 22082
    death, 5481
Prince, Ebenezer, 1700-1779. Sermon, 5480?
Prince, John, 1751-1836
    Discourse, 34414-16
    Part of a discourse, 38323
    hand of fellowship, 17995
    ordained, 17073
Prince, Joseph, d. 1791, death, 23584
Prince, Nathan, 1698-1748
    Answer to Lesley, 2581
    Constitutions and government, 5041-42
    Essay to solve, 3830
Prince, Samuel, d. 1728, death, 3095
Prince, Thomas, 1687-1758
    Abstract of the author's life, 5214-15
    Account of a strange, 2068
    Annals of New England, 7301, 7546-47
    Be followers, 7548
    Case of Heman, 7769
    Character of Caleb, 7770
    Christ abolishing, 4067
    Chronological history, 4068
    Civil rulers, 3093
    Conclusion to the whole, 8285
    Departure of Elijah, 3094
    Dying prayer, 3596
    Earthquakes, 2945-46, 7549
    Extract of a sermon, 13558, 15036
    Extraordinary events, 5681, 6057
    Faithful servant, 3597
    Fulness of life, 6228
    Funeral sermon, 4306
    God brings, 1925
    God destroyeth, 6766
    Grave and death, 3095
    Great and solemn, 2256
    Improvement of the doctrine, 7550
    Morning health, 2947-48
    Natural and moral, 6408, 6596
    People of New England, 3343
    Pious cry, 5855
    Postscript, 7330
    Precious in the sight, 3955
    (ed.) Psalms, hymns, 8082, 12678
    Salvation, 5856
    Sermon, (1718) 1996, (1727) 2949, (1730) 3344,
        (1746) 5857
    Sovereign God, 5481
    Vade mecum, 3470, 3598
    Young Abel, 3599
    achieves publication of Willard's work, 2828
    answered, 7820
    appendix by, 13081, 13773, 15221, 26485, 29893
    daughter's meditations, 22082
    death, 8257

VOL.	ITEMS	VOL.	ITEMS
1	1-3244	8	22298-25074
2	3245-6623	9	25075-28145
3	6624-9891	10	28146-30832
4	9892-13091	11	30833-33261
5	13092-16176	12	33262-25854
6	16177-19448	13	35855-39162
7	19449-22297		

VOL.	ITEMS	VOL.	ITEMS
1	1-3244	8	22298-25074
2	3245-6623	9	25075-28145
3	6624-9891	10	28146-30832
4	9892-13091	11	30833-33261
5	13092-16176	12	33262-25854
6	16177-19448	13	35855-39162
7	19449-22297		

olic Christian) 13142, (Colles) 21740, (Cullen) 13143, (Gentlemen and ladies . . .
military closet) 8475, (Gregory) 13830, (Hebrew grammar) 3798, (History of the publick life) 8763, (Lee papers) 19029, (Leland)
12669, (Lyman) 36169, (Lyons) 22627, (Martel) 30741, (Maxcy) 23560, (Morse) 30828,
(Pennsylvania chronicle) 10319 (Psalterium) 1904, (public laws) 21867, (W. Smith)
22150, (Trowel) 10519, (Tufts) 8052
  for publishing a large, 22924
        a tri-weekly, 27083
     by subscription, (Benyowsky) 36170,
        (Campbell) 33488, (Trumbull) 31318
  for reprinting, (Ferguson) 11983, (Hume)
        11984
  for securing, 7767
  for the preservation, 1093
  for the speedy, 18960
  for traffick, 1942
  made by Isaac Collins, 18961
  made by the president, 689
  of some things, 3553, 13336
  offered, 3717
  relating, 6321
  to amend, 17679
  to prevent, 7551
  touching, 1647
Proposed appendix, 15825
  ordinance, 14992
  plan, 14993
Propositions concerning, 68
  made by the Five, 819
  made by the sachems, 545
  respecting the coinage, 19328, 23906
Proprietor of lands on the Scioto. Address, 22298
Proprietors of the locks and canals
  Act incorporating, 24714
  By-laws, 24715
  To the inhabitants, 27567
Propriety of singing, 13395
Prosody made easy, 19867
Prospect before us, 37083-84
  from the Congress gallery, 30229-30, 31948
  Hill, 14414
  of death, 28978
  of exterminating, 39022
  of peace, a poetical, 15729, 20952
  of peace; from the New York, 17967
  of Philadelphia, 28845, 30571
  of the city, 5066
  of the times, 13334
Prospective plan, 7363
Prospects on the war, 27465
Prospectus; c'est appeller, 28491
  of a lottery, 3045
  of a plan, 35626
  of a series, 31237
  of explanatory, 3776
  of The country, 33400
  of The nightingale, 30907
Protesilaus, character of, 3784
Protest against popery, 5615
  entered into, 14090
  of divers, 15016
  of the Lords, 14091
Protestant Episcopal church
  At a convention, 18744
  Body now assembled, 18745
  Book of common prayer, (1785) 19940, (1790)
    22821, (1791) 23721, (1793) 26042-43, (1794)

27575-76, 27578, (1795) 29362-63, (1797) 32727,
    (1798) 34420, (1799) 36175, (1800) 38334-37
  Catechism, (1792) 24721, (1795) 29366, (1797)
    32728, (1798) 33519, (1799) 36176, (1800) 38338
  Constitution, (1791) 23722, (1794) 27579, (1800)
    38332
  Form and manner of making, 26044
  Journal of a convention, (1785) 19209, (1786)
    19941-42, (1789) 22084
  Journal of the proceedings, (1789) 22822, (1792)
    24722, (1795) 29364, (1799) 36177
  Morning and evening prayer, 29365
  Selections from the Book, 26045
  To the members, 26046
Protestant Episcopal church. Carolinas
  Pastoral letter, 22820
Protestant Episcopal church. Connecticut
  Address, 19207
  Journal of conventions, 29358
Protestant Episcopal church. Delaware
  Journal of the proceedings, (1791) 23718, (1792)
    24716
Protestant Episcopal church. Maryland
  Abstract of the proceedings, 32724
  Address, 18742
  Convention of the Protestant, 27569
  Journal of a convention, 36171, 38331
  Journal of the proceedings, (1791) 23719, (1792)
    24717, (1793) 26039, (1794) 27568
Protestant Episcopal church. Massachusetts
  At a convention, 22818
  Journal of the proceedings, 24718
Protestant Episcopal church. New Jersey
  Proceedings of a convention, (1791) 23720, (1792)
    24719, 26040, (1793) 26041, (1794) 27570, (1796)
    31057, (1797) 32725, (1798) 34419, (1799) 36172,
    (1800) 38333
  Proceedings of a special convention, 36173
  Proceedings of the convention, (1787) 20666,
    (1788) 21408, (1795) 29359
Protestant Episcopal church. New York
  Journal of the convention, (1787-91) 24720
  Journal of the proceedings, (1792) 27571-73,
    (1796) 31058, (1797) 32726
  Proceedings of the convention, 20667
Protestant Episcopal church. Pennsylvania
  A.B.C. with the catechism, 21409
  A.B.C. with the Church of England, 19208
  At a meeting, 18743
  Journal of the fifteenth convention, 36174
  Journal of the meetings, 22819
  Journals of five conventions, (1791-95) 29360
  Minutes of the proceedings, 27574
Protestant Episcopal church. South Carolina
  Rules of the Society, 21410
Protestant Episcopal church. Vermont
  True copy of the proceedings, 29361
Protestant Episcopal church. Virginia
  Journal of a convention, 36178
Protestant Episcopal church catechism, 32728
Protestant tutor, 387
Protestant's danger, 7552
Protestant's solution, 5858
Protestation (Campbell), 3638
Protestation gegen, 9668, 9803
  of the members, 5043
  presented, 4704, 4932
  shewing, 4092
Protestations des colons, 27665
Proteus ecclesiasticus, 1144
Proud, Joseph. Hymns and spiritual songs, 24599
Proud, Robert, 1728-1813. History of Pennsylvania,

VOL.	ITEMS	VOL.	ITEMS
1	1-3244	8	22298-25074
2	3245-6623	9	25075-28145
3	6624-9891	10	28146-30832
4	9892-13091	11	30833-33261
5	13092-16176	12	33262-25854
6	16177-19448	13	35855-39162
7	19449-22297		

Q

Quaedam ex colloquiis, 21771
Quaestiones discutiendae, 443
Quaestiones duae, 140
Quaestiones in philosophia see under college, e.g.
   Harvard college. Quaestiones . . .
Quaestiones pro modulo see under college, e.g.
   Yale college. Quaestiones . . .
Quaker, a comic opera, (1794) 26558, 26880, 27449
Quaker in politics. Maxims, 36162
Quaker of Rhode Island see Wilkinson, Edward,
   1727-1809
Quaker unmask'd, 9646-47
Quaker vindicated, 9805
Quakerism a judicial, 3489
Quakers assisting, 9806-807
Quakers grace, 10150
Qualifications and duties, 28223
   characters, 7409
   commission, 23220
   of rulers, 30112
Quantity of books, 38257
Quarle, Francis, poems by, 447
Quarll, Philip, adventures of, 28297-98, 31822-23,
   35203, 36187
Quashy, 32507, 34141
Quasson, Joseph, d. 1726, executed, 2782
Queen's rangers, 15837
Queries addressed, 16331
   concerning, 24834
   humbly offered, 6597
   respecting, 28257
   selected, 31845
   to the voters, 22087
   to the Whigs, 16482
Querist. Queries to the Whigs, 16482
Querist, or a letter, 7228
Querist; to the freeholders, 11431-32
Querists, (1740) 4586-88, (1741) 4791-92, (1754)
   7302
Querno, Camillo see Boucher, Jonathan, 1738-1804

Question answered, 18204
   are we obliged, 3209
   whether God is not, 2479
   whether God wills, 26266
Quevedo de Alcala see Salas Barbadillo, Alonso
   Jerónimo, 1580-1635
Quick, John, 1636-1706. Young man's claim, (1700)
   949, (1728) 3097, (1741) 4793, (1746) 5859
Quickened soul, 2141
Quickening word, 152
Quicksilver, James see Puglia, Santiago Felipe
Quimby, Darius, d. 1791?, murdered, 23814-15,
   24836-38, 27767, 32899
Quinby, Josiah
   Correspondence, 3718
   Short history, 4589
Quince, Peter see Story, Isaac, 1774-1803
Quincy, ——, treason of, 13840
Quincy, Edmund, 1681-1738
   daughter's death, 738
   death, 4251
Quincy, Edmund, 1703-1788, Treatise, 10151
Quincy, Edmund, 1733?-1768, elegy on, 10855
Quincy, Josiah, 1744-1775
   Observations on the act, 13561-62
   treason of, 13840?
Quincy, Josiah, 1772-1864. Oration, 34429-31
Quincy, Samuel. Twenty sermons, 6598
Quinney, John, tr. Assembly's catechism, 29879

VOL.	ITEMS	VOL.	ITEMS
1	1-3244	8	22298-25074
2	3245-6623	9	25075-28145
3	6624-9891	10	28146-30832
4	9892-13091	11	30833-33261
5	13092-16176	12	33262-25854
6	16177-19448	13	35855-39162
7	19449-22297		

R

Randolph, Peyton, 1721-1775
  Letter (to a gentleman), 8476
  letter (from Gage), 13738, 13741
  letters (from Grotius), 14094
Ranger (ship), in Portsmouth, 15648
Rankin, Adam, 1755-1827
  Reply to a narrative, 27598
  trial, 27545
Ranlet, Henry
  Complete New Hampshire register, 31073
  New Hampshire register, 29386
  Youth's instructor, 24726, 27599
Rape of Bethesda, 24436
Raphael, 1905
Rare jewel, 3399, 4907
Raspe, Rudolf Erich, 1737-1794. Gulliver revived,
  (1787) 20670-72, (1792) 24727, (1795) 29387,
  (1797) 32740
Rasselas, 10939, 28904
Rastel, Philippe François de. Invitation serieuse,
  12421
Ratcliffe, Ann see **Radcliffe, Anne Ward, 1764-1822**
Rates of porterage, 13563
  of toll; the directors, 33207
  of toll to be received, 33208
Rathbun, Daniel. Letter (to Whittacor), 19212
Rathbun, Reuben. Reasons offered, 38359
Rathbun, Valentine, b. 1723
  Account of the matter, 17318
  Brief account, 17681
  Some brief hints, (1781) 17319-21, (1782) 17682-
  83, (1783) 18145
Ratification of the constitution, 22848-49
Ratifications of the new, 21529
Ratio disciplinae, 2775
Rational explanation, 13368
Rational method, 32625
Ratzer, Bernard. To his excellency, 11434
Ravara, Joseph. Statement of facts, 26053
Rawle, Francis, 1660-1727
  Just rebuke, 2807
  Some remedies, 2287
  Ways and means, 2697
Rawle, William. Opinions, 34001
Rawlet, John, 1642-1686. Christian monitor, 3719,
  5279
Rawson, Edward
  (ed.) Book of the general lawes, 60
  preface by, 12973
  secy. Mass. Bay, 68, 81, 88, 103, 109, 124-25, 141-
  42, 149, 168-69, 177-78, 190-91, 200-205, 216,
  219, 235-36, 250, 253, 271-72, 289-91, 305, 317-
  18, 349-50, 367-69, 389
Rawson, Grindall, 1658-1715
  Miles Christianus, 1145
  (tr.) Nashuanittue, 550
  Necessity of a speedy, 1429
  (ed.) Sampwutteahae, 497
  memorials of, 1757
Rawson, Grindall, fl. 1751-1755
  (ed.) Old man's calendar, 25530
  installation, 7670, 25529
  ordained, 6784
Rawson, Jonathan
  Compendium, 26054
  Instructor generalis, 26055
Ray, ———, medical observations, 6783
Ray, James
  Acts of the rebels, 6058-60
  Lamentations, 6061
Ray, Nicholas. Importance of the colonies, 10471

Raymond, Lord ———, additions from, 10935
Raynal, Guillaume Thomas François, 1711-1796
  Revolution of America, (1781) 17322-23, (1782)
  17684-87, (1792) 24728, (1794) 27328, (1796)
  31172
  Sentiments, 14417, 18352
  extracts from, 17096
  letter (from Benezet), 22330
  letter (from Paine), 17651-54, 24658, 27466, 32633
Raynolds, Freegrace, ordained, 28223
Rea, ———, sings ode, 29590
Read, ———, grammarian, 6928, 8728, 10758, 16982-
  83, 27639-40
Read, Benjamin, baptized, 2575
Read, Charles, 1715-1780. Copy of a letter, 9809-
  811
Read, Collinson, 1751-1815
  Lancaster, Jan. 6, 1800, 38360
  Precedents, 27600
Read, Daniel, 1757-1841
  American musical magazine, 19945
  American singing-book, (1785) 19213, (1788)
  21416, (1792) 24729, (1793) 26056, (1795) 29388
  Columbian harmonist, 26057, 29389-91
  Introduction to psalmody, 22829, 29392
  Supplement to the American singing-book, 20673
Read, George
  Laws of the state, 32030
  attack on, 21498
  pres. convention, 14732
Read, J., method of raising hemp, 22906-907
Read, Jacob, 1751-1816
  reports on Conn. expenses, 18838
  reports on Indian affairs, 18830, 19294
  reports on Penobscot expedition, 19312
  reports on post office, 19298
  reports on sundry motions, 19307
Read, John
  Latin grammar, 4071
  heirs of, 6784
Read, John, 1769-1854. Observations, 34906
Read, John K., 1746-1805
  Commemorative oration, 38361
  New Ahimon Rezon, 23727
  conduct of, 37811, 38957
Read, Joseph. Baltimore, May 1, 1775, 13820
Reader, W., tr. Count Bergowsky, 35695
Reading, Philip. Protestant's danger, 7552
Reading, Pa. Moral and historical play, 34435
Reading made easy, 19946, 29393
Reading no preaching, (1757) 8015, (1761) 8987,
  (1797) 32408
Ready reckoner, (1774) 13274, (1789) 21822, (1792)
  24316, (1794) 26967-68, (1797) 32127, (1798)
  33730, (1799) 35477
Ready way, 17447
Real advantages, 9302
  and genuine, 17720
  beauty, 12061
  Christian, 4952, 5593
  Christian hope, 7825

VOL.	ITEMS	VOL.	ITEMS
1	1-3244	8	22298-25074
2	3245-6623	9	25075-28145
3	6624-9891	10	28146-30832
4	9892-13091	11	30833-33261
5	13092-16176	12	33262-25854
6	16177-19448	13	35855-39162
7	19449-22297		

treasure, 32741, 36191
union, 9626
Reason against coition, 6600
    and faith, 23728
    satisfied, 1555
    the only, 18322
    why, 2030
Reasonable religion, 931
Reasonable service, 25229
Reasonableness and importance, 27102
    of Christianity, 3527
    of nonconformity, 4237
    of personal, 2634
    of regular singing, 2183
Reasons against a separation, 23978
    against any, 11435
    against the renewal, 9812
    and design, 15607
    for adhering, 3600, 3831
    for his conduct, 3069
    for not signing, 9265
    for quiting, 18525
    for repealing, 20130
    for the inditement, 294
        necessity, (1780) 16724, (1786) 19924-25,
          (1795) 28346-47
        present glorious, 11436
    for writing, 4590
    in support, 24730
    of dissent, 8562, 8617
    of my withdrawing, 1332
    of the Christian's, 37942
    offered by Mr. Nathanael, 5609
    offered for leaving, 38359
    why Mr. Byles, 11035
    why the British, 9658
    why the people, 12257
Rebuker rebuked, 1113
Recantation, 32153-54
Receipt to make, 10472
Receipts and expenditures, (1797) 34333, (1798)
    36066, (1799) 37218, (1800) 37219
Received and read, 32966
Received the 13th of January, 31407
    the 14th December, 31460, 31466
    the 18th December, 31462
    the 20th of January, 31468
Receiving the cup, 21162
Recherches et observations, 26873
Reciprocal duties, 33875
Reckett, William, 1706-1769. Some account, 18146
Recommendation from the convention, 22417
Recommendation of inoculation, 14891
Reconciliation or the triumph, 22638
Reconciliation with an offended, 4470
Record of death, 35942
Record of the family, 35602
Recovery from sickness, 11095, 27809
Rector detected, 9613
Red and black, 31075
Rede, Carteret. Token for youth, 4795, 10473
Rede bei der feier, 27355
    gehalten den 6th, 21274
    gehalten in dem hause, 9643
    herrn Joseph Galloways, 9673
    von den absichten, 17570
    von der incorporirten, 29126

Redeemed captive, (1707) 1340, (1720) 2197, (1748)
    6211, (1758) 8285, (1773) 13081, (1774) 13773,
    (1776) 15221, (1793) 26485, (1795) 29893, (1800)
    39104
Redemption from death, 10295
Redfield, Amanda, d. 1783, death, 18213
Redfield Levi, 1745-   Succinct account, **34436**
Redfield, Nathan. Treatise, 31076
Redick, John. Detection, 10152
Redman, John, 1722-1807
    Defence of inoculation, 8477
    letter (from Rush), 26111
Redstone association. Minutes, (1790-93) 26058-61
Redwood, Abraham, establishes library, 9764
Redwood, William, referee, 11614
Redwood library. Laws, &c., 9764
Reed, ———, grammarian see **Read, ———, grammarian**
Reed, ———, satire on, 16697
Reed, Abner, 1771-1866. First step, 38362-63
Reed, Albert, engraver, 26819
Reed, Jesse. Sermon, 26062
Reed, John, of Phila.
    Explanation of the map, 13564
    plaintiff, 11053
Reed, John, 1751-1831
    Sermon, (1787) 21417, (1792) 26063
    hand of fellowship, 26135
Reed, Joseph, 1723-1787. Register office, 9250
Reed, Joseph, 1741-1785
    Dissertation III, 10400
    Following paper, 17324
    In council, 17288
    Joseph Reed, defendant, 11053
    My late engagements, 17325
    Proclamation, (1779) 16433-35, 16437, (1780)
        16925-27, (1781) 17283-84
    Remarks on a late, 18147-48
    Remarks on Gov. Johnstone, 16483
    reply to, 17867
    satirized, 16697?
Reed, Richard, recants, 14194
Rees, Thomas. New system, 38364
Reese, Thomas, 1742-1796. Essay on the influence,
    21418
Reeve, ———. The purse, 32003
Reeve, Clara, 1729-1807. Old English baron, 32742
Reeve, John, 1608-1658. Transcendent spiritual,
    32743
Reeve, Joseph, tr. History of the Old, 18471
Reeves, Elizabeth, d. 1792?, murdered, 24672
Reference not only, 33305
Reflection and prospect, 20316
    on death, 9608
    on the seven days, 38601
Reflections and maxims, 6392-93
    critical, 16802
    of a few, 15041
    on a wonderful, 26064
    on courtship, (1746) 5772-73, (1758) 8132,
        (1793) 25501
    on death, (1773) 12754, (1793) 25407, (1796)
        30356
    on education, 32197
    on extortion, 15859
    on French atheism, 30724

on hypocrisy, 4799
on love, 38365
on Monroe's, 34675
on political, 32318a
on taxes, 27601
on the goodness, 18670
  inconsistency, 31077
  Observations, 19804
  policy, 19214, 20036
  present, 2169
  proposition, 32744
  Revolution, 23238, 24157
upon Mr. Wetmore, 5377
upon reflections, 2111
Reflexiones, 36192
Reflexions on the present, 16027
  on the state, 24230
  sur la doctrine, 32720
  sur la guerre, 33928
Reformation of manners, 13388
Reformation the great duty, 713
Reformed Dutch church
  Acts and proceedings, (1797) 32745, (1800) 38366
  Articles of faith, 33412
  Bekanntmachung, 5280
  Constitution, 26065, 27602
  Extracts of the proceedings, 37392
  Heidelbergh catechism, 22091-92
  Proceedings, 19215
  Psalms, hymns, 30071
  Whole book of forms, 6230
Reformed German church
  Catechismus, (1777) 15558, (1786) 19947, (1788) 21419, (1790) 22830
  Geistreiche lieder, 6917
  Lutherische und reformirte, 16028
  Neu-vermehrt und vollständiges gesang-buch, (1753) 7102, (1763) 9495, (1772) 12534, (1774) 13565
  Neue und verbesserte gesang-buch, 36193
  Psalms of David, 10561
Reformed German church lottery, 12535
Reformers and intercessors, 7989
Reformierten kirchen, 6098
Reformirter oder Heidelberger, 6853
Refreshment, 30119-20
Refutation of a dangerous, 1053
Refutation of three opposers, 516
Regards due, 3379
Regeln der incorporirten, 25994, 27507
  der Teutschen gesellschaft, 9795, 10453
  für die ordnung, 26361
  und articuls, 8016
Regeneration, a sermon, 18074
  and the testimony, (1740) 4514, (1741) 4720, (1742) 4959
  stated, 26432
  the most important, 10523
Regierungsverfassung, 18690-91, 22761
Regiment to consist, 37364
Regimental orders, 13884
Regiments-verfassung, 14996
Register and pocket almanack, 15794
  for the state, 18433, 19596
  of New Hampshire, 27740
  of the southern, (1769) 11111, (1770) 11523, (1771) 11930, (1772) 12279, (1773) 12612, (1774) 13072, (1775) 13761, (1776) 14617
  office, 9250
Règlement militaire, 15190
Regular and skilful, 13503

English syntax, (1780) 16725, (1783) 17858, (1786) 19526, (1788) 20985, (1792) 24153
singing, 3006, 12716
Regulation for the government, 35866
Regulation of Massachusetts, 13303
Regulations ascertaining, 30547, 32237
  for the exercise, 22038
  government, 31852
  order and discipline, (1779) 16627-28, (1782) 17773-74, (1783) 18267, (1784) 18843, (1785) 19267, 19329, (1787) 20780-82, 20832, (1788) 21530-31, (1790) 22990-92, (1791) 23907, (1792) 2419-20, (1793) 26356-60, (1794) 27957-65, 27967-70, 27972-73, (1795) 29778-79, (1796) 31469-70, (1798) 34898-901, (1800) 38806
  quarter master, 17775
 of the Grand lodge, 35508
  Grand royal arch, 35505
  market, 891
 respecting, 38807
 to be observed, 33097
Regulator for Crazy Will, 8988
Regulus
  To the freemen, 12970
  see also **Husbands, Herman, d. 1795**
Reiche, Carl Christoph. Fifteen discourses, 23729
Reichel, Carl Gotthold, ed. Lesebuch, 29258
Reiche, F., woodcut by, 35864
Reid, James. Sermon, 9496
Reid, John. American atlas, 31078
Reid, Thomas, 1710-1796. Essays, 24731, 26066
Reid, Thomas, 1739-1802. Essay, 19216
Reigart, Adam, receives linen, 14817
Reign of grace, (1793) 25212, (1795) 28313, (1798) 33434
Reinagle, Alexander, 1756-1809
  America, 27647
  Chorus sung, 22093
  Collection of favorite, 21420, 22095
  Federal march, 21421
  Music in the historical, 36194
  My soul is thine, 22096
  New song, 27648
  Select collection, 20674
  Sonata, 22094
  Tantive back, 22097
  'Tis not the bloom, 22098
  arranges music, 22069, 22142
  benefit for, 36101
Reinhard, Brother, prophecies by, 9318
Reinholdt, Georg Christoph. George Christoph Reinholdt, 12971
Reintzell, D. List of the prizes, 26430
Reise nach Jerusalem, 25358
Reitz, Johann Heinrich. Fürbilde der heilsamen, 21422
Rejoinder, being a defence, 24378
Rejoinder to the Reverend, 8224
Relapse, 7303
Relation of a remarkable, 7553

paragraphs, (1772) 12328, (1773) 12684, (1774) 13154
points, 5890
principles, 35671
on that part, 18488
on the address of sixteen, 20871
  address of the committee, 35714
  American universal, 25510
  assertions, 37197
  bill of rights, 30549
  book of Daniel, 26663
  contents, 3900
  death, 33501
  doings, 17533
  essays, 22476
  first part, 35423
  gaseous oxyd, 29089
  insidious letter, 33529
  introduction, 11437
  Jacobiniad, 28726, 33779
  land bill, 30550
  late printed, 8814
  late proceedings, 3098
  leading sentiments, 27195
  letter, 8751
  manufacturing, 22832, 23731-32
  nature, 13831
  observations, 3705
  opinions, 15730
  organization, 36201
  pamphlet, 29396
  plan, 7098
  preface, 4190
  proceedings, 19495
  proposed plan of a federal, 21131
  proposed plan of an emission, 20403
  Quaker unmask'd, 9813
  report, 22833
  result, 4065, 13171
  revenue, 31166
  Rev. Mr. Cooper, 4947-49
  Revd. Mr. Croswell, 9340
  Rev. Mr. Emmons's, 27110
  Rev. Mr. Hopkins's, 13325
  Rev'd Mr. James, 11099
  Rev. Mr. Joshua, 5392
  review, 11976
  signs, 37733
  treaty, 30255
on Zenger's trial, 4118-20
on Zenger's tryal, 11573
upon a discourse intituled, 3156
  discourse preached, 13825
  message sent, 9497
  pamphlet entitled, 3897
  pamphlet intitled, 17440
  protestation, 4820
upon education, 28594
upon Mr. Gales, 2215
upon Mr. George, 5405
upon Paul's, 30133
upon the advice, 2951
  bishop, 4594
  defence, 3917
  delineated, 9814
  manner, 7388
  navigation, 22509
  postscript, 2526
  resolves, 13244
which the author, 5108
Remedy against despair, 964

Remember now, 393
Remembrance of Christ, 12900
Remembrance of former, 784
Remembrancer. To the freemen, 14501
Remembrancer, for Lord's day, 32747
Remington, E. Short account, 10747
Remington, Samuel, d. 1766, death, 10747
Reminiscence of Washington, 37492
Remmele, John. Design and nature, 19948
Remmey, John. Account of the present, 36202
Remonstrance (Marin ben Jesse), 7457
Remonstrance addressed, 35717
  and petition of a county, 20457
  and petition of the legislature, 32980-81
  of Obadiah, 7914-15
  of several, 846
  of the General assembly, 1325
Remsen, Henry
  To the respectable publick, 13681
  chairman comm. for affairs in N.Y.C., 13483
  chairman comm. of correspondence, 13482
  chairman comm. of observation, 14328, 14330-31, 14333, 14335
  motion by, 13481, 14511
Renatus, 2672
Render, W., tr. Count Benyowsky, 37745
Rending of the vail, 1875, 2326
Renewal of covenant, 239
Rennell, James, appendix by, 38188
Renovation of man, 24692
Renowned history of Giles Gingerbread, 19949, 20675
Renowned history of Valentine, (1794) 27605, (1795) 29783, (1800) 38368
Rensselaerville association. Minutes, (1798) 36203, (1799) 36204, (1800) 38369
Renty, —— de, life of, 29459
Reparation, a comedy, 28195
Reparation, or the school, 37784
Repeated admonitions, 2359, 2673
  bereavements, 6134
  warnings, 1556
Repent and be converted, (1778) 15796, (1780) 16777, (1783) 17932, (1784) 18476, (1792) 24327
Repentance and faith, 4684
  and remission, 18809
  of passion, 28977
  the sure way, 2958
Reply of a Roman Catholic, 30125
  of William Cunningham, 34906
  to a book, 4926
  to a defence, 10316
    few observations, 11476
    letter, 6618
    narrative, 27598
    pamphlet entitled, (Considerations) 18149, (The answer) 7424
    piece called, 9640
    piece wrote, 12317
  to Alexander, 38370

VOL.	ITEMS	VOL.	ITEMS
1	1-3244	8	22298-25074
2	3245-6623	9	25075-28145
3	6624-9891	10	28146-30832
4	9892-13091	11	30833-33261
5	13092-16176	12	33262-25854
6	16177-19448	13	35855-39162
7	19449-22297		

to an address to the author, 14060
    address to the Roman, 19382
    address written, 34439
    apology, 38527
to Col. Clap's, 8719
to Dr. Chandler's, 11598
to Dr. Mayhew's, 9932
to Dr. Priestley's, (1772) 12328, (1773) 12684, (1774) 13154
to General Joseph, 17867
to Gov. Cornbury, 1326
to Mr. Clark's, 7205
to Mr. Increase, 1109
to Sir Henry, 18208
to some essays, 12984
to some remarks, 3471
to the address, 29024
    Church of England, 11830
    Correspondent, 28058
    declaration, 4927-28
    false reasoning, 30423
    objections, 3268-70
    observations, 20382
    principal, 2027
    remarks, 10932
    Rev. Mr. Chandler's, 11100
    Reverend Mr. Eells, 8749
    Reverend Mr. George, 11279
    speech, 3841
    strictures, 18804
Réponse du général, 32773
Report, &c.; the secretary, 38808
    concerning the town, 2413
    from the commissioners, 24921
    from the committee appointed to prepare, 31368
        committee of revisal, 38809
        committee to whom was referred on the 22d, 33040
        committee to whom was referred on the 29th, 34772
        committee to whom was referred the bill, 36562
        department of war, 31468
        lords of the committee, 9388
        secretary, 38810
    in part of the committee appointed, (9th of Dec.) 38811, (18th instant) 34789, (24th of Dec.) 38812
        of the committee of elections, 38813
        of the committee of privileges, 38814
        of the committee of revisal, 38815
        of the committee to whom was referred, (on the 28th) 38816, (on the 29th) 34769
        of the committee to whom was referred so much, 36563
        of the committee to whom were referred, 38817
    of a case decided, 27777
        case lately decided, 30743
        committee appointed, (to consider) 20078, (to explore) 24604, (to propose) 16630
        committee chosen, 31854
        committee of the First, 6975
        committee of the inhabitants, 12331
        committee of the select, 30996
        constitution, 16352
    of an action for a libel, 37103
    of an action of assault, (Forsey) 9660, (Torrey) 10190
    of commissioners, 16631

of committee of South Carolina, 26183
of committee on amendments, 34778
of committee on the letters, 34779
of Manhattan committee, 35950
of the arrears, 36067
    attorney general of fees, 29761
    attorney general read, 23908-909
    attorney general to Congress, 31431
    board of trustees, 26364
    case between Field and Harrison, 31667
    case between Jos. Wilkins, 31670
    case between William Fowler, 31668
    case between William Yates, 31671
    case in the court, 34220
    case of Love against Donelson, 31669
    case upon statute, 31672
    commissioners appointed by the General assembly, 13214
    commissioners appointed by the President, 27977
    commissioners for purchasing, 27947
    commissioners of the sinking fund, (1794) 27948, (1795) 31462, (1796) 31463, (1797) 33089-90, (1798) 34881, (1799) 36564, (1800) 38818
    commissioners of Virginia, 19274
    commissioners on the accounts, 24922
    commissioners to execute, 27949
    committee, alterations, 34777
of the committee appointed by the directors, 24635
    appointed by the Medical, 35933
    appointed, (on the 4th instant) 36565, (on the 5th instant) 32987, 38819, (on the 10th December) 38820, (on the 10th instant) 34776, (on the 20th) 38821, (on the 22d) 38822, (on the 24th) 32982
    appointed the sixteenth, 32988
    appointed to enquire concerning, 38220
    appointed to enquire if any, 31387
    appointed to enquire, (into the actual state) 31378, (into the expediency) 38823, (into the operation of the act) 32989, (into the operation of the acts) 38824, (into the state) 32986, (into the truth) 31391
    appointed to enquire whether any and if any, 38825
    appointed to enquire whether any and what alterations, 31386, 32984
    appointed to enquire whether any and what amendments, 32985
    appointed to examine, (into the proceedings) 4082, (into the state) 27909
    appointed to inspect, 19771
    appointed to prepare, 32983
    appointed to take, 31394
    directed to report, 27905
    for regulating, 16632
    for the sale, 29043-44
of the committee of both houses, 5063
of the committee of claims instructed, 38826
of the committee of claims on a motion of the 11th, 31376
    on a motion relative, 34727
    on a resolution, 34728
    on copies, 32994
    on the memorial, (Alexander) 34729, (Fowler) 31393, (Perry) 34733
    on the memorials and petitions, 34731, 36566

VOL.	ITEMS	VOL.	ITEMS
1	1-3244	8	22298-25074
2	3245-6623	9	25075-28145
3	6624-9891	10	28146-30832
4	9892-13091	11	30833-33261
5	13092-16176	12	33262-25854
6	16177-19448	13	35855-39162
7	19449-22297		

33032, (on the 14th) 38869, (on the 18th) 38870, (on the 19th) 36578, (on the 20th) 33034-35, (on the 21st) 38871-72, (on the 23d) 34773, (on the 26th) 38873, (on the 29th of November) 34770-71, (on the 29th ultimo) 33039, (on the 30th) 34784

to whom was referred so much of the President's, 38874-76

to whom was referred so much of the speech, 33031

to whom was referred the act for the relief, 34774

to whom was referred the act providing, 34780

to whom was referred the bill, (Feb. 15, 1799) 36579, (Dec. 23, 1799) 36580, (Jan. 21, 1800) 38879, (Feb. 17, 1800) 38878, 38885, (Mar. 28, 1800) 38883, (Mar. 31, 1800) 38877, (Apr. 2, 1800) 38890, (Apr. 4, 1800) 38881, (Apr. 9, 1800) 38880, (Apr. 12, 1800) 38884, (Apr. 16, 1800) 38882, (Apr. 22, 1800) 38888, (Apr. 25, 1800) 38887, (Apr. 28, 1800) 38886, 38889, 38891

to whom was referred the letter, 38892

to whom was referred the memorial, (Neufville) 33033, (Smith) 38893

to whom was referred the memorial, and petition, 34781

to whom was referred the memorial of the representatives, 27906

to whom was referred the message from the President, 31383

to whom was referred the message of the President, (1795) 29727, (1796) 31388

to whom was referred, (the motion), 34783, (the petition) 38894, (the remonstrance) 33038, (the report) 38895, (the resolution) 38896, (the resolutions) 33036, (the several petitions) 27904

to whom were re-committed, 33024

to whom were referred, (on the 12th) 36581, (on the 24th) 38897

to whom were referred so much, 31390

to whom were referred sundry, 38898

to whom were referred the petitions, 38899

to whom were referred the reports, 31370

of the comptroller-general, 38221

of the directors (Missionary soc.), 35738

of the directors of the Western, 31623, 35012

of the extraordinary, 35424

of the inspectors, 35930

of the intendant, 18580

of the joint committee, 34350, 36089-90

of the lords commissioners, 2640

of the opinions, 29284

of the register-general, (1792) 25974, (1794) 29293, (1795) 30981-82, (1796) 32657, (1797) 34334, (1798) 36068, (1799) 38222

of the register of the treasury, 22993

of the secretary of state, (assays and experiments) 26338, (fisheries) 23911-12, 24924, (lands unclaimed) 23913, (memorial of A. Carmichael) 33069-70, (memorial of citizens) 33071, (privileges) 26339, (weights) 22994-97, 23910

of the secretary of state; to the President, 25648

of the secretary of the navy, 36582, 38900

of the secretary of the South Carolina, 23783

of the secretary of the treasury, (duties on spirits) 24925, (Kosciusko claim) 34873, (manufactures) 23914, (public credt) 22998, (public debt) 24926-27

of the secretary of the treasury accompanied with estimates, 33075
> **for the improvement,** 29773
> **read in the House,** 29772
> **relative to the loans,** 26347
> **respecting the tonnage,** 27946

of the secretary of war (July 3, 1797), 33054

of the secretary of war, (on 35 petitions) 26363, (on 47 petitions) 26362, (on 60 petitions) 27955, (on the petition) 33099

of the trial, (Bedlow) 26513, (Croucher) 38373, (Rowan) 27643, (Weeks) 38372

of the trustees, 257

of Thomas Davis, 27292

of ways and means, 19253

on alterations, 34767

on privileges, 23915

on the institution, 28697
> **petition,** (Bell) 38901, (Carr) 33030
> **practicability,** 36709
> **state of the mint,** 29774
> **Virginia resolutions,** 35795

on weights, 26348

printed by order, 31849

to the select, 36091

Reports and dissertations, 25296

of cases adjudged, (1789) 21914, (1798) 34485, (1799) 35607
> **argued and determined in the court of appeals,** 34958, 36670
> **argued and determined in the superior courts,** 33382
> **determined by the judges,** 37086
> **in the county courts,** 36763-64
> **... in the high court,** 38414
> **ruled and adjudged,** 22445, 33598, 35374

of committees in Congress, 36205, 36583

of committees on the petitions, 33041

of divine kindness, (1758) 8285, (1773) 13081, (1774) 13773, (1776) 15221

of sundry, 23679

of the board, 16633

of the secretary of state, 33048

Repräsentanten der Vereinigten, 15174

Representation and petition of divers, 34335
and petition of your majesty's, 9786
and remonstrance, 32183
of facts, 10748
of the figures, 16959
of the General assembly, 6032
to the president, 17167
to the public, 9591

Representations of Governor Hutchinson, 12820

Representative for the 7th, 38374

Representative reform assn. Address, 26784

Representatives of the United States, 15173

Reprimander reprimanded, 17086

Reprover doing his duty, 1174

Republic of reason, 32224

Republic of the Israelites, 21192

Republican
Election of President, 37348
Fellow citizens, 30411
Observations, 15950
Public notice, 30984
To the electors, 29642

Republican dissected, 14626
Republican farmer. To the citizens, 38645
Republican gazetteer, 32789
    government, 27024
    harmonist, 37343
    harmony, 28300
    magazine, 34028
    rush-light, 38378
Res sacrae, 21069
Reserches sur la medicine, 36987
Residence in France, 33797, 35030
Resident of New York see Burgher, John
Resignation, a funeral sermon, 12422
    a poem, 20171, 29938-39
    in two parts, (1764) 9888, (1791) 24020, (1794)
        27071, (1799) 36746
    of his excellency, 31535
    to the afflictive, 35134
Resistance to tyrants, 13935-43
Resolution of the high court, 19164
Resolution (ship), in Pacific, 17921
Resolutions, acts and orders, 20079
    agreed to, 36211
    adopted, 15151
    and articles, 36103
    and extracts, 20080
    and proceedings, 36212-13
    directing, 14368, 14994
    of Congress, 20783
    of the Provincial, 14938
    of the stockholders, 30330
    on adopting, 35468
    regulating, 30107
    that the General assembly, 36647
Resolve appointing, 32451
    confirming, 19088
    for districting, 24524-26
    of committee, 15934
    of his majesty's, 8414
Resolved Christian, 933
    that it be, 17396
    that the following, 30895
Resolves and orders of the Congress, 15892
    and orders of the Council, 16496
    &c. of the General court, 35796, 37922-23
    of a meeting, 12961
    of Congress, 15688
    of the General assembly, (1776) 14879-81,
        (1777) 15412-17, (1778) 15893-96, (1779)
        16353-57, (1780) 16848-49
    of the General court, (1780) 16850, (1781)
        17230-34, (1782) 17598-601, (1784) 18601-603,
        (1785) 19089-92, (1786) 19791-93, (1787)
        20514-17, (1788) 21246-48, (1789) 21951-52,
        (1790) 22656-59, (1791) 23554-55, (1792)
        24527-29, (1793) 25782-85, (1794) 27289-90,
        (1795) 29045-46, (1796) 30764-66, (1797)
        32449-50, (1798) 34072-73, (1799) 35797,
        (1800) 37924
    respecting the militia, 14467
Resort and remedy, 4712
Resort of piety, 1830
Respectable member of the community. Extract
    from an address, 16773
Responsary, 28370
Rest which remaineth, 16090
Restitution, 9393
Restitutus, 2917
Restraints merciful, 1619, 1656
Result of a council of churches, 5156
    of a council of nine churches, 6577
        of ten churches, 5391

    of the consociated, 6083
of an ecclesiastical, (1735) 3915, (1744) 5407,
    (1770) 11858, (1773) 12687
    of the convention, 15858
    of the council, 6974
    of the deliberations, 20810
Results of the deliberations, 20811
Results of three synods, 2661
Resurrection of good men, 36300
    of Jesus, 19702
    of Laurent Ricci, 21706-707
    of the saints, 37810
Retired Christian, 1129
Retort, Jack see Hunt, Isacc, 1751-1809
Return of duties, 24928
    of seamen, 34851
    of the several, 36099
    of the whole number, 23916, 34905
Returned captive, (1787) 20676-77, (1790) 22834,
    (1800) 38381
Returning unto God, 293
Reuben and Rachel, 34490
Revealed knowledge, (1795) 28355-61, (1796) 30126,
    (1797) 31877
Revelation a guide, 13003
    of nature, 29567, 31238
    of politics, 31325
Revenge, a tragedy, (1761) 9046, (1794) 26559,
    28145
Revere, Paul, 1735-1818
    engraver, 9659, 11572, 12352, 16979
    messenger from Boston, 13674?
    pres. board of health, 35220, 36995
    worshipful master, 31799
Rev. Aaron Hutchinson's reply, 11101
Reverend association. Plain narrative, 5281
Rev. brother Ripley's prayer, 34150
    Dr. N. Whitaker's neighbour, 18404
    Mr. Pickering's letters, 5037
    Mr. . . . Sir, 26595
    Mr. Smith, 7793
    Peres Fobes, 22851
    sir, and respected, 24211
Review (1754), 7304
Review of school, 19590
    of the administration, 33066
        constitution, 20678
        life and character, 12960
        military operations, 8163, 11701
        question, 31086
    of The rector detected, 9612
        revenue system, 26973
        subject, 24138
Revisal of the intreagues, 3210
Revised discipline, 27023
Revised laws, 18276
Reviving cordial, 13134
Reviving thoughts, 4110
Revolution in France, 28053
    in New England, 575, 12973
    of America. (1781) 17322-23, (1782) 17684-87,

VOL.	ITEMS	VOL.	ITEMS
1	1-3244	8	22298-25074
2	3245-6623	9	25075-28145
3	6624-9891	10	28146-30832
4	9892-13091	11	30833-33261
5	13092-16176	12	33262-25854
6	16177-19448	13	35855-39162
7	19449-22297		

Act (1789), (convention) 22109, (credit) 22110, (impost) 22108, (tax) 22107, (topic not given) 22111
Act (1790), (Abolition society) 22842, (convention) 22840, (election of senators) 22841
Act (1791), (Providence bank) 23738, (tax) 23737
Act (1792), (election of representatives) 24737-38
Act (1793), (militia) 26075
Act (1794), (granting £6000) 27615, (highways) 27612
Act (1795), (charter to United library co.) 29403, (St. John's church incorporated) 29368
Act (1796), (choosing representatives) 31093, (tax) 31094
Act (1797), (militia) 32755, (tax) 32756
Act (1798), (militia) 34448, (tax) 34450
Act (1799), (Newport insurance co. incorporated) 36215, (Washington lodge incorporated) 36214
Bill to prevent, 7110
Following is a copy of a bill, 22110
Rhode Island and Providence plantations united, 22847
Rhode Island college
Act for the establishment, 9823
Catalogue, (1775) 14424, (1778) 16049, (1781) 17347, (1786) 19960, (1789) 22112, (1792) 24739, (1795) 29406, (1798) 34456, (1800) 38395
Catalogue of books, 26077
Commencement, (1795) 29407, (1796) 31097, (1797) 32760, (1798) 34457, (1799) 36226, (1800) 38396
Exhibition, 5 December, 34459
Exhibition in College chapel, 34458
Laws, 26078
Order of the exercises, 27617
Supplement to the laws, 26079
Theses, (1769) 11444, (1776) 15060, (1788) 21432, (1789) 22113, (1790) 22850, (1791) 23739, (1792) 24740, (1793) 26080, (1794) 27618, (1795) 29408, (1796) 31098, (1797) 32761, (1798) 34460, (1799) 36227, (1800) 38397
petition by, 33003-4
Rhode Island district, &c., 34908
Rhode Island museum, 27619
Rhode-Island register, 28066
Rhodes, John, fl. 1727
dispute with Baptist church, 2209
publishes work by Penn, 2941, 20617
Rhodes, John, b. 1755. Surprising adventures, 34461, 36228
Rhodes, William. Directions for sailing, 10882
Rhymer, Merlin. Almanac see **Almanacs (Rhymer)**
Rhymes relating, 10159
Ricci, Laurent, resurrection, 21706-707
Rice, ——, tavern keeper, 21349
Rice, David, 1733-1816
Essay on baptism, 22115
Slavery, 24741-42
Rich Elisha
Number of the beast, 14425
Poem on the bloody, 14426
Poem on the late, 15061
Poetical remarks, 14427
Rich, John, 1691-1761. Spirit of contradiction, 9258
Rich cabinet, 2766
Rich treasure, 339, 9372
Richard E. Lee's letter, 37811

Richards, George, d. 1814
The accepted, 38399
Hymns composed, 37675, 38400
Psalms, hymns, 24952
Solemn dirge, 36229
Richards, George, 1769-1837
Cry of the watchmen, 29410
Declaration, 26084
Operative and speculative, 26087
Oration, 29411
Political passing bell, 22116
Richards, Hannah, d. 1770, death, 11681
Richards, John, memorial of, 31373
Richards, Peter, accounts, 18121
Richards, William. Reflections, 30724
Richardson, ——, pastor in Lime-street, 5372
Richardson, Gideon, ordained, 7231
Richardson, John, 1647-1696
Almanac see **Almanacs (Richardson)**
Necessity of a well experienced, 276, 307
Richardson, John, 1666-1753. Account of the life, 8308, 18158
Richardson, Joseph, 1755-1803. The fugitive, 29412
Richardson, Joseph, 1778-1871. Oration, 38401
Richardson, Luther, 1774-1811. Oration, 38402
Richardson, Rebecca, widow, 7414
Richardson, Samuel, 1689-1761
Clarissa, (1795) 29413, (1798) 34463, (1800) 38403
History of Clarissa, (1786) 19961, (1796) 31100
History of Miss Clarissa, 34464
History of Pamela, (1792) 24744, (1794) 27622, (1796) 31101, (1797) 32763, (1799) 36230-31
History of Sir Charles, (1786) 19962, (1790) 22852, (1794) 27623, (1795) 29415, (1797) 32764, (1798) 34465
Pamela, 5485, 5487, 19963
Paths of virtue, 23740, 29414
Pleasing history of Pamela, 26088
proposals to publish Sir Charles Grandison, 34466
Richardson, Sibyl, d. 1799, death, 36024
Richardson, Thomas, jeweller, 11381
Richardson, William, of Boston. William Richardson imports, 37023
Richardson, William, fl. 1692. Letter, 611
Richardson, William, fl. 1753. Liberty of the laity, 7111
Richardson, William, 1743-1814
Cacique of Ontario, 36232
Philosophical analysis, 21433, 27624
Richmond, Charles Lennox, 1st duke, 1672-1723, death of heir, 1280
Richmond, Charles Lennox, 3d duke, 1735-1806
defended, 17650
protests, 14090
Richmond, Edward, 1767-1842
Sermon, 34467
ordained, 25573
Richmond, Va.
By-laws of St. John's, 32765

VOL.	ITEMS	VOL.	ITEMS
1	1-3244	8	22298-25074
2	3245-6623	9	25075-28145
3	6624-9891	10	28146-30832
4	9892-13091	11	30833-33261
5	13092-16176	12	33262-25854
6	16177-19448	13	35855-39162
7	19449-22297		

Robbins, Ammi Ruhamah, 1740-1813
   Calamity, 32820
   Empires, 22118
   To treat, 12543
   ordained, 9260
Robbins, Asher, election favored, 38652
Robbins, Chandler, 1738-1799
   Account of a late, 27637
   Address, 26102
   Century sermon, 27630
   Character of Dorcas, 12215
   Discourse, 31110
   Reply to some, 12984
   Sermon, (1791) 23741, (1793) 27629, 31111,
     (1794) 27631, (1795) 29423, (1797) 32772
   Some brief remarks, 13581
   To please Christ, 12544
   Ways of God, 10755
   death, 36300
   ordained, 8727
   reply to, 12739
Robbins, Ephraim. Friendly letter, 31112
Robbins, Jane, d. 1800, death, 37721
Robbins, Jonathan
   case of, 36121-24
   motion concerning, 38787, 38791
   report concerning, 38782
Robbins, Nathaniel, 1727-1795
   Charge, 27180
   Jerusalem's peace, 12545
   Sermon, 12216, 12985
   death, 31286
   ordained, 6654
Robbins, Philemon, 1710-1781
   Plain narrative, 5281, 6063
   Sermon, 8727, 9260
   answer to, 6250
Robbins, Robert, 1741-1804. Divine sovereignity,
   24750
Robbins, Thomas, 1777-1856. Oration, 38411
Robe, James, 1688-1753. Short narrative, 5046-47
Roberdeau, Daniel
   chairman meeting, 16463
   satirized, 16697
Roberdeau, Isaac, 1763-1829. Oration, 38412
Robert Barclays Apologie, 14659
Robert B. Thomas has for sale, 31295
Robert Campbell and Co's. catalogue, 31913
Robert Campbell's catalogue for 1796, 30153
   catalogue of books, 26727
   sale catalogue, 23244
Robert G. Cranch, sadlers ironmonger, 13233
Roberts, Daniel, 1658-1726. Some memoirs, (1751)
   6774, (1752) 6926, (1753) 7113, (1766) 10482,
   (1773) 12986, (1783) 18166, (1790) 22855
Roberts, David. Some memoirs, 6774
Roberts, George, 1776-1827. Strictures, 27632
Roberts, John, memoirs of, 6774, 6926, 7113, 10482,
   12986, 18166, 22855
Roberts, Joseph, ordained, 7189
Roberts, R. Seven rational, 15584
Roberts, Thomas. Catalogue, 19966
Roberts, William, 1767-1849
   (ed.) Looker-on, 30702
   Too high, 34475
Robertson, Alexander
   New-York, June 23, 1769, 11445
   reply to, 11137
Robertson, David. Proceedings and debates, 22037
Robertson, George. Charge, 36874
Robertson, James

Account of the trial, 27633-35
   Proclamation, 17963
Robertson, John, 1712-1776
   Tables of difference, (1790) 22856, (1799) 35670,
     36236
   Tables of latitude, 24357
Robertson, Joseph, 1726-1802
   Clear and practical, 24751, 31113
   Essay on punctuation, 22119
Robertson, William, 1721-1793
   Historical disquisition, 24752
   History of America, 34476, 36237, 38413
   History of the reign, 11837
Robespierre, Maximilien
   Important state paper, 27003
   National convention, 27002
   Report, 28697
   dictatorship of, 28265, 31635
   extracts from, 26015
   government of, 31106
Robie, Thomas, 1689-1729
   Almanac see **Almanacs (Robie)**
   Knowledge of Christ, 2288
   Letter, 2171
Robin, Claude C., b. 1750. New travels, 18167,
   18765
Robin Hood, 37827
Robin Hood society. Debates, 13486
Robin Red Breast, 20461, 35735
Robineau, Alexander B. Tell truth, 32066
Robins, Ezekeil, candidate, 35934
Robinson, Sir Christopher, 1766-1833. Reports of
   cases, 38414
Robinson, George, hand of fellowship, 28227
Robinson, J. Yorker's stratagem, 26103
Robinson, James. Philadelphia register, 36238
Robinson, John, ordained, 21810
Robinson, Joseph, letter (from Clinton), 6026
Robinson, Levi, baptized, 25056
Robinson, Matthew, baron Rokeby see **Rokeby,**
   Matthew Robinson, 2d baron, 1713-1800
Robinson, Moses
   Proclamation, 23014
   on committee, 17842
Robinson, Robert, 1735-1790. Ecclesiastical re-
   searches, 29424
Robinson, William. Epistle, 911
Robinson, Crusoe, (1775) 14004, (1776) 14730,
   (1777) 15283, (1786) 19599, (1788) 21045, (1789)
   21787-88, (1791) 23320, (1792) 24253-54, (1793)
   25386, (1794) 26864-66, (1795) 28552-55, (1796)
   30325, (1798) 33617, (1799) 36445, (1800) 37303-
   305
Robinson's Philadelphia register, 36238
Robison, John, 1739-1805
   Proofs, 34477-78
   extracts from, 35181, 35307, 36239
Robson, John C. Scriptural view, 34479
Roby, Joseph, 1724-1803
   Sermon, 17356, 27636
   hand of fellowship, 9506?

VOL.	ITEMS	VOL.	ITEMS
1	1-3244	8	22298-25074
2	3245-6623	9	25075-28145
3	6624-9891	10	28146-30832
4	9892-13091	11	30833-33261
5	13092-16176	12	33262-25854
6	16177-19448	13	35855-39162
7	19449-22297		

Roman Catholic church see Catholic church
Roman Catholic primer, 19967
  history, 28755, 33805
  stories, 29466, 31176
Romance of an hour, 15377, 28918
  of real life, 36316
  of the forest, 29379-80
Romans, Bernard, 1720-1784
  Annals, 16059, 17707
  Chart containing part, 14441
  Chart containing the peninsula, 14442
  Concise natural history, 14440, 15069
  It is proposed, 14443
  Map of the state, 15585
  To the Hon'l, 14444
Romans in Greece, 35160
Romayne, Jeremiah, 1768-1818. American Israel,
  29429
Romayne, Nicholas, dedication to, 28193
Romeo and Judiet [playbill], 10573
Romeyn, James C. V., installation, 37257
Romeyn, John Brodhead, 1777-1825. Funeral ora-
  tion, 38421
Romilly, Sampel, tr. Considerations, 19803
Romp, a musical, 24111, 25192
Romulus (ship), at Charleston, 29128
Ronde, Lambertus de
  (tr.) Constitutie, 21522
  Gekruicigde Christus, 6776
  System containing, 9507
  True spiritual, 10757
  Ware gedagt'nis, 6927
Ronde chanté, 27228
Roney, James. To the inhabitants, 16547
Roosen, Gerhard, 1612-1711. Christliches gemüths-
  gespräch, (1769) 11446, (1770) 11648, (1790)
  22858
Roosevelt, Nicholas I.
  Papers, 31473
  petition, 33987
Root, Erastus, 1773-1846. Introduction to arith-
  metic, (1795) 29430, (1796) 31119, (1799) 36244
Root, Jesse, 1736-1822. Reports of cases, 34485
Roots, Benajah, 1726-1787. Few brief remarks,
  11838
Roots, Peter Philanthropos, 1764-1828. Letter,
  27637
Rosa, 28978
Rosamond, mistress of Henry II, 30563
Rosary, 30569
Roscoe, William. The nurse, 38604
Roscoe, William, 1753-1831
  Strictures on Mr. Burke, 32778
  Wrongs of Africa, 21435
Roscommon. To the author, 3722
Rose, Aquila, 1695-1723
  Poems, 4593
  elegy on, 2436
Rose, Charles, d. 1787
  Narrative of the life, 20974
  executed, 21598-99
Rose, Henry. Inaugural dissertation, 27638
Rose, Joseph, publishes father's poems, 4593
Rose of Sharon, 21436
Rosencrantz, Herman, d. 1770. Life and confession,
  11839
Rosina, a comic opera, 20243-44, 28348
Rosina, or love, 23223
Roslin Castle, 16508
Ross, ——, remarks upon, 10621
Ross, Capt. ——, sermon before, 13861-62

Ross, David, b. 1750
  Address, 24756
  reply to, 24538
Ross, Ezra, d. 1778, executed, 15872-73
Ross, George
  At a meeting, 14821
  In committee, 14817
Ross, James, 1744-1827
  Plain, short, 34486
  Practical new, 36245
Ross, James, 1762-1847
  accounts, 19179?
  election favored, 35450, 35081-82
  election opposed, 35631, 36422-23
  infidel, 35674
Ross, Robert, d. 1782
  American grammar, 17708
  American Latin grammar, (1770) 11840, (1780)
    16982-83, (1793) 26105, (1794) 27639-40
  Complete introduction, (1752) 6928, (1760) 8728,
    (1767) 10758
  Plain address, 9261
  Sermon, 12987, 15070
  extracts from, 15072
  reply to, 13360
Ross, Robert, d. 1799
  New American spelling, 19927, 19968
  New primer, 21437, 22859
Ross, William Morrey. Chemico-physiological in-
  augural, 29431
Ross, Zephaniah
  Defence of the divinity, 29432
  Oration, 29433
Ross & Douglas
  Catalogue, 38237
  booksellers, 35419
Rossell, Zechariah, subscribes to sports book,
  23785-86
Rotch, ——, shipowner, 12913
Rotheram, John, d. 1788
  (ed.) Edinburgh new dispensatory, 30692-93
  Essay, 10759
  notes by, 24236, 25359
Rou, Lewis
  Collection of some, 2698
  True state, 2811
Rouelle, John. Complete treatise, 24757
Rouget de Lisle, Claude Joseph, 1760-1836
  Hymne des Marseillais, 26106
  Marseilles-march, 26107
Rough Hewer see Yates, Abraham, Jr.
Round hand copies, 27641
Round text copies, 20257
Roupell, George, case of, 10945
Rousby, Gezelena
  New-York, January, 11448
  To the freeholders, 11447
Rousby, William, imprisonment, 11447
Rouso, Charles Dennis D'Eres. Memoirs, 38422
Rousseau, Jean Jacques, 1712-1778
  Confessions, 31121

VOL.	ITEMS	VOL.	ITEMS
1	1-3244	8	22298-25074
2	3245-6623	9	25075-28145
3	6624-9891	10	28146-30832
4	9892-13091	11	30833-33261
5	13092-16176	12	33262-25854
6	16177-19448	13	35855-39162
7	19449-22297		

VOL.	ITEMS	VOL.	ITEMS
1	1-3244	8	22298-25074
2	3245-6623	9	25075-28145
3	6624-9891	10	28146-30832
4	9892-13091	11	30833-33261
5	13092-16176	12	33262-25854
6	16177-19448	13	35855-39162
7	19449-22297		

Rumford, Benjamin Thompson, count, 1753-1814
  Essays political, 34656, 36251
Rumpus, Roger, at a meeting in N.Y., 13126
Rumsey, James, 1743-1792
  Explanation of a steam engine, 21439
  Plan wherein the power, 21092, 21440
  Short treatise, 21441-42
  defended, 20954
  false datings, 21093
  given manufacturing rights, 22051
  plan of steamboat, 21032
Rural economy, 25061
    felicity, 34493
    harmony, 25695, 30662
    magazine, (1795) 29450, (1796) 31141, (1798)
      34494, (1799) 36252
    oeconomy, 15226
    Socrates, (1776) 15226, (1792) 25061, (1800)
      38923
    walks, 29525
Rush, Benjamin, 1745-1813
  Account of the bilious, 27658-59
  Account of the sugar maple, 24761
  Address to the inhabitants, 12990-94, 14447
  Considerations on the injustice, 24762
  Considerations upon the present, 18770, 19230
  Directions for preserving, 16064-65
  Directions for the use, 19971
  Enquiry into the effects, 20689
  Enquiry into the origin, 26111
  Essays literary, 34495
  Eulogium in honor, 22862-63
  Eulogium intended, 31143
  Experiments, 12995
  (ed.) First lines, 17129
  Inquiry into the effects, (1787) 20690, (1790)
    22864-65, (1791) 23415
  Inquiry into the natural, 22122
  Medical inquiries, (1789) 22123, (1793) 26112,
    (1794) 27660, (1796) 31144, (1797) 32784,
    (1798) 34496
  New method, 17362
  Observations on, 11449
  Observations upon the cause, 19231
  Observations upon the origin, 36253
  Observations upon the present, 15589, 18172
  Oration delivered Feb. 4, 1774, 13592
  Oration delivered before the American, 19972-73
  Plan for the establishment, 19974
  Second address, 36254
  Sermons to gentlemen, 12547
  Syllabus, 18173, 34497
  Thoughts on female education, 23790
  Thoughts upon female, 20691-92, 23747
  To the citizens, 17743
  Three lectures, 36255
  dedication to, 24138
  observations on, 25254, 31172
  plaintiff, 37103
  plans cure for yellow fever, 28761
  recommends book, 33718
  reply to, 26836
Rush, Jacob, 1746-1820
  Address, 23748
  Charge, 34498
Rush light, 27661, 37198
Rushton, Edward, 1756-1814. Expostulatory letter,
  32785-86
Russ, D. Uranian harmony, 23749
Russel, ——, reply to, 1635
Russel, Chambers. Journal, 6861

Russel, Joseph, petition, 38899
Russel, Nathaniel, lodges complaint, 34908
Russel, Noadiah, 1659-1713
  Cambridge ephemeris see Almanacs (Russell)
  death, 1670
Russel, Noadiah, d. 1795, death, 31630
Russel, Robert. Seven sermons, (1701) 1021, (1727)
  2953, (1728) 3101, (1766) 10484-85, (1767) 10762-
  63, (1772) 12548-49, (1774) 13593, (1784) 18772,
  (1788) 21443, (1792) 24763, (1793) 26113-16,
  (1795) 29452, (1797) 32787-88, (1798) 34499
Russel, William, demandent, 11614
Russell, ——, tr. Essay on the character, 13650
Russell, Benjamin, 1761-1845. Society of the Cin-
  cinnati, 18771
Russell, David. Vermont university, 38933
Russell, Edward, earl of Oxford see Oxford,
  Edward Russell, earl of, 1653-1727
Russell, Ezekiel. Life and character, 22270
Russell, James, warning to, 459
Russell, James, d. 1798, death, 34144
Russell, John, 1774?-1795, death, 28330, 29605
Russell, John, fl. 1786, ed. Miscellaneous collec-
  tion, 19751
Russell, John Miller, 1768-1840
  Funeral oration, 38435
  Oration, 32790-91
  Pastoral songs, 36356
  Poem, 34500
  Poems, 36625
Russell, Jonathan, 1655-1711. Plea, 1193
Russell, Jonathan, 1771-1832
  Oration, 38436-37
  To the freemen, 38438
  Tribute to the memory, 22867
Russell, Joseph, of Boston. To all people, 26690
Russell, Joseph, 1775-1861
  Oration, 36257
  Sermon, 34501
  hand of fellowship, 36019
  ordained, 30008
Russell, Robert see Russel, Robert
Russell, S., petition, 34743
Russell, Samuel, 1661-1731. Connecticut election
  sermon, 895
Russell, Samuel, 1693-1746
  Man's liableness, 5050
  death, 6065
Russell, Thomas, d. 1796
  Information for immigrants, 28321
  death, 30604-605, 30825, 31284
  eulogy of, 31522
Russell, William, 1690-1761
  Decay of love, 3473
  Duty of an army, 8729
Russell, William, 1741-1793. History of modern,
  38439
Russell & Clap, auctioneers, 21204
Russell's gazette. Boston, Jan. 1, 1800, 38441
Russian slaves, 28494-95
Rustic festivity, 29610, 34633
Rusticus
  Friendly debate, 2386
  Good of the community, 7312
  Letter from the country, 12652
  Liberty, a poem, (1768) 11061, (1769) 11323,
    (1770) 11844-45
  see also Dickinson, John, 1732-1808
Rutgers, Anthony. City of New-York, 11284
Rutgers, Elizabeth
  Arguments and judgment, 18773

plaintiff, 18320
Rutgers, H. G., & co.
Catalogue of books, 35946
Large catalogue, 35948
Large consignment, 35947
Rutherford, ——. Exercises of mind, 29905
Rutherford, Thomas, 1712-1771. Institutes of natural, 36260
Rutherford, Walter. Brief of the claim, 11356
Ruth's resolution, 8589
Rutland co. To the representatives, 36434
Rutledge, Edward, 1749-1800
War office, 15192
on committee to meet Howe, 15168

Rutledge, John, 1739-1800
observations on, 17861
reports on Northwest Territory, 18264
Rutter, Thomas, rebuked, 811
Rutty, John, 1698-1775. Liberty, 8486
Ryan, James. Pedantic pedagogue, 16513
Rycaut, Sir Paul, d. 1700. Counterfeit Messiah, 29454, 30301, 32793
Ryer, John, d. 1793
Narrative of the life, 26118
reward for, 25906
Ryland, John, 1753-1825. Northampton letter, 36799
Rymnikski, Alexander Suworow, campaigns, 36845
Ryther, John, 1634-1681. Best friend, 2289

S

S., F. Sentiments, 4074
S., F., 1737?-1763, prostitute, 9717, 10047, 12242
S., G., fl. 1756, editor, 7650
S., G., fl. 1793. New introduction to reading, (1793) 26119, (1794) 27663, (1795) 29455-56, (1796) 31146
S. . ., G. . . H. . see Spierin, George Hartwell
S., H. History of the Davenport, 34505
S., J.
Almanac see **Almanacs (Sherman)**
(ed.) Brief view, 9916-17
Second Spira, 681, 2290, 14448
see also **Scottow, Joshua, 1618-1698; Searson, John; Sherman, John, 1624-1695**
S., J. G., tr. Elegia, 28620
S., John see Sechia, John
S., L. Porcupine, 18774
S., M. see Menno Simons
S., R.
Jachin and Boaz, (1796) 31147, (1798) 34506, (1799) 36263
see also **Sandeman, Robert, 1718-1771; Steere, Richard**
S., S. see Sewall, Samuell
S., T.
Almanac see **Almanacs (S., T.)**
Divine breathings, 29457
see also **Peters, Samuel Andrew, 1735-1826**
S., W.
Mysterious nothing, 4075
To Mrs. Margaret, 5268
see also **Shirley, William, 1693-1771**
S——a, Miss ——. Letter, 23501
S. . .h, W. see Smith, William, 1727-1803
S——t, J——s, moves to Philadelphia, 11507
Sabbath-day's rest, 2664
Sabbath profanity, 8773

Sackett, Nathaniel. Memorial, 19232
Sackville, George Germaine, 1st viscount see Germaine, George, 1st viscount Sackville
Saco Indians, conference, 4976
Sacrament of the Lord's supper, 4519
Sacramental catechism, 23654
controversy, 11566
exercises, (1715) 1739, (1725) 2628, (1729) 3158, (1756) 7649
meditations and advices, 28104-105
on the sufferings, 4483, 24170
upon divers, 1351, 1543
sermon, 21670
Sacred architecture, 26201
baptism, 2907
biography, 27146, 28870
concert, 38108
dignity, 6870
dirges, 37635
dramas chiefly intended, 20534
dramas written, 32179
harmony, (anon.) 21453, (Cole) 35319, (Lee) 22615, 38446
lines, 25562
minister, 12864
music, 25951

platform, 13155
poetry, 28258, 31793
to the memory, 35664, 36265
Sacrifice of the wicked, 17508
Sacrificer, 1698
Sad effects, 1626
estate, 4076
tendency, 6797
Safe conduct, 29458
Safety of appearing, (1687) 434, (1729) 3220, (1742) 5068
Saffin, John. Brief and candid, 1022
Sagasity, ———. Whiteoak anthum, 10211
Sage, Sylvester, 1765-1841
Sermon, 34507
ordained, 23367
Sagesse; no. 2660, 35838-39
Sagittarius's letters, 14255
Sailor boy, 25613
Sailor lov'd, 30203
Sailor's medley, 38447
Sailor's return, 23204
Sailours companion, 1406
St. André, Jean Bon. Summary journal, 27664
St. Andrew's society, N.Y. Rules, 11777, 19135
St. Andrew's society, Phila.
Constitution, 11416, 23698
Rules, 6756
St. Asaph, Jonathan, bp. of see Shipley, Jonathan, 1714-1788
St. Caecilia society. Rules, 13196
St. Clair, Alexander. Staunton, Sept. 3d, 1793, 26204
St. Clair, Arthur
Letter, 38753
Speech, 21538
address to his brigade, 15229
compensated, 27858
court martial, 16141
defeat by Indians, 23474, 24474, 24865
defeat investigated, 24909
expedition, 25665-71, 28907
investigation of Harmar's conduct, 23905
memorial of, 27907
reports on courts-martial, 20061
reports on currency, 20051
reports on emoluments, 20090
retreat, 16217-18
witnesses treaty, 20789
St. Clair's defeat, 24474
St. David's, Charles, bp. of see Moss, Charles, 1711-1802
St. Domingo
Particular account, 24765-66
Protestations, 27665
St. Francis Indians, conference, 3916, 4976
St. George (ship), scene of court martial, 7892
St. Hubert, 38448
Saint indeed, 2869, 28676
St. John, Buckingham, d. 1771, death, 12255
St. John, Henry viscount Bolingbroke see Bolingbroke, Henry St. John, viscount, 1678-1751
St. John, J. Hector see Crèvecoeur, Michel Guillaume St. Jean de, 1735-1813
St. John, Nathan, letters patent, 3454
St. John, Peter
Death of Abel, 26120
Poetical relation, 23750
St. John, Samuel. American taxation, 18174
St. John's church, incorporated, 29368
St. John's college. Address of the visitors, 27666

St. John's Indians, conference with, 4976
St. John's lodge. By-laws, 32765
St. John's vision, 10310
St. Joseph (snow), suit against, 6832
Saint-Jure, Jean Baptiste, 1588-1657. Extract of the life, 29459
St. Lambert, Jean François de, 1716-1803. Story of Sarah, 32794
St. Leger, Miss ———. Youthful imprudence, 34525
St. Louis (pilot boat), seized, 15877
St. Patrick, song to, 22591
St. Paul's example, 25952
St. Paul's manner, 33960
St. Peter's exhortation, 15596
St. Pierre, Jacques Henri Bernardin de, 1737-1814
Beauties of the studies, 36266
Botanical harmony, 32795
Indian cottage, 38449
Paul and Mary, 27667, 29460
Paul and Virginia, (1796) 31150, (1799) 36267, (1800) 38450
Paul et Virginie, 31148-49
Studies of nature, 32796, 34508
Vindication of divine, 32797
Voyages of Amasis, 29461
St. Preux to Eloisa, 17605
St. Sauveur, J. Grasset. Twenty five precepts, 27463-64
St. Tammany's society. Constitution, 22019
St. Vellum, ———. Collection of country dances, 29462
Saint's daily assistant, (1791) 23516, (1793) 25737, (1796) 30711
everlasting rest, (1763) 9335, (1776) 14661, (1790) 22331, (1791) 23161, (1794) 26626-27, (1796) 30040, (1800) 36910
jewel, 5289
prayer, 1791
victory, 774
Salas Barbadillo, Alonso Jerónimo, 1580-1635
Lucky idiot, 32798
Sale catalogue for 1786, 19538
catalogue for 1787, 20260
catalogue of a collection, 12670
calalogue of books, (Campbell) 26728, 35267, (Keatinge) 30652
catalogue of the books, 22399
Salem, Mass.
Articles for the Old fire club, 22125
Articles of the Amity fire club, 31152
Articles of the Social fire club, 26125
By-laws and regulations of the East India, 38454
Bylaws and regulations of the incorporated, 32800
Catalogue of books (Dutch), 38456
Copy of the church-covenants, 295
Direction for a publick, 100
Essex, ss. To either, 23751
Large collection, 36268
Last night of performing, 36269
Laws of the Marine society, 18775, 22868
List of prices, 16514
Medicine chests, 38455
Memorial to United States, 31151
Price act, 15590
Proposal for printing, 38453
Remainder of a large catalogue, 36270
Rules and regulations of the proprietors, 32799
Rules and regulations to be observed, 34509
Salem, Nov. 18, 1800, 38451
Tribute to the memory, 38452

VOL.	ITEMS	VOL.	ITEMS
1	1-3244	8	22298-25074
2	3245-6623	9	25075-28145
3	6624-9891	10	28146-30832
4	9892-13091	11	30833-33261
5	13092-16176	12	33262-25854
6	16177-19448	13	35855-39162
7	19449-22297		

agent of Ohio company, 20604
letter (from Henderson), 38892?
Sarjeant, Thomas
(ed.) Easy and compendious, 21869, 24370, 35578
Elementary principles, 21445
Federal arithmetician, 22870, 26137
Introduction to the counting house, 22127
Paradigm of inflections, 21446
Select arithmetical exercises, 26138
Select arithmetical tables, 21447, 22128
Synopsis, 21448
Twenty arithmetical, 19977
Sarrazin, M., engraver of maps, 5063
Sartorius, Christoph Friderich, preface by, 14021
Sarum, Robert, bp. of see **Drummond, Robert Hay, 1711-1776**
Sasse, Bernhard Heinrich. Geistliche lieder, 36276
Satan strip'd, 5180-81
Satan's harbinger, 948
Saturday, (Mar. 18, 1775) 13968-69, (Mar. 25, 1775) 13971, (Apr. 1, 1775) 13973, (Apr. 8, 1775) 13975, (Apr. 15, 1775) 13977, (Apr. 22, 1775) 13979, (Apr. 29, 1775) 13981
Satyr on the sweepers, 13595
Saul, an apostle, 16515
Saunders, ——, ship's captain, 27819
Saunders, Daniel. Journal, 27671, 32804
Saunders, Richard. Almanac see **Almanacs (Pocket); Almanacs (Poor Richard)**
Saunders, Tracy, plaintiff, 31668
Saunders, William, 1743-1817
Observations, 18178
Treatise, 32805
Saur, Christoph, 1693-1758
Abgenöthigter bericht, 4420
Bekanntmachung, 4796
Verschiedene Christliche, 6233
Zu dieser zeit, 7564, 9828
Saur, Christoph, 1721-1784
Einfältiges reim-gedichte, 17367
Nuetzliche anweisung, (1751) 6777, (1762) 9264, (1772) 12552, (1792) 24771
Wertheste landes-leute, 10162
aspersions by, 9902
books for sale by, 11339
Saur, Samuel. Almanac see **Almanacs (Saur)**
Savage, Edward, 1761-1817
Liberty, 31159-60
portrait by, 30392, 37951
Savage, Ezekiel, 1760-1837. Eulogy, 38466
Savage, Thomas, d. 1681?, death, 380
Savannah
At a meeting, 29469
Fire ordinance, 32806
Rules and regulations for the Dancing assembly, 22873
Savary, ——, travels of, 31692, 33466
Savery, William, 1750-1804. Three sermons, 32807
Sawney
Dialogue, 2339
Paradise regain'd, 11849
answer to, 2333
Sawney, Scots. Letter (to Wilkes), 9489
Sawyer, Edmund, town clerk Newbury, 15484
Sawyer, Lanah, raped, 26513
Sawyer, Matthias E. Inaugural dissertation, 26140
Saxe, Count ——, excerpts from, 26054
Say, Benjamin, 1756-1813
Annual oration, 36278
Short compilation, 31161
Say, Thomas, 1709-1796
Visions, 13598

life and writings of, 31161
Saybrook synod. Confession of faith, 1486, 8733
Sayre, Francis Bowes. Inaugural dissertation, 22874
Sayre, James
Address, 22130
Candid narrative, 21450
letter (from Bowden), 24139
reply to, 21709
Sayre, John
From the New York journal, 15078
Sermon, 12998
Sayre, Stephen, 1736-1818
Englishman deceived, 11065-66
Reasons for not signing, 9265
Short narrative, 27673
petition, 36567, 38828
Scaevola. To the commissioners, 12999
Scale of depreciation, 17235
Scales, William. Confusion, 16989
Scanyawtauragahrooote Indians, adventures with, 38422
Scarce and valuable books, 38258
Scarecrow, being an infamous, 30231-33, 31948
Scautacook Indians, conference with, 3916
Scene in the first, 9829
Schabalie, Jan Philipsen. Wandlende seel, (1763) 9511, (1768) 11067, (1771) 12221, (1794) 27674
Schaffer, David. To the public, 16990
Schaffer, Francis C. Pocket companion, 34516
Schedule of requisitions, 20081, 20784-85
of the expenses of the town, 35219, 38339
French, 20082
requisitions, 21532
whole number, 23917
Scheel, Henri Othon de, 1745-1807. Treatise, 38467
Schell, Alexander, anecdotes of, 31313
Schema sacrum, 14665
Scheme by striking, 4194
for the revival, 7115
of a convention, 19330
of a lottery for disposing, 13000-1
for raising, 13002
for the purpose, 22721
granted, 13559, 28026
to be drawn, 8031
to raise 39,900, 27675
to raise 40,800, 26141
to raise the sum, 23754
of Christ-church lottery, 12160
of the exercises, 36743
of the exhibitions, (1796) 35060, (1797) 35061, (1798) 35062, (1800) 39154
of the Irish state, 22585
to drive, 7377
Schenck, Abraham
At a meeting, 33276
To the electors, 34669
Schenck, William. Attempt to delineate, 31162
Schenectady
Charter, 34517
Constitution of the Social society, 38468
Schenectady, April 13th, 1799, 36279
Schenectady academy. Rules, 26142
La Schiava overture, 22069
Schiller, Johann Christoph Friedrich von, 1759-1805
Cabal and love, 29470
Ghost-seer, 31163-64
Robbers, 26143, 29471
Schinck, A., tr. The stranger, 35705
Schmiedlein, Jacob. Kurtze beschreibung, 6234
Schneeberger, Andrew

VOL.	ITEMS	VOL.	ITEMS
1	1-3244	8	22298-25074
2	3245-6623	9	25075-28145
3	6624-9891	10	28146-30832
4	9892-13091	11	30833-33261
5	13092-16176	12	33262-25854
6	16177-19448	13	35855-39162
7	19449-22297		

verses on, 11249
Scott, Joseph
At his shop, 31168
Blue shop, 31065
New and universal gazetteer, (1798) 34519,
(1799) 36282, (1800) 38473
United States gazetteer, 29476
Scott, Joseph Warren, 1778-1871. Oration, 34520
Scott, Mary, life, 30096
Scott, Obadiah, petition, 38763
Scott, R., engraver, 36757
Scott, Sarah Robinson, 1723-1795
Man of real, 20696, 38474
Man of sensibility, 32812
Scott, Thomas, excerpts from, 30371
Scott, Thomas, of Annapolis. Sermon, 24773
Scott, Thomas, 1747-1821
Force of truth, 26147, 29475
Vindication of the divine, 32813
Scott, Sir William, judgments by, 38414
Scott, William, 1750-1804
Introduction to the reading, 20697
Lessons in elocution, (1786) 19980, (1788) 21451,
(1790) 22879, (1794) 27680, (1795) 29477,
(1797) 32814, (1798) 34521, (1799) 36283-85,
(1800) 38475
O tempora, 13599-600
Scottow, Joshua, 1618-1698
Massachusetts, 773
Narrative, 709
Old men's tears, (1691) 576, (1715) 1779, (1732)
3604, (1749) 6413, (1769) 11457
(tr.) Rise, spring, 119
Scougal, Henry, 1650-1678
Leben Gottes, 7565, 7787
Life of God, (1766) 10489-90, (1789) 22131,
(1795) 29478
Sermon, 4195
Vital Christianity, (1725) 2700, (1730) 3350,
(1741) 4797
Scourge, Humphrey. Tit for tat, 8256
Scourge, in two numbers, 12222
Scourge of fashion, 38476
Scribler, 9831
Scribner, Rev. ———, conference with, 17449
Scriptural account, 16814
and allegorical, 31308
answer, 12412
catechism, 565
cautions, 18310
comment on the Athanasian, 23396
comment upon the thirty-nine, 12443
doctrine of atonement, 19381
of future, 32342
of water baptism, 35560
enquiry, 27695
grounds, 12076
light, 4264
researches, 22555
view, 34479
Scripture account, 27689
bishop, or the divine, 3528, 3636
bishop vindicated, 3651
catechism, 6603
characters, 4910
doctrine concerning predestination, 5881
of original sin, 8103
of predestination, 21961, 29479
of regeneration, 36872
of the appropriation, 25109
of the reconciliation, 7806

grounds, 3885
history, 31178
instruction, 7198
manual, (1763) 9546, (1772) 12620, (1795)
29905
prophesies, 7870
songs, being a translation, 12554
songs for Zion's, 12619
truths and precepts, 23838
truths demonstrated, 20309
warning, 34522
Scriptures the only, 2491
Scripturista see **Hart, William, 1713-1784**
Scrivener's guide, 32212
Scudder, William. Journal, 27681
Scull, Nicholas, 1700-1761
Kawanio che, 7788-89
Plan of the city, 15593
Plan of the improved, 9267
To the honourable, 8489
surveyor, 7209?
Scull, William. To the honourable, 11850
Seabury, Samuel, d. 1764
Modest reply, 8490
Sermon, 5051
Seabury, Samuel, 1729-1796
Address to the ministers, 22880, 32815
Alarm, 14453
Bishop Seabury's second charge, 19981
Communion-office, 19982
Congress canvassed, 13601
Discourse delivered before an assembly, 29480
Discourse delivered before the triennial, 24774
Discourse delivered in St. James, 29481
Discourse delivered in St. John's, 23650, 23755
Discourse on brotherly, 15594
Discourse on II. Tim., 15595
Discourses on several important, 34523
Discourses on several subjects, 26148
Duty of considering, 22132
Earnest persuasive, 22133
Free thoughts, 13602
St. Peter's exhortation, 15596
Sermon, 18180, 21452
View of the controversy, 13603
address to, 19207
approves psalter, 28282
death, 30636
sermon before, 26175
Seagrave, Robert, 1693-1760
Remarks, 4594
True Protestant, 6235-36
Seaman, Valentine, 1770-1817
Account of the epidemic, (1796) 31169, 31593,
(1797) 32816
Dissertation, 26149
Inaugural dissertation, 24775
Midwives monitor, 38477
Seaman's articles, 24913
daily assistant, 15360, 16301
journal, (1786) 19534, (1788) 20988, (1800)
38478
Search after happiness, (1773) 12872, (1774) 13449,
(1775) 14263, (1786) 19811-12, (1787) 20535,
(1791) 23575-76, (1793) 25846, (1795) 29105,
(1796) 30815, (1797) 32502
Seares, Alexander. Account of the reasons, 2174
Searl, John, 1721-1787
Character and reward, 16069
Funeral sermon, 12223, 16425
Revelation, 13003

Searl, Jonathan, ordained, 13353
Sears, Isaac, 1729-1786
  Advertisement, 11458
  Letter, 13820
  New York, Oct. 1, 1774, 13484
  affidavit by, 14336
  candidate, 14674
  destroys manuscript, 14626
  letter (from a lady), 14032
  nominated, 14331
  satirized, 13656?
  tries to buy vote, 11322
Searson, John, 1750-
  Art of contentment, 31170
  Mount Vernon, 38479
  Poems, 32817
  Seven hints, 11851
  Two discourses, 11852
Seasonable account, 950
  advertisement, 11459
  advice concerning, 2780
    to a neighbour, 8982
    to the inhabitants, 3213
  and earnest, 8626
  caveat, 3975
  discourse, 325
  meditations both, 1566-67
  meditations for the last, 3146
  memento, 5947
  motives, 463
  plea, 11556
  testimony to good order, 2149
  testimony to the glorious, 1074
  thoughts on the state, 5151
  thoughts upon mortality, 1557
  warning against bad, 2824-25
  warning to these, 5757
  watch-word, 243
Seasons (Lovell), 10043
Seasons (Thomson), (1777) 15613, (1788) 21495, (1790) 22930-31, (1791) 23827, (1792) 24849, (1793) 26255, (1795) 29628, (1797) 32927, (1800) 38634
Seaver, Comfort, letter (from Hibbard), 28830
Seaward, William, d. 1782, death, 17746
Sebastian, Benjamin, reply to, 29024
Seccombe, John, 1708-1792
  Father Ab—y's will, 3474-75
  Eine zu Halifax, 11853
  Sermon, 12555
Seccombe, Joseph, 1706-1760
  Business and diversion, 5285
  Essay, 4798
  Plain and brief, 4595
  Reflections, 4799
  Some occasional, 5052
  Specimen, 5286
  Ways of pleasure, 9268
  ordained, 3723
Sechia, John, tr. Everlasting gospel, 7033
Sechs und zwanzig, 9874
Secker, Thomas, 1693-1768
  Answer to Dr. Mayhew, 9832
  Blessing of peace, 29668
  commentary on, 13193
  correspondence with Whitefield, 10803
  letter (from 18 ministers), 8807, 8819, 9003, 9027, 9288
  life, 12960, 13191-92
  reply to, 11995
Secker, William, d. 1681. Wedding ring, 6604, 13004

Second address to the citizens, 36254
  to the freemen, 22599
  to the members, 6693
  to the Reverend, 31259
  American edition; farriery, 33449
  Baptist church in New York, 25913
  catechism, 21577
  charge, 19981
  commandment, 5056
2d December 1800, 38907
Second defence of the episcopal, 11698
  defence of the old, 5930
  dialogue, 11490
  edition; a New Year's gift, 30216, 30234, 31174
  edition of An oration, 28109
  edition of the Ohio, 33915-16
  essay, 16671
  familiar conference, 9910
  holiday, 26826
  inquiry, 31244
  letter, (Bowden to Stiles), 21711, (Chauncy to Whitefield) 5153, (Devotion to Bellamy) 11631, (Kinnersley to friend), 4537, (Phocion to citizens) 18516
  letter from a gentleman, 8032
    from a minister, 3784
    from one in the country, 3214-15
    on the subject, 10238
    to a friend, 7382
    to —— —— merchant, 4800
    to the congregations, 9003
  Norwich edition, 13734
  part of South-Sea, 2291
    of the catalogue, 14392
    of the memorial, 19056
Second Philadelphia city troop of horse. Articles, 36109
Second publication, 6023
  reply, 11468
  section, 15838
  sermon, 37064
  sett of catechisms, 5708, 6265
  Spira, (1693) 681, (1721) 2290, (1775) 14448
  supplement, 27509
  treatise, 12715
  vindication of God's, 6094, 6123
  warning, 15555
Secrecy, or the ruin, 28667-68
Secret, a comedy, 38001
Secret history, 36286
  prayer explained, 12901
  prayer inculcated, 2086
  tribunal, 31839
Secretary of state, to whom was referred . . . the letter, 23001
Secretary of state, to whom was referred . . . the petition, 23919
Secretary of the treasury having attentively, 23920
  pursuant to a resolution, 24929
  sir, 27919
  to whom the House, 24930

VOL.	ITEMS	VOL.	ITEMS
1	1-3244	8	22298-25074
2	3245-6623	9	25075-28145
3	6624-9891	10	28146-30832
4	9892-13091	11	30833-33261
5	13092-16176	12	33262-25854
6	16177-19448	13	35855-39162
7	19449-22297		

to whom was referred, 24931
to whom were referred by the House, 24932
to whom were referred certain, 24933
Secretary of the U.S. for the Dept. of foreign affairs, 19323, 27929
Secretary of the U.S. for the Dept. of war, 20786
Secretary of war and the secretary, 38808
Secretary's guide, (1698) 818, (1705) 1201, (1714) 1668, (1728) 2997, (1729) 3139, (1737) 4127
Secrets of Masonry, 35310
Secrets worth knowing, 35845
Secundus. Animadversions, 16519
Security of Englishmen's lives, 2178, 13024
Security of the rights, 24776
Sedaine, Michel Jean, 1719-1797. The deserter, 29482-83, 31171
Sedgwick, John
Impartial narrative, 18181
reply to, 17957
Sedgwick, Theodore, 1746-1813
dedication to, 38663?
political testament, 37645
Sedgwick & co., or a key, 33484
See brother see, 29119
Seed of the woman, 17441
Seelige creutz-schule, 9315
Seely, Bazaleel. Letter, 16991
Seged of Ethiopia, 28978
Seguenot. Letter from a Romish priest, 3216
Seidel, Christoph, tr. Christen reise, 7163, 30137
Seigneux de Correvon, Gabriel, d. 1776, essay by, 37382
Seiner königlichen, 9833
Seip, Frederic. Inaugural dissertation, 38481
Seitel, Christoph see **Seidel, Christoph**
Seixas, Gershom Mendez, 1745-1816
Discourse, 34524
Religious discourse, 22134
Seixas, Moses, cashier, 30896
Sejanus, character of, 3784
Sel spécifique, 32195
Selby, William, d. 1800
Apollo, 22881
Two anthems, 22882
Selden, Andrew, 1762?-1825. Young child's easy, 38482
Seleced [!] catalogue, 25587
Select arithmetical exercises, 26138
arithmetical tables, 21447, 22128
collection of historical, 13604
of poems, 31027
of the most, 20674
dialogues, 21927, 28991
discourses, 34638
essays, containing, 15597
essays with some, 1715
fables of Aesop, (1777) 15232, (1786) 19455, (1790) 22300
fables of Esop, (1791) 24027, (1794) 26539, (1798) 33274
harmony (Brownson), 17857, **23227**
harmony (Law), (1779) 16318, (1784) 18553, (1786) 19754, (1791) 23492, (1792) 24467
letters, 16078
number of plain tunes, (1767) 10662, (1772) 12427, (1781) 17097-98, (1782) 17475, (1785) 18930, (1794) 27208
pamphlets, 29484, 31172-74
pamphlets respecting, 36287
passages, 28272

pieces, 18081, 31521
plays, 31175, 35701
poems, (Fry) 20381, 37479, (Humphreys) 20420
poems on various, 20698
psalms and hymns, 20181, 26660
religious, 37188
remains (Mason), (1743) 5234, (1793) 25768, (1799) 35783, (1800) 37900
sermons, 28306
songster, 19750
stories (Berquin), 26646, 31804
stories for the instruction, 29485
stories or miscellaneous, 34525
verses, 22883
Selectae e profanis, 20227
e Veteri Testamento et e profanis, 21683
e Veteri Testamento historiae, (1787) 20226, (1795) 28272, (1796) 30069
Selected catalogue, 25587
Selected pronouncing, 37355-56
Selection of fables, 34112
hymns and spiritual, 33460
hymns from the best, 24749
miscellaneous, 24777
orations, 36859
psalms and hymns, 22593, 33939
psalms with occasional, 24108, 26661
sacred harmony, (1788) 21453, (1790) 22884, (1797) 32818
the patriotic, 33345
Selections from the Book, 26045
Selections from the correspondence, 38997
Selectmen of the town, 25215
Self-defensive war, 13861-62
Self disclaimed, 8070
Self-employment, 357, 19587
Self-examination, 5787
Self immolation, 35702, 37759
Self-interpreting Bible, (1790) 22348, (1791) 23181, (1792) 24099
Self-justiciary, 1322, 4561
Self knowledge, (1789) 21942, (1793) 25769, (1800) 37901
Seliger marter-stand, 6964
Selima & Azore, 24500
Selkirk, Alexander, verses by, 32501
Sellers, Richard, sufferings of, 12556, 38519
Selling of Joseph, 951, 4149
Semi-annual oration, 35263
Semi-Virgilian husbandry, 9808
Semper radiantes, 19845, 20571
Semple, ——, violates agreement, 11888
Semple, James George, swindler, 38291
Senator of the U. S. Review of the question, 31086
Senators, a poem, 12372
Seneca. Morals, (1792) 24778, (1794) 27682-83, (1800) 37818
Seneca Indians
Documents relative, 28886
conferences, 8156
propositions by, 819?
treaty, (1694) 702?, (1696) 743?, (1758) 8157
Senior see **Austin, William, 1778-1841**
Senneke Indians, treaty, 702
Sensibility, a drama, 34526
Sensibility, a poetical, 19102
Sensible sinners, 3977
Sententiae pueriles, 1045, 2427
Senter, Isaac, d. 1800
death, 38196
proposal to print sermon by, 38113

Sentimental and literary, 32819
    journey, (1771) 12237, (1790) 22909, (1791)
      23800, (1792) 24818, (1793) 26210, (1795)
      29565
    lucubrations, 25980
    sailor, 17605
Sentiments and plan of the Stonington, 20731
    and plan of the Warren, 11519
    and resolutions, 5668
    concerning the coming, 31225
    of a British, 9851
      foreigner, 14417
      free, 12224
      principal, 4074
    of an American, 16992
    of the humours, 9551
    on education, 16070
    upon the religion, 29486-88
Sentinel
    To the inhabitants of New York, 15107
    To the inhabitants of the city, 14757, 15108
Separation of the Jewish, 15317
Separation of the tares, 5926
September 27th, 1794, 26731
Sept. 30, 1796, 30060
Seraphical young, 25270-71
Seraphina, a novel, 32467
Sergeant, John, 1710-1749
    Causes and danger, 5287
    Letter (to Colman), 5288
    Morning prayer, 4596
Sergeant, John, fl. 1735
    missionary, 7023, 7916-17, 29879
    ordained, 3867?
Sergeant, John D., opinion of, 24421
Sergeant, Thomas, ed. Gurney's Easy, 35578
Sergeant-major of grenadiers. Journal, 8381
Series of Indostan letters, 22380
    of letters on courtship, 34527
      on education, 33236
      on missions, 28857
Serious address and farewell, 20835
    address of a minister, 24196
      on the dangerous, 30551
      to Christian, 18896
      to godfathers, 27684
      to part, 10851
      to such of the inhabitants, 9834-37
      to such of the people, 15843-45
      to the candid, 24779
      to the clergy, 7765
      to the freeholders, 8237
      to the inhabitants, 13605
      to the members, 5208, 6158
      to the people, 7028
      to the rulers, 17839
      to those, 2780
      to unbaptized, 6579
      to young people, 9488
      upon the subject, 19744
    advice to a sick, 3243
      to delivered ones, 261-62
      to persons, 7015
    and earnest, 5861
    appeal, 605
    call from the city, 8033-35
      in Christian, 3552, 28850
      to Christian, 18529
      to such, 30034
      to the Quakers, 1392
    consideration, 4326
    considerations on absolute, 5310

    on several, 15737
    on the election, 37835-36
    on the present, 7223-24, 7692
exhortation, 162, 254
exhortations, 3525
expostulation, 25820-22, 27319
facts, 38486
letter, 18033
poem, 26150
poem on various, 11233
reflections affectionately, 15738
    on late, 3838
    on the times, 8036
thoughts on the infallible, 21961
thoughts on the miseries, 3559
word, 3238
Serjeant, Winthrop, letter (from Henderson),
  38892
Serjent, Abel. Humble address, 24780
Serle, Ambrose, 1742-1812
    Christian parent, 23756, 29489
    Christian remembrancer, (1791) 23757, (1795)
      29490, (1799) 36288
    Horae solitariae, 36289
Sermon . . . see under author of the sermon
  (unless anonymous)
Sermon delivered by the Rev. Mr. N-o-y-e-s, 19149
    delivered on the death, 12503
    in praise of swearing, 10766, 22885
    on Luke VIII, 4801
    on Luke XIX, 25575
    on natural religion, 12225
    on sacrifices, 24488
    on tea, 13606
    on the evacuation, 18182
      present situation, 12557, 17717
      religious, 33237
      resurrection, 5053
    preached at Litchfield, 11551
      at the anniversary, 11460
      on the 25th, 4195
    to the bucks, 21454
Sermons on important, 32820
    on sacramental, 4438
    on several occasions, 28060, 39068
    on some, 37370
    on the cross, 19765
      religious, 26905
      security, 27551
    on various important, 35583
    on various subjects, doctrinal, 38579
    on various subjects, evangelical, 30679
    or declarations, 10868
    preached in London, 32384
    to asses, 11347-48, 11751-52
    to children, 32821
    to gentlemen, 12547
    to the rich, 23758
    to young persons, 26906
    to young women, 21831, 30435-36
    upon the following, 8081
Sero sapiunt, 13985

VOL.	ITEMS	VOL.	ITEMS
1	1-3244	8	22298-25074
2	3245-6623	9	25075-28145
3	6624-9891	10	28146-30832
4	9892-13091	11	30833-33261
5	13092-16176	12	33262-25854
6	16177-19448	13	35855-39162
7	19449-22297		

Servant man turned soldier, 35298
    of Abraham, 1831
    of God dismissed, 7861, 8097
    of the Lord, 1177
Servant's actual readiness, 6810, 6956
Servants' directory, 8607
Servants of the Lord, 5317
Service funèbre, 27685
    of God, 2740, 3007
    of the Lord, 4263
Services of an useful, 2357
Set of anatomical, 26166, 32221
    eight, 21152
    propositions, 10891
    round hand, 33188
    signals, 36899
    six, 27176
    tables, 29491
Sethona, a tragedy, 13255, 28586
Seton, James, in commercial firm, 26151
Seton, William, 1746-1798. New-York, June 1, 1793, 26151
Seton, William M., in commercial firm, 26151
Settle, Elkanah, 1648-1724, extract from, 27384
Settled ministry, 32394
Seven champions
    Illustrious and renowned, 36291
    Most illustrious, 27686
Seven hints, 11851
    letters, 10438
    rational, 15584
    sermons, (Eaton) 12756, (Hemmenway) 10643, (Mayhew) 6365
    sermons (Russel), (1701) 1021, (1727) 2953, (1728) 3101, (1766) 10484-85, (1767) 10762-63, (1772) 12548-49, (1774) 13593, (1784) 18772, (1788) 21443, (1792) 24763, (1793) 26113-16, (1795) 29452, (1797) 32787-88, (1798) 34499
    voyages, 28205
    wise masters, (1794) 27669-70, (1795) 29466-67, (1797) 32803
    wise mistresses, (1795) 29492, (1796) 31176, (1797) 32285-86
Seventeen discourses, 25757
1794; his excellency, 27616
1799; his excellency, 36222-23
1799; John Brown, 36224
Seventeenth jewel, 32269
Seventh essay, 19367
Sever, Thomas. Ode, 34528
Sever, William
    consents to proclamation, 14839
    consents to resolve, 14212
Several acts, 34876
Several assemblies, 14583
Several gentlemen. Revolution in New England, 12973
Several gentlemen of this country. Virginia miscellany, 3483
Several laws, 1328
    methods by which, 30385
    methods of making, 14584-85
    poems, 244, 8091
    reasons, 2258, 2781
    rules, orders, 1040, 2843
    sermons (Mather), 1767
    sermons on Heb. XI, 3240
    texts, 27687, 28289
Severals relating, 337
Sevier, John. Proclamation, 31282, 34637
Sewall, ——
    favors Croswell, 4926

sermons before, 10456
Sewall, Abigail, d. 1720, death, 2145
Sewall, Daniel
    Almanac see Almanacs (Sewall)
    This is to give, 24017
Sewall, Daniel, 1755-1842. Eulogy, 38488
Sewall, Hannah, d. 1717, death, 1909
Sewall, Jonathan, 1728-1796
    Americans roused, 14455
    Cure for the spleen, 14454
    Massachusettensis, 14157
Sewall, Jonathan Mitchel, 1748-1808
    Eulogy, 37383, 38489
    Oration, 21456
    Verses, 32823
    Versification, 34532
    War and Washington, 16520
Sewall, Joseph, 1688-1769
    All flesh, 4802
    Believers, 1852
    Caveat, 1997
    Certainty, 1853
    Character and blessedness, 1927
    Character and reward, 9513
    Charge, (1746) 5753, (1753) 6955, (1761) 8830
    Christ victorious, 3723
    Desires, 1854
    Duty, character, 8257
    Duty of a people, 2954-55
    Duty of every man, 2956
    Faithful narrative, 3958
    First and great, 5054
    God's people, 5055
    He that would keep, 3102
    Holy Spirit convincing, 4803
    Holy Spirit the gift, 3103
    Jehovah, 2957
    Lamb slain, 5685
    Nineveh's repentance, 4597
    Orphan's best legacy, 3351
    Precious treasure, 1928
    Repentance, 2958
    Rulers must be, 2583
    Second commandment, 5056
    Sermon, 9269
    Sober-mindedness, 2256
    Tender heart, 7790
    Thirsty invited, 5057
    When the godly, 4196
    at South church, 1996
    death, 11206
    favors Croswell, 4926?
    letter (from March), 8166
    preface by, 7748
    publishes Willard's work, 2828
    sermon before, 7096, 10456?
Sewall, Rebekah, 1704-1710, death, 1489
Sewall, Samuel, 1652-1730
    Memorial relating, 2292
    Mrs. Judith Hull, 738
    Phaenomena quaedam, 813, 2959
    Proposals, 1647
    Selling of Joseph, 951, 4149
    Tuesday, 1332
    Upon Mr. Samuel Willard, 952
    Wednesday, 1023
    appendix by, 2406, 2977
    death, 3344, 3351
    preface by, 12973
    wife's death, 1909
Sewall, Stephen, 1704-1760
    Character of the late, 6778

From the Boston, 6779
  death, 8666
Sewall, Stephen, 1734-1804
  Carmina, 22136
  Hebrew grammar, 9514
  (tr.) Nocte cogitata, 20170
  Oratio funebris, 11461
  Oration, 16521
  Scripture account, 27689
  Scripture history, 31178
Sewall, Thomas, d. 1716, death, 1840
Seward, Anna, 1747-1809
  Louisa, 22137
  Monody, (1781) 17368, (1782) 17719, (1788)
    21457-58, (1790) 22888, (1792) 24782, (1794)
    27690, (1798) 33290, 33841, 34533
  letters to, 33652
Seward, Stephen, birth in family, 1730
Seward, William, 1712-1782
  Brotherly love, 12226
  Due consideration, 12558
Seward, William, fl. 1740. Journal, 4598
Sewel, William, 1650-1725
  History of the rise, (1728) 3104, (1774) 13607,
    (1776) 15081
  excerpts from, 24261
Seybert, Adam, 1773-1825. Inaugural dissertation,
  26153
Seymour, Mrs. ———, sings song, 33252
Seymour, Israel, d. 1784, death, 18370
Seymour, Joseph H., engraver, 22486, 23186, 26481,
  29129, 36363
Seymour, William, relief of, 29685
Sèze, Raymond, comte de, 1748-1828. Defence of
  Louis, 24783
El-Shaddai, 2669
Shade of Alexander, 37937, 37941
Shades or profiles, 23667
Shadwell, Thomas, 1642-1692. Don Juan, 29494
Shaftsbury association. Minutes, (1786) 19984,
  (1788) 21459, (1789) 22138, (1790) 22889, (1791)
  23760, (1792) 24784, (1793) 26154, (1794)
  27691, (1795) 29495, (1796) 31179, (1797) 32824,
  (1798) 34534, (1799) 36295
Shakespeare, William
  Catharine and Petruchio, 9270
  Hamlet, 26559, 27692
  King Lear, 9004
  Plays and poems, 29496, 31180
  Tempest, 9005
  Twelfth night, 26559, 27693
  Twins, or which is which, 20700
  analysis, 27624
  songs by, 19105, 29122, 35847
Shakespeare's jests, 13608
Shaking dispensations, 1763
Shalome ben Shalomoh, conversion, 989
Sham beggar, 9271
Shangar, Marcus. Letter (to Tucker), 14456
Shannon & Poalk
  Auction of very select, 38256
  Quantity of books, 38257
  Scarce and valuable, 38258
Sharp, ———, reports on debts, 20773
Sharp, Anthony. Almanac see **Almanacs (Sharp)**
Sharp, Granville, 1735-1813
  Declaration, 13609-613
  Essay on slavery, 13005
  Extract from a representation, 11985
  Letter (to Maryland soc.), 26155-56
  Remarks, 15730
Sharp, John, 1644-1714. Sermon, 1280

Sharp, Joshua. Almanac see **Almanacs (Sharp)**
Sharpe, Horatio, address to, 7044
Shattuck, Benjamin, d. 1794, death, 29553
Shaveblock, Pasquin see **Macgowan, John, 1726-
  1780**
Shaver see **Macgowan, John, 1726-1780**
Shaver's new sermon, 30722-24
Shaw, Dr. ———, travels, 33466
Shaw, Jeremiah. Charge, 25090
Shaw, John, 1707-1791
  Character of a pastor, 7116
  Holding forth, 9006
Shaw, Josiah Crocker, d. 1847
  Oration, 34536
  ordained, 26157
Shaw, Oakes, d. 1807
  Charge, 31866
  Sermon, 10491
  ordained, 9006
Shaw, Robert. Gentleman's amusement, (1794)
  27694, (1795) 29498, (1796) 31181-82
Shaw, Robert G., & co.
  Large, valuable, 36299
  Stock of new books, 37012
  Valuable books, 37013
  Valuable collection, 37014
Shaw, Samuel, ed. Interestive narrative, 23228
Shaw, Samuel, 1635-1696
  Angelical life, 5488
  Farewel life, 10163
  Immanuel, 4804, 5489
  Voice of one, 5862
Shaw, Thomas. Proclamation, 13994
Shaw, William, 1743-1816
  Insurrection, 36300
  Sermon, 21460, 26157
  hand of fellowship, 37467
  ordained, 10491
Shaw, William, d. 1770, executed, 11973-75, 12200
Shawnee Indians
  Articles of a treaty, 20041
  prisoners of, 28931
  treaty, 3041?, 7925-26?, 29742?
Shays, Daniel, 1747-1825
  rebellion, 19789, 20500, 20505, 20829, 21259
  reward for apprehension of, 20623
She left me, 31183
  stoops to conquer, (1773) 12794-95, (1793)
    26559, (1794) 27059
  would, 8815
Shebbeare, John, 1709-1788. Letter from Batista,
  9838-39
Sheed, William. Account of the births, 8714
Sheehan, Bryan, d. 1772
  Life, 12559
  executed, 12375
Sheehan, Daniel, brother's death, 20701
Sheehan, John, d. 1787
  Lamentation, 20701
  True narrative, 20702
Sheffield, John Baker Holroyd, earl of, 1735-1821

VOL.	ITEMS	VOL.	ITEMS
1	1-3244	8	22298-25074
2	3245-6623	9	25075-28145
3	6624-9891	10	28146-30832
4	9892-13091	11	30833-33261
5	13092-16176	12	33262-25854
6	16177-19448	13	35855-39162
7	19449-22297		

Observations, 17975-76
reply to, 18367, 23294-95
Shelburne, William Petty, earl of, 1737-1805
  Letter (to Bernard), 10970
  letter (from Paine), 27466
  reply to, 17650
Sheldon, ——, captain of Warren (ship), 22846
Sheldon, Col. ——, insinuations, 16210
Sheldon, Elisha, court martial, 17048
Sheldon, William. Cursory remarks, 34537
Shenstone, William, 1714-1763
  Elegy, 13005
  The shipwreck, 24440
  excerpts from, 23246, 34112
Shepard, Jeremiah, 1648-1720
  Early offerings, 1583
  Ephemeris see **Almanacs (Shepard)**
  God's conduct, 1780
  Sort of believers, 1527
Shepard, Jonathan, d. 1792, death, 24364
Shepard, Samuel, of Lenox, ordained, 29578
Shepard, Samuel, of Virginia. List of pensioners, 33130
Shepard, Samuel, 1739-1815
  Answer to the publications, 26158
  Principle of universal, 34538
  Scriptural enquiry, 27695
  Three letters, 23761
  observations on, 25233
  ordained, 12569
  reply to, 36118
Shepard, Thomas, behavior toward, 1022
Shepard, Thomas, 1605-1649
  Church-membership, (1663) 82, (1669) 145, (1762) 9272, (1769) 11462, (1786) 19985
  Penitential cries, (1769) 11326, (1783) 18019, (1787) 20495, (1790) 22649, (1791) 23546
  Saints' jewel, 5289
  Sampwutteahae, 497
  Sincere convert, (1664) 93, (1742) 5058, (1743) 5290-91
  Sound believer, 4077, 5059
  Three valuable, 6067
  Two questions, 814
  Wine for gospel, 130
  death, 240
Shepard, Thomas, 1635-1677. Eye-salve, 182
Shepherd, E. Columbian accountant, 38494
Shepherd, Job. Almanac see **Almanacs (Poor Job)**
Shepherd, Nathanael, dying testimony, 7145
Shepherd of Salisbury, 37128-29
Shepherdess of the Alps, 29021, 32420
Shepherd's barometer, 27755
  dog, 28977
  week, 38977
Sherburne, Col. ——, chaplain's sermon, 15726
Sherburne, Henry, 1709-1767, death, 10640
Sherburne, Henry, d. 1824, state treasurer R.I., 27616
Sherburne, Henry, 1741-1825. Oriental philanthropist, 38495
Sherburne, Samuel, speaker NH House, 25878
Sheridan, Richard Brinsley Butler, 1751-1816
  The critic, 20703, 29499
  The duenna, 16522
  The governess, 29500
  (tr.) Pizarro, 35698-701, 37758
  Real and genuine School, 17720
  School for scandal, (1786) 19986, (1789) 22139, (1792) 24785
  Verses, 28978
Sheridan, Thomas, of Baltimore. Short but partic-

ular, 23762
Sheridan, Thomas, 1719-1788
  Complete dictionary, 22140, 31184-85
  Course of lectures, 31186
  Rhetorical grammar, 18184
Sheriff's sale, 36718
Sherlock, Martin, 1750-1797, travels of, 31692?
Sherlock, Thomas, 1678-1761
  Letter from the lord bishop, 6607
  Memorial, 13193
  Trial of the witnesses, 21461, 38496
  Tryal of the witnesses, 7314
Sherman, John, 1624-1695. Almanac see **Almanacs (Sherman)**
Sherman, Josiah, 1734-1789
  Administration of parochial, 22141
  Christ the true, 20704
  God in no sense, 18781
  History of Melchizedek, 19987
  Nature of moral, 20705
  Oracles, 20706
  Sermon to swine, 20707
  letter (from Bowden), 21710
Sherman, Nathaniel, installation, 10873
Sherman, Roger, 1721-1793
  Astronomical diary see **Almanacs (Sherman)**
  Caveat, 6933
  Remarks, 18782
  death, 25434
  reports on accounts, 18833
  reports on Conn. expenses, 18838
  reports on Penobscot expedition, 19312
  reports on representation, 18827
Sherwin, Thomas. Divine breathings, (1792) 24786, (1797) 32828, (1799) 35412, 36301
Sherwood, Samuel, 1730-1783
  Church's flight, 15082
  Sermon, 13614
Sheward, Caleb, secretary, 10034
Shewell, W. Several methods, 14584-85
Shewen, William, 1631-1695
  Brief testimony, 1024
  Counsel, 13006, 26159
  Good advice, 1025
Shield, William, 1748-1829
  Amidst the illusions, 29501
  Fame, let thy trumpet, 16523
  Green Mountain farmer, 34302
  Heaving of the lead, 25967
  How can I forget, 29502
  Johnny and Mary, 34539
  Morning is up, 34540
  Overture to the new opera, 22142
  What are the boasted, 34541
  selections from, 31182, 34516
Shields, John. Advertisement, 18783
Ship Dutchess of Gordon, 14298
Ship Revolution; articles, 17369
Shipley, Jonathan, 1714-1788
  Sermon, 13007-12, 19238
  Speech intended, 13615-23
  Whole of the celebrated, 13624
  Whole speech, 13625
Shipmaster's assistant, 32829
Shippen, John
  Observations, 27696
  Oration, 27697
  Story of Palemon, 31187
Shippen, William, 1736-1808, reply to, 17240
Shipping articles
  Articles of agreement, 31188

It is agreed, 29503
Shipwreck (Falconer), 37393
Shipwreck, a poem, 21080, 30399
Shipwreck, a sentimental, 13257, 21081
Shipwreck and adventures, 35425
Shipwreck'd seaman's ghost, 26160
Shirley, Rev. ———, reply to, 12821
Shirley, Frances, d. 1746, death, 5754
Shirley, James, 1596-1666
  Gamester, 9007
  excerpts from poetry, 23246?
Shirley, William, 1693-1771
  Antigonian and Bostonian, 7317
  Conference, 4976
  Journal of the proceedings, 7222
  Letter (to Duke of Newcastle), 5863-65
  Memoirs of the principal, 8258
  Proclamation, (1741) 4747, (1742) 5005, (1743)
    5245, (1744) 5434-35, (1745) 5632-34, (1746)
    5805-809, (1747) 6001, (1748) 6002, 6185-88,
    (1749) 6358-59, (1753) 7057, (1754) 7251-52,
    (1755) 7476-77
  appoints commissioners, 7025
  at Oswego, 7652
  dedication to, 5204, 5408, 5607, 5786, 5963, 6156,
    6330, 6514, 6852, 7021, 7208, 7363, 7390, 7429,
    7681, 7910
  sermon before, 4695, 4881, 5173, 5326, 5602, 5737,
    5919, 6175, 6280, 7256, 7383
  vindicated, 8163
  wife's death, 5754
Shirtliff, Roswell see **Shurtleff, Roswell, 1773-1861**
Shitz, Francis, d. 1797, murdered, 34040
Shocking narrative, 31995
Shoemaker, Abraham. Almanac see **Almanacs**
  (Shoemaker)
Shoemaker, Isaac, d. 1779, death, 16528, 26895
Shoemaker, John, son's death, 16528, 26895
Shoemaker, Samuel, furniture confiscated, 16092
Shopkeeper turned sailor, 37158
Shore, Jane
  concubine of Edward IV, 30563
  history of, 27121, 32255
Short, Matthew. Thankful memorial, 3217
Short, Thomas, 1690-1772. Medicina Britannica,
  6783
Short abridgement, 34484
  account of a northwest, 33936
    of a remedy, 21123
    of Algiers, 26732-33
    of Ann Rogers, 27168
    of Philadelphia, 31235
    of that part, 9066-67, 9341
  account of the apostolic, 23763
    city, 27090
    convincement, 17457
    death, 38500
    establishment, 23703
    exemplary, 27054
    experience, 5580
    honourable, 24395
    last sickness, 23822
    life and character, 11463
    life and death, (Fletcher) 29863, (Scott)
      30096
    malignant fever, (1793) 25255-57, (1794)
      26735-37, (1796) 31172
    origin, 30574
    people, (1780) 16712-13, (1783) 17840,
      (1799) 35178
    plague, 25075, 25385

  principal, 33838
  solar system, 21721-22
  state of Mendon, 12658
  yellow fever, 27108, 33890-91
  three young, 10747
address, 7815-18
advice, 13772
and accurate, 29507
  candid, 23995, 31625
  easie method, 3675, 5619
  easy guide, 27700
  easy method of surveying, 35406
  easy method with the deists, (1785) 17999,
    (1797) 32373, (1798) 33993
  faithful, 5342
  plain but faithful, 4258
  plain narrative, 10581
  practical essay, 33974
  sincere, 14256
  true account, 11069
but comprehensive grammar, 32870, 38555
  story, 31948
  system, (1795) 28606-609, (1796) 30372-73,
    (1797) 32068, (1798) 33653-54, (1799)
    35428, (1800) 37338
but particular, 23762
but serious, 11854
catechism agreed upon, 7
  composed, (1661) 67, (1676) 222, (1694)
    707, (1714) 1708, (1797) 32604
  drawn out, 378, 2181
  for children, 37033
  for some congregations, 4890
  for young children, (1753) 7030, (1761)
    8893, (1765) 10026
  particularly designed, 34424
  wherein the chief, 10504
  wherein the principles, 5691
collection, 35764
compendium, 38510
confession, 3476, 3823
conversations, 26161, 29508
compilation, 31161
description of Pennsilvania, 594
  of the difference, 7613, 11557
  of the state, 31199-200
  of the Tennassee, 26168
detail, 10178
dialogue, 419
direction, 4421
discourse delivered, 6625
  proving, 3190
  shewing, 1839
easy and comprehensive, 8895, 9414
essay on civil, 14036
  on scriptural, 38354
  on the rattles, 3614
extract, 26050
-hand book, 3105, 3218
history of a long journey, 4589

VOL.	ITEMS	VOL.	ITEMS
1	1-3244	8	22298-25074
2	3245-6623	9	25075-28145
3	6624-9891	10	28146-30832
4	9892-13091	11	30833-33261
5	13092-16176	12	33262-25854
6	16177-19448	13	35855-39162
7	19449-22297		

a long travel, (1724) 2518, (1751) 6656,
   (1753) 6986, (1754) 7177, (1765) 9944,
   (1770) 11616, (1788) 21031, (1794) 26831,
   (1797) 32002
Mr. Thomas, 29509
New England, 700
the British, 27529
the grand, 5866
the late, 36006
the nature, 28383-84, 31174
the treatment, 20006
the war, 20382
the yellow fever, 32138, 33742
introduction to Christian, 24328
   to English grammar, (1780) 16822, (1783)
      18005, (1795) 28990, (1799) 35749, (1800)
      37857
   to grammar, 9309, 13080
   to Latin grammar, (1781) 17370, (1783)
      18185, (1786) 19988, (1789) 22143,
      (1790) 22890, (1792) 24787, (1794) 27701,
      (1797) 32835, (1799) 36309, (1800) 38501
   to moral philosophy, 21164
   to the Latin tongue, (1709) 1384, (1724)
      2511, (1737) 4197, (1749) 6417, (1755)
      7567-68, (1761) 9008, (1766) 10492,
      (1767) 10767, (1768) 11070, (1769) 11464,
      (1770) 11855-56, (1771) 12227, (1773)
      13013, (1783) 18186, (1785) 19239-42
   to the Spanish, 6741
life, 1699
method, 29237
narrative of mischief, 6488
   the claim, 3106
   the extraordinary, 5046-47
   the horrid, 11580-81
   the life and character, 27673
   the life and sufferings, 31890
   the massacre, 11582
observations, 17096
relation, (1769) 11465, (1770) 11857, (1774)
   13200, (1785) 19402
reply, 4805
review, 20899
scriptural catechism, 29075-76, 30789-90
sketch of the evidence, 24233, 24292
sketch of the life, 33827
state of the proceedings, 14285
stories, 38502
system, 32316
though true, 5382
treatise of church discipline, 5124
   on divine, 34374
   on rice machinery, 19483
   on the application, 21441-42
   on the Christian's, 3034
   on the visible, 6338, 6521
view and defence, 30992
   of . . . medicine, 37264
   of the whole scripture, 33166
vindication of the conduct, 10614
vindication of the religious, 16780
Shorter catechism, (1665) 105, (1683) 354, (1691)
   579, (1698) 855, (1729) 3234, (1734) 3973, (1739)
   4422, 4445, (1740) 4625, (1745) 5709, (1746) 5882,
   (1749) 6443, (1751) 6795, (1754) 7335, 7337,
   (1757) 8063, (1759) 8519, (1760) 8767, (1762)
   9306-307, (1765) 10206, (1768) 11115, (1770)
   11935, (1781) 17089, (1782) 17798-99, (1788)
   21600, (1790) 23076, (1792) 25030, (1794) 28077,
   (1795) 29880, (1797) 33211-12, (1799) 35119,

(1800) 39079
Shortness and afflictions, 20008
Shotwell, Samuel, d. 1790?, murdered, 23475
Shove, Edward, referee, 11614
Shower, John, 1657-1715. Some account, 1194, 2175
Shreeve, Thomas, ridicule of, 12356
Shrubsole, William, 1729-1797. Christian memoirs,
   31190
Shultess, Gaspard, d. 1800, death, 37125
Shultz, Benjamin
   Inaugural botanico-medical, 29510
   Oration, 29511
Shumway, Nehemiah, 1761-1843. American har-
   mony, 26162
Shurtleff, James, 1745-1832
   Concise review, 34548
   preface by, 38584
Shurtleff, Roswell, 1773-1861. Oration, 38504
Shurtleff, William, 1689-1747
   Distressing dangers, 2960
   Faith and prayer, 4599
   Gospel ministers, 4423
   Labour that attends, 2961
   Letter to those, 5686
   Obligations, 4806
Shurtlieff, Robert, female soldier, 32417
Shute, Daniel, 1722-1802
   Compendious and plain, 27702
   Sermon, (1767) 10768, (1768) 11071, (1787) 20708
   hand of fellowship, 26134
Shute, Samuel, 1662-1742
   Proclamation, 2240
   Speech, 1818
   character of, 2042
   gives imprimatur, 2008
   report on his memorial, 2640
   sermon before, 2265, 2340
   speech before, 1906
Shute, Thomas, letter concerning, 2643
Shuttlesworth, Samuel, 1750-1834
   Discourse, 24788
   ordained, 22325
Siamese tales, 32836
Sibbes, Richard, 1577-1635. Divine meditations,
   31191
Sibley, Solomon, 1769-1846. Oration, 31192
Sibly, Job
   Three sermons, 32807
   Trial of Richard Parker, 32837
Sibyllae Americanae, 17721
Sicard, ————. New constitution march, 21462
Sicilian romance, (1794) 27703, (1795) 29381, 29512
Sicilius. Letters, 28889
Sick and dying-bed exercises, 21063
Siddons, Henry, 1774-1815. Sicilian romance, 27703,
   29381, 29512
Sidney, Fanny, history of, 36196
Sidney, John
   Nullum tempus, 3608
   Reply, 3841
Siege of Calais, 25733
   Lyons, 28265
   Meaux, 29376
Siegenische katechismus, 6237
Siegvolck, George Paul
   Everlasting gospel, 7033
   (ed.) Das von Jesu, 10942, 11304
Sierra Leone company. Substance of the report,
   29513-14, 36310
Sieyès, Emmanuel Joseph, comte, 1748-1836, letter
   (from Paine), 24658, 27466, 32633

VOL.	ITEMS	VOL.	ITEMS
1	1-3244	8	22298-25074
2	3245-6623	9	25075-28145
3	6624-9891	10	28146-30832
4	9892-13091	11	30833-33261
5	13092-16176	12	33262-25854
6	16177-19448	13	35855-39162
7	19449-22297		

dialogue, 8735
discourses on different, 12077
discourses or sermons, 30899
essays, 8848
Friends (ship), expedition to Port-Royal, 513
letters (Garden to Whitefield), 4515
letters on the spiritual, 28682
Six Nations
  Treaty, (1736) 4146, (1742) 5216, (1744) 5416-17,
    (1745) 5790, (1746) 5791, (1748) 6169, (1784)
    18817
  deed Indiana, 15219
  grant from, 17437
  message to Gates, 15642
Six political, 15748
    sermons, (Blake) 12330, (Buskirk) 33111,
      (McKnight) 22631, (Worcester) 39147
    sketches, 14801
Sixteen sermons, (Love) 24482, (Muir) 21275
16th December, 1799, 36585-87
Sixth essay on field-husbandry, 8344
Sixth essay on free trade, 18301
Sixth Massachusetts turnpike corporation. By
  laws, 35803
Sixty sermons, 16425, 16921
Skaniadaradigrono Indians, conferences, 8156
Sketch of the black, 26800
  of the denominations, 30395, 32101
        history of the life, 29330
        history of the war, 34551
        life and confession, 20300
        life and death, 28692
        life of James, 26164
        manners, 26001
        present state, 32115
        revolutions, 34559
        rise, 37274
        soil, 31071
        times, 15598
Sketches from nature, 25680
  of American, 19366
  of French, 31803
  of Masonic, 34091
  of the finances, 30469
        history, genius, 31688, 38508
        history of America, 33485
        life, 22441
        principles, 25297-98
        reciprocal, 34132
  on rotation(s), (1792) 24129, (1796) 30103,
    (1797) 31846
Skillman, Isaac, 1740-1799
  American alarm, 13014
  Oration, (1773) 13015-18, (1774) 13627, (1775)
    14457
Skinner, Cortland, speaker NJ House, 14287
Skinner, Ichabod Lord, 1767-1852
  Discourse, 31195
  Farewell discourse, 36313
  ordained, 27752
Skinner, Mary, d. 1745, death, 5867
Skinner, Thomas, 1710-1762
  Faithful minister's trials, 6784
  Mourner admonished, 5867
  wife's death, 5867
Skinner, Thomas, fl. 1796. Connecticut harmony,
  30521
Skipwith, Fulmar, expenses paid, 27854
Skull, Nicholas, surveyor, 7209
Sky-lark, 29517, 32839
Slack, Mrs. ——

American instructor, (1748) 6238, (1753) 7120,
  (1760) 8736, (1766) 10495, (1770) 11859, (1775)
  14458, (1778) 16071, (1779) 16524, (1785) 19243,
  (1787) 20709, (1792) 24790
Instructor, (1785) 19244, (1786) 19990, (1794)
  27706, (1797) 32840
Pleasing instructor, 29518
Slator, Lionel
  Instructions, 3959
  book criticized, 3911
Slatter, Michael
  appendix by, 6160
  circular by, 6828
Slavery, a poem, 21269-70
    inconsistent, 24741-42
    not forbidden, 12903
Slaves in Algiers, 27655, 31130
Slee, Isaac. Two discourses, 22146-47
Sleeper, Samuel. Divine hymns, 29530, 32848
Sleepy dead sinners, 25155
Slender, Robert see Freneau, Philip, 1752-1832
Sloan, James. Address of the Republican, 36767
Sloop for Halifax, 18816
Slothful servants, 12070
Slothfulness reproved, 12407
Slover, John, escape, 17993
Slow and sure. Philadelphia, 16950
Small broom, 1277
    but very valuable, 37007
    catechism, 8907
    collection of questions, 36315
    collection of sentimental, 26165
    sketch, 25576
    offers, 487
Smalley, John, 1734-1820
  Consistency, 11467
  Eternal salvation, 19245
  Inability of the sinner, 12560
  Law in all, 19991
  On the evils, 38509
  Perfection, 20710
Smallwood, Isaac, meeting at house of, 37526
Smallwood, William, orders court martial, 16334
Smalridge, George, 1663-1719. Art of preaching,
  (1739) 4424, (1741) 4807, (1747) 6068, (1751)
  6785, (1762) 9273
Smart, ——. World displayed, 29926, 31664
Smart, Christopher, 1722-1771
  Hymns, 23765, 29519
  (tr.) Works of Horace, 37647
  excerpts from, 34112
Smellie, William, 1697-1763
  Abridgement of the practice, 19992
  Set of anatomical, 26166, 32221
Smellie, William, 1740-1795. Philosophy, 23766
Smibert, Nathanael, death, 7845
Smile from the youth, 34552
Smith, ——
  Animadversions, 5060
  State of the embarrassments, 11478
  reports on accounts, 20062
  reports on commerce, 20053
  reports on Indian affairs, 20052, 20770
  reports on new states, 20058, 20769
  reports on prisoners, 17383
  reports on supplies, 19308
  selections from, 31959, 32741, 36191
Smith, Col. ——
  at Lexington, 14679
  bully, 13987
Smith, Miss ——, d. 1794, death, 29085

VOL.	ITEMS	VOL.	ITEMS
1	1-3244	8	22298-25074
2	3245-6623	9	25075-28145
3	6624-9891	10	28146-30832
4	9892-13091	11	30833-33261
5	13092-16176	12	33262-25854
6	16177-19448	13	35855-39162
7	19449-22297		

VOL.	ITEMS	VOL.	ITEMS
1	1-3244	8	22298-25074
2	3245-6623	9	25075-28145
3	6624-9891	10	28146-30832
4	9892-13091	11	30833-33261
5	13092-16176	12	33262-25854
6	16177-19448	13	35855-39162
7	19449-22297		

Querists, 7302
Some considerations about baptism, 2082
    considerations of, or a brief, 3960
        on the bills, 566
        on the consequences, 2176
        on the keeping, 7341
        propounded, 19435
        relating, (1731) 3388, (1732) 3500-501,
          (1738) 4218
        upon the several, 1855
    critical observations, 6611
    deductions, 17728-29
    difficulties, 20158, 26503
    distinguishing, 7338
    doubts, 34569
    evidences, 7592
    excellent verses, 4810
    expressions, 13999, 14722
    extracts, 29543
    facts, 34284
    farraginous, 25593
    few reasons, 7675
    few remarks, 975
    friendly remarks, 6472
    fruits of solitude, 6392-93, 7285
    fugitive thoughts, 13630
    further account, 2259
    gospel treasures, 7889
    helps, 52-53
    hints, 23583
    historical account, 11985
    important cases, (1757) 8009, (1759) 8470,
      (1760) 8716, (1764) 9798, (1786) 19707
        observations, 10346
        truths, 374, 2260
    meditations, 11716
    melancholy, 26457
    memoirs of the life (Roberts), (1751) 6774,
      (1752) 6926, (1763) 7113, (1766) 10482,
      (1773) 12986, (1783) 18166, (1790) 22855
    memoirs of the life (Tryon), 9028
    miscellaneous observations, 34570
    miscellaneous remarks, 15234
    miscellany observations, 631
    modern directions, 24802
    more friendly, 6646
    motives, 34555
    necessary and important, (1728) 3035, (1733)
      3663, (1736) 4023, (1759) 8361
        precautions, 2964
        remarks, 15739
    new thoughts, 37169
    observations and directions, 14166
        made, 4188
        of consequence, 11073
        on the bill, 7319
        on the charge, 3835
        on the constitution, 21263
        on the doctrines, 23078
        on the new, 2211
        on the proceedings, 3904-905
        on the Reverend, 4602-603
        on the scheme, 4308
        on the situation, 18356
        on the two, 9243
        relating to the establishment, 15802, 22151
        relating to the present, 6612
        upon a late, 8137
    occasional thoughts, 5052
    of the dying, 2814
        honours, 1737

    many false, 1111
  plain and necessary, 3231, 4835
  principles, (1753) 7005, (1765) 9976, (1769)
    11268, (1783) 17939, (1795) 28923
  proposals, 2177
  queries concerning, 4604
    sent to the Rev. G., 6303
    sent up, 944
  reasons and arguments, 2019
    and causes, 606
    given, 5643
    that influenced, 10297
  reflections on the disputes, 9889
  reflections on the law, 7495
  remarkable particulars, 35771
    passages, (1748) 6125, (1765) 9952, (1789)
      21799, (1792) 24274, (1795) 28577-78
    proceedings, 2702
  remarks and observations, 2508
  remarks upon a late pamphlet, 1231, 3660
    on a late sermon, 1078
    on a pamphlet intituled, (All men) 18215,
      (The enthusiasm) 6445-46
    on Abel, 6419
    on Mr. Ebenezer, 4605
    on Mr. President, 7881
    on religion, 8885
    on the great, 16993
    on the memorial, 19249
  remarks upon a late charge, 5713
  remarks upon a late pamphlet, 1231, 3660
    a second, 4019
    the claims, 9061
    the times, 4811
  remedies, 2287
  rude & indigested, 3359
  seasonable advice, 1832, 2776
    considerations, 688
    enquiries, 2459
    observations, 14462
    thoughts, 4510
  select cases, 6067
  serious and awful, 11175
    remarks, 8342
    thoughts concerning, 3553
    thoughts on the design, 6366
  short account, 12756
    and easy, 2096
    observations, 2293, 2584
    remarks, 21334
  strictures, 14352
  temporal advantages, 6418
  thoughts concerning, (1742) 4939, (1768) 10888-
    89, (1784) 18453
    on Christianity, 9824
    on education, 6935
    on the call, 9275
    on the gloomy, 24803, 26181
    upon the names, 12230
    upon the spirit, 8064
  transactions, 24333

VOL.	ITEMS	VOL.	ITEMS
1	1-3244	8	22298-25074
2	3245-6623	9	25075-28145
3	6624-9891	10	28146-30832
4	9892-13091	11	30833-33261
5	13092-16176	12	33262-25854
6	16177-19448	13	35855-39162
7	19449-22297		

unregenerate, 9326
Somers, John, baron, 1650-1716
  Judgment of whole, 13023, 13631-33
  Security, 2178, 13024
Somervell, James, memorial of, 38835
Somerville, William, 1675-1742, excerpts from, 34112?
Somerville & Noble
  Advertisement, 14463
  Prices current, 14464
Somes, Nehemiah, petition, 31380
Something new, 35266
Sommaire de considérations, 27198
Sommers, Lord see **Somers, John, baron, 1650-1716**
Sommers, Simon, petition, 38850
Sommersett, James, argument for, 13318
Son of freedom. Following anonymous, 14031
Son of liberty
  Salvation of American, 11846
  To the inhabitants, 13653
  To the Sons of liberty, 14516
  Union, activity and freedom, 11508
    see also **Church, Benjamin, 1734-1776; Downer, Silas; McDougall, Alexander, 1731-1786**
Son of Martin-Mar-Prelate see **Walter, Thomas, 1696-1728**
Son of Tammany see **Workman, Benjamin**
Son of the Church of England see **Browne, Arthur, 1700-1773**
Sonata for the pianoforte, 32911
Sonata sung by a number, 22094
Sonatina, op. 71, 33863
Song adapted, 33895
  book containing, 34571
  composed by the British, 14465
  composed for the fraternity, 23784
  made on the taking, 15599
  made upon the election, 3836
  of deliverance, 297
  of praise, 4929
  of the angels, 21467
  on the surrender, 16529
  on vacation, 31301
  to the tune, 11472
Songs and lullabies, 36335
  &c., 32482
  comic, 15603
  duets, and chorusses, 29120
  duets, etc., 22748
  duetts, trios, 27436
  for the amusement, 22894
  from the rock, 32368
  in Rosina, 26702
  in The castle, 27438
  in the comic opera, 27256
  in The deserter, 26882
  in The flitch of bacon, 26916
  in The highland reel, 27444
  in the musical drama, 33423
  in The purse, 26832
  in The son-in-law, 27446
  naval and military, 16530
  of Robin Hood, 6613
  of Tammany, 27100
  of The farmer, 27440
  of the redeemed, 794
  of victory, 8290
  orations, odes, 32439
  sung at the first, 32947
Songster's companion, 23634
Songster's magazine, 29542

Sonmans, Peter. Answer, &c., 1431
Sonnet by a husband, 28978
Sonnet; for the fourteenth, 25563
Sonnets for the cradle, 29122
Sons of Coke and Littleton, 20136
Sons of liberty. New York, July 7, 1769, 11379
Sons of St. George. Rules and constitutions, 12528
Son's patrimony, 26970
Sophia, electress of Hanover, settlement on, 2703
Sophist unmasked, 33158
Sophronistes. Some extracts, 29543
Soren, John, b. 1757. Narrative, 38531
Sorge, ——. Authentic account, 8494
Sorlie, Sholto. Treatise, 34572
Sorrow balanced, 22504
Sorrow turned, 8750
Sorrowful Sam, 35297, 37137
Sorrowful spectacle, 1764
Sorrows and sympathetic, 18501
Sorrows of Werter, (1786) 19688, (1789) 21859, (1794) 27056, (1795) 28753, (1796) 30494-95
Sort of believers, 1527
Sotweed redivivus, 3266
Soul-saving gospel, (1703) 1134, (1712) 1569, (1743) 5249
Soul upon the wing, 2361
Soul well-anchored, 1558
Soulanges, ——, correspondence with Jay, 19325
Souldier defended, 1016
  taught, 1407
  told, 1315
Souldiers counselled, 488
Souldiery spiritualized, 193
Soule, Olive, d. 1795, death, 32802
Souls flying, 4490
Sound believer, 4077, 5059
  repentance, 398
  words, 1065
Source of virtue, 24624
South Carolina
  Account of importations, 4079, 4309
  Account of the importations, 4198, 4426
  Address and rules of the South Carolina society, 19254
  At a court, 4812
  Bill for establishing, 20716
  By the mail which, 21469
  Constitution, 22896
  Debates which arose, 21470
  Extracts from the journals, 14466, 15090-91
  Grand lodge, Antient York Masons, 36338
  In the House of representatives, 36337
  Letter from the honourable William Bull, 4480
  Report of committee of legislature, 26183
  Report of the committee appointed, 4082
  Report of the committee of both, 5063
  Report of ways and means, 19253
  Resolves respecting, 14467
  Rules and orders of the courts, 31220, 38535
  South Carolina; in a Congress, 15092
  South Carolina; in the Senate, 26184
  State of South Carolina; an ordinance, 22898
South Carolina. Governor
  Message, 19252
  Proclamation, 5492
South Carolina. Laws (collective)
  Acts and resolutions, (1795-97) 34575
  Laws and regulations, 27720
  Laws of the province, 4080
  Public laws, 22897
South Carolina. Laws (session)
  Acts, (1736-37) 4199, (1760) 8738, (1764) 10168,

(1765) 10169, (1768) 11074, (1782) 17724-25,
(1783) 18190, (1784) 18789, (1785) 19250-51,
(1786) 19998, (1787) 20715, (1788) 21468, 22152,
(1789) 22153, (1790) 22895, (1791) 23781, 24804,
(1792) 26182, (1793) 27718, (1794) 27719, 29544,
34573-74, (1795) 31219, (1796) 32856, (1797)
34576, (1798) 36336, 38532, (1799) 38533

South Carolina. Laws (separates)
Act (1744), (beasts) 5492, (debtors) 5491
Act, (1764) 9843, (1765) 10170, (1766) 10498,
(1778) 16073, (1779) 16531, (1786) 19997,
(1787) 20717, (1800) 38534, 38536

South Carolina. Legislature
Proceedings, 27721

South Carolina Federalist see **Desaussure, Henry
William, 1763-1839**

South Carolina; in a Congress, 15092
in the Senate, 26184
justice of peace, 21472, 30519

South Carolina society
Information, 28411
Rules, 28410

**South Carolina society for promoting and improv-
ing agriculture**
Address and rules, 34577
Letters and observations, 21471

South Carolina weekly museum, 32860, 34581

South Carolina Yazoo co. Extract from the proceedings, 23783

South Kentucky district association. Minutes,
26187-93

Southampton, ——, earl, letter (from Essex),
13832

Southeby, William
Anti-slavery tract, 1781, 1929
Testimony, 953

Southerland, Thomas, d. 1692, execution, 588

Southern territorial co. Plan of association, 29550

Southern Territory. Governor
Proclamation, 27725

Southern Territory. Laws (session)
Acts, (1793) 26195, (1794) 27724, (1795) 29551

Southern Territory. Legislative council
Journal, 27726, 29552

Southerne, Thomas, 1660-1746. Oroonoko, 27727

Southey, Robert, 1774-1843
Joan of Arc, 34583-86
Poems, 36345

Southmayd, Daniel, d. 1754, death, 7226

Southwark, Eng. Declaration of the faith, 24481

Southwark theater see under title of playbill, or
under **Philadelphia**

Southwick, Remington. Almanac see **Almanacs
(Southwick)**

Soveraign efficacy, 326

Soveraignty & goodness, 331-32, 2173

Sovereign decrees, 12656
God acknowledged, 5481
grace, 12725

Sovereignty of God in determining, 10628, 18468

Sovereignty of God in the exercises, 4863

Sower going forth, 10821

Spaight, Richard Dobbs, 1758-1802
reports on accounts, 18833
reports on Indian affairs, 18830

Spain, Capt. ——, arrival at Philadelphia, 13858

Spain
Definitive treaty, 9397
Letter to Timothy Pickering, 32863

Spalding, Alva, d. 1796, death, 30576

Spalding, James, defendant, 24353

Spalding, John, 1765-1795
Few serious queries, 35518
Some account, 36346

Spalding, Joshua, 1760-1825
Sentiments, 31225
Sermon, 20721, 38540

Spalding, Josiah, 1751-1823
Duty and importance, 38541
Sermon, 18194

Spalding, Lyman, 1775-1821
Inaugural dissertation, 32864
New nomenclature, 36347

Spangenberg, Augustus Gottlieb, 1704-1792
Account, 22155
Preaching of the cross, 26196

Spanish fryar, 8844

Sparhawk, Ebenezer, d. 1805
Charge, 20999
Discourse, 29553
ordained, 9080

Sparhawk, John, ordained, 4111

Sparhawk, Thomas Stearns, 1769-1807. Oration,
34587

Sparrow, T., engraver, 13742

Spaulding, Benjamin, daughter's illness, 29554-55

Spaulding, Joshua see **Spalding, Joshua, 1760-1825**

Spaulding, Josiah see **Spalding, Josiah, 1751-1823**

Spaulding, Mary. Remarkable narrative, 29554-55

Spaven, J. Christian's defence, 5381

Speaker, or miscellaneous, (1795) 28630, (1798)
33694, (1799) 35446

Special verdict, 32369

Specimen of a plan, 22029
of divine truths, (1765) 10001, 10174, (1787)
20411, (1791) 23438, (1794) 27106, (1797)
32244
of Isaiah Thomas's, 19272
of the confession, 37225
harmony, 5286
patriotism, 28941
unrelenting, 7795

Spectacle nouveaux, 29162

Speech delivered from the bench, 2937

Speech of . . . see under name of speaker, or under
his official position

Speech of a Creek Indian, 7321
of a member, 13848
of Joseph T..sd..e, 10780
of the speaker of the House, 4523
of the statue, 11868
of Th-ma- P-wn-ll, 11423-26
of William Tr..n, 15095
said to have been delivered, 7573
to the Assembly, 1705

Speeches and addresses, 2270
in the General assembly, 2366
in the last session, 14092
of Charles Pinckney, 38270
of Messrs. Erskine and Kydd, 33698
of Mr. Smith, 27714
of the Hon. Thomas Erskine, 32093

VOL.	ITEMS	VOL.	ITEMS
1	1-3244	8	22298-25074
2	3245-6623	9	25075-28145
3	6624-9891	10	28146-30832
4	9892-13091	11	30833-33261
5	13092-16176	12	33262-25854
6	16177-19448	13	35855-39162
7	19449-22297		

of the right honourable, 10463
Speed the plough, 38006-7
Speedy repentance, 539
Speedy return, 2728
Spelling book (1643), 13
Spelling book improved, 30346-48
    book, or a guide, 15789
        or a new guide, 21796
        or the first, 35579
Spencer, ——, of New York, submits report, 38091
Spencer, Abigail, d. 1788, death, 21198
Spencer, Joseph, sermon before, 8121
Spencer, Philip, wife's death, 21198
Spencer, Thomas. New vade mecum, 27728
Sperry, Benjamin. Vindication of the proceedings, 9846
Spicer, ——
    Philadelphia harmony, 21629
    address by, 21695
Spicer, Jacob. Grants, concessions, 8205
Spiegel der eheleute, 8262
    der self-kennes, 2120
    der tauffe, 5400
    für alle menschen, 35202
Spierin, George Hartwell
    Sermon, 22900
    Song, 23784
Spiess, Christian Heinrich, 1755-1799. Mountain cottager, 38544
Spikeman, Capt. ——, killed, 8557-58
Spindleshanks, Peter. Battle of the two, 36350
Spira, Francis, apostate, 310, 338, 9059, 11558, 12657, 14448, 30012, 33356-57
Spirit of contradiction, 9258
    of despotism, 28936, 35691
    of God, 2962
    of independence, 37067
    of liberty, 12501
    of life, 1195, 1316
    of man, 661
    of Masonry, 37671
    of prayer, 1098
    of railing, 1110
    of '76, 38545
    of the hat, 662
        martyrs, 8085
        times, 11500
Spirits of the present, 4992-93
Spirit's teaching, 3244
Spiritual anatomizing, 1661
    desertions, (1699) 901, (1713) 1659, (1741) 4868
    food, 24807
    ignorance, 9330
    improvement, 18935
    inability, 10635
    journey, 4814
    knowledge, 12002
    liberty, 11141
    milk for babes, 120
    milk for Boston, 42, 506
    presence, 12464
    retreat, 28865
    songs, (1742) 4996-97, (1743) 5235, (1769) 11326, (1771) 12114, (1783) 18019, (1787) 20495, (1790) 22649, (1791) 23546
    temple, 28959
    warfare, 2121
    watchman's character, 28519
Spoil'd child, 30568-69

Spooner, Bathshua, d. 1778, execution, 15872-73
Spooner, John Jonas. Discourse, 29556
Spooner, Joshua, d. 1778, murdered, 15793, 15872-73
Spooner, Paul, sermon before, 18566, 19536
Spooner, Polly, d. 1782, death, 19443
Spooner, W., pres. convention, 16229
Sportsman's companion, 23785-86, 24809
Spotswood, William
    Catalogue, 29558
    Stock of new books, 37012
Spotsylvania county. Address, 29559
Spouse of Christ, 165
Sprague, Edward, ordained, 15863
Sprigg, Richard. Theological works, 7322
Spring, Alpheus, d. 1791, death, 23518
Spring, Paul, d. 1772, suicide, 12499
Spring, Samuel, 1746-1819
    Christian knowledge, 19257
    Discourse, 27730
    Exemplary pastor, 23787
    Friendly dialogue, 18792
    God the author, 38547
    Moral disquisitions, 22156
    Nature and importance, 18793
    Sermon, (1777) 16076, (1780) 16995-96, (1792) 24810, (1793) 27731
    Substance of a discourse, 16997
    Thanksgiving sermon, 34590
    Three sermons, 18195, 22901
    letters (from Tappan), 19270
Springfield library co. Catalogue, 31227
Sprinkling a scriptural mode, 12829, 21917
Sprinkling the proper mode, 28626-27
Sproat, James, d. 1793
    Address, 14411
    Discourse, 12234
    death, 27065
    moves to Philadelphia, 11507
Sproutt, James. Discourse, 12234
Spunkey, Simon see **Fessenden, Thomas Green, 1771-1807**
Spunkiad, 35052
Spuren der güte, 23697
Spurrier, John. Practical farmer, 26198
Squabble, a pastoral, 9564-65
Squibb, Robert
    Gardener's calendar, 34592, 35234
    Gardener's kalendar, 20722
Squier, Andrew, wife's death, 18406
Squier, Huldah, d. 1783, death, 18406
Squier, Truman
    secy. Vermont, 31487, 33120-21, 34921
    signs proclamation, 29788
Squire, Francis. Answer to some late, 7123
Staats, Samuel. To the honourable, 852
Stability of Christ's church, 30021
Stacey, Joseph, ordained, 2129
Stackhouse, Thomas, 1677-1752
    Lehrbegriff, 27732
    commentary on Bible, 20960, 21680, 22347
Stafford, Cornelius William. Philadelphia directory, (1797) 32868, (1798) 34593, (1799) 36353, (1800) 38549
Stafford, Joseph. Almanac see **Almanacs (Stafford)**
Stair, John Dalrymple, 3d earl, reply to, 6808
Stall, John, d. 1782, death, 19443
Stamford, Lord ——, protests, 14090
Stamp act, (1755) 7476, (1764) 9681-82, 9723, (1765) 9986-93, (1797) 32956
Stamp act repealed, 10529-32
Stamp duties, 34877-78

VOL.	ITEMS	VOL.	ITEMS
1	1-3244	8	22298-25074
2	3245-6623	9	25075-28145
3	6624-9891	10	28146-30832
4	9892-13091	11	30833-33261
5	13092-16176	12	33262-25854
6	16177-19448	13	35855-39162
7	19449-22297		

VOL.	ITEMS	VOL.	ITEMS
1	1-3244	8	22298-25074
2	3245-6623	9	25075-28145
3	6624-9891	10	28146-30832
4	9892-13091	11	30833-33261
5	13092-16176	12	33262-25854
6	16177-19448	13	35855-39162
7	19449-22297		

Nature of saving, 11873
Necessity of acknowledgment, 1026
Presence of Christ, 1999
Question whether, 2479
Safety of appearing, (1687) 434, (1729) 3220, (1742) 5068
Sufficiency, 1147
Those taught, 1584-85
Three sermons, 1930
Treatise, 2072
Tryal of assurance, 853
Way for a people, 1148
Way to know, 2073
death, 3149, 3239
reply to, 1366
Stoddard, Thomas, sermon before, 7384
Stoddart, John. Report, 4042
Stoddert, Benjamin, 1751-1813, letter (from Talbot), 38602
Stokes, George
Account of births, 17675
Account of the births, (1768) 11036, (1769) 11414, (1770) 11819, (1771) 12522, 12524, (1773) 12950, (1774) 13541, (1775) 14388
Stokes, William. Tentamen medicum, 26214
Stolwood, Benjamin, d. 1713, murdered, 1626
Stone, ——
reports on Conn. expenses, 18838
reports on Penobscot expedition, 19312
Stone, Abner, d. 1774?, death, 13129
Stone, Daniel, ordained, 30508
Stone, Eliab, 1737-1822
Discourse, 36373, 38564
Sermon, (1783) 18199, (1793) 27745, (1798) 34605
ordained, 8806
Stone, F. Lancaster county, to wit, 12828
Stone, Hugh, d. 1689, execution, 539
Stone, James. How Christ, 5870
Stone, John Hoskins. Proclamation, 30746
Stone, John Hurford, 1763-1818. Copies of original, 34606
Stone, Joseph. Columbian harmony, 26215
Stone, Nathan, fl. 1730-1765
If ministers, 10177
Two discourses, 9019
ordained, 3427
Stone, Nathan, fl. 1764-1797
hand of fellowship, 31866
ordained, 10177
Stone, Nathanael, 1667-1755
Additional proposals, 3221
Caution, 4312
Concio ad magistratum, 3107
Lecture sermon, 2179
Letter, 3839
On account of pleas, 4429
Postscript, 3840
Rulers are a terror, 2180
Serious reflections, 3838
Veracity, 2480
Very brief account, 3478
Way to attain, 2000
advice to Whitefield, 5668
reply to, 4365
Stone, Nathaniel, d. 1848
Duty of worshipping, 31240
hand of fellowship, 31866?
Stone, Samuel, 1600-1663. Short catechism, 378, 2181
Stone, Seth, manages lottery, 33861
Stone, Thomas, 1743-1787

reports on Conn. expenses, 18838?
reports on Penobscot expedition, 19312?
Stone, Timothy, 1742-1797
Nature and evil, 16084-85
Sermon, 24820, 27746
Victory, 17000
death, 33850
ordained, 10900
Stone cut out, 1833
Stonhouse, Sir James, 1716-1795
Christ's temptations, 11874
Universal restitution, 11875
Stonington association
Minutes, (1789) 22167, (1790) 22911, (1791) 23803, (1792) 24821, (1793) 26216, (1794) 27747, (1795) 29570, (1796) 31241, (1797) 32885, (1798) 34607, (1799) 36374, (1800) 38565
Sentiments and plan, 20731
Storace, Stephen, 1763-1796
Ah can I cease, 26217
Captivity, 26218
Sweet little Barbara, 36375
The willow, 34608
composes song, 25306-308, 27126, 30203
Storer, Miss ——, benefit for, 11867
Storm, a poem, 21081
Storm, or the American syren, 13032
Storrs, Andrew, d. 1785, death, 18950
Storrs, Eleazer, ordained, 10486
Storrs, John, 1735-1799. Sermon, 20010
Storrs, Richard Salter
ordained, 20010
wife's death, 33354
Storrs, Sarah, d. 1798, death, 33354
Story, Daniel, ordained, 34609
Story, Enoch. Philadelpha, Jan. 14, 1775, 14476
Story, Isaac, 1749-1816
Discourse, 29571
Love of our country, 13643
Sermon, 29571, 34609
ordained, 12174
Story, Isaac, 1774-1803
All the world's a stage, 31242
Consolatory odes, 36376
Epistle from Yarico, 24822, 27748
Eulogy, 38567
Liberty, 29572
Yarico to Inkle, 28202
Story, Joseph, 1779-1845
Eulogy, 38568
Power of solitude, 38569
Story, Thomas, 1662-1742
Two discourses, 11483
case of, 2502?
Story of a very remarkable, 29573
Aeneas, 13743-44
Albany, 28978
Chambert, 28978
Edward and Maria, 33533
Edwards, 28978
Eugenio, 34475

VOL.	ITEMS	VOL.	ITEMS
1	1-3244	8	22298-25074
2	3245-6623	9	25075-28145
3	6624-9891	10	28146-30832
4	9892-13091	11	30833-33261
5	13092-16176	12	33262-25854
6	16177-19448	13	35855-39162
7	19449-22297		

Frank, 33533
Joseph, 36377, 37151-53
Le Fevre, 28978
Melissa, 28977-78
Palaemon, 31187
poor Trickett, 35298
Sarah, 32794
Seymour, 28978
the cruel giant, 11082
the dreamer, 31080
the innocent Amelia, 36378
Story teller, 29574
Stothard, ——, drawings by, 24437, 25672, 27174, 28910, 37393
Stouffer, Henry, petition, 38854
Stoughton, Willam, 1631-1701
New England's true interest(s), (1670) 155-56, (1722) 2363, (1774) 13445
Proclamation, 987
Speech, 907
death, 1035
lieutenant governor, 3287
Stout, Benjamin. Narrative, 32886, 38570-71
Stoutenburgh, Jacobus. Short detail, 10178
Stover, John, captivity, 35689
Stover, William Lilly. Almanac see **Almanacs (Stover)**
Stowers, John, innholder, 19390
Strahan, William, letter (from Smith), 28867
Strait gate, 3167, 35298
Strange, Lord ——, **fl. 1766,** speech by, 10463
Strange, James, petition, 31380
Strange, Sir John, 1696-1754, quotations from, 10935?
Strange account, 577, 10778
and remarkable, 14680
and wonderful Indian dream, 12969
and wonderful predictions, 8499-501, 23509
relation, 5692
The stranger see **Story, Isaac, 1774-1803**
The stranger, a comedy, 35705
The stranger, or misanthropy, 35703-704
Stranger's assistant and school-boy's, 29576
Stranger's assistant, being a collection, 29575
Strawberry district association
Met at Gill's-creek, 26226
Minutes, 26219-25
Strawbridge, Thomas, accounts, 18700
Strawbridge, Jackson & Dexter, deed of trust to, 38613
Strebeck, George
Collection, 32567
Sermon, 31243, 38572
Street, Nicholas, 1730-1806. American states, 15604
Street, Thomas George. Aura, 21479
Strength and weakness, 2815
Strephon. Panegyrick, 9280
Stretch, L. M. Beauties of history, 29577, 27749-51
Strictures and observations, 24513
on a pamphlet entitled, (A friendly address) 13372-73, 13824, 14151-55, (The case of George) 15605
on a sermon, 27632
on Bishop Watson's, 30027
on female education, (1792) 24094, (1793) 25161, (1795) 28263
on Harvard, 33344
on Mr. Burke's, 31876, 32778
on national, 16176
on the Elementa, 28816
friendly, 13863-65

landed, 19921
love of power, 29374
modern, 37995-96
Philadelphia, 16868
remarks, 26697
Rev. Mr., 18800, 19265
second part, 32105
upon an essay, 22540
upon the letter imputed, 37265
letter of General, 37637
Observations, 24823
Striving to enter, 8926
Strolling gentlemen, 25940-42
Strong, ——, grammarian, 4011, 5762, 6485, 7884, 10603
Strong, Anna, 1759?-1789, death, 21733
Strong, Caleb
Proclamation, 37913
dedication to, 37593
Strong, Cyprian, 1743-1811
Animadversions, 22168, 26227
Christian system, 34610
Discourses delivered, 36379
Discourse on Acts, 17001, 23804
God's care, 15606
Inquiry, 26228
Kingdom, 36380
Nature and design, 29578
Second inquiry, 31244
Sermon, 20011, 38574-75
reply to, 28071, 35006
Strong, Esther, d. 1793, death, 25641
Strong, Jedidiah, clerk of meeting, 16746
Strong, Job, ordained, 6492
Strong, Jonathan, 1764-1814
Sermon, 29579, 34611
ordained, 21908
Strong, Joseph, 1729-1803
Christian religion, 35583
Church of Christ, 18200
Duty of singing, 13033
Importance of duly, 12570
Office of the ministers, 14478
That Presbyterian ministers, 11083
reply to, 18672
Strong, Joseph, 1753-1834
Sermon, 31245, 38576
ordained, 16086
Strong, Nathan, relief of, 27854
Strong, Nathan, 1717-1795
Sermon, 13644
death, 31636
ordained, 5781
wife's death, 25641
Strong, Nathan, 1748-1816
Agency, 17002
Discourse, 38577
Doctrine, 31246
Hartford selection, 36382
Political instruction, 34612, 36381
Reasons and design, 15607
Sermon, (1778) 16086, (1790) 22913, (1794) 27752, (1797) 32887-89, 34613, (1798) 34614, (1800) 38578
Sermons, (v.1) 34615, (v.2) 38579
Thanksgiving sermon, 38580
ordained, 13644?
wife's death, 21733?
Strong, Nathaniel. England's perfect, 1487
Strong, Nehemiah, 1729-1807
Almanac see **Almanacs (Strong)**

Astronomy, 18797
Watson's register, 13645
addresses association, 33828
Strong, Simeon. Paraphrase, 28284
Strong rod, 6130
Strother, John
Map of the state, 31047
Treatise, 31251
Struensee, Count ——, conversion, 12874
Stuart, Archibald. Staunton, 26204
Stuart, David. Oration, 12571
Stuart, George, reply to, 10253
Stuart, Gilbert, portrait by, 38152-53?
Stuart, James. Dissertation, 34619
Stuart, William
Oration, 27758
election favored, 38649
Stubbe, Henry, 1606-1678. Conscience, 954, 1717
Stubs, I., dispute with Roger Williams, 228
Studdiford, Peter
Funeral sermon, 23811
pres. Queen's college, 25350
Student and pastor, 27275
Student at Yale college. Almanac see **Almanacs (Huntington)**
Student in a college in this state. Elegies, 37350
Student in physic see **Minor, Jehu, 1743-1808**
Student of Dickinson college see **Shippen, John**
Student of Harvard university see **Harris, Thaddeus Mason, 1768-1842**
Student of law. Fellow citizens, 12765
Student of the College of Philadelphia see **Duché, Jacob, 1739-1798**
Student of Yale-college. Almanac see **Almanacs (College)**
Studies of nature, 32796, 34508
Stueber, Henry, continues Franklin's Autobiography, 33756
Stulta est, 2965
Stumbling stone, 8364, 8577
Stump, Frederick, reward for, 11024
Sturgeon, Robert. Trespass-offering, 2704
Sturm, Christoph Christian, 1740-1786. Beauties of nature, 38583
Styles, E. Oration, 17733, 19437
Subjects for painters, 22288
Sublime and beautiful, 29348
Sublimity and devotion, 34964
Submission, 18315
Subscriber being engaged, 22335
Subscriber takes, 23142
Subscribers, proprietors, 30988
to Malden, 20480
to the non-importation, (New York) 11780, (Philadelphia) 11876
Subscription assembly, 30109
Substance and scope, 6426
of a council, 9848
of a discourse delivered at the dedication, 31840
delivered at Westford, 16997
delivered on the day, 10647-51
on . . . Washington, 39116
preached, 33359
of a late, 38584
of a sermon preached at the ordination, 12569
preached at Baltimore, 18959
preached before, 31841
of a speech delivered by James, 20889
of a speech delivered in the House, 31271

of a thanksgiving, 29131
of an address delivered, 24498
to a meeting, 21028
to an assembly, 16196-97
of an exercise, 10015
of General Burgoyne's, 15752
of the evidence, 14067
report delivered, 29513
report of the court, 29514
reports, 36310
of two sermons, 16414
of two speeches, 35531
Subtensial plain, 8777
Success of the preach'd, 5988
Successful minister, 9657
Succession of generations, 24406
Successive generations, 1765
Succinct account, 34436
Such as have, 5781
Sudler, Emory, petition, 38849
Sufferings of the family, 37761-62
Sufficiency and excellency, 28054
of a worm, 5782
of one, 1147
of the spirit's, 9410
Suffolk, Lord ——, address to, 13960-66
Suffolk county. At a meeting, 13646
Suffolk harmony, 19512
Suffolk ss., 13426
Sugar plumb, 20735
Suicide, 32019
Sullivan, George, 1771-1838. Oration, 38585
Sullivan, James, 1744-1808
Altar of Baal, 29585-88
Biographical sketch, 26234-35
History of the district, 29589
Impartial review, 34620
Observations, 23812
Ode, 29590
Path to riches, 24829
Strictures, 18800, 19265
Thoughts, 21173
observations on, 24324
reply to, 18804
satire on, 19662
Sullivan, John, 1740-1795
Address, 19266
Following plan, 19823
Regulations, 19267
aide-de-camp's book, 26054
campaign against Indians, 31952
letter (from Washington), 30392
pres. NH Senate, 21291
Sullivan, John, d. 1784
confession, 18324, 18559
execution, 19037
Sulpitius, Joannes Verulanus. De moribus, 15035
Sum of religion, 4524
Sum of saving, 5709, 35119
Summary account, 2782

VOL.	ITEMS	VOL.	ITEMS
1	1-3244	8	22298-25074
2	3245-6623	9	25075-28145
3	6624-9891	10	28146-30832
4	9892-13091	11	30833-33261
5	13092-16176	12	33262-25854
6	16177-19448	13	35855-39162
7	19449-22297		

and comparative, 18581
arguments, 27759
declaration, 6421, 33371
historical and political, (1747) 5936, (1748) 6126, (1749) 6306-307, (1750) 6490, (1751) 6662-63, (1753) 6992, (1757) 7885
history, 35075
journal, 27664
of Christian faith, 10944
of church discipline, 17826, 26759
of the law of nations, 29025
   laws, 10935
   principal, 38308
statement, 27951-52
view of the courses, 18373
   of the heavenly, 20737
   of the rights, 13350-52
Summe of certain sermons, 35
Summer, a pastorale, 34634
Sumner, Charles Pinckney, 1776-1836
   Compass, 29591
   Eulogy, 37383, 38586
Sumner, Clement. Oration, 22918
Sumner, Increase, d. 1799
   Proclamation, 32443, 35789
   approves law, 34067
   approves resolve, 34065-66
   death, 35629, 36142, 36405
   dedication to, 32234, 33853
   funeral, 35792-93, 36017
   sermon before, 33675
Sumner, Jane, dying words, 30362
Sumner, Jezaniah. Masonic ode, 35023
Sumner, John, sermon requested by, 8729
Sumner, Joseph, 1739-1824
   Ministers, 23813
   Sermon, 38587
   ordained, 9493
Sumner, Samuel, fl. 1791, ordained, 23813
Sumter, Thomas, 1734-1832, message referred to, 34807
Sun-beams, 35370-71
Sun fire society. Association and articles, 26689
Sunday reading, 37149, 37151-53
   school, 35298
   service, 19098
Sundry anthems, 21484
   estimates, (1793) 26349, (1794) 27953, (1796) 31460
   false hopes, 1581
   letters, 36389
   resolutions and proceedings, 36591
   resolutions of the board, 34907
   rules, 3633
   statements by the secretary, 26351
   statements respecting, 26350
   votes, 13254
Superannuated horse, 28978
Superiour dignity, 7773
Superiour skill, 4111
Superlative love, 6225
Supernumary crisis, 18078-79
Suple, Nathan
   To the electors, 36390
   reply to, 36433
Supplement extraordinary, 21172
   to a memoir, 36904
   to a piece, 6052
   to an ordinance, 20788, 21515, 21533
   to the act . . . see under state, e.g. **Pennsylvania. Laws.** Supplement to the act . . .

to the American singing-book, (1787) 20673, (1793) 26056, (1795) 29388
   catalogue, 25995
   chorister's, 24434
   Daily advertiser, 20088
   encylopaedia, 38593
   essay, 22368
   Independent journal, 20812, 21559
   laws, 26079
   militia act, 35778
   Norfolk, 20813
   Pennsylvania, 11922
   resolves, 19091
   vindication, 3514
Supplementary catalogue consisting, 38098
   catalogue of the books, 38099
   notes, 33934
Supplication of J. R***,** 38594
Supplications of Peter, 33933
Support under trials, 29903
Supreme deity, 7862, 23242
   influence, 8879
   judicial court, 36225
Sure and certain, 25349
   guide, 6643-44, 10568
   way, 3003
Surest way to advance, 2207
Surest way to the greatest, 880
Surgeon of Norfolk. Treatise, 20752
Surgical works, 28909
Surprising account of the captivity, (1787) 20472, (1788) 21210, (1794) 27248, (1796) 30713, (1797) 32401
   account of the devil's, 18954, 30187
   account of the life, 23837
   adventures, 34461, 36228
   dream, 15318
   life and death, 28655
   narrative, (1787) 20616, (1795) 29276, (1797) 32638, (1799) 36035-36
   variety, 5095
   voyages, 28349
Surprizing account of an old, 19529-30
   account of the captivity, 36391
   instance, 13870
   though true, 19545
   yet real, 13257
Surr, Thomas Skinner, 1770-1847. New work, 38596
Survey of man, 8744, 22171
Survey of the roads, 21741
Surviving servants, 2591
Suspected daughter, 6790
Suspicious husband, 23443, 31175
Suspiria vinctorum, 2777
Susquehannah case, 18971
Susquehannah title, 30091
Sutter, Petter. Eight dollars, 11484
Sutton, Abraham, petition, 33005
Sutton, Mass. Inhabitants of the town, 15610
Swan, Abraham. Collection of designs, 14481
Swan, Godfried, murderer, 10042
Swan, James, 1754-1831
   Dissuasion, 12572, 13034
   National arithmetick, 20016
   On the fisheries, 18801
Swan, Timothy, 1758-1842. Federal harmony, (1785) 19268, (1788) 21485, (1790) 22919, (1792) 24831, (1794) 27762
Swanwick, John, 1760-1798
   British honour, 31255

VOL.	ITEMS	VOL.	ITEMS
1	1-3244	8	22298-25074
2	3245-6623	9	25075-28145
3	6624-9891	10	28146-30832
4	9892-13091	11	30833-33261
5	13092-16176	12	33262-25854
6	16177-19448	13	35855-39162
7	19449-22297		

of vocal, 32901
System containing, 9507
for the discipline, 32878
of astronomy, 26678
of chemistry, 23817
of doctrines, 25634
of exchange, 37696
of mineralogy, 29601
of public education, 21702

of rhetorick, 21477
of seamanship, 36393
of short-hand, 25252
of surgery, 23168-70
of the law of marine, (1789) 22048, (1799) 36040, (1800) 38186-87
of the laws of the state, 29600, 31260
Systematic arrangement, 29913

T

T. Extracts of private, 13273, 13307
T., A. see **Witherspoon, John,** 1722-1974
T., B. see **Tompson, Benjamin,** 1642-1714
T., E., tr. Adventures, 35183
T., E. see **Turell, Ebenezer,** 1701-1778
T., J. see **Tomkins, John,** 1663-1706
T., R. Old Mr. Dod's, (1673) 174, (1731) 3412, (1760) 8583, (1768) 10884
T., T. Almanac see **Almanacs (T. T.)**
T., T. Suspected daughter, 6790
T., W. Counterpoise, 7127
T----sd---e, Joseph. Boston, Dec. 23, 1767, 10780
T***t., T.** Be merry, 9285
Taber, Joseph. Address, 18802
Tabitha rediviva, 1627
Table calculated to shew in an instant, 20740
calculated to shew the contents, 12239, 22921
exhibiting a plan, 27954
for receiving, (1792) 24070, (1795) 26365-66, (1796) 31263
for the payment of principal, 17049, 18271-72
payment of the second, 17050
ready turning, 6615-16
for turning, 6422
for understanding, 23818
of an analytical, 36759
of discount, 38427
of duties, 23894
of exchange, 19549
of fees, 29405
of French, 16730
of interest at five per cent, 7378
at six per cent, 23819
on lawful, 8044
of latitude, 32639
of post offices and rates, 38908
of post-offices in the U.S., 24935
of the fees, 22016
first, 16634
kings, 10781
sums, 16635

value of foreign, 26368
value of the lawful, 9521
variations, 30917
weight, 18604
or list, 34879-80
shewing the distance, 22922
the value of any, 31136
the value of 100, 33574
to bring, 29602
Tableau de son & accens, 26743
des F. F., 33765
syllabique, 33249
Tables and instructions, 31264
and plates, 38467
exhibiting, 37193
for calculating, 22173
for readily, 23300
of difference, 22856, 35670, 36236
of discount, 38426
of latitude, 24357
of the port, 14586
shewing, 31265-66
Tablet, a miscellaneous, 29603
Täglichen loosungen, (1764) 9529, (1765) 9860, (1766) 10513, (1767) 10793, (1768) 10794, 11102, (1769) 11103, (1770) 11510, (1771) 11907, (1772) 12261, (1773) 12588, (1774) 13055, (1775) 13700, (1776) 14531, (1780) 16551, (1781) 17012, (1782) 17382, (1783) 17754, (1784) 18222, (1796) 29673, (1797) 31330, (1798) 32948, (1800) 36395, (1801) 38600

Taft, Moses, ordained, 7116
Tag, Tommy. Collection of pretty, 9281
Tagebuch der convention, 21372
der General assembly, (1787) 19889, (1788) 21373, (1789) 22056, (1790) 22779
des achten, 34327-28
des raths, 18713
des sechsten, 30979
des Senats, (1794) 27486, (1797) 32654, (1798) 34330, (1799) 36069

des siebenten, 32652
des vierten, 27481
Taggart, Samuel, 1754-1825
  Calm impartial, 22174
  Discourse, 38599
Tailer, William, d. 1732
  death, 3524
  dedication to, 3287
Tailfer, Patrick. True and historical, 4816-17
Take heed, 4721, 4959
Talapoins, maxims by, 32836
Talbot, Catherine, 1721-1770. Reflections, **38601**
Talbot, John
  Great mistery, 1235
  proposal unanswered, 1192
  remarks on, 1231
  reply to, 1230
Talbot, Silas
  Explanatory, 38602
  plaintiff, 19164, 22053
Talcott, Joseph, 1669-1741
  Proclamation, 3649
  dedication to, 3383, 3496, 3619, 3729, 3859, 3978, 4106, 4213, 4329, 4465, 4661, 4873
Tales of passed times, 29300
Tales of the hermitage, 38269
Talleyrand-Périgord, Charles Maurice de, 1754-1838, reply to, 34363
Talleyrand dissected, 33738
Tallmadge, Benjamin, ordained, 7371
Tame stag, 28147
Tammanial Tontine association. Plan, 24612
Tammany, Indian chief, 29088
Tammany, Jr. see **Workman, Benjamin**
Tammany society. American museum, 23619
Tancred and Sigismunda, 27794
Tanguy de La Boissière, C. C., d. 1799
  Observations on the dispatch, 32905
  Observations sur la depeche, 32904
  Observer of Europe, 28970
  Philadelphia, 27770
  death, 37126
Tanner, ———, engraver, 36202
Tansillo, Luigi, 1510-1568. The nurse, 38604
Tans'ur, William, 1699-1783
  American harmony, (1769) 11489, (1771) 12240-41, (1773) 13035, (1774) 13647
  Royal melody, (1761) 9021, (1764) 9598-600, (1766) 10236, (1767) 10782, (1768) 10829, 11085
Tantive back, 22097
Taplin, William, d. 1807
  Compendium, 32906
  Gentleman's stable directory, 27771
Tappan, Benjamin, d. 1790, death, 22504
Tappan, David, 1752-1803
  Beauty, 38605
  Character and best, 17734
  Character and death, 18803
  Christian thankfulness, 29604
  Connexion, 24840
  Copy of an address, 27772
  Discourse delivered at the third, 18203
  Discourse delivered in the chapel, (1794) 27773-74, (1795) 29605, (1798) 34629
  Discourse delivered to the religious, 34627-28
  Discourse delivered to the students, 31267
  Discourse in English, 38999, 39100-101
  Duty of private, 16089
  Friendly dialogue, 18792

Minister's solemn, 26243
  Question answered, 18204
  Sermon, (1789) 22175, (1792) 24841, (1793) 26244, (1794) 27775-76, (1797) 32907, (1800) 38606
  To friendly letters, 19270
  ordained, 13354?
  reply to, 28340
  strictures on, 22156
Tappan, John, ordained, 30028
Tappin, John, 1653?-1672, death, 183
Tardiveau, ———, presents petition, 21521
The task, (1787) 20303, (1791) 23293, (1795) 28497, (1796) 30290-92
Tasker, Benjamin, address to, 6872
Tate, James. Major est veritas, 22923
Tate, Nahum
  New version, (1710) 1444, (1713) 1594-95, (1720) 2094, (1725) 2603, (1733) 2625, (1737) 4114, (1740) 4471, (1754) 7149, (1755) 7358, (1757) 7846, (1760) 8544, (1762) 9068-69, (1763) 9344-45, (1765) 9913-14, (1766) 10241, (1767) 10557-58, (1769) 11180, (1770) 11569-70, (1771) 11988-91, (1773) 12673-77, (1774) 13149-51, (1775) 13835, (1787) 20228, (1788) 20962, (1790) 22351, (1791) 23187, (1793) 25176, (1795) 28274
  selections from, 35222
Tatem, William. Evidence, 36396
Tatham, William, 1752-1819
  Political economy, 36397
  Proposals for publishing, 22924
  Report, 27777
  Topographical analysis, 23820-21
Tatom, Absalom, 1742-1802, message referred to, 31406
Taunton, Mass. Testimony of a number, 5693
Tavern rates, 21667
Taverner, William, d. 1731
  Maid the mistress, 9022
  adaptation from, 30732
Tawney Rachel, 34133
Tax-act and estimate, 10498
Tax for the year, (1798) 34074-75, (1799) 35798-99, (1800) 37925
Tax no. 4, 18597, **(no. 5)** 19093, 19795, **(no. 6)** 21249, **(no. 7)** 21950, **(no. 8)** 22660, **(no. 9)** 23556, **(no. 10)** 25787, **(no. 11)** 27294, **(no. 12)** 29047-48, **(no. 13)** 30767-68, **(no. 14)** 32452
Taxation royal tyranny, 16541
Tayler, Thomas. Observation, 24842
Taylor, ———, actor, 30569
Taylor, Capt. ———, sermon before, 14758
Taylor, Dr. ———. Letters (to Webster), 31593
Taylor, ———, of Deerfield, appendix by, 26485, 29893, 39104
Taylor, Abraham, 1727-1740. Insufficience, 7578
Taylor, Amos
  American babes, 17736
  Genuine experience, 31268-69
  Narrative, 17735

VOL.	ITEMS	VOL.	ITEMS
1	1-3244	8	22298-25074
2	3245-6623	9	25075-28145
3	6624-9891	10	28146-30832
4	9892-13091	11	30833-33261
5	13092-16176	12	33262-25854
6	16177-19448	13	35855-39162
7	19449-22297		

29193-95, (1796) 30878
precepts, 22158
sermons, 29886, 33218
Tench, Watkin, 1759-1833. Narrative, 22176
Tender counsel, 18082
heart, 7790
salutation, 28443
Tenessee company to Messrs., 38613
Tennent, Charles. Letter to the printer, 4791
Tennent, Gilbert, 1703-1764
All things, 5695
Blessedness, 10181
Brotherly love, 6243
Danger of an unconverted, 4609-10, 5070-71
Danger of forgetting, 3964
Danger of spiritual, 5696
Discourses on several, 5697, 5871
Divine government, 6940
Divinity, 4431
Duty of self examination, 4432
Espousals, 3965, 4819
Examiner examined, 5297-98
Expostulary address, 3968
Funeral sermon, 5698
Gefahr, 4611
Good mans character, 7797
Happiness, 7798-99
Irenicum, 6423
Late association, 6244-47
Legal bow, 4433
Love to Christ, 5497
Necessity of holding, 5299
Necessity of keeping, 5699
Necessity of praising, 5700
Necessity of religious, 3966
Necessity of studying, 5498
Necessity of thankfulness, 5499
Preciousness, 4434
Persuasive, 8745
Remarks, 4820
Righteousness, 4821
Sermon, (1741) 4822-26, (1746) 5872, (1748) 6248, 6425, (1749) 6424, (1761) 9023
Sermons on important, 8266
Sermons on Psalm XIV, 4436
Sermons on sacramental, 4438
Solemn scene, 4435
Solemn warning, 3967, 4612
Substance and scope, 6426
Terrors, 6427
Three letters, 4354
Twenty-three sermons, 5500
Two sermons, (1741) 5072-73, (1742) 5299, (1749) 6428
Unsearchable riches, 4437
death, 9657
extract from, 4792
preface by, 5883-85, 8116-17
refuted, 4946, 5200
remarks on, 4509
reply to, 4581, 6239-40
vindicated, 4862
Tennent, John, M.D.
Essay on pleurisy, 5074
Essay on the pleurisy, 4085
Every man his own doctor, (1734) 3843-44, (1736) 4086, (1737) 4202
Jeder sein eigener, 6340
Tennent, John, 1706-1732
Nature of regeneration, 3968
Two sermons, 4612
life, 4612

Tennent, William, 1705-1777
Exhortations, 4439
God's sovereignty, 10182
Sermon, 11491
Sermons on sacramental, 4438
Three letters, 4354
Tennent, William, 1740-1777
Address, 13649
Speech, 15612
death, 15233, 15357
Tennessee
Constitution, 31278-79, 36404
Journal of the proceedings, 31280
Remonstrance and petition, 32980-81
Tennessee. Governor
Proclamation, 31282, 34637
Tennessee. House of representatives
Journal, 31281
Tennessee. Laws (collective)
Laws relative to lands, 38612
Tennessee. Laws (session)
Acts, (1796) 31277, (1797) 32913, (1798-99) 36402-403
Tenny, Joseph. Brief illustration, 27785
Tenntamen medicum inaugurale de epilespsia, 24198
medicum inaugurale de scarlatina, 21575
medicum inaugurale quaedam, 26214
varia, 26914
Tenth edition; the minister, 23254
Terms, conditions, 34882
of Christianity, 7807
of enlistment, 15839
of Richard Folwell, 35489
Terra beata, 2778
Terrell, Job, d. 1756, death, 7821
Terribilia Dei, 795
Territorial assembly. Acts, 27224
Terror of the Lord, 2919-21
Terrors of death, 29085
Terrors of the Lord, 6427
Terry, Mary, death, 1645
Tersteegen, Gerhard, 1697-1769
Anhagen, 9850
Frommen lotterie, 5501, 6791
Geistliches blumen-gärtlein, (1747) 6073, (1769) 11492, (1773) 13036, (1791) 23823, (1800) 38615
Glückliche genügsamkeit, 6074
Kraft der liebe, 12573
, Lebens beschreibung, 26247
Vom Christlichen gebrauch, 24843
Von der mystik, 24755
Warnungs-schreiben, 6249
Test of the religious, 37704-706
Testament abridged, 36959
of the twelve, (1709) 1426, (1714) 1710, (1716) 1849
und abschrift, 23199
Testamentary system, 32431
Testimony against evil, 2051
against prophaneness, 953

VOL.	ITEMS	VOL.	ITEMS
1	1-3244	8	22298-25074
2	3245-6623	9	25075-28145
3	6624-9891	10	28146-30832
4	9892-13091	11	30833-33261
5	13092-16176	12	33262-25854
6	16177-19448	13	35855-39162
7	19449-22297		

several prophane, 451
that false, 607
the antichristian, 3644
the prophaness, 8574
and advice of a number, 5176, 5300
advice of an assembly, 5136
caution, 637
concerning acceptable, (1794) 27050, (1799)
35545, (1800) 37512
from the scripture, 151, 2676
given before a committee, 34760
given forth, 15302
of a number of ministers, 5693
of a number of New-England, 5544
of an association of ministers, 5678
of an association or club, 5701
of conscience, 12745
of the authenticity, (1795) 28790-91, (1796)
30126, 30530, (1797) 31877
monthly meetings, 33768
North association, 5605
pastors, 5135
people, 14052
president, 5409
two witnesses, 19485, 25131
to the order, (1701) 978, (1717) 1941, (1772)
12626
Teucro duce, 15352
Teutsch und englische, 6075
Teutsche gesellschaft
Erste frucht, 10138
Regeln, 9795, 10453
Schreiben des evangelisch, 14394
Teutsche pilgrim see **Almanacs (Teutsche)**
Teutscher handwercksmann. Klare und gewisse,
5982
Tevebaugh, George, petition, 38753
Thacher, George, 1754-1824, message referred to,
31406?
Thacher, Oxenbridge, 1720-1765
Considerations, 9146, 9283
Sentiments, 9851
Thacher, Peter, 1651-1727
Alsufficient, 1529
Cases of conscience, 2485
Christ's forgiveness, 1587
Divine riddle, 2484
Funeral sermon, 2076
Perpetual covenant, 1653
Saints' victory, 774
Signal and most gracious, 1374
Unbelief, 1375
death, 3016, 3059, 30777, 31286
successor, 5757
Thacher, Peter, 1678-1739
Brief declaration, 2187
Man's frailty, 3362
Vindication, 2186
Wise & good, 2816
death, 4351, 4357, 4444
difficulty in Weymouth, 2089
ordained, 2104
ordination disputed, 2174
Thacher, Peter, 1688-1744. Fear of God, 2188
Thacher, Peter, 1715-1785
Prayer, 17739
Select discourses, 34638
Thacher, Peter, 1752-1802
Brief account of the present, 28322
Brief account of the Society, 34639
Nature and effects, 27786

Observations, 18206
Oration, 15101
Reply, 18804
Rest which remaineth, 16090
Sermon, (1788) 21489-90, (June 2, 1790) 22925,
(Nov. 14, 1790) 23824-25, (1793) 26248-49,
(1794) 27787, (1795) 29616, (1796) 31283-84,
(1797) 32914, (1798) 34641-42, (June 12, 1799)
36405, (Dec. 29, 1799) 38619, (1800) 38618
That the punishment, 18207
To the members, 34640
hand of fellowship, 36409
installation, 19157
ordained, 12216
remarks on, 18488?
reply to, 18800, 30604-605
strictures on, 19265
Thacher, Samuel. Oration, 31285
Thacher, Thomas, 1620-1678
Brief rule, 242, 1096
Fast, 258
Thacher, Thomas, 1756-1812
Discourse, (1795) 29617, (1800) 38620-21
Eulogy, 38622
Sermon, (1784) 18805, (1795) 31286, (1797) 34645
Thacher, Thomas Cushing, 1771-1849
Eulogy, 38623
Sermon, 27788, 29618
ordained, 27787
Thackara, James
Young ladies' and gentlemen's, 34643
engraver, 22486, 23008, 26543, 27005, 27209, 28978,
38467
Thackeray, Rev. —— visitation, 7691
Thane, Daniel, ordained, 6457
Thankefull remembrance, 226
Thankful Christian, 1907
Thankful memorial, 3217
Thanks of the public, 13184
Thanksgiving and praise, 35264
and prayer, 28674
discourse, 19709
ode, 28601
sermon, (Appleton) 10230, (Bradley) 35228,
(Cumings) 10596, (Emerson) 8592, 10293,
(Fränkel) 8126-28, 9390, (Kellogg) 32331,
(Moore) 32498, (Spring) 34590, (Strong)
38580, (Throop) 10506, (Treat) 9287, (Wil-
lard) 18887, (Worcester) 31659
Tharp, Peter
Elegy, 38624-25
New and complete, 34644
That Jesus Christ, 7800
ministers, 4058
people, 7617
Presbyterian, 11083
the commissioners, 20083
gospel, 24279
publick, 25276
punishment, 18207
there is, 11174
Thatcher, ——, message referred to, 31406
Thatcher, Peter see **Thacher, Peter**
Thatcher, Thomas, 1756-1812 see **Thacher, Thomas,
1756-1812**
Thaumatographia, 995
Thayer, Atherton, d. 1798, death, 34997
Thayer, Cornelius, d. 1745, death, 5556
Thayer, Ebenezer, 1688-1733
Christ, 2391
Jerusalem, 2709

Ministers, 2967
Thayer, Ebenezer, 1734-1792
  Family worship, 36406
  ordained, 10290
Thayer, Elihu, 1747-1812
  Charge, 36050
  Funeral discourse, 29619
  Faithful watchman, 22926
Thayer, John, 1758-1815
  Account, 21491
  Controversy, 26250-51, 29620
  Discourse, 34646-47
Thayer, Nathaniel, 1769-1840
  Anthems, 36407
  Character of St. John, 32915
  Preaching, 36408
  Sermon, (1795) 29621, 31287, (1798) 34648, (1799) 36409
  hand of fellowship, 33368
  ordained, 25952
Thayer, Simeon, relief of, 26326
Thayer, Zechariah, ordained, 3421
Theatre, a poem, 24844
    Newport, 38114
    of education, 20744
    on Wednesday, 33364
Thecla, martyr, 9863
Their majesties colony, 686
Thellen, Wilhelm, poem on, 11068
Themistocles. Reply, 18208
Then say, 27789
Theobald, John. Every man, (1767) 10783, (1794) 27790, (1800) 38626
Theocrat. Brush of sound reason, 30131
Theodosius, or the force, 8902
Theological dissertation, 35772
    magazine, (1795) 29622, (1796) 31288-89, (1797) 32916, (1798) 34649, (1799) 36410
    preceptor, 12497
    system, 18408
    theses, 10493
    works, 7322
Theologisches bedenken, 11953
Theophilanthropy, 36411
Theophilus
    Letters, 5985
    see also **Dickinson, Jonathan, 1688-1747**
Theopolis Americana, 1469
Theory and practice, 14098
Theory of agency, 12188
Theosebes, Bereanus see **Hazlitt, William, 1737-1820**
Theosophischen lectionen, 6840
Theosophischer entwurf, 24755
There is a snake, 34650
There shall be, 15191
Thermometrical navigation, 36722
Theron, Paulinus and Aspasio, 8297, 33396
Thespian chaple, 33627
Thespian oracle, 34651
Theus, James, petition, 33012
They steer, 25498
Thickness, Philip, case of, 13953-59
Things as they are, 28752
    for a distress'd, 755
    lovely, 27260
    that young, 934
    to be look'd for, 567
    to be more, 1628
Think well on't, 23253, 37116
Third and last letter, 31215

Third and last voyage, 28476-77, 30275-76
Third Congress of the U.S. . . . An act . . . see under **U. S. Laws (separates)** Act . . .
Third Congress of the U.S. . . . Resolved . . . see under **U. S. Congress.** Resolve . . .
Third edition; the Democratiad, 30589, 31173
    extraordinary budget, 11177
    letter, 4148
    supplement, 31001
Thirsty invited, 5057
Thirteen hymns, 15222-23
Thirteen sermons, 31310
13th February, 1800, 38909
Thirty dollars reward; ran away, 23314
    dollars reward; this evening, 15440
    important cases, 878
This day is published, 14015
    day was published, 19439
    evening, 11009
    indenture made, 9212, 22205
    is to give, 11778, 24017
    night, 29623
    oration, 37205
    poem, 10143
    twenty fourth day, 37916
    week, 16008
Thoma Wilcocks köstlicher, 13771
Thomas à Kempis
    Christian pattern, 6342
    Extract of the Christian's pattern, 27179, 37717
    Following of Christ, 37718
    Imitation of Christ, 114
    Kleine A.B.C., 4982
    Kleine Kempis, (1750) 6523, (1751) 6698, (1773) 12824, (1788) 21183, (1795) 28920
    Of the imitation, 17992, 23480
    Soliloquy of the soul, 37719-20
    Vier bücher, 6342
Thomas, Alexander, 1775-1809. Orator's assistant, 32917
Thomas, Antoine Léonard, 1732-1785. Essay, 13650
Thomas, Benjamin, d. 1800, death, 36892
Thomas, David
    Novelty, 17740
    Virginia Baptist, 13651
Thomas, Elisha, verses to, 21545
Thomas, Eliza, d. 1799. Vision, 38627
Thomas, Evan, tr. Shepherdess, 29021
Thomas, Sir George, 1695?-1774
    Letter, 4613
    Notice is hereby, 4783
    Proclamation, (1741) 4781, (1742) 5032, (1744) 5473, (1746) 5847
    Speech, 4298
    Treaty held, 5416
Thomas, Isaiah, 1749-1831
    Catalogue of books, (1787) 20745, (1792) 24845, (1793) 26252, (1796) 31290
    (ed.) Laus Deo, 27202
    Literary proposal, 21492
    New American spelling, 19271

VOL.	ITEMS	VOL.	ITEMS
1	1-3244	8	22298-25074
2	3245-6623	9	25075-28145
3	6624-9891	10	28146-30832
4	9892-13091	11	30833-33261
5	13092-16176	12	33262-25854
6	16177-19448	13	35855-39162
7	19449-22297		

concerning the bank, with some, 19591
concerning the nature, 27799
for a Lord's, 14409
for the day, 1559
in prison, (1779) 16261, (1786) 19610, (1794) 26898
of a dying, 796
of the heart, 4832
on agency, 10130
    Christian baptism, 30923
    Christian holiness, 24851
    conversation, 32928
    divine, 27497
    education addressed, 20736
    education tending, 6294
    emigration, 25648
    government, 14639-40, 20911
    repentance, 21803
    some important, 23468
    taxation, 18436
on the atonement, 23459
    Christian, 32929
    doctrine, 22934
    entertainments, 26259
    erection, 26260
    examinations, 10223
    five per cent, 17742
    French, 29569
    importance of the manners, (1788) 21271, (1795) 29106, (1797) 32503
    late proceedings, 18452
    late transactions, 12088
    lawfulness, 31299
    letter, 15740-41
    love, 28240
    nature, 10505, 14662
    present state, 14965
    state, 28126
    subject, 38635
upon female education, 20691-92, 23747
    several, 23324
    slavery, (1774) 13145-46, 13762, (1792) 25014
    the amusements, 22866
    the political, 21173
    the state, 5302
Three ballads, 35283
    brothers, 32930
    choice and profitable, 90
    curious pieces, 17447
    dialogues, 33139
    discourses, (Beach) 10830, (Cooper) 3526, (Loring) 3437, (S. Smith) 24798
    duetts, 27712
    instructive dialogues, 23952
    lectures, 36255
    letters, (Beeman) 26631, (Colman) 4354, (Daggett) 37281-83, (Pinckney) 36122-24, (White) 6444, (Whitefield) 4651
    letters addressed, 18219
    letters; letter first, 23761
    letters on Theron, 9825
Three millions. Extracts, 14028
Three new marches, 34660
    plain practical, 3091
    practical discourses, 1746, 2887
    remarkable, 22320
    rondos, 20246
    sermons, (Doddridge) 21800, (Gill) 7674, 15312, 32193, (Rogers) 7785, (Savery) 32807, (R. Smith) 23770, 24797, (Spring) 18195,

22901, (Stoddard) 1930
sisters, 32930
treatises, 11661, 18083
valuable pieces, 6067
voyages, 31982-83
woe trumpets, 28113, 39118
years travels through the interior, (1784) 18391, (1789) 21728, (1792) 24181, (1796) 30169
years travels throughout, 26745, 31920
Throne established, 3745
Throop, Amos, ordained, 2967
Throop, Benjamin, 1712-1785
    Religion, 8267
    Thanksgiving sermon, 10506
    death, 19756
Throop, John Dixwell, b. 1793, beneficiary, 27743
Throop, William, 1720-1756. Sermon, 7129
Thrum, Tam. Look before ye loup, 34661
Thumb, Thomas see Waterhouse, Samuel
Thumb, Tom
    Bag of nuts, 20748, 34662
    Exhibition, 20749, 29632
    Tom Thumb's folio, (1786) 20020, (1787) 20750, (1794) 27800, (1795) 29633-34, (1796) 31300
    Tom Thumb's little book, 27801, 29635-36
    Tom Thumb's play book, 20021-22
    history of, 32931
Thumb Bible, 10179, 11086
Thunder and earthquake, 2833-34
Thunderstorm, 18671
Thurber, John, tavern owner, 30298
Thurber, Laban
    Composition, 24852
    Young ladies' & gentlemen's, 32932
Thurman, John
    To the freemen, 14500
    conduct of, 13809, 14518
    makes motion, 13475?
    statement by, 14502
Thurman, Ralph
    To the inhabitants, 14484
    supplies Gen. Gage, 14505
Thursday, (Sept. 20, 1770) 11878, (Sept. 27, 1770) 11879-80
Thurston, Benjamin, 1756-1804
    Discourse, 22181
    Four sermons, 23831
    Sermon, 29637
    Two sermons, 24853, 26261
    ordained, 19459
    reply to, 26158
Thurston, James, ordained, 37965
Thurston, Pearson, ordained, 24810
Thy name, 13916-25
Tiberius Gracchus see Hay, John
Tichenor, Isaac
    At a meeting, 17842
    Illustrious and beloved, 36419
    Proclamation, (1797) 33121, (1798) 34921-22, (1800) 38929

VOL.	ITEMS	VOL.	ITEMS
1	1-3244	8	22298-25074
2	3245-6623	9	25075-28145
3	6624-9891	10	28146-30832
4	9892-13091	11	30833-33261
5	13092-16176	12	33262-25854
6	16177-19448	13	35855-39162
7	19449-22297		

To our friends, 14770
To please Christ, 12544
To Robert Jordan, 4740
To Robert Lemmon, 16330
To Samuel Allinson, 13753
To sing of mercy, 25528
To . . . Sir, 28403
To Sir Timothy, 32695
To supplication, 13982
To the advocates, 12727
  agents, 13037
  associators, 14487
  august, 16331
  author of a letter, 18034
    of the book, 29661
    of those, 3722
  betrayed, 11319
  candid gentlemen, 13038
  children, 14968
  citizens and freemen, 15917
  citizens of Accomack, 34291
    America, 17743
    Annapolis, (Jan. 11, 1775) 14488, (Jan. 13, 1775) 14489
    Baltimore, 26762
    Burlington, 38643
    New York; Dec. 30, 1775, 14490
    New York; keep, 21500
    New York, on the present, 13118
    Pennsylvania, (1780) 16949, (1784) 18714, (1799) 36421
    Philadelphia, (1771) 12244, (1779) 16377, (1787) 20358
    Portsmouth, 29345
    of the county, 36422
    of the electoral, 38301
    of the U.S., 38645
    of Virginia, 38646
  claimants, 36327
  clergymen, 34985
  commissioners and assessors, 9852
  commissioners appointed, 12999
  committee, 34668
  Congress, 15499
  curious and benevolent, 22375
  curious; Tuesday, 29018
  Delaware pilots, 12942
  detestable author, 38647
  dissenting electors, 11494
  disunited, 16545
  editor, 33072
  elders, 126
  electors and freeholders, (1774) 13654, (1776) 15104
  electors at the ensuing, 21732
    of Baltimore, 18757
    of Dutchess county, 32936, 34669
    of New York, 15039
    of Pennsylvania, 36423-24, 36390, 36425
    of Philadelphia, 15753, 36426
    of the borough, 12828
    of the city, 36427
    of the county, 27807
    of the eastern, 33278
    of the Kennebec, 36428
    of the state of New York, (1795) 29641-42, (1798) 33275, 33277, (1800) 38648
    of the tenth district, 38649
  encouragers of literature, 12321
To the federal electors, 38650
    free Africans, 29948
    free and independent citizens, 31302

    independent electors of the city, 15028
    independent electors of the county, 36430
    independent electors of the several, 24856
    independent voters, 34670
    loyal inhabitants, 11588, 13180
    patriotic inhabitants, 11882
    respectable, 14491
  free electors of Kings county, 38407
  free electors of the city, 22936
  freeborn citizens, 13655
  freeholders and electors of the city, 9853
    electors of the province, 9915
    freemen; a further, 2969
    freemen in Pennsylvania, 13039
  freeholders and freemen of New York, 14492
    of the city and colony, 11710, 12103
    of the city and county of New York, (anon.) 11375, (Cruger) 11228-29, (Livingston) 11311-12, (Philanthropos) 11040, (Scott) 11454, 11456
    of the city and county of New York, (as the last) 14317, (fellow citizens) 14493, (gentlement, many arts) 14494, (gentlemen, the important) 11883, (in communion) 11495, (many) 13689, (the following) 11088, (the querist) 11431-32, (whereas) 11496
    of the city and province, 11497, 13040
    of the city of New York, (De Lancey) 11234, (Rousby) 11447
    of the city of New York, (electors) 11017, (fellow-citizens, a survey) 14495, (fellow citizens, several) 13809
    of the north ward, 15211
    of this city, 11198
  freeholders and other electors for the city, 9854
    and electors of assembly men, 10184
    and other inhabitants of the towns, 14222
    and others, inhabitants, 8862
  freeholders, freemen and inhabitants of the city and county, (1774) 13389, (1775) 14496-97
    freemen and inhabitants of the city of New York, 13656
    merchants, tradesmen, 11884
    of New-Town, 14498
    of the county, 8046
    of the district, 27808
    of the province, 5075
    of the town of Boston, 8747
    of the town of Jamaica, 14499
    to prevent mistakes, 2970
To the freemen and electors, 18321
  freemen and freeholders of New York, 15105
    of the city and county of New-York, (1768) 11089-90, (1775) 14500-501
    of the city of New York, 10507
    of the east ward, 13846, 15106
  freemen, citizens, 12946-47
    freeholders and other inhabitants of the

VOL.	ITEMS	VOL.	ITEMS
1	1-3244	8	22298-25074
2	3245-6623	9	25075-28145
3	6624-9891	10	28146-30832
4	9892-13091	11	30833-33261
5	13092-16176	12	33262-25854
6	16177-19448	13	35855-39162
7	19449-22297		

manufacturers, 13664
members of the Free, 29645
    of the General assembly, 18519
    of the Protestant, 26046
    of the Society, 34640
merchants and inhabitants, 12246
    and manufacturers, 10185
    and traders, 11886
    committee, 11887
militia, 15919
military, 14241
[mutilated] . . . At a meeting, 37775
non-commissioned, 14507
officers, 15465
patrons of the Independent, 37686
    of the Newburyport, 34232
    of the Salem gazette, 34511, 36273
people called freeholders, 12578
people of America, 14509
    Cecil, 38655
    England, 13896-905
    Great Britain, 13707
    Kentucky, 28706
    Maryland; gentlemen, 15111
    Maryland; give me, 15112
    New Jersey, 38656
    New York, 13665
    Oneida, 38281
    Pennsylvania, 18784, 20248-49
    the American, 37812
    the county, 37528
    the state, (1798) 33277, (1800) 38657
    the United States, 31539
philharmonical, 11280
planters, 21969
president and council, 15500
    and executive, 17166
    of the United States; the address, 21844
    of the United States; the secretary, 36592
    Senate and House, 22517
printer of the Maryland, 29646
printers of the Pennsylvania, 10308
printur of the Penselvaney, 12579
privates, 15113
Provincial congress, 13446
To the public, (1764) 9654, 9674, (1767) 10627,
    (July 16, 1768) 11018, (July 25, 1768) 11019,
    (1769) 11500, (July 21, 1769) 11224, (Dec. 23,
    1769) 11350, (Dec. 28, 1769) 11499, 11501, (1770)
    11823, 11890, 11896, (Jan. 9, 1770) 11829, (Jan.
    15, 1770) 11589, (Mar. 8, 1770) 11889, (June 30,
    1770) 11888, (1771) 12053, 12288, (Aug. 1, 1771)
    12084, (Aug. 13, 1771) 12247, (Jan. 15, 1772)
    12580, (Jan. 28, 1772) 12336, (Oct. 12, 1772)
    12589, (1774) 13673, (Apr. 19, 1774) 13671, (Apr.
    21, 1774) 13672, (May 17, 1774) 13669, (June 20,
    1774) 13670, (Sept. 14, 1774) 13668, (Sept. 28,
    1774) 13667, (Oct. 5, 1774) 13674, (Oct. 27, 1774)
    13675, (Nov. 16, 1774) 13677, (Nov. 21, 1774)
    13676, (Dec. 30, 1774) 13666, (1775) 14512, (Jan.
    18, 1775) 14314, (Mar. 13, 1775) 14511, (Mar. 18,
    1775) 14266, (Mar. 21, 1775) 14267, (Mar. 22,
    1775) 14513, (Mar. 24, 1775) 14514, (Apr. 29,
    1775) 14624, (June 3, 1775) 14436, (June 12,
    1775) 14510, (Aug. 4, 1775) 14589, (1776) 14967,
    15114, (Aug. 19, 1779) 16329, (Sept. 18, 1779)
    16320, (1780) 17007, (July 29, 1780) 16990, (Jan.
    12, 1782) 17779, (Jan. 22, 1785) 19274, (Feb. 15,
    1786) 19830, (Apr. 21, 1786) 20025, (May 17,
    1786) 19449, (Dec. 31, 1788) 21478, (1789) 21970,
    (Jan. 9, 1789) 22222, (1791) 23834, (Mar. 1, 1791)

23421, (1792) 26265, (1795) 28643, (Nov. 14, 1796)
    30160, (1797) 32252, (Sept. 28, 1797) 33243, (Apr.
    17, 1798) 34674, (Oct. 7, 1799) 36433, (Oct. 27,
    1800) 37266, (Nov. 8, 1800) 38659, (Nov. 15, 1809,
    i.e. 1800) 38658
To the public, (Aged Friend) 17007, (An elector)
    26265, (Esten) 9654, (Evans) 28643, (Furman)
    12053, (Galloway) 9674, (Gardiner) 10627, (Hil-
    lard) 32252, (Legion) 11500, 13673, (Montfort)
    21970, (Paine) 14967, (Philadelphus) 11823,
    (Towne) 11896, (Wikoff) 12288
To the public (on officers of the navy), 15114
To the public (on taxing the counties), 11890
To the public; stop him, 13676
    public; the Crisis, 14512
    publick, (1766) 10253, (1775) 14095, 14514
    real patriots, 18807
    religious, 21503
    representatives of the freemen of the common-
      wealth, 17164-65
        freemen of the counties, 13678
        freemen of the United States, 36434
        freemen of this province, 628
        people of the state, 38094-95
    Republican citizens, 38660
    Republicans of Pennsylvania, 36435
    respectable body, 13483
      inhabitants of the city and county, 14320
      inhabitants of the city of New York, 14515
      public (Symmes), 20738-39
      public; a publication, 14167
      public; have a good end, 13679
      public; we conceive, 13680
      publick; certain, 13681
    Reverend James, 5011
      Mr. Pitkin, 12518
      Mr. Vesey, 3611
      Mr. William, 4950
    quarterly, 6671
    right honourable, (Feb. 16, 1775) 13953-59,
      (Mar. 6, 1775) 13970
    right worshipful, 3779
    selectmen . . . (Mass.), 25781
    selectmen of . . . as all, 16880
      of the town of ———, 27285
      of the town of Lynnfield, 31306
      pursuant, 27377
    Senate and House (Penna.) (1793) 25520,
      25987, (1799) 36104
    Senate and House (U.S.), 30458, 32163
    Senate and Representatives, 33313
    Senate and the House, 30363
    several battalions, 15115
    several persons, 10720
    Society, 31687
    Sons of liberty in this city, 11891
      of liberty of New York, 14516
      of science, 12671
    speaker, 29647
    supervisors, 22185
    supporters, 16093

VOL.	ITEMS	VOL.	ITEMS
1	1-3244	8	22298-25074
2	3245-6623	9	25075-28145
3	6624-9891	10	28146-30832
4	9892-13091	11	30833-33261
5	13092-16176	12	33262-25854
6	16177-19448	13	35855-39162
7	19449-22297		

VOL.	ITEMS	VOL.	ITEMS
1	1-3244	8	22298-25074
2	3245-6623	9	25075-28145
3	6624-9891	10	28146-30832
4	9892-13091	11	30833-33261
5	13092-16176	12	33262-25854
6	16177-19448	13	35855-39162
7	19449-22297		

on universal redemption, 23839
　　restoration, 25210
　　salvation, 30609
on . . . yellow fever, 37058
proving, 6253
shewing, 6254
upon husbandry, 7356
upon the typhus, 21717
Treaty and convention, 8348, 15353
　　between his excellency, 5791
　　　　the government, 7688
　　　　the president, 6168
　　　　the U.S., 31419
　　held at the town, 5416
　　　　with the Catawba, 7689
　　　　with the Indians, (1742) 5216, (1744) 5417
　　　　with the Ohio Indians, 7026
　　its merits, 31312
　　of amity and commerce, 20089, 36597
　　of amity, commerce, 29743-56, 31414
　　of commerce, 31413
　　of friendship, 4146
　　of peace and amity, 31410
　　of peace and friendship, 2343
Tree of knowledge, 37792-93
Tree planted, 1178
Tremenda, 2251-52
Trenchard, E., engraver, 32018, 30313
Trenchard, J., engraver, 22486, 23454, 24412, 29474
Trenchard, John. Independent Whig, 2537, 4522
Trenck, Friedrich, freiherr von der, 1726-1794
　　History, 27813
　　Life, (1789) 22187, (1792) 24439, 24861-62, (1793)
　　　　26277-79, (1794) 27812, 27814, (1796) 31313,
　　　　(1798) 34678, (1799) 36446-47
Trent, Joseph. Inquiry, 38666
Trenton, N.J.
　　Acts and ordinances, 36448
　　Order of the funeral, 38667
　　Verses composed, 38668
Trenton, Dec. 22, 1794, 27388
Trenton library company. Laws, 34679
Trésor des consolations, 775
Trespass-offering, 2704
Treuhertzige erinnerung, 7443, 7805
Treuhertzige und einfältige, 6433
Treutlen, John Adam. Proclamation, 15291, 15309
Trevett, ———, plaintiff, 20825
Treziulney, ———. Letter (to Washington), 31314-15, 32940
Trial and defense, 13047
Trial of a false, 12683
　　of Abraham, 15711
　　of Alice Clifton, 20275
　　of Daniel Disney, 10958
　　of Daniel Isaac Eaton, 26930-31
　　of Frederick Calvert, 10919
　　of his R. H., 11898
　　of Jeremiah Hill, 25603
　　of John Fries, 35282
　　of Joseph Gerrald, 27591
　　of Louis XVI, 25499
　　of Maurice Margarot, 27592-96, 31173
　　of Mr. Whitefield, 4837
　　of Nathaniel Price, 32712
　　of Renwick Williams, 23445
　　of Richard Parker, 32837
　　of spirits, 8578
　　of the king, 25500
　　　　spirits, 9308, 10279
　　　　witnesses, 21461, 38496

of Thomas Paine, 26280-81
of time, 37240
of William Orr, 34281
of William Wemms, 11683
Trials at large, 27815-16
　　of eight, 2003
　　of five, 2818
　　of John Fries, 35281
　　of sixteen, 2819
　　of the human heart, 29439
Tribe of Asher, 1908
Tribulations of Junius, 33486
Tribunus populi. Reply, 6618
Tribute to Caesar, 1572
　　to the memory of Catherine, 38670
　　　　memory of Nathan, 22867
　　　　memory of Washington, 38452
　　　　swinish, (1794) 27795, (1795) 29629, (1796) 30952
　　　　United States, 33609
　　to Washington, 37852
Trifle-hunter, 36450
Trimmer, Sarah Kirby, 1741-1810
　　Easy introduction, 31316
　　Fabulous histories, 27817
Trimmer, Tim. Life and adventures, 10433
Trinity church, New York see under New York
Trip, Tommy
　　Natural history, 29656
　　Pictures, 26282
Triplett, Thomas. Inaugural dissertation, 34680
Tripp, John, 1761-1847
　　Bible the word, 38672
　　Cherubims, 29657
Tripp, Tommy see Jones, Giles
Tristitiae, 5667
Triumph (cutter), at Philadelphia, 18234-37
Triumph der Christlichen, 33941
　　of infidelity, 21065-66
　　of mercy, 1961
　　of perseverance, 29264
　　of reason, 23336
　　of the Whigs, 14523
　　of truth, 23207
Triumphant Christian, (1736) 4087, (1755) 7580,
　　(1774) 13688, (1800) 38673
Triumphs of grace, 1933, 28944
　　of love, 29129
　　of superstition, 22556
　　of temper, (1781) 17185, (1787) 20410, (1792)
　　　　24387, (1794) 27104
　　of the reformed, 568
　　over troubles, 996
Triumvirate, 2712
Troil, ———, travels of, 31692
Trois hymnes, 28409
Trot, Benjamin, d. 1734, death, 3890, 4245
Trott, Nicholas. Laws of the province, 4080-81
Trotter, Thomas, 1761-1832. Observations, 26283
Troubles of life, (1799) 35297, (1800) 37159
Troup, R.

VOL.	ITEMS	VOL.	ITEMS
1	1-3244	8	22298-25074
2	3245-6623	9	25075-28145
3	6624-9891	10	28146-30832
4	9892-13091	11	30833-33261
5	13092-16176	12	33262-25854
6	16177-19448	13	35855-39162
7	19449-22297		

Trumbull, John, 1715?-1787, death, 21574
Trumbull, John, 1750-1831
 Elegy on the death, 12255
 Elegy on the times, 13693, 14525
 Epithalamium, 11504
 Essay, 11901
 M'Fingal, (1775) 14528, (1782) 17750-52, (1785) 19277, (1787) 20754, (1791) 23841, (1795) 29659, (1799) 36456
 New proclamation, 14526
 Progress of dulness, (1772) 12585, (1773) 13050-52, (1794) 27822, (1797) 32943
 Thomas Gage's proclamation, 14527
 excerpts from, 31959
Trumbull, John, 1756-1843
 Proposals, 22946
 arrives in Boston, 17849?
Trumbull, Jonathan, 1710-1785
 Address, 17885
 (ed.) Journal of the transactions, 23086
 Proclamation, (1769) 11220, (1770) 11606-607, (1771) 12017-18, (1772) 12363-64, (1773) 12733-34, (1774) 13210-12, (1775) 13878-81, (1776) 14711-13, (1777) 15267-73, (1778) 15768-70, (1779) 16241, (1780) 16747-48, (1781) 17123-24, (1782) 17500-501, (1783) 17886-88, (1784) 18416
 daughter's death, 15712
 death, 19620
 dedication to, 13785, 16059, 17445, 17805, 18316
 express from, 15245, 15355
 orders address published, 16639
 sermon before, 18198, 19261
 wife's death, 17000
Trumbull, Jonathan, 1740-1809
 Proclamation, (1798) 33559, (1799) 35343, (1800) 37229-30
 dedication to, 31675, 33253
Trumbull, Joseph, d. 1778, death, 16680
Trusdell, William, plaintiff, 3848
Trusler, John, 1735-1820, ed. Principles of politeness, (1778) 15914, 16077, (1785) 19258, (1786) 20003, (1791) 23790, (1792) 24813, (1793) 26202, (1794) 27736-37, (1796) 31229, (1798) 34595, (1800) 38553
Trust in God, 11599
Trust reposed, 30128
Trustaff, Sir George Jeoffery. Foreigner's scribble, 26288
Truth advanced, 691
 and faithfulness, 23713
 and innocency, 609
 held forth, 730
 is great, 17083
 its own test, 37550
 of the Bible, 32145
 rescued, 865
 triumphant, 11505
 vindicated and the doctrine, 6148
 vindicated, or a spiritual, 26971
 will out, 33648
Truxton's victory, 35114, 36247
Truxtun, Thomas, 1755-1822. Remarks, 27823
Tryal of assurance, 853
Tryal of the witnesses, 7314
Tryals of sixteen, 2819
Tryed professor, 2047
Tryon, Thomas, 1634-1703
 Some memoirs, 9028
 Way of health, 8271
Tryon, William
 Address to the inhabitants, 16291
 Draft of a bill, 15827

 Proclamation, (1771) 12156-57, (1774) 13461, (1775) 14078, (1776) 14919
 Ship Dutchess of Gordon, 14298
 Speech (1773), 12890
 Speech of William Tr . . n, 15095
 To the inhabitants, 14920
 address left with, 14296
 address to, 12891, 13468-70, 14486, 16212
 sermon before, 10977
 sermon requested by, 15596
 warning against, 15107
Tschudy, Jean Baptiste Louis Theodore, baron de
 Grand pantomime, 29660
Tubbs, Benjamin, d. 1799, death, 36621
Tucke, John, ordained, 3539
Tucker, Benjamin. To the author, 29661
Tucker, John, 1719-1792
 Brief account, 10788-89
 Example of Christ, 6792
 Four sermons, 7806
 God's goodness, 8049
 Letter (to Chandler), 10790
 Ministers considered, 11098
 Ministers of the gospel, 10791
 Observations, 8050
 Remarks on a discourse, 13694
 Remarks on a sermon, 10792
 Remarks on the Rev'd, 11099
 Reply to the Rev., 11100
 Rev. Aaron Hutchinson's, 11101
 Sermon, (1765) 10512, (1771) 12256, (1788) 21507
 Two following, 11506
 Validity, 16096
 death, 24285, 26453
 letter (from Shangar), 14456
 reply to, 10576, 10851, 10932
Tucker, Josiah, 1711-1799. True interest, 15119-20
Tucker, Nathaniel. Bermudian, a poem, 13695
Tucker, St. George, 1752-1827
 Dissertation, 31319
 Knight and friars, 20035
 Letter, (to member of Congress) 36457, (to Morse) 29662
 Liberty, 21508
 Probationary odes, 31320
 Reflections, 20036
Tucker, Thomas Tudor, 1745-1828
 Oration, 29663
 reports on ratification, 21520
Tuckerman, Joseph, 1778-1840. Funeral oration, 38680
Tuckey, ——, sings anthem, 7350
Tudor, William, 1750-1819
 Discourse, 34683
 Gratulatory address, 22947
 Oration, 16550
Türck, Johann de, conference at house of, 5082
Tuesday, Nov. 25, 1707, 1332
Tuesday, the 24th of May, 13746
Tufts, Cotton, 1731-1815. Oration, 38681
Tufts, James, ordained, 32084

VOL.	ITEMS	VOL.	ITEMS
1	1-3244	8	22298-25074
2	3245-6623	9	25075-28145
3	6624-9891	10	28146-30832
4	9892-13091	11	30833-33261
5	13092-16176	12	33262-25854
6	16177-19448	13	35855-39162
7	19449-22297		

Two funeral discourses, 6625
    Indian treaties, 3041
    interests, 3363
    last sermons, 4186
    lectures, (combustion) 32412, (comets) 8522,
      (parallax) 11536, (prophecies) 25049
    letters, (Burke) 31895, (Crisp) 2330, 9098,
      (Lord) 4377, (Wheelwright) 3853, (Williams
      & Wheelock) 5523
    letters; a circular, 11903
    letters to a friend on the present, 7400
    letters to a friend on the removal, 11507
    mothers, 8506
    ordination sermons, 8244
    patriotic, 33903
    plans, 18375
    practical discourses, 2835, 29265
    questions, 814
    reports, 7276
    sermons, (Andrews) 20933, (Avery) 23137,
      30007, (Baker) 2988, (Balch) 23143, (Barn-
      ard) 1665, (Beckwith) 5334, (Bradford)
      28334, 33450, Bradstreet) 26699, (Cheever)
      2736, (Colton) 3889, (Cradock) 5928, (Dana)
      35376, (Ely) 12036, (Fitch) 4015, (Foxcroft)
      2336, (Livingston) 35738, (Loring) 2545,
      (Manners) 27262, (Mayhew) 9443, (Potter)
      12202-203, (Priestley) 27559, (Smith) 22149,
      (Stearns) 15602, (Stillman) 13030-31
    sermons (Tennent), (1741) 5072-73, (1743)
      5299, (1749) 6428
    sermons, (Thurston) 24853, 26261, (Whitaker)
      11938, (Whitefield) 28080, (Woods) 36738
    shoemakers, 32501, 35297
    short discourses, 19409
Two Sisters (schooner), seized, 14541
Two soldiers, 35297
    songs, 36462
    treatises, 12257
    trials, 37104
    vast enjoyments, 3016
    very circumstantial, 7653-54
    wealthy farmers, 35297, 37132-36

witnesses, 4013
Tylee, Nathaniel, chairman mechanicks, 14940
Tyler, ——, sings song, 30243, 30370, 30582, 36246
Tyler, Andrew, d. 1775. Terms of Christianity,
    7807
Tyler, John, 1742-1823
    Blessing, 29668
    Discourse, 36363-64
    Eulogy, 38683
    Sanctity, 12258
    Sermon, 31327
    Universal damnation, 34685
Tyler, Lemuel, ordained, 26285
Tyler, Royall, fl. 1755, imprisoned, 7481
Tyler, Royall, 1757-1826
    Algerine captive, 32945
    Contrast, 22948
    Georgia spec, 32946
    Oration, 38684
    Origin of evil, 26290
    clerk U.S. commissioners, 34709
Tyng, Dudley Atkins see Atkins, Dudley, 1760-
    1829
Typographia, 3298
Tyrannical liberty, 29669
Tyranny and slavery, 5125
Tyrany and Toryism, 17316
Tytler, James, 1747-1805
    Paine's second part, 31328
    Rising of the sun, 29670
    Treatise, 36465
    proposals for printing Treatise, 34030

VOL.	ITEMS	VOL.	ITEMS
1	1-3244	8	22298-25074
2	3245-6623	9	25075-28145
3	6624-9891	10	28146-30832
4	9892-13091	11	30833-33261
5	13092-16176	12	33262-25854
6	16177-19448	13	35855-39162
7	19449-22297		

U

In Congress, Saturday, 15132-34
In Congress; the delegates, 15129
In Congress, Wednesday, 15137
Journal of the proceedings of the Congress, (1774) 13737-39, (1775) 14569-71, (1776) 15144-45
Letter of the two commanders-in-chief, 14559
Lettre addressee, 13740, 14575
List of the delegates, 14576
9th article of the association, 13706
Par son excellence, 14543
Petition, 13741, 14555
Philadelphia; in Congress, May 21, 1776, 15142
Philadelphia; in Congress, Monday, 14560
Philadelphia; in Congress, Thursday, 13702
Philadelphia, Sept. 29, 1775, 14558
Proceedings of the general Congress, 13701
Rules and articles, 14577-81
Rules for the regulation, 14582
Second Norwich edition of extracts, 13734
Several assemblies, 14583
Several methods, 14584-85
Tables of the port, 14586
To the inhabitants, 15146
To the people, 13707
Tory act, 15147
Twelve United Colonies, 14532-34
Whereas the government, 14588
Whole proceedings, 14552
United endeavours, 4883
United library co., incorporated, 29403
United sons of liberty. New York, July 7, 1769, 11379
United States
March 18, 1783, 18268
Apr. 18, 1783, 18269
23d February, 1796, 31381
25th February, 1796, 31382
11th March, 1796, 31349
14th March, 1796, 31350
12th April, 1796, 31389
19th June, 1797, 33098
12th December, 1797, 32964
16th December, 1799, 36585-87
4th February, 1800, 38732
11th February, 1800, 38730
13th February, 1800, 38909
2d December, 1800, 38907
Abstract of cases, 36467, 38687
Abstract of goods, 26340, 29762
Abstract of the duty law, 23889
Accompanying the report, 38688
Account of payments, 26353
Account of receipts, 33073
Account of the receipts, (1791) 26341, (1792) 27930, (1793) 27931, (1794) 29763, (1795) 31434, (1797) 34847, (1798) 36468, (1799) 38689-90
Accounts of the treasurer, (1794) 27932, (1795) 31435, (1796) 33074, (1797) 34848, (1798) 36469, (1800) 38691
Accounts of the U.S., 20037
Accurate list of duties, 27933
Address and recommendations, 18223-28
Address and remonstrance, 38705
Address from the United States, 20039
Address in answer, 32961
Address of the Congress, 16097-104
Advertisement, by General Mifflin, 15618
Alphabetical list of the duties, 20040, 27934-35
Alterations to be made, 36489
Amendment in committee of the whole, 34694

Amendment proposed, 38706
Amendments agreed to, 36490
Amendments, &c., 38707
Amendments of the Senate to the bill, (defence of merchant vessels) 34698, (direct tax) 34702, (Georgia boundaries) 38708-712, (marine corps) 34691, (naval armament) 34703
Amendments proposed by Mr. Otis, 34714
Amendments proposed in the committee, 27898
Amendments proposed to be added, 22953
Amendments proposed to the bill, 38713
Amendments to the bill, (appropriations) 34696, (collection of revenue) 34693
America and France, 34815
Amour paternel, 17038
Articles agreed upon, 20791
Articles de confederation, 15628
Articles of a treaty, (Oct. 22, 1784) 18817, (Jan. 21, 1785) 19278, (Nov. 28, 1785) 19279, (Jan. 31, 1786) 20041, (Jan. 15, 1799) 36491-92
Articles of agreement made, 34849
Articles of agreement of the convention, 38714
Articles of confederation, (1776) 15148-49, (1777) 15619-27, (1778) 16105, (1784) 18818
Articles published, 16145
Artikel des bundes, 16106
Artykelen die geaccordeerd, 20792
At a conference, 15150
At a meeting of the board, 36493-94
At a treaty held, 36495
Baltimore, Jan. 29; extract, 15629
Baltimore, Sept. 13; we are, 15630
Baltimore, Dec. 31, 1776, 15152
Baron Steuben's regulations, 20077, 20780-82
Bey seiner excellenz, 15635
Bill of rights, 22845
Board of treasury, (1777) 15631, (Aug. 27, 1785) 19280, (Apr. 8, 1786) 20042, (June 22, 1786) 20043
Board of treasury, to whom it was, 20756
Board of treasury, to whom was referred, (a motion) 20755, (their letter) 20044
By his excellency, 15634, 18230
By the Congress of the U.S., 16132
By the honourable, 19441
By the U. S. in Congress assembled, (Mar. 3, 1781) 17383, (Apr. 7, 1781) 17384, (Jan. 3, 1782) 17755, (Jan. 10, 1782) 17756, (Feb. 20, 1782) 17757-58, (Aug. 7, 1782) 17759, (Sept. 4, 1782) 17760, (Oct. 4, 1782) 17761, (Feb. 17, 1783) 18232, (Nov. 1, 1783) 18246, 18827, (Mar. 23, 1784) 18824, (Apr. 23, 1784) 19283, (Apr. 30, 1784) 18825, (June 3, 1784) 18826, (Feb. 23, 1785) 19281, (Mar. 31, 1785) 19282, (June 7, 1785) 19284, (July 27, 1785) 19285, (Aug. 17, 1785) 19286, (Sept. 27, 1785) 19287, (Sept. 30, 1785) 19288-89, (Oct. 3, 1785) 19290, (Oct. 12, 1785) 19291, (Nov. 2, 1785) 19292, (Jan. 2, 1786) 20045, (June 27, 1786) 20046, (July 14, 1786) 20047, (Aug. 2, 1786) 20048, (Aug. 7, 1786) 20049, (Aug. 8, 1786) 20050, (Sept. 18,

VOL.	ITEMS	VOL.	ITEMS
1	1-3244	8	22298-25074
2	3245-6623	9	25075-28145
3	6624-9891	10	28146-30832
4	9892-13091	11	30833-33261
5	13092-16176	12	33262-25854
6	16177-19448	13	35855-39162
7	19449-22297		

VOL.	ITEMS	VOL.	ITEMS
1	1-3244	8	22298-25074
2	3245-6623	9	25075-28145
3	6624-9891	10	28146-30832
4	9892-13091	11	30833-33261
5	13092-16176	12	33262-25854
6	16177-19448	13	35855-39162
7	19449-22297		

Ordinance for, (amending) 17769, (ascertaining the mode of disposing) 19326, (ascertaining the mode of locating) 18842, (establishing) 20072, (further amending) 17770, (regulating) 20777

Ordinance for the, (better distribution) 17771, (establishment) 20073-74, (government of the Territory) 20779, (government of the Western Territory) 20778, (relative to the capture) 17394, (to amend) 20075

Papers relative, 31473

Passport and roll of equipage, 34842, 34844, 34846

Passport & roll d'equipage, 34843

Peace, liberty, 18235

Petition of Cato West, 38799

Philadelphia, (Mar. 24) 18234, (Sept. 17) 15168

Philadelphia, (May 1, 1777) 15647, (Aug. 22, 1777) 15686, (Jan. 21, 1794) 27927, (Dec. 21, 1799) 38800

Philadelphia, Wednesday, 22986

Plan for conducting, (the hospital department) 17040, (the inspector's department) 17041, (the quartermaster general's department) 17042

Plan for establishing, 17395

Plan for the general arrangement, 20076, 22987-88

Plan of the foederal, 20806

Post office law, 38801

Postscript to the Carlisle, 20807

Postscript to the Mercury, 34811

Proceedings in the House, 24916-17

Proceedings of a board, 17043-46

Proceedings of a court of enquiry, 23905

Proceedings of a general court martial, (André) 17047, (Henley) 16139, 16626, (Howe) 17772, (Lee) 16140, (St. Clair) 16141, (Schuyler) 16142, (Sheldon) 17048

Proceedings of the accounting, 29771

Proceedings of the executive, 29738

Proceedings of the foederal, 20808

Proceedings of the grand federal, 20809

Proceedings of the House, 31364, 36560

Proceedings on the impeachment, 36561

Proclamation, (Aug. 16, 1776) 15153, (Jan. 25, 1777) 15632-33, (Nov. 1, 1777) 15680, (Nov. 16, 1777) 15687, (Mar. 7, 1778) 16117, (May 9, 1778) 16121, (June 17, 1778) 16107, (June 19, 1778) 16108, (Nov. 9, 1778) 16122, (Nov. 17, 1778) 16134-35, (Mar. 20, 1779) 16552-53, (Dec. 9, 1779) 16554-57, (Apr. 26, 1780) 17013-14, (Sept. 1, 1780) 17016, (Oct. 18, 1780) 17017-18, (Mar. 20, 1781) 17385-87, (Oct. 26, 1781) 17388-89, (Oct. 11, 1782) 17762-63, (Jan. 23, 1783) 18231, (Apr. 11, 1783) 18238-39, (June 24, 1783) 18229, (Sept. 3, 1783) 18249, 18819, (Sept. 25, 1783) 18245, (Dec. 11, 1783) 18247, (1784) 18821, 18823, (Jan. 14, 1784) 18819, (Jan. 20, 1784) 18820, (Jan. 22, 1784) 18822, (Feb. 2, 1785) 19327, (Sept. 1, 1788) 21517, (Nov. 26, 1789) 22211

see also **U.S. President.** Proclamation

Propositions respecting the coinage, 19328, 23906

Pursuant to the order, 24918

Ratifications of the new foederal, 21529

Received and read 19th May, 32966

Regeln für die ordnung, 26361

Reglement militaire, 15190

Regulations for the order and discipline, (1779) 16627-28, (1782) 17773-74, (1783) 18267, (1784)

18843, (1785) 19329, (1788) 21530-31, (1790) 22990-92, (1791) 23907, (1792) 24919-20, (1793) 26356-60, (1794) 27957-65, 27967-70, 27972-73, (1795) 29778-79, (1796) 31469-70, (1798) 34898-901, (1800) 38806

Regulations for the quarter master, 17775

Regulations respecting, 38807

Regulations to be observed, 33097

Remonstrance and petition, 32980-81

Report, &c.; the secretary, 38808

Report from the commissioners, 24921

Report from the committee appointed, 31368

Report from the committee of revisal, 38809

Report from the committee to whom was referred, (on the 22d) 33040, (on the 23d) 34773, (on the 29th) 34772

Report from the committee to whom was referred the bill, 36562

Report from the department of war, 31468

Report from the secretary, 38810

Report in part of the committee appointed, (on the 9th) 38811, (on the 18th) 34789, (on the 24th) 38812

Report in part of the committee, (of elections) 38813, (of privileges) 38814, (of revisal) 38815

Report in part of the committee to whom was referred, (on the 28th) 38816, (on the 29th) 34769, (so much) 36563

Report in part of the committee to whom were referred, 38817

Report of a committee appointed, (to consider) 20078, (to propose) 16630

Report of commissioners for settling, 16631

Report of committee on amendments, 34778

Report of the attorney general, (1790) 23908-909, (1795) 29761, (1796) 31431

Report of the board, 26364

Report of the commissioners appointed, 27977

Report of the commissioners for purchasing, 27947

Report of the commissioners of the sinking fund, (1794) 27948, (1795) 31462, (1796) 31463, (1797) 33089-90, (1798) 34881, (1799) 36564, (1800) 38818

Report of the commissioners on the accounts, 24922

Report of the commissioners to execute, 27949

Report of the committee, alterations, 34777

Report of the committee appointed, (on the 4th) 36565, (on the 5th instant to enquire into the expediency) 38819, (on the 5th instant to enquire into the progress) 32987, (on the 10th December) 38820, (on the 10th instant) 34776, (on the 20th) 38821, (on the 22d) 38822, (on the 24th) 32982

Report of the committee appointed the 16th, 32988

Report of the committee appointed to enquire, (if any) 31387, (into the actual state) 31378, (into the expediency) 38823, (into the opera-

VOL.	ITEMS	VOL.	ITEMS
1	1-3244	8	22298-25074
2	3245-6623	9	25075-28145
3	6624-9891	10	28146-30832
4	9892-13091	11	30833-33261
5	13092-16176	12	33262-25854
6	16177-19448	13	35855-39162
7	19449-22297		

VOL.	ITEMS	VOL.	ITEMS
1	1-3244	8	22298-25074
2	3245-6623	9	25075-28145
3	6624-9891	10	28146-30832
4	9892-13091	11	30833-33261
5	13092-16176	12	33262-25854
6	16177-19448	13	35855-39162
7	19449-22297		

U. S. President
Address of George Washington, 31527-29, 31540-41, 31550
Address of his excellency, 31525
Address of the President, 31533, 31536
Address to the people, 31532, 31534
Bericht, 34818
Collection of the speeches, 31402
Columbia's legacy, 31538, 31545
Confidential message, 33054
George Washington, President, 31409
George Washington's resignation, 31552
Legacy of the father of his country, 31530, 31551
Message (Dec. 5, 1793), 26334, 29735-36
Message (1794), (commercial laws abroad) 27918, (letters from U.S. minister) 27916, (spoliations) 27917, (threats to territories of Spain) 27913
Message, (May 22, 1794) 27914, (May 23, 1794) 27915, (Jan. 8, 1796) 31406, (Jan. 13, 1796) 31407, (Mar. 1, 1796) 31411, (Mar. 8, 1796) 31408, (Mar. 25, 1796) 31421, (Mar. 29, 1796) 31418, (Mar. 30, 1796) 31415-17, 31420, (Jan. 19, 1797) 33048-49, (Feb. 15, 1797) 33051, (June 12, 1797) 33052, (June 22, 1797) 33053, (July 3, 1797) 33055, (July 5, 1797) 34798, (Jan. 1, 1798) 34799, (Jan. 18, 1798) 34800, (Feb. 2, 1798) 34802, (Feb. 5, 1798) 34803, (Feb. 12, 1798) 34804, (Feb. 19, 1798) 34805, (Feb. 20, 1798) 34806, (Feb. 23, 1798) 34807-808, (Mar. 5, 1798) 34809, (Mar. 19, 1798) 34810-11, (Apr. 3, 1798) 34812, 34814, (May 4, 1798) 34819, (June 5, 1798) 34821-22, (June 18, 1798) 34823-24, (June 21, 1798) 34825, (June 27, 1798) 34826, (July 17, 1798) 34827, (Dec. 31, 1798) 36549, (Jan. 8, 1799) 36550, 36553, (Jan. 18, 1799) 36551, (Jan. 21, 1799) 36546-48, (Jan. 22, 1799) 36552, (Jan. 28, 1799) 36545, (Jan. 31, 1799, 36555, (Feb. 15, 1799) 36554, (Mar. 1, 1799) 36556, (Dec. 5, 1799) 36557, (1800) 38785, (Jan. 8, 1800) 38780, 38784, (Jan. 13, 1800) 38783, (Jan. 20, 1800) 38778, (Jan. 23, 1800) 38779, (Feb. 7, 1800) 38782, (Apr. 17, 1800) 38781
President Washington's resignation, 31537
President's address, 31526, 31531, 31542-44, 31546-48
President's answer, 34836
President's message, 31415-16, 31420
President's speech, (1796) 31427, (1798) 34833, 34835, (1800) 38802
Proclamation, (Aug. 14, 1790) 22989, (Apr. 22, 1793) 26335-36, (Oct. 10, 1793) 26337, (Sept. 25, 1794) 27912, (Jan. 1, 1795) 29730-33, (July 10, 1795) 29734, (Feb. 29, 1796) 31412, (May 9, 1797) 33046, (May 15, 1797) 33047, (Mar. 23, 1798) 34797, (1799) 36500, (Apr. 25, 1799) 36497, (June 26, 1799) 36498, (July 17, 1799) 36499, (Jan. 6, 1800) 37921, 38805
Secretary of the treasury; sir, 27919
Speech, (1789) 22212, (Oct. 25, 1791) 23921, (Nov. 6, 1792) 24934, (Nov. 19, 1794) 27923, (Dec. 8, 1795) 29739-41, (Dec. 7, 1796) 31424-27, (May 16, 1797) 33056-57, (Nov. 23, 1797) 33058-59, (Dec. 8, 1798) 34831-32, 34835, (Dec. 15, 1798) 34833, (Dec. 3, 1799) 36589, (Nov. 22, 1800) 38802, 38906
To the people of the U.S., 31539
United States, (15th January) 27920, (16th January) 27921, (22d January) 27922
U. S. Senate
Journal, (1789) 22207, (1790) 22982, (1791) 23900-

901, (1792) 24911, (1793) 26333, (1794) 27911, (1795) 29724, (1796) 31355, (1797) 32971-72, (1798) 34720, (1799) 36521, (1800) 38749
Resolve, 27890
United States, (Jan. 16, 1792) 24944, (Nov. 22, 1792) 24925, (Jan. 15, 1794) 27920, (Jan. 16, 1794) 27921, (Jan. 22, 1794) 27922, (Dec. 30, 1794) 29776
United States and New Hampshire register, 31474
United States calendar, 38913
   Christian magazine, 29781, 31475
   country dances, 37336
   court kalendar, 36601
   elevated, 18198, 19261
United States (frigate), letter concerning, 33096
United States gazetteer, 29476
United States in Congress assembled, (Apr. 27, 1784) 18845-46, (Feb. 15, 1786) 20084, (Mar. 3, 1786) 20086, (Apr. 13, 1787) 20776, (May 22, 1788) 21534
   in Congress assembled, Friday, 20790
   in Congress assembled; to all who shall, 18233
   in Congress assembled; to all whom these, 20087
   in Senate, 24943
United States lottery. List of the fortunate, (1778) 16150, (1779) 16646, (1780) 17051, (1781) 17398
United States lottery, no. . . . class, 15194
United States lottery; the scheme, (1776) 15193, (1778) 16149, (1779) 16647
United States magazine, (1779) 16648, (1794) 27982
United States of America in Congress assembled, 20789
United States register, 27983-84
   repository, 37578
   sacred harmony, 36119
United States theatre. On Friday, 39009
Unitie our dutie, 19
Unity and peace, 27029
Unius labor, 314
Universal annual register, 30001
   asylum, (1790) 23008, (1791) 23930-31, (1792) 24948-49
   damnation, 34685
   dream-book, 33103
   friend, 19435
   friends' advice, 18849
Universal gazette. Circular, 36603
Universal geography, 29521
   interpreter, 28635
   love, a sermon, 8240
   love recommended, 7370
   merchant, 31710-11
   peace-maker, 9797
   preacher, 33308
   register of the Baptist, 26584-85
   register, or Columbian, 19016
   restitution, 11875
   restoration, (1792) 25050, (1793) 26493, (1794) 28114-16, (1795) 29910
   right, 36604
   spelling book, (1769) 11255, (1772) 12388,

VOL.	ITEMS	VOL.	ITEMS
1	1-3244	8	22298-25074
2	3245-6623	9	25075-28145
3	6624-9891	10	28146-30832
4	9892-13091	11	30833-33261
5	13092-16176	12	33262-25854
6	16177-19448	13	35855-39162
7	19449-22297		

(1786) 19643, (1787) 20354, (1788) 21090, (1793) 26371, (1797) 33105, (1799) 35478
Universal Tontine. Articles of association, 24950
Universalism contrary, 27985
Universalism vindicated, 34161
Universalist. Letter (to friend), 23502
Universalist; in seven letters, 20713, 21466
Universalists
    Articles of faith, 23009
    Circular, 26372
    Elders and messengers, 33106
    Evangelical psalms, 24951
    Psalms, hymns, 24951
Universe, a miscellany, 17777
University of Pennsylvania
    Account of the commencement, 14395
    Additional charter, 7540
    Exercise containing, 14396
    Exercise performed, 22798
    Exercises containing, 9484
    General heads and plan, 15994
    Morning prayer, 16935
    Philosophemata, (1761) 8981, (1762) 9239, (1763) 9485
    Plan of a performance, 10140
    Prayers for the use, 7093
Unmasked nabob, 31477
Unparalleled sufferings, 31998-99
Unpartheyische gedancken, 6890
Unpartheyisches zeugnüss, 5196
Unprofitableness, 3516
Unsearchable riches, 4437, 19157
Unsex'd females, 38293
Unspeakable gift, 4352
Unteachable, 7623
Untimely death, 5403
Unum necessarium, 654
Up-bookum Psalmes, 74
Updike, Daniel, secy. convention, 22845, 22848
Upham, Caleb, d. 1786, death, 20147
Upham, Timothy, 1748-1811
    Discourse, 27986
    Sermon, 26373
Upon Mr. Samuel, 952
Upon the peace, 9409

Upright lives, 4660
Upsher, Thomas. To Friends in Ireland, 956
Upton, John. ed. Enchiridion, 24302, 25452
Upton, William. To the maid, 34912
Urania, (1761) 8908, (1767) 10666, (1773) 12839
Uranian harmony, 23749
Uranian society
    First Uranian concert, 20646
    Introductory lessons, 19194, 19920
Urban, Americanus, edits almanac, 35239
Urbanus Filter. New England magazine, 8200
Urquhart, James, names given to, 14089
Ursinus, Z. Catechismus, 9135
Urständliche, 5538
Use and excellency, 11601
Useful and correct, 20093
    and entertaining, 20340
    information, 29769
    instructions and evangelical, 17485, 17859
    instructions for a professor, 184
    knowledge, 35486
    miscellanies, 6993
    questions, 6952
    tables, 12262
Usefulness and experience, 4193
    and importance, 19866
    and necessity, 5733
    of consideration, 5702
    of reveal'd religion, 3260
Usher, Bridget, d. 1723
    death, 2431
    dedication to, 286
Usher, John, ordained, 26175
Usher, comprising, 35734
Ussher, George Neville. Elements of English, 23010, 31480
Ussher, James, 1581-1656, extracts from, 27564-66
Ustick, Stephen C., superintends printing of mintes, 38244
Ustick, Messrs., conduct of, 14505
Ut fluctus, 574
Utile dulci, 2481
Utilia, 1834
Utility, 35937

VOL.	ITEMS	VOL.	ITEMS
1	1-3244	8	22298-25074
2	3245-6623	9	25075-28145
3	6624-9891	10	28146-30832
4	9892-13091	11	30833-33261
5	13092-16176	12	33262-25854
6	16177-19448	13	35855-39162
7	19449-22297		

(1798) 34921-22, (1800) 38929
Vermont. Laws (collective)
  Laws, 34925
  Statutes (1787-91), 23939
Vermont. Laws (session)
  Acts, (1778-79) 16649-50, (1779-80) 17052-54,
    (1781) 17399-402, (1782) 17778, 18276, (1783)
    18274-75, (1784) 18852, 19340, (1785) 19341-42,
    (1787) 20827-28, (1788) 21540, (1789) 22217,
    (1790) 23013, (1791) 23933-34, (1792) 24955,
    (1793) 26376, (1794) 27993, (1795) 29787, (1796)
    31486, (1797) 33117-18, 34920, (1798) 36613,
    (1799) 36614, (1800) 38927
Vermont. Laws (separates)
  Act, (fees) 34919, (militia) 26375, 33116, (tax)
    33115
Vermont association. Minutes, (1790) 23153, 26381,
  (1791-93) 26382-84, (1795) 29791, (1800) 38931
Vermont repository, 29450
Vermont university; the subscribers, 38933
Vermonters unmasked, 17674
Vermont's appeal, 16722
Vernon, Edward, 1684-1757
  Genuine speech, 4830
  verses on, 4810
Versamelinge, 5954
Verschiedene alte(r), (1744) 5503, (1748) 6258,
  (1755) 7582, (1792) 24961
Verschiedene Christliche, 6233
Verses addressed, 21545
    composed, 38668
    dedicated, 308
    for the New Year, 21380
    made, 19443
    occasioned, 32823
    of the printer's boy, 5478
    of the printers' lads, 11031
    on Doctor, 9327
    . . . on his marriage, 30901
    written, 36621
Versification, 34532
Version of the book, 30078
Vertitude (privateer), outrages by, 34803
Verus see **Yrujo, Philip Fatis**
Very brief, 3478
    entertaining, 37431
    extraordinary, 24838
    important, 34353
    needful, 1318
    plain, 2297
    remarkable account, 25364-65, 28509
    surprising narrative, (1796) 30956-57, (1797)
      32637, (1798) 34305, (1800) 38182-83
Vesey, William
  Sermon, 1436
  letter to, 3611
  protest against, 3638
Vetch, Col. ——, instructions to, 1353
Veteran see **Prescott, Robert, 1725-1816**
Veterans, 30345
Veterona, 28978
Vezey, ——, of Charleston, petition, 33013-14
Vial poured out, 2779
Viaud, Pierre see **Dubois-Fontanelle, Jean Gaspard,
  1737-1812**
Vicar of Wakefield, (1772) 12405, (1773) 12796,
  (1780) 16787, (1791) 23417, (1792) 24360-61,
  (1794) 27060, (1795) 28758-59
Vice in its proper, 22221
Vicious courses, 2083, 5506
Vico, Galeazzo Caracciolo, marquis of, 1517-1586,
  life of, 6633, 26601

Victor, Benjamin. Voyages, 22402
Victor, H. B. Compleat instructor, 16152
Victorina, 1911, 2922
Victory is the Lord's, 9269
Victory over sin, 17000
Vidal, ——, auctioneer, 6650
Vier bücher von der nachfolge, 6343
Vierte general-versammlung, 5082
Viets, Roger, 1738-1811
  Serious address, 20835
  Sermon, (1784) 20836, (1789) 22223, (1800)
    38936-37
View of a Christian, 17553
    of a most magnificent, 29652
    of ecclesiastical, 34234
    of religions, 23102
    of society, 18036, 24553-54
    of the administration, 34928
        calumnies, 3227
        Calvinistic, 36008
        causes, 32094-99
        conduct, 32491
        controversy between, 13603
        controversy subsisting, 14474
        debts, 19904
        evidences, 29273-74
        inestimable, 5889
        internal evidence, (1780) 16812, (1787)
          20431, (1789) 21904, (1791) 23471, (1793)
          25659
        life, 26542-43
        mutual duties, 18558
        New England, 35269-70, 36009-10
        practicability, 35715
        principles, 21546
        proposed, 20591
        public debt, 37485
        quarterly, 31493
        rights, 32409
        rise, 37650
        scandals, 3228
        science, 33254
        title, 15219
        United States, 26829
Vigil, 34929
Vigilant (warship), at Philadelphia, 15321
Vigilantius, 1265
Vigilius, 2048
Vile prophanations, 1154
Village, a poem, 22433, 23297
    curate, 25642, 30613
    harmony, (1795) 29793, (1796) 31494, (1797)
      33123, (1798) 34930, (1800) 38938
    holiday, 29794
    merchant, 27019
    orphan, 38940
    recruit, 34932
    wedding, 30311
Villaret, Claude, extracts from, 30489, 32189-90
**Villaret de Joyeuse, Louis Thomas, comte, 1750-
  1812,** commands convoy, 27664

VOL.	ITEMS	VOL.	ITEMS
1	1-3244	8	22298-25074
2	3245-6623	9	25075-28145
3	6624-9891	10	28146-30832
4	9892-13091	11	30833-33261
5	13092-16176	12	33262-25854
6	16177-19448	13	35855-39162
7	19449-22297		

1795) 31504, (for 1796) 33130, (for 1797) **34940**,
(for 1798) 36644, (for 1799) 38958
List of pensioners provided for, 26395
Memorial and remonstrance, 20109
Minutes of the Baptist general committee, 36648
Ordinances passed at a convention, 14595-96
Ordinances passed at a general convention, 15199
Proceedings of the convention, (1775) 14597-98,
(1776) 15197-98
Report of the committee, (of revisors) 18863,
(on the state) 36646, (to whom was committed) 38961
Resolutions that the General assembly, 36647
Richmond, Jan. 30, 1800, 38962
Richmond, state of Va., 21552-53
Sir, as the committee, 14600
Some remarkable proceedings, 2702
Supplement to the Independent journal, 21559
To the honorable the General assembly, 20108
To the hon. the speaker, 26396
To the worshipful, 31505
Tuesday, the 24th of May, 13746
Virginia; in the high court, 38963
Virginia; in the House of delegates, 31501, 34941
Virginia to wit, 34942
War office, Williamsburg, 16663
We his majesty's most dutiful, 13748
We the underwritten, 18864
Williamsburg, Saturday, 14602
Williamsburg, Wednesday, 11513
Virginia. Assembly
Proceedings, 38959-60
Virginia. Governor
Proclamation, (1774) 13745, (1775) 14591-92,
(1776) 15196
Speech, (1758) 8277, (1775) 14601
Virginia. House of burgesses
Journal, (1732) 3612, (1736) 4094, (1738) 4318,
(1740) 4618-19, (1742) 5083, (1744) 5504, (1746)
5873-74, (1747) 6077, (1748-49) 6435, (1752)
6943, (1753) 7131, (1754) 7325-27, (1755) 7584-
86, (1756) 7810-11, (1757) 8055, (1758) 8274-
76, (1759) 8511-12, (1760) 8757-58, (1761)
9032-33, (1762) 9293-95, (1763) 9530, (1764)
9861, (1765) 10193, (1769-70) 11910, (1772)
12592, (1773) 13058, (1774) 13749, (1775) 14599
Resolves, 11512
Virginia. House of delegates
Journal, (1776) 15204, (1777) 15696, (1778)
16155-56, (1779) 16658-59, (1780) 17056-57,
(1781) 17414-16, (1782) 17783-84, (1783) 18284-
85, (1784) 18859-60, (1785) 19353, (1786) 20106,
(1787) 20840, (1788) 21556-57, 22226, (1789)
23018, (1790) 23944, (1791) 24966, (1792) 26390,
(1793) 28002, (1794) 29799, (1795) 31502,
(1796) 33128, (1797-98) 34936, (1799) 36642,
(1800) 38954
Resolve, (1793) 26391, (1798) 34941-42
Virginia. Laws (collective)
Abridgment of the public, 31497
Acts of Assembly, (to 1733) 3728, (to 1752) 6941,
(to 1769) 11511
Acts, (1768-85) 19351, (1784-85) 26386
Acts (James River), 26387
Acts (regulating pilots), 31500
Akten, 29797
Certain acts (militia), 26389
Collection of all such acts, 27999
Continuation of the abridgment, 4441
Exact abridgment, 4204
Virginia. Laws (session)
Acts, (1680) 334, (1730) 3369, (1734) 3849, (1736)

4094, (1738) 4317, (1740) 4616-17, (1752) 6942,
(1756-57) 7808-809, 8054, (1758-61) 8273, 8509-
510, 8754-56, 9030-31, (1761-62) 9290-92, (1766)
10515, (1768) 11105, (1770) 11909, (1771) 12264-
65, (1772) 12591, (1773) 13056, (1776) 15203,
(1777) 15694-95, (1778) 16153-54, (1779) 16654-
55, (1780) 17055, 17407, (1781) 17408-409,
17781, (1782) 17782, 18281, (1783) 18282-83,
(1784) 18858, 19348, (1785) 20104, (1786) 20837,
(1787) 21548-49, (1788) 21550, 22224, (1789)
23017, (1790) 23943, (1791) 24963, (1792) 26388,
(1793) 27997-98, (1794) 29796, (1795) 31499,
(1796) 33126, (1797-98) 34934, 36629, (1799)
38948
Virginia. Laws (separates)
Act (1776), 15202
Act (1777), (allegiance) 15693, (troop quota)
15692, (volunteers) 15691
Act, (1782) 17780, (1784) 18857, 20103, (1786)
20101-102, (1787) 20842, (1793) 26389, (1794)
29416, (1796) 31498
Act (1799), (elections) 36626, (taxes) 36627-28
Bill concerning, 38950
Bill for establishing, 19350
Bill to amend, 38951
Militia law, 36645
New tobacco law, 3371
Virginia. Senate
Journal, (1776) 15205, (1777) 15697, (1778)
16157, (1779) 16660-62, (1780) 17058-59, (1781)
17412-13, (1782) 17785-86, (1783) 18286-87,
(1784) 18861-62, (1785) 19354, (1786) 20107,
(1787) 20841, (1788) 21558, 22227, (1789)
23019, (1790) 23945, (1791) 24967, (1792)
26392, (1793) 28003, (1794) 29800, (1795)
31503, (1796) 33129, (1797-98) 34937, (1799)
36643, (1800) 38955
Virginia: a pastoral, 19717
Virginia Baptist association. Minutes, (1790-93)
26397-400, (1794) 28006
Virginia chronicle, 21920, 22616-17
Virginia farmer see **Palmer, Robert F.**
Virginia gazette. From the Virginia gazette, 13287
Virginia; in the high court, 38963
in the House of delegates, Thursday, 26391
in the House of delegates, Tuesday, (1796)
31501, (1798) 34941
Virginia justice, 13637
Virginia miscellany, 3483
Virginia Portsmouth association. Minutes, 26025-27
**Virginia society for promoting the abolition of
slavery.** Constitution, 29803
Virginia to wit, 34942
Virginian
Letter (to members of Congress), 13167-70
Political address, 34390
Virginian Baptist, a view, 13651
Virginian born and bred see **Hay, James**
Virginia's danger, 7644
Virginiensis see **Lee, Charles, 1758-1815**
Virgin's advice, 3368

VOL.	ITEMS	VOL.	ITEMS
1	1-3244	8	22298-25074
2	3245-6623	9	25075-28145
3	6624-9891	10	28146-30832
4	9892-13091	11	30833-33261
5	13092-16176	12	33262-25854
6	16177-19448	13	35855-39162
7	19449-22297		

W

W., A.
  Friendly address, 13224-26
    reply to, 13313
      see also **Seabury, Samuel, 1729-1796**
W., E. see **Ward, Edward, 1667-1731**
W., G.
  Elegy, 30558
  Memoirs, 32249
W., H. Answer to a piece, 10195
W., J.
  Address to the freeholders, 9532
  Mode of elections, 11517
  letter (from Gale), 11243, 11269-70
    see also **Wyeth, Joseph**
W***, J*****
  Baseness and perniciousness, 11518
  Meditations, 9313
W., N. Almanac see **Almanacs (Whittemore)**
W., S. see **Webster, Samuel; Willard, Samuel, 1640-1707**
W., T.
  Letter to a friend, 7381
  Second letter, 7382
  preface by, 17489
    see also **Chauncy, Charles, 1705-1787; Wilcocks, Thomas, b. 1622**
W., W. gent. see **Winstanley, William, 1628-1690**
W., W. R. see **Wild, W. R.**
W., Z. Melancholy case, 12596
Waare deught, 7432
Waarschouwing tegens, 4097
Wadaijahun, 35201
Waddell, William. To the freeholders, 15211
Waddington, Joshua
  defendant, 18320
  dispute with Rutgers, 18773
Wadsworth, Col. ——, in battle, 14338
Wadsworth, Benjamin, 1669-1737
  Advice, 2078
  Assembling, 1532
  Benefits, 2079
  Blameless Christian, 1335
  Bonds, 1934
  Christian advice, 1720
  Christ's fan, 2397
  Churches, 1935
  Considerations, 1282
  Constant preparedness, 2004
  Danger of hypocrisy, 1533
  Dialogue, 2590, 12597

  Early seeking, 1786
  Essay for the charitable, 2005
  Essay on the Decalogue, 2080, 2298
  Essay to do good, 1491
  Exhortations, 1099
  Faithful reprover, 1534
  Faithful warnings, 2398
  Fervent zeal, 2006
  Five sermons, 1721, 2299
  Fraud, 1590
  Funeral sermon, 1492
  Good souldiers, 958
  Gospel not opposed, 2081
  Great and last, 1437, 1655
  Guide, 1787-88, 2191
  Hearty submission, 1860, 2192
  Highest dwelling, 1535
  Help to get, 1722
  Imitation, 2399
  Invitations, 1789
  It's honourable, 2715
  King William lamented, 1100
  Letter of wholesome, 1438
  Letter to a friend, 1439
  Letter to those towns, 1440
  Lord Jesus, 2251-52, 2300
  Lord's day, 2193
  Men self-condemned, 1283
  Ministers, 1790
  Mutual love, 1029
  Publick worship, 1197
  Restraints, 1656
  Rulers, 1861
  Saints prayer, 1791
  Sermon, 1792, 2256
  Some considerations, 2082
  Surviving servants, 2591
  Testimony, 2051
  True piety, 2400
  Twelve sermons, 2301

VOL.	ITEMS	VOL.	ITEMS
1	1-3244	8	22298-25074
2	3245-6623	9	25075-28145
3	6624-9891	10	28146-30832
4	9892-13091	11	30833-33261
5	13092-16176	12	33262-25854
6	16177-19448	13	35855-39162
7	19449-22297		

Twelve single sermons, 1936
Unchast practices, 1862
Vicious courses, 2083, 5506
Well-ordered family, 1591, 2084
death, 4110, 4139-40, 4196, 4209
preface by, 1956, 2431, 2987
pres. Harvard, 3287, 3428, 3548, 3666, 3780, 3914, 4025
reply to, 2315
Wadsworth, Benjamin, 1750-1826
America invoked, 29825
Eulogy, 38972
Sermon, 17789
Social thanksgiving, 31519
hand of fellowship, 34609
ordained, 12985
Wadsworth, Daniel, 1704-1747. Christ's presence, 4621
Wadsworth, J. Boston, Mar. 29, 1783, 17849
Wadsworth, Jeremiah, 1743-1804, reports on Illinois petition, 21521
Wadsworth, Lemuel, ordained, 34467
Wadsworth, Recompence, memorial to, 1621
Wadsworth, William, engraver, 33329, 36686
Wächter-stimm, 6937
Waere genade, 7188
Wager (ship), lost in South Seas, 7859
Waggon load, 20118
Waggoner, 26885
Wagner, Tobias. Abschieds-rede, 8514
Wagstaffe, John, poem on, 8762
Wahre brant(e)wein, 33142, 33851
Wahre und wahrscheinliche, 10517
Wahrer bericht, 5102
Wahrheit, 18291
Wainwright, Elizabeth, 1700-1714, death, 1671
Wainwright, John, clerk, 3916
Wake, Baldwin. To Samuel Allinson, 13753
Wakefield, Gilbert, 1756-1801
Examination of the Age, 28016-19
Examination of the work, 27464
Plain account, 26412
remarks on, 28338
Wakefield, Priscilla Bell, 1751-1832. Mental improvement, 36664
Wakeman, Samuel
Sound repentance, 398
Young man's legacy, 183
Walden, ———, advertisement, 32743
Walden, Isaac. Narrative, 13062
Waldo, Albigence, 1750-1794. Oration, 18868
Waldo, Lucy, d. 1741, death, 4687
Waldo, Samuel, 1696-1759
Defence, 4098
grant to, 19088
lands taxed, 21249, 21950, 22660, 23556
wife's death, 4687
Waldron, William, d. 1727
death, 2848, 2872, 2912, 2971-72
ordained, 2356
Wale, Samuel, engraver, 21766, 29927
Wales, Prince of, letter to, 28968
Wales, Atherton, colleague ordained, 21829
Wales, Ebenezer. Counsels and directions, 13754
Wales, Samuel, 1748-1794. Dangers, 19359
Wales, Samuel, 1773?-1790, death, 23489
Walk and conversation, 28020
Walk of the upright, 7061
Walker, George, 1772-1847. Vagabond, 38973
Walker, James, of Baltimore. Directory, 31297
Walker, James, of Virginia. Inquiry, 33143
Walker, James L. Painting, 24979

Walker, Jeremiah, d. 1793. Fourfold foundation, 23953, 26413
Walker, John, 1732-1807. Elements of gesture, (1793) 25841, (1794) 27680, (1795) 29477, (1797) 32494-95, 32814, (1798) 34521, (1799) 35835
Walker, Patrick. Great Scots prophet, 8279
Walker, Robert, 1716-1783. Sermons, (1772) 12598, (1790) 23029, (1796) 31520, (1797) 33144
Walker, Thomas, maimed, 10958
Walker, Thomas, trial of, 27076
Walker, Timothy, 1705-1782
Letter (to a friend), 7381
Second letter, 7382
Those who have, 12599
Way to try, 5306
ordained, 3390
Walker, Timothy, 1737-1822. Address, 16163
Walker, Timothy P. Flaming sword, 36665
Walking with God, 1036, 24285
Wall, ———, reflections on, 2215
Wall, George. Description, 21568
Wall, George, accounts, 18104-105
Wall, Rachel, d. 1789
Life, last words, 22235
Lives and confessions, 22236
confession, 22083
Wallace, Andrew, petition, 38854
Wallace, James Westwood. Inaugural physiological, 26414
Wallace, Jonathan. Carlisle, October, 1798, 34951
Waller, ———, meeting at house of, 36648
Waller, Edmund, 1606-1687, excerpts from, 23246
Waller, John, d. 1711, death, 1577
Walley, Thomas, 1618-1670. Balm of Gilead, 146, 157
Wallin, Benjamin, 1711-1782. Evangelical hymns, 9297
Walling, William. Wonderful providence, 3373
Wallingford case, 9035
Wallis, David, d. 1713, execution, 1601, 1626
Wallis, George, 1740-1802
Art of preventing, 28021
extracts from, 9066-67, 9341-42
Wallis, Hugh, ordained, 28749
Wallis, James. Oration, 38974
Wallis, John. Geographical, 23104
Walpole, Horatio, 1678-1757, letter (from Secker), 11995, 13193
Walpoole, Edward, publishes cases, 25702
Walsh, Thomas, 1730-1759. Whole armour, 34952
Walter, Mrs. ———, daughter's evil courses, 29671
Walter, Nathanael, 1709-1776
Character of a Christian, 5877
Character of a true, 5706
Heavenly, 5085
Thoughts, 4832
Walter, Nehemiah, 1663-1750
Body of death, 1336-37, 4099
(tr.) Charitable Samaritan, 464
Discourse, 1657
Discourses, 7588
Faithfulness, 2489
Letter, 1224
Massachusetts artillery, 1536
Plain discourse, 2302
Practical discourses, 2822
Sermons, 2401
Unfaithful hearers, 777, 7330
opinion of Whitefield, 5668
Walter, Thomas, 1696-1728
Choice dialogue, 2194
Essay, 2592

Friendly debate, 2339
Grounds and rules of musick, (1721) 2303, (1723)
   2490, (1740) 4622, (1746) 5878, (1760) 8760,
   (1764) 9598-600, (1766) 10236, (1768) 10829
Scriptures the only, 2491
Sweet psalmist, 2402-403
death, 2666
ordained, 1982
remarks on, 2510
Walter, William, 1737-1800
   Charge, 25147
   Discourse, 34953
Walton, George, 1740-1804. Observations, 17419
Walton, Gerald. Rates of toll, 33207-208
Walton, Gerard. At a meeting, 35011
Walton, Jacob
   To the freeholders, 11234
   Whereas a paper, 11230
   candidate, 11228-29, 11263-64, 11390, 11529
   dispute over, 11376
   letter (from Aristides), 11968, 13121
Walton, John. Essay on fevers, 3614
Walton, John, d. 1764
   Religion of Jesus, 4100
   Remarks, 3484
   Vindication, 4320
   controversy on baptism, 3885
Walton, William, ed. Narrative, 18497
Wame ketoohomae, 72-73, 75, 85, 312, 385
Wandel eines einsamen, 5579
Wandering infants, 28827
Wandering Jew, 8761
Wandlende seel, (1763) 9511, (1768) 11067, (1771)
   12221, (1794) 27674
Wand'ring village maid, 29612
Want, Hannah, marriage, 11504
Wante, Charles Etienne Pierre. Memoire, 26415
Wanted by the barrack-master, 15840
Wanton, Abigail, d. 1771, death, 11994
Wanton, Joseph
   Proclamation, 13573
   wife's death, 11994
Wanton wife, 29826
Wappinger Indians
   conferences, 8156
   land controversy, 10911
   treaty, 8157
War, an heroic poem, 9091, 9933
   and Washington, 16520
   between Michael, 22558
   department, (Aug. 6, 1792) 24946, (May 19,
      1794) 27979
   inconsistent, 36281, 38472
   is lawful, 4389
   necessary, 35255
   office, (Nov. 14, 1776) 15192, (Apr. 25, 1785)
      19334, (Sept. 12, 1785) 19335, (Apr. 25, 1786)
      20090
   office, Williamsburg, 16663
   temporal, 9298
   with the devil, 1207, 1682
Warbling songster, 29827
Warburton, William
   (ed.) Essay on man, 8718
   observations on, 9872-73, 10869
   reply to, 9539
Ward, Capt. ——, oration to his company, 36990
Ward, Benjamin M. Essay, 23030
Ward, Edmund, ordained, 3775
Ward, Edward, 1667-1731
   Female detected, (1742) 5086, (1786) 20119,
      (1793) 26416, (1794) 28022, (1795) 29828-29,

(1798) 34954
Nuptial dialogues, 7133
Ward, Ephraim, 1741-1818
   Fidelity, 38976
   ordained, 12069
Ward, Henry, 1732-1797
   Letter to the freemen, 22237
   moderator Newport town meeting, 13498
   secy. Rhode Island, 8989-90, 8992, 8994-97, 9251-
      57, 9498-502, 9815-22, 10750, 13573, 18241, 21431,
      22840-41, 22843-44, 23737-38, 24737-38, 27616,
      29404, 32757
Ward, James, d. 1792, death, 24364
Ward, Jonathan, 1769-1860
   Brief statement, 36666
   reply to, 38607
Ward, Nathaniel, 1570-1653
   Liberties, 6
   Simple cobler, 1658
Ward, Richard. Proclamation, 5045
Ward, Samuel, excerpts from, 5991
Ward, Samuel, 1725-1776
   Letter (to Hopkins), 8057
   Proclamation, 10480
   conduct of, 9370
   death, 15097
Ward, Stephen, candidate, 21350
Ward, Thomas, 1652-1708. Demonstration, 10518
Ward, Thomas, fl. 1751-1761, secy. Rhode Island,
   6770-73, 6920-25, 7104, 7106-109, 7305-309, 7555,
   7558-62, 7774, 7776-83, 8018, 8020-21, 8023-24,
   8247, 8249-53, 8478, 8480-82, 8720-21, 8724-26
Warden, Hugh. Whereas, 15874
Ware, Henry. Compendious and plain, 27702
Ware, Henry, 1764-1845
   Continuance, 29830
   Sermon, 38977
   hand of fellowship, 39096
   ordained, 21143
Ware, Timothy, d. 1784, death, 18473
Ware gadagt'nis, 6927
Ware vryheyt, 8639, 9158
Wareham social library. Catalogue, 34955
Wareing, Elijah. On the death, 8762
Waring, William
   Almanac see **Almanacs (Waring)**
   American tutor's assistant, 31731-32
   Journal for lunar, 23954
   preface by, 36824
Warnende, 6345
Warner, Edmund, dispute with Fenwick, 9970
Warner, Effingham. Select pieces, 3152
Warner, George James. Means for the preserva-
   tion, 33145
Warning of the presbytery, 7300
   piece, 16718
   piece; a poetical, 17062
   piece to all, 5507
   to God's covenant, 3626
   to little children, 30362
   to the flocks, 935

VOL.	ITEMS	VOL.	ITEMS
1	1-3244	8	22298-25074
2	3245-6623	9	25075-28145
3	6624-9891	10	28146-30832
4	9892-13091	11	30833-33261
5	13092-16176	12	33262-25854
6	16177-19448	13	35855-39162
7	19449-22297		

VOL.	ITEMS	VOL.	ITEMS
1	1-3244	8	22298-25074
2	3245-6623	9	25075-28145
3	6624-9891	10	28146-30832
4	9892-13091	11	30833-33261
5	13092-16176	12	33262-25854
6	16177-19448	13	35855-39162
7	19449-22297		

funeral, 35937, 35940, 35951, 36840, 37285, 37302, 38097, 38780
gift to, 23396
heroic youth, 7403
hymn to, 37492, 37495, 37673-75, 38400
intelligence from, 14343
intercepted letters, 18208
letter, (from Duché) 15292, (from Dwight) 31314-15, 32940, (from Paine) 30951, 32631, 32871, 33947, (from Rushton) 32785-86
mausoleum for, 38735, 38907
medal, 22857
memorial to, 15446, 30448, 36399, 36996, 37500, 38399, 38747
memorial service for, 35945, 36419, 36785, 36999, 37008, 37105, 37120-21, 37453-54, 37457, 37460, 37598, 37920, 37961, 38260, 38452, 38667-68, 38686
militia for, 16237
music sung before, 22093-94
observations on, 31042-43
orders court martial, 16140-42, 17043-47, 17772
orders military law, 16108
papers relative to, 39017-19
paraphased in verse, 34532
petition to, 30060
poem on, 16677, 19650, 37633, 37852, 37927
poetical epistle to, 17435-36, 17801
portrait, 15705, 16053, 16415, 16480, 16765, 16796, 16979, 17434, 18163, 21584-85, 22498, 23667, 23980-81, 26771, 28938, 29520, 32309-310, 32584, 34581, 35637, 36114, 37543, 37951, 38479
pres. convention, 20791, 20807
proclamation concerning, 36500, 37921, 38805
rebel, 17076
recommends book, 13851, 36697-98
recruiting for, 15103
requests, (firearms) 14857, (militia) 17222, (recruits) 14241, (reinforcements) 14200
requisition by, 16860
resolution on reinforcing, 15172
satirized, 16697
sends message, 31365
sketch of life, 17131
song about, 16520, 34301
song sung on birthday, 32198
subscribes to Bible, 24099
subscribes to book, 22380
testimonial by, 30282
treaty with Algiers, 31410
tribute to, 37235
troops commanded by, 37031
troops ordered to join, 15654
Washington, Martha
Letter (to Adams), 38780
condolence for, 36965
dedication to, 22093, 39061-63
Washington, D.C.
Letter from the commissioners, 35525
On Friday evening, 39009
Washington and independence, 34959
Washington (canal boat), in Middlesex canal, 35819
Washington city, July 21, 1800, 39013
Washington county. At a numerous meeting, 36857
Washington hall theatre. Last night, 36269
Washington hotel lottery
Correct list, 28029
List of the prizes, 26430
Washington insurance co. Charter, 38344
Washington military society. Constitution, 30887, 34227
Washington society, Alexandria. Constitution,

36795
Washingtoniana, a collection, 39017
Washingtoniana, containing, 39018-19
Washingtons ankunft, 39020
Washington's march, 29834, 31553, 31555
Washington's monuments, 39021
Washington's political legacies, 38998-99
Watch for a wise, 898
Watch-tower, (1754) 7229, (1756) 7698
Watch-word, 20449
Watchman
To the inhabitants, 15109
Whoever has candidly, 13770
Watchman, No. I-V, 11916-22
Watchman's alarm, 13757
Watchman's answer, 7674, 7863-64
Water-baptism, 498
Waterhouse, Benjamin, 1754-1846
On the principle, 23038
Prospect of exterminating, 39022
Rise, progress, 24987
Synopsis of a course, 20123
Waterhouse, Samuel
Monster, 7532
Proposals for printing, (T. Brazen) 8763, (T. Trowel) 10519
Watering of the olive, 45
Waterland, Daniel, 1638-1740
Discourse, 25837
Regeneration, 26432
remarks on, 5163-64, 5513-14
Waterman, Elijah, 1769-1825
Oration, 28031
ordained, 26846
Waterman, Foster, d. 1843. Child's instructor, (1793) 26433, (1794) 28032, (1795) 29837, (1799) 36671
Waterman, Nehemiah, d. 1802
Impartial relation, 35650
Oration, 39023
Waterman, Simon, 1737-1813. Death chosen, 21574
Waters, Nicolaus Baker, 1764-1796
(ed.) System of surgery, 23170
Tentamen medicum, 21575
Waters, Samuel. Meditations, 26434
Watertown, Mass. True and genuine account, 2492
Watertown, July 6, 1775, 14239
Watertown, Aug. 14, 1775, 14207
Watervliet, N.Y. At a meeting, 36672
Watkins, George. Digest of the laws, 37505
Watkins, John. Essay, 29838
Watkins, John W. Oration, 26435
Watkins, Robert
Digest of the laws, 37505
Examination of the executive, 36673
Watkinson, Edward. Essay, 10196-99
Watson, Elizabeth, d. 1767, death, 10755
Watson, Elkanah, 1758-1842
Land for sale, 31560
Tour in Holland, 23039
Watson, George, wife's death, 10755
Watson, Richard, 1737-1816
Address to the people, 34961-62
Address to young, 33153
Apology for Christianity, 28033, 31561-63
Apology for the Bible, (1796) 31564-73, (1797) 32373, 32633, 33154-57
Christian panoply, 33158
defended, 30305
reply to, 30027, 30603
Watson, Samuel, ordained, 34514
Watson, Thomas, d. 1686

VOL.	ITEMS	VOL.	ITEMS
1	1-3244	8	22298-25074
2	3245-6623	9	25075-28145
3	6624-9891	10	28146-30832
4	9892-13091	11	30833-33261
5	13092-16176	12	33262-25854
6	16177-19448	13	35855-39162
7	19449-22297		

Grammatical institute, (1783) 18297-98, (1784) 18870-71, (1785) 19361-64, (1787) 20866-69, (1789) 22260, (1790) 23054-55, (1791) 23966, (1792) 25001-2, (1794) 28047-48, (1796) 31594-96, (1797) 33184, (1798) 34980, (1800) 39043-44
(ed.) Journal of the transactions, 23086
Letter (to governors), 34981
Little reader's assistant, (1790) 23056, (1791) 23967-68, (1793) 26449, (1798) 34982-83
(ed.) New England primer amended, (1787) 20546, (1789) 21989, (1793) 25866, (1796) 34180
Oration, 34984, 39049
The prompter, (1791) 23969, (1792) 25003-7, (1793) 26450-52, (1794) 28049-52, (1795) 29856, (1796) 31597-99, (1797) 33185-87, (1799) 36688, (1800) 39050-51
Revolution in France, 28053
Rod for the fool's back, 39052-55
Rudiments of English, 23057-59
Sketches, 19366
Ten letters, 39056
Three letters, 37281-83
To the clergymen, 34985
Vindication of the treaty, 29752, 29757
attacks Cobbett, 31947
Webster, Pelatiah, 1725-1795
Address, 23970-71
Dissertation, 18299-300
Enquiry, 20870
Essay on credit, 20129
Essay on free trade, 16670
Essay on the seat, 22262
Fifth essay, 17065
Fourth essay, 17064
Plea, 23060-61
Political essays, 23972
Reasons for repealing, 20130
Remarks, 20871
Second essay, 16671
Seventh essay, 19367
Sixth essay, 18301
Weaknesses, 20872
reply to, 18782
Webster, Samuel, 1719-1796
Blessedness, 26453
Justification, 10204
Ministers, 12609
Misery, 13758
Sermon, 15703
Soldiers, 7813
Sufficiency, 28054
Winter evening's conversation, 8060-61
Winter evening's conversation vindicated, 8283
Young children, 13071, 17066
death, 30170
letter (from March), 8166
ordained, 4776
Webster, Samuel, 1743-1777
Rabshakeh's proposals, 14615
ordained, 12609
Webster, Stephen, sermon before, 7813
Webster, Zephaniah. Almanac see **Almanacs (Webster)**
Wedderburne, Alexander
conduct of, 13670
epitaph, 13268
Wedding, an epic, 31600
Wedding-day, 25630
Wedding ring, 6604, 13004
Wednesday, (Jan. 1, 1701) 1023, (July 14, 1779) 16683

Wednesday afternoon, 26974
Weea Indians, treaty, 29742
Weed, Enos. American orthographer, 34986-88
Weeden, ———, defendant, 20825
Weedon, Gen. ———. Headquarters, 15645
Weedon, J. Set of round hand, 33188
Weegshale, 2219
Weekes, George. Ebenezer, 3117
Weekly magazine, 34991-93, 36691
museum (Baltimore), 33193
museum (N.Y.), (1790) 23063, (1791) 23973, (1792) 25008, (1793) 26454, (1794) 28055, (1795) 29857, (1796) 31603, (1797) 33191, (1798) 34995
Weekly museum, N.Y.
Address to the carrier, (1796) 31604, (1797) 33192, (1799) 36693
Address to the generous, 29858
Carrier of the Weekly museum, 39059
Weeks, Levi, trial, 37576, 38372
Weems, Mason Locke, 1759-1825
Almanac see **Almanacs (Weems)**
(ed.) Beauties of the late, 31574
History of the life, 39061-63
Hymen's recruiting, 39064
Life and memorable actions, 39065
Philanthropist, 36694-98
Weenpauk, Indian chief, 3916
Weeping, 39095
Weg der gottseligkeit, 12278
Weg zum glück, 30445
Wege und werke, 25010
Wehkomaonganoo, 84, 440
Weichenhan, Erasmus, d. 1594. Christliche betrachtungen, 23975
Weiser, Conrad
Translation of a German letter, 8062
Wohlgemeindter und ernstlicher, 4836
favors proprietary government, 9799
Weiss, Georg Michael. Da in der Americanischen, 3233
Weiss, Ludwig, 1717-1796
Getreue warnung, 9865
Zuschrift, 15471
Weissheit Gottes, 4211
Welch, Benjamin. Humble address, 16835
Welch, Moses Cook, 1754-1824
Addressor addressed, 31607
Eulogy, 31608
Glorious resurrection, 28057
Hope, 22263
Reply to the Correspondent, 28058
Sermon, 39066
reply to, 27769, 31259
Welch, William, d. 1754. Last speech, 7333
Weld, Ezra, 1736-1816
Discourse, 36699
Funeral address, 34997
Sermon, (1771) 12610, (1772) 12611, (1788) 22264, (1792) 26456, (1794) 28059
ordained, 9540

VOL.	ITEMS	VOL.	ITEMS
1	1-3244	8	22298-25074
2	3245-6623	9	25075-28145
3	6624-9891	10	28146-30832
4	9892-13091	11	30833-33261
5	13092-16176	12	33262-25854
6	16177-19448	13	35855-39162
7	19449-22297		

VOL.	ITEMS	VOL.	ITEMS
1	1-3244	8	22298-25074
2	3245-6623	9	25075-28145
3	6624-9891	10	28146-30832
4	9892-13091	11	30833-33261
5	13092-16176	12	33262-25854
6	16177-19448	13	35855-39162
7	19449-22297		

the state, 34219
these **United States,** 16564
this **Assembly,** 14702
we the subscribers, 14268
Where's the harm, 32280
Wheten, George. Almanac see **Almanacs (Wheten)**
Whido (ship), wrecked, 1901
Whig. To the inhabitants, 14506
Whigg, Christopher. Choice dialogue, 2194
Whipple, ———, escorts Burgoyne, 15438
Whipple, Enoch, 1755-c.1840
Importance of early, 36712
ordained, 20912
Whiston, ———, answered, 3466
Whiston, William, ed. Genuine works of Flavius, 27173
Whitaker, Jonathan, ordained, 35630
Whitaker, Nathaniel, 1710-1795
Antidote, 15709
Brief history, 18885
Charge, 12174
Confutation, 13768
Funeral sermon, 11937
Mutual care, 19384
Reward, 18312
Trial of the spirits, 9308
Two sermons, 11938
installation, 8905
letter (from Hart), 12066
reply to, 11285, 15805, 18404
Whitcomb, Chapman, 1765-1833. Miscellaneous poems, 29884
Whitcomb, Elihu, ordained, 36408
White, ———, dismissal, 9846
White, ———, reports on Illinois petition, 21521
White, ———, traitor, 14028
White, Capt. ———
murdered, 18886
on Harlequin, 18076
White, Dr. ———, reply to, 13687
White, Alexander, 1761-1784
Narrative, 18886
confession, 18324
execution, 19037
last words, 18559
White, Anthony Walton, 1750-1813. Military system, 26474
White, Broughton, 1773-1861. Lines adapted, 38504
White, Charles, 1728-1813. Treatise, 26475
White, Charles, fl. 1740, murderer, 4681
White, Daniel. Short confession, 3476
White, Daniel Appleton, 1776-1861. Eulogy, 39088
White, Ebenezer, 1709-1779
Brief narrative, 9871
dismissal, 9846?
White, Elizabeth, d. 1660. Experiences, 4841
White, Elizabeth, d. 1798, death, 33286, 35095
White, Francis. Philadelphia directory, 19385
White, Henry. To the public, 14624
White, Hugh, trial, 11683
White, Hugh Lawson, petition, 33024, 33092
White, J., engraver, 37816
White, James, of Boston. Catalogue of books, 33215
White, James, 1749-1809
franking privilege, 27887
reports on Illinois petition, 21521?
White, John, 1677-1760
Gospel treasure, 2717
New England's lamentations, 3854-55
Secret prayer, 2086
Three letters, 6444
defended, 6268
extract from, 12626

reply to, 6251, 11094
White, John, fl. 1785. Annapolis, 19070
White, Joseph, of Williamsburg. Interesting intelligence, 16312
White, Joseph, 1745-1814. Sermons, 26476
White, Joseph, d. 1779?, memorial of, 16223
White, Levi, ordained, 34611
White, Mary, d. 1797, death, 34042
White, Moses, petition, 36572, 38846
White, Robert, d. 1773?, murdered, 12936
White, Robert, fl. 1790?, captivity, 23066
White, Samuel, 1770-1809. Oration, 38686
White, Stephen, 1718-1894
Civil rulers, 9538
Death dissolves, 16680
death, 28057
White, Thomas, sees mermaid, 6904
White, Tom, history of, 34134
White, William, 1748-1836
Case of the episcopal, 17802
Sermon, (1786) 20145-46, (1795) 29885, (1799) 36713
To the members, 26046
presides at convention, 19940
wife's death, 34042, 35095
White, William Charles, 1777-1818. Orlando, 33216
White, William P., wife's death, 33286
White, Wright, petition, 31372
White oak. Riddle, 11836
White Plains, July 9, 1776, 15158
Whitefield, George, 1714-1770
Account of the money, 4842-43
Almost Christian, 4446
Answer to the bishop, 4457
Answer to the first, 5515-17
Answer to the queries, 4791
Brief account of some, 7590-91
Brief account of the occasion, 5518
Brief and general, 4626-29, 4844
Britain's mercies, 5883-84
Christmas, 4447, 12617
Collection of hymns, (1765) 10209, (1766) 10361, (1768) 11116
Continuation, 4633-36, 4846-55
Directions, 4637-38
Doctrine of election, 23998
Duty, 4448
Eighteen sermons, 33217
Expostulatory letter, 7136
Extent and reasonableness, 4449
Extract of a letter, 21361
Fifteen sermons, 28078-79
Five sermons, 4639, 5885
Free grace, 4857
Further account, 5886-87
Great duty, 4450
Heinous sin, 4640
Hymn composed, 23079
Indwelling of the spirit, (1739) 4451, (1740) 4641, (1741) 4858
Intercession, 4452
Journal, from London to Gibraltar, 4845

VOL.	ITEMS	VOL.	ITEMS
1	1-3244	8	22298-25074
2	3245-6623	9	25075-28145
3	6624-9891	10	28146-30832
4	9892-13091	11	30833-33261
5	13092-16176	12	33262-25854
6	16177-19448	13	35855-39162
7	19449-22297		

Journal of a voyage from Gibraltar, 4453, 4632
Journal of a voyage from London, 4454, 4630-31
Knowledge of Jesus, 26477
Last will, 12285
Lecture on the prodigal, 5089
Letter, (to Chauncy) 5710-11, (to church members) 4644-46, 4859, (to divine in Boston) 6269, (to Durell) 11117, (to friend in London) 4642-43, (to Harvard) 5712, (to religious societies) 4455, (to Wesley) 4647, 4856, 22278, (to Wright) 10803
Lord our righteousness, 5090
Marks of the new, 4456
Marriage of Cana, 5091
Nature and necessity, 4648
Nine sermons, 5311
Observations, 9539, 9872-73
Predigten, 4653-55
Querists, 4586-88, 7302
Sermon, (1739) 4458-59, (1740) 4649
Sermon on Luke 8th, 25033
Sermons on various, 4650, 4860
Short address, 7815-18
Some remarks on a late, 5312-13
Some remarks on a pamphlet, 6445-46
Some remarks upon a late, 5713
Ten sermons, 29886, 33218
Three letters, 4651
Two first parts, 10210
Two sermons, 28080
Voorbidding, 4656-57
What think ye, 4458, 4861
Worldly business, 4652
acrostic on, 12131
admission to pulpits, 5569, 5583, 5609, 5686
apology for, 5594
character, 4486, 4600-601, 10165
conduct, 4862, 5621
death, 11798-99, 11862, 11937, 11954, 12234, 12280, 26458
declaration concerning, 5534, 5690, 5719
dedication to, 11347-48
defended, 4705, 5563
design on ministers, 5560
elegy for, 11600, 11645, 11662, 11812-15
examined, 5551
imitated, 5616
in New England, 5233
invitations to, 5591
itinerancy, 5608, 5610, 5670
letter, (from Chauncy) 5152-53, 5557, (from Dutton) 5169, (from Erskine) 4714, (from Franklin) 5187, (from Garden) 4516, (from L. K.) 5420-21, 5617, (from Prescott) 5680, (from C. Wesley) 23064, 26459, (from Wigglesworth) 5715
letters, (from Garden) 4705, 4957-58, (from Tennent) 4354
life, 33799
memoirs of, 13298
mode of preaching, 30668
observations on, 4602-603
ode to, 11794
portrait, 12031, 13547
preaches in Cambridge, 7338
preaching of, 4510, 4669, 5643
preface by, 5372
queries of, 6303
reception in Scotland, 5224
recommends book, 8494
remarks on, 4509, 4591, 4721, 5405

reply to, 4499, 4690
resolutions concerning, 5668
satirized, 5177
sermons by, 10391
short reply to, 4805
soliloquy, 5644
testimony against, 5409, 5605, 5678
testimony for, 5693
trial, 4837
views on, 5581-82, 5592
vindicated, 4508, 4594, 5704
Whitefield and Tennent, their conduct, 4862
Whitehaven parish. Introduction to the knowledge, 36714
Whitehead, ———, excerpts from, 34112
Whitehead, George, 1636-1723
    Christian epistle, 580
    defended, 822, 1578
Whitehead, John, 1740-1804. Discourse, 23999-24000
Whitehead, Matthew
    Account of the baptisms, 29309
    Account of the births, 12950, 13541, 14388
Whitelaw, James
    Correct map, 29887, 31626
    Map of the state, 26478, 28094
Whiteoak anthum, 10211
Whitfield, Charles. Ananias's reprehension, 22146-47
Whither my love, 25309
Whiting, Calvin, d. 1795, death, 29275
Whiting, John, 1635?-1689. Way of Israels welfare, 421
Whiting, Nathan, sermon before, 7576
Whiting, Samuel, 1597-1679
    Abraham's humble, 111
    Discourse, 94
    Oratio, 29, 1441
Whiting, Samuel, 1670-1725. Sermon, 36755
Whiting, Samuel, 1744-1819
    Discourse, 33220
    Oration, 31628
Whiting, Thurston, 1752-1829
    Discourse, 35021
    Oration, 35022
Whiting, William
    appendix by, 14585
    sent to Connecticut, 14208
Whitman, Benjamin, 1768-1840
    Index to the laws, 33221
    Oration, 35023
Whitman, Elizabeth, love affair, 32142
Whitman, Elnathan, 1709-1777
    Able and faithful, 13079
    Character and qualifications, 5714
    Death of good men, 12286
Whitman, Kilborn, 1764-1835
    Oration, 35024
    Sermon, 31629
    ordained, 21417
Whitman, Levi, 1748-1838
    Jesus Christ, 20147
    Sermon, 20885, 39091
    Twenty sermons, 29888
    ordained, 19096
Whitman, Samuel, 1676-1751
    Discourse, 3733
    Practical godliness, 1723
    Sermon, 2974
Whitman, Samuel, 1752-1827
    Dissertation, 33222
    Doctrine of Christ, 23080
    God the author, 28082

Nature and design, 39092
Perfection, 26480
Two sermons, 25034
reply to, 38513
Whitney, ———, method of making compost, 28875
Whitney, Abel, memorial of, 34867
Whitney, Charles, case of, 31364
Whitney, Eli, 1765-1825. Oration, 25035
Whitney, Joshua, petition, 33005
Whitney, Josiah, 1731-1824
  Christian minister, 9540
  Essential requisites, 21601
  Sermon, (1790) 23081, (1795) 31630, (1799) 39093
  ordained, 7875
  wife's death, 22408
Whitney, Lois, d. 1789, death, 22408
Whitney, Nicholas Bowes, ordained, 39096
Whitney, Peter, Jr., ordained, 39094
Whitney, Peter, 1744-1816
  American independence, 15710
  Charge, 32772
  Christ's ambassadors, 39094
  Duty of praising, 31631
  History of the county, 26481
  Transgression, 13769
  Weeping, 39095
Whitney, Phineas, 1740-1819. Sermon, 39096
Whitney, R., secy. Vermont, 34922
Whitsuntide gift, 20148
Whittacor, James, letter (from Rathbun), 19212
Whittaker, James, 1751-1787
  Concise statement, 19386, 23082
  Letter, 22664
  letter (from Rathbun), 19212?
Whittelsey, Charles, d. 1764, death, 9628
Whittelsey, Chauncey, 1717-1787
  Brief discourse, 8768
  Discourse, 11530
  Importance of religion, 16170
  Sermon, (1744) 5519, (1768) 11118, (1769) 11531
  death, 20316, 20729
Whittelsey, Samuel, Jr., ordained, 4460
Whittelsey, Samuel, 1686-1751
  Publick spirit, 3490
  Regards due, 3379
  Sermon, 4460
  Woful condition, 3491
Whittemore, Joseph
  Joseph Whittemore presents, 31632, 35025
  To the generous, 33223
Whittemore, Nathaniel. Almanac see Almanacs (Whittemore)
Whittenhall, Edward see Wetenhall, Edward, 1636-1713
Whittington, Sir Richard, d. 1423
  Famous history, (1788) 21602, (1790) 23083, (1796) 31633
  Remarkable history, 28083
  history, 37395
Whitwell, Benjamin, 1772-1825. Eulogy, 39097
Whitwell, Samuel, d. 1791. Oration, 22279
Whitwell, William, 1737-1781
  Discourse delivered, 11940
  Discourse occasioned, 11939
  hand of fellowship, 12174
  ordained, 9060
Whoever has, 13770
Whole armour, 34952
  book of forms, 6230
  book of Psalms faithfully, 4, 20
  book of Psalms in metre, (1790) 22356, (1791) 23721, (1793) 25187-88, 26042-43, (1794)

27575-78, (1795) 29363, (1796) 30079, (1797) 32727, (1798) 34420, (1800) 36960
  correspondence, 20430
  duty of man, 5888
  duty of woman, (1761) 8896, (1762) 9152, (1768) 10941, (1788) 21184, (1790) 22601, (1793) 25686, (1794) 27181-82, (1797) 32335, (1798) 33948-49
  genuine and complete works (Josephus), (1792) 24437, (1793) 25672, (1794) 27174, (1795) 28910, (1799) 35675
  of the celebrated, 13624
  proceedings of the American, 14552
  proceedings of the trial, 27076
  speech, 13625
  story, 26211
  system, 7262, 7351
Wholesome words, 1130, 1630
Why, huntress, why, 30370
Wiandot Indians, treaty, 19278
Wicked mans portion, 210
Wickham, John, 1763-1839. Substance of an argument, 29889
Widder, Philip. Sechs und zwanzig, 9874
Widerlegung, 21603-604
Widow of Malabar, 23791, 24049
  of Nain, 3062
  of the village, (1797) 32421, (1798) 34045, (1799) 35769
Widowed mourner, 23400
Widow's vow, 20425
Wiederdarstellung, 5537
Wieer, William, execution, 7168
Wieland, Christoph Martin, 1733-1813
  Socrates, 33224
  Trial of Abraham, 15711
Wieland, 33461, 35247
Wier, Daniel. It being expedient, 15821
Wiggin, Mrs. ———, d. 1794, death, 29085
Wigglesworth, ———. Charge, 9506
Wigglesworth, A. Extract from an eulogium, 39098
Wigglesworth, Edward, 1693-1765
  Blessedness, 3493
  Charge, 9506?
  Discourse, 3236
  Doctrine of reprobation, 9541
  Enquiry, 4324
  Faithful servant, 4209
  Letter (to Whitefield), 5715
  Seasonable caveat, 3975
  Sober remarks, 2594-95
  Some distinguishing, 7338
  Some evidences, 7592
  Some thoughts, 8064
  Sovereignty, 4863
  death, 9905
  reply to, 2510
Wigglesworth, Edward, 1732-1794
  Authority, 16171
  Boston, Nov. 10, 1785, 18901
  Calculations, 14625

VOL.	ITEMS	VOL.	ITEMS
1	1-3244	8	22298-25074
2	3245-6623	9	25075-28145
3	6624-9891	10	28146-30832
4	9892-13091	11	30833-33261
5	13092-16176	12	33262-25854
6	16177-19448	13	35855-39162
7	19449-22297		

Hope of immortality, 16681
   dedication to, 17183
   vice-pres. Harvard, 17184
Wigglesworth, Katherine, address to, 24698
Wigglesworth, Michael, 1631-1705
   Day of doom, (1662) 71, (1666) 112, (1683) 355,
      (1701) 1030, (1715) 1794, (1751) 6796
   Massachusetts election sermon, 422
   Meat out of the eater, (1670) 158, (1689) 500,
      (1706) 1285, (1717) 1938, (1721) 2305, (1770)
      11941
   described, 1212-13
Wigglesworth, Samuel, 1688-1768
   Blessedness, 7593
   Essay, 3735
   God's promise, 7594
   Pleasures, 3120
   Religious fear, 3121
   Remarks, 5890
   Sermon, 3736
   View of the inestimable, 5889
   reply to, 5734
Wight, Elnathan. Sermon, 7595
Wight, Henry, 1752-1837
   Sermon, 28084
   ordained, 19198
Wight, Jabez, ordained, 2894, 6867
Wightman, Valentine, 1681-1747
   Infant baptism, 3237
   Letter to the elders, 2719
   Sermon, 4462
   Some brief remarks, 3494
   dispute with Rogers, 2209
Wignell, Thomas
   benefit for, 21804
   publishes play, 22948
Wijnpersse, Dionijsius van de, 1724-1808. Proof,
   31666
Wikoff, Isaac
   Address, 12287
   To the public, 12288
   controversy, 12170
   reply to, 12053, 12084
Wilberforce, pseud. To the freemen, 29890
Wilberforce, William, 1759-1833
   Practical view, 35026, 36716
   letters (from Cogan), 35318
   submits propositions, 21864
Wilcocke, Samuel H., tr. Essay, 36750
Wilcocks, Thomas, b. 1622
   Choice drop of honey, (1667) 118, (1734) 3857,
      (1741) 4864-67, (1743) 5314, (1770) 11942,
      (1794) 28085
   Guide, (1702) 1101, (1757) 8065, (1759) 8521
   Köstlicher honig-troppen, 13771
Wilcox, Elijah, son's death, 21072
Wilcox, Reuben, d. 1788, death, 21072
Wilcox, Thomas see **Wilcocks, Thomas, b. 1622**
Wilcoxson, David B. Song on vacation, 31301
Wild, Daniel
   Large and general, 37004-5
   Large and well assorted, 37006
   Small but very valuable, 37007
Wild, W. R. Letter, 24485, 27239
Wild-goose chase, 37766
Wild oats, 25940-42, 31175
Wild youth, 37767
Wilde, Samuel Sumner, 1771-1855. Oration, (1797)
   33225, (1799) 36717
Wilder, Dorothy, d. 1790, death, 22438
Wilder, John, 1759-1836
   Blessedness, 23084

Discourse, 35027
   hand of fellowship, 26136, 35624
   ordained, 22558
Wilder, Samuel, wife's death, 22438
Wilderness shall blossom, 11211
Wildfire, Athanasius. Traditions, 3618
Wiles of popery, 5716
Wilkes, John, 1727-1797
   Authentick account, 9542-44
   North Briton, 11532
   North Briton no. 45, 9545
   Speech, 16682
   Works, 11119
   intercession for, 11191
   letter (from Sawney), 9489
   portrait, 11112-14
Wilkesbare, Pa. Sheriff's sale, 36718
Wilkie, ——, excerpts from, 34112
Wilkins, Henry
   Family adviser, 26482, 29891
   Inaugural dissertation, 26483
   Original essay, 25036
   (tr.) Synopsis of methodical, 25361, 28508
Wilkins, Isaac, 1742-1830
   Republican dissected, 14626
   Short advice, 13772
   fugitive, 14509
   reply to Hamilton, 14096
Wilkins, John, 1614-1672. Discourse, 2009, 2196
Wilkins, Joseph, case of, 31670
Wilkinson, Edward, 1727-1809. Wisdom, a poem,
   (1787) 20886, (1788) 21605-606, (1792) 25037,
   (1794) 28086, (1798) 35029
Wilkinson, Eliab. Almanac see **Almanacs (Wilkin-
son)**
Wilkinson, George, d. 1796?, murdered, 30424
Wilkinson, James. Estimate, 16563
Wilkinson, Peter, adventures of, 25080, 26540, 36779
Wilkinson, Tate, remarks on, 25758
Wilkinson, Thomas, appendix by, 33768
Wilkinson, Thomas, 1751-1836. Appeal to England,
   28087
Wilkinson, William. Catalogue of books, 28396
Wilkinson, William, reply to, 2027
Will, P., tr. Sufferings of the family, 37761-62
Will of a father, 1631
Will of General George, 39000-7
Willard, ——. Ode for independence, 26487
Willard, Abigail, d. 1721, death, 2250
Willard, John, ordained (1757), 7901
Willard, John, ordained (1786), 19721
Willard, Joseph, of Boxborough, installation, 19934
Willard, Joseph, of Wilbraham, dismission, 27199
Willard, Joseph, of Swampfield, ordained, 1999
Willard, Joseph, d. 1723, killed by Indians, 2545
Willard, Joseph, 1738-1804
   Address in Latin, 39100-101
   Almanac see **Almanacs (Willard)**
   Duty of the good, 17438
   Remarks, 34642
   Sermon, (1785) 19387, (1790) 23085, (1793) 28088
   Thanksgiving sermon, 18887
   ordained, 12760
   examines medical candidate, 21915, 22049, 28572,
      28679, 29056, 31881, 32864
   pres. Harvard, 17557-58, 17970-71, 18521-22,
      19035-36, 19703-704, 20408-409, 21136-37, 21879-
      80, 22560, 22562, 23431, 23433, 24384, 25589,
      27098, 28809, 30545, 32234, 33853, 35598
Willard, Josiah, d. 1756
   death, 7770, 7790

poem on, 7988
Willard, Katharin, 1690?-1725, death, 2669
Willard, Samuel, 1640-1707
  Barren fig, 581
  Best priviledge, 1031
  Brief directions, 3976
  Brief discourse, 423
  Brief reply, 1150
  Character of a good, 711
  Checkered state, 1032
  Child's portion, 380
  Christian's exercise, 1033, 2306
  Compleat body, 2828
  Covenant-keeping, 335
  Danger of taking, 582
  Doctrine of the covenant, 684
  Duty, 296
  Fear of an oath, 1034
  Fiery tryal, 336
  Fountain opened, (1700) 960, (1722) 2406, (1727)
    2959, 2977
  Heart garrisoned, 227
  Heavenly merchandize, 424
  High esteem, 356
  Impenitent, 856
  Israel's true safety, 1198
  Just man's perogative, 1286
  Law established, 712
  Love's pedigree, 961
  Man of war, 899-900
  Mercy magnified, 379
  Morality, 962
  Mourners cordial, 583
  Ne sutor, 309
  Peril, 963
  Principles of the Protestant, 502
  Prognostics, 1035
  Promise-keeping, 584
  Reformation, 713
  Remedy, 964
  Rules, 685
  Sermon, 277
  Sinfulness, 585
  Some brief sacramental, 1537, 5315
  Some miscellany, 631
  Spiritual desertions, (1699) 901, (1713) 1659,
    (1741) 4868
  Truly blessed, 965
  Walking with God, 1036
  death, 1295, 1329
  defended, 1150
  illness, 952
  preface by, 7330
  refuted, 1053
  reply to, 515, 1160
Willard, Samuel, 1705-1741
  Minister of God, 5316
  death, 5301, 5316
  ordained, 3460
Willes, Henry, d. 1758, death, 8387
Willes, Martha, d. 1773, death, 13383
William III
  Letter to the Lords, 501
  address to, 453
  death, 1100
  deliverance by, 461
  escape from plot, 764
  grant to, 678
  petition to, 471
  safe return to England, 759
William Augustus, duke of Cumberland, 1721-1765

Address, 5891
Extract of orders, 7904
New rules, 8142
chronicles of, 5732
victory, 5842, 5857, 5866
William and Mary college. Charter, 8284
William Beadles lebenschreibung, 30042
William C. Bradley's oration, 35229
William Coates takes, 12354
William Cunningham's life, 23303
William Hall at the new, 13312
William Jackson, an importer, 11120
William of the ferry, 30587
William Richardson imports, 37023
William Riley's courtship, 39103
William (ship), off Norfolk, 14592
William Spotswood's catalogue, 29558
William Young's catalogue, 20173
Williams, ——, meeting-house in Wrentham,
  19360
Williams, Capt. ——, arrival in Philadelphia,
  14942
Williams, Col. ——, death, 7700
Williams, Dr. ——. Dr. Williams' last legacy,
  22280
Williams, Mrs. ——, history of, 30596
Williams, Rev. ——, of Bristol, Eng., preaches
  sermon, 27563
Williams, A. American harmony, (1769) 11489,
  (1771) 12240-41, (1773) 13035, (1774) 13647
Williams, Abraham, 1726-1784
  Sermon, (1762) 9310, (1766) 10522, (1771) 12289
  ordained, 6410
Williams, Benjamin, 1754-1814. Newbern, 28089
Williams, Caleb, adventures, 28752
Williams, Chester
  Letter (to Hobby), 6645
  answered, 6694
Williams, David, 1738-1816. Lessons to a young,
  24001-2, 31172
Williams, Ebenezer, d. 1753, death, 7340
Williams, Edward. Five strange, 3858
Williams, Eleazar, 1688-1742
  Essay, 2495
  Sensible sinners, 3977
  death, 5317
Williams, Eliphalet, 1727-1803
  Charge, 20407
  Duty of a people, 7819
  God's wonderful, 8769
  Ruler's duty, 11943
  Sermon, 11533
  Some extracts, 29543
  wife's death, 38578
Williams, Elisha, 1694-1755
  Death the advantage, 3122
  Divine grace, 3123
  Essential rights, 5520
  rector Yale, 3383, 3496, 3619, 3729, 3859, 3978,
    4106, 4213, 4329, 4465
Williams, Eunice, captivity, 5094

VOL.	ITEMS	VOL.	ITEMS
1	1-3244	8	22298-25074
2	3245-6623	9	25075-28145
3	6624-9891	10	28146-30832
4	9892-13091	11	30833-33261
5	13092-16176	12	33262-25854
6	16177-19448	13	35855-39162
7	19449-22297		

VOL.	ITEMS	VOL.	ITEMS
1	1-3244	8	22298-25074
2	3245-6623	9	25075-28145
3	6624-9891	10	28146-30832
4	9892-13091	11	30833-33261
5	13092-16176	12	33262-25854
6	16177-19448	13	35855-39162
7	19449-22297		

Peace, 21614
Utility, 35037
Wilson, James, 1760-1839
   Apostolic church, 35038
   Oration, 28108-109
   Proceedings of seven, 26491
   Second edition of An oration, 28109
   Substance of a discourse, 39116
   ordained, 26135
Wilson, John, 1688-1667
   Copy of verses, 48
   Seasonable watch-word, 243
   Song of deliverance, 297?
   death, 725
Wilson, John, fl. 1796. Inaugural experimental, 31644
Wilson, Peter, compiles index, 18632
Wilson, Rachel. Discourse, 11534-35, 25047
Wilson, Samuel. Kentucky English grammar, 35039
Wilson, Samuel, 1703-1750. Scripture manual, (1763) 9546, (1772) 12620, (1795) 29905
Wilson, William, accounts, 19900
Wily, John. Treatise, 10214
Winch, Silas. Age of superstition, 29906
Winchester, Benjamin, bp. of see **Hoadly, Benjamin, 1676-1761**
Winchester, Elhanan, 1751-1797
   Attempt to collect, 20150
   Collection of psalms, 12621
   Collection of hymns, 20890
   Course of lectures, (1794) 28110, (1795) 29907, (1800) 39117
   Discourse, 29908
   Divinity of Christ, (1784) 18889, (1786) 20151, (1794) 28111
   Elegy, 25048
   Face of Moses, 20152, 20891
   Four discourses, 20152
   Gospel of Christ, 18314, 26492
   (tr.) Merkwürdige lebenslauf, 33404
   Mystic's plea, 17439
   New book, 13084
   Outcasts, 17083
   Plain political, 31645-46
   Remarks, 17440
   Seed of the woman, 17441
   Ten letters (to Paine), 28112, 29909
   Thirteen hymns, 15222-23
   Three woe trumpets, 28113, 39118
   Two lectures, 25049
   Universal restoration, (1792) 25050, (1793) 26493, (1794) 28114-16, (1795) 29910
   Wisdom learnt, 20892
   Wisdom taught, 29911
   reply to, 17464, 17740, 36838
Winchilsea, Heneage Finch, earl of, d. 1689. True and exact, 139
Wind Mill Island cash lottery, 13776
Windham, William, 1717-1761. Plan of exercise, (1768) 11121, (1771) 12290, (1772) 12622-24, (1774) 13777
Windham, Conn. Answer of the pastor, 6082
Windham county
   Letter from the associated, 5717
   Minister of the county, 17074
   Plan of consociation, 39121
   Result of a council, 6083
Wine for gospel wantons, 130
Wingate, ——, reports on Illinois tract, 21514
Wingate, ——, **of Amesbury.** Charge, 10825
Wingfield, Unca Eliza. Female American, 39123
Winlove, Solomon. Approved collection, 22283,

26494
Winn, Timothy, agent for Whitney, 33005
Winship, Josiah. Charge, 30508
Winslow, Gen. ——, man-servant of, 8611
Winslow, John. commissioner, 7025
Winslow, Josiah, d. 1724, death, 2668
Winslow, Samuel. Register, 27740
Winstanley, William, 1628-1690. New help, 2408
Winston, Isaac. Inaugural dissertation, 35042
Winter, Joseph, secy. committee of safety, 14926
Winter, a ballad, 28978
   displayed, 18562
   evening's conversation, 8060-61, 8283
   -meditations, 656
   piece, 17554
   piety, 1563
Winterbotham, William, 1763-1829
   Historical, geographical and philosophical, 31648
   Historical, geographical, commercial, 29912, 31647
   plagiarism by, 30050
Wintersted, ——, **tr.** Socrates, 33224
Winthrop, James, 1752-1821
   (tr.) Attempt to translate, 26669
   Catalogus librorum, 12805
   Systematic arrangement, 29913
Winthrop, John, 1587-1649
   Declaration, 17
   Journal, 23086
Winthrop, John, 1606-1676
   death, 224-25
   real estate of, 8031
Winthrop, John, d. 1707, death, 1365
Winthrop, John, 1714-1779
   Lecture, 7597
   Letter to the publisher, 7820
   Relation, 9040
   Two lectures, (on comets) 8522, (on the parallax) 11536
   death, 16306, 16315, 16521, 16681
Winthrop, Samuel, clerk, 7837
Winthrop, Wait, 1641?-1717
   At the town-house, 458
   death, 1899, 1927
Winthropi justa, 1365
Wirt, William, 1772-1834. Oration, 39124
Wisdom, a poem, (1787) 20886, (1788) 21605-606, (1792) 25037, (1794) 28086, (1798) 35029
   an essential, 8468
   in miniature, (1795) 29914, (1796) 31650-51, (1798) 35045, (1800) 39125-26
   is justified, 4943
   justified, 5028
   knowledge, 6985
   learnt, 20892
   no. 2660, 35838-40
   of angels, (1794) 27766, (1795) 29597, (1796) 31258
   of Crop the conjuror, 20153, 28117
   of God as exhibited, 32402
      crying, 4212
      in the gospel, 8385
      in the permission, 8081, 8541
      in the redemption, 2987
   taught, 29911
Wise, Jeremiah, d. 1756
   Funeral sermon, 2720
   Prayer, 3495
   Rulers, 3242
Wise, John, 1652-1725
   Churches quarrel, 1660, 1795
   Deplorable state, 2214

Friendly check, 2310
Vindication of the government, 1941, 12625-26
Word of comfort, 2311
 death, 2717
 defended, 15805
 reply to, 13768
Wise and foolish, 4649
 & good, 2816
 ruler, 6151
Wiseman, Billy. Puzzling cap, 39127
Wishart, Thomas, claim, 26308
Wishart, Williams, claim, 26312
Wisshart, William, preface by, 7565
Wister, Johannes. Bekanntmachung, 9880
Wiswall, Samuel, successor to, 5902
With rage, 13976
Wither, George, 1588-1667. Abuses, 447
Wither'd hand, 4353, 4491
Withers, John. Plain reasons, 2721
Witherspoon, John, 1722-1794
 Address to the inhabitants, 12627
 Address to the reader, 23184
 Christian magnanimity, 20893
 Dominion, 15224
 Draught of a plan, 19935
 Ecclesiastical characteristics, 10804
 Essay on money, 20154-55, 20894
 Humble confession, (1778) 15914, 16173, (1783) 18039
 Letter from a blacksmith, (1764) 9881-82, (1765) 10215, (1785) 19389, (1787) 20418, (1800) 37819
 Letters on marriage, 34527
 Pastoral letter, 14410
 Practical discourses, 11944
 Series of letters, 33236
 Sermon, 22284-85, 33237
 Works, 39128
 death, 29425
 preface by, 21275
 remarks on, 12346
 satirized, 16697
Witness of the spirit, (1740) 4504, (1743) 5165-66, (1744) 5364, (1799) 35404
Witness to truth see **Graham, John, 1694-1773**
Wits of Westminster, 13085
Witsius, Hermann, 1636-1708. Oeconomy, 35046
Witt, C., tr. Short, easy and comprehensive, 8895, 9414
Witter, Ezra
 Gratitude, 35134
 Resignation, 35134
Wives, as they were, 32304-305
Wo and a warning, 10216
Wo to drunkards, 179, 1570
Wo to sleepy, 2136
Woburn, Mass. Council of six churches, 6084
Wöchentliche Pennsylvanische staatsbote. Des herumträgers, 11946
Wöchentliche Philadelphische staatsbote. Neujahrs-verse, 10218, 10525
Woful condition, 3491
Woful effects, 1452
Woglog. Aesop's fables, 9049
Wohl eingerichtetes deutsches A.B.C., (1791) 24008-9, (1792) 25051, (1794) 28118, (1796) 31652
Wohl-eingerichtetes vieh-arzney-buch, 12292
Wohlerfahrne baum-gärtner, 36735
Wohlfahrt, Michael, 1684-1741
 Weissheit, 4211
 Wisdom, 4212
Wohlgegründetes bedenken, 5207
Wohlgemeindter, 4836

Wolcot, John, 1738-1819
 Expostulatory odes, 22287
 Hair powder, 29915
 Instructions, 21615
 Lousiad, 20156, 22286
 Peter Pindar's new gypsy song, 26495
 Pindariana, 28119
 Poetical works, (1789) 22288, (1790) 23087-88, (1792) 25052, (1794) 28120, (1797) 33238
 Romish priest, 30857
 Subjects for painters, 22288
 Works of Peter Pindar, 28120-21
 character, 38293
 excerpts from poetry, 23246, 34112
Wolcott, Erastus, 1722-1793, death, 27245
Wolcott, Josiah. Meditations, 9313
Wolcott, Oliver, d. 1797
 Articles of agreement, 34849
 Pretensions, 31212-13
 Proclamation, 30266-67, 31975-76
 Treasury department, Trenton, 34884
 certifies subscriptions, 28403
 concludes treaty, 18817
 corrects authorship attribution, 26973
 death, 31761
 dedication to, 20166, 20900, 21621, 22297, 23096, 24016, 25060, 26519, 28142, 29932, 31675, 33253
 reports on debts, 20773
 sermon before, 21601, 30738
Wolcott, Roger, 1679-1767
 Letter (to Hobart), 9041
 Poetical meditations, 2722
 death, 10736
 dedication to, 6801, 6948, 7138
 poem on, 8629
Wolcott, Solomon, installation, 19911
Wolcott, William, 1753-1825
 Devout wish, 17442
 Grateful reflections, 16684
 dedication to, 8629
Wolfe, James, 1727-1759
 Instructions to young officers, 14104, 16174
 life, 8702-703
 poem on, 35389
 poem to, 8471
 song about, 16285
Wolfe, John C. Anecdotes of the elephant, 20444
Wollstonecraft, Mary, 1759-1797
 (tr.) Elements of morality, 29464, 31156-57
 Historical and moral, 29916
 Letters written, 31653
 Maria, 35555
 Vindication of the rights, (1792) 25053-54, (1794) 28122-23
 burlesque on, 29613
 memoirs of, 35556
A woman see **Fenwick, Mrs. E.**
Woman, a poem, 30116
Woman's labour, 25421
Women invited, 20895
Wonder of wonders, 13779-80

VOL.	ITEMS	VOL.	ITEMS
1	1-3244	8	22298-25074
2	3245-6623	9	25075-28145
3	6624-9891	10	28146-30832
4	9892-13091	11	30833-33261
5	13092-16176	12	33262-25854
6	16177-19448	13	35855-39162
7	19449-22297		

Woolman, Jacob, son murdered, 9996
Woolman, John, 1720-1773
  Considerations on keeping, 9314
  Considerations on pure wisdom, 11124
  Considerations on the true, 11948
  Epistle, 12630
  Extract from John Woolman's, 11949
  First book, 11538, 33248
  Journal, 23090
  Some considerations, 7341
  Works, (1774) 13782, (1775) 14631, (1800) 39142
Woolsey, Melancton Lloyd. Address, 39143
Woolston, Thomas, 1669-1733
  Free gift, 2597
  reply to, 21461, 38496
Woolverton, Charles
  Christ's the eternal, 4327
  Spirit's teaching, 3244
  Upright lives, 4660
Woolworth, Aaron, ordained, 20986
Woolworth, Samuel Buell, d. 1794, death, 26709
Wooster, David
  New York, Aug. 29, 1775, 14343
  address to, 14121
  sermon before, 8299
  widow's petition, 38838
Wooster, Mary, petition, 38838
Worcester, Francis, 1698-1783
  Bridle, 9548, 17804
  Rise, travils, 9549
  Sabbath profanity, 8773
Worcester, Isaac, bp. of see **Maddox, Isaac, 1697-1759**
Worcester, Leonard, 1767-1846
  Letters, 29921
  Oration, 39144
  ordained, 36870
  reply to, 29661
Worcester, Noah, 1758-1837
  Candid discussion, 28130
  Charge, 36870
  Election sermon, 39145
  Familiar dialogue, 26502
  Friendly letter, 24011
  Gospel ministry, 24012
  Impartial inquiries, 28031
  Letter (to Murray), 20158
  Natural teacher, 35053
  Polemic essay, 36739
  Sermon, (1794) 28132, (1796) 31657
  Some difficulties, 26503
  hand of fellowship, 37323
  remarried, 35055
  reply to, 26602-603, 35143
Worcester, Samuel, 1770-1821
  Oration, (1795) 29922, (1796) 31658, (1800) 39146
  Six sermons, 39147
  ordained, 33342
Worcester, Thomas, 1768-1831
  Dialogue, 28133
  Oration, 35054
  Solemnity, 35055
  Thanksgiving sermon, 31659
  hand of fellowship, 36870
  ordained, 24012
Worcester, Mass.
  House lots for sale, 19390
  Public auction, 39148
  Worcester, (Jan. 3, 1793) 26504, (Jan. 4, 1793) 26505
  Worcester county convention, 19447

Worcester associate library company. Rules, 26506
Worcester collection, (1786) 19752, (1787) 20452, (1788) 21193, (1791) 23490, (1792) 24461, (1794) 27202, (1797) 32363, (1800) 37786
Worcester county convention, 19447
Worcester fire society. Articles, 26507, 35056
Worcester, January 3d, 26504
Worcester, January 4th, 26505
Worcester magazine, (1786) 20159, (1787) 20896, (1788) 21616
Worcester news-paper, 19440
Word in season; fellow citizens, 4104
  in season, or the duty, 2944
    to all Protestants, 9550
    to all true, 6140
  in Zion's behalf, 10005
  of advice; beware, 11125
    mark well, 11126
    to such, 4463
  of comfort, 2311
  of counsel, 16207
  of God, 7340
  to the aged, 264
  to the well-wishers, 4953
  to the wise is sufficient, 15649
  to the wise, or the bishop, 6463
  to the world, 27262
  to those, 4244
Words of Moses, 20453
  of sundry, 21686
  of understanding, 2562
Work of a Christian, 1044, 4008
  of a gospel minister, 7425, 9493
  of God, 34033
  of ministers and the duty, 3737
  of ministers represented, 4007
  of the gospel ministry, 6990, 34625
    Lord, 3024
    ministry, 1981
  upon the Ark, 489
  within-doors, 1409
Workman, Benjamin
  Almanac see **Almanacs (Workman)**
  American accountant, (1789) 22290, (1793) 26508, (1796) 31660
  Elements of geography, (1789) 22291, (1790) 23091-92, (1791) 24013, (1793) 26509, (1795) 29924, (1796) 31661, (1799) 36740
  Guaging, 21618
  (ed.) Treatise of arithmetic, (1788) 21116, (1793) 25561, (1796) 31663
  (ed.) Treatise on arithmetic, 30503
Workman, Hugh, swindler, 38291
Workman's practical, 25956
Works, Samuel, d. 1795, death, 28981
Works and reward, 15865
Works of Aristotle, 33312
  Flavius Josephus, 12822, 13357, 14135
  Horace, 37647
  John Woolman, (1774) 13782, (1775) 14631, (1800) 39142

VOL.	ITEMS	VOL.	ITEMS
1	1-3244	8	22298-25074
2	3245-6623	9	25075-28145
3	6624-9891	10	28146-30832
4	9892-13091	11	30833-33261
5	13092-16176	12	33262-25854
6	16177-19448	13	35855-39162
7	19449-22297		

X

X. Y. Z. see **Williamson, Hugh, 1735-1819**

Xavier, Francisco, 1506-1552. Life of Francis Xavier, 33754

Y

Y. Observations, 34264
Y dull o fedyddio, 3336
Yadkin association. Minutes, 26514-17
Yale college
Catalogue, (1724) 2598, (1730) 3382, (1733) 3738, (1736) 4105, (1739) 4464, (1742) 5097, (1745) 5718, (1748) 6270, (1751) 6800, (1754) 7342, (1757) 8066, (1760) 8774, (1763) 9552, (1765) 10262, (1766) 10526, (1769) 11539, (1772) 12631, (1775) 14633, (1778) 16175, (1780) 17075, (1781) 17443-44, (1784) 18891, (1787) 20901, (1790) 23095, (1793) 26518, (1794) 28141, (1796) 31673, (1797) 35058, (1798) 35059, (1799) 36741, (1800) 39152
Catalogue of books, 24015
Catalogue of the library, 5320
Catalogue of the most valuable, 7598
Catalogus senatus, (1796) 31674, (1800) 36742
Collegii Yalensis . . . statuta see **Yale college. Statuta**
Declaration of the rector, 5719
Front view of Yale, 20165
Judgment of the rector, 5720-21
Laws of Yale, (1774) 13783, (1787) 20902, (1795) 29931, (1800) 39153
Proceedings of the council, 19394
Quaestiones, (1740) 4662, (1741) 4874, (1742) 5099, (1743) 5322, (1744) 5526, (1745) 5723, (1746) 5896, (1747) 6086, (1748) 6273, (1749) 6448, (1750) 6623, (1751) 6802, (1752) 6949, (1753) 7139, (1754) 7344, (1755) 7601, (1756) 7823, (1757) 8068, (1758) 8287, (1759) 8525, (1760) 8776, (1761) 9045, (1762) 9316, (1763) 9553, (1764) 9886, (1765) 10219, (1766) 10527, (1767) 10806, (1768) 11127, (1769) 11540, (1770) 11950, (1771) 12294, (1772) 12632, (1773) 13087, (1774) 13784, (1781) 17446, (1782) 17806, (1783) 18317, (1784) 18003, (1785) 19395, (1786) 20167, (1787) 20903, (1788) 21622, (1789) 22297, (1790) 23097
Scheme of the exercises, 36743
Scheme of the exhibitions, (1796) 35060, (1797-98) 35061-62, (1800) 39154
Statuta, (1749) 6271, (1755) 7599, (1759) 8523, (1764) 9885

VOL.	ITEMS	VOL.	ITEMS
1	1-3244	8	22298-25074
2	3245-6623	9	25075-28145
3	6624-9891	10	28146-30832
4	9892-13091	11	30833-33261
5	13092-16176	12	33262-25854
6	16177-19448	13	35855-39162
7	19449-22297		

Young gentleman and lady's assistant, (1791) 23387, (1794) 27011, (1796) 30447
  gentleman and lady's entertaining, 24559, 25844
  gentleman and lady's magazine, (1798) 35045, (1800) 39125
  gentleman and lady's monitor, (1789) 21972, (1790) 22676-77, (1792) 24556, (1793) 25841, (1794) 27345, (1795) 29097-98, (1797) 32494-95, (1798) 34130, (1799) 35835, (1800) 37992
  gentleman and lady's pleasing instructor, 29914, 39126
Young gentleman of New York see **Linn, John Blair, 1777-1804**
Young gentleman of Philadelphia. Funeral eulogy, 9657
Young gentleman's parental monitor, 25064-65
  gentlemen and ladies accidence, 25066
  gentlemen and ladies' instructor, 31708
  gentlemen and lady's monitor, 20531
  Jemmy, 36747
Young ladies' academy, Philadelphia. Rise and progress, 27514
Young ladies' & gentlemen's complete, 34643
  ladies & gentlemen's preceptor, 32932
  ladies' and gentlemen's spelling book, 31709, 33257, 35093
Young lady see **Whalley, Thomas Sedgwick, 1746-1828**
Young lady of the state of New-York. Fortunate discovery, 33744
Young lady's accidence, (1785) 18934, (1789) 21692, (1790) 22363, (1791) 23206, (1792) 24114, (1793) 25197, (1794) 26675, (1796) 30095, (1797) 31828, (1799) 35209
  lady's arithmetic, 32333
    instructor, 29130
    parental monitor, 25067-69
  man spoken to, 1564
  man warn'd, 3358
  man's claim, (1700) 949, (1728) 3097, (1741) 4793, (1746) 5859
    duty, 2007, 2716
    glory, 534
    guide, 4962
    legacy, 183
    magazine, 18895, 20174
    monitor, 134, 937
    preservative, 997
Mason's monitor, (1789) 22164, (1791) 23996, (1792) 24819
  men are dead, 34407
  mill-wright, 28644
  misses' magazine, (1787) 20907, (1792) 24472, (1800) 38324
  people called, 12238

  people warned, 4829
  piper's pleasant, 26007
  Quaker, 27448
  secretary's guide, (1708) 1354, (1713) 1609, (1717) 1885, (1718) 1957, (1727) 2879, (1730) 3288, (1750) 6517
  secretary's instructor, 8840
  Simon, 29121
  Willy, 33252
Young woman in England
  New-Years gift, 25894
  New-Year's letter, 25895
Young's vocal and instrumental, 26522
Your attendance, 10135
  committee beg leave, 20091
  committee to whom, 16129
Youth advised, 2050
  and hope, 28784
  in its brightest, 1410
Youth of his parish. Elegy, 13264
Youth of this city. Thoughts, 22934
Youth under a good conduct, 1181
Youthful jester, 39160
Youthful pleasures, 4727
Youth's assistant, (1785) 19066, (1789) 21928, (1791) 23521, (1793) 25740, 26524, (1795) 29004, (1796) 29793, (1798) 34930
  entertaining, 7181
  friendly monitor, 20256
  instructor, (1731) 3411, (1746) 5762, (1750) 6485, (1753) 7082, (1757) 7884, (1760) 8582, (1767) 10603, (1792) 24726, (1794) 27599
  library, 36947, 37248
  monitor, 36748
  news paper, 33258
  warning, 25070-71
Yrujo, Carlos Martínez de, 1763-1824
  Letter (to Pickering), 32863
  Letters (to committee), 34788
  Observations, 38142
  letter (from Pickering), 33067
Yrujo, Philip Fatis
  Letters of Verus, 33259
  Lettres de Verus, 33260

VOL.	ITEMS	VOL.	ITEMS
1	1-3244	8	22298-25074
2	3245-6623	9	25075-28145
3	6624-9891	10	28146-30832
4	9892-13091	11	30833-33261
5	13092-16176	12	33262-25854
6	16177-19448	13	35855-39162
7	19449-22297		

Z